Theory of Neural Information Processing Systems

Theory of Neural Information Processing Systems

A. C. C. Coolen, R. Kühn, P. Sollich

King's College, London

OXFORD
UNIVERSITY PRESS

This book has been printed digitally and produced in a standard specification in order to ensure its continuing availability

OXFORD
UNIVERSITY PRESS

Great Clarendon Street, Oxford OX2 6DP

Oxford University Press is a department of the University of Oxford.
It furthers the University's objective of excellence in research, scholarship,
and education by publishing worldwide in

Oxford New York

Auckland Cape Town Dar es Salaam Hong Kong Karachi
Kuala Lumpur Madrid Melbourne Mexico City Nairobi
New Delhi Shanghai Taipei Toronto
With offices in
Argentina Austria Brazil Chile Czech Republic France Greece
Guatemala Hungary Italy Japan South Korea Poland Portugal
Singapore Switzerland Thailand Turkey Ukraine Vietnam

Oxford is a registered trade mark of Oxford University Press
in the UK and in certain other countries

Published in the United States
by Oxford University Press Inc., New York

Reprinted 2006

ISBN 978-0-19-853023-7

Printed and bound by CPI Antony Rowe Eastbourne

Preface

The study of the principles behind information processing in complex networks of simple interacting decision-making units, be these units cells ('neurons') in brains or in other nervous tissue, or electronic processors (or even software) in artificial systems inspired by biological neural networks, is one of the few truly interdisciplinary scientific enterprises. The field involves biologists (and psychologists), computer scientists, engineers, physicists, and mathematicians; over the years these have all moved in and out of the centre stage in various combinations and permutations, modulated and triggered by advances in experimental, mathematical, or computational techniques. The reason for its unique interdisciplinary character is that this multifaceted area of research, which from now on we will simply denote as the study of 'neural information processing systems', is one of the few which meets the fundamental requirement of fruitful interdisciplinary science: all disciplines get something interesting and worthwhile out of the collaboration. The biologist benefits from tapping into the mathematical techniques offered by the more quantitative sciences, the computer scientist or engineer who is interested in machine learning finds inspiration in biology, and the theoretical physicist or applied mathematician finds new and challenging application domains for newly developed mathematical techniques.

We owe the knowledge that brain tissue consists of complicated networks of interacting brain cells mainly to the work (carried out towards the end of the nineteenth century) of two individuals, who shared the 1906 Nobel Prize in medicine in recognition of this achievement: Camillo Golgi, who invented a revolutionary staining method that for the first time enabled us to actually *see* neurons and their connections under a microscope, and Santiago Ramón y Cajal, who used this new technique to map out systematically and draw in meticulous and artful detail the various cell types and network structures which were now being revealed (in fact Cajal had originally wanted to be an artist). Initially and for several decades neural networks continued to be regarded as a branch of medicine and biology. This situation changed, however, with the birth of programmable computing machines around the time of the Second World War, when the word 'computer' was still used to denote a *person* doing computations. It came to be realized that programmable machines might be made to 'think', and, conversely, that human thinking could perhaps be understood in the language of programmable machines. This period also saw the conception of 'information theory', which was largely the brain child of Claude Shannon. Probably the first to focus systematically on the information processing capabilities of neural networks were Warren McCulloch and Walter Pitts, who published in 1943 a paper ('A Logical Calculus of the Ideas Immanent in Nervous Activity') that can safely be regarded as the starting point of our research field. Looking back, one cannot help observing that McCulloch and Pitts were surprisingly typical of the kind of scientist that henceforth would tend to be drawn into this area. McCulloch had studied philosophy and psychology, then moved into medicine, and ended up in a laboratory of electronic engineering. Pitts, who was only 20 at the time when 'A Logical Calculus' was published, initially studied mathematics and also ended up in electronic engineering, but he never received a formal academic degree. It is not unreasonable to take the view that bringing together these disparate scientific backgrounds and interests was crucial to the achievement of McCulloch and Pitts.

The field never lost the interdisciplinary flavour with which it was born. Since the 1940s its popularity peaked at (roughly) 20-year intervals, with a second wave in the 1960s (the launch of the perceptron, and the exploration of learning rules for individual neurons), and a more recent wave in the 1980s (which saw the development of learning rules for multilayer neural networks, and the extensive application of statistical mechanics techniques to recurrent ones). Extrapolation of this trend would suggest that interesting times might soon be upon us. However, the interdisciplinary character of neural network research was also found to have drawbacks: it is neither a trivial matter to keep the disciplines involved connected (due to language barriers, motivation differences, lack of appropriate journals etc.), nor to execute effective quality control (which here requires both depth and unusual breadth). As a result, several important discoveries had to be made more than once, before they found themselves recognized as such (and hence credit was not always allocated where in retrospect it should have been). In this context one may appreciate the special role of textbooks, which allow those interested in contributing towards this field to avoid first having to study discipline specific research papers from fields in which they have not been trained.

Following the most recent wave of activity in the theory of neural information processing systems, several excellent textbooks intended specifically for an interdisciplinary audience were published around 1990. Since then, however, the connectivity between disciplines has again decreased. Neural network research still continues with energy and passion, but now mostly according to the individual scientific agendas, the style, and the notation of the traditional stake-holding disciplines. As a consequence, those neural network theory textbooks which deal with the progress which has been achieved since (roughly) 1990, tend to be of a different character.

They are excellent expositions, but often quite specialized, and focused primarily on the questions and methods of a single discipline.

The present textbook aims to partly remedy this situation, by giving an explicit, coherent, and up-to-date account of the modern theory of neural information processing systems, aimed at students with an undergraduate degree in any quantitative discipline (e.g. computer science, physics, engineering, biology, or mathematics). The book tries to cover all the major theoretical developments from the 1940s right up to the present day, as they have been contributed over the years by the different disciplines, within a uniform style of presentation and of mathematical notation. It starts with simple model neurons in the spirit of McCulloch and Pitts, and includes not only the mainstream topics of the 1960s and 1980s (perceptrons, multilayer networks, learning rules and learning dynamics, Boltzmann machines, statistical mechanics of recurrent networks etc.) but also the more recent developments of, say, the last 15 years (such as the application of Bayesian methods, Gaussian processes and support vector machines) and an introduction to Amari's information geometry. The text is fully self-contained, including introductions to the various discipline-specific mathematical tools (e.g. information theory, or statistical mechanics), and with multiple exercises on each topic. It does not assume prior familiarity with neural networks; only the basic elements of calculus and linear algebra, and an open mind. The book is pitched at the typical postgraduate student: it hopes to bring students with an undergraduate degree to the level where they can actually contribute to research in an academic or industrial environment. As such, the book could be used either in the classroom as a textbook for postgraduate lecture courses, or for the training of individual PhD students in the first phase of their studies, or as a reference text for those who are already involved in neural information processing research. The material has been developed, used, and tested by the authors over a period of some 8 years, split into four individual one semester lecture courses, in the context of a one-year inter-disciplinary Master's programme in Information Processing and Neural Networks at King's College London.

London, January 2005 Ton Coolen, Reimer Kühn, Peter Sollich

Acknowledgements

It is our great pleasure to thank all those colleagues who, through discussions, joint research, joint teaching, or otherwise, have directly or indirectly contributed towards this textbook. Especially we would like to thank (in alphabetical order): David Barber, Michael Biehl, Siegfried Bös, Zoubin Ghahramani, Dieter Grensing, Leo van Hemmen, Heinz Horner, Wolfgang Kinzel, Charles Mace, Jort van Mourik, Hidetoshi Nishimori, Manfred Opper, Hamish Rae, David Saad, David Sherrington, Nikos Skantzos, Chris Williams, and Annette Zippelius.

Contents

Part I Introduction to neural networks

This first part of the text more or less covers the main principles and developments in neural information processing theory from its beginnings in the 1940s up to the mid-1980s (albeit expanded in places with further calculations, examples, and pointers to later developments, in order to link the material to that in subsequent chapters). The particular cutoff point chosen more or less marks the stage where the field became significantly more mathematical in nature. As a result, this first part is mathematically less demanding than the others.

We start with an introduction to the basic characteristics and principles of information processing by networks of interacting nerve cells (neurons), as observed in biology. The next stage is to use this knowledge to define simplified versions (mathematical models) of neuron-type information processing units and their connections, hopefully capturing the essence of their functioning, followed by a demonstration of the universality (in information processing terms) of one specific important neuron model: the McCulloch–Pitts neuron.

We then turn to the so-called perceptrons (McCulloch–Pitts neurons equipped with clever 'learning rules'), proving convergence and also presenting a preliminary analysis of the dynamics of these learning rules, and to the so-called error backpropagation learning algorithm for multilayer feed-forward networks of model neurons. In addition we explore via a number of simple examples the dynamical properties and the possible use in information processing tasks of recurrent neural networks, including a brief discussion of the crucial role of synaptic symmetry.

1 General introduction

1.1 Principles of neural information processing

The brain is a piece of hardware that performs quite sophisticated information processing tasks, using microscopic elements and operations which are fundamentally different from the ones on which present-day computers are based. The microscopic processors in the brain, the nerve cells or *neurons* (see Figure 1.1), are excitable brain cells which can be triggered to produce electrical pulses (*spikes*), by which they communicate with neighbouring cells. These neurons are rather noisy elements, which operate in parallel. They do not execute a fixed 'program' on a given set of 'data', but they communicate signals through relay stations (the *synapses*), located at the junctions where the output channel (*axon*) of one neuron meets an input channel (*dendrite*) or the cell body of another. The strengths of these relay stations, or *synaptic efficacies*, are continuously being updated, albeit slowly. The neurons of each given brain region are organized and wired in a specific network, the structure of which can vary from very regular (especially in regions responsible for pre-processing of sensory data) to almost amorphous (especially in the 'higher' regions of the brain, where cognitive functions are performed), see Figure 1.2. The dynamic relay stations, or synapses, in combination with some adjustable intrinsic neuron properties, represent both 'data' and 'program' of the network. Hence program and data change all the time.

We can roughly summarize the main similarities and differences between conventional computer systems and biological neural networks in the following table:

Computers (specifications as of 2004)	Biological neural networks
Processors	Neurons
operation speed $\sim 10^9$ Hz	*operation speed* $\sim 10^2$ Hz
signal/noise $\gg 1$	*signal/noise* ~ 1
signal velocity $\sim 10^8$ m/s	*signal velocity* ~ 1 m/s
connections ~ 10	*connections* $\sim 10^4$
Sequential operation	Parallel operation
Program and data	Connections and neuron characteristics
External programming	Self-programming and adaptation
Not robust against hardware failure	Robust against hardware failure
Cannot deal with unforeseen data	Messy, unforeseen, and inconsistent data

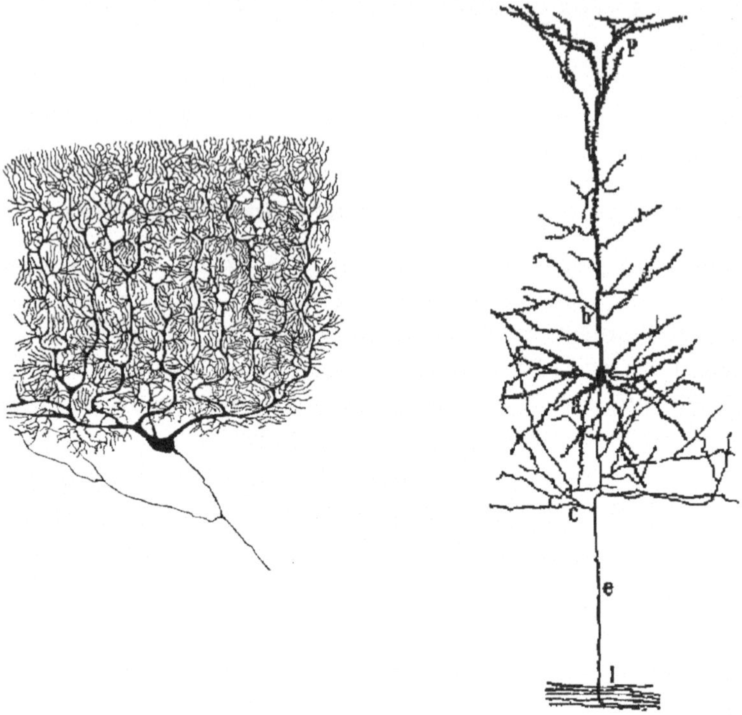

Figure 1.1 Left: a Purkinje neuron in the human cerebellum (a brain region responsible for smooth movement control). Right: a Pyramidal neuron in the rabbit cortex (the region of cognitive functions). Both pictures are due to Ramon y Cajal (1880), obtained from a chemical staining method invented by Golgi. The black blobs are the neuron cell bodies, the trees of wires fanning out constitute the input channels (or dendrites) through which signals are received, sent off by other firing neurons. The lines at the bottom of the pictures, bifurcating only modestly, are the output channels (or axons).

From an engineering point of view the neurons are clearly extremely poor substitutes for processors; they are slower and less reliable by several orders of magnitude. In the brain this setback is overcome by redundancy: that is, by making sure that a very *large* number of neurons are always involved in any process, and by having them operate in *parallel*. This is in contrast to conventional computers, where individual operations are as a rule performed sequentially, that is, one after the other, so that failure of any part of this chain of operations is mostly fatal. The other fundamental difference is that conventional computers can only execute a detailed specification of orders, the program, requiring the programmer to know exactly which data can be expected and how to respond. Any subsequent change in the actual situation, not foreseen by the programmer, leads to trouble. Neural networks, as we know from everyday experience, can adapt quite well to changing circumstances. We can recognize objects also if they are deformed

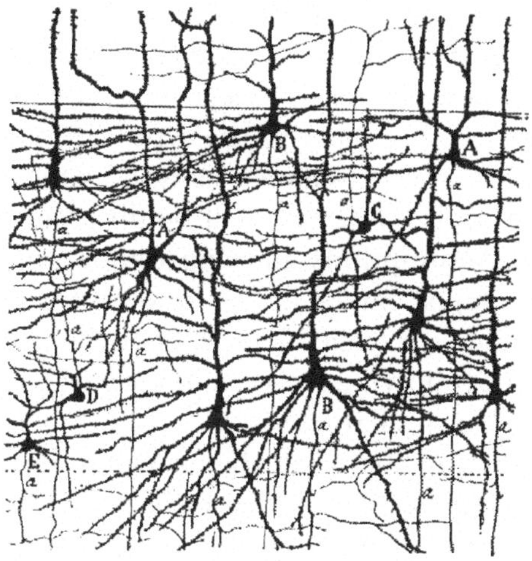

Figure 1.2 Pyramidal neurons in the visual area of the cortex, taken from Ramon y Cajal (1880). Golgi's staining method colours only a fraction of the neurons, so in reality the network is more dense than the picture suggests.

or only partly visible; our visual system can adapt to the strangest deformations of the image on our retina (for instance: everything upside down), and we can even re-wire the nerve fibres coming from arms and legs and again learn how to control movements. Finally, there is the robustness against physical hardware failure. In our brain large numbers of neurons end their careers each day unnoticed. Compare this to what happens if we randomly cut a few wires in our workstation.

We know what the brain and its neural network building blocks can do, the question now is: how do they do these things? It was suggested already in 1957 by von Neumann that, in view of the large number of interacting neurons, (on the order of 10^{11}, each of which communicating with roughly 10^4 colleagues) and the stochastic nature of neural processes, statistical theories might well be the appropriate language for describing the operation of the brain.[1] Later such ideas were given a more precise meaning in terms of stochastic processes and statistical mechanics. Roughly speaking, one can distinguish three types of motivation for studying neural networks. Biologists aim at understanding information processing in real biological nervous tissue. Engineers and computer scientists would like to use the principles behind neural information processing for designing adaptive software and artificial information processing systems which can learn and which are structured in such a way that the processors can operate efficiently in parallel. Such devices would clearly be

[1] The numbers quoted here are estimates and are not to be taken too literally; estimates vary among sources.

quite complementary to the conventional types of computers. Theoretical physicists and mathematicians are challenged by the fundamental new problems posed by neural network models, which exhibit a rich and highly non-trivial behaviour. Consequently, the types of model studied and the language in which they are formulated, as well as the role of experiments in guiding and constraining research will be different in the different scientific communities. Assumptions and approximations which are fruitful and natural to the biologist can be useless or even forbidden in the context of artificial systems, and vice versa. Neural networks are rather complex systems to analyse, for the following reasons: (i) the large number of interacting elements, (ii) the non-linear character of the operation of the individual elements, (iii) the interactions between the elements are not identical, or at least regular in space, but usually different in strength for each individual pair of elements, (iv) two given neurons can operate on one another in a different way (there is not even pairwise symmetry), and (v) the interactions and firing thresholds change all the time. In response to these hurdles, two distinct strategies have largely been followed in order to simplify analysis. The first is to look at *layered networks*, where no interaction loops are present, so that the states of the neurons can be calculated iteratively, layer by layer. The second is to describe the system statistically at a *macroscopic* level of global quantities, and to forget about the microscopic details at the level of the behaviour of individual neurons.

Biological modelling

Here there is still a huge gap between theory and experiment. It is not yet clear even which are the full microscopic laws. Of those microscopic processes that have been identified, mostly relating to the operation of individual neurons, we do not know which degrees of freedom are relevant and which are 'accidental' (i.e. non-productive artifacts of evolution). Last but not least, one often does not know how to quantify the macroscopic processes, that is, what to look for. In order to arrive nevertheless at a level of description where mathematical analysis becomes possible, specific choices of simplifications have been made in model studies of neural networks. In the typical model, instantaneous neuron states are represented by scalar variables[2] that evolve stochastically in time, driven by so-called postsynaptic potentials, which are usually taken to depend linearly on the states of the neurons. In recurrent networks there is no simple feedforward-only or even layered operation, but the neurons drive one another collectively and repeatedly without particular directionality. In these networks the interest is in the global behaviour of all the neurons and the associative retrieval

[2] Especially among psychologists, the scalar information processing units in idealized neural network models are assumed not to represent individual neurons, but rather groups of neurons.

of memorized states from initializations in noisy versions of these states. They are often referred to as *attractor* neural networks.[3] They are idealizations of amorphous parts of the brain, such as cerebral cortex. The study of this type of model has resulted in a thorough quantitative understanding of the functioning of nervous tissue as associative memories for static and dynamic patterns, but also led to insight into typically biological phenomena like memory disorders induced by damage, phase-locked neural oscillations and chemical modulation. The simplifications made in order to arrive at solvable models are more or less ad hoc, motivated by experience, intuition, and the desire to quantify the problem. However, the last two decades have shown that significant progress has been made in incorporating more biological detail into analytically solvable models.

Artificial neural networks

Here one is not particularly interested in the electro-chemical details of neural information processing, but rather in understanding the two building blocks of learning and massive parallellism, on which the remarkable computational power of the brain is based. Biological experiments are only relevant in that they may hint at possible mechanisms for achieving the aim, but they play no role as constraints on model definitions. Rather than a necessary simplification, to the computer scientists representing neuron states as binary variables is a welcome translation into familiar language. The preferred architecture of many artificial neural networks for application as expert systems is that of layers. Many input neurons drive various numbers of hidden units eventually to one or few output neurons, with signals progressing only forward from layer to layer, never backwards or sideways. The interest lies in training and operating the networks for the deduction of appropriate inferences from the simultaneous input of many, possibly corrupted, pieces of data.

1.2 Biological neurons and model neurons

Some biology

Neurons come in all kinds of shapes and sizes but, roughly speaking, they all operate more or less in the following way (see Figure 1.3). The lipidic cell membrane of a neuron maintains concentration differences between the inside and the outside of the cell, of various ions (the main ones are Na^+, K^+, and Cl^-), by a combination of the action of active ion pumps and

[3] They are often abbreviated as ANN, but we avoid this notation since it is also commonly used for *artificial* neural networks.

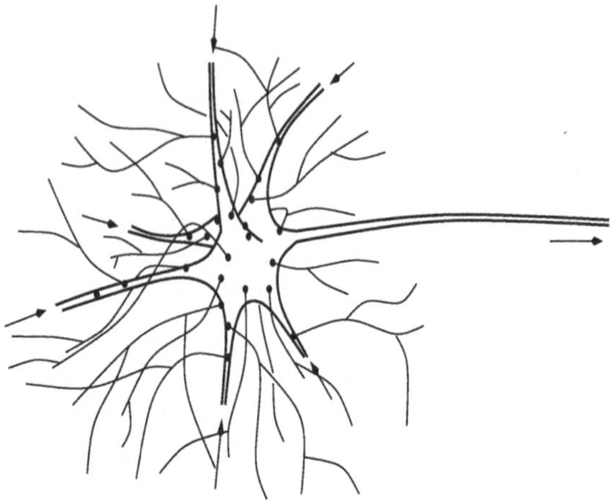

Figure 1.3 Schematic drawing of a simple neuron, with its dendritic tree (branching from the cell body), the incoming axons from other neurons (incoming solid lines) with their points of contact (synapses; dark blobs), and its own axon (outgoing branch at the right).

controllable ion channels. When the neuron is at rest, these channels are closed, and due to the activity of the pumps and the resultant concentration difference the inside of the neuron has a stable net negative electric potential of around –70 mV, compared to the fluid outside.

Equilibrium concentrations (mmol/l)	Na^+	K^+	Cl^-
Outside the cell	143	5	103
Inside the cell	24	133	7

The occurrence of a sufficiently strong local electric excitation, making the cell potential temporarily less negative, leads to the opening of specific ion channels, which in turn causes a chain reaction of other channels opening and/or closing. This results in the generation of an electrical peak of height +40 mV, with a duration of about 1 ms, which will propagate along the membrane at a speed of about 5 m/s: the so-called *action potential*. After this electro-chemical avalanche it takes a few milliseconds to restore peace and order. During this period, the so-called *refractory period*, the membrane can only be forced to generate an action potential by extremely strong excitation. The action potential serves as an electrical communication signal, propagating and bifurcating along the output channel of the neuron, the *axon*, to other neurons. Since the propagation of an action potential along an axon is the result of an active electro-chemical process, the signal will retain shape and strength, even after bifurcation, much like a chain of tumbling domino stones.

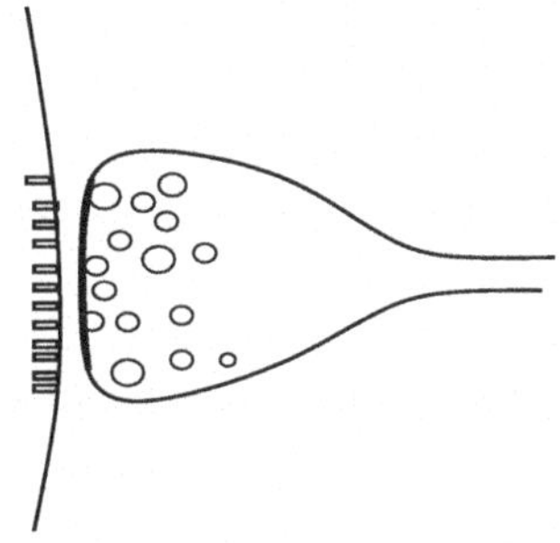

Figure 1.4 Schematic drawing of a simple synapse. Right part: terminal of the axon of the sending neuron, left part: surface of a dendrite of the receiving neuron. The two are separated by the so-called synaptic cleft. Circles: pockets of neurotransmitter, to be released into the synaptic cleft upon the arrival of an action potential along the axon.

The junction between an output channel (axon) of one neuron and an input channel (dendrite) of another neuron, is called *synapse* (see Figure 1.4). The arrival of an action potential at a synapse can trigger the release of a specific chemical, the *neurotransmitter*, into the so-called *synaptic cleft* which separates the cell membranes of the two neurons. The neurotransmitter in turn acts to open selectively ion channels in the membrane of the dendrite of the receiving neuron. If these happen to be Na^+ channels the result is a local increase of the potential at the receiving end of the synapse, while if they are Cl^- or K^+ channels the result is a decrease. In the first case the arriving signal will thus increase the probability of the receiving neuron to start firing itself, therefore such a synapse is called *excitatory*. In the second case the arriving signal will decrease the probability of the receiving neuron being triggered, and the synapse is called *inhibitory*. The main neurotransmitters are now believed to be glutamate, operating in excitatory synapses, and gamma-amino butyric acid (GABA) and glycine, operating in inhibitory synapses. However, there is also the possibility that the arriving action potential will not succeed in releasing neurotransmitter; neurons are not perfect. This introduces an element of uncertainty, or noise, into the operation of the machinery. A general rule (Dale's Law) is that every neuron can have only one type of synapse attached to the branches of its axon; it either excites all neurons that it sends signals to, in which case it is called an *excitatory neuron*, or it inhibits all neurons that it sends signals to, in which case it is called an *inhibitory neuron*.

Whether or not the receiving neuron will actually be triggered will depend on cumulative effect of all excitatory and inhibitory signals arriving, a detailed analysis of which requires also taking into account the electrochemical details of the dendrite. The region of the neuron membrane that is most sensitive to being triggered into generating an action potential is the so-called *hillock zone*, near the root of the axon. If the potential in this region, the *postsynaptic potential* exceeds some neuron-specific threshold (of the order of -30 mV), the neuron will fire an action potential. However, the firing threshold is not a strict constant, but can vary randomly around some average value (so that there will always be some nonzero probability of a neuron not doing what we would expect it to do with a given postsynaptic potential), which introduces the second main source of uncertainty into the operation.

Let us inspect some typical numbers to get an idea of dimensions:

Characteristic time-scales		Typical sizes	
Duration of action potential:	~1 ms	Neuron cell body:	~50 μm
Refractory period:	~3 ms	Axon diameter:	~1 μm
Synaptic signal transmission:	~1 ms	Synapse size:	~1 μm
Axonal signal transport:	~5 m/s	Synaptic cleft:	~0.05 μm

The key to the adaptive and self-programming properties of neural tissue and its ability to store information is that the strengths of the synapses and the levels of the firing thresholds are not fixed, but are being updated all the time. It is not entirely clear how this is realized at the electro-chemical level. It appears that both the amount of neurotransmitter in a synapse available for release and the effective contact surface of a synapse are modified.

Model neurons—common simplifications

Although we can never be sure beforehand to which level of microscopic detail we will have do descend in order to understand the emergent global properties of neural networks, there are reasons for not trying to analyse in all detail all chemical and electrical processes involved in the operation of a given neural system. First, we would just end up with a huge set of nasty equations that are impossible to handle, and consequently learn very little. Second, the experiments involved are so complicated that the details we would wish to translate into equations are still frequently being updated. Let us now therefore try to construct a simple mathematical neuron model. Not all of the simplifications that we will make along the way are strictly necessary, and some can be removed later. Note that what follows is certainly not a strict derivation, but rather a rough sketch of how various neuron models can be related to biological reality. Our neuron is assumed to be embedded in a network of N neurons, which will be labelled with the index $i = 1, \ldots, N$. The postsynaptic potential of our neuron at time t will be called $V(t)$.

First of all, we forget about the details of the avalanche creating an action potential, and concentrate only on the presence/absence of an action potential, denoted by the variable $S \in \{0, 1\}$:

$$S(t) = \begin{cases} 1: & \text{neuron fires an action potential at time } t \\ 0: & \text{neuron is at rest at time } t \end{cases} \tag{1.1}$$

with

$$
\begin{aligned}
&J_{ik} \in (-\infty, \infty): \quad \text{synapse connecting } k \to i \\
&\tau_{ik} \in [0, \infty): \quad \text{time for signals to travel from } k \to i \\
&p_{ik}(t) \in \{0, 1\}: \quad \text{success/failure of transmitter release at } k \to i \\
&S_k(t) = \theta(U_k(t) - U_k^\star(t)): \quad \text{firing state of neuron } k
\end{aligned}
\tag{1.13}
$$

Equation (1.12) would appear to describe many of the neuron characteristics which seem relevant. However, it contains the synaptic noise and threshold noise variables $\{p_{ij}(t), U_i^\star(t)\}$, and, although sufficiently simple to simulate on a computer, it is still too complicated to allow us to proceed analytically.

The next stages in the argument are therefore, first to work out the effect of the random variables describing transmitter release $\{p_{ij}(t)\}$ and threshold noise $\{U_i^\star(t)\}$ for individual connections and neurons, followed by estimating their combined effect on the dynamics of large networks:

- At each time and for each synapse the $p_{ik}(t)$ are assumed to be completely independently distributed, without correlations with either potentials, synaptic strengths, thresholds or transmission delays, according to

$$
\begin{aligned}
\text{Prob}[p_{ij}(t) = 1] &= p \\
\text{Prob}[p_{ij}(t) = 0] &= 1 - p
\end{aligned}
\tag{1.14}
$$

  We thus also take all synapses to be identical in their average failure/success rate. It now follows, in particular (after writing averages over the $\{p_{ij}(t)\}$ and, shortly, the $\{U_i^\star(t)\}$, as $\overline{\cdots}$), that

$$
\overline{p_{ij}(t)} = p \tag{1.15}
$$

$$
\overline{p_{ij}(t)p_{k\ell}(t)} = p\delta_{ik}\delta_{j\ell} + p^2\left(1 - \delta_{ik}\delta_{j\ell}\right) = p^2 + p(1-p)\delta_{ik}\delta_{j\ell} \tag{1.16}
$$

  where we have used the Kronecker symbol δ_{ij}, defined as

$$
\delta_{ij} = \begin{cases} 1, & \text{if } i = j \\ 0, & \text{otherwise} \end{cases}
$$

- Similarly, at each time and for each neuron the thresholds $U_i^\star(t)$ are assumed to be completely independently distributed around some average value $U_i^\star$, according to a probability density $P(u)$:

$$\text{Prob}\big[U_i^\star(t) - U_i^\star \in [u, u + du)\big] = P(u)\,du \quad (0 < du \ll 1) \quad (1.17)$$

It then follows that

$$\overline{S_i(t)} = \int_{-\infty}^{\infty} du\, P(u)\theta(U_i(t) - U_i^\star - u) = \int_{-\infty}^{U_i(t)-U_i^\star} du\, P(u) \tag{1.18}$$

$$\begin{aligned}\overline{S_i(t)S_k(t')} &= \delta_{ik}\overline{S_i(t)S_k(t')} + (1 - \delta_{ik})\overline{S_i(t)}\;\overline{S_k(t')} \\ &= \overline{S_i(t)}\;\overline{S_k(t')} + \delta_{ik}\left[\overline{S_i(t)S_k(t')} - \overline{S_i(t)}\;\overline{S_k(t')}\right]\end{aligned} \tag{1.19}$$

Note that $dt\,\overline{S_i(t)} = dt \int_{-\infty}^{U_i(t)-U_i^\star} du\, P(u)$ is precisely the probability that neuron i fires in the infinitesimal time interval $[t, t + dt)$. For situations where the potential $U_i(t)$ does not vary too much with time (apart from a regular reset due to neuron i itself firing), this probability can be regarded as roughly proportional to the firing frequency $f_i(t)$ of neuron i:

$$f_i(t) = \frac{\text{number of firings in } [t - dt, t + dt]}{2\,dt} \sim \frac{\overline{S_i(t)}2\,dt/\Delta}{2\,dt} = \frac{1}{\Delta}\overline{S_i(t)} \tag{1.20}$$

where we have taken into account the refractory period Δ.

- For sufficiently large systems, that is, $N \gg 1$, the outcome of the summation over k in equation (1.12) will be described by a Gaussian probability distribution, due to the central limit theorem (CLT),[5] the average and variance of which are given by:

$$\begin{aligned}\text{av} &= \overline{\sum_{k=1}^{N} J_{ik}p_{ik}(t)S_k(t - \tau_{ik})} = \sum_{k=1}^{N} J_{ik}\overline{p_{ik}(t)}\;\overline{S_k(t - \tau_{ik})} \\ &= p\sum_{k=1}^{N} J_{ik}\overline{S_k(t - \tau_{ik})}\end{aligned} \tag{1.21}$$

[5] For the CLT to apply we would in principle have to check whether a number of specific technical conditions are met; having a sum of a large number of independent random variables is in itself not enough. To these technical subtleties we will return later.

$$
\begin{aligned}
\text{var} &= \overline{\left[\sum_{k=1}^{N} J_{ik} p_{ik}(t) S_k(t-\tau_{ik})\right]^2} - \text{av}^2 \\
&= \sum_{k,\ell=1}^{N} J_{ik} J_{i\ell} \overline{p_{ik}(t) p_{i\ell}(t)}\; \overline{S_k(t-\tau_{ik}) S_\ell(t-\tau_{i\ell})} - \text{av}^2 \\
&= p^2 \sum_{k,\ell=1}^{N} J_{ik} J_{i\ell} \left[\overline{S_k(t-\tau_{ik}) S_\ell(t-\tau_{i\ell})} - \overline{S_k(t-\tau_{ik})}\; \overline{S_\ell(t-\tau_{i\ell})}\right] \\
&\quad + p(1-p) \sum_{k=1}^{N} J_{ik}^2 \overline{S_k^2(t-\tau_{ik})} \\
&= p \sum_{k=1}^{N} J_{ik}^2 \left[\overline{S_k(t-\tau_{ik})} - p\overline{S_k(t-\tau_{ik})}^2\right]
\end{aligned}
\tag{1.22}
$$

In going to the last line we have used that $S_k^2(t) = S_k(t)$ for all k and t.

- We now use a crude scaling argument to suggest that for densely interacting networks we can ignore the width of the Gaussian distribution describing the summation over k in equation (1.12). We assume that each neuron receives input from about $\mathcal{N}$ of the N neurons present, where both $N \gg 1$ and $\mathcal{N} \gg 1$. A measure for the relative uncertainty in the outcome of the summation, due to the randomness, is given by

$$
\begin{aligned}
\text{Relative uncertainty} &= \frac{\sqrt{\text{variance}}}{\text{average}} \\
&= \frac{\sqrt{\sum_{k=1}^{N} J_{ik}^2 \overline{S_k(t-\tau_{ik})}\left\{1 - p\overline{S_k(t-\tau_{ik})}\right\}}}{\sqrt{p}\sum_{k=1}^{N} J_{ik}\overline{S_k(t-\tau_{ik})}} \sim \frac{1}{\sqrt{\mathcal{N}}}
\end{aligned}
$$

If the network is sufficiently densely interacting, that is, $\mathcal{N} \to \infty$, this implies that to a first approximation we can replace the summation in (1.12) by its average, and forget about the uncertainty; in this case all that remains of the random variables $\{p_{ij}(t)\}$ describing synaptic operation is the prefactor p. Note, however, that no such reasoning applies to the probability of any individual neuron firing.

Replacing the summation in (1.12) by its average over the noise variables, we now obtain the following simplified dynamic equation:

$$
\begin{aligned}
\tau \frac{\mathrm{d}}{\mathrm{d}t} U_i(t) &= \frac{p}{\rho} \sum_{k=1}^{N} J_{ik} g\big(U_k(t-\tau_{ik}) - U_k^\star\big) \\
&\quad - U_i(t)\left[1 + \frac{\tau}{\Delta}\theta\left(\int_0^\Delta \mathrm{d}s\, S_i(t-s)\right)\right]
\end{aligned}
\tag{1.23}
$$

with

$$S_i(t) = \theta(U_i(t) - U_i^\star) \qquad g(x) = \int_{-\infty}^{x} \mathrm{d}u\, P(u) \tag{1.24}$$

Model neurons—specific examples

From the starting point (1.23) we can obtain directly most of the model neurons that have been used as starting points of analytical studies, as specific limits or approximations. We will concentrate on the most common ones.

Graded response neurons

Here we discard the delays, $\tau_{ij} = 0$ for all (i, j), and the reset term in (1.23), assuming that the fluctuations of the neuron potential due to the reset mechanism are not relevant. Our basic equations now become (after a redefinition of our variables to get rid of irrelevant prefactors):

$$\tau \frac{\mathrm{d}}{\mathrm{d}t} U_i(t) = \sum_{k=1}^{N} J_{ik} g(U_k(t) - U_k^\star) - U_i(t) \tag{1.25}$$

$$g(U - U^\star) = \int_{-\infty}^{U-U^\star} \mathrm{d}u\, P(u): \quad \text{proportional to firing frequency} \tag{1.26}$$

We note that the (non-linear) function $g(x)$ has the following properties:

$$\text{(i)}\ \lim_{x\to-\infty} g(x) = 0 \qquad \lim_{x\to\infty} g(x) = 1$$
$$\text{(ii)}\ g'(x) \geq 0 \quad (\forall x \in \mathbb{R}) \tag{1.27}$$

Often one adds to (1.25) a noise term, in order to account for both the possibility that the randomness in the potentials $U_i(t)$ is not negligible (in cases where our naïve scaling argument is wrong) and for the fluctuations due to the reset mechanism. Contrary to what common sense might suggest, we will find that having some degree of noise will often improve the operation of neural networks.

McCulloch–Pitts neurons

Here we forget about delays, reset mechanisms, and noise. In the absence of noise the variables $U_k^\star(t)$ reduce to fixed numbers $U_k^\star$, that is, $g(x) = \theta(x)$. We also neglect the time it takes for electric currents to build up the postsynaptic potential: we put $\tau \to 0$ in equation (1.23) (from which the reset term has been eliminated and in which all $\tau_{ij} = 0$). As a result the postsynaptic potential becomes, after elimination of distracting prefactors:

$$U_i(t) = \sum_{k=1}^{N} J_{ik} S_k(t)$$

Since we have now lost, in a sense, the intrinsic clock of the system because all time constants have been thrown out, we have to restore the dynamics by writing the neuron states in terms of the *previous* value of the postsynaptic potential, that is,

$$S_k(t + \Delta) = \theta(U_k(t) - U_k^\star)$$

Time is now discretized in units of the refractory period Δ, and we obtain the so-called McCulloch–Pitts neurons[6]:

$$S_i(t + \Delta) = \theta\left(\sum_{k=1}^{N} J_{ik} S_k(t) - U_i^\star\right) \tag{1.28}$$

In spite of their simplicity, we will see that networks of McCulloch–Pitts neurons are already universal in the sense that the operation of any (finite) digital machine can be emulated by an appropriately constructed network of such units.

Stochastic binary neurons

In the case where we do wish to take into account noise in systems with McCulloch–Pitts type neurons, so that the $U_k^\star(t)$ are truly random, it is often convenient to choose the latter to all have the same variance and write them in a form where the average and the variance are explicit:

$$U_i^\star(t) = U_i^\star - \tfrac{1}{2} T z_i(t)$$

with

$$\frac{1}{4} T^2 = \overline{[U_k^\star(t) - U_k^\star]^2} = \int du\, u^2 P(u) \qquad \overline{z_i(t)} = 0 \qquad \overline{z_i^2(t)} = 1$$

The reason for this specific notation will become apparent below. The parameter T measures the amount of noise in the system; for $T = 0$ we return to our previous deterministic laws, while for $T \to \infty$ the system behaves in a completely random manner. A second convenient translation is to redefine the neuron state variables, such that the two neuron states 'firing' and 'rest' will be represented by the numbers '$\sigma = +1$' and '$\sigma = -1$', respectively, as opposed to '$S = +1$' and '$S = 0$'. This allows us to make use of symmetry

[6] The actual neuron model proposed by McCulloch and Pitts in 1943 was even simpler!

properties and of a strong similarity between neural dynamics and the physics of magnetic materials; although we need not make this connection explicit, it has led the way in many analytical studies. The translation is simple if we also express the $U_i^\star$ in terms of suitably transformed quantities ϑ_i:

$$S_i(t) = \tfrac{1}{2}[\sigma_i(t) + 1] \qquad U_i^\star = \tfrac{1}{2}\Big(\sum_k J_{ik} - \vartheta_i\Big)$$

The stochastic version of the McCulloch–Pitts recipe (1.28), viz.

$$S_i(t+\Delta) = \theta\left(\sum_{k=1}^N J_{ik} S_k(t) - U_i^\star + \frac{1}{2} T z_i(t)\right)$$

thereby becomes

$$\frac{1}{2}[\sigma_i(t+\Delta) + 1] = \theta\left(\frac{1}{2}\sum_{k=1}^N J_{ik}\sigma_k(t) + \frac{1}{2}\vartheta_i + \frac{1}{2} T z_i(t)\right)$$

giving

$$\sigma_i(t+\Delta) = \mathrm{sgn}(h_i(t) + T z_i(t)) \qquad h_i(t) = \sum_{k=1}^N J_{ik}\sigma_k(t) + \vartheta_i \tag{1.29}$$

with the sign function $\mathrm{sgn}(x) = 2\theta(x) - 1$. So $\mathrm{sgn}(x > 0) = 1$, $\mathrm{sgn}(x < 0) = -1$; $\mathrm{sgn}(0)$ is drawn randomly from $\{-1, 1\}$. The quantity $h_i(t)$ is called the 'local field'. The probability to find a neuron state $\sigma_i(t+\Delta)$ can be expressed in terms of the distribution $P(z)$ of the remaining (independent) noise variables $z_i(t)$. For *symmetric* noise distributions, that is, $P(z) = P(-z)\ \forall z$, this probability can be written in a very compact way:

$$\mathrm{Prob}\big[\sigma_i(t+\Delta) = 1\big] = \mathrm{Prob}\,[h_i(t) + T z_i(t) > 0] = \int_{-h_i(t)/T}^{\infty} \mathrm{d}z\, P(z)$$

$$\mathrm{Prob}\big[\sigma_i(t+\Delta) = -1\big] = \int_{-\infty}^{-h_i(t)/T} \mathrm{d}z\, P(z) = \int_{h_i(t)/T}^{\infty} \mathrm{d}z\, P(z)$$

We can now combine the two probabilities into the single expression:

$$\mathrm{Prob}[\sigma_i(t+\Delta)] = g(\sigma_i(t+\Delta) h_i(t)/T) \tag{1.30}$$

with

$$g(x) = \int_{-\infty}^{x} \mathrm{d}z\, P(z) = \frac{1}{2} + \int_0^x \mathrm{d}z\, P(z)$$

The function $g(x)$ is seen to have the following properties:

(i) $g(x) + g(-x) = 1$

(ii) $\lim_{x\to-\infty} g(x) = 0,\ g(0) = \frac{1}{2},\ \lim_{x\to\infty} g(x) = 1$ (1.31)

(iii) $g'(x) = P(x)$: $g'(x) \geq 0\ \forall x,\ g'(-x) = g'(x)\ \forall x,\ \lim_{x\to\pm\infty} g'(x) = 0$

A natural choice for the distribution $P(z)$ of the noise variables z_i is the Gaussian rule

$$P(z) = (2\pi)^{-1/2}\,\mathrm{e}^{-z^2/2} \qquad \text{with } \overline{z} = 0,\ \overline{z^2} = 1$$

$$g(x) = \frac{1}{2} + \int_0^x \frac{\mathrm{d}z}{\sqrt{2\pi}}\,\mathrm{e}^{-z^2/2} = \frac{1}{2} + \int_0^{x/\sqrt{2}} \frac{\mathrm{d}z}{\sqrt{\pi}}\,\mathrm{e}^{-z^2} = \frac{1}{2}\left[1 + \mathrm{erf}\left(\frac{x}{\sqrt{2}}\right)\right]$$

Here $\mathrm{erf}(u)$ denotes the error function, see, for example, [1]. An alternative choice that will simplify considerably many of our subsequent calculations, is to replace the above function $g(x)$ by the following (qualitatively similar) one:

$$g(x) = \tfrac{1}{2}[1 + \tanh(x)] \tag{1.32}$$

This function satisfies our general requirements (1.31), and corresponds to the noise distribution

$$P(z) = \tfrac{1}{2}[1 - \tanh^2(z)]$$

In a network of such units, updates can be carried out either synchronously (in parallel) or randomly asynchronously (one after the other). In the first case, since all noise variables are independent, the combined probability to find state $\boldsymbol{\sigma}(t+\Delta) = (\sigma_1(t+\Delta), \ldots, \sigma_N(t+\Delta)) \in \{-1, 1\}^N$ equals the product of the individual probabilities, so

$$\text{parallel:} \quad \mathrm{Prob}[\boldsymbol{\sigma}(t+\Delta)] = \prod_{i=1}^{N} g(\sigma_i(t+\Delta)h_i(t)/T) \tag{1.33}$$

In the second case we have to take into account that only one neuron changes its state at a time. The candidate is drawn at random with probability N^{-1}, resulting in

$$\text{sequential:} \quad \begin{cases} \text{choose } i \text{ randomly from } \{1, \ldots, N\} \\ \mathrm{Prob}[\sigma_i(t+\Delta)] = g(\sigma_i(t+\Delta)h_i(t)/T) \end{cases} \tag{1.34}$$

Coupled oscillators

One might well speculate that, even though knowledge of the exact details of the action potentials might not be relevant, going to a description involving only firing frequencies is too crude an approximation in that the degree of synchrony with the neurons fire might be important. This has led to the proposal to study so-called coupled oscillator models. Essentially one incorporates the voltage reset mechanism by saying that the potentials are *periodic* functions of some underlying *phase variables*:

$$U_i(t) = f(\phi_i(t)) \qquad f(\phi + 2\pi) = f(\phi)$$

If all phases $\phi_i(t)$ are identical (mod 2π), the neurons fire action potentials coherently. In the absence of mutual interaction all neurons are assumed to oscillate at some neuron-specific basic frequency ω_i. Excitatory synapses are assumed to induce a more coherent firing of the two neurons involved; inhibitory synapses are assumed to lead to incoherent firing. The simplest phenomenological model to have such properties is

$$\frac{\mathrm{d}}{\mathrm{d}t}\phi_i(t) = \omega_i + \sum_{k=1}^{N} J_{ik} \sin(\phi_k(t) - \phi_i(t)) \tag{1.35}$$

In order to see that this model indeed has the desired properties, let us concentrate on the interaction between a given pair of identical oscillators, say number 1 and number 2 ($\omega_1 = \omega_2$). Here we observe

$$\frac{\mathrm{d}}{\mathrm{d}t}[\phi_1(t) - \phi_2(t)] = (J_{12} + J_{21}) \sin(\phi_2(t) - \phi_1(t))$$

The solution of this equation is shown in Figure 1.5, for the two choices $J_1 + J_2 = 1$ and $J_1 + J_2 = -1$. In the first case the system always evolves towards a synchronized situation, with $\phi_1 - \phi_2 = 2m\pi$ (m integer); in the

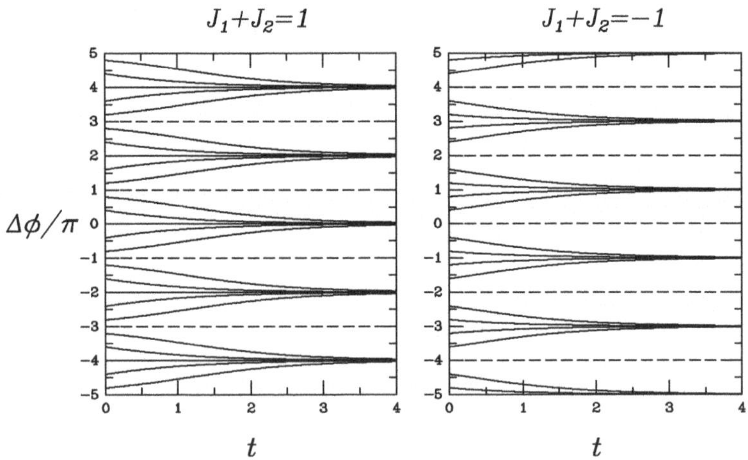

Figure 1.5 Evolution in time of the phase difference $\Delta\phi = \phi_1 - \phi_2$ for $J_1 + J_2 = 1$ (left) and $J_1 + J_2 = -1$ (right). In the first case the two oscillators will always synchronize; their action potentials will eventually be fired simultaneously. In the second case they will do the opposite.

second case towards an anti-synchronized state, with $\phi_1 - \phi_2 = \pi + 2m\pi$ (m integer). Indeed, for small differences between the two phases, $\phi_1(t) - \phi_2(t) = 2m\pi + \epsilon(t)$ with $|\epsilon(t)| \ll 1$, we can linearize our equation, giving:

$$\frac{\mathrm{d}}{\mathrm{d}t}\epsilon(t) = -(J_{12} + J_{21})\epsilon(t) + \mathcal{O}(\epsilon^3(t))$$

For $J_{12}+J_{21} > 0$ the phase difference $\epsilon(t)$ will decrease further (the coherent state $\phi_1(t) = \phi_2(t)$ is stable), whereas for $J_{12}+J_{21} < 0$ the phase difference will increase (now the coherent state $\phi_1(t) = \phi_2(t)$ is unstable). As with the graded response neurons, one often adds to (1.35) a noise term, to account for the possibility that the randomness in the potentials $U_i(t)$ is not negligible.

1.3 Universality of McCulloch–Pitts neurons

The simplest of the neuron models that we described in the previous section was the McCulloch–Pitts neuron (1.28). Here we will show that networks of such neurons have universal computational capabilities in the sense that the operation of any finite deterministic digital information processing machine can be emulated by a properly constructed network of McCulloch–Pitts neurons. Since the basic logical units of digital machines can all be built with McCulloch–Pitts neurons, all theorems of computer science (on computability, Turing machines, etc.) that apply to such digital machines will apply to networks of McCulloch–Pitts neurons as well. Here we will not dig too deep, and just prove some simple statements.

Reduction to single-output binary operations

First we demonstrate how any such machine can be reduced to a collection of simpler single-output binary machines:

- Finite digital machines can by definition only handle finite-precision representations of real numbers, that is,

  $$\pi \to 3.141592653589793238462643$$

  Every finite-precision representation of a real number can, in turn, be expressed in terms of integers:

  $$\pi \to \Big(\overbrace{3141592653589793238462643}^{\text{digits}};\ \overbrace{1}^{\text{decimal point}}\Big)$$

Every integer can, in turn, be expressed as a (so-called Boolean) string of binary numbers $\in \{0, 1\}$, for example,

$$
\begin{aligned}
1239 &= 1 \cdot 2^{10} + 0 \cdot 2^9 + 0 \cdot 2^8 + 1 \cdot 2^7 + 1 \cdot 2^6 + 0 \cdot 2^5 + 1 \cdot 2^4 + 0 \cdot 2^3 \\
&\quad + 1 \cdot 2^2 + 1 \cdot 2^1 + 1 \cdot 2^0 \\
&= 1024 + 128 + 64 + 16 + 4 + 2 + 1 = (10011010111)
\end{aligned}
$$

- It follows that every finite digital machine can be regarded as a device that maps finite-dimensional binary input vectors $\boldsymbol{S} \in \Omega \subseteq \{0, 1\}^N$ (representing characters, numbers, keys typed on a keyboard, camera images, etc.) onto finite dimensional binary output vectors $\boldsymbol{S}' \in \{0, 1\}^K$ (characters, numbers, reply text on a screen, control signals for other equipment, etc.). Deterministic machines will by definition always reply in exactly the same manner to identical input data. Therefore every finite deterministic digital machine can be specified in full by specifying the output vector $\boldsymbol{S}'(\boldsymbol{S})$ for every possible input vector $\boldsymbol{S} \in \Omega$, that is, by specifying the mapping M:

$$M\colon \quad \Omega \to \{0, 1\}^K \quad M\boldsymbol{S} = \boldsymbol{S}'(\boldsymbol{S}) \ \ \forall \boldsymbol{S} \in \Omega$$

- Finally, we can always construct K independent sub-machines M_ℓ ($\ell = 1, \ldots, K$), each of which takes care of one of the K output bits of the full mapping M:

$$M_\ell\colon \quad \Omega \to \{0, 1\} \quad M_\ell \boldsymbol{S} = S'_\ell(\boldsymbol{S}) \ \ \forall \boldsymbol{S} \in \Omega$$

We conclude that we are allowed to concentrate only on the question of whether it is possible to perform any single-ouput mapping $M : \Omega \subseteq \{0, 1\}^N \to \{0, 1\}$ with networks of McCulloch–Pitts neurons. This question will be answered in the affirmative in two steps: (i) we first show that any such single-output Boolean function of N variables can be expressed in terms of combinations of three logical operations performed on the inputs (these three logical operations can be even further reduced to one), (ii) it is then demonstrated that all three elementary logical operations can be performed by McCulloch–Pitts neurons.

Reduction to three elementary operations

For the purpose of achieving the envisaged reduction, we first introduce a partitioning of the set Ω of input vectors into two subsets, depending on the corresponding desired output value:

$$\Omega = \Omega^+ \cup \Omega^- \qquad \begin{aligned} \Omega^+ &= \{\boldsymbol{S} \in \Omega \mid M\boldsymbol{S} = 1\} \\ \Omega^- &= \{\boldsymbol{S} \in \Omega \mid M\boldsymbol{S} = 0\} \end{aligned} \tag{1.36}$$

We now label the elements in Ω^+. The number of elements in Ω^+, denoted by P, obviously cannot exceed 2^N, which is the total number of vectors in $\{0,1\}^N$.

$$\Omega^+ = \{\boldsymbol{S}^1, \boldsymbol{S}^2, \ldots, \boldsymbol{S}^{P-1}, \boldsymbol{S}^P\} \qquad \boldsymbol{S}^\mu \in \{0,1\}^N$$

Evaluation of M thus amounts to identifying whether or not an input vector belongs to Ω^+. This identification can be performed using only the three logical operators $\wedge$ (AND), $\vee$ (OR) and $\neg$ (NOT) which are defined by their output tables:

$\wedge:\{0,1\}^2 \to \{0,1\}$ $\qquad$ $\vee:\{0,1\}^2 \to \{0,1\}$ $\qquad$ $\neg:\{0,1\} \to \{0,1\}$

x	y	$x \wedge y$
0	0	0
0	1	0
1	0	0
1	1	1

x	y	$x \vee y$
0	0	0
0	1	1
1	0	1
1	1	1

x	$\neg x$
0	1
1	0

We can use these basic operations to construct the operator SAME(x, y), which tells us whether two binary variables have the same value:

$$\text{SAME}(x, y) = (x \wedge y) \vee ((\neg x) \wedge (\neg y))$$

The definitions of AND and OR can be extended to cover more than two argument variables in the usual way:

$$x_1 \wedge x_2 \wedge \cdots \wedge x_{L-1} \wedge x_L = x_1 \wedge (x_2 \wedge (\cdots \wedge (x_{L-1} \wedge x_L) \cdots))$$

$$x_1 \vee x_2 \vee \cdots \vee x_{L-1} \vee x_L = x_1 \vee (x_2 \vee (\cdots \vee (x_{L-1} \vee x_L) \cdots))$$

Checking whether or not the input vector $\boldsymbol{S}$ is identical to any of the vectors $\boldsymbol{S}^\mu$ in the set Ω^+ (defined above) is then performed by evaluation of

$$\begin{aligned} M\boldsymbol{S} = &\big(\text{SAME}(S_1, S_1^1) \wedge \text{SAME}(S_2, S_2^1) \wedge \cdots \wedge \text{SAME}(S_N, S_N^1)\big) \\ &\vee\big(\text{SAME}(S_1, S_1^2) \wedge \text{SAME}(S_2, S_2^2) \wedge \cdots \wedge \text{SAME}(S_N, S_N^2)\big) \\ &\qquad\vdots \\ &\vee\big(\text{SAME}(S_1, S_1^P) \wedge \text{SAME}(S_2, S_2^P) \wedge \cdots \wedge \text{SAME}(S_N, S_N^P)\big) \end{aligned}$$

and since this latter expression can be constructed entirely with the three basic operations $\{\wedge, \vee, \neg\}$, we know that every operation $M:\Omega \subseteq \{0,1\}^N \to \{0,1\}$, and therefore the operation of every finite deterministic digital machine, can be reduced to a combination of these three basic operations.

We can reduce the set of required operations further, since the operation $\vee$ (OR) can be written in terms of $\neg$ (NOT) and $\wedge$ (AND), as $x \vee y = \neg((\neg x) \wedge (\neg y))$:

x	y	$x \vee y$	$\neg x$	$\neg y$	$(\neg x) \wedge (\neg y)$
0	0	0	1	1	1
0	1	1	1	0	0
1	0	1	0	1	0
1	1	1	0	0	0

In fact we can reduce the set of operations yet further, since the operations $\{\wedge, \neg\}$ can, in turn, be written in terms of a single operation NAND (NOT-AND) as $\neg x = \text{NAND}(x, x)$ and $x \wedge y = \text{NAND}(\text{NAND}(x, y), \text{NAND}(x, y))$:

x	y	$\text{NAND}(x, y)$	$\text{NAND}((\text{NAND}(x, y), \text{NAND}(x, y))$
0	0	1	0
0	1	1	0
1	0	1	0
1	1	0	1

x	$\text{NAND}(x, x)$
0	1
1	0

Elementary operations via McCulloch–Pitts neurons

Finally we have to show that each of the three elementary logical operations $\{\wedge, \vee, \neg\}$ can be realized with our simple McCulloch–Pitts neurons

$$S_i(t + \Delta) = \theta\left(\sum_{k=1}^{N} J_{ik} S_k(t) - U_i^\star\right)$$

provided we choose appropriate values of the parameters $\{J_{ik}, U_i^\star\}$. This we do by construction. Note that, in order to prove universality, we only have to construct the operation NAND with McCulloch–Pitts neurons (see above); however, by way of illustration we also construct the operations $\{\wedge, \vee, \neg\}$:

x	y	$x \wedge y$	$x+y-3/2$	$\theta[x+y-3/2]$
0	0	0	$-3/2$	0
0	1	0	$-1/2$	0
1	0	0	$-1/2$	0
1	1	1	$1/2$	1

x	y	$x \vee y$	$x+y-1/2$	$\theta[x+y-1/2]$
0	0	0	$-1/2$	0
0	1	1	$1/2$	1
1	0	1	$1/2$	1
1	1	1	$3/2$	1

x	$\neg x$	$-x+1/2$	$\theta[-x+1/2]$
0	1	$1/2$	1
1	0	$-1/2$	0

x	y	NAND(x,y)	$-x-y+3/2$	$\theta[-x-y+3/2]$
0	0	1	$3/2$	1
0	1	1	$1/2$	1
1	0	1	$1/2$	1
1	1	0	$-1/2$	0

1.4 Exercises

Exercise 1.1. (Higher order synapses.) It is known that there also exist synapses which operate in a more complicated way than the simple ones discussed so far. We now try to see how our equations would change if we were to take into account so-called higher-order synapses, like the one in Figure 1.6. The new type of synapse requires the simultaneous arrival of *two* action potentials to release neurotransmitter, so that equation (1.4) will be replaced by:

$$I_k(t) = p_k(t) J_k S_k(t-\tau_k) + \sum_{\ell=1}^{N} \hat{p}_{k\ell}(t) \hat{J}_{k\ell} S_k(t-\tau_k) S_\ell(t-\tau_\ell)$$

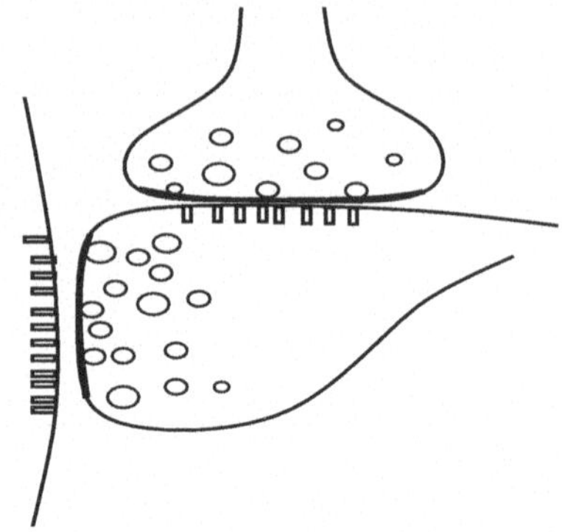

Figure 1.6 Schematic drawing of a higher-order synapse. Right part: terminals of the axons of two sending neurons, left: surface of a dendrite of the receiving neuron.

in which the new variables have the following meaning: $\hat{p}_{k\ell}(t)$ is a random variable deciding whether two simultaneously arriving action potentials from neurons k and ℓ are successful in releasing neurotransmitter, $\hat{J}_{k\ell}$ defines the resulting current induced by the second-order synapse, if transmitter release takes place. Assume $\hat{J}_{kk} = 0$ for all k. Which will be the new equation to replace equation (1.12), if we take into account the existence of the above type of higher order synapse? Assume (without proof) that the simple scaling argument again applies that allowed us to replace all summations over different current contributions by their noise averages. Which equation do we find to replace (1.23)? Perform the simplifications that led us to the graded response neurons. What form will these equations now take? Answer the same question for McCulloch–Pitts neurons.

Exercise 1.2. (Graded response neurons.) Consider two identical coupled graded response neurons, without self-interactions, with $\tau = \rho = 1$:

$$\frac{\mathrm{d}}{\mathrm{d}t}U_1 = J_a\, g(U_2 - U^\star) - U_1 \qquad \frac{\mathrm{d}}{\mathrm{d}t}U_2 = J_b\, g(U_1 - U^\star) - U_2$$

Assume that $g(x) > 0 \quad \forall x \in \mathbb{R}$, as for e.g. $g(x) = \frac{1}{2}[1 + \mathrm{erf}(x)]$. Show that:

(a) if $J_a = J_b$ there exists a solution of the form $U_1(t) = U_2(t)\ \forall t \geq 0$.

(b) if $J_a \neq J_b$ there is no solution of the form $U_1(t) = U_2(t)\ \ \forall t \geq 0$.

Now choose $g(x) = \theta(x)$, that is, no noise, and $J_a = J_b = J \neq 0$. Simplify the above equations by transforming to new variables:

$$U_1 = Ju_1 \quad U_2 = Ju_2 \quad U^\star = Ju^\star$$

so that the new equations become

$$\frac{\mathrm{d}}{\mathrm{d}t}u_1 = \theta(u_2 - u^\star) - u_1 \qquad \frac{\mathrm{d}}{\mathrm{d}t}u_2 = \theta(u_1 - u^\star) - u_2$$

Solve these equations separately in the four relevant regions of the (u_1, u_2) plane, (I) $u_1 > u^\star$, $u_2 > u^\star$ (II) $u_1 < u^\star$, $u_2 > u^\star$ (III) $u_1 < u^\star$, $u_2 < u^\star$, and (IV) $u_1 > u^\star$, $u_2 < u^\star$, and draw the trajectories in the (u_1, u_2) plane, for $u^\star < 1$. Do the same for $u^\star > 1$. What can you conclude about the dependence of the system's behaviour on the height of the neural threshold?

Exercise 1.3. (Coupled oscillators.) Consider three coupled oscillators, without self-interactions, described by the following equations:

$$\frac{\mathrm{d}}{\mathrm{d}t}\phi_1 = \omega_1 + J_{12}\sin(\phi_2 - \phi_1) + J_{13}\sin(\phi_3 - \phi_1)$$

$$\frac{\mathrm{d}}{\mathrm{d}t}\phi_2 = \omega_2 + J_{21}\sin(\phi_1 - \phi_2) + J_{23}\sin(\phi_3 - \phi_2)$$

$$\frac{\mathrm{d}}{\mathrm{d}t}\phi_3 = \omega_3 + J_{31}\sin(\phi_1 - \phi_3) + J_{32}\sin(\phi_2 - \phi_3)$$

Explain the meaning and relevance of the various quantities which occur in these equations. Assume from now on that $\omega_1 = \omega_2 = \omega_3 = \omega$. Show that the above system of equations admits solutions such that

$$\phi_3 - \phi_2 = m\pi \qquad m = 0, \pm 1, \pm 2, \ldots$$

if and only if $J_{31} = (-1)^m J_{21}$. What do these solutions represent in terms of firing coherence? Assume that the above condition holds for some *even* integer m, and that $J_{ik} = J$ for all i, k. Show that

$$\frac{\mathrm{d}}{\mathrm{d}t}(\phi_1 + 2\phi_2) = 3\omega \qquad \frac{\mathrm{d}}{\mathrm{d}t}(\phi_1 - \phi_2) = -3J\sin(\phi_1 - \phi_2)$$

Finally, suppose that $J > 0$ and that *initially* the difference $\phi_1 - \phi_2$ is not a multiple of π. Show, by considering the phase diagram pertaining to the above differential equation for $\phi_1 - \phi_2$, or otherwise, that as $t \to \infty$ all three oscillators will fire coherently, that is, synchronously. What happens if $J < 0$?

2 Layered networks

2.1 Linear separability

All elementary logical operations that we encountered in the previous chapter could not only be realized with McCulloch–Pitts neurons, but even with a *single*, McCulloch–Pitts neuron. The question naturally arises whether all operations $\{0,1\}^N \to \{0,1\}$ can be performed with a single McCulloch–Pitts neuron. For $N = 1$, that is, the trivial case of only one input variable $x \in \{0,1\}$, we can simply check all possible operations $M : \{0,1\} \to \{0,1\}$ (of which there are four, to be denoted by M_a, M_b, M_c, and M_d), and verify that one can always construct an equivalent McCulloch–Pitts neuron $S(x) = \theta(Jx - U)$:

x	$M_a(x)$	$\theta(-1)$	$M_b(x)$	$\theta(-x+1/2)$	$M_c(x)$	$\theta(x-1/2)$	M_d	$\theta(1)$
0	0	0	1	1	0	0	1	1
1	0	0	0	0	1	1	1	1

For $N > 1$, however, the answer is no. There are several ways of showing this. The simplest is to give first a counterexample for $N = 2$, which can subsequently be used to generate counterexamples for any $N \geq 2$, the so-called XOR operation (exclusive OR):

x	y	$\mathrm{XOR}(x,y)$
0	0	0
0	1	1
1	0	1
1	1	0

Proposition. No set of real numbers $\{J_x, J_y, U\}$ exists such that

$$\theta(J_x x + J_y y - U) = \mathrm{XOR}(x,y) \qquad \forall (x,y) \in \{0,1\}^2$$

Proof. By contradiction. Assume the above statement were false, this would imply:

$$
\begin{array}{llll}
(x,y)=(0,0): & -U<0 & \Rightarrow & U>0 \\
(x,y)=(0,1): & J_y-U>0 & \Rightarrow & J_y>U \\
(x,y)=(1,0): & J_x-U>0 & \Rightarrow & J_x>U \\
(x,y)=(1,1): & J_y+J_y-U<0 & \Rightarrow & J_x+J_y<U
\end{array}
$$

This contradiction shows that the above statement can never be false, which completes our proof. □

For $N > 2$ we can construct a similar operation M by just applying the XOR operation to the first two of the N input variables:

$$M: \{0,1\}^N \to \{0,1\} \quad M(x_1,\ldots,x_N) = \mathrm{XOR}(x_1,x_2)$$

to which the same proof applies as to the $N = 2$ case discussed above. As a result we know that indeed for all $N \geq 2$ there exist operations that cannot be performed by a single McCulloch–Pitts neuron.

We can also give a geometric picture of the situation. The set of all possible operations $M : \{0,1\}^N \to \{0,1\}$ consists of all possible ways to fill the right column of the corresponding table with ones or zeros:

x_1	x_2	$\cdots$	$\cdots$	x_{N-1}	x_N	$M(\boldsymbol{x})$
0	0	$\cdots$	$\cdots$	0	0	$*$
1	0	$\cdots$	$\cdots$	0	0	$*$
$\vdots$	$\vdots$	$\vdots$	$\vdots$	$\vdots$	$\vdots$	$\vdots$
$\vdots$	$\vdots$	$\vdots$	$\vdots$	$\vdots$	$\vdots$	$\vdots$
1	1	$\cdots$	$\cdots$	1	0	$*$
1	1	$\cdots$	$\cdots$	1	1	$*$

The total number of possible operations $M : \{0,1\}^N \to \{0,1\}$ is the number of possible ways to fill the right column of the above table. There are 2^N entries in this column, with two possible values for each, so

$$\text{number of operations } M: \{0,1\}^N \to \{0,1\} = 2^{2^N}$$

The set $\{0,1\}^N$ of possible binary input vectors consists of the corners of the unit hyper-cube in $\mathbb{R}^N$. A McCulloch–Pitts neuron, performing the operation

$$S: \{0,1\}^N \to \{0,1\} \qquad S(\boldsymbol{x}) = \theta\left(\sum_{k=1}^{N} J_k x_k - U\right)$$

can be seen as dividing the space $\mathbb{R}^N$ into two subsets which are separated by the hyper-plane $\sum_{k=1}^N J_k x_k = U$. The information conveyed by the outcome of the operation of a McCulloch–Pitts neuron, given an input $\boldsymbol{x} \in \{0,1\}^N$, is simply in which of the two subsets the corner $\boldsymbol{x}$ of the hyper-cube is located. $S(\boldsymbol{x}) = 1$ if $\boldsymbol{x}$ is in the subset $\sum_{k=1}^N J_k x_k > U$, whereas $S(\boldsymbol{x}) = 0$ if $\boldsymbol{x}$ is in the subset $\sum_{k=1}^N J_k x_k < U$; let us not yet worry about the pathological case where $\boldsymbol{x}$ is *on* the separating plane for the moment. Note that this division of $\{0,1\}^N$ into subsets, here separated by a plane, is identical to the division which we already introduced earlier through the subsets Ω^+ and Ω^-. In terms of the above table, Ω^+ is the set of all hyper-cube corners $\boldsymbol{x} \in \{0,1\}^N$ for which $* = 1$; Ω^- is the set of corners $\boldsymbol{x} \in \{0,1\}^N$ with $* = 0$. Since each of these 2^{2^N} operations M is characterized uniquely by its associated set Ω^+, each can be pictured uniquely by drawing the hyper-cube in $\mathbb{R}^N$ in which corners in Ω^+ are coloured black, and corners in Ω^- are white.

For $N = 1$ the hyper-cube reduces simply to a line segment with $2^1 = 2$ 'corners'. There are $2^{2^1} = 4$ operations $M: \{0,1\} \to \{0,1\}$, that is, four ways of colouring the two corners:

$N = 1$: $\boldsymbol{x} \in \{0,1\}$ •: $\boldsymbol{x} \in \Omega^+,\ M(\boldsymbol{x}) = 1$ o: $\boldsymbol{x} \in \Omega^-,\ M(\boldsymbol{x}) = 0$

For $N = 2$ the hyper-cube is a square (with $2^2 = 4$ corners). There are $2^{2^2} = 16$ operations $M : \{0,1\}^2 \to \{0,1\}$, that is, sixteen ways of colouring the four corners:

$N = 2$: $\boldsymbol{x} \in \{0,1\}^2$ •: $\boldsymbol{x} \in \Omega^+,\ M(\boldsymbol{x}) = 1$ o: $\boldsymbol{x} \in \Omega^-,\ M(\boldsymbol{x}) = 0$

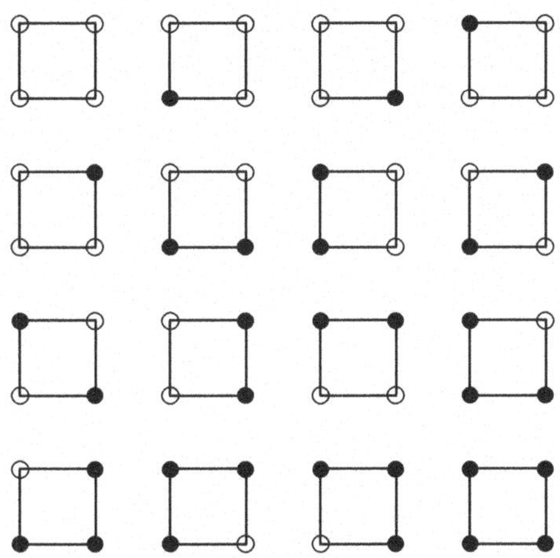

For $N = 3$ the hyper-cube is a cube (with eight corners). There are $2^{2^3} = 256$ operations M: $\{0,1\}^3 \to \{0,1\}$, that is, 256 ways of colouring the eight corners, etc. Of all these operations, McCulloch–Pitts neurons can only perform those for which the Ω^+ corners $\boldsymbol{x}$ (the black ones), can be separated from the Ω^- corners $\boldsymbol{x}$ (the white ones) by one *single* plane $\boldsymbol{x} \cdot \boldsymbol{J} = U$. Such operations are called *linearly separable*. It is now immediately clear for the above examples $N = 1$ and $N = 2$, simply by looking at the graphs, which operations are linearly separable:

$N = 1$:

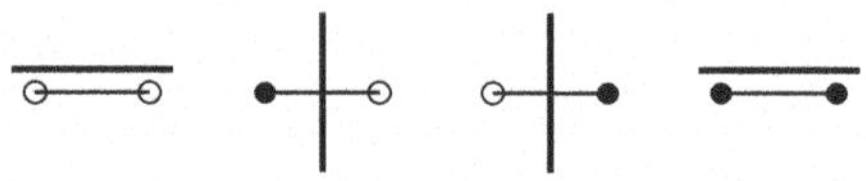

$N = 2$:

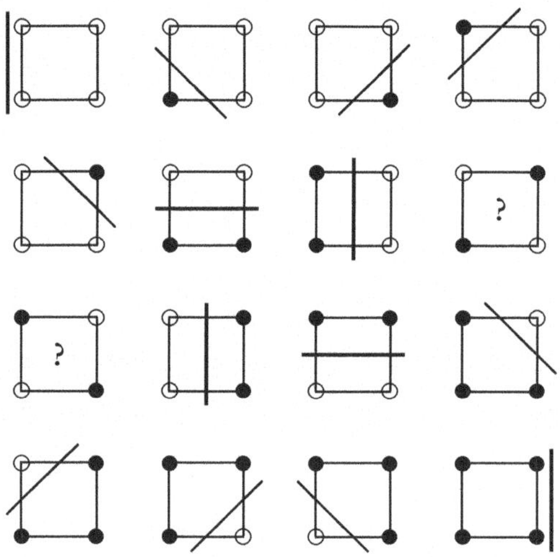

For $N = 1$ we recover our earlier result that all operations are linearly separable (i.e. can be performed by a suitably constructed McCulloch–Pitts neuron). For $N = 2$ we find that of the sixteen possible operations, the following two are *not* linearly separable:

x	y	$M_a(x, y)$
0	0	0
0	1	1
1	0	1
1	1	0

x	y	$M_b(x, y)$
0	0	1
0	1	0
1	0	0
1	1	1

in these we recognize the two operations XOR (as expected) and $\neg$(XOR).

2.2 Multilayer networks

Having seen that a single McCulloch–Pitts neuron cannot realize every mapping M: $\{0,1\}^N \to \{0,1\}$, we now set out to demonstrate that every such mapping M can at least be performed by a two-layer feed-forward network of such neurons, with only one neuron in the second layer. This will in fact be a specific neural realization of the look-up table for elements of the set Ω^+, as introduced earlier in demonstrating the universality of McCulloch–Pitts neurons.

As a simple explicit example we will now illustrate how a multilayer perceptron can be designed to perform a linearly non-separable task such as XOR. Here the set of vectors Ω^+, for which the XOR operation is to give as output the value 1, is

$$\Omega^+ = \{\boldsymbol{x}^1, \boldsymbol{x}^2\} \quad \text{with} \quad \boldsymbol{x}^1 = (1,0), \quad \boldsymbol{x}^2 = (0,1)$$

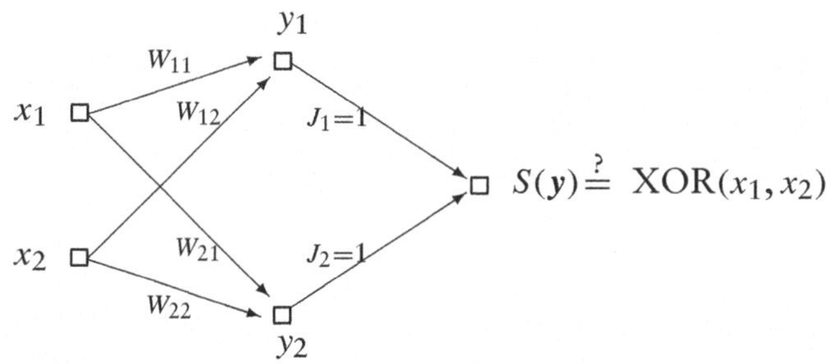

Our solution is based on a so-called 'grandmother-cell' construction for the neurons of the hidden layer. It uses our knowledge of Ω^+, and is designed in such a way that for each of the vectors $\boldsymbol{x}^i$ in Ω^+ there is precisely one neuron i in the middle (or 'hidden') layer which produces an output $+1$ for this (and only for this) input vector, thereby signaling that the state of the output neuron is to be $+1$ when $\boldsymbol{x}^i$ occurs as input. The weights W_{ij} and firing thresholds V_i for the hidden neurons which achieve this follow from the observation that for $\boldsymbol{x}^i \in \Omega^+$ and $\boldsymbol{x} \in \{0,1\}^2$ the sum $\sum_{j=1}^{2}(2x_j^i - 1)(2x_j - 1) = \sum_{j=1}^{2} 2(2x_j^i - 1)x_j - \sum_{j=1}^{2}(2x_j^i - 1)$ will be +2 if $\boldsymbol{x} = \boldsymbol{x}^i$, and less than or equal to 0 otherwise. From this one reads off that suitable weights and thresholds of the hidden neurons to achieve the desired action

$$y_i(\boldsymbol{x}) = \theta\left(\sum_{j=1}^{2} W_{ij}x_j - V_i\right) = \delta_{\boldsymbol{x},\boldsymbol{x}^i}$$

are $W_{ij} = 2(2x_j^i - 1)$ and $V_i = 1 + \sum_{j=1}^{2}(2x_j^i - 1)$. For the two relevant input vectors in Ω^+ this implies, more specifically

$$W_{11} = 2(2x_1^1 - 1) = +2 \qquad W_{12} = 2(2x_2^1 - 1) = -2$$
$$W_{21} = 2(2x_1^2 - 1) = -2 \qquad W_{22} = 2(2x_2^2 - 1) = +2 \qquad V_1 = V_2 = 1$$

Having set the values of our parameters to the above values, one can check directly that the XOR operation is now indeed implemented correctly:

$$\boldsymbol{x} = (0,0): \quad S(\boldsymbol{y}) = \theta(y_1 + y_2 - 1/2) = \theta(0 + 0 - 1/2) = 0$$
$$\boldsymbol{x} = (1,0): \quad S(\boldsymbol{y}) = \theta(y_1 + y_2 - 1/2) = \theta(1 + 0 - 1/2) = 1$$
$$\boldsymbol{x} = (0,1): \quad S(\boldsymbol{y}) = \theta(y_1 + y_2 - 1/2) = \theta(0 + 1 - 1/2) = 1$$
$$\boldsymbol{x} = (1,1): \quad S(\boldsymbol{y}) = \theta(y_1 + y_2 - 1/2) = \theta(0 + 0 - 1/2) = 0$$

We now give the general construction, which works for arbitrary input dimensions N and for arbitrary operations M: $\{0,1\}^N \to \{0,1\}$. We choose L to be the size of the set $\Omega^+ = \{\boldsymbol{x} \in \{0,1\}^N | M(\boldsymbol{x}) = 1\}$, and construct the neurons y_i in the hidden layer such that the operation of each of them is defined as determining whether the input vector $\boldsymbol{x}$ equals a neuron-specific prototype vector from Ω^+. The construction of the associated grandmother neurons follows the above pattern used in dealing with XOR. First we define the building block G:

$$\boldsymbol{x}, \boldsymbol{x}^* \in \{0,1\}^N: \quad G(\boldsymbol{x}^*; \boldsymbol{x}) = \theta\left(\sum_{i=1}^{N}(2x_i - 1)(2x_i^* - 1) - N + 1\right) \qquad (2.1)$$

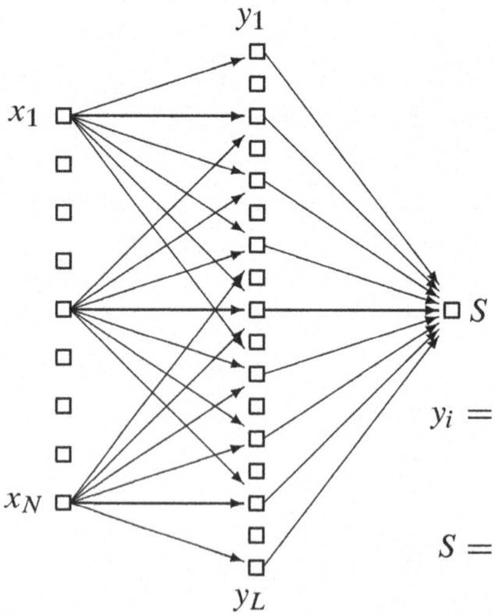

$$y_i = \theta\left(\sum_{j=1}^{N} W_{ij} x_j - V_i\right)$$

$$S = \theta\left(\sum_{i=1}^{L} J_i y_i - U\right)$$

Proposition. $G(\boldsymbol{x}^*;\boldsymbol{x}) = 1$ if and only if $\boldsymbol{x} = \boldsymbol{x}^*$.

Proof. We first turn to the trivial 'if' part of the proof:

$$G(\boldsymbol{x};\boldsymbol{x}) = \theta\left(\sum_{i=1}^{N}(2x_i - 1)^2 - N + 1\right) = \theta\left(\sum_{i=1}^{N} 1 - N + 1\right) = 1$$

Next we show that $G(\boldsymbol{x}^*;\boldsymbol{x}) = 0$ as soon as $\boldsymbol{x} \neq \boldsymbol{x}^*$.

$$\forall x_i, x_i^* \in \{0,1\}: \quad (2x_i - 1)(2x_i^* - 1) = \begin{cases} 1, & \text{if } x_i = x_i^* \\ -1, & \text{if } x_i \neq x_i^* \end{cases}$$

Consequently:

$$\sum_{i=1}^{N}(2x_i - 1)(2x_i^* - 1) = N - 2 \times (\text{number of indices } i \text{ with } x_i \neq x_i^*)$$

so that:

$$\boldsymbol{x} \neq \boldsymbol{x}^* \Rightarrow \sum_{i=1}^{N}(2x_i - 1)(2x_i^* - 1) \leq N - 2 \Rightarrow G(\boldsymbol{x}^*;\boldsymbol{x}) = 0$$

which completes the proof. □

The expression $G(\boldsymbol{x}^*;\boldsymbol{x})$, interpreted as an operation performed on the variable $\boldsymbol{x}$ (for fixed $\boldsymbol{x}^*$), is clearly of the McCulloch–Pitts form:

$$G(\boldsymbol{x}^*;\boldsymbol{x}) = \theta\left(2\sum_{i=1}^{N}(2x_i^* - 1)x_i - 2\sum_{i=1}^{N} x_i^* + 1\right)$$

We can now construct our two-layer network from these building blocks, by assigning to each vector $\boldsymbol{x}^\star \in \Omega^+$ a hidden neuron of the form $G(\boldsymbol{x}^*;\boldsymbol{x})$:

$$\Omega^+ = \{\boldsymbol{x} \in \{0,1\}^N \mid M(\boldsymbol{x}) = 1\} = \{\boldsymbol{x}^1, \boldsymbol{x}^2, \ldots, \boldsymbol{x}^{L-1}, \boldsymbol{x}^L\}$$

$$\forall i \in \{1,\ldots,L\}: \qquad y_i\colon \{0,1\}^N \to \{0,1\} \quad y_i = G(\boldsymbol{x}^i;\boldsymbol{x})$$

The required operation of the output neuron S, finally, is to simply detect whether or not any of the hidden layer neuron states y_i equals one. Our final result is the following network:

$$y_i(\boldsymbol{x}) = \theta\Big(\sum_{j=1}^{N} W_{ij}x_j - V_i\Big) \qquad S(\boldsymbol{y}) = \theta\Big(\sum_{i=1}^{L} y_i - \frac{1}{2}\Big) \tag{2.2}$$

$$W_{ij} = 2(2x_j^i - 1) \qquad V_i = 2\sum_{j=1}^{N} x_j^i - 1 \tag{2.3}$$

This construction will exactly perform the required operation M. The state of each hidden neuron indicates whether ($y_i = 1$) or not ($y_i = 0$) element number i of the set Ω^+ equals the actual input $\boldsymbol{x}$; output neuron S subsequently tells us whether ($S = 1$) or not ($S = 0$) there is a $+1$ state in the hidden layer, that is, whether $\boldsymbol{x}$ is in the set Ω^+. Since the size of Ω^+ can scale exponentially in N, this is usually not an efficient way of realizing an operation M with McCulloch–Pitts neurons, but efficiency was not our aim. At least we know now that a two-layer feed-forward architecture is capable of realizing any operation, if properly constructed. It also proves *en passant* that any mapping M: $\{0,1\}^N \to \{0,1\}^K$ can be performed by a two-layer feed-forward network.

2.3 The perceptron

Here we turn to the question of how to model and understand the process of learning. In the simple context of a McCulloch–Pitts neuron $S(\boldsymbol{x}) = \theta(\boldsymbol{J}\cdot\boldsymbol{x} - U)$ this means the adaptation of the set of connections $\{J_i\}$ and the threshold U, in order to improve the accuracy in the execution of a given task M: $\Omega \subseteq \{0,1\}^N \to \{0,1\}$. We assume that we do not know M explicitly; we only have examples provided by some 'teacher' of 'questions' (input vectors $\boldsymbol{x} \in \{0,1\}^N$) with corresponding 'answers' (the associated output values $M(\boldsymbol{x})$).

The starting point of the training session is a neuron with, say, randomly chosen parameters $\{J_i\}$ and U. A so-called 'online' training session consists of iterating the following procedure:

step 1: Draw at random a question $\boldsymbol{x} \in \Omega$

step 2: Check whether teacher and student agree on the answer:

$M(\boldsymbol{x}) = S(\boldsymbol{x})$: do nothing, return to 1

$M(\boldsymbol{x}) \neq S(\boldsymbol{x})$: modify parameters, then return to 1

modify parameters:

$$\begin{array}{lcl} \boldsymbol{J} & \to & \boldsymbol{J} + \Delta\boldsymbol{J}(\boldsymbol{J}, U; \boldsymbol{x}, M(\boldsymbol{x})) \\ U & \to & U + \Delta U(\boldsymbol{J}, U; \boldsymbol{x}, M(\boldsymbol{x})) \end{array}$$

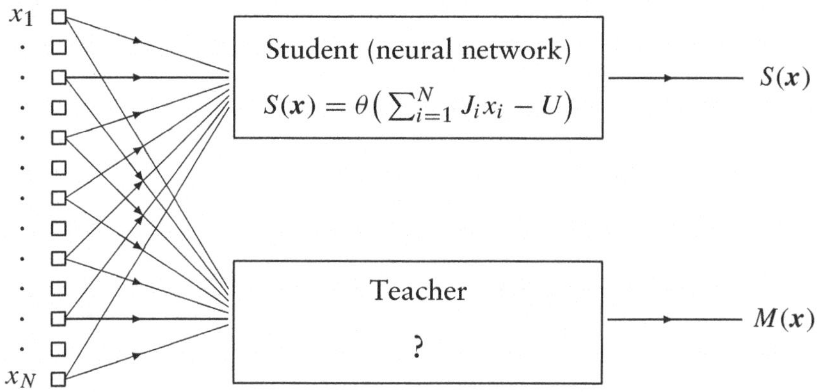

The input vectors $\boldsymbol{x}$ need not all have the same probability of being drawn. The ultimate goal is to end up with a neuron that has learned to perform the task M perfectly, that is, to have $M(\boldsymbol{x}) = S(\boldsymbol{x}) = \theta(\boldsymbol{J} \cdot \boldsymbol{x} - U)\ \forall \boldsymbol{x} \in \Omega$ (which, of course, is only possible if the task M is itself linearly separable). The problem one faces is how to choose an appropriate recipe $(\Delta\boldsymbol{J}, \Delta U)$ for updating the neuron's parameters that will achieve this.

A perceptron is defined as a McCulloch–Pitts neuron, learning in an online fashion, according to the following rule for updating its parameters:

$$\text{perceptron learning rule:} \quad \begin{cases} M(\boldsymbol{x}) = 0, \ \ S(\boldsymbol{x}) = 1: & \Delta\boldsymbol{J} = -\boldsymbol{x}, \ \ \Delta U = 1 \\ M(\boldsymbol{x}) = 1, \ \ S(\boldsymbol{x}) = 0: & \Delta\boldsymbol{J} = \boldsymbol{x}, \ \ \Delta U = -1 \end{cases} \tag{2.4}$$

Upon some reflection, this recipe is rather transparent. If $S(\boldsymbol{x}) = 1$ but should have been 0, the effect of the modification is to *decrease* the local field $h = \boldsymbol{J} \cdot \boldsymbol{x} - U$ so that the next time question $\boldsymbol{x}$ appears the perceptron is more likely to give the (correct) answer $S(\boldsymbol{x}) = 0$. Conversely, if $S(\boldsymbol{x}) = 0$ but should have been 1, the modification causes an *increase* of the local field so that the perceptron is more likely to give the (correct) answer $S(\boldsymbol{x}) = 1$ in the future.

Perceptron convergence theorem

The nice and powerful property of the specific recipe (2.4) is the existence of the following associated perceptron convergence theorem.

Proposition. If the task M is linearly separable, then the above procedure will converge in a finite number of modification steps to a stationary configuration, where $\forall \boldsymbol{x} \in \Omega$: $S(\boldsymbol{x}) = M(\boldsymbol{x})$.

Proof. We first simplify our equations by introducing an additional dummy input variable, which is simply constant: $x_0 = 1$. This allows us, together with the identification $J_0 = -U$, to write the perceptron and its learning rule in the compact form

$$S(\boldsymbol{x}) = \theta(\boldsymbol{J} \cdot \boldsymbol{x}) \qquad \begin{aligned} \boldsymbol{x} &= (x_0, x_1, \ldots, x_N) \in \{0,1\}^{N+1}, \\ \boldsymbol{J} &= (J_0, J_1, \ldots, J_N) \in \mathbb{R}^{N+1} \end{aligned}$$

$$\text{learning rule:} \quad \begin{aligned} M(\boldsymbol{x}) = 0,\ S(\boldsymbol{x}) = 1{:} \quad \Delta \boldsymbol{J} &= -\boldsymbol{x} \\ M(\boldsymbol{x}) = 1,\ S(\boldsymbol{x}) = 0{:} \quad \Delta \boldsymbol{J} &= \boldsymbol{x} \end{aligned} \quad \Leftrightarrow \Delta \boldsymbol{J} = [2M(\boldsymbol{x}) - 1]\boldsymbol{x}$$

The new set Ω now consists of all vectors $(x_0, x_1, \ldots, x_N)$ with $x_0 = 1$ and with $(x_1, \ldots, x_N)$ as in the original input set.

- The first step of the proof is to translate the linear separability of the operation M into the following statement:

$$\exists \boldsymbol{B} \in \mathbb{R}^{N+1} \quad \text{such that } \forall \boldsymbol{x} \in \Omega: \quad M(\boldsymbol{x}) = \theta(\boldsymbol{B} \cdot \boldsymbol{x})$$

and, since the argument of the step function $\theta(\cdots)$ can here never be zero (since we know that $M(\boldsymbol{x}) \in \{0, 1\}$):

$$\exists \delta > 0: \quad \text{such that } \forall \boldsymbol{x} \in \Omega: \quad |\boldsymbol{B} \cdot \boldsymbol{x}| > \delta$$

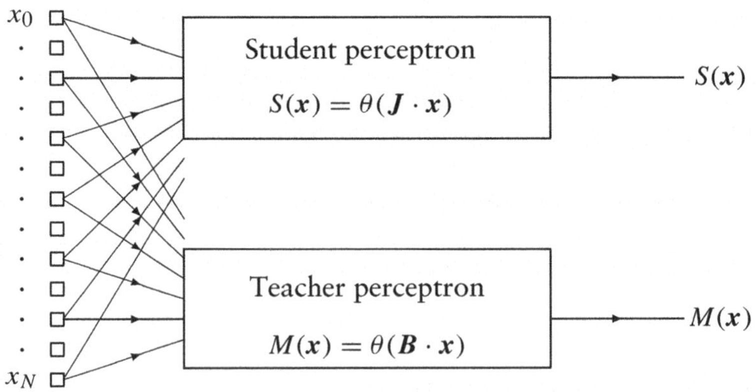

We may consequently view the task operation M as generated by a teacher perceptron, equipped with weights/threshold $\boldsymbol{B}$ (which, of course, the student perceptron does not know). Since $|\boldsymbol{B}|$ can be rescaled arbitrarily without affecting the associated operation M, we may choose $|\boldsymbol{B}| = 1$.

- Any modification step, where $\boldsymbol{J} \to \boldsymbol{J}' = \boldsymbol{J} + \Delta\boldsymbol{J}$, is seen to obey the following two inequalities:

$$\begin{aligned}
\boldsymbol{J}' \cdot \boldsymbol{B} &= \boldsymbol{J} \cdot \boldsymbol{B} + [2M(\boldsymbol{x}) - 1]\boldsymbol{x} \cdot \boldsymbol{B} \\
&= \boldsymbol{J} \cdot \boldsymbol{B} + [2\theta(\boldsymbol{x} \cdot \boldsymbol{B}) - 1]\boldsymbol{x} \cdot \boldsymbol{B} \\
&= \boldsymbol{J} \cdot \boldsymbol{B} + |\boldsymbol{x} \cdot \boldsymbol{B}| \\
&\geq \boldsymbol{J} \cdot \boldsymbol{B} + \delta
\end{aligned} \tag{2.5}$$

and

$$\begin{aligned}
|\boldsymbol{J}'|^2 &= \{\boldsymbol{J} + [2M(\boldsymbol{x}) - 1]\boldsymbol{x}\}^2 \\
&= \boldsymbol{J}^2 + 2\,\text{sgn}(\boldsymbol{B} \cdot \boldsymbol{x})\boldsymbol{J} \cdot \boldsymbol{x} + \boldsymbol{x}^2 \\
&\leq \boldsymbol{J}^2 - 2\,\text{sgn}(\boldsymbol{J} \cdot \boldsymbol{x})\boldsymbol{J} \cdot \boldsymbol{x} + N + 1 \\
&\leq \boldsymbol{J}^2 + N + 1
\end{aligned} \tag{2.6}$$

After n such modification steps, repeated usage of the above inequalities gives:

$$\boldsymbol{J}(n) \cdot \boldsymbol{B} \geq \boldsymbol{J}(0) \cdot \boldsymbol{B} + n\delta \qquad |\boldsymbol{J}(n)|^2 \leq |\boldsymbol{J}(0)|^2 + n(N+1) \tag{2.7}$$

- We now define

$$\omega = \frac{\boldsymbol{J} \cdot \boldsymbol{B}}{|\boldsymbol{J}|}$$

Due to the Schwarz inequality $|\boldsymbol{x} \cdot \boldsymbol{y}| \leq |\boldsymbol{x}||\boldsymbol{y}|$ we know that always $|\omega| \leq |\boldsymbol{B}| = 1$. After n modifications, however, it follows from (2.7) that we must have

$$\omega(n) = \frac{\boldsymbol{J}(n) \cdot \boldsymbol{B}}{|\boldsymbol{J}(n)|} \geq \frac{\boldsymbol{J}(0) \cdot \boldsymbol{B} + n\delta}{\sqrt{|\boldsymbol{J}(0)|^2 + n(N+1)}} \tag{2.8}$$

From this we conclude that there can be only a *finite* number of modification steps n. The algorithm will have to stop at some stage, since otherwise we would run into a conflict with $|\omega(n)| \leq 1$:

$$\lim_{n\to\infty} \omega(n) \geq \lim_{n\to\infty} \frac{\boldsymbol{J}(0) \cdot \boldsymbol{B} + n\delta}{\sqrt{|\boldsymbol{J}(0)|^2 + n(N+1)}} = \infty$$

If no more modifications can take place, the system must by definition be in a configuration where $M(\boldsymbol{x}) = S(\boldsymbol{x})\ \forall \boldsymbol{x} \in \Omega$, which completes the proof. □

The perceptron convergence theorem is a very strong statement, as it depends only on the linear separability of the task M being learned. In particular it does not depend on the probability distribution of the input vectors $\boldsymbol{x}$. An upper bound $n_{\max}$ for the number n of modification steps required for convergence can be obtained by checking at what stage (in the worst case) we actually run into conflict with $|\omega(n)| \leq 1$:

$$\frac{[\boldsymbol{J}(0) \cdot \boldsymbol{B} + n_{\max}\delta]^2}{|\boldsymbol{J}(0)|^2 + n_{\max}(N+1)} = 1$$

For zero initial connections, that is, for $\boldsymbol{J}(0) = (0, \ldots, 0)$, we obtain:

$$n_{\max} = \frac{N+1}{\delta^2}$$

Although this is of limited practical value, as we usually have no information about δ, it is consistent with our geometrical picture of the linearly separable operations: the more complicated the operation M, the closer the separating plane will be to the corners of the hyper-cube, the smaller δ, and therefore the larger the number of adaptation steps that the perceptron needs to obtain perfect performance.

Note that the number n is not the same as the number of times we have to present an example input vector $\boldsymbol{x}$, but rather the number of actual parameter modifications. It could happen that the number of times we need to draw at random a question $\boldsymbol{x}$ is still very large, simply due to the small probability of some particular relevant questions to be selected. Alternatively, we could also draw the example vectors $\boldsymbol{x}$ in a fixed order, since the perceptron convergence theorem does not require them to be drawn at random. In the latter case the number of times we present a question $\boldsymbol{x}$ will also be bounded. However, as we will see later, the number of randomly drawn questions $\boldsymbol{x} \in \{0,1\}^N$ needed to obtain convergence (for a linearly separable task) normally scales linearly with N for large N. It is therefore usually more efficient to draw the examples at random; indeed, making a single full sweep through the set $\{0,1\}^N$ of possible questions involves many more trials, namely 2^N.

Ising perceptrons

The only property of the input vector space $\Omega \subseteq \{0,1\}^N$ that is actually used in proving convergence of the perceptron learning rule is the existence of an upper bound for the norm of $\boldsymbol{x}$:

$$\exists C > 0: \quad \text{such that} \quad \forall \boldsymbol{x} \in \Omega: \quad \boldsymbol{x}^2 \leq C$$

and the constant C will then simply replace the factor $N+1$ in equation (2.7). In particular, we can therefore apply the same procedure to $\boldsymbol{x} \in \Omega \subseteq \{-1, 1\}^N$. If we also transform the perceptron output and the task definition in the familiar way from the $\{0, 1\}$ representation to the so-called 'Ising spin' variables $\{-1, 1\}$, we obtain the Ising perceptron:

$$\begin{array}{ll} \text{task:} & T\colon \Omega \subseteq \{-1, 1\}^N \to \{-1, 1\} \\ \text{Ising perceptron:} & \sigma\colon \Omega \subseteq \{-1, 1\}^N \to \{-1, 1\} \\ & \sigma(\boldsymbol{x}) = \text{sgn}(\boldsymbol{J} \cdot \boldsymbol{x} + \vartheta) \end{array} \tag{2.9}$$

equipped with the following learning rule:

step 1: Draw at random a question $\boldsymbol{x} \in \Omega$

step 2: Check whether teacher and student agree on the answer:

$$\begin{array}{lll} T(\boldsymbol{x}) = \sigma(\boldsymbol{x}): & \text{do nothing} & \text{return to step 1} \\ T(\boldsymbol{x}) \neq \sigma(\boldsymbol{x}): & \Delta \boldsymbol{J} = T(\boldsymbol{x})\boldsymbol{x}, \ \Delta\vartheta = T(\boldsymbol{x}) & \text{then return to step 1} \end{array}$$

Note that this learning procedure, like the original $\{0, 1\}$ version, can be written in an even more compact way, without the explicit check on whether or not perceptron and teacher give the same answer to a given question $\boldsymbol{x}$. With the convention $x_0 = 1 \ \forall \boldsymbol{x} \in \Omega$ and $J_0 = \vartheta$ (as before, the dummy variable x_0 takes care of the threshold) we may simply write:

$$\text{draw at random an} \quad \boldsymbol{x} \in \Omega, \quad \Delta \boldsymbol{J} = \tfrac{1}{2}[T(\boldsymbol{x}) - \text{sgn}(\boldsymbol{J} \cdot \boldsymbol{x})]\boldsymbol{x} \tag{2.10}$$

We can now run through the perceptron convergence proof, much like before. We simply replace $M(\boldsymbol{x}) \to \frac{1}{2}[T(\boldsymbol{x}) + 1]$ and use for the extended input vector $\boldsymbol{x} \in \{-1, 1\}^{N+1}$ the inequality $\boldsymbol{x}^2 \leq N + 1$.

The advantage of the $\{-1, 1\}$ formulation over the previous $\{0, 1\}$ one is a significant simplification of subsequent calculations. For instance, for randomly and uniformly drawn vectors $\boldsymbol{x} = (x_1, \ldots, x_N)$ we find the expectation values:

$$\begin{array}{lll} \boldsymbol{x} \in \{0, 1\}^N: & \langle x_i \rangle = \frac{1}{2} & \langle x_i x_j \rangle = \frac{1}{4} + \frac{1}{4}\delta_{ij} \\ \boldsymbol{x} \in \{-1, 1\}^N: & \langle x_i \rangle = 0 & \langle x_i x_j \rangle = \delta_{ij} \end{array}$$

The continuous time limit

With the familiar convention $x_0 = 1\ \forall \boldsymbol{x} \in \Omega \subseteq \{0,1\}^N$ we can also write the learning rule of the original $\{0,1\}$ representation of the perceptron in the compact form

$$\text{draw at random an} \quad \boldsymbol{x} \in \Omega, \quad \Delta\boldsymbol{J} = \epsilon\boldsymbol{x}[M(\boldsymbol{x}) - \theta(\boldsymbol{J}\cdot\boldsymbol{x})] \tag{2.11}$$

without the need for checking explicitly whether $M(\boldsymbol{x}) = \theta(\boldsymbol{J}\cdot\boldsymbol{x})$. We have now inserted a prefactor ϵ, with $0 < \epsilon \ll 1$, which controls the rate at which the parameters $\boldsymbol{J}$ change. Note that with this modification the perceptron convergence theorem still applies. We will now derive, in a specific limit, a differential equation to describe the evolution in time of the parameters $\boldsymbol{J}$. A more thorough and general analysis will be given in Part IV of this book; here we will restrict ourselves to a reasonably simple derivation. The resulting differential equation is considerably more convenient for describing the learning process than the above original iterative map (2.11).

Let us define a time variable such that each update corresponds to a time interval of length ϵ, so

$$\Delta\boldsymbol{J} = \boldsymbol{J}(t+\epsilon) - \boldsymbol{J}(t)$$

After a modest number $n \ll \epsilon^{-1}$ of iteration steps the vector $\boldsymbol{J}$ will have changed only a little,

$$\boldsymbol{J}(t+n\epsilon) = \boldsymbol{J}(t) + \mathcal{O}(n\epsilon)$$

For intermediate stages $\ell < n$ we may therefore write:

$$\boldsymbol{J}(t+\ell\epsilon+\epsilon) - \boldsymbol{J}(t+\ell\epsilon) = \epsilon\boldsymbol{x}_\ell[M(\boldsymbol{x}_\ell) - \theta(\boldsymbol{J}(t)\cdot\boldsymbol{x}_\ell + \mathcal{O}(n\epsilon))]$$

in which $\boldsymbol{x}_\ell$ denotes the input vector that is drawn from Ω at iteration step ℓ. We now sum the left- and the right-hand side of this equation over the iteration index $\ell = 0, \ldots, n-1$:

$$\sum_{\ell=0}^{n-1}\boldsymbol{J}(t+\ell\epsilon+\epsilon) - \sum_{\ell=0}^{n-1}\boldsymbol{J}(t+\ell\epsilon) = \epsilon\sum_{\ell=0}^{n-1}\boldsymbol{x}_\ell[M(\boldsymbol{x}_\ell) - \theta(\boldsymbol{J}(t)\cdot\boldsymbol{x}_\ell + \mathcal{O}(n\epsilon))]$$

which gives

$$\frac{\boldsymbol{J}(t+n\epsilon) - \boldsymbol{J}(t)}{n\epsilon} = \frac{1}{n}\sum_{\ell=0}^{n-1}\boldsymbol{x}_\ell[M(\boldsymbol{x}_\ell) - \theta(\boldsymbol{J}(t)\cdot\boldsymbol{x}_\ell + \mathcal{O}(n\epsilon))]$$

We now take a limit where $n\epsilon \to 0$ and $n \to \infty$ (e.g. $n = \epsilon^{-\gamma}$ with $0 < \gamma < 1$). As a result, for $\epsilon \to 0$ the left-hand side of the above equation becomes a time derivative, whereas on the right-hand side we obtain an average over the input set Ω:

$$\frac{\mathrm{d}}{\mathrm{d}t}\boldsymbol{J}(t) = \langle \boldsymbol{x}[M(\boldsymbol{x}) - \theta(\boldsymbol{J}(t) \cdot \boldsymbol{x})]\rangle_\Omega \tag{2.12}$$

with $\langle f(\boldsymbol{x})\rangle_\Omega = \sum_{\boldsymbol{x}\in\Omega} p(\boldsymbol{x})f(\boldsymbol{x})$ and with $p(\boldsymbol{x})$ denoting the probability that input vector $\boldsymbol{x}$ is drawn from Ω during the learning process. Equation (2.12) is valid for times measured in units of the learning rate ϵ, in the limit $\epsilon \to 0$.

If we apply this derivation to the Ising perceptron (2.9, 2.10), we find the same continuous time equation for $\boldsymbol{J}(t)$, but now written in the form

$$\frac{\mathrm{d}}{\mathrm{d}t}\boldsymbol{J}(t) = \frac{1}{2}\langle \boldsymbol{x}[T(\boldsymbol{x}) - \mathrm{sgn}(\boldsymbol{J}(t) \cdot \boldsymbol{x})]\rangle_\Omega \tag{2.13}$$

At first sight it might seem that the continuous time process (2.12) is weaker than the discrete time version (2.11), as it is derived in a specific temporal limit and involves only averages over the distribution Ω. Nevertheless we can still prove that, provided the task is linearly separable, the continuous time equation will converge towards the desired state. This can even be shown to happen in a finite time. We restrict ourselves for simplicity to discrete and finite input sets.

Proposition. If the task M is linearly separable over a discrete and finite input set Ω, then equation (2.12) will converge to a fixed point $\boldsymbol{J}$ such that $\theta(\boldsymbol{J} \cdot \boldsymbol{x}) = M(\boldsymbol{x})\ \forall \boldsymbol{x} \in \Omega$.

Proof. First we demonstrate that the dynamical equation (2.12) must lead to a fixed point. Then we show that this fixed point corresponds to a state where the perceptron performs the task M perfectly.

- To see that (2.12) must lead to a fixed point, we first note that the differential equation (2.12) describes a so-called gradient descent dynamics in an 'error-landscape' $E(\boldsymbol{J})$,

$$\frac{\mathrm{d}}{\mathrm{d}t}J_i = -\frac{\partial}{\partial J_i}E(\boldsymbol{J})$$

  with

$$E(\boldsymbol{J}) = \langle (\boldsymbol{J} \cdot \boldsymbol{x})[\theta(\boldsymbol{J} \cdot \boldsymbol{x}) - M(\boldsymbol{x})]\rangle_\Omega \tag{2.14}$$

(which can be verified easily by explicit derivation). As a result we know that during the process (2.12) the quantity E can only decrease:

$$\frac{\mathrm{d}}{\mathrm{d}t}E(\boldsymbol{J}) = \sum_i \frac{\partial E}{\partial J_i}\frac{\mathrm{d}}{\mathrm{d}t}J_i = -\sum_i \left(\frac{\partial E}{\partial J_i}\right)^2 \leq 0$$

- Since M is linearly separable, $\exists \boldsymbol{B}$ (with $|\boldsymbol{B}| = 1$) such that $M(\boldsymbol{x}) = \theta(\boldsymbol{B}\cdot\boldsymbol{x})$ $\forall \boldsymbol{x} \in \Omega$. We can use this property to show (i) that $E(\boldsymbol{J}) \geq 0$ for all $\boldsymbol{J}$ and, for finite Ω, (ii) that there is a positive lower bound for $|\mathrm{d}E(\boldsymbol{J})/\mathrm{d}t|$ as long as $E > 0$. Together these results imply convergence to a fixed point in finite time.
  (i) To see that $E(\boldsymbol{J}) \geq 0$, we use $M(\boldsymbol{x}) = \theta(\boldsymbol{B}\cdot\boldsymbol{x})$, and $\theta(x) = \frac{1}{2}\times[\mathrm{sgn}(x)+1]$ to rewrite equation (2.14) as

$$\begin{aligned} E(\boldsymbol{J}) &= \tfrac{1}{2}\langle(\boldsymbol{J}\cdot\boldsymbol{x})[\mathrm{sgn}(\boldsymbol{J}\cdot\boldsymbol{x}) - \mathrm{sgn}(\boldsymbol{B}\cdot\boldsymbol{x})]\rangle_\Omega \\ &= \tfrac{1}{2}\langle|\boldsymbol{J}\cdot\boldsymbol{x}|[1 - \mathrm{sgn}(\boldsymbol{J}\cdot\boldsymbol{x})\mathrm{sgn}(\boldsymbol{B}\cdot\boldsymbol{x})]\rangle_\Omega \end{aligned}$$

  from which the required result $E(\boldsymbol{J}) \geq 0$ follows immediately.
  (ii) To establish a positive lower bound for $|\mathrm{d}E(\boldsymbol{J})/\mathrm{d}t|$ which holds as long as $E > 0$, we use the Schwarz inequality $\boldsymbol{y}^2 \geq (\boldsymbol{B}\cdot\boldsymbol{y})^2$ (for $|\boldsymbol{B}| = 1$). This gives us the inequality

$$\begin{aligned} \frac{\mathrm{d}}{\mathrm{d}t}E(\boldsymbol{J}) = -\left(\frac{\mathrm{d}}{\mathrm{d}t}\boldsymbol{J}\right)^2 &= -\langle\boldsymbol{x}[\theta(\boldsymbol{B}\cdot\boldsymbol{x}) - \theta(\boldsymbol{J}\cdot\boldsymbol{x})]\rangle_\Omega^2 \\ &\leq -\langle(\boldsymbol{B}\cdot\boldsymbol{x})[\theta(\boldsymbol{B}\cdot\boldsymbol{x}) - \theta(\boldsymbol{J}\cdot\boldsymbol{x})]\rangle_\Omega^2 \\ &= -\langle|\boldsymbol{B}\cdot\boldsymbol{x}|\theta(-(\boldsymbol{J}\cdot\boldsymbol{x})(\boldsymbol{B}\cdot\boldsymbol{x}))\rangle_\Omega^2 \\ &\leq -\big[\min_{\boldsymbol{x}\in\Omega^*(\boldsymbol{J})} p(\boldsymbol{x})|\boldsymbol{B}\cdot\boldsymbol{x}|\big]^2 \end{aligned}$$

  in which $\Omega^*(\boldsymbol{J}) = \{\boldsymbol{x}\in\Omega \mid (\boldsymbol{J}\cdot\boldsymbol{x})(\boldsymbol{B}\cdot\boldsymbol{x}) < 0\}$. This set is not empty if $E > 0$. Using the finiteness of Ω to define the constant[7] $K > 0$ as

$$K = \min_{\boldsymbol{x}\in\Omega} p(\boldsymbol{x})|\boldsymbol{B}\cdot\boldsymbol{x}|$$

  we now immediately arrive at

$$E(\boldsymbol{J}) > 0: \quad \frac{\mathrm{d}}{\mathrm{d}t}E(\boldsymbol{J}) \leq -\big\{\min_{\boldsymbol{x}\in\Omega} p(\boldsymbol{x})|\boldsymbol{B}\cdot\boldsymbol{x}|\big\}^2 = -K^2 \qquad (2.15)$$

- This last inequality (2.15) subsequently implies

$$E(t) = E(\boldsymbol{J}(t)) \leq 0 \quad \text{for } t > E(0)/K^2$$

[7] A similar proof can be set up for the case where the input set is not discrete and finite; there one will need some additional assumptions such as $(\exists\delta > 0)$: $|\boldsymbol{B}\cdot\boldsymbol{x}| > \delta|\boldsymbol{x}|$ for all $\boldsymbol{x}\in\Omega$.

As a consequence we know that $E(t) = 0$ for $t \geq E(0)/K^2$, which, in turn, implies that $\mathrm{d}J_i/\mathrm{d}t = 0\ \forall i$ as soon as $t > E(0)/K^2$. Therefore the vector $\boldsymbol{J}(t)$ evolves in a finite time towards a fixed point.[8]

- Finally we show that any fixed point of (2.12) will have the stated property, $\theta(\boldsymbol{J} \cdot \boldsymbol{x}) = M(\boldsymbol{x})\ \forall \boldsymbol{x} \in \Omega$. A fixed point $\boldsymbol{J}$ satisfies

$$\langle \boldsymbol{x}[\mathrm{sgn}(\boldsymbol{B} \cdot \boldsymbol{x}) - \mathrm{sgn}(\boldsymbol{J} \cdot \boldsymbol{x})]\rangle_\Omega = 0$$

Taking the inner product with the teacher vector $\boldsymbol{B}$ gives:

$$\langle (\boldsymbol{B} \cdot \boldsymbol{x})[\mathrm{sgn}(\boldsymbol{B} \cdot \boldsymbol{x}) - \mathrm{sgn}(\boldsymbol{J} \cdot \boldsymbol{x})]\rangle_\Omega = 0$$
$$\langle |\boldsymbol{B} \cdot \boldsymbol{x}|[1 - \mathrm{sgn}(\boldsymbol{B} \cdot \boldsymbol{x})\mathrm{sgn}(\boldsymbol{J} \cdot \boldsymbol{x})]\rangle_\Omega = 0$$

so, since $|\boldsymbol{B} \cdot \boldsymbol{x}| > 0\ \forall \boldsymbol{x} \in \Omega$:

$$\forall \boldsymbol{x} \in \Omega: \quad \mathrm{sgn}(\boldsymbol{B} \cdot \boldsymbol{x}) = \mathrm{sgn}(\boldsymbol{J} \cdot \boldsymbol{x})$$

which is equivalent to saying that $M(\boldsymbol{x}) = \theta(\boldsymbol{J} \cdot \boldsymbol{x})\ \forall \boldsymbol{x} \in \Omega$. This completes our proof. □

The quantity $E(\boldsymbol{J})$ (2.14) that is minimized by the process (2.12) has a clear interpretation. By using the identity $\frac{1}{2}[1 - \mathrm{sgn}(A)\mathrm{sgn}(B)] = \theta(-AB)$, we can write $E(\boldsymbol{J})$ as

$$E(\boldsymbol{J}) = \langle |\boldsymbol{J} \cdot \boldsymbol{x}|\theta(-(\boldsymbol{J} \cdot \boldsymbol{x})(\boldsymbol{B} \cdot \boldsymbol{x}))\rangle_\Omega \qquad (2.16)$$

This shows that $E(\boldsymbol{J})$ measures the average distance to the separating plane $\boldsymbol{J} \cdot \boldsymbol{x} = 0$ of all those input vectors $\boldsymbol{x} \in \Omega$ that are at the wrong side of this plane. Minimizing E is therefore equivalent to moving the plane in such a way that this average distance goes down. At the minimum of E, the number of vectors at the wrong side of the plane is indeed zero.

Our interpretation of the learning rule as a gradient descent minimization of some error measure (at least in the continuous time limit (2.12)) is an important one. First, it allows us to build systematically other learning rules for our perceptron, by specifying alternative error measures, deriving the corresponding gradient descent equation, and subsequently performing the translation from the continuous time formulation back to the original discrete time version. Second, this interpretation also allows us to derive learning rules for the more complicated layered networks.

[8] A function E of a dynamical variable with these properties, bounded from below and decreasing monotonically with time, is called a Lyapunov function.

2.4 Learning in layered networks: error backpropagation

For feed-forward layered networks, where the state of any neuron cannot feed back to influence its input, the difference between graded response neurons and McCulloch–Pitts neurons is not too large. Just consider two subsequent layers of graded response neurons, $\{U_i\}$ $(i = 1, \ldots, N)$ and $\{U'_j\}$ $(j = 1, \ldots, L)$, respectively. If the states in the first layer $\{U_i\}$ are stationary, the equations for the second layer are solved easily:

$$\tau \frac{\mathrm{d}}{\mathrm{d}t} U'_i(t) = \sum_k J_{ik} g(U_k - U_k^{\star}) - U'_i(t)$$

$$U'_i(t) = U'_i(0)\, e^{-t/\tau} + \sum_k J_{ik} g(U_k - U_k^{\star})(1 - e^{-t/\tau})$$

$$U'_i(\infty) = \sum_k J_{ik} g(U_k - U_k^{\star})$$

Therefore, if we simply wait until all layers have relaxed towards their stationary states $\{U'_i(\infty)\}$, one layer after the other, then for both McCulloch–Pitts neurons and graded response neurons the effective equations can eventually be written in the general form

$$S'_i = g\Big(\sum_k J_{ik} S_k - U_i^{\star}\Big) \tag{2.17}$$

with McCulloch–Pitts neurons corresponding to the special choice $g(x) = \theta(x)$.

Single-output feed-forward two-layer networks

Let us now build a two-layer feed-forward network of such graded response units:

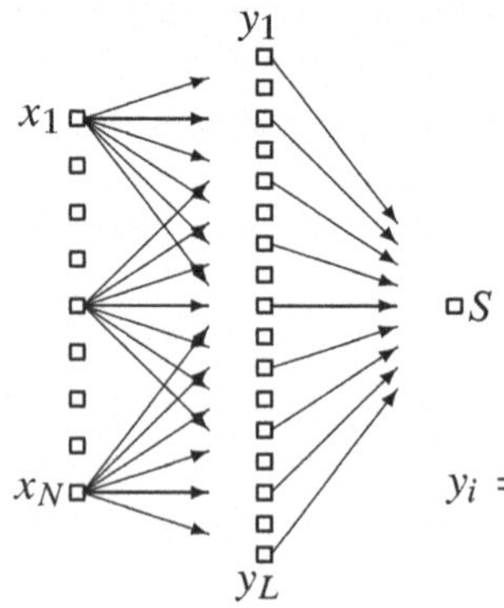

$$y_i = g\Big(\sum_{j=1}^{N} W_{ij} x_j - V_i\Big)$$

$$S = g\Big(\sum_{i=1}^{L} J_i y_i - U\Big)$$

Upon using the by now familiar trick of adding the dummy variables $x_0 = y_0 = 1$ and defining $W_{i0} = -V_i$ and $J_0 = -U$, we can write our equations in their simpler form

$$y_i = g\left(\sum_{j=0}^{N} W_{ij}x_j\right) \qquad S = g\left(\sum_{i=0}^{L} J_i y_i\right) \tag{2.18}$$

or, in combination:

$$S(\boldsymbol{x}) = g\left(J_0 + \sum_{i=1}^{L} J_i\, g\left(\sum_{j=0}^{N} W_{ij}x_j\right)\right) \tag{2.19}$$

The operation M to be learned need no longer be formulated in terms of binary variables since our present graded response neurons produce real-valued outputs, so we write more generally:

$$M: \quad \Omega \subseteq \mathbb{R}^N \to [0,1] \tag{2.20}$$

We note, however, that the universality proof of two-layer feed-forward networks was given only for binary input and output variables.

The aim of a learning procedure is to achieve $S(\boldsymbol{x}) = M(\boldsymbol{x})\ \forall \boldsymbol{x} \in \Omega$. In the spirit of the situation we encountered with the continuous time version of the perceptron learning rule, we now define the dynamics of the weights by gradient descent on an error surface $E(\boldsymbol{B}, \boldsymbol{J})$, for which one usually chooses

$$E(\boldsymbol{B}, \boldsymbol{J}) = \tfrac{1}{2}\langle [S(\boldsymbol{x}) - M(\boldsymbol{x})]^2 \rangle_\Omega \tag{2.21}$$

Clearly E is bounded from below. Supposing that the operation M *can* in principle be realized with the given neurons and network architecture, the minimum is $E = 0$ and corresponds to the desired situation where $S(\boldsymbol{x}) = M(\boldsymbol{x})\ \forall \boldsymbol{x} \in \Omega$. The learning rule thereby becomes:

$$\frac{\mathrm{d}}{\mathrm{d}t}W_{ij} = -\frac{\partial}{\partial W_{ij}}E(\boldsymbol{B}, \boldsymbol{J}) \qquad \frac{\mathrm{d}}{\mathrm{d}t}J_i = -\frac{\partial}{\partial J_i}E(\boldsymbol{B}, \boldsymbol{J}) \tag{2.22}$$

which guarantees, as before, that

$$\frac{\mathrm{d}}{\mathrm{d}t}E = \sum_{ij}\frac{\partial E}{\partial W_{ij}}\frac{\mathrm{d}}{\mathrm{d}t}W_{ij} + \sum_i \frac{\partial E}{\partial J_i}\frac{\mathrm{d}}{\mathrm{d}t}J_i = -\sum_{ij}\left(\frac{\partial E}{\partial W_{ij}}\right)^2 - \sum_i\left(\frac{\partial E}{\partial J_i}\right)^2 \leq 0 \tag{2.23}$$

The overall error E will always go down, however, we have no guarantee that we will end up at the absolute minimum $E = 0$. A simple one-dimensional example will illustrate what could happen:

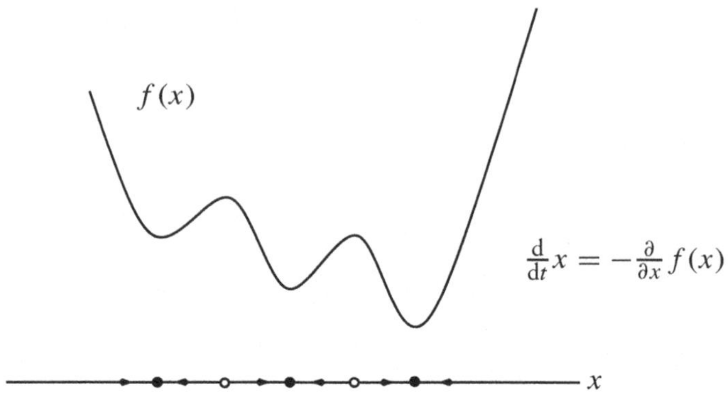

There are three local minima of $f(x)$ (indicated by •), of which one is the global minimum, and two unstable fixed points (indicated by ∘). The dynamic equation $dx/dt = -\partial f(x)/\partial x$ will lead to the desired minimum only for initial values $x(0)$ in a restricted segment of the x-axis. If $x(0)$ happens to be close to one of the other two (local) minima, the system will evolve towards a suboptimal local minimum instead.

We can now simply use the chain rule for differentiation to work out the learning rules (2.22). We introduce the output error $\Delta(\boldsymbol{x}) = M(\boldsymbol{x}) - S(\boldsymbol{x})$ that the network makes upon presentation of input vector $\boldsymbol{x} \in \Omega$, allowing us to write

$$\frac{d}{dt}J_i = \left\langle \Delta(\boldsymbol{x})\frac{\partial S(\boldsymbol{x})}{\partial J_i}\right\rangle_\Omega = \left\langle \Delta(\boldsymbol{x})g'\left(\sum_{j=0}^{L} J_j y_j\right) y_i\right\rangle_\Omega \tag{2.24}$$

$$\begin{aligned}\frac{d}{dt}W_{ij} &= \left\langle \Delta(\boldsymbol{x})\frac{\partial S(\boldsymbol{x})}{\partial W_{ij}}\right\rangle_\Omega \\ &= \left\langle \Delta(\boldsymbol{x})g'\left(\sum_{k=0}^{L} J_k y_k\right) J_i g'\left(\sum_{m=0}^{N} W_{im}x_m\right)x_j\right\rangle_\Omega \end{aligned}\tag{2.25}$$

A convenient choice for the non-linear function $g(x)$ is $g(x) = \frac{1}{2}[1 + \tanh(x)]$, which has the nice property that the derivative of $g(x)$ is a simple function of $g(x)$ itself, $g'(x) = G(g(x)) = 2g(x)[1 - g(x)]$; this property can be exploited to reduce the number of numerical function evaluations in applications of the scheme considerably. In that case the learning rule simplifies to:

$$\frac{\mathrm{d}}{\mathrm{d}t}J_i = \langle \Delta(\boldsymbol{x}) G(S(\boldsymbol{x})) y_i \rangle_\Omega \tag{2.26}$$

$$\frac{\mathrm{d}}{\mathrm{d}t}W_{ij} = \langle \Delta(\boldsymbol{x}) G(S(\boldsymbol{x})) J_i G(y_i(\boldsymbol{x})) x_j \rangle_\Omega \tag{2.27}$$

Returning to the derivation of the continuous time version of the perceptron learning rule, the evolution equations (2.26, 2.27)—usually referred to as batch-learning equations as they involve (averaging over) the complete set Ω of inputs—can be identified as the continuous-time limit of the online learning process:

$$J_i(t+\epsilon) = J_i(t) + \epsilon \Delta(\boldsymbol{x}) G(S(\boldsymbol{x})) y_i \tag{2.28}$$

$$W_{ij}(t+\epsilon) = W_{ij}(t) + \epsilon \Delta(\boldsymbol{x}) G(S(\boldsymbol{x})) J_i G(y_i(\boldsymbol{x})) x_j \tag{2.29}$$

In the online equations (2.28, 2.29), the vectors $\boldsymbol{x} \in \Omega$ are drawn at random at each iteration step. This discrete formulation, with the understanding that $\epsilon \ll 1$, is called 'learning by error backpropagation'. In the limit $\epsilon \to 0$ the online equations become fully equivalent to (2.26, 2.27).

The term error backpropagation stems from the property that, for the online formulation (2.28, 2.29), by performing the chain rule differentiations we are essentially linking all variations in parameters appearing in an earlier layer of neurons to the resulting changes in the error $\Delta(\boldsymbol{x})$ in the final layer. This will become more transparent in a generalization to arbitrary feed-forward architectures to which we turn now.

Generalization to arbitrary feed-forward networks

The above construction can be generalized quite easily to an arbitrary number of output variables and an arbitrary number of hidden layers, as long as the architecture remains of a strictly feed-forward nature. We imagine a structure with N input variables and L output neurons. In between the input and output layers one has m hidden layers, labelled by $\ell = 1, \ldots, m$; each of these contains N_ℓ neurons, the states of which are written as y_i^ℓ ($i = 1, \ldots, N_\ell$). The weight (or synapse) connecting neuron j in layer $\ell - 1$ to neuron i in layer ℓ is denoted by J_{ij}^ℓ. The equations giving the neuron states then become (with the usual convention of the extra dummy neurons to take care of thresholds):

$$M\colon\ \Omega \subseteq \mathbb{R}^N \to [0,1]^L \qquad S\colon\ \Omega \subseteq \mathbb{R}^N \to [0,1]^L \tag{2.30}$$

$$y_i^1 = g\Big(\sum_{j=0}^{N} J_{ij}^1 x_j\Big) \qquad y_i^\ell = g\Big(\sum_{j=0}^{N_{\ell-1}} J_{ij}^\ell y_j^{\ell-1}\Big) \quad (\ell > 1) \tag{2.31}$$

$$S_i = g\left(\sum_{j=0}^{N_m} J_{ij}^{m+1} y_j^m\right) \tag{2.32}$$

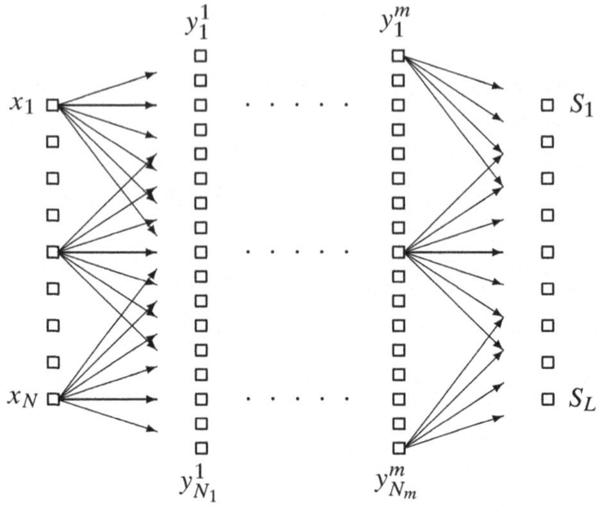

The overall error measure is now defined as the sum of the squared errors of the L individual output neurons:

$$E(\boldsymbol{J}) = \frac{1}{2}\sum_{i=1}^{L}\langle[S_i(\boldsymbol{x}) - M_i(\boldsymbol{x})]^2\rangle_\Omega \tag{2.33}$$

E is bounded from below; its minimum[9] $E = 0$ corresponds to the desired situation where $S_i(\boldsymbol{x}) = M_i(\boldsymbol{x})\ \forall \boldsymbol{x} \in \Omega$ and $\forall i \in \{1, \ldots, L\}$. The gradient descent learning rule generalizes to:

$$\frac{\mathrm{d}}{\mathrm{d}t}J_{ij}^{\ell} = -\frac{\partial}{\partial J_{ij}^{\ell}}E(\boldsymbol{J}) \quad \forall(i, j, \ell) \tag{2.34}$$

which guarantees that

$$\frac{\mathrm{d}}{\mathrm{d}t}E = \sum_{ij}\sum_{\ell}\frac{\partial E}{\partial J_{ij}^{\ell}}\frac{\mathrm{d}}{\mathrm{d}t}J_{ij}^{\ell} = -\sum_{ij}\sum_{\ell}\left(\frac{\partial E}{\partial J_{ij}^{\ell}}\right)^2 \leq 0 \tag{2.35}$$

To work out the learning rules (2.34) we again define output errors $\Delta_i(\boldsymbol{x}) = M_i(\boldsymbol{x}) - S_i(\boldsymbol{x})$; there are now L of these. We also simplify our equations by

[9] We are once more assuming that the task is realizable by the given architecture.

writing $g'(x) = G(g(x))$. This allows us to write for $\ell = m + 1$:

$$\frac{\mathrm{d}}{\mathrm{d}t} J_{ij}^{m+1} = \sum_{k=1}^{L} \left\langle \Delta_k \frac{\partial S_k}{\partial J_{ij}^{m+1}} \right\rangle_{\Omega} = \langle \Delta_i G(S_i) y_j^m \rangle_{\Omega} \tag{2.36}$$

whereas for $1 < \ell \leq m$ one finds

$$\begin{aligned}
\frac{\mathrm{d}}{\mathrm{d}t} J_{ij}^{\ell} &= \sum_{k=1}^{L} \left\langle \frac{\partial S_k}{\partial J_{ij}^{\ell}} \Delta_k \right\rangle_{\Omega} \\
&= \sum_{k=1}^{L} \sum_{i_\ell=0}^{N_\ell} \cdots \sum_{i_m=0}^{N_m} \left\langle \Delta_k \frac{\partial S_k}{\partial y_{i_m}^m} \frac{\partial y_{i_m}^m}{\partial y_{i_{m-1}}^{m-1}} \cdots \frac{\partial y_{i_{\ell+1}}^{\ell+1}}{\partial y_{i_\ell}^{\ell}} \frac{\partial y_{i_\ell}^{\ell}}{\partial J_{ij}^{\ell}} \right\rangle_{\Omega} \\
&= \sum_{k=1}^{L} \sum_{i_{\ell+1}=0}^{N_{\ell+1}} \cdots \sum_{i_m=0}^{N_m} \big\langle \Delta_k G(S_k) J_{k i_m}^{m+1} G(y_{i_m}^m) J_{i_m i_{m-1}}^m \\
&\quad \times \cdots \times G\big(y_{i_{\ell+1}}^{\ell+1}\big) J_{i_{\ell+1} i_\ell}^{\ell+1} G(y_i^\ell) y_j^{\ell-1} \big\rangle_{\Omega}
\end{aligned} \tag{2.37}$$

Finally, for $\ell = 1$ we only have to change the last derivative in the previous line:

$$\begin{aligned}
\frac{\mathrm{d}}{\mathrm{d}t} J_{ij}^{1} &= \sum_{k=1}^{L} \sum_{i_2=0}^{N_2} \cdots \sum_{i_m=0}^{N_m} \big\langle \Delta_k G(S_k) J_{k i_m}^{m+1} G(y_{i_m}^m) J_{i_m i_{m-1}}^m \\
&\quad \times \cdots \times G(y_{i_2}^2) J_{i_2 i_1}^2 G(y_i^1) x_j \big\rangle_{\Omega}
\end{aligned} \tag{2.38}$$

These equations illustrate more clearly than in the two-layer case the interpretation of output-errors propagating backwards through the network to the parameter that is being modified. We can make this interpretation even more explicit by introducing 'scaled' output errors

$$\delta_k^{m+1} = \Delta_k G(S_k) \quad 1 \leq k \leq L$$

Using the last layer of connections in a direction opposite to that of the forward signal propagation as given by (2.31, 2.32), these define scaled back-propagated errors for the last hidden layer via

$$\delta_{i_m}^m = \left(\sum_{k=1}^{L} \delta_k^{m+1} J_{k i_m}^{m+1} \right) G(y_{i_m}^m) \quad 1 \leq i_m \leq N_m$$

This procedure of backpropagating and rescaling errors can be iterated from layer to layer. Thus for $m \geq \ell \geq 1$ backpropagation $\ell + 1 \to \ell$ with rescaling reads

$$\delta_{i_\ell}^\ell = \left(\sum_{i_{\ell+1}=1}^{N_{\ell+1}} \delta_{i_{\ell+1}}^{\ell+1} J_{i_{\ell+1}i_\ell}^{\ell+1} \right) G(y_{i_\ell}^\ell), \quad 1 \leq i_\ell \leq N_\ell$$

In terms of these backpropagated and rescaled errors, the dynamic equations for the connections take a very simple and transparent form, pairing scaled errors at the output side of a connection with signal at the input side, namely

$$\frac{\mathrm{d}}{\mathrm{d}t} J_{ij}^\ell = \langle \delta_i^\ell y_j^{\ell-1} \rangle_\Omega, \; 2 \leq \ell \leq m+1 \quad \text{and} \quad \frac{\mathrm{d}}{\mathrm{d}t} J_{ij}^1 = \langle \delta_i^1 x_j \rangle_\Omega \tag{2.39}$$

The discrete-time online version of the above procedure is obtained in the by now familiar manner. The average over the set Ω is removed and at each iteration step an input vector $\boldsymbol{x} \in \Omega$ is drawn at random instead:

$$J_{ij}^{m+1}(t+\epsilon) = J_{ij}^{m+1}(t) + \epsilon \Delta_i G(S_i) y_j^m \tag{2.40}$$

with for $1 < \ell \leq m$:

$$J_{ij}^\ell(t+\epsilon) = J_{ij}^\ell(t) + \epsilon \sum_{k=1}^{L} \sum_{i_{\ell+1}=0}^{N_{\ell+1}} \cdots \sum_{i_m=0}^{N_m} \Delta_k G(S_k) J_{ki_m}^{m+1} G(y_{i_m}^m) J_{i_m i_{m-1}}^m \\ \times \cdots \times G\big(y_{i_{\ell+1}}^{\ell+1}\big) J_{i_{\ell+1}i_\ell}^{\ell+1} G(y_i^\ell) y_j^{\ell-1} \tag{2.41}$$

and for $\ell = 1$:

$$J_{ij}^1(t+\epsilon) = J_{ij}^1 + \epsilon \sum_{k=1}^{L} \sum_{i_2=0}^{N_2} \cdots \sum_{i_m=0}^{N_m} \Delta_k G(S_k) J_{ki_m}^{m+1} G(y_{i_m}^m) J_{i_m i_{m-1}}^m \\ \times \cdots \times G(y_{i_2}^2) J_{i_2 i_1}^2 G(y_i^1) x_j \tag{2.42}$$

with the discretization step $\epsilon \ll 1$.

2.5 Learning dynamics in small learning rate perceptrons

As a prelude to a more general analysis later in this book, we now show how for large perceptrons with small learning rates (i.e. upon taking the limit $N \to \infty$ after the limit $\epsilon \to 0$) and simple probability distributions for the input vectors $\boldsymbol{x} \in \Omega$, the dynamical equation for the connections $\boldsymbol{J}(t)$ can be reduced to just two coupled non-linear differential equations, which contain all the relevant information on the learning process and on the performance of the perceptron at any time. From these one can calculate the generalization error of our perceptron as a function of time; conversely, given the desired reliability of the system's operation one can then predict the required duration of the learning process.

Macroscopic observables

Our starting point is the Ising perceptron with infinitesimal learning rates, as described by the continuous time equation (2.13), with a linearly separable task $T(\boldsymbol{x}) = \mathrm{sgn}(\boldsymbol{B} \cdot \boldsymbol{x})$. By taking the inner product on both sides with $\boldsymbol{J}$ and $\boldsymbol{B}$ we obtain from (2.13) the following two equations:

$$\frac{\mathrm{d}}{\mathrm{d}t}\boldsymbol{J}^2 = 2\boldsymbol{J} \cdot \frac{\mathrm{d}}{\mathrm{d}t}\boldsymbol{J} \tag{2.43}$$

$$= \langle(\boldsymbol{J} \cdot \boldsymbol{x})[\mathrm{sgn}(\boldsymbol{B} \cdot \boldsymbol{x}) - \mathrm{sgn}(\boldsymbol{J} \cdot \boldsymbol{x})]\rangle_\Omega \tag{2.44}$$

$$\frac{\mathrm{d}}{\mathrm{d}t}(\boldsymbol{B} \cdot \boldsymbol{J}) = \frac{1}{2}\langle(\boldsymbol{B} \cdot \boldsymbol{x})[\mathrm{sgn}(\boldsymbol{B} \cdot \boldsymbol{x}) - \mathrm{sgn}(\boldsymbol{J} \cdot \boldsymbol{x})]\rangle_\Omega \tag{2.45}$$

We now define $\boldsymbol{J} = J\hat{\boldsymbol{J}}$, with $|\hat{\boldsymbol{J}}| = 1$, and $\omega = \boldsymbol{B} \cdot \hat{\boldsymbol{J}}$. Using relations such as $\mathrm{d}(\boldsymbol{B} \cdot \boldsymbol{J})/\mathrm{d}t = J(\mathrm{d}\omega/\mathrm{d}t) + \omega(\mathrm{d}J/\mathrm{d}t)$, one immediately obtains from (2.44, 2.45) the following two equations in terms of the macroscopic observables (J, ω):

$$\frac{\mathrm{d}}{\mathrm{d}t}J = \frac{1}{2}\langle(\hat{\boldsymbol{J}} \cdot \boldsymbol{x})[\mathrm{sgn}(\boldsymbol{B} \cdot \boldsymbol{x}) - \mathrm{sgn}(\hat{\boldsymbol{J}} \cdot \boldsymbol{x})]\rangle_\Omega$$

$$J\frac{\mathrm{d}}{\mathrm{d}t}\omega = \frac{1}{2}\langle[(\boldsymbol{B} \cdot \boldsymbol{x}) - \omega(\hat{\boldsymbol{J}} \cdot \boldsymbol{x})][\mathrm{sgn}(\boldsymbol{B} \cdot \boldsymbol{x}) - \mathrm{sgn}(\hat{\boldsymbol{J}} \cdot \boldsymbol{x})]\rangle_\Omega$$

We note that the statistics of the input vectors $\boldsymbol{x}$ enter into these equations only through the two quantities $u = \boldsymbol{B} \cdot \boldsymbol{x}$ and $v = \hat{\boldsymbol{J}} \cdot \boldsymbol{x}$, so that we can write

$$\frac{\mathrm{d}}{\mathrm{d}t}J = \frac{1}{2}\int \mathrm{d}u\mathrm{d}v\, P(u,v)v[\mathrm{sgn}(u) - \mathrm{sgn}(v)]$$

$$J\frac{\mathrm{d}}{\mathrm{d}t}\omega = \frac{1}{2}\int \mathrm{d}u\mathrm{d}v\, P(u,v)(u - \omega v)[\mathrm{sgn}(u) - \mathrm{sgn}(v)]$$

in which $P(u, v)$ denotes the joint probability distribution of u and v for randomly drawn input vectors $\boldsymbol{x} \in \Omega$ with probabilities $p(\boldsymbol{x})$. This distribution depends on time through the evolving vector $\hat{\boldsymbol{J}}$.

By working out the effect of the sgn() functions for the various integration regimes, the above differential equations can be written in the simple form

$$\frac{d}{dt}J = -\int_0^\infty\int_0^\infty du dv\ v[P(u,-v) + P(-u,v)] \tag{2.46}$$

$$\frac{d}{dt}\omega = \frac{1}{J}\int_0^\infty\int_0^\infty du dv\ (u+\omega v)[P(u,-v) + P(-u,v)] \tag{2.47}$$

Clearly $dJ/dt \leq 0$ and $d\omega/dt \geq 0$ at all times. In order to quantify the degree to which the perceptron has learned the task at hand, and to interpret the dynamic equations (2.46, 2.47), we can define and calculate error measures. The quantity $E(\boldsymbol{J})$ from (2.14), for instance, can be rewritten in terms of the above variables as

$$E = J\int_0^\infty\int_0^\infty du dv\ v[P(u,-v) + P(-u,v)] \tag{2.48}$$

Another relevant quantity is the so-called *generalization error* E_g, defined as the probability of finding an input vector $\boldsymbol{x} \in \Omega$ such that $\text{sgn}(\boldsymbol{B}\cdot\boldsymbol{x}) \neq \text{sgn}(\boldsymbol{J}\cdot\boldsymbol{x})$. Its definition $E_g = \langle\theta(-(\boldsymbol{B}\cdot\boldsymbol{x})(\boldsymbol{J}\cdot\boldsymbol{x}))\rangle_\Omega$ translates immediately into

$$E_g = \int_0^\infty\int_0^\infty du dv\ [P(u,-v) + P(-u,v)] \tag{2.49}$$

The details of the task T, the size N, and the statistics $p(\boldsymbol{x})$ of input vectors are all concentrated in the distribution $P(u,v)$. According to (2.46), the length of the evolving vector $\boldsymbol{J}$ always decreases monotonically. As soon as $J = 0$, we will have to define in the original dynamical rules what we want sgn(0) to be (as also in the original perceptron learning rule); the natural choice is $\text{sgn}(0) = 0$.

Large perceptrons with uniformly distributed input vectors

We now restrict ourselves to large perceptrons (i.e. $N \to \infty$) with uniformly distributed input vectors (i.e. $\Omega = \{-1,1\}^N$ with $p(\boldsymbol{x}) = 2^{-N}\ \forall \boldsymbol{x} \in \Omega$). Here we benefit from the following simplifications: one can calculate $P(u,v)$, the latter turns out to be a rather simple function, and in addition it depends on time only through ω. In combination, this means that the two equations (2.46, 2.47) will close, that is, their right-hand sides can be expressed solely as functions of (ω, J). Instead of N coupled non-linear differential equations (for the N components of the weight vector $\boldsymbol{J}$) we will have reduced the problem of solving the learning dynamics to the analysis of just two coupled non-linear differential equations, which in fact can be reduced further to only one. Not all of the properties assumed here to arrive at this simplification are, strictly speaking, necessary. In fact we only need $N \to \infty$ and $p(\boldsymbol{x}) = \prod_i p_i(x_i)$; here we will only illustrate the ideas for the simplest case.

For $N \to \infty$ and $\Omega = \{-1, 1\}^N$, with $p(\boldsymbol{x}) = 2^{-N}\ \forall \boldsymbol{x} \in \Omega$ (so that all components of $\boldsymbol{x}$ are distributed independently according to $p(x_i) = \frac{1}{2}$ for $x_i = \pm 1$), we may try to apply the central limit theorem (CLT) to the two stochastic quantities $u = \boldsymbol{B} \cdot \boldsymbol{x}$ and $v = \hat{\boldsymbol{J}} \cdot \boldsymbol{x}$, which suggests that they will be described by a Gaussian probability distribution $P(u, v)$. This will usually be true, but not always; one simple counterexample is the case where $\boldsymbol{B}$ or $\hat{\boldsymbol{J}}$ has only a *finite* number of nonzero components. The conditions for an inner product $\boldsymbol{B} \cdot \boldsymbol{x}$ of N-component vectors to acquire a Gaussian probability distribution for $N \to \infty$, given statistically independent random components $x_i \in \{-1, 1\}$ (with equal probabilities), are rather subtle. A sufficient condition is

$$\forall \epsilon > 0: \quad \lim_{N\to\infty} \sum_{i=1}^{N} \theta\left(B_i^2 - \epsilon \sum_{k=1}^{N} B_k^2\right) = 0 \tag{2.50}$$

A necessary condition is

$$\lim_{N\to\infty} \frac{\sum_{i=1}^{N} B_i^4}{\left(\sum_{i=1}^{N} B_i^2\right)^2} = 0 \tag{2.51}$$

For a derivation of these conditions see Appendix B. Both conditions state that for large N the inner product $\boldsymbol{B} \cdot \boldsymbol{x}$ should not be dominated by just a small number of components of $\boldsymbol{B}$.

In the generic case, both conditions (2.50, 2.51) will usually be met, and $P(u, v)$ is indeed a Gaussian distribution. In Appendix D we derive some general results for Gaussian distributions of more than one variable. For the present problem we can calculate directly the first few moments of $P(u, v)$, by noting that $\langle x_i \rangle_\Omega = 0$ and $\langle x_i x_j \rangle_\Omega = \delta_{ij}$:

$$\begin{aligned}
\int \mathrm{d}u\mathrm{d}v\, uP(u, v) &= \langle u \rangle_\Omega = \sum_{i=1}^{N} B_i \langle x_i \rangle_\Omega = 0 \\
\int \mathrm{d}u\mathrm{d}v\, vP(u, v) &= \langle v \rangle_\Omega = \sum_{i=1}^{N} \hat{J}_i \langle x_i \rangle_\Omega = 0 \\
\int \mathrm{d}u\mathrm{d}v\, u^2 P(u, v) &= \langle u^2 \rangle_\Omega = \sum_{ij=1}^{N} B_i B_j \langle x_i x_j \rangle_\Omega = \sum_{i=1}^{N} B_i^2 = 1 \qquad (2.52) \\
\int \mathrm{d}u\mathrm{d}v\, v^2 P(u, v) &= \langle v^2 \rangle_\Omega = \sum_{ij=1}^{N} \hat{J}_i \hat{J}_j \langle x_i x_j \rangle_\Omega = \sum_{i=1}^{N} \hat{J}_i^2 = 1 \\
\int \mathrm{d}u\mathrm{d}v\, uvP(u, v) &= \langle uv \rangle_\Omega = \sum_{ij=1}^{N} B_i \hat{J}_j \langle x_i x_j \rangle_\Omega = \sum_{i=1}^{N} B_i \hat{J}_i = \omega
\end{aligned}$$

Using the results of Appendix D, we know that the values of the moments (2.52) completely determine the distribution $P(u, v)$, so that we may write directly

$$P(u, v) = \frac{\sqrt{\det \boldsymbol{A}}}{2\pi} \exp\left[-\frac{1}{2}\begin{pmatrix} u \\ v \end{pmatrix} \cdot \boldsymbol{A}\begin{pmatrix} u \\ v \end{pmatrix}\right]$$

$$\boldsymbol{A}^{-1} = \begin{pmatrix} \langle u^2 \rangle & \langle uv \rangle \\ \langle uv \rangle & \langle v^2 \rangle \end{pmatrix} = \begin{pmatrix} 1 & \omega \\ \omega & 1 \end{pmatrix}$$

All we need to do is to invert the matrix $\boldsymbol{A}^{-1}$, which gives us the desired result:

$$\boldsymbol{A} = \frac{1}{1-\omega^2}\begin{pmatrix} 1 & -\omega \\ -\omega & 1 \end{pmatrix} \qquad \det \boldsymbol{A} = \frac{1}{1-\omega^2}$$

$$P(u, v) = \frac{1}{2\pi\sqrt{1-\omega^2}}\, e^{-(u^2+v^2-2\omega uv)/2(1-\omega^2)} \tag{2.53}$$

Without even having to calculate any integrals, we can already draw important conclusions on the solution of the differential equations (2.46, 2.47), by simply exploiting that (2.53) remains the same if we change the sign of both u and v or if we interchange u and v. This leads to the identities $P(u, -v) = P(-u, v)$ and

$$\int_0^\infty\!\!\int_0^\infty \mathrm{d}u\mathrm{d}v\; v[P(u, -v) + P(-u, v)] = \int_0^\infty\!\!\int_0^\infty \mathrm{d}u\mathrm{d}v\; u[P(u, -v) + P(-u, v)]$$

In particular, we can simplify (2.46, 2.47) to

$$\frac{\mathrm{d}}{\mathrm{d}t}J = -K(\omega) \qquad \frac{\mathrm{d}}{\mathrm{d}t}\omega = \frac{1+\omega}{J}K(\omega) \tag{2.54}$$

$$K(\omega) = \int_0^\infty\!\!\int_0^\infty \frac{\mathrm{d}u\mathrm{d}v}{\pi\sqrt{1-\omega^2}}\, v\, e^{-(u^2+v^2+2\omega uv)/2(1-\omega^2)} \tag{2.55}$$

Elimination of $K(\omega)$ from the two equations (2.54) gives $(1+\omega)^{-1}(\mathrm{d}\omega/\mathrm{d}t) + J^{-1}(\mathrm{d}J/\mathrm{d}t) = 0$, or

$$\frac{\mathrm{d}}{\mathrm{d}t}[\ln(1+\omega) + \ln(J)] = 0 \;\Rightarrow\; J(t) = \frac{C}{1+\omega(t)} \tag{2.56}$$

in which the constant can be determined by inserting the details of the initial state: $C = J(0)[1+\omega(0)]$. The curves (2.56), for various values of C, are shown in Figure 2.1.

In order to go further, and find the values of the macroscopic observables explicitly as functions of time, we calculate in Appendix D the integral $K(\omega)$

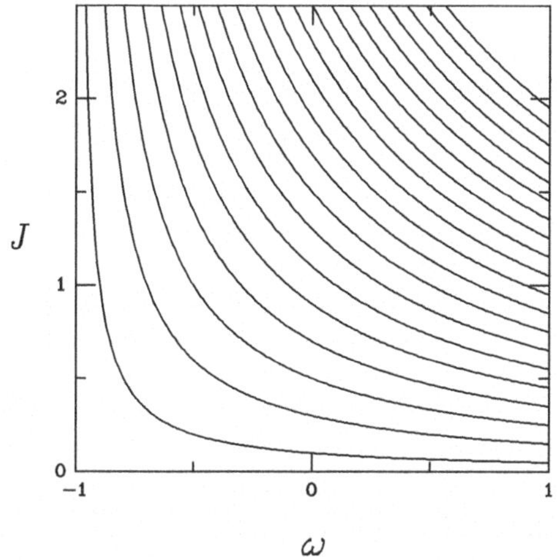

Figure 2.1 The relation between $J(t) = |\boldsymbol{J}|$ and $\omega(t) = \boldsymbol{B} \cdot \hat{\boldsymbol{J}}(t)$ during the training of large perceptrons with infinitesimal learning rates, on linearly separable tasks. Different curves refer to different initial conditions $(\omega(0), J(0))$. The flow through these trajectories is from the left to the right.

defined by (2.55). The result is (see integral I_5 of the appendix) $K(\omega) = (1-\omega)/\sqrt{2\pi}$, with which we obtain for (2.54)

$$\frac{\mathrm{d}}{\mathrm{d}t}J = -\frac{1-\omega}{\sqrt{2\pi}} \qquad \frac{\mathrm{d}}{\mathrm{d}t}\omega = \frac{1-\omega^2}{J\sqrt{2\pi}} \tag{2.57}$$

Finally we can use the relation between J and ω (2.56) to reduce the set (2.57) to just a single equation for $\omega(t)$. We achieve this simplification by simply substituting $J(t) = J(0)[1+\omega(0)]/[1+\omega(t)]$ into the differential equation for $\omega(t)$:

$$\frac{\mathrm{d}}{\mathrm{d}t}\omega = \frac{1}{D}(1+\omega)(1-\omega^2) \qquad D = J(0)[1+\omega(0)]\sqrt{2\pi} \tag{2.58}$$

This equation is solved using separation of variables. We get

$$\begin{aligned}
\frac{\mathrm{d}}{\mathrm{d}\omega}t &= \frac{D}{(1+\omega)(1-\omega^2)} = \frac{D}{2(1+\omega)}\left(\frac{1}{1+\omega} + \frac{1}{1-\omega}\right) \\
&= \frac{1}{2}D\left[\frac{1}{(1+\omega)^2} + \frac{1}{1-\omega^2}\right] \\
&= \frac{1}{4}D\left[\frac{2}{(1+\omega)^2} + \frac{1}{1+\omega} + \frac{1}{1-\omega}\right] \\
&= \frac{1}{4}D\frac{\mathrm{d}}{\mathrm{d}\omega}\left[-\frac{2}{1+\omega} + \ln(1+\omega) - \ln(1-\omega)\right]
\end{aligned} \tag{2.59}$$

so that

$$t = J(0)[1+\omega(0)]\sqrt{\frac{\pi}{2}}\left[\frac{1}{2}\ln\left(\frac{1+\omega}{1-\omega}\right) - \frac{1}{1+\omega} + A\right] \tag{2.60}$$

with the constant A determined by initial conditions:

$$A = \frac{1}{1+\omega(0)} - \frac{1}{2}\ln\left[\frac{1+\omega(0)}{1-\omega(0)}\right] \tag{2.61}$$

In particular, for the simple and common case where the initial student vector $\boldsymbol{J}(0)$ is drawn at random, we typically have $\omega(0) = 0$. In that case, the solution (2.60) takes a simple form:

$$\omega(0) = 0: \quad t = J(0)\sqrt{\frac{\pi}{2}}\left[\frac{1}{2}\ln\left(\frac{1+\omega}{1-\omega}\right) + \frac{\omega}{1+\omega}\right] \tag{2.62}$$

For large perceptrons, that is, for $N \to \infty$ as in the above analysis of the closed dynamical equations for ω and J, we can also work out the precise relation (2.49) between ω and the generalization error E_g (2.49) (see integral I_3 in Appendix D), which gives us

$$E_g = \frac{1}{\pi}\arccos(\omega) \qquad \omega = \cos(\pi E_g) \tag{2.63}$$

This one-to-one relation enables us to write the equations for ω (2.58, 2.60) in terms of E_g. For instance, by using standard relations like $\cos(2\alpha) = \cos^2(\alpha) - \sin^2(\alpha)$, we can transform the result (2.62) for initial conditions characterized by $\omega(0) = 0$ (so $E_g(0) = \frac{1}{2}$) into

$$t = \frac{1}{2}\sqrt{\frac{\pi}{2}}J(0)\left[1 - \tan^2\left(\frac{1}{2}\pi E_g\right) - 2\ln\tan\left(\frac{1}{2}\pi Eg\right)\right] \tag{2.64}$$

This relation is drawn in Figure 2.2, for different values of $J(0)$.

2.6 Numerical simulations

We end this chapter with some numerical simulations of the learning procedures and network architectures discussed so far. We will illustrate some general trends and, where possible, make comparisons with our theoretical results.

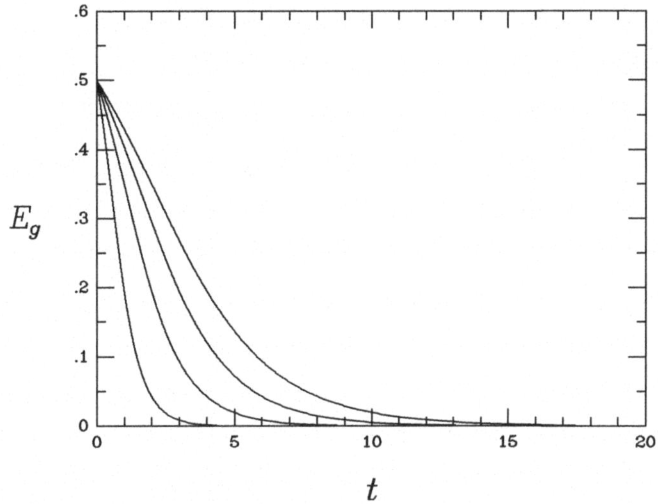

Figure 2.2 The generalization error E_g as a function of time, following a random initial weight configuration, that is, $E_g(0) = \frac{1}{2}$. The different curves refer to $J(0) = 2, \frac{3}{2}, 1, \frac{1}{2}$ (from top to bottom).

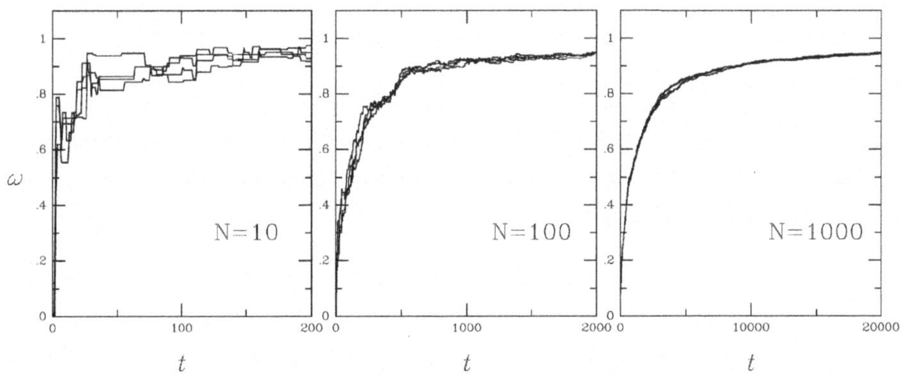

Figure 2.3 Evolution in time of the macroscopic observable $\omega = \boldsymbol{B} \cdot \hat{\boldsymbol{J}}$ for numerical simulations of the standard discrete-time perceptron learning rule, for different system sizes N, always with a randomly drawn but normalized task vector $\boldsymbol{B}$ and learning rate $\epsilon = 1$. For each picture, $\boldsymbol{J}$ was initialized randomly, with four different lengths $J(0) \in \{2, \frac{3}{2}, 1, \frac{1}{2}\}$.

Numerical simulations of perceptrons

We first simulate numerically the original discrete perceptron learning procedure (2.4), for different choices of the input space dimension N and of the initial length $J(0) = |\boldsymbol{J}(0)|$ of the student vector. For simplicity we choose $\Omega = \{-1, 1\}^N$, $p(\boldsymbol{x}) = 2^{-N}\ \forall \boldsymbol{x} \in \Omega$, and a randomly drawn (but normalized) teacher vector $\boldsymbol{B}$. We measure the observable $\omega = \boldsymbol{B} \cdot \hat{\boldsymbol{J}}$, where $\hat{\boldsymbol{J}} = \boldsymbol{J}/|\boldsymbol{J}|$. The results are shown in Figure 2.3. Several conclusions can be drawn from such experiments, while keeping in mind that for specifically constructed pathological teacher vectors the picture might be different:

- The duration of the learning process scales *linearly* with N.
- If viewed on the relevant N-dependent timescale (as in the figure), the fluctuations in ω as caused by the randomness in the selection of input vectors $\boldsymbol{x}$ become negligible as $N \to \infty$; this is the main property that enabled the derivation of the deterministic continuous time equation.
- In contrast to the situation with small learning rates, for $\epsilon = 1$ all differences in the initial length $J(0)$ which are $\mathcal{O}(1)$ are irrelevant. The reason is clear: they can be wiped out in just a few iteration steps.

Next we show that for $N \to \infty$ and $\epsilon \to 0$ the learning dynamics is indeed described by equation (2.60). We have to keep in mind that in the derivation we have taken the two limits in a specific order: $\lim_{\epsilon \to 0}$ first, followed by $\lim_{N \to \infty}$. The required ϵ needed to find oneself in the scaling regime described by the earlier dynamical analysis may therefore generally depend on N: $\epsilon = \epsilon(N)$. Since ϵ defines the unit of time in the process $\boldsymbol{J}(t + \epsilon) = \boldsymbol{J}(t) + \epsilon \Delta \boldsymbol{J}(\ldots)$, and since the learning time is found to scale linearly with N, we are led to the scaling relation

$$\epsilon(N) = \eta/N \qquad \eta \ll 1 \tag{2.65}$$

According to the simulation experiments for small ϵ, as shown in Figures 2.4 and 2.5, this is indeed the appropriate scaling of the learning rate. Note that the time can now no longer be identified with the number of iteration steps (as in the $\epsilon = 1$ case); for $\epsilon < 1$ the relation is $t = n_{\text{steps}}\epsilon$. Equivalently,

$$n_{\text{steps}} = Nt/\eta$$

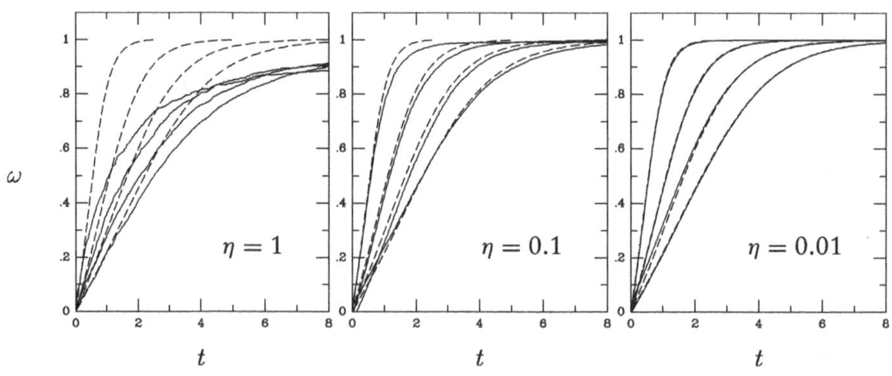

Figure 2.4 Evolution of ω in an Ising perceptron (with $N = 1000$ and a randomly drawn but normalized task vector $\boldsymbol{B}$), for $\eta = \epsilon N \in \{1, 0.1, 0.01\}$, following random initialization. Solid lines correspond to numerical simulations, and dashed lines to the theory, with $J(0) \in \{2, \frac{3}{2}, 1, \frac{1}{2}\}$, from top to bottom.

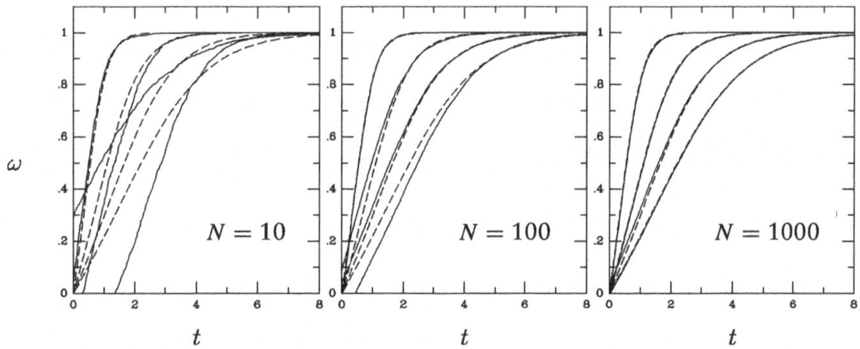

Figure 2.5 Evolution of ω in an Ising perceptron (with $\eta = \epsilon N = 0.01$ and a randomly drawn but normalized task vector $\boldsymbol{B}$), for $N \in \{10, 100, 1000\}$, following random initialization. Solid lines correspond to numerical simulations, and dashed lines to the theory, with $J(0) \in \{2, \frac{3}{2}, 1, \frac{1}{2}\}$, from top to bottom.

Note also that the figures illustrate the different roles played by the two limits $N \to \infty$ and $\eta \to 0$. Decreasing η moves the experimental curves towards the theoretical ones; increasing N reduces the fluctuations (mainly triggered by initial conditions).

Numerical simulations of error backpropagation

In the case of multilayer networks, trained with the online version of error backpropagation (i.e. the version where at each iteration step an input vector is drawn at random), there is as yet little theory to compare with. The exception are results on the so-called 'committee machines'; these are two-layer networks in which only the weights feeding into the hidden layer evolve in time. Therefore we will just show how the learning procedure works out in practice, by measuring as a function of time, for a network with two layers and a single output neuron, the output error $E = \frac{1}{2}\langle [S(\boldsymbol{x}) - M(\boldsymbol{x})]^2 \rangle_\Omega$. We consider two simple tasks, the parity operation (in ± 1 representation) and a linearly separable operation (with a randomly drawn teacher vector):

$$\boldsymbol{x} \in \Omega = \{-1, 1\}^N \qquad \begin{array}{ll} \text{task I:} & M(\boldsymbol{x}) = \prod_{i=1}^{N} x_i \in \{-1, 1\} \\ \text{task II:} & M(\boldsymbol{x}) = \text{sgn}(\boldsymbol{B} \cdot \boldsymbol{x}) \in \{-1, 1\} \end{array} \tag{2.66}$$

to be learned by the two-layer network

$$S(\boldsymbol{x}) = g\left(\sum_{i=0}^{L} J_i y_i(\boldsymbol{x})\right) \qquad y_i(\boldsymbol{x}) = g\left(\sum_{j=0}^{N} W_{ij} x_j\right) \tag{2.67}$$

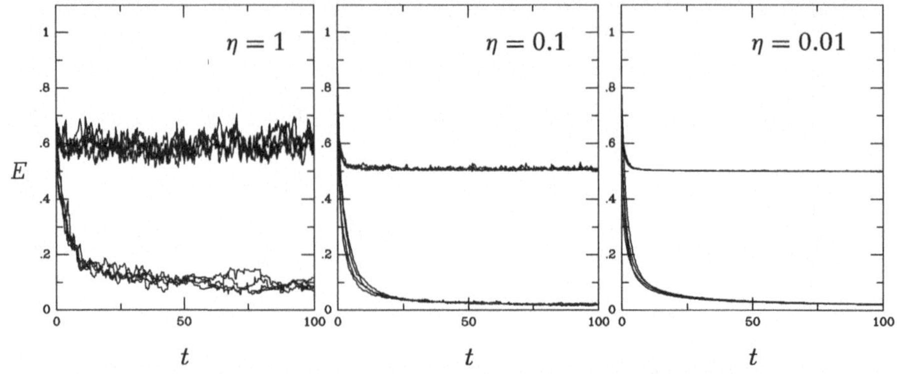

Figure 2.6 Evolution of the overall error E in a two-layer feed-forward network trained by error backpropagation, with $N = 15$ input neurons, $L = 10$ hidden neurons, and a single output neuron. The results refer to independent experiments involving either a linearly separable task (with random teacher vector, lower curves) or the parity operation (upper curves), with learning rates $\eta = \epsilon N \in \{1,\ 0.1,\ 0.01\}$, following random initialization.

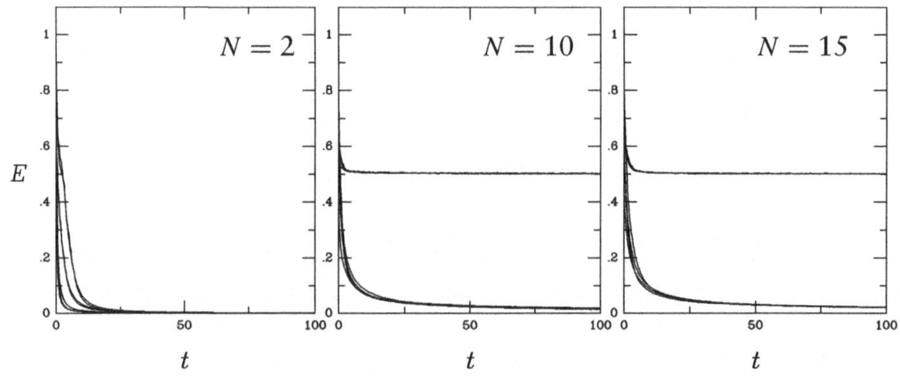

Figure 2.7 Evolution of the overall error E in a two-layer feed-forward network trained by error backpropagation, with $\eta = \epsilon N = 0.01$, $L = 10$ hidden neurons, and a single output neuron. The results refer to independent experiments involving either a linearly separable task (with random teacher vector, lower curves) or the parity operation (upper curves), with input size $N \in \{2,\ 10,\ 15\}$, following random initialization.

in which the transfer function is chosen to be $g(x) = \tanh(x) \in (-1, 1)$ and we use the usual dummy variables $x_0 = y_0 = 1$. Perfect performance would obviously correspond to $E = 0$. On the other hand, for a task $M(\boldsymbol{x}) \in \{-1, 1\}$ a trivial multilayer perceptron with all parameters (weights and thresholds) set to zero would produce $E = \frac{1}{2}\langle M^2(\boldsymbol{x})\rangle_\Omega = \frac{1}{2}$.

The results of numerical simulations are shown in Figures 2.6, 2.7, and 2.8; we performed four independent trials for each parameter combination and each task. For the online version of error backpropagation to approach the desired learning equations involving *averages* over the input set (the batch version, corresponding to gradient descent on the error surface), we again have to take the limit $\epsilon \to 0$ for every (N, L) combination,

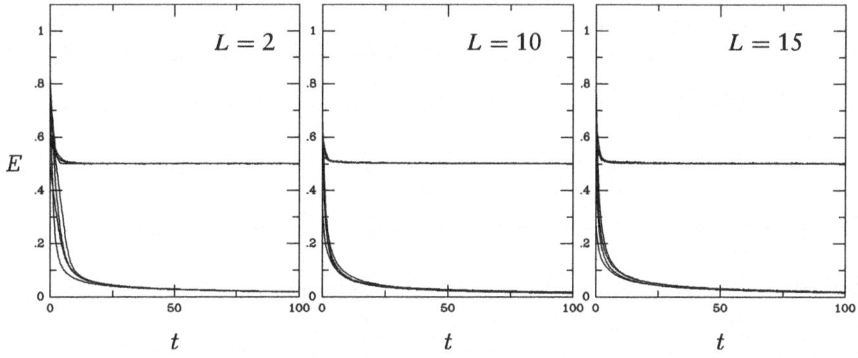

Figure 2.8 Evolution of the overall error E in a two-layer feed-forward network trained by error backpropagation, with $\eta = \epsilon N = 0.01$, $N = 10$ inputs, and a single output neuron. The results refer to independent experiments involving either a linearly separable task (with random teacher vector, lower curves) or the parity operation (upper curves), with hidden layer size $L \in \{2, 10, 15\}$, following random initialization.

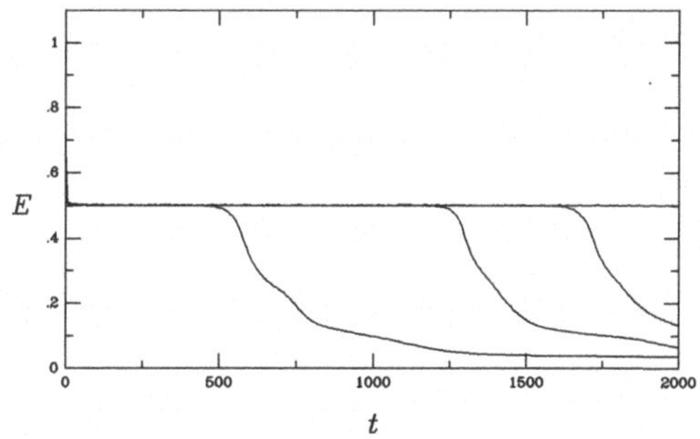

Figure 2.9 Evolution of the overall error E in a two-layer feed-forward network, trained by error backpropagation on the parity operation (with $\eta = \epsilon N = 0.01$, $N = 10$ inputs, $L = 10$ hidden neurons, and a single output neuron), following random initialization.

so we should expect $\epsilon = \epsilon(N, L)$. The simulation results indicate the appropriate scaling to be

$$\epsilon(N, L) = \eta/N \qquad \eta \ll 1 \tag{2.68}$$

We have to be careful, however, in drawing conclusions about whether the network succeeds in solving the problem from simulations experiments such as the ones in Figures 2.6, 2.7, and 2.8. A learning session can involve several distinct stages and timescales, possibly dependent on initial conditions.

For instance, the experiments done in the time window $0 < t < 100$ suggest that the network does not succeed in performing the parity operation for $(N, L) \in \{(10, 10), (10, 15)\}$, whereas we know it is perfectly capable of doing so for $L \geq N$. However, if we enlarge the time window of our experiments we do find a certain fraction of our trials being successful after all, if we are prepared to wait longer, as illustrated by Figure 2.9. The system is seen to spend a significant amount of time in a transient so-called 'plateau' phase, where the error E does not change much, before it discovers the rule underlying the training examples.

2.7 Exercises

Exercise 2.1. (Elementary logical operations and model neurons.) Consider the task $f\colon \{0,1\}^3 \to \{0,1\}$ that is defined by

$$f(x_1,x_2,x_3) = \begin{cases} 1, & \text{if } (x_1,x_2,x_3) = (1,0,1) \\ 1, & \text{if } (x_1,x_2,x_3) = (1,1,1) \\ 0, & \text{otherwise} \end{cases}$$

Show, via geometrical considerations or otherwise, that the function f can be realized by a single McCulloch–Pitts neuron. Give suitable values for synaptic weights and the threshold. If we take into account higher order synapses, the operation of a McCulloch–Pitts neuron is known to become somewhat more sophisticated:

$$S(\boldsymbol{x}) = \theta\Big(\sum_k J_k x_k + \sum_{k,\ell} \hat{J}_{k\ell} x_k x_\ell - U\Big)$$

Can we perform the so-called XOR operation, that is, $(x_1,x_2) \to \text{XOR}(x_1,x_2)$ with $(x_1,x_2) \in \{0,1\}^2$, which a McCulloch–Pitts neuron cannot realize, with a single neuron like this?

Exercise 2.2. (The parity operation.) Define the so-called parity operation

$$M\colon \{0,1\}^N \to \{0,1\} \qquad M(\boldsymbol{x}) = \tfrac{1}{2}[1 + (-1)^{\sum_{i=1}^N x_i}]$$

The function M indicates whether ($M = 1$) or not ($M = 0$) the number of '+1' components of the input vector $\boldsymbol{x}$ is even. Show that for $N = 2$ one has $M(x_1,x_2) = \neg\text{XOR}(x_1,x_2)$. Prove that for $N \geq 2$ the parity operation cannot be performed by a single McCulloch–Pitts neuron of the standard form

$$S(\boldsymbol{x}) = \theta\Big(\sum_{i=1}^N J_i x_i - U\Big)$$

Exercise 2.3. (Symmetries.) We know that a two-layer feed-forward network of McCulloch–Pitts neurons, with $L = |\Omega^+| \leq 2^N$ neurons in the hidden layer can perform any operation M: $\{0,1\}^N \to \{0,1\}$, provided all connections and thresholds are properly chosen. Here $|\Omega^+|$ denotes the number of input vectors in the set Ω^+. However, in the case where there are symmetries in the task M, the number L of required hidden neurons can be considerably smaller. An example of such an operation is the parity operation (see above). Here M is invariant under all permutations of the indices $\{1,\ldots,N\}$ of the input vector $\boldsymbol{x}$. We take $N = 2$. Now $\Omega^+ = \{(0,0),(1,1)\}$, so the upper bound for L is 2. Construct a two-layer feed-forward network of McCulloch–Pitts neurons with $L = 2$ that performs the parity operation, not as a realization of a look-up table, but by using the fact that, due to the permutation symmetry, $M(\boldsymbol{x})$ can be written as a function only of $x_1 + x_2$. Hints: write $y_i(\boldsymbol{x}) = \theta(x_1 + x_2 - U_i)$, and use a graphical representation of what the output neuron $S(y_1, y_2)$ is required to do in order to find an appropriate separating plane.

Next choose $N = 3$. Since here $\Omega^+ = \{(0,0,0),(0,1,1),(1,0,1),(1,1,0)\}$, the upper bound for L is 4. Construct a two-layer feed-forward network of McCulloch–Pitts neurons with $L = 3$ that performs the parity operation. Give the network construction for general $N \geq 2$ (without proof), by generalizing the previous results obtained for $N \in \{2,3\}$. Show that we need only N hidden neurons. More demanding: give the proof, for general N, that the above construction indeed performs the task M.

Exercise 2.4. (Learning the unlearnable.) We now study what happens when a perceptron is being trained on a task that is not linearly separable, such as $\text{XOR}(x_1, x_2)$. In ± 1 (i.e. Ising) representation, and with the convention of $x_0 = 1$ as the dummy input, the task T and the Ising perceptron σ are defined as

$$T\colon \{-1,1\}^3 \to \{-1,1\} \qquad T(x_0,x_1,x_2) = -x_1 x_2$$

$$\sigma\colon \{-1,1\}^3 \to \{-1,1\} \qquad \sigma(x_0,x_1,x_2) = \text{sgn}(\boldsymbol{J}\cdot\boldsymbol{x}) \quad \boldsymbol{J} = (J_0,J_1,J_2)$$

with $\Omega = \{\boldsymbol{x} \in \{-1,1\}^3 \mid x_0 = 1\}$ and $p(\boldsymbol{x}) = \frac{1}{4}\ \forall \boldsymbol{x} \in \Omega$ (note: there are four input vectors in Ω). In the limit of small learning rate $\epsilon \to 0$ the learning process is described by equation (2.13):

$$\frac{\mathrm{d}}{\mathrm{d}t}\boldsymbol{J} = \frac{1}{2}\langle \boldsymbol{x}[T(\boldsymbol{x}) - \text{sgn}(\boldsymbol{J}\cdot\boldsymbol{x})]\rangle_\Omega$$

Calculate $\langle \boldsymbol{x}T(\boldsymbol{x})\rangle_\Omega$. Prove that $|\boldsymbol{J}|$ decreases monotonically with time. Show that the dynamic equation (2.13) describes a gradient descent on a surface $E(\boldsymbol{J})$. What is the meaning of $E(\boldsymbol{J})$? Prove that $\lim_{t\to\infty} |\boldsymbol{J}(t)| = 0$.

Exercise 2.5. (Application of the CLT to $\boldsymbol{B}\cdot\boldsymbol{x}$.) Appendix B gives a discussion of the conditions required for the CLT to apply to the inner product

$u = \boldsymbol{B} \cdot \boldsymbol{x}$, with $\boldsymbol{x} \in \{-1, 1\}^N$ and $p(\boldsymbol{x}) = 2^{-N}\ \forall \boldsymbol{x} \in \{-1, 1\}^N$. A sufficient (although not necessary) condition for u to acquire a Gaussian probability distribution in the limit $N \to \infty$ is Lindeberg's Condition:

$$\forall \epsilon > 0: \quad \lim_{N\to\infty} \sum_{i=1}^{N} \theta\left(B_i^2 - \epsilon \sum_{k=1}^{N} B_k^2\right) = 0$$

A necessary (although not sufficient) condition for u to acquire a Gaussian probability distribution in the limit $N \to \infty$ is

$$\lim_{N\to\infty} \frac{\sum_{i=1}^{N} B_i^4}{(\sum_{i=1}^{N} B_i^2)^2} = 0$$

Here we inspect trivial and non-trivial teacher vectors $\boldsymbol{B} = (B_1, \ldots, B_N)$ for which the CLT does not apply. Show that both conditions above are violated if $B_1 = 1$ and $B_i = 0\ \forall i > 1$. Answer the same question for $B_i = 1$ for $i \leq n$ and $B_i = 0\ \forall i > n$, for every fixed $n \geq 1$ (i.e. n not dependent on N). Similarly for the two cases $B_k = e^{-k}$ and $B_k = 1/k$. Show that both conditions above are satisfied for $B_k = 1/\sqrt{k}$. Use the results on summations given in Appendix C.

Exercise 2.6. (Forgetful perceptrons.) Consider next an Ising perceptron σ with N ordinary input variables in ± 1 representation and with the convention of the dummy input $x_0 = 1$, so $\boldsymbol{J} = (J_0, \ldots, J_N) \in \mathbb{R}^{N+1}$, learning a task T:

$$T: \{-1, 1\}^{N+1} \to \{-1, 1\}$$

$$\sigma: \{-1, 1\}^{N+1} \to \{-1, 1\} \qquad \sigma(x_0, \ldots, x_N) = \text{sgn}(\boldsymbol{J} \cdot \boldsymbol{x})$$

Assume $\Omega = \{\boldsymbol{x} \in \{-1, 1\}^{N+1} |\ x_0 = 1\}$ and $p(\boldsymbol{x}) = 2^{-N}\ \forall \boldsymbol{x} \in \Omega$ (so there are 2^N input vectors in Ω). In the original perceptron learning rule we now add a decay term, which tends to erase previously accumulated information:

$$\Delta \boldsymbol{J} = \tfrac{1}{2}\boldsymbol{x}[T(\boldsymbol{x}) - \text{sgn}(\boldsymbol{J} \cdot \boldsymbol{x})] - \gamma \boldsymbol{J}$$

Introduce a time discretization ϵ in the usual way: $\boldsymbol{J}(t + \epsilon) = \boldsymbol{J}(t) + \epsilon \Delta \boldsymbol{J}$. Derive the new continuous-time equation to replace (2.13), by taking the limit $\epsilon \to 0$. Show that this equation describes gradient descent on a surface $E(\boldsymbol{J})$, and prove that $E(\boldsymbol{J})$ is bounded from below. Assume that T is linearly separable, that is, $T(\boldsymbol{x}) = \text{sgn}(\boldsymbol{B} \cdot \boldsymbol{x})\ \forall \boldsymbol{x} \in \Omega$. Show that $\lim_{t\to\infty} \boldsymbol{B} \cdot \boldsymbol{J}(t) \geq 0$. From now on consider only tasks and perceptrons without thresholds, that is, $B_0 = J_0 = 0$, and choose $|\boldsymbol{B}| = 1$. Define, following Section 2.5, the two quantities $J = |\boldsymbol{J}|$ and $\omega = \hat{\boldsymbol{J}} \cdot \boldsymbol{B}$, with $\boldsymbol{J} = J\hat{\boldsymbol{J}}$. Derive the differential equations that replace (2.46) and (2.47). Show that (2.47) is not affected by the decay term. Assume that the two inner products $u = \boldsymbol{B} \cdot \boldsymbol{x}$ and $v = \hat{\boldsymbol{J}} \cdot \boldsymbol{x}$ have a Gaussian joint probability distribution, and find the equations that replace (2.54) and (2.55). Show that (2.56) is replaced by $e^{\gamma t} J(t)[1 + \omega(t)] = J(0)[1 + \omega(0)]$. Show that the evolution in time of the macroscopic observable ω, following $\omega(0) = 0$, is now given by

$$\frac{1}{\gamma}(e^{\gamma t} - 1) = J(0)\sqrt{\frac{\pi}{2}}\left[\frac{1}{2}\ln\left(\frac{1+\omega}{1-\omega}\right) + \frac{\omega}{1+\omega}\right]$$

Use the expansion $e^x = 1 + x + \mathcal{O}(x^2)$ to show how for times $t \ll 1/\gamma$ one recovers the old result (2.62). Show that for any $\gamma > 0$: $\lim_{t\to\infty} \omega(t) = 1$ and $\lim_{t\to\infty} J(t) = 0$. Which are the advantages and disadvantages of forgetting by weight decay?

3 Recurrent networks with binary neurons

We now turn to recurrent networks of binary (Ising) neurons $\sigma_i \in \{-1, 1\}$, with fixed synaptic interactions $\{J_{ij}\}$ and fixed thresholds $\{\vartheta_i\}$. We still have explicit (stochastic) rules (1.29) that determine the evolution in time of our system, namely

$$\sigma_i(t+\Delta) = \text{sgn}(h_i(t) + Tz_i(t)) \qquad h_i(t) = \sum_{k=1}^{N} J_{ik}\sigma_k(t) + \vartheta_i \tag{3.1}$$

with the independent random noise variables $z_i(t)$, but in contrast to the situation with layered networks, we can no longer write down explicitly the future states of our neurons in terms of given input signals, due to the feedback present. Recurrent systems operate and are used in a manner fundamentally different from layered ones. We really have to solve the dynamics. Written in terms of probabilities, with $P(z)$ denoting the distribution of the noise variables, our dynamical rules become

$$\text{Prob}[\sigma_i(t+\Delta)] = g(\sigma_i(t+\Delta)h_i(t)/T) \qquad g(x) = \int_{-\infty}^{x} dz\, P(z) \tag{3.2}$$

Here we have assumed that the noise distribution is symmetric, that is, $P(z) = P(-z)$; see (1.30). For recurrent systems we also have to specify in which order the neurons states are updated; for layered networks the update order did not make a difference. We restrict ourselves to two extreme cases for the update order:

$$\text{parallel:} \quad \text{Prob}[\boldsymbol{\sigma}(t+\Delta)] = \prod_{i=1}^{N} g(\sigma_i(t+\Delta)h_i(t)/T)$$

$$\text{sequential:} \quad \begin{cases} \text{choose } i \text{ randomly from } \{1, \ldots, N\} \\ \text{Prob}[\sigma_i(t+\Delta)] = g(\sigma_i(t+\Delta)h_i(t)/T) \end{cases}$$

so that after making the simple choice

$$P(z) = \frac{1}{2}[1 - \tanh^2(z)] \;\Rightarrow\; g(x) = \frac{1}{2}[1 + \tanh(x)] = \frac{e^x}{2\cosh(x)} \tag{3.3}$$

we get, using $\cosh(-x) = \cosh(x)$:

$$\text{parallel:} \quad \text{Prob}[\boldsymbol{\sigma}(t+\Delta)] = \frac{e^{\sum_i \sigma_i(t+\Delta)h_i(t)/T}}{\prod_i [2\cosh(h_i(t)/T)]} \tag{3.4}$$

$$\text{sequential:} \quad \begin{cases} \text{choose } i \text{ randomly from } \{1,\ldots,N\} \\ \text{Prob}[\sigma_i(t+\Delta)] = \frac{1}{2}[1+\sigma_i(t+\Delta)\tanh(h_i(t)/T)] \end{cases} \tag{3.5}$$

The particularly simple dependence of the state probabilities in the above expressions on the state variables $\sigma_i(t+\Delta)$, which is a result of the choice (3.3), will enable a detailed analysis later. In order to obtain an idea of what to expect for such systems, however, we first turn to the deterministic (noiseless) case, $T = 0$.

3.1 Noiseless recurrent networks

Let us forget for the moment about the pathological case where for certain system states the postsynaptic potentials h_i can become zero. In such cases, $h_i(t) = 0$, we would have to take the limit $T \to 0$ in the stochastic laws, which means that $\sigma_i(t+\Delta)$ is chosen at random from $\{-1, 1\}$ with equal probabilities. The dynamical rules now reduce to:

$$\text{parallel:} \quad \sigma_i(t+\Delta) = \text{sgn}\Big(\sum_j J_{ij}\sigma_j(t) + \vartheta_i\Big) \quad (\forall i) \tag{3.6}$$

$$\text{sequential:} \quad \begin{cases} \text{choose } i \text{ randomly from } \{1,\ldots,N\} \\ \sigma_i(t+\Delta) = \text{sgn}\Big(\sum_j J_{ij}\sigma_j(t) + \vartheta_i\Big) \end{cases} \tag{3.7}$$

For parallel dynamics we now generate a deterministic chain of successive network states

$$\boldsymbol{\sigma}(0) \to \boldsymbol{\sigma}(\Delta) \to \boldsymbol{\sigma}(2\Delta) \to \boldsymbol{\sigma}(3\Delta) \to \cdots$$

Since the number of different configurations is finite (2^N), at some stage we must obtain in this chain a configuration $\boldsymbol{\sigma}^\star$ that has already appeared earlier. Because the process is deterministic, the configurations following $\boldsymbol{\sigma}^\star$ will be exactly the same as those that followed $\boldsymbol{\sigma}^\star$ after its earlier occurrence. Thus the deterministic network with parallel dynamics will always evolve into a limit cycle with period $\leq 2^N$.

For sequential dynamics with random selection of the neuron to be updated, the above statement will not be true: a repeated occurrence of any state $\boldsymbol{\sigma}^\star$ does not permit more than probabilistic statements on the expected future path of states. However, if we were to choose the neurons to be sequentially updated in a fixed (as opposed to random) order, the dynamics once more becomes deterministic, so that the reasoning above applies and the system must evolve into a limit cycle with period $\leq 2^N$.

Simple model examples with parallel dynamics

We start by inspecting (and solving) a number of simple recurrent model examples with parallel dynamics, of increasing complexity. The system will be prepared in some initial microscopic state $\boldsymbol{\sigma}(0)$. For simplicity we choose $\Delta = 1$ (the duration of the elementary time-steps), so that $t \in \{0, 1, 2, \ldots\}$.

Example 1. $J_{ij} = 0$, $\vartheta_i \neq 0$
The dynamics (3.6) now becomes:

$$\sigma_i(t+1) = \text{sgn}(\vartheta_i) \quad (\forall i) \quad (\forall t \geq 0)$$

which gives the trivial solution $\sigma_i(t) = \text{sgn}(\vartheta_i)$ $(\forall t > 0)$. In one time-step the system moves into a unique fixed point attractor. Associated with an attractor is an attraction domain $\mathcal{D}$: the set of all initial configurations $\boldsymbol{\sigma}(0)$ that are attracted by it. The size $|\mathcal{D}|$ is the number of configurations in $\mathcal{D}$. Here $\mathcal{D} = \{-1, 1\}^N$, so $|\mathcal{D}| = 2^N$. The dynamical flow corresponding to the present example is depicted schematically in the following diagram:

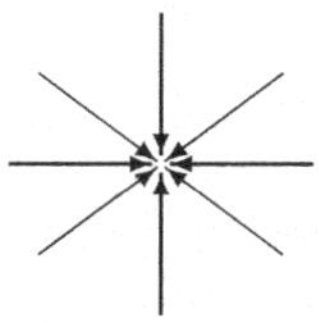

Example 2. $J_{ij} = J/N$, $\vartheta_i = 0$
We choose the system size N to be odd (so that the average activity can never be zero), and $J \neq 0$. The dynamics (3.6) now becomes:

$$\sigma_i(t+1) = \text{sgn}(J)\,\text{sgn}\left(\frac{1}{N}\sum_j \sigma_j(t)\right) \quad (\forall i) \quad (\forall t \geq 0)$$

We introduce the average neuronal activity $m(t) = N^{-1}\sum_j \sigma_j(t) \in [-1, 1]$, in terms of which the dynamics simplifies to

$$m(t+1) = \text{sgn}(J)\,\text{sgn}(m(t)) \quad (\forall i) \quad (\forall t \geq 0)$$

We have to distinguish between the two cases $J > 0$ and $J < 0$:

$$J > 0: \quad m(t) = \text{sgn}(m(0)) \qquad (\forall t > 0)$$
$$J < 0: \quad m(t) = (-1)^t \,\text{sgn}(m(0)) \quad (\forall t > 0)$$

Note that $m(t) = 1$ implies that $\boldsymbol{\sigma}(t) = (1, \ldots, 1)$, whereas $m(t) = -1$ implies that $\boldsymbol{\sigma}(t) = (-1, \ldots, -1)$. Hence, for $J > 0$ the system moves in one time-step into one of two fixed point attractors: $\boldsymbol{\sigma}^+ = (1, \ldots, 1)$, with $\mathcal{D}^+ = \{\boldsymbol{\sigma} \in \{-1, 1\}^N \mid N^{-1} \sum_i \sigma_i > 0\}$, and $\boldsymbol{\sigma}^- = (-1, \ldots, -1)$, with $\mathcal{D}^- = \{\boldsymbol{\sigma} \in \{-1, 1\}^N \mid N^{-1} \sum_i \sigma_i < 0\}$, as illustrated in the following diagram:

$J > 0$:

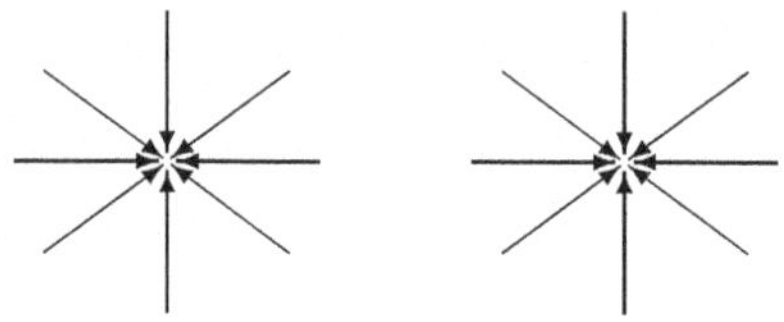

For $J < 0$, on the other hand, the system is seen to move in one time-step into a unique period-2 limit cycle attractor, $\boldsymbol{\sigma}^+ \to \boldsymbol{\sigma}^- \to \boldsymbol{\sigma}^+ \to \boldsymbol{\sigma}^- \to \cdots$, with $\mathcal{D} = \{-1, 1\}^N$, as depicted below.

$J < 0$:

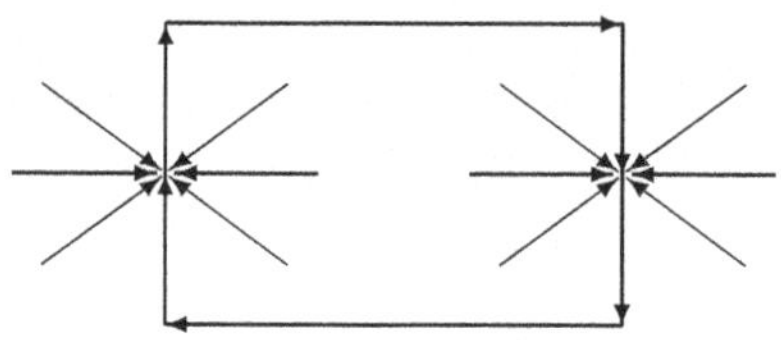

Example 3. $J_{ij} = J/N$, $\vartheta_i = \vartheta \neq 0$
In order to make sure that the thresholds ϑ_i will not completely dominate the behaviour, we choose $|\vartheta| < |J|$. The dynamics (3.6) now becomes:

$$\sigma_i(t+1) = \text{sgn}\left(\frac{J}{N} \sum_j \sigma_j(t) + \vartheta\right) \quad (\forall i) \ (\forall t \geq 0)$$

In terms of the average activity $m(t) = N^{-1} \sum_j \sigma_j(t)$ we then find:

$$m(t+1) = \text{sgn}(Jm(t) + \vartheta) \quad (\forall t \geq 0)$$

Let us again distinguish between $J > 0$ and $J < 0$:

$$J > 0: \ m(t+1) = \text{sgn}(m(t) + \vartheta/J) \quad \begin{cases} m(0) > -\vartheta/J: & m(t > 0) = 1 \\ m(0) < -\vartheta/J: & m(t > 0) = -1 \end{cases}$$

For $J > 0$ the system once more moves in one time-step into one of two fixed point attractors: $\boldsymbol{\sigma}^+ = (1,\ldots,1)$, with attraction domain $\mathcal{D}^+ = \{\boldsymbol{\sigma} \in \{-1,1\}^N \mid N^{-1}\sum_i \sigma_i > -\vartheta/J\}$, and $\boldsymbol{\sigma}^- = (-1,\ldots,-1)$, with $\mathcal{D}^- = \{\boldsymbol{\sigma} \in \{-1,1\}^N \mid N^{-1}\sum_i \sigma_i < -\vartheta/J\}$. Note, however, that the boundaries and relative sizes of the two attraction domains are now controlled by the quantity ϑ/J. Only for $\vartheta = 0$ do we recover the previous situation, where the two attractors were equally strong. The following diagram illustrates the situation:

$J > 0$:

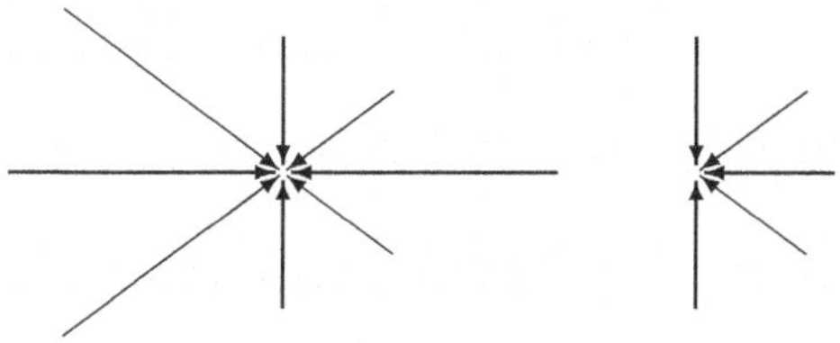

For $J < 0$, on the other hand, we find:

$J < 0$:

$$m(t+1) = -\text{sgn}(m(t) - \vartheta/|J|) \qquad \begin{cases} m(0) > \vartheta/|J|: & m(t>0) = (-1)^t \\ m(0) < \vartheta/|J|: & m(t>0) = (-1)^{t+1} \end{cases}$$

For $J < 0$ the system again moves in one time-step into the period-2 limit cycle attractor $\boldsymbol{\sigma}^+ \to \boldsymbol{\sigma}^- \to \boldsymbol{\sigma}^+ \to \boldsymbol{\sigma}^- \to \cdots$, with $\mathcal{D} = \{-1,1\}^N$. The only difference with the previous example is that we are now more likely to enter the attractor in one point than the other, to an extent controlled by ϑ/J.

$J < 0$:

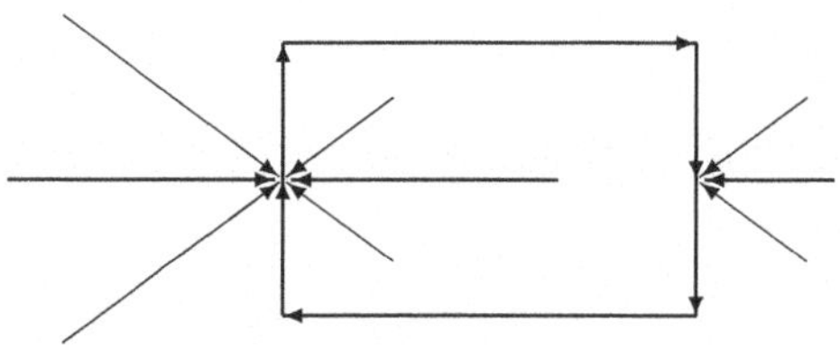

Example 4. $J_{ij} = J/N$, $\vartheta_i \in \{-\vartheta, \vartheta\}$, $\vartheta \neq 0$
In order to make sure that the thresholds will not completely dominate the behaviour, we choose $|\vartheta| < |J|$. For simplicity we assume that one half of the neurons in the system have $\vartheta_i = \vartheta$, and the other half have $\vartheta_i = -\vartheta$. The dynamics (3.6) now becomes:

$$\sigma_i(t+1) = \text{sgn}\left(\frac{J}{N}\sum_j \sigma_j(t) + \vartheta_i\right) \quad (\forall i) \;\; (\forall t \geq 0)$$

In terms of the average activity $m(t) = N^{-1}\sum_j \sigma_j(t)$ we then find:

$$m(t+1) = \tfrac{1}{2}\,\text{sgn}(Jm(t)+\vartheta) + \tfrac{1}{2}\,\text{sgn}(Jm(t)-\vartheta) \quad (\forall t \geq 0)$$

As before we distinguish between $J > 0$ and $J < 0$:

$$J > 0: \quad m(t+1) = \frac{1}{2}\text{sgn}\left(m(t)+\frac{\vartheta}{J}\right) + \frac{1}{2}\text{sgn}\left(m(t)-\frac{\vartheta}{J}\right)$$

$$\begin{cases} m(0) > |\vartheta/J|: & m(t) = 1 \quad (t > 0) \\ |m(0)| < |\vartheta/J|: & m(t) = 0 \quad (t > 0) \\ m(0) < -|\vartheta/J|: & m(t) = -1 \quad (t > 0) \end{cases}$$

Note that for the stationary situation $m = 0$ we find from the dynamic laws that $\sigma_i = \text{sgn}(\vartheta_i)$ for all i (a microscopic fixed point, to be denoted by $\boldsymbol{\sigma}^0$). We conclude that for $J > 0$ the system moves in one time step into one of three fixed point attractors: $\boldsymbol{\sigma}^+ = (1,\ldots,1)$, with $\mathcal{D}^+ = \{\boldsymbol{\sigma} \in \{-1,1\}^N \,|\, N^{-1}\sum_i \sigma_i > |\vartheta/J|\}$, $\boldsymbol{\sigma}^0$, with $\mathcal{D}^0 = \{\boldsymbol{\sigma} \in \{-1,1\}^N \,|\, |N^{-1}\sum_i \sigma_i| < |\vartheta/J|\}$, and $\boldsymbol{\sigma}^- = (-1,\ldots,-1)$, with $\mathcal{D}^- = \{\boldsymbol{\sigma} \in \{-1,1\}^N \,|\, N^{-1}\sum_i \sigma_i < -|\vartheta/J|\}$. The boundaries and relative sizes of the three attraction domains are now controlled by the quantity ϑ/J; the two $m = \pm 1$ attractors are always equally strong. For $\vartheta \to 0$ the attractor $\boldsymbol{\sigma}^0$ is removed, and we return to the previously studied case with only two attractors.

$J > 0$:

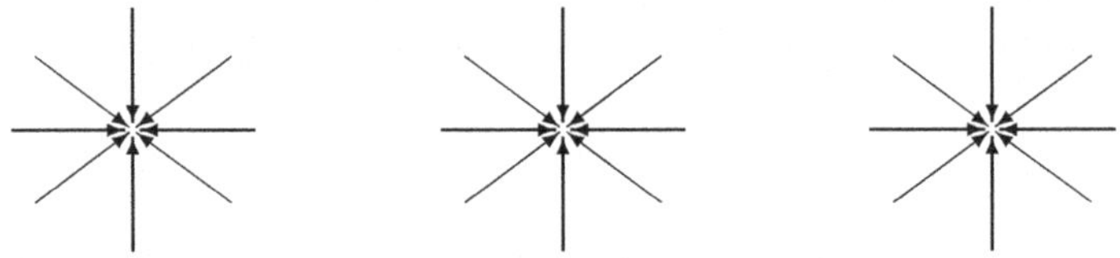

For $J < 0$, on the other hand, we obtain:

$$J < 0: \quad m(t+1) = -\frac{1}{2}\text{sgn}\left(m(t)+\frac{\vartheta}{J}\right) - \frac{1}{2}\text{sgn}\left(m(t)-\frac{\vartheta}{J}\right)$$

$$\begin{cases} m(0) > |\vartheta/J|: & m(t) = (-1)^t \quad (t > 0) \\ |m(0)| < |\vartheta/J|: & m(t) = 0 \quad (t > 0) \\ m(0) < -|\vartheta/J|: & m(t) = (-1)^{t+1} \quad (t > 0) \end{cases}$$

Here we see that the system moves in one time-step either into the period-2 limit cycle attractor $\boldsymbol{\sigma}^+ \to \boldsymbol{\sigma}^- \to \boldsymbol{\sigma}^+ \to \boldsymbol{\sigma}^- \to \cdots$, with $\mathcal{D} = \{\boldsymbol{\sigma} \in \{-1,1\}^N \,|\, N^{-1}\sum_i \sigma_i > |\vartheta/J|\}$, or into the fixed point attractor $\boldsymbol{\sigma}^0$, with $\mathcal{D}^0 = \{\boldsymbol{\sigma} \in \{-1,1\}^N \,|\, |N^{-1}\sum_i \sigma_i| < |\vartheta/J|\}$. The boundaries and relative sizes of the two attraction domains are again controlled by the quantity ϑ/J. For $\vartheta \to 0$ the attractor $\boldsymbol{\sigma}^0$ is removed, and we return to the previously studied case with only the limit cycle attractor. In a diagram:

$J < 0$:

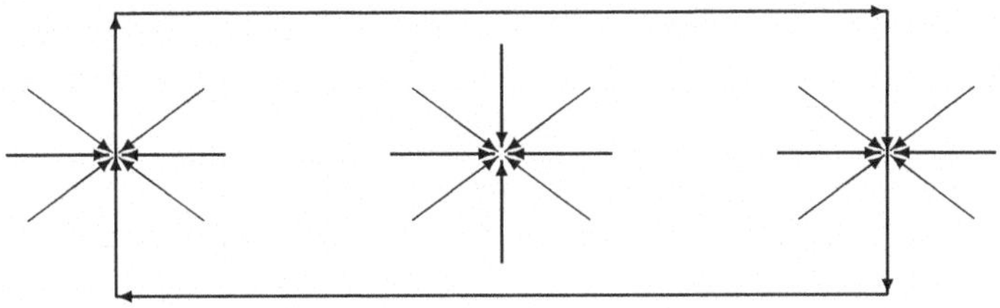

Example 5. $J_{ij} = \frac{1}{N}(\xi_i - \xi_j)$, $\vartheta_i = 0$
For simplicity we choose $\xi_i \in \{-1, 1\}$ for all i such that half of the neurons in the system will have $\xi_i = 1$ and the other half will have $\xi_i = -1$. We will write $\boldsymbol{\xi} = (\xi_1, \ldots, \xi_N)$. The dynamics (3.6) now becomes:

$$\sigma_i(t+1) = \text{sgn}\left(\xi_i \frac{1}{N}\sum_j \sigma_j(t) - \frac{1}{N}\sum_j \xi_j \sigma_j(t)\right) \quad (\forall i) \;\; (\forall t \geq 0)$$

The relevant macroscopic quantities to inspect now turn out to be

$$m_1(t) = \frac{1}{N}\sum_j \sigma_j(t) \qquad m_2(t) = \frac{1}{N}\sum_j \xi_j \sigma_j(t)$$

in terms of which we can write, for all $t \geq 0$:

$$\begin{aligned}
m_1(t+1) &= \frac{1}{N}\sum_i \text{sgn}(\xi_i m_1(t) - m_2(t)) \\
&= \frac{1}{2}\text{sgn}(m_1(t) - m_2(t)) - \frac{1}{2}\text{sgn}(m_1(t) + m_2(t)) \\
m_2(t+1) &= \frac{1}{N}\sum_i \text{sgn}(m_1(t) - \xi_i m_2(t)) \\
&= \frac{1}{2}\text{sgn}(m_1(t) - m_2(t)) + \frac{1}{2}\text{sgn}(m_1(t) + m_2(t))
\end{aligned}$$

At this stage it is convenient to switch to new variables:

$$m_\pm(t) = m_1(t) \pm m_2(t)$$

which leads to the simple equations:

$$m_+(t+1) = \text{sgn}(m_-(t)) \qquad m_-(t+1) = -\text{sgn}(m_+(t))$$

From this it follows, in turn, that:

$$\begin{pmatrix} m_+(t+2) \\ m_-(t+2) \end{pmatrix} = -\begin{pmatrix} \text{sgn}(m_+(t)) \\ \text{sgn}(m_-(t)) \end{pmatrix} \Rightarrow \begin{pmatrix} m_+(t+4) \\ m_-(t+4) \end{pmatrix} = \begin{pmatrix} \text{sgn}(m_+(t)) \\ \text{sgn}(m_-(t)) \end{pmatrix}$$
$$\Rightarrow \begin{pmatrix} m_+(t+8) \\ m_-(t+8) \end{pmatrix} = \begin{pmatrix} m_+(t+4) \\ m_-(t+4) \end{pmatrix}$$

In at most four time-steps the system will have entered a period-4 limit cycle solution. If $m_+(0) \neq 0$ and $m_-(0) \neq 0$, this solution is

$$\begin{pmatrix} m_+ \\ m_- \end{pmatrix}: \begin{pmatrix} 1 \\ 1 \end{pmatrix} \to \begin{pmatrix} 1 \\ -1 \end{pmatrix} \to \begin{pmatrix} -1 \\ -1 \end{pmatrix} \to \begin{pmatrix} -1 \\ 1 \end{pmatrix} \to \begin{pmatrix} 1 \\ 1 \end{pmatrix} \to \cdots$$

When translated back into m_1 and m_2, this implies:

$$\begin{pmatrix} m_1 \\ m_2 \end{pmatrix}: \begin{pmatrix} 1 \\ 0 \end{pmatrix} \to \begin{pmatrix} 0 \\ 1 \end{pmatrix} \to \begin{pmatrix} -1 \\ 0 \end{pmatrix} \to \begin{pmatrix} 0 \\ -1 \end{pmatrix} \to \begin{pmatrix} 1 \\ 0 \end{pmatrix} \to \cdots$$

Note that $m_1 = \pm 1$ means that $\boldsymbol{\sigma} = \boldsymbol{\sigma}^{\pm} = \pm(1, \ldots, 1)$, whereas $m_2 = \pm 1$ means that $\boldsymbol{\sigma} = \pm\boldsymbol{\xi}$. As a result we find that at the microscopic level we have the following period-4 limit cycle attractor:

$$\boldsymbol{\sigma}^+ \to \boldsymbol{\xi} \to \boldsymbol{\sigma}^- \to -\boldsymbol{\xi} \to \boldsymbol{\sigma}^+ \to \cdots$$

The remaining periodic solutions, obtained when at least one of the $m_\pm(0)$ is zero, turn out to be unstable. The resulting picture is therefore as follows:

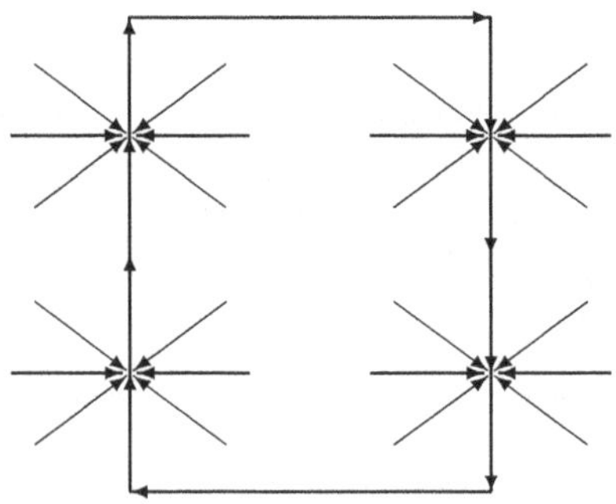

Example 6. $J_{ij} = \delta_{\pi(i),j}$, $\vartheta_i = 0$
Our final simple example illustrates the occurrence of even larger periods. Here π is a mapping on the set of neuron indices:

$$\pi\colon \quad \{1, \ldots, N\} \to \{1, \ldots, N\}$$

The dynamical rules (3.6) reduce to

$$\sigma_i(t+1) = \text{sgn}(\sigma_{\pi(i)}(t)) = \sigma_{\pi(i)}(t) \quad (\forall i) \;\; (\forall t \geq 0)$$

At each time step each neuron i determines its new state by simply copying the present state of some specific colleague $\pi(i)$. One can find quite a wide range of periods, by variation of the index operation π. Some examples are:

- $\pi(i) = k$ $(\forall i)$: Here all neurons copy their new state from the same location k. This leads to

$$\sigma_i(t+1) = \sigma_k(t) \;(\forall i) \quad \Rightarrow \quad \sigma_i(t) = \sigma_k(0) \;(\forall i)\; (\forall t > 0)$$

  The system thus ends up in one of two fixed point attractors: $\boldsymbol{\sigma}^+ = (1, \ldots, 1)$, with attraction domain $\mathcal{D}^+ = \{\boldsymbol{\sigma} \in \{-1,1\}^N \mid \sigma_k(0) = 1\}$ and $\boldsymbol{\sigma}^- = (-1, \ldots, -1)$, with $\mathcal{D}^- = \{\boldsymbol{\sigma} \in \{-1,1\}^N \mid \sigma_k(0) = -1\}$.
- $\pi(i) = N + 1 - i$ $(\forall i)$: Note that the mapping π now obeys $\pi(\pi(i)) = \pi(N+1-i) = i$ $(\forall i)$. As a result the dynamics is itself 2-periodic, since for each i we find

$$\sigma_i(t+1) = \sigma_{N+1-i}(t) \quad \Rightarrow \quad \begin{cases} \sigma_i(t) = \sigma_i(0) & (\forall t > 0 \text{ even}) \\ \sigma_i(t) = \sigma_{N+1-i}(0) & (\forall t > 0 \text{ odd}) \end{cases}$$

  There are many fixed points (corresponding to those states with $\sigma_i = \sigma_{N+1-i}$ for all i), and period-2 cycles, which together cover the whole state space $\{-1,1\}^N$.
- $\pi(i) = i + 1 \pmod N$ $(\forall i)$: This is just an N-periodic index shift. One simply finds for all i (where we define indices periodically, that is, i is taken mod N, for simplicity):

$$\sigma_i(t+1) = \sigma_{i+1}(t) \quad \Rightarrow \quad \sigma_i(t) = \sigma_{i+t}(0) \quad (\forall t > 0)$$

  Here we find many limit cycles with periods up to N. Some have smaller periods, due to periodicities in the initial state $\boldsymbol{\sigma}(0)$ (for instance, $\boldsymbol{\sigma}(0) = (1, \ldots, 1)$ gives a period-1 solution).

3.2 Synaptic symmetry and Lyapunov functions

It is clear that the diversity in the possible modes of operation in these recurrent systems is quite large. If we were to repeat the above exercise of solving simple models for the case of sequential dynamics, we would again find qualitative differences. We clearly need some tools for classification. It turns out that a relevant feature for distinguishing between various systems is whether or not the matrix of synaptic interactions is symmetric, that is, whether or not $J_{ij} = J_{ji}$ for all (i, j). As always we exclude the pathological cases where local fields $h_i(\boldsymbol{\sigma})$ can be *exactly* zero.

Proposition. If the synaptic matrix $\boldsymbol{J}$ is symmetric, that is, if $J_{ij} = J_{ji}$ for all (i, j), then the quantity

$$L(\boldsymbol{\sigma}) = -\sum_i \Big|\sum_j J_{ij}\sigma_j + \vartheta_i\Big| - \sum_i \sigma_i\vartheta_i \tag{3.8}$$

is a Lyapunov function for the deterministic parallel dynamics

$$\sigma_i(t+1) = \operatorname{sgn}\Big(\sum_j J_{ij}\sigma_j + \vartheta_i\Big) \quad (\forall i) \tag{3.9}$$

and the system will evolve either towards a fixed point or into a period-2 limit cycle.

Proof. Clearly $L(\boldsymbol{\sigma})$ is bounded from below: $L(\boldsymbol{\sigma}) \geq -\sum_{ij} |J_{ij}| - 2\sum_i |\vartheta_i|$. The non-trivial part of the proof is to show that it decreases monotonically with time, and that it implies evolution towards a period-2 limit cycle (of which a fixed point is a special case). Consider a transition $\boldsymbol{\sigma} \to \boldsymbol{\sigma}'$, described by the dynamical rules (3.9). The resulting change in L is given by:

$$\begin{aligned}\Delta L &= L(\boldsymbol{\sigma}') - L(\boldsymbol{\sigma}) \\ &= -\sum_i \Big|\sum_j J_{ij}\sigma'_j + \vartheta_i\Big| + \sum_i \Big|\sum_j J_{ij}\sigma_j + \vartheta_i\Big| + \sum_i \vartheta_i(\sigma_i - \sigma'_i)\end{aligned}$$

We first use (3.9) to rewrite the second contribution,

$$\begin{aligned}\Delta L &= -\sum_i \Big|\sum_j J_{ij}\sigma'_j + \vartheta_i\Big| + \sum_i \sigma'_i\Big(\sum_j J_{ij}\sigma_j + \vartheta_i\Big) + \sum_i \vartheta_i(\sigma_i - \sigma'_i) \\ &= -\sum_i \Big|\sum_j J_{ij}\sigma'_j + \vartheta_i\Big| + \sum_{ij} \sigma'_i J_{ij}\sigma_j + \sum_i \vartheta_i\sigma_i\end{aligned}$$

and then exploit the interaction symmetry, to obtain

$$\begin{aligned}\Delta L &= -\sum_i \Big|\sum_j J_{ij}\sigma'_j + \vartheta_i\Big| + \sum_{ij} \sigma_i J_{ij}\sigma'_j + \sum_i \vartheta_i\sigma_i \\ &= -\sum_i \Big|\sum_j J_{ij}\sigma'_j + \vartheta_i\Big| + \sum_i \sigma_i\Big(\sum_j J_{ij}\sigma'_j + \vartheta_i\Big) \\ &= -\sum_i \Big|\sum_j J_{ij}\sigma'_j + \vartheta_i\Big|\Big[1 - \sigma_i \,\mathrm{sgn}\Big(\sum_j J_{ij}\sigma'_j + \vartheta_i\Big)\Big] \leq 0.\end{aligned} \tag{3.10}$$

Note that $\Delta L \neq 0$ implies that $\Delta L \leq -\kappa$, where

$$\kappa = 2 \min_{\boldsymbol{\sigma}} \min_i \Big|\sum_j J_{ij}\sigma_j + \vartheta_i\Big| > 0$$

Since L is bounded from below, the number of iteration steps for which one observes $\Delta L \neq 0$ must be finite. So L decreases monotonically, until at some time $t^\star < \infty$ a stage is reached where $L(\boldsymbol{\sigma}(t+1)) = L(\boldsymbol{\sigma}(t))$ $\forall t > t^\star$. From then on it follows from (3.10) that

$$(\forall i)\ (\forall t > t^\star)\colon \quad \sigma_i(t) = \mathrm{sgn}\Big(\sum_j J_{ij}\sigma_j(t+1) + \vartheta_i\Big) = \sigma_i(t+2)$$

a condition characterizing either a fixed point or a period-2 limit cycle. This completes the proof. □

For sequential dynamics we find that, apart from requiring synaptic symmetry, we need to impose an additional requirement to construct a Lyapunov function, namely: $J_{ii} \geq 0$ $(\forall i)$. Under these conditions we can prove the following:

Proposition. If the synaptic matrix $\boldsymbol{J}$ is symmetric, that is, if $J_{ij} = J_{ji}$ for all (i, j), and if $J_{ii} \geq 0$ for all i, then the quantity

$$L(\boldsymbol{\sigma}) = -\frac{1}{2}\sum_{ij} \sigma_i J_{ij}\sigma_j - \sum_i \sigma_i\vartheta_i \tag{3.11}$$

is a Lyapunov function for the sequential dynamics

$$\begin{aligned}\sigma_i(t+1) &= \mathrm{sgn}\Big(\sum_j J_{ij}\sigma_j(t) + \vartheta_i\Big) \\ \sigma_k(t+1) &= \sigma_k(t) \quad (\forall k \neq i)\end{aligned} \tag{3.12}$$

and the system will evolve into a fixed point. The sites $i(t)$ to be updated at the various times t can be drawn either at random or in a fixed order; the order is not relevant for the proof.

Proof. Clearly $L(\boldsymbol{\sigma})$ is bounded from below: $L(\boldsymbol{\sigma}) \geq -\frac{1}{2}\sum_{ij}|J_{ij}| - \sum_i |\vartheta_i|$. If the neuron to be updated at a given time step does not change its state, that is, if $\sigma_i' = \sigma_i$, then L will obviously remain the same. On the other hand, consider a transition $\boldsymbol{\sigma} \to \boldsymbol{\sigma}'$, described by the dynamical rules (3.12), in which $\sigma_i' = -\sigma_i$, so that

$$\sigma_i' = \operatorname{sgn}\Big(\sum_j J_{ij}\sigma_j + \vartheta_i\Big) = -\sigma_i \qquad \sigma_k' = \sigma_k \quad \text{for all } k \neq i \tag{3.13}$$

The resulting change in L is then given by:

$$\begin{aligned}\Delta L = L(\boldsymbol{\sigma}') - L(\boldsymbol{\sigma}) &= -\frac{1}{2}\sum_{k\ell} J_{k\ell}(\sigma_k'\sigma_\ell' - \sigma_k\sigma_\ell) - \sum_k \vartheta_k(\sigma_k' - \sigma_k) \\ &= \sigma_i \sum_\ell J_{i\ell}\sigma_\ell + \sigma_i \sum_k J_{ki}\sigma_k - 2J_{ii} + 2\vartheta_i\sigma_i\end{aligned}$$

Using both interaction symmetry and the sign restriction on self-interactions J_{ii} one obtains

$$\Delta L = 2\sigma_i\Big(\sum_j J_{ij}\sigma_j + \vartheta_i\Big) - 2J_{ii} = -2\Big|\sum_j J_{ij}\sigma_j + \vartheta_i\Big| - 2J_{ii} < 0 \tag{3.14}$$

Note that $\Delta L \neq 0$ implies that $\Delta L \leq -\kappa$, where

$$\kappa = 2\min_{\boldsymbol{\sigma}}\min_i \Big\{\Big|\sum_j J_{ij}\sigma_j + \vartheta_i\Big| + J_{ii}\Big\} > 0$$

Again, due to L being bounded from below, it follows that only a finite number of iterations can give $\Delta L \neq 0$. So L decreases monotonically until at some time $t^\star < \infty$ a stage is reached where $L(\boldsymbol{\sigma}(t+1)) = L(\boldsymbol{\sigma}(t))$ $\forall t > t^\star$. From then on it follows from (3.14) that for every site i to be updated: $\sigma_i' = \sigma_i$, which implies

$$(\forall i)\ (\forall t > t^\star): \quad \sigma_i(t+1) = \operatorname{sgn}\Big(\sum_j J_{ij}\sigma_j(t) + \vartheta_i\Big)$$

This completes the proof. □

One might think that the need for excluding negative self-interactions in the above proof is just an artifact of the particular Lyapunov function used, and that one might in principle also be able to prove that sequential systems with negative self-interactions evolve to a fixed point (by using an alternative method). This is not the case, as a simple example illustrates. Consider neurons with negative self-interactions only: $J_{ij} = J\delta_{ij}$, $J < 0$, $\vartheta_i = 0$. Here one has, if at time t we update the state of neuron i:

$$\sigma_i(t+1) = \text{sgn}(J)\sigma_i(t) = -\sigma_i(t)$$
$$\sigma_k(t+1) = \sigma_k(t) \quad (\forall k \neq i)$$

Each update will now result in a state change, for all times. Therefore, the absence of negative self-interactions is indeed a relevant factor in determining whether or not the sequential systems will evolve towards a fixed point.

3.3 Information processing in recurrent networks

Let us now turn to the question of how recurrent neural networks can actually be used to process information. The basic recipe will be the creation of attractors in the space $\{-1, 1\}^N$ of network states, through appropriate modification of synaptic interactions and thresholds (i.e. through learning). The previous model examples gave us an impression of which types of dynamical behaviour can be obtained by making specific choices for the system parameters. Now we are interested in the inverse problem: given a required operation, how should we choose (or modify) the parameters?

The simplest class of attractors are fixed points. Let us first illustrate how, through the creation of fixed point attractors, recurrent networks can be used as so-called 'associative memories' for storing patterns (words, pictures, abstract relations, whatever). The basic ideas will carry over in a natural way to the more general case of creating limit cycle attractors of arbitrary length, in order to store pattern sequences.

- Represent each of the p items or patterns to be stored (pictures, words, etc.) as an N-bit vector $\boldsymbol{\xi}^\mu = (\xi_1^\mu, \ldots, \xi_N^\mu) \in \{-1, 1\}^N$, $\mu = 1, \ldots, p$.
- Construct synaptic interactions $\{J_{ij}\}$ and thresholds $\{\vartheta_i\}$ such that fixed point attractors are created at the p locations of the pattern vectors $\boldsymbol{\xi}^\mu$ in state space.
- If now we are given an input to be recognized, we choose this input to be the initial microscopic network configuration $\boldsymbol{\sigma}(0)$. From this initial state the neuron state vector $\boldsymbol{\sigma}(t)$ is allowed to evolve in time autonomously, driven by the network dynamics, which will by definition lead to the nearest attractor (in some topological sense).

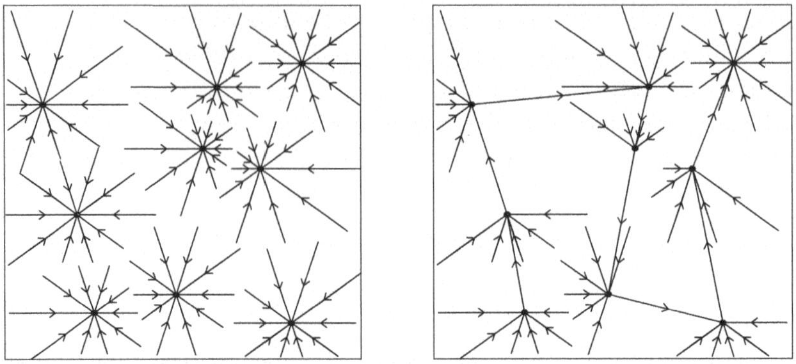

Figure 3.1 Information storage and retrieval in recurrent neural networks through the creation of attractors in phase space. Patterns $\boldsymbol{\xi}^{\mu}$ to be retrieved are marked as •. Left picture: if the interactions J_{ij} are chosen to be symmetric, the attractors will be fixed points or period-2 limit cycles (the latter for parallel dynamics only). Right picture: in order to store pattern sequences of length > 2, the interactions J_{ij} will have to be non-symmetric.

- The final state reached $\boldsymbol{\sigma}(\infty)$ can be interpreted as the pattern recognized by the network from the input $\boldsymbol{\sigma}(0)$.

The idea is illustrated in Figure 3.1 (left picture). It is, however, far from clear a priori whether all this can actually be done. For such a programme to work, we need to be able to create systems with many attractors with nonzero attraction domains. Furthermore, in biology (and to some degree also in engineering) we are constrained in our choice of learning rules, in the sense that only 'local' rules will be realizable and/or cost-effective. Local rules are modification recipes that involve only information available at the junction or neuron that is updated:

$$\Delta J_{ij} = \mathcal{F}(J_{ij}; \sigma_i; \sigma_j; h_i; \vartheta_i, \vartheta_j) \qquad \Delta\vartheta_i = \mathcal{G}(\sigma_i; h_i; \vartheta_i)$$

Finally, it is clear that the basic idea will in due course need some refining. For instance, if only the p patterns to be stored are attractors, each initial state will eventually lead to pattern recognition (also nonsensical or random ones), so we will also need an attractor that can act as a rubbish bin, attracting all initial states that we would not like to see recognized.

To illustrate the fundamental features of the idea, let us first consider the simplest case and try to store just a single pattern $\boldsymbol{\xi} = (\xi_1, \ldots, \xi_N) \in \{-1, 1\}^N$ in a noiseless and fully recurrent network with *tabula rasa* initial wiring, that is, $J_{ij} = 0$ for all (i, j), and with uniform thresholds. A biologically motivated rule for suitable interaction modification is the so-called Hebbian rule:

$$\Delta J_{ij} \sim \xi_i \xi_j \tag{3.15}$$

In other words, if two neurons are required to be in the same state ($\xi_i = \xi_j$) we increase their mutual interaction strength J_{ij}, otherwise (i.e. when $\xi_i = -\xi_j$) we decrease J_{ij}. This rule is also similar to the perceptron learning rule, the only difference being that in the case of the perceptron we only modify if the system makes an error. The resulting network is (with appropriate scaling):

$$J_{ij} = \frac{1}{N}\xi_i\xi_j \qquad \vartheta_i = \vartheta \tag{3.16}$$

with $|\vartheta| < 1$. We introduce new variables $\tau_i = \xi_i\sigma_i$ and $v_i = \xi_i\vartheta$, in terms of which the parallel dynamical laws can be written as

$$\tau_i(t+\Delta) = \text{sgn}\left(\frac{1}{N}\sum_j \tau_j(t) + v_i\right) \quad (\forall i) \tag{3.17}$$

with $v_i \in \{-\vartheta, \vartheta\}$. This is precisely Example (4) studied earlier, with $J = 1$. If the fraction of neurons with $\xi_i = 1$ equals the fraction of neurons with $\xi_i = -1$, we can use the result obtained for Example (4). Translated back into the original variables σ_i this leads, with $m = N^{-1}\sum_i \xi_i\sigma_i$, to:

$$\begin{array}{lll} m(0) > |\vartheta|: & m(t) = 1 & (t > 0) \\ |m(0)| < |\vartheta|: & m(t) = 0 & (t > 0) \\ m(0) < -|\vartheta|: & m(t) = -1 & (t > 0) \end{array}$$

For $m = \pm 1$ we have a microscopic state where $\sigma_i = \pm\xi_i$ ($\forall i$). For $m = 0$ we have, according to the dynamic laws, $\sigma_i = \text{sgn}(\vartheta)$; if furthermore we choose $\vartheta < 0$, we get $\sigma_i = -1$ for this latter state. At a microscopic level the picture thus becomes:

$$\begin{array}{lll} \frac{1}{N}\sum_i \xi_i\sigma_i(0) > |\vartheta|: & \boldsymbol{\sigma}(t) = \boldsymbol{\xi} & (t > 0) \\ -|\vartheta| < \frac{1}{N}\sum_i \xi_i\sigma_i(0) < |\vartheta|: & \boldsymbol{\sigma}(t) = (-1, \ldots, -1) & (t > 0) \\ \frac{1}{N}\sum_i \xi_i\sigma_i(0) < -|\vartheta|: & \boldsymbol{\sigma}(t) = -\boldsymbol{\xi} & (t > 0) \end{array}$$

We see that this system can indeed reconstruct dynamically and autonomously the original pattern $\boldsymbol{\xi}$ from an input vector $\boldsymbol{\sigma}(0)$. Note that the network only reconstructs the pattern if the initial state shows a sufficient resemblance; a random initial state will not evoke pattern recall, but lead to an attractor with zero activity. We also realize, however, that *en passant* we have created an additional attractor: the microscopic state $-\boldsymbol{\xi} = (-\xi_1, \ldots, -\xi_N)$.

The boundaries and relative sizes of the three attraction domains are controlled by the threshold ϑ; the two $m = \pm 1$ attractors are always equally strong (this will be different if the fraction of neurons with $\xi_i = 1$ is different from the fraction with $\xi_i = -1$). For $\vartheta \to 0$ the 'rubbish bin' attractor $(-1, \ldots, -1)$ is removed. For sequential dynamics the picture is qualitatively the same, the only difference being that the various attractors are not reached in a single time-step but are approached gradually.

Finally, let us investigate what happens if we attempt to store more than just a single pattern and apply the Hebbian learning rule (3.15) to a set of p patterns $\{\boldsymbol{\xi}^\mu\}$, with $\boldsymbol{\xi}^\mu = (\xi_1^\mu, \ldots, \xi_N^\mu)$ $(\mu = 1, \ldots, p)$. Let us, furthermore, assume for simplicity that these patterns are mutually orthogonal:

$$\frac{1}{N}\sum_i \xi_i^\mu \xi_i^\nu = \delta_{\mu\nu}$$

This obviously requires $p \leq N$. Let us also choose sequential dynamics and remove the self-interactions ($J_{ii} \to 0$). The resulting neural network model is the so-called Hopfield model (for simplicity we take $\vartheta_i = 0$ for all i):

$$J_{ij} = \frac{1}{N}(1 - \delta_{ij}) \sum_{\mu=1}^{p} \xi_i^\mu \xi_j^\mu \qquad \vartheta_i = 0 \tag{3.18}$$

We can now show that all p patterns must be stationary states of the dynamics. The Lyapunov function (3.11), which will be our tool, can here be written as:

$$L(\boldsymbol{\sigma}) = \frac{1}{2}p - \frac{1}{2}\sum_{\mu=1}^{p}\left(\frac{1}{\sqrt{N}}\sum_i \xi_i^\mu \sigma_i\right)^2$$

We can now choose the normalized pattern vectors $\hat{\boldsymbol{e}}^\mu = \boldsymbol{\xi}^\mu/\sqrt{N}$ as orthogonal and normalized basis vectors in the space $\mathbb{R}^N$, and then use the general relation $\boldsymbol{x}^2 \geq \sum_\mu (\hat{\boldsymbol{e}}^\mu \cdot \boldsymbol{x})^2$ to obtain a lower bound for the Lyapunov function:

$$L(\boldsymbol{\sigma}) \geq \tfrac{1}{2}p - \tfrac{1}{2}\boldsymbol{\sigma}^2 = \tfrac{1}{2}(p - N)$$

On the other hand, if we choose the state $\boldsymbol{\sigma}$ to be exactly one of the patterns, that is, $\boldsymbol{\sigma} = \boldsymbol{\xi}^\mu$ for some μ, we see that we satisfy exactly the lower bound:

$$L(\boldsymbol{\xi}^\mu) = \tfrac{1}{2}(p - N)$$

Since we know that any state change must decrease the value of L (which here is clearly impossible), we find that each of the patterns must correspond to a fixed point of the dynamics. It will turn out that they are also attractors. However, we will find once more that additional attractors are created by the Hopfield recipe (3.18), in addition to the patterns $\boldsymbol{\xi}^{\mu}$ and their inverses $-\boldsymbol{\xi}^{\mu}$, which correspond to *mixtures* of the p fundamental patterns. These mixtures can be eliminated by adding noise to the dynamics, as will be shown in Chapter 21.

Simulation examples (including neuronal noise)

Here we will only illustrate with numerical simulations the functioning of the Hopfield model (3.18) as an associative memory, and the quantitative description of the pattern recall process in terms of so-called overlaps:

$$m_{\mu}(\boldsymbol{\sigma}) = \frac{1}{N}\sum_{i} \xi_i^{\mu}\sigma_i \tag{3.19}$$

Clearly, if $m_{\mu}(\boldsymbol{\sigma}) = \pm 1$ one has $\boldsymbol{\sigma} = \pm\boldsymbol{\xi}^{\mu}$, whereas randomly drawn states $\boldsymbol{\sigma}$ would simply give $m_{\mu}(\boldsymbol{\sigma}) = 0$. Our simulated system is an $N = 841$ Hopfield model, in which $p = 10$ patterns have been stored (see Figure 3.2) according to the prescription (3.18). The state of each neuron σ_i is represented by a pixel (e.g. black for $\sigma_i = 1$, white for $\sigma_i = -1$). The two-dimensional arrangement of the neurons in this example is just a guide to the eye; since the model is fully connected, the spatial arrangement of the neurons in the network is irrelevant. The dynamics is taken to be a sequential stochastic alignment to the postsynaptic potentials $h_i(\boldsymbol{\sigma})$, as defined by the rule (3.5), with noise level $T = 0.1$.

In Figure 3.3 we show the result of letting the states of the neurons in the network evolve in time from an initial state, which is chosen to be a noisy version of one of the stored patterns. Here 40% of the neurons (or pixels) were 'flipped', that is, subjected to $\sigma_i \to -\sigma_i$. The top row of graphs shows snapshots of the microscopic configuration as the system evolves. The bottom row shows the corresponding values of the $p = 10$ overlaps m_{μ} as defined in (3.19), measured as functions of time; the one

Figure 3.2 Information storage with the Hopfield model: $p = 10$ patterns represented as specific microscopic configurations in an $N = 841$ recurrent neural network.

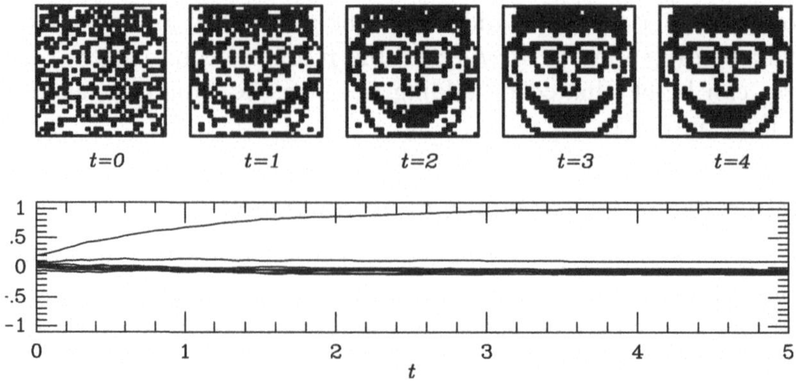

Figure 3.3 Dynamic reconstruction (at neuronal noise level $T = 0.1$) of a stored pattern, following an initial microscopic network state which is a corrupted version thereof. Top row: snapshots of the microscopic system state at times $t = 0, 1, 2, 3, 4$ iterations/neuron. Bottom: the corresponding values of the $p = 10$ overlaps m_μ as functions of time.

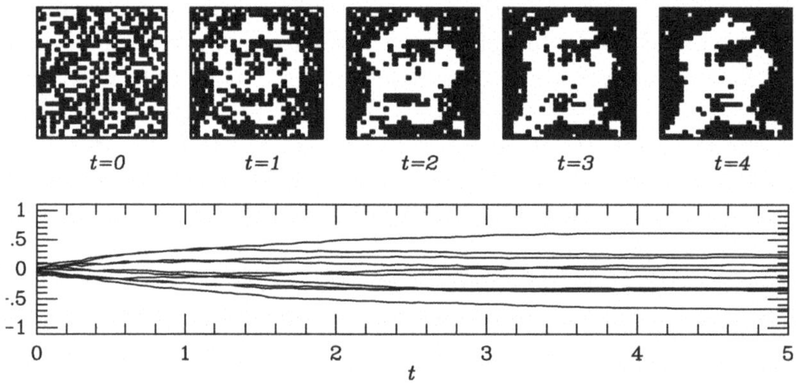

Figure 3.4 Evolution (at neuronal noise level $T = 0.1$) towards a spurious (mixture) state, following a randomly drawn initial microscopic network state. Top row: snapshots of the microscopic system state at times $t = 0, 1, 2, 3, 4$ iterations/neuron. Bottom: the corresponding values of the $p = 10$ overlaps m_μ as functions of time.

which evolves towards the value 1 belongs to the pattern that is being reconstructed. Figure 3.4 shows a similar experiment, in which now the initial state is drawn at random, rather than as a corrupted version of a stored pattern. The system subsequently evolves towards some mixture of the stored patterns. Note that the patterns involved are not uncorrelated; see Figure 3.2.

The particular way of storing and recalling information described here, which is based on *association* and on exploiting the actual content of the stored patterns rather than on comparing labels (or pointers) which refer to the physical locations where the patterns are stored in the underlying hardware, is denoted as *associative memory* or *content-addressable memory*. It will be clear from our simple simulation examples above that the idea of information storage in recurrent neural networks via the creation of attractors by modification of local parameters certainly works. More rigorous analytical studies of the recall dynamics in these networks will be described later, in Part IV of this book.

3.4 Exercises

Exercise 3.1. (Examples for noiseless parallel dynamics.) Consider noiseless recurrent networks with parallel dynamics. Assume that the local fields (or postsynaptic potentials) $h_i = \sum_j J_{ij}\sigma_j + \vartheta_i$ are always nonzero. Consider Example (2) in this chapter, that is, $J_{ij} = J/N$, $\vartheta_i = 0$. Write the Lyapunov function L (3.8) in terms of the average activity $m(\boldsymbol{\sigma}) = N^{-1}\sum_i \sigma_i$, and verify that L decreases monotonically. Which values for L are obtained in the different attractors? Same questions for Example (3): $J_{ij} = J/N$, $\vartheta_i = \vartheta \neq 0$. Now turn to Example (4): $J_{ij} = J/N$, $\vartheta_i \in \{-\vartheta, \vartheta\}$. Define the two sub-networks $I_+ = \{i \mid \vartheta_i = \vartheta\}$ and $I_- = \{i \mid \vartheta_i = -\vartheta\}$, and assume these to be equally large: $|I_+| = |I_-| = \frac{1}{2}N$. Define also the corresponding average activities

$$m_+(\boldsymbol{\sigma}) = \frac{2}{N}\sum_{i\in I_+}\sigma_i \qquad m_-(\boldsymbol{\sigma}) = \frac{2}{N}\sum_{i\in I_-}\sigma_i$$

Calculate $m_+(t)$ and $m_-(t)$ for $t > 0$, along the lines of the analysis in the various examples. Write the Lyapunov function L (3.8) in terms of the two average activities $m_\pm(\boldsymbol{\sigma})$ in the sub-networks, and verify that L decreases monotonically. Which values for L are obtained in the different attractors?

Exercise 3.2. (Examples for noiseless sequential dynamics.) Consider noiseless recurrent networks with sequential dynamics. Choose $J_{ij} = J/N$, $\vartheta_i = 0$ and N odd. The average activity in the system is defined as usual: $m(t) = N^{-1}\sum_i \sigma_i(t)$. Show that for $J > 0$: $m(\infty) = \lim_{t\to\infty} m(t) = \text{sgn}(m(0))$ (as for parallel dynamics). Show that for $J < 0$, on the other hand, the behaviour is completely different from the corresponding system with parallel dynamics. Calculate $\lim_{N\to\infty} m(t \to \infty)$ for $J < 0$.

Exercise 3.3. (Lyapunov functions.) Next consider networks with *anti-symmetric* synaptic interactions, that is, with $J_{ij} = -J_{ji}$ for all (i, j), with $\vartheta_i = 0$ for all i and with parallel deterministic dynamics. Show that $L(\boldsymbol{\sigma})$ (3.8) is also a Lyapunov function for such networks. Prove that these networks will always evolve into a period-4 limit cycle.

Exercise 3.4. (Information storage through the creation of attractors.) Consider noiseless recurrent networks with parallel dynamics: $\sigma_i(t+1) = \text{sgn}(\sum_j J_{ij}\sigma_j(t))$ for all i. Let the p vectors $\boldsymbol{\xi}^\mu = (\xi_1^\mu, \ldots, \xi_N^\mu) \in \{-1, 1\}^N$ ($\mu = 1, \ldots, p$) represent patterns (information) to be stored and retrieved. Assume these patterns to be mutually orthogonal and p to be finite. We define the p pattern overlaps $m_\mu(\boldsymbol{\sigma}) = N^{-1}\sum_i \xi_i^\mu \sigma_i \in [-1, 1]$. Choose the synaptic interactions corresponding to the Hopfield model:

$$J_{ij} = \frac{1}{N}\sum_{\mu=1}^{p} \xi_i^\mu \xi_j^\mu$$

Give a condition on the initial overlaps $\{m_\mu(0)\}$ sufficient to guarantee that $\boldsymbol{\sigma}(1) = \boldsymbol{\xi}^\lambda$. Show that for $N \to \infty$ all pattern vectors $\boldsymbol{\xi}^\mu$ are fixed point attractors, by demonstrating that the above condition is fulfilled for a set of states close to these patterns. Now choose

$$J_{ij} = \frac{1}{N}\sum_{\mu=1}^{p-1} \xi_i^{\mu+1} \xi_j^\mu + \frac{1}{N}\xi_i^1 \xi_j^p$$

Give a condition on the initial overlaps $\{m_\mu(0)\}$ sufficient to guarantee that $\boldsymbol{\sigma}(1) = \boldsymbol{\xi}^\lambda$. Show that for $N \to \infty$ there exists a stable period-p limit cycle attractor of the form $\boldsymbol{\xi}^1 \to \boldsymbol{\xi}^2 \to \cdots \to \boldsymbol{\xi}^{p-1} \to \boldsymbol{\xi}^p \to \boldsymbol{\xi}^1 \to \cdots$

Exercise 3.5. (Attractor networks storing patterns with unequal embedding strengths.) Again we consider noiseless recurrent networks with parallel dynamics: $\sigma_i(t+1) = \text{sgn}\big(\sum_j J_{ij}\sigma_j(t)\big)$ for all i, in which p orthogonal vectors $\boldsymbol{\xi}^\mu = (\xi_1^\mu, \ldots, \xi_N^\mu) \in \{-1, 1\}^N$ ($\mu = 1, \ldots, p$) are to be stored and retrieved (with p finite). We now store these patterns according to a Hebbian rule, but with different (positive) embedding strengths w_μ:

$$J_{ij} = \frac{1}{N}\sum_{\mu=1}^{p} w_\mu \xi_i^\mu \xi_j^\mu$$

Given a condition on the initial overlaps $\{m_\mu(0)\}$ sufficient to guarantee that $\boldsymbol{\sigma}(1) = \boldsymbol{\xi}^\lambda$. Show that for $N \to \infty$ all pattern vectors $\boldsymbol{\xi}^\mu$ are fixed point attractors, by demonstrating that the above condition is fulfilled for a set of states close to these patterns. Describe the effects of having unequal embedding strengths on the attraction domains of the p stored patterns.

4 Notes and suggestions for further reading

The idea that brain operation and reasoning can be analysed scientifically, with mathematical tools, took rather a long time to emerge. Neurons were only discovered in 1880 by Ramon y Cajal, using a novel staining method developed by Golgi. Until then there had been two scientific camps: *neuronists* believed that the brain consisted of interconnected information processing cells, whereas *reticularists* saw the brain as a continuous uninterrupted network of fibres only. In 1936, Turing [2] contributed significantly to the further demystification of the concept of 'intelligence' and proved statements about computability by machines. This more or less marked the start of the field of 'artificial intelligence'. McCulloch and Pitts [3] were the first to introduce a very simple discrete mathematical neuron model, in 1943, and they subsequently proved its universality. In 1949 the psychologist Hebb [4] introduced the idea that biological neural networks store information in the strengths of their interactions (the synapses). Learning is then by definition the modification of synapses, for which Hebb made a specific proposal. Rosenblatt [5] defined a learning rule in 1958 according to which a McCulloch–Pitts neuron updates its interaction strengths on the basis of examples of input–output relations which correspond to a given information processing task that the neuron is to perform. They called their systems *perceptrons*, and proved the perceptron convergence theorem [6]. A thorough mathematical analysis of the potential and restrictions of perceptrons was carried out by Minsky and Papert [7] in 1969. They showed that single perceptrons could unfortunately not perform all information processing tasks; some tasks require *layers* of perceptrons, for which no learning rule was known at that time.

Minsky and Papert's beautiful book seems to have dampened the existing enthusiasm for neural network research, and diverted attention temporarily away from the study of natural and synthetic learning machines towards the rule-based domain of artificial intelligence. Neural computation ceased to be fashionable, and remained in that state for some 20 years. Nevertheless, progress continued away from the central stages. In 1974 Little [8] introduced concepts from the statistical physics of magnetic systems (such as temperature) into the study of recurrent neural networks, building on earlier work by Cragg and Temperley [9] in 1955. The mechanisms underlying neuronal firing and spike transmission in real neurons were only firmly established in 1952, through the discovery of the relevant dynamical equations by Hodgkin and Huxley [10]. In 1972 Kohonen [11] and Amari [12] introduced the idea of building associative memories with recurrent neural networks, where one creates specific stable microscopic network states by manipulation of the interaction strengths, that is, the synapses. In retrospect this was found to have been proposed already in 1956 by Taylor [13]. Such systems were brought into the domain of statistical mechanics by the work of Hopfield [14] in 1982 (see also [15], written in that period). More or less in parallel with these developments in the study of recurrent neural networks, a learning rule for multilayer feed-forward networks of graded-response neurons was derived by Rumelhart and McClelland in 1986 [16]. The same rule, it turned out, had already been proposed by Werbos [17] in 1974. This development coincided with a spectacular increase in the power and availability of computers, which enabled numerical experimentation on a scale that had not been possible before. By this time, the study of natural and synthetic neural networks had once more become very fashionable, also due to additional developments in the application of techniques from statistical mechanics (to network operation) and from information theory (to learning), of which more later.

Since the late 1980s, artificial neural information processing systems have become standard tools in computer science and information engineering, especially in dealing with real-world (i.e. messy, partly inconsistent, or incompletely defined) tasks, where deductive logical problem solving is not an option. Neural network models and principles have diffused across many discipline boundaries, and the field is now paying the price of its success by becoming increasingly disconnected. At the computer science and applied mathematics interface, neural network type methods have merged with more traditional Bayesian parameter estimation theory (see Chapter 6). Here the developments have been in the direction of alternative formulations of neural information processing, where the modifiable connections between elements and specific choices of pre-processing are 'integrated out', in favour of more direct representation in terms of the resulting input–output operations (leading to the so-called Gaussian processes and support vector machines, discussed in Chapters 7 and 8). In statistical mechanics, attention largely shifted towards the analysis of the dynamics of learning processes (or algorithms). In biology, emphasis now appears to be on the study of timing aspects of neural communication (e.g. see [18] for coupled oscillator models as such, or [19] for more recent work on the mathematical modelling of real spiking neurons) and of synaptic modification rules, the role of chemical modulators, and on understanding the role of specific network architectures in specific brain regions.

Some suggestions for further reading on the developments up until, say, the mid-1980s, are the following books. In the interdisciplinary compilation [20] one finds reprints of original papers from 1890 to 1987;

the volume [21] gives introductions to the various aspects of modern day neural information processing, written by selected experts. The original book by Minsky and Papert [7] is simply a pleasure to read, and a great window on the spirit of the period in which it was written. Several excellent textbooks were written around 1990, such as [22–25]. However, the reader should be aware that they were produced in a period of accelerated research activity, and that much has happened since then.

Part II Advanced neural networks

In this second part of the book we expand both in breadth and in depth the material covered so far. Apart from its first chapter (and in contrast to most of Part I), the material presented and developed here will involve rather novel research results, which go back less than around 10 years.

Expansion in breadth refers to the addition of new neural network classes and new learning rules, such as competitive unsupervised learning processes (e.g. different versions of Vector Quantization, and Self-Organizing Maps—this material is still not too mathematical because there is little theory on these systems), and Support Vector Machines. The latter are part of a wider family of information processing tools referred to as 'kernel methods', and we only give an introduction here to what is now a research area in its own right.

Expansion in depth refers to a more solid statistical understanding, interpretation, and also increased potential for analysis and prediction of the most popular neural network types (e.g. Bayesian techniques in supervised learning, and their application to Gaussian processes). These latter subjects, although more mathematical in nature, have generated the main progress in industrial and commercial neural network applications over the last 10 years, since they have removed in a rigorous way the problems related to data noise and to the quantification of the reliability of neural network decisions.

5 Competitive unsupervised learning processes

In this chapter, we introduce and study two so-called 'unsupervised' learning processes, where the problem is not to learn to associate some correct response to each possible incoming signal (specified by a teacher or supervisor signal, as in, for example, feed-forward networks of the perceptron or multilayer perceptron type), but rather to build some alternative (more efficient, more compact, or more structured) representation of the data vectors fed into the system. The first two procedures to do this, vector quantization (VQ) and soft vector quantization (SVQ), aim to achieve data reduction for initially unknown data distributions. They find typical applications in communication, where compact representations are obviously cheaper to transmit than non-compact ones, allowing more signals to be communicated via the same channel. Methods in a third class—self-organizing maps (SOM), also known as feature maps or Kohonen maps—aim to create a topologically correct but low-dimensional internal representation of a given data distribution. This has applications in, for example, biology (the brain is known to create such maps for sensory signals), data-base mining, medical diagnostics, etc.

5.1 Vector quantization

Data reduction via code-book vectors

Imagine we have a source of real-valued data vectors $\boldsymbol{x} = (x_1, \ldots, x_n) \in \mathbb{R}^n$, with statistics described by some probability density $p(\boldsymbol{x})$ (with $\int d\boldsymbol{x}\; p(\boldsymbol{x}) = 1$, and with averages given by $\langle f(\boldsymbol{x})\rangle = \int d\boldsymbol{x}\; p(\boldsymbol{x}) f(\boldsymbol{x})$). Alternatively, if the data can only take values from a discrete set, we would have $p(\boldsymbol{x})$ representing probabilities, with $\sum_{\boldsymbol{x}} p(\boldsymbol{x}) = 1$ and $\langle f(\boldsymbol{x})\rangle = \sum_{\boldsymbol{x}} p(\boldsymbol{x}) f(\boldsymbol{x})$; see also Appendix A on elementary probability theory. Especially if n is very large, we would like to represent the real data $\boldsymbol{x}$ by alternative (and simpler) signals from which the $\boldsymbol{x}$ can be re-constructed, with some loss of accuracy, but with a reduction in dimensionality. One way to achieve this is the following:

- We 'cover' the data space by a suitable (small) set of characteristic data points, the so-called 'code-book vectors' $\boldsymbol{m}_i \in \mathbb{R}^n$. Here i labels the individual code-book vectors, that is, if we have N code-book vectors then $i = 1, \ldots, N$.

- We then approximate (or 'round off') each data point $\boldsymbol{x}$ by the *nearest* code-book vector, that is, by that particular $\boldsymbol{m}_i$ for which $|\boldsymbol{x} - \boldsymbol{m}_i|$ is minimal.

It will be clear why in communication this might be desirable: instead of the n real numbers $(x_1, \ldots, x_n)$ we would now need to send only a single integer number: the index i. The price we pay for this is a reduction in accuracy; after all we have approximated $\boldsymbol{x}$ by $\boldsymbol{m}_i$, and have thereby lost information. We can no longer be sure of the exact value of $\boldsymbol{x}$, since many other data points $\boldsymbol{x}$ would have been replaced by $\boldsymbol{m}_i$ (all those which are close to $\boldsymbol{m}_i$). The amount of information lost will obviously be smaller if we have a larger number or a more efficiently distributed set of code-book vectors.

The above procedure gives us what is known as a Voronoi tessalation of data space. This is a partitioning into convex subsets $V_i[\{\boldsymbol{m}\}]$, controlled by the choice $\{\boldsymbol{m}\}$ made for the N code-book vectors, which are defined as

$$V_i[\{\boldsymbol{m}\}] = \{\boldsymbol{x} \in \mathbb{R}^n \mid \forall j \neq i \colon |\boldsymbol{x} - \boldsymbol{m}_i| < |\boldsymbol{x} - \boldsymbol{m}_j|\} \tag{5.1}$$

(see Figure 5.1).

A good set of code-book vectors is one with the property that the density of code-book vectors in a given region of $\mathbb{R}^n$ is proportional to the density of data points in that region. In other words, given the statistics of the data and given the number N of code-book vectors we are willing to invest,

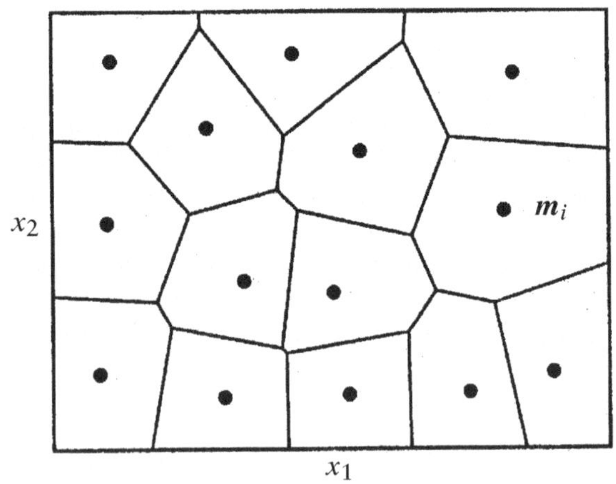

Figure 5.1 Example of a Voronoi tessalation of data space for $n = 2$, that is, $\boldsymbol{x} = (x_1, x_2)$. The points • represent the code-book vectors. The Voronoi cell associated with code-book vector $\boldsymbol{m}_i$, $V_i[\{\boldsymbol{m}\}]$, is the compartment surrounding point $\boldsymbol{m}_i$.

we aim for a set $\{\boldsymbol{m}\}$ such that for all i and j:

$$\text{Prob}(\boldsymbol{x} \in V_i[\{\boldsymbol{m}\}]) = \text{Prob}(\boldsymbol{x} \in V_j[\{\boldsymbol{m}\}]) \tag{5.2}$$

In this way all code-book vectors are used equally often, and no resources are wasted. The problem addressed by the VQ and SVQ algorithms is how to find a proper set of code-book vectors via an adaptive process, that is, both are based on gradually learning a proper positioning of the code-book vectors by observing the data.

The VQ algorithm and its properties

The Vector Quantization (VQ) algorithm is defined as follows. First we initialize the N code-book vectors $\boldsymbol{m}_i \in \mathbb{R}^n$ (randomly, or according to a recipe to be given below). Then we iterate the following stochastic process:

step 1: pick a data point $\boldsymbol{x}$ at random, according to the probability density $p(\boldsymbol{x})$

step 2: find the Voronoi cell containing $\boldsymbol{x}$, that is, find i such that $|\boldsymbol{x} - \boldsymbol{m}_i| < |\boldsymbol{x} - \boldsymbol{m}_j|$ for all $j \neq i$

step 3: move $\boldsymbol{m}_i$ towards $\boldsymbol{x}$: $\boldsymbol{m}_i \to \boldsymbol{m}_i + \eta(\boldsymbol{x} - \boldsymbol{m}_i)$

step 4: return to 1

The parameter $\eta > 0$ is the learning rate and controls the magnitude of the changes; one takes $\eta \ll 1$ to suppress fluctuations. The uncertainty (stochasticity) of the process is only in the realization of the sequence of data points we draw. Note that there would be a problem with data points $\boldsymbol{x}$ which are exactly on the border of two Voronoi cells. In practice this is not an issue: first, the probability for this to happen is generally very small (unless we have a pathological distribution $p(\boldsymbol{x})$), and second, one could simply decide in those instances not to make a change.

The VQ algorithm can be seen to have the following properties:

(*i*) A code-book vector will only become mobile when we pick a data point in its Voronoi cell, that is, sufficiently close to it. Hence the process of moving the $\boldsymbol{m}_i$ will proceed slowly in areas where the data density $p(\boldsymbol{x})$ is low.

(*ii*) Unless we reduce η during the process, the code-book vectors will continue to move stochastically, although the *density* of code-book vectors in any given region should become stationary.

(*iii*) VQ is very simple and (as we will see below) effective, and has just three tunable parameters: N, η, and the duration of the process.

As a consequence of (*i*) we also conclude that it is not necessarily optimal to initialize the N code-book vectors randomly: those which are initialized in regions where $p(\boldsymbol{x})$ is zero are in danger of *never* being used. Alternatively one could initialize the $\boldsymbol{m}_i$ by putting them at the locations of the first N observed data points. By construction they can then never be initialized in regions where there are no data.

Examples of VQ in action

The figures below illustrate the functioning of the VQ algorithm for a number of simple examples with $n = 2$ (i.e. where one has data points $\boldsymbol{x} = (x_1, x_2)$ in a plane) and $N = 100$ (i.e. a population of 100 code-book vectors), but for different choices of the data distribution $p(\boldsymbol{x})$ and with different initialization strategies. First, Figures 5.2 and 5.3 show examples of simple data distributions and random initialization, where the process is still seen to work fine, simply because in this case no code-book vector happens to have been initialized in data-free regions. Figures 5.4, 5.5, and 5.6 refer to strongly non-uniform data distributions, but now with non-random initialization (so that the non-uniformities cannot disrupt the functioning of VQ). The process is again seen to work fine. In contrast, in Figures 5.7, 5.8, and 5.9 the same three non-uniform distributions are considered, but now with random (i.e. inappropriate) initialization of the code-book vectors. The resulting locations of the code-book vectors illustrate quite clearly how for random initialization and non-uniform data distributions the VQ process fails to use its resources effectively.

5.2 Soft vector quantization

The SVQ algorithm and its properties

The SVQ algorithm, which can be regarded as a smooth version of VQ, is defined as follows. First we initialize the N code-book vectors $\boldsymbol{m}_i \in \mathbb{R}^n$ randomly (in contrast to VQ, random initialization poses no problem for SVQ, as we will see). Then we iterate the following stochastic process:

step 1: pick a data point $\boldsymbol{x}$ at random, according to the probability density $p(\boldsymbol{x})$

step 2: calculate, for *all* i:

$$F_i(\boldsymbol{x}, \{\boldsymbol{m}\}) = \frac{e^{-\beta(\boldsymbol{x}-\boldsymbol{m}_i)^2}}{\sum_{j=1}^{N} e^{-\beta(\boldsymbol{x}-\boldsymbol{m}_j)^2}} \tag{5.3}$$

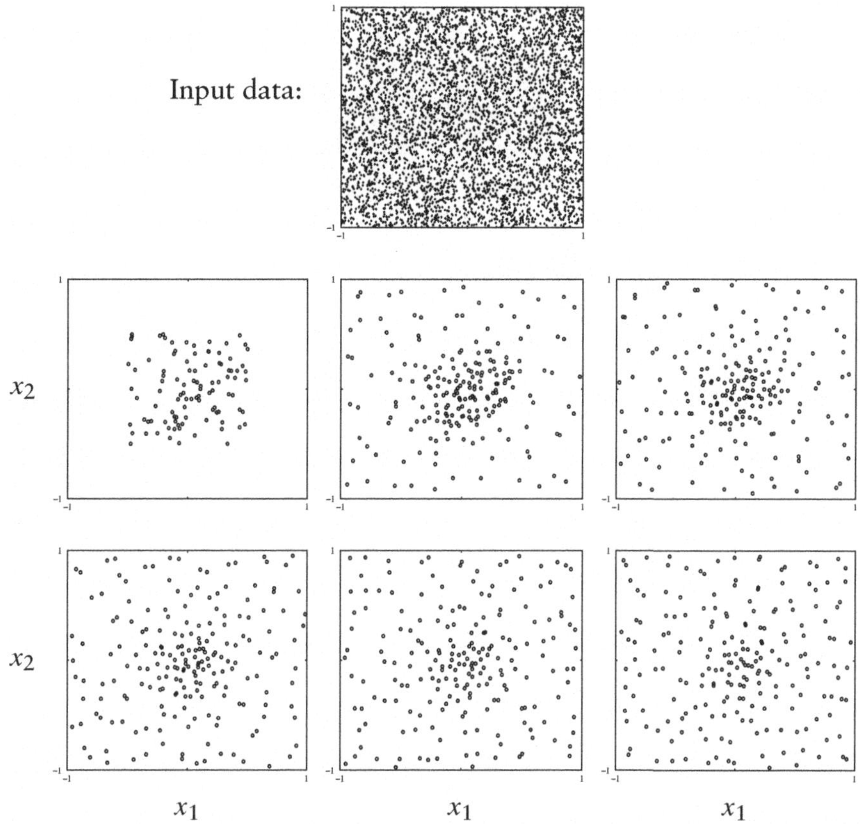

Figure 5.2 Numerical simulation of VQ, with $n = 2$, $\eta = 0.5$, and $N = 100$. Top graph: data distribution $p(\boldsymbol{x})$, uniform over the square $[-1, 1] \times [-1, 1]$. Bottom six graphs: locations of the code-book vectors $\boldsymbol{m}_i$ during the course of the process ($i = 1, \ldots, 100$), at times $t = 0$ (middle row, left), $t = 1000$ (middle row, centre), $t = 2000$ (middle row, right), $t = 3000$ (bottom row, left), $t = 4000$ (bottom row, middle), and $t = 5000$ (bottom row, right). Times are measured in the number of iterations. Code-book vectors are initially allocated randomly in the square $[-\frac{1}{2}, \frac{1}{2}] \times [-\frac{1}{2}, \frac{1}{2}]$.

step 3: move *all* $\boldsymbol{m}_i$ towards $\boldsymbol{x}$: $\quad \boldsymbol{m}_i \rightarrow \boldsymbol{m}_i + \eta(\boldsymbol{x} - \boldsymbol{m}_i)F_i(\boldsymbol{x}, \{\boldsymbol{m}\})$

step 4: return to 1

The parameter $0 < \eta \ll 1$ (the learning rate) again controls the overall magnitude of the changes. Note that, by construction, $\sum_i F_i(\boldsymbol{x}, \{\boldsymbol{m}\}) = 1$ and $0 \leq F_i(\boldsymbol{x}, \{\boldsymbol{m}\}) \leq 1$.

The SVQ algorithm can be seen to have the following general properties:

1. All code-book vectors are moved towards $\boldsymbol{x}$ at every iteration step, but those which are closest to $\boldsymbol{x}$ are moved most.

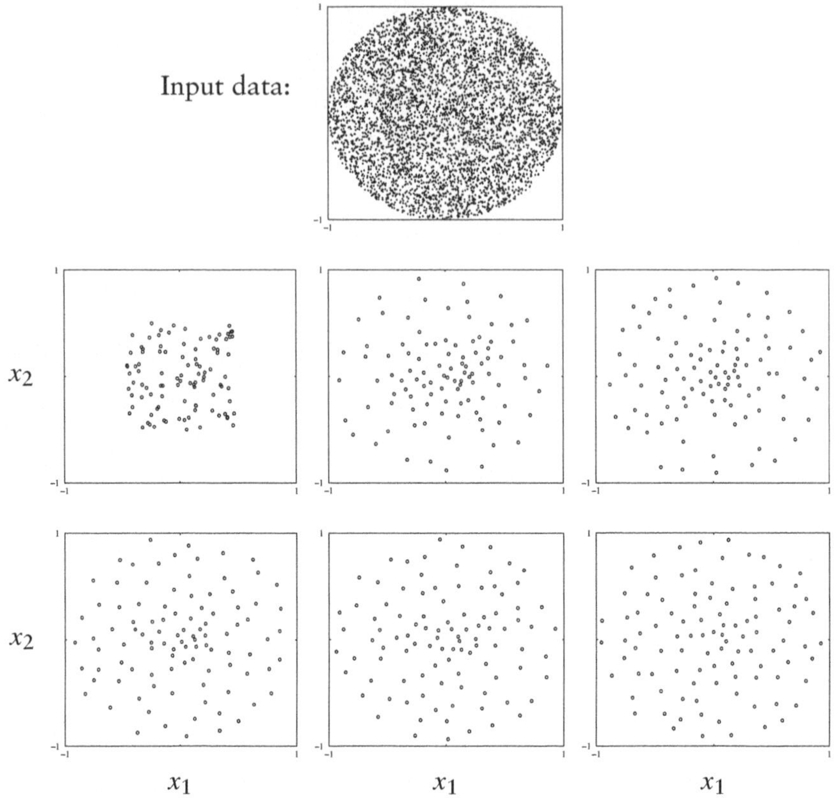

Figure 5.3 Numerical simulation of VQ, with $n = 2$, $\eta = 0.5$, and $N = 100$. Top graph: data distribution $p(\boldsymbol{x})$, uniform over the disk $|\boldsymbol{x}| < 1$. Bottom six graphs: locations of the code-book vectors $\boldsymbol{m}_i$ during the course of the process ($i = 1, \ldots, 100$), at times $t = 0$ (middle row, left), $t = 1000$ (middle row, centre), $t = 2000$ (middle row, right), $t = 3000$ (bottom row, left), $t = 4000$ (bottom row, middle), and $t = 5000$ (bottom row, right). Code-book vectors are initially allocated randomly in the square $[-\frac{1}{2}, \frac{1}{2}] \times [-\frac{1}{2}, \frac{1}{2}]$.

2. Unless we reduce η during the process, the code-book vectors will continue to move stochastically, although the *density* of code-book vectors in any given region should become stationary.
3. SVQ is still simple, but it has one more parameter than VQ. This extra parameter, β, defines a characteristic distance in data space: code-book vectors with $|\boldsymbol{x} - \boldsymbol{m}_i| > 1/\sqrt{\beta}$ will move only weakly, in contrast to those with $|\boldsymbol{x} - \boldsymbol{m}_i| < 1/\sqrt{\beta}$. Hence $1/\sqrt{\beta}$ defines the distance over which code-book vectors tend to exert an influence. Since the characteristic distance between the code-book vectors will also strongly depend on N, one should expect the optimal value of β to depend on N.
4. SVQ has an advantage over VQ when data distributions $p(\boldsymbol{x})$ can (slowly) change over time. Although we can ensure in VQ, by appropriate initialization, that the code-book vectors cannot get stuck in

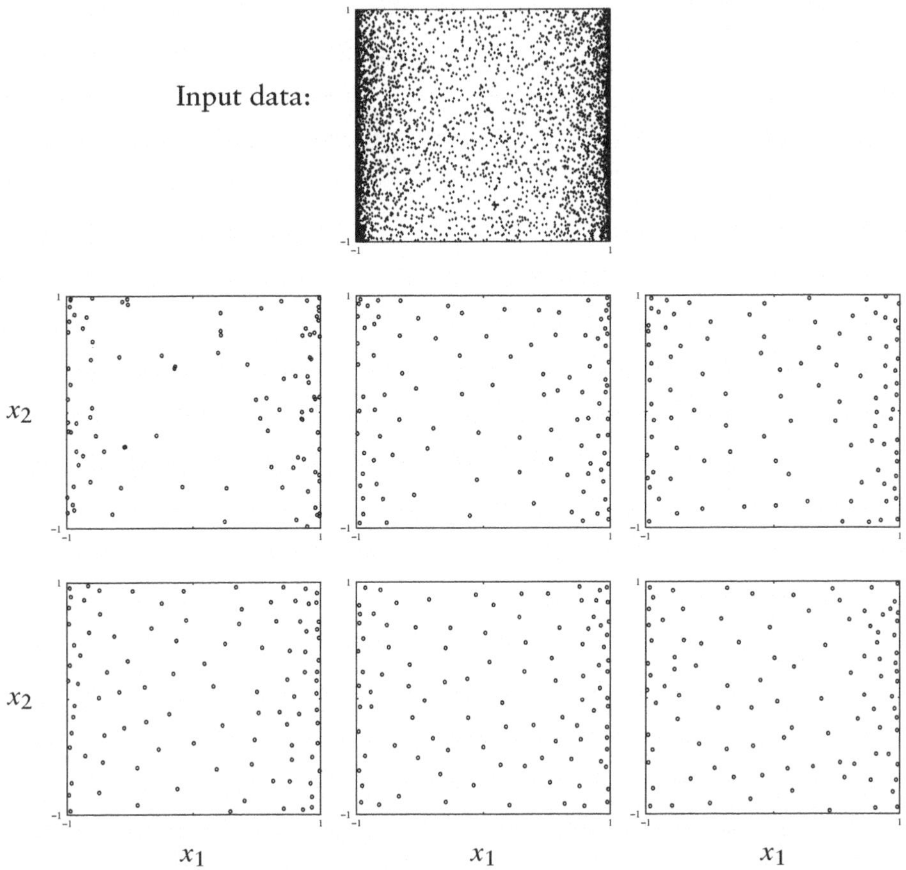

Figure 5.4 Numerical simulation of VQ, with $n = 2$, $\eta = 0.5$, and $N = 100$. Top graph: data distribution $p(\boldsymbol{x})$, non-uniform over the square $[-1, 1] \times [-1, 1]$, with highest data density near the borders $|x_1| = 1$. Bottom six graphs: locations of the code-book vectors $\boldsymbol{m}_i$ during the course of the process ($i = 1, \ldots, 100$), at times $t = 0$ (middle row, left), $t = 1000$ (middle row, centre), $t = 2000$ (middle row, right), $t = 3000$ (bottom row, left), $t = 4000$ (bottom row, middle), and $t = 5000$ (bottom row, right). Code-book vectors are initially positioned at the locations of the first 100 data points picked by the process.

data-poor regions, this will no longer be guaranteed if $p(\boldsymbol{x})$ can change over time: regions which are data-rich now, and which attract code-book vectors, might become data-poor later. In SVQ the system will always be able to adapt to the new data environment, since all code-book vectors are updated all the time.

Let us next investigate the action of the SVQ algorithm for the two extreme values of the new parameter β: $\beta = \infty$ and $\beta = 0$.

Proposition 1. $\lim_{\beta\to\infty} \text{SVQ} = \text{VQ}$.

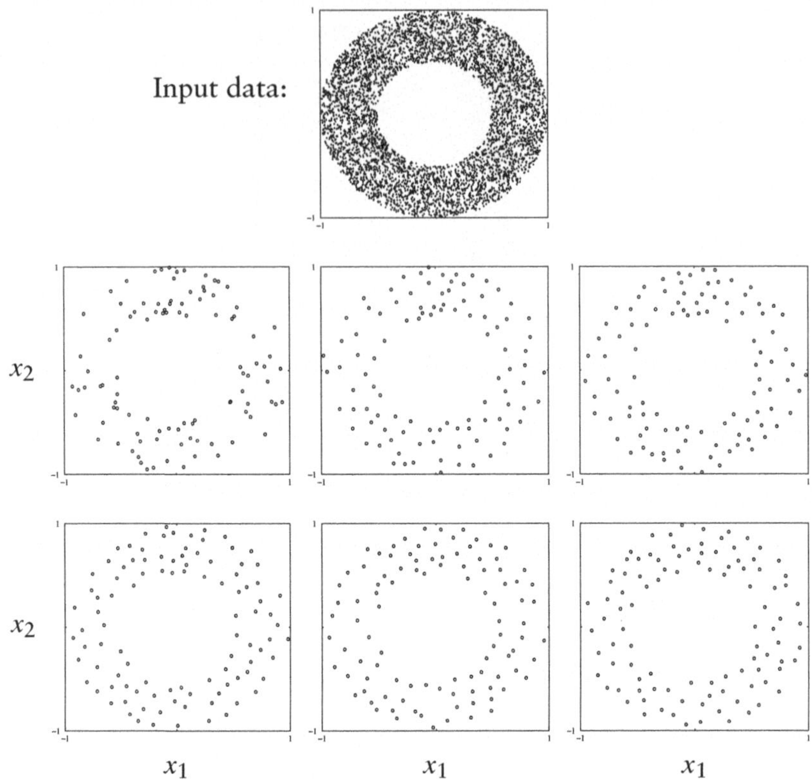

Figure 5.5 Numerical simulation of VQ, with $n = 2$, $\eta = 0.5$, and $N = 100$. Top graph: data distribution $p(\boldsymbol{x})$, uniform over the region $\frac{1}{2} < |\boldsymbol{x}| < 1$. Bottom six graphs: locations of the code-book vectors $\boldsymbol{m}_i$ during the course of the process ($i = 1, \ldots, 100$), at times $t = 0$ (middle row, left), $t = 1000$ (middle row, centre), $t = 2000$ (middle row, right), $t = 3000$ (bottom row, left), $t = 4000$ (bottom row, middle), and $t = 5000$ (bottom row, right). Code-book vectors are initially positioned at the locations of the first 100 data points picked by the process.

Proof. Define the Voronoi tessalation of data space induced by the code-book vectors $\{\boldsymbol{m}\}$. Consider an SVQ iteration step, where we pick data point $\boldsymbol{x}$. Assume $\boldsymbol{x} \in V_k[\{\boldsymbol{m}\}]$, that is, $\boldsymbol{x}$ is found to be in the Voronoi cell of code-book vector k. We again exclude the pathological cases where $\boldsymbol{x}$ is at the boundary of Voronoi cells; see the section on VQ. Now multiply numerator and denominator of (5.3) by $\exp(\beta(\boldsymbol{x} - \boldsymbol{m}_k)^2)$, and use the property that $|\boldsymbol{x} - \boldsymbol{m}_i| > |\boldsymbol{x} - \boldsymbol{m}_k|$ for all $i \neq k$:

$$\lim_{\beta\to\infty} F_i(\boldsymbol{x}, \{\boldsymbol{m}\}) = \lim_{\beta\to\infty} \frac{e^{-\beta[(\boldsymbol{x}-\boldsymbol{m}_i)^2-(\boldsymbol{x}-\boldsymbol{m}_k)^2]}}{\sum_{j=1}^{N} e^{-\beta[(\boldsymbol{x}-\boldsymbol{m}_j)^2-(\boldsymbol{x}-\boldsymbol{m}_k)^2]}}$$

$$= \lim_{\beta\to\infty} \frac{e^{-\beta[(\boldsymbol{x}-\boldsymbol{m}_i)^2-(\boldsymbol{x}-\boldsymbol{m}_k)^2]}}{1 + \sum_{j\neq k} e^{-\beta[(\boldsymbol{x}-\boldsymbol{m}_j)^2-(\boldsymbol{x}-\boldsymbol{m}_k)^2]}} = \begin{cases} 1, & \text{for } i = k \\ 0, & \text{for } i \neq k \end{cases}$$

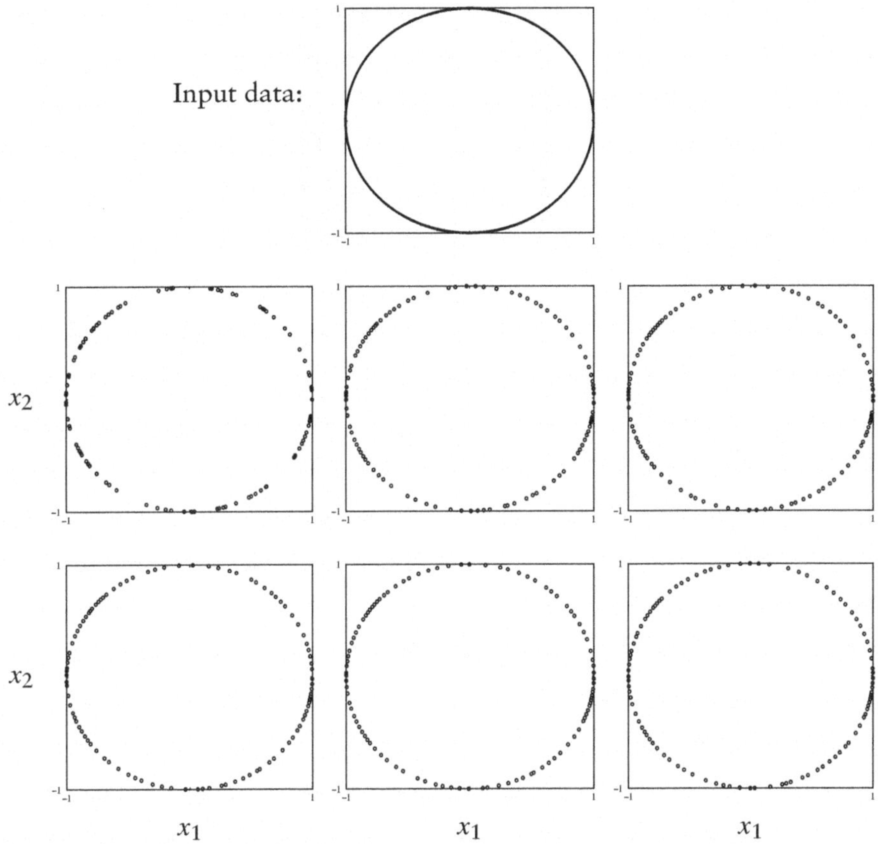

Figure 5.6 Numerical simulation of VQ, with $n = 2$, $\eta = 0.5$, and $N = 100$. Top graph: data distribution $p(\boldsymbol{x})$, uniform over the circle $|\boldsymbol{x}| = 1$. Bottom six graphs: locations of the code-book vectors $\boldsymbol{m}_i$ during the course of the process ($i = 1, \ldots, 100$), at times $t = 0$ (middle row, left), $t = 1000$ (middle row, centre), $t = 2000$ (middle row, right), $t = 3000$ (bottom row, left), $t = 4000$ (bottom row, middle), and $t = 5000$ (bottom row, right). Code-book vectors are initially positioned at the locations of the first 100 data points picked by the process.

The denominator in the fraction tends to one for $\beta \to \infty$ for any i, because all exponents in the sum are large and negative; the difference between $i = k$ and $i \neq k$ arises from the numerator, which is one in the former case and tends to zero in the latter. This result shows that for $\beta \to \infty$ the SVQ modification of the code-book vectors in a single iteration reduces to

$$\boldsymbol{m}_k \to \boldsymbol{m}_k + \eta(\boldsymbol{x} - \boldsymbol{m}_k)$$

$$\boldsymbol{m}_i \to \boldsymbol{m}_i \quad \text{for all } i \neq k$$

which is identical to that of VQ. □

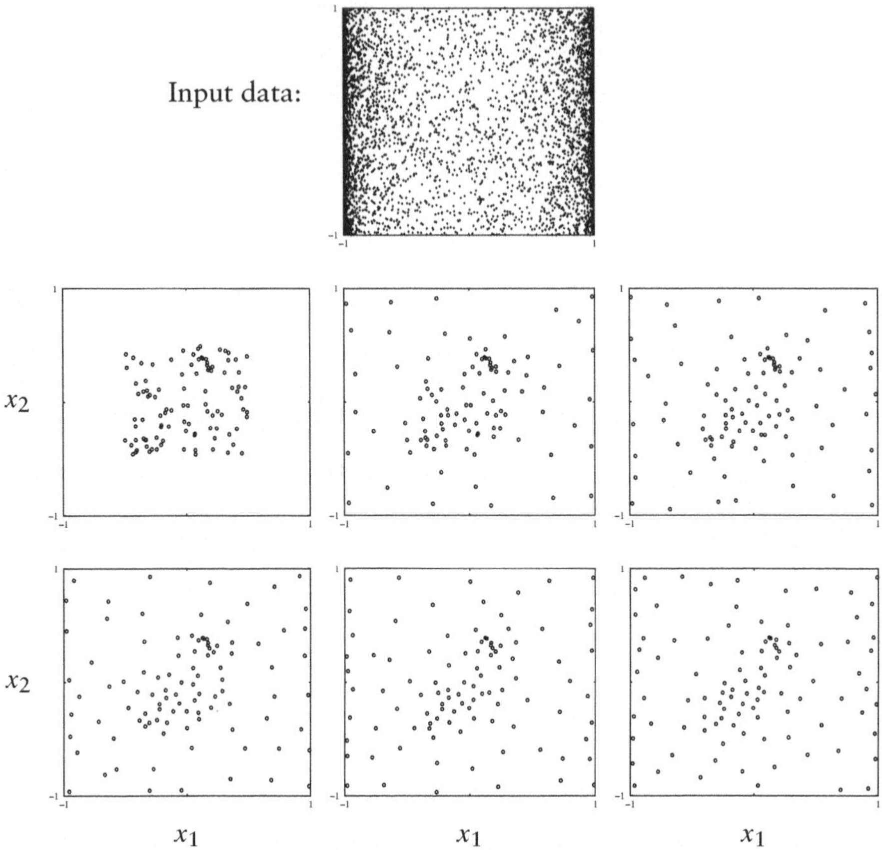

Figure 5.7 Numerical simulation of VQ, with $n = 2$, $\eta = 0.5$, and $N = 100$. Top graph: data distribution $p(\boldsymbol{x})$, non-uniform across the square $[-1, 1] \times [-1, 1]$, with highest data density near the borders $|x_1| = 1$. Bottom six graphs: locations of the code-book vectors $\boldsymbol{m}_i$ during the course of the process ($i = 1, \ldots, 100$), at times $t = 0$ (middle row, left), $t = 1000$ (middle row, centre), $t = 2000$ (middle row, right), $t = 3000$ (bottom row, left), $t = 4000$ (bottom row, middle), and $t = 5000$ (bottom row, right). Code-book vector are initially allocated randomly in the square $[-\frac{1}{2}, \frac{1}{2}] \times [-\frac{1}{2}, \frac{1}{2}]$. Comparison with Figure 5.4 shows that code-book vectors initialized in data regions where $p(\boldsymbol{x})$ is small tend to get stuck.

Proposition 2. For $\beta \to 0$ all code-book vectors $\boldsymbol{m}_i$ will ultimately collapse to a single point, which will fluctuate around the average data-point $\langle \boldsymbol{x} \rangle = \int d\boldsymbol{x}\, \boldsymbol{x}\, p(\boldsymbol{x})$.

Proof. For $\beta \to 0$ we find $F_i(\boldsymbol{x}, \{\boldsymbol{m}\}) = N^{-1}$ (for any $\boldsymbol{x}$, any i and any $\{\boldsymbol{m}\}$) and the SVQ modifications simply reduce to

$$\boldsymbol{m}_i \to \boldsymbol{m}_i + \frac{\eta}{N}(\boldsymbol{x} - \boldsymbol{m}_i) \quad \text{for all } i$$

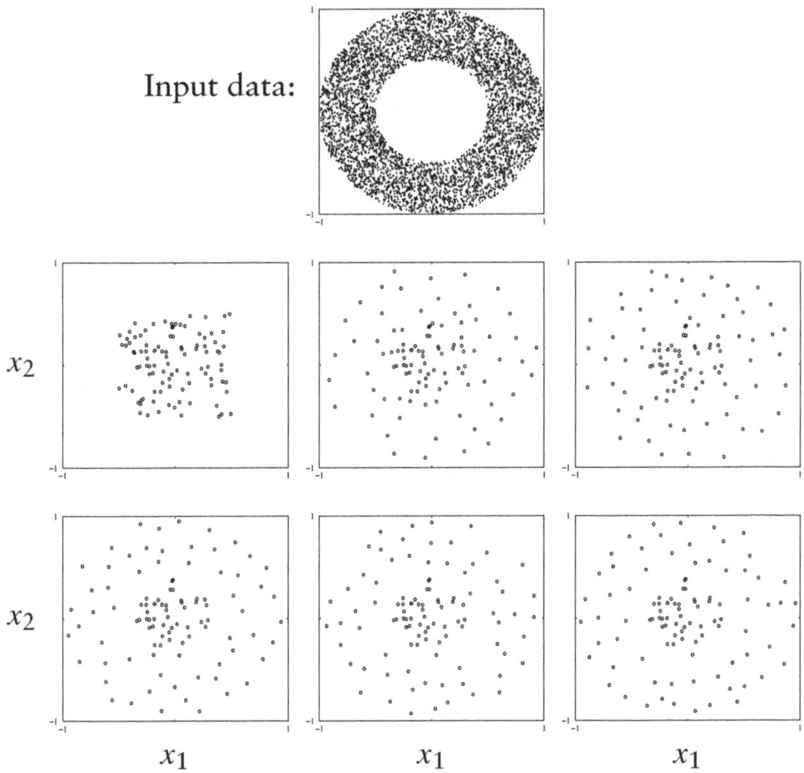

Figure 5.8 Numerical simulation of VQ, with $n = 2$, $\eta = 0.5$, and $N = 100$. Top graph: data distribution $p(\boldsymbol{x})$, uniform over the region $\frac{1}{2} < |\boldsymbol{x}| < 1$. Bottom six graphs: locations of the code-book vectors $\boldsymbol{m}_i$ during the course of the process ($i = 1, \ldots, 100$), at times $t = 0$ (middle row, left), $t = 1000$ (middle row, centre), $t = 2000$ (middle row, right), $t = 3000$ (bottom row, left), $t = 4000$ (bottom row, middle), and $t = 5000$ (bottom row, right). Code-book vector are initially allocated randomly in the square $[-\frac{1}{2}, \frac{1}{2}] \times [-\frac{1}{2}, \frac{1}{2}]$. Comparison with Figure 5.5 shows that code-book vectors initialized in data regions where $p(\boldsymbol{x})$ is zero tend to get stuck.

Now consider the difference between any two code-book vectors. If we label the iterations of the algorithm by $\ell = 0, 1, 2, \ldots$, we find

$$\boldsymbol{m}_i(\ell + 1) - \boldsymbol{m}_j(\ell + 1) = \left(1 - \frac{\eta}{N}\right)[\boldsymbol{m}_i(\ell) - \boldsymbol{m}_j(\ell)]$$

hence

$$\boldsymbol{m}_i(\ell) - \boldsymbol{m}_j(\ell) = \left(1 - \frac{\eta}{N}\right)^{\ell}[\boldsymbol{m}_i(0) - \boldsymbol{m}_j(0)]$$

so $\lim_{\ell\to\infty}[\boldsymbol{m}_i(\ell) - \boldsymbol{m}_j(\ell)] = 0$, as claimed.

To find out *where* all the code-book vectors will go collectively, we only need to inspect the dynamics of the average $\boldsymbol{m} = N^{-1}\sum_i \boldsymbol{m}_i$ (since $\lim_{\ell\to\infty}[\boldsymbol{m}(\ell) - \boldsymbol{m}_i(\ell)] = 0$). Writing the data point drawn at iteration ℓ as $\boldsymbol{x}(\ell)$, we get $\boldsymbol{m}(\ell + 1) = (1 - \eta/N)\boldsymbol{m}(\ell) + (\eta/N)\boldsymbol{x}(\ell)$. Hence, upon

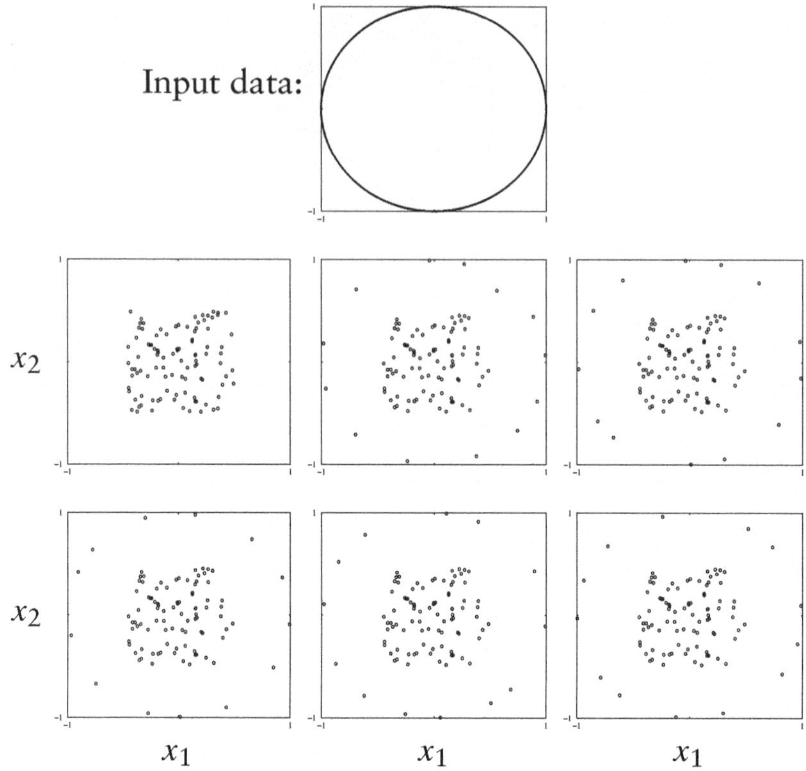

Figure 5.9 Numerical simulation of VQ, with $n = 2$, $\eta = 0.5$, and $N = 100$. Top graph: data distribution $p(\boldsymbol{x})$, uniform over the circle $|\boldsymbol{x}| = 1$. Bottom six graphs: locations of the code-book vectors $\boldsymbol{m}_i$ during the course of the process ($i = 1, \ldots, 100$), at times $t = 0$ (middle row, left), $t = 1000$ (middle row, centre), $t = 2000$ (middle row, right), $t = 3000$ (bottom row, left), $t = 4000$ (bottom row, middle), and $t = 5000$ (bottom row, right). Code-book vector are initially allocated randomly in the square $[-\frac{1}{2}, \frac{1}{2}] \times [-\frac{1}{2}, \frac{1}{2}]$. Comparison with Figure 5.6 shows that code-book vectors initialized in data regions where $p(\boldsymbol{x})$ is zero tend to get stuck.

abbreviating the factor $1 - \eta/N$ as z,

$$\begin{aligned}
\boldsymbol{m}(1) &= z\,\boldsymbol{m}(0) + \frac{\eta}{N}\boldsymbol{x}(0) \\
\boldsymbol{m}(2) &= z\left[z\boldsymbol{m}(0) + \frac{\eta}{N}\boldsymbol{x}(0)\right] + \frac{\eta}{N}\boldsymbol{x}(1) \\
&= z^2\boldsymbol{m}(0) + \frac{\eta}{N}[z\,\boldsymbol{x}(0) + \boldsymbol{x}(1)] \\
\boldsymbol{m}(3) &= z\left[z^2\boldsymbol{m}(0) + \frac{\eta}{N}z\,\boldsymbol{x}(0) + \frac{\eta}{N}\boldsymbol{x}(1)\right] + \frac{\eta}{N}\boldsymbol{x}(2) \\
&= z^3\boldsymbol{m}(0) + \frac{\eta}{N}[z^2\boldsymbol{x}(0) + z\,\boldsymbol{x}(1) + \boldsymbol{x}(2)] \\
\vdots\; &= \qquad \vdots \\
\boldsymbol{m}(\ell) &= z^{\ell}\boldsymbol{m}(0) + \frac{\eta}{N}\sum_{k=0}^{\ell-1} z^{\ell-1-k}\boldsymbol{x}(k)
\end{aligned}$$

We can now average over the possible choices of data, using $\langle \boldsymbol{x}(k)\rangle = \langle \boldsymbol{x}\rangle$, the average of the distribution $p(\boldsymbol{x})$ (assuming this average to be finite). Together with $\sum_{k\geq 0} z^k = 1/(1-z)$, which holds generally whenever $|z| < 1$, this gives us

$$\begin{aligned}\lim_{\ell\to\infty} \langle \boldsymbol{m}(\ell)\rangle &= \lim_{\ell\to\infty} \left(z^{\ell}\boldsymbol{m}(0) + \frac{\eta}{N}\langle \boldsymbol{x}\rangle \sum_{k\geq 0}^{\ell-1} z^k \right) \\ &= \frac{\eta}{N}(1-z)^{-1}\langle \boldsymbol{x}\rangle = \langle \boldsymbol{x}\rangle\end{aligned}$$

as claimed. □

One can show similarly that the fluctuations of $\boldsymbol{m}$ around $\langle \boldsymbol{x}\rangle$ remain finite, provided the width of the data distribution is finite, that is, $\langle \boldsymbol{x}^2\rangle < \infty$.

Thus VQ can be regarded as a special case of SVQ, obtained by putting $\beta \to \infty$. Second we infer from inspection of the extreme case $\beta = 0$ that one of the effects of the smoothing of SVQ, relative to VQ, is for code-vectors to 'drag one another along'.

A Lyapunov function for small learning rates

Our understanding of SVQ (and thus also of VQ) would greatly improve if we could recognize the process as the minimization of some error measure. For finite η this is not possible, but for $\eta \to 0$ it is. Labelling the different iterations with $\ell = 0, 1, 2, \ldots$, and writing the data point drawn at stage ℓ as $\boldsymbol{x}(\ell)$, we can cast both VQ and SVQ in the following compact form:

$$\boldsymbol{m}_i(\ell+1) = \boldsymbol{m}_i(\ell) + \eta[\boldsymbol{x}(\ell) - \boldsymbol{m}_i(\ell)]F_i(\boldsymbol{x}(\ell), \{\boldsymbol{m}(\ell)\}) \tag{5.4}$$

with

$$F_i^{\mathrm{SVQ}}(\boldsymbol{x}, \{\boldsymbol{m}\}) = \frac{e^{-\beta(\boldsymbol{x}-\boldsymbol{m}_i)^2}}{\sum_{j=1}^{N} e^{-\beta(\boldsymbol{x}-\boldsymbol{m}_j)^2}} \tag{5.5}$$

$$F_i^{\mathrm{VQ}}(\boldsymbol{x}, \{\boldsymbol{m}\}) = \begin{cases} 1, & \text{if } \boldsymbol{x} \in V_i[\{\boldsymbol{m}\}] \\ 0, & \text{otherwise} \end{cases} \tag{5.6}$$

For small learning rates we follow the procedure introduced to derive deterministic equations for online learning in layered neural networks (see Section 2.3), and define a new time variable $t = \eta\ell$. We then take the $\eta \to 0$ limit and find the stochastic process (5.4) being replaced by the deterministic equation

$$\frac{\mathrm{d}}{\mathrm{d}t}\boldsymbol{m}_i = \langle (\boldsymbol{x} - \boldsymbol{m}_i)F_i(\boldsymbol{x}, \{\boldsymbol{m}\})\rangle \tag{5.7}$$

with the average $\langle\cdots\rangle$ taken over $p(\boldsymbol{x})$ as before. Let us first look at SVQ, $F_i(\boldsymbol{x},\{\boldsymbol{m}\}) = F_i^{\mathrm{SVQ}}(\boldsymbol{x},\{\boldsymbol{m}\})$. We will show that the small η-limit (5.7) of the SVQ-algorithm attempts to approximate the data distribution $p(\boldsymbol{x})$ by a mixture of Gaussian distributions, each centred at one of the code-book vectors,

$$q(\boldsymbol{x}|\{\boldsymbol{m}\}) = \frac{1}{N}\sum_i \frac{e^{-\beta(\boldsymbol{x}-\boldsymbol{m}_i)^2}}{(\pi/\beta)^{n/2}} \tag{5.8}$$

This is demonstrated by proving the following proposition.

Proposition 3. For $F_i(\boldsymbol{x},\{\boldsymbol{m}\}) = F_i^{\mathrm{SVQ}}(\boldsymbol{x},\{\boldsymbol{m}\})$, equation (5.7) describes a gradient descent dynamics for an error measure $E[\{\boldsymbol{m}\}]$ given by the Kullback–Leibler distance between the data distribution p and the Gaussian mixture (5.8) parametrized by the set $\{\boldsymbol{m}\}$ of code-book vectors:

$$\frac{\mathrm{d}}{\mathrm{d}t}\boldsymbol{m}_i = -\frac{1}{2\beta}\nabla_{\boldsymbol{m}_i} E[\{\boldsymbol{m}\}], \quad E[\{\boldsymbol{m}\}] = \int \mathrm{d}\boldsymbol{x}\, p(\boldsymbol{x}) \ln\left[\frac{p(\boldsymbol{x})}{q(\boldsymbol{x}|\{\boldsymbol{m}\})}\right] \tag{5.9}$$

Proof. We just work out the relevant partial derivatives of $E[\{\boldsymbol{m}\}]$:

$$\begin{aligned}
-\frac{1}{2\beta}\nabla_{\boldsymbol{m}_i} E[\{\boldsymbol{m}\}] &= \frac{1}{2\beta}\int \mathrm{d}\boldsymbol{x}\, p(\boldsymbol{x}) \nabla_{\boldsymbol{m}_i} \ln q(\boldsymbol{x}|\{\boldsymbol{m}\}) \\
&= \frac{1}{2\beta}\int \mathrm{d}\boldsymbol{x}\, p(\boldsymbol{x}) \nabla_{\boldsymbol{m}_i} \ln \sum_j e^{-\beta(\boldsymbol{x}-\boldsymbol{m}_j)^2} \\
&= \frac{1}{2\beta}\int \mathrm{d}\boldsymbol{x}\, p(\boldsymbol{x}) \left[\frac{\nabla_{\boldsymbol{m}_i} e^{-\beta(\boldsymbol{x}-\boldsymbol{m}_i)^2}}{\sum_j e^{-\beta(\boldsymbol{x}-\boldsymbol{m}_j)^2}}\right] \\
&= \int \mathrm{d}\boldsymbol{x}\, p(\boldsymbol{x}) \left[\frac{(\boldsymbol{x}-\boldsymbol{m}_i) e^{-\beta(\boldsymbol{x}-\boldsymbol{m}_i)^2}}{\sum_j e^{-\beta(\boldsymbol{x}-\boldsymbol{m}_j)^2}}\right] \\
&= \left\langle (\boldsymbol{x}-\boldsymbol{m}_i) F_i^{\mathrm{SVQ}}(\boldsymbol{x},\{\boldsymbol{m}\}) \right\rangle
\end{aligned}$$

Comparison with (5.7) gives the desired result. □

The error measure $E[\{\boldsymbol{m}\}]$ in (5.9) is indeed the Kullback–Leibler distance $D(p\|q)$ between the data distribution p and the Gaussian mixture q introduced in (5.8). It is an information-theoretic measure of the deviation between the two distributions. Properties of this measure will be discussed in greater detail in Part III of this book. What is needed here is that $D(p\|q) \geq 0$ for any two distributions p and q, with equality only if $p(\boldsymbol{x}) = q(\boldsymbol{x})$ (in a distributional sense). From the inequality $D(p\|q) \geq 0$, hence $E[\{\boldsymbol{m}\}] \geq 0$, in combination with the gradient descent equation in (5.9) which ensures that $\mathrm{d}E/\mathrm{d}t \leq 0$, we may conclude that $D(p\|q) = E[\{\boldsymbol{m}\}]$ introduced in (5.9) is a Lyapunov function for the SVQ process (5.4). Hence we can interpret SVQ, at least for small η, as approximating the data distribution $p(\boldsymbol{x})$ optimally by a mixture of Gaussians of the form (5.8), via adaptation of the centres $\boldsymbol{m}_i$ of these Gaussians.

Similarly, since $\lim_{\beta\to\infty}\text{SVQ} = \text{VQ}$ and since $\lim_{\beta\to\infty}(\beta/\pi)^{n/2} \times e^{-\beta(\boldsymbol{x}-\boldsymbol{m}_i)^2} = \delta(\boldsymbol{x}-\boldsymbol{m}_i)$ (see Appendix F for definition and properties of the delta distribution), we may for small η interpret VQ as approximating the data distribution $p(\boldsymbol{x})$ optimally by a mixture of delta-distributions, via adaptation of the centres of these delta-distributions:

$$\eta \ll 1,\ \text{SVQ}: \quad \text{finds } \{\boldsymbol{m}\} \text{ such that} \quad p(\boldsymbol{x}) \approx \frac{1}{N}\sum_i \frac{e^{-\beta(\boldsymbol{x}-\boldsymbol{m}_i)^2}}{(\pi/\beta)^{n/2}}$$

$$\eta \ll 1,\ \text{VQ}: \quad \text{finds } \{\boldsymbol{m}\} \text{ such that} \quad p(\boldsymbol{x}) \approx \frac{1}{N}\sum_i \delta(\boldsymbol{x}-\boldsymbol{m}_i)$$

The characteristic distance which we already identified above is now recognized as the width $\sigma = 1/\sqrt{2\beta}$ of the individual Gaussians with which SVQ aims to match the data distribution $p(\boldsymbol{x})$. For finite (but not too large) η we may regard SVQ and VQ as noisy versions of the above gradient descent processes.

Finally we note briefly that the stationary state of the $\eta \to 0$ equation (5.7), given by $\langle(\boldsymbol{x}-\boldsymbol{m}_i)F_i(\boldsymbol{x},\{\boldsymbol{m}\})\rangle = 0$, translates into

$$\boldsymbol{m}_i = \frac{\int \mathrm{d}\boldsymbol{x}\, \boldsymbol{x} F_i(\boldsymbol{x},\{\boldsymbol{m}\})p(\boldsymbol{x})}{\int \mathrm{d}\boldsymbol{x}\, F_i(\boldsymbol{x},\{\boldsymbol{m}\})p(\boldsymbol{x})}, \quad \text{so for VQ:} \quad \boldsymbol{m}_i = \frac{\int_{V_i[\{\boldsymbol{m}\}]} \mathrm{d}\boldsymbol{x}\, \boldsymbol{x}\, p(\boldsymbol{x})}{\int_{V_i[\{\boldsymbol{m}\}]} \mathrm{d}\boldsymbol{x}\, p(\boldsymbol{x})} \tag{5.10}$$

For VQ we thus have the transparent result that, in equilibrium and for η sufficiently small, the location of code-book vector $\boldsymbol{m}_i$ will be the centre of gravity of the data distribution within its associated Voronoi cell $V_i[\{\boldsymbol{m}\}]$.

Examples of SVQ in action

The figures on the following two pages illustrate the functioning of the SVQ algorithm for a number of simple examples with $n = 2$ (i.e. where one has data points $\boldsymbol{x} = (x_1, x_2)$ in a plane) and $N = 100$ (i.e. a population of 100 code-book vectors), but for different choices of the data distribution $p(\boldsymbol{x})$. Figure 5.10 shows the locations of the code-book vectors at different times, for $\beta = 10$, where the characteristic width of the data covering Gaussians is $\sigma = 1/\sqrt{2\beta} \approx 0.22$. We observe that code-book vectors indeed no longer get stuck in data-poor regions even if they are initialized randomly, and that they keep a distance of the order of σ from the boundaries of the data region. Because the width of the data strip is $\frac{1}{2}$, here this essentially sends all

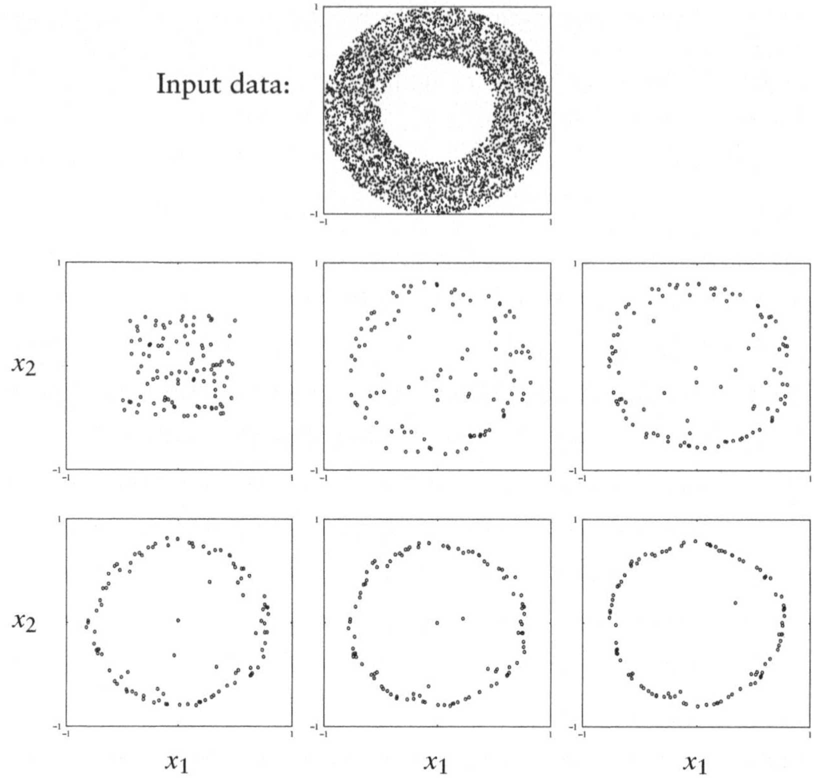

Figure 5.10 Numerical simulation of SVQ, with $n = 2$, $\eta = 0.1$, $\beta = 10$, and $N = 100$. Top graph: data distribution $p(\boldsymbol{x})$, uniform over the region $\frac{1}{2} < |\boldsymbol{x}| < 1$. Bottom six graphs: locations of the code-book vectors $\boldsymbol{m}_i$ during the course of the process ($i = 1, \ldots, 100$), at times $t = 0$ (middle row, left), $t = 1000$ (middle row, centre), $t = 2000$ (middle row, right), $t = 3000$ (bottom row, left), $t = 4000$ (bottom row, middle), and $t = 5000$ (bottom row, right). Times are measured in the number of iterations. Code-book vector are initially allocated randomly in the square $[-\frac{1}{2}, \frac{1}{2}] \times [-\frac{1}{2}, \frac{1}{2}]$.

code-book vectors to the circle $|\boldsymbol{x}| = \frac{3}{4}$. Figure 5.11 shows the asymptotic locations (after 10,000 iterations) of the code-book vectors for four different values of β. The corresponding values of σ are: $\sigma = 0.1$ ($\beta = 50$), $\sigma \approx 0.22$ ($\beta = 10$), $\sigma \approx 0.32$ ($\beta = 5$), and $\sigma \approx 0.71$ ($\beta = 1$). With these values one can understand perfectly the observed clustering properties of the code-book vectors; this underlines the power of theoretical results such as those above (i.e. Proposition 3).

5.3 Time-dependent learning rates

We have seen that for finite η the processes of the type (5.4) can be regarded as noisy versions of the deterministic equation (5.7). For SVQ and VQ the

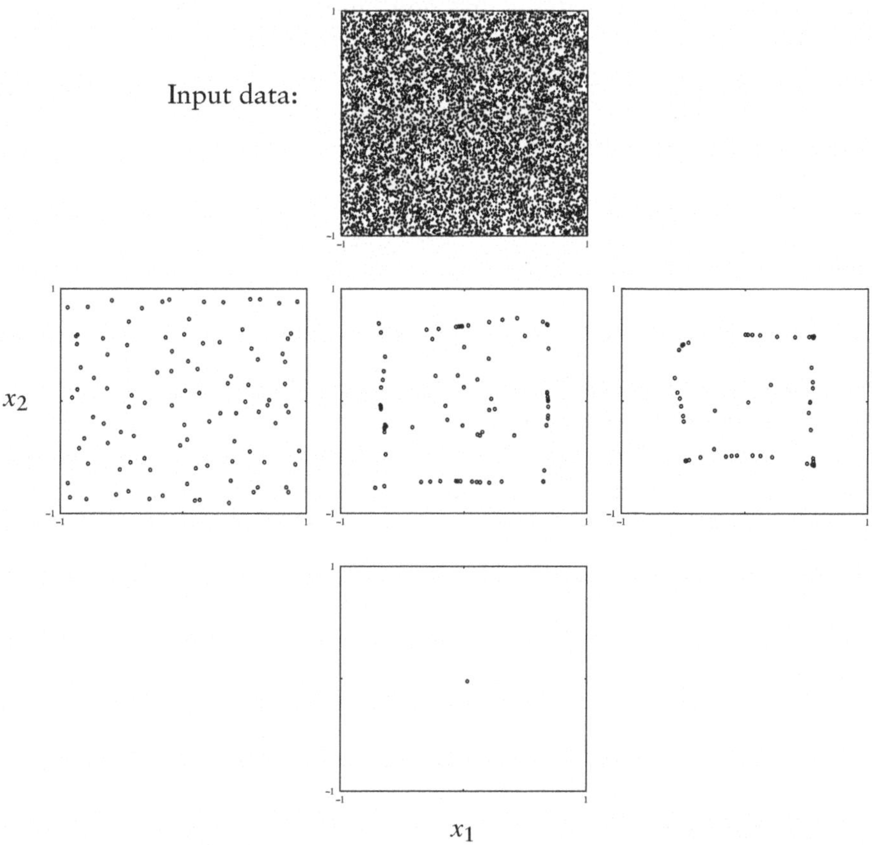

Figure 5.11 Numerical simulation of SVQ, with $n = 2$, $\eta = 0.5$, and $N = 100$. Top graph: data distribution $p(\boldsymbol{x})$, uniform over the square $[-1, 1] \times [-1, 1]$. Bottom four graphs: locations of the code-book vectors $\boldsymbol{m}_i$ after 10,000 iteration steps ($i = 1, \ldots, 100$), for different choices of the parameter β: $\beta = 50$ (middle row, left), $\beta = 10$ (middle row, middle), $\beta = 5$ (middle row, right), and $\beta = 1$ (bottom row). Code-book vector are initially allocated randomly in the square $[-\frac{1}{2}, \frac{1}{2}] \times [-\frac{1}{2}, \frac{1}{2}]$.

latter minimize a transparent and sensible error measure. In the initial stages of these processes it is then preferable to have a finite η: the added randomness may prevent the system from going to a suboptimal local minimum of the error measure. Asymptotically, on the other hand, one would prefer a fluctuation-free and unique (reproducible) final state, that is, $\eta \to 0$. It is therefore natural to choose a slowly but monotonically decreasing time-dependent learning rate $\eta(\ell)$, where ℓ labels the iterations of the algorithm (5.4). The question then is how to determine the optimal rate of decay for $\eta(\ell)$. Too fast a reduction of $\eta(\ell)$ might cause evolution to local minima, or might prevent the code-book vectors from travelling over sufficiently large distances to take up their optimal positions in the data space, whose size we do not know beforehand. Too slow a decrease in $\eta(\ell)$, on the other hand, might cause fluctuations and non-uniqueness of the final state to persist too long for us to achieve the desired stationary state within the time-scales of our experiments. We will always choose our $\eta(\ell)$ such that $0 < \eta(\ell+1) \leq \eta(\ell)$ and $\eta(0) < N$. Below we show that sensible criteria to be met by the decay of $\eta(\ell)$ are

$$\text{not too fast: } \sum_{\ell=0}^{\infty} \eta(\ell) = \infty, \qquad \text{not too slow: } \sum_{\ell=0}^{\infty} \eta^2(\ell) < \infty \tag{5.11}$$

Proposition 1. The learning rate must obey $\sum_{\ell=0}^{\infty} \eta(\ell) = \infty$, otherwise there will be an undesirable a priori bound on the possible distance to be covered by the code-book vectors.

Proof. We deduce from the following alternative way of writing equation (5.4),

$$\boldsymbol{m}_i(\ell+1) = \boldsymbol{m}_i(\ell)[1 - \eta F_i(\boldsymbol{x}(\ell), \{\boldsymbol{m}(\ell)\})] + \eta F_i(\boldsymbol{x}(\ell), \{\boldsymbol{m}(\ell)\})\boldsymbol{x}(\ell),$$

together with the properties $F_i(\boldsymbol{x}, \{\boldsymbol{m}\}) \in [0, 1]$ and $0 \leq \eta \leq 1$, that

$$|\boldsymbol{m}_i(\ell+1)| \leq |\boldsymbol{m}_i(\ell)| + \eta(\ell)|\boldsymbol{x}(\ell)|$$

Hence, by iteration:

$$|\boldsymbol{m}_i(\ell)| \leq |\boldsymbol{m}_i(0)| + \sum_{k=0}^{\ell-1} \eta(k)|\boldsymbol{x}(k)|$$

so

$$\lim_{\ell\to\infty} \langle|\boldsymbol{m}_i(\ell)|\rangle \leq |\boldsymbol{m}_i(0)| + \langle|\boldsymbol{x}|\rangle \sum_{k=0}^{\infty} \eta(k)$$

Thus, unless $\sum_{k=0}^{\infty} \eta(k) = \infty$, we have an a priori bound on the distance which can be travelled by any code-book vector, which could prevent parts of the data distribution from being reached. □

Proposition 2. If the learning rate obeys $\sum_{\ell=0}^{\infty} \eta^2(\ell) < \infty$, then we can at least be sure that for the simplest process of the class (5.4) the uncertainty in the location of the average code-book vector cannot diverge.

Proof. The simplest process of the class (5.4) is the $\beta \to 0$ limit of SVQ: $F_i(\boldsymbol{x}, \{\boldsymbol{m}\}) = 1/N$, so $\boldsymbol{m}(\ell+1) = \boldsymbol{m}(\ell) + (\eta(\ell)/N)[\boldsymbol{x}(\ell) - \boldsymbol{m}(\ell)]$, where

$\boldsymbol{m}(\ell) = N^{-1}\sum_i \boldsymbol{m}_i(\ell)$. We now write $\boldsymbol{m}(\ell) = \langle \boldsymbol{m}(\ell)\rangle + \boldsymbol{v}(\ell)$, so that $\langle \boldsymbol{v}(\ell)\rangle = 0$ and

$$\boldsymbol{v}(\ell+1) = \left(1 - \frac{\eta(\ell)}{N}\right)\boldsymbol{v}(\ell) + \frac{\eta(\ell)}{N}[\boldsymbol{x}(\ell) - \langle \boldsymbol{x}\rangle]$$

Note that $\boldsymbol{v}(\ell)$ is statistically independent of all $\boldsymbol{x}(\ell')$ with $\ell' \geq \ell$. Note also that, since at $\ell = 0$ there are no fluctuations yet, $\boldsymbol{v}(0) = 0$. Hence

$$\langle \boldsymbol{v}^2(\ell+1)\rangle = \left(1 - \frac{\eta(\ell)}{N}\right)^2 \langle \boldsymbol{v}^2(\ell)\rangle + \frac{\eta^2(\ell)}{N^2}\langle[\boldsymbol{x} - \langle \boldsymbol{x}\rangle]^2\rangle$$

Further iteration gives

$$\langle \boldsymbol{v}^2(\ell+2)\rangle = \left(1 - \frac{\eta(\ell+1)}{N}\right)^2 \left(1 - \frac{\eta(\ell)}{N}\right)^2 \langle \boldsymbol{v}^2(\ell)\rangle + \left(1 - \frac{\eta(\ell+1)}{N}\right)^2$$
$$\times \frac{\eta^2(\ell)}{N^2}\langle(\boldsymbol{x} - \langle \boldsymbol{x}\rangle)^2\rangle + \frac{\eta^2(\ell+1)}{N^2}\langle(\boldsymbol{x} - \langle \boldsymbol{x}\rangle)^2\rangle$$

We see that this iteration leads us to the following general expression

$$\frac{\langle \boldsymbol{v}^2(\ell)\rangle}{\langle(\boldsymbol{x} - \langle \boldsymbol{x}\rangle)^2\rangle} = \sum_{k=0}^{\ell-1} \left(1 - \frac{\eta(\ell-1)}{N}\right)^2 \left(1 - \frac{\eta(\ell-2)}{N}\right)^2 \cdots$$
$$\times \left(1 - \frac{\eta(k+1)}{N}\right)^2 \frac{\eta^2(k)}{N^2} \qquad (5.12)$$

It is clear that $\langle \boldsymbol{v}^2(\ell)\rangle \leq N^{-2}\langle(\boldsymbol{x} - \langle \boldsymbol{x}\rangle)^2\rangle \sum_{k=0}^{\ell-1} \eta^2(k)$, from which our claim follows immediately. One could try to go somewhat further for those situations where N is large, and use (5.12) to infer

$$\langle \boldsymbol{v}^2(\ell)\rangle = N^{-2}\langle(\boldsymbol{x} - \langle \boldsymbol{x}\rangle)^2\rangle \sum_{k=0}^{\ell-1} \eta^2(k) + \mathcal{O}(N^{-3})$$

Here the above-bound would also be the leading order for large N and ℓ finite.[10] □

[10] For $\ell \to \infty$, so that terms of order ℓ/N can no longer be discarded, matters are more subtle: one would have to check carefully whether the leading order in N remains identical to the above one. We will not carry out this analysis here.

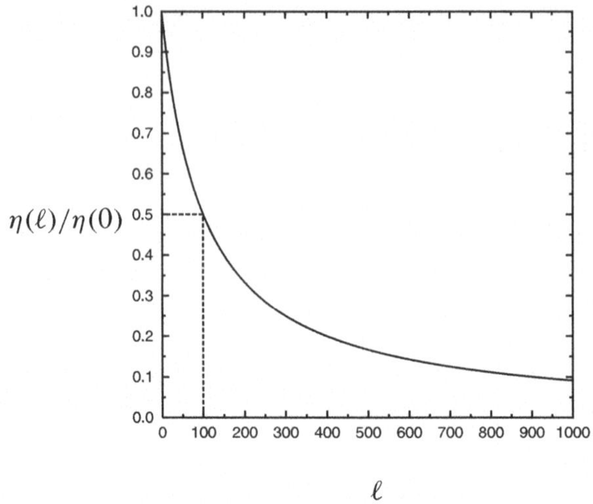

Figure 5.12 The time-dependent learning rate defined in (5.13), which meets the conditions (5.11) on the asymptotic rate of decay to zero. The 'half-way point' $(\tau, \frac{1}{2})$ is marked by dashed lines (here $\tau = 100$).

The most commonly used asymptotic form of decay for $\eta(\ell)$ that meets the above two requirements is $\eta(\ell) \sim \ell^{-1}$ as $\ell \to \infty$. For instance:

$$\eta(\ell) = \frac{\eta(0)}{1+\ell/\tau} \quad \text{which obeys} \quad \begin{array}{ll} \ell \ll \tau: & \eta(\ell) \approx \eta(0)[1-\ell/\tau] \\ \ell \approx \tau: & \eta(\ell) \approx \frac{1}{2}\eta(0) \\ \ell \gg \tau: & \eta(\ell) \approx \eta(0)\tau/\ell \end{array} \tag{5.13}$$

This dependence is drawn in Figure 5.12.

5.4 Self-organizing maps

Any flexible and robust autonomous system, whether living or robotic, will have to be able to create or at least update an internal map or representation of its environment. Information on the environment, however, is usually obtained in an indirect manner, through a redundant set of highly non-linear sensors, each of which provide only partial and indirect information.

The system responsible for forming this map needs to be adaptive, as both environment and sensors can change their characteristics during the system's lifetime. Our brain performs re-calibration of sensors all the time. For example, simply because we grow, the neuronal information about limb positions, generated by sensors which measure the stretch of muscles, has to be reinterpreted continually. Anatomical changes, and even acquisition of new skills, such as playing an instrument, are found to induce modifications of internal maps.

At a more abstract level, the neural system responsible for building the internal representation is confronted with a complicated non-linear mapping from a relatively low-dimensional and more or less flat space (the 'physical world' $\mathcal{W}$, with D dimensions) into a high-dimensional one (the space of sensory signals, of which there are $n \gg D$), and the aim is to extract the properties of the original space $\mathcal{W}$ from the sensory signals alone, that is, to 'invert' the operation which maps world states to sensory signals.

$$\begin{array}{ccc} \text{world coordinates:} & \text{sensory signals:} & \text{internal representation:} \\ \boldsymbol{X} = (X_1, \ldots, X_D) \in \mathcal{W} \longrightarrow & \boldsymbol{x} = (x_1, \ldots, x_n) \longrightarrow & \text{reconstruction of } \mathcal{W}? \end{array}$$

The definition of the 'world' depends on the specific degrees of freedom of the system at hand, and D, for example, need not be three. The sensory signals are usually non-linear functions of the world coordinates; they are indirect and noisy, but also highly redundant to compensate for their individual inadequacies.

The key to achieving the objective of forming an internal representation of the world is to exploit continuity and correlations in sensory signals, assuming similar sensory signals to represent similar positions in the environment, which therefore must correspond to similar positions in the internal map: if $\boldsymbol{X}' = \boldsymbol{X} + \Delta\boldsymbol{X}$ for small $\Delta\boldsymbol{X}$, then also $\boldsymbol{x}(\boldsymbol{X}') \approx \boldsymbol{x}(\boldsymbol{X}) + \boldsymbol{A}(\boldsymbol{X}) \cdot \Delta\boldsymbol{X}$, for some $\boldsymbol{A}(\boldsymbol{X})$ (the Jacobian matrix of the mapping $\boldsymbol{X} \to \boldsymbol{x}$).

Before turning to the learning process which is to carry out the construction task, we first explain in more detail the type of representation one aims for, which is inspired by biological systems. Let us give a simple example (see also Figure 5.13). Imagine a system operating in a simple two-dimensional world, where positions are represented by Cartesian coordinates $\boldsymbol{X} = (X_1, X_2)$, observed by sensors and fed into a neural network as input signals. For simplicity we will consider trivial sensors, and just put $x_1 = X_1$, $x_2 = X_2$. Each neuron i receives information on the input signals (x_1, x_2) in the usual way, via modifiable synapses $\{m_{ij}\}$; its activity on receiving input $\boldsymbol{x}$ will be $y_i(\boldsymbol{x}) = g(m_{i1}x_1 + m_{i2}x_2)$, for some monotonically increasing non-linear function $g(z)$.

We denote the *physical* location of neuron i within the map-forming array by $\boldsymbol{r}_i$. If this network is to become an internal coordinate system, faithfully reflecting the events $\boldsymbol{x} = (x_1, x_2)$ observed in the outside world—and therefore, in the present example, with the topology of a two-dimensional array—the following objectives are to be met:

1. Each neuron y_i is more or less 'tuned' to a specific type of signal $\boldsymbol{x}_i$, that is, $y_i(\boldsymbol{x})$ should be large only when $|\boldsymbol{x} - \boldsymbol{x}_i|$ is sufficiently small.

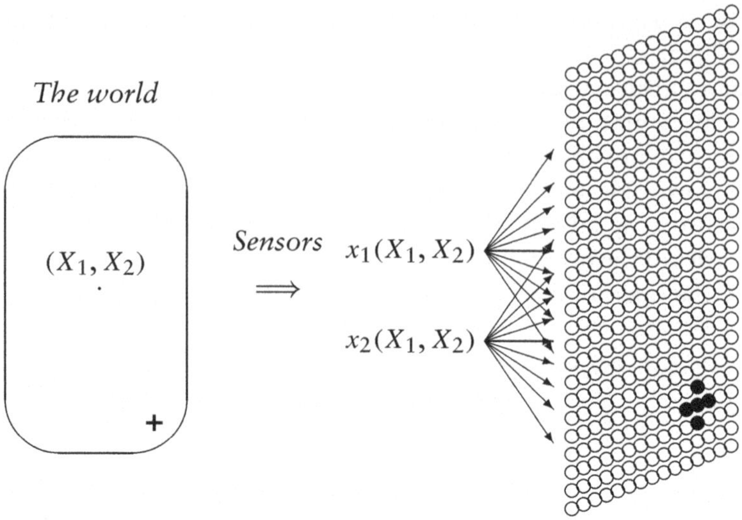

Figure 5.13 Simple two-dimensional example of the internal representation ('map') of the environment as built in biological systems. The brain has no direct access to the world coordinates (X_1, X_2), it is only given sensory signals $x_1(X_1, X_2)$ and $x_2(X_1, X_2)$. Many different representations of the coordinates (X_1, X_2) would have been possible; in the specific one aimed for here, each indirectly observed position (X_1, X_2) is supposed to give rise to a specific localized area of firing activity in a sheet of neurons. Compare this to driving a car with blinded windows, but with electronic sensors observing the environment. The sensory information is to be converted back into world coordinates, and to make a light flash up in a road map inside the car, exactly at the car's current location. This is the information used by the driver. The question discussed in this section is how to *construct* the road map, that is, the conversion of sensory to world coordinates, solely on the basis of structure in the sensory signals $x_1(X_1, X_2)$ and $x_2(X_1, X_2)$.

2. Neighbouring neurons in the array are tuned to similar signals, that is, if $|\boldsymbol{r}_i - \boldsymbol{r}_j|$ is small then $|\boldsymbol{x}_i - \boldsymbol{x}_j|$ is small.
3. External distance is monotonically related to internal distance, that is, if $|\boldsymbol{r}_i - \boldsymbol{r}_j| < |\boldsymbol{r}_i - \boldsymbol{r}_k|$ then $|\boldsymbol{x}_i - \boldsymbol{x}_j| < |\boldsymbol{x}_i - \boldsymbol{x}_k|$.

How to learn a topologically correct map

It turns out that in order to achieve these objectives one needs learning rules where neurons effectively compete to have input signals $\boldsymbol{x}_i$ 'allocated' to them, whereby neighbouring neurons stimulate one another to develop similar synaptic interactions and distant neurons are prevented from developing similar interactions. Let us try to construct the simplest such learning rule (see Figure 5.14).

Initially, before learning has taken place, input signals just evoke random firing patterns in the neuronal array. After learning we wish to see localized firing patterns, as shown above. Our equations take their simplest

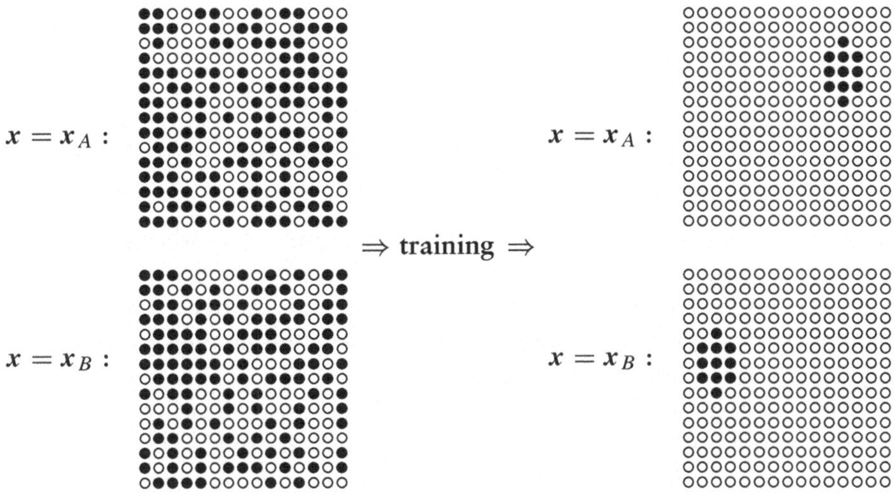

Figure 5.14 Illustration of the desired outcome of training a topological map. Before training (left), two distinct input signals elicit random (de-localized) firing patterns. After training (right), the same input signals produce distinct localized firing patterns in the map-forming array.

form in the case where the input signals are normalized, so we define $(x_1, x_2) \in [-1/\sqrt{2}, 1/\sqrt{2}]^2$ and add a dummy variable $x_3 = \sqrt{1 - x_1^2 - x_2^2}$, together with a dummy synaptic interaction m_{i3} for every neuron. If we write the synapses of neuron i as $\boldsymbol{m}_i = (m_{i1}, m_{i2}, m_{i3})$, and normalize them according to $|\boldsymbol{m}_i| = 1$, we simply get

$$y_i(\boldsymbol{x}) = g(\boldsymbol{m}_i \cdot \boldsymbol{x}), \qquad |\boldsymbol{m}_i| = |\boldsymbol{x}| = 1 \tag{5.14}$$

Learning now implies rotating the vectors $\boldsymbol{m}_i$.

By construction, since $g(z)$ is a monotonically increasing function a given neuron is triggered most when $\boldsymbol{m}_i \cdot \boldsymbol{x}$ is maximal, which is for the input signal $\boldsymbol{x} = \boldsymbol{m}_i$. This has two important implications: one can now interpret $\boldsymbol{m}_i$ as the input signal to which neuron i is tuned, corresponding to $\boldsymbol{x}_i$ in our earlier notation; and tuning neuron i to a given signal $\boldsymbol{x}$ is found to be equivalent to rotating $\boldsymbol{m}_i$ towards $\boldsymbol{x}$. As a result one finds that a learning rule with the desired effect is as follows.

Starting from random (normalized) synaptic vectors $\boldsymbol{m}_i$, iterate the following recipe until a more or less stable situation is reached:

step 1: pick a data point $\boldsymbol{x}$ with $|\boldsymbol{x}| = 1$ at random

step 2: find the most active neuron, that is, the i such that $|\boldsymbol{m}_i \cdot \boldsymbol{x}| > |\boldsymbol{m}_j \cdot \boldsymbol{x}|$ for all $j \neq i$

step 3: rotate the synaptic vector of neuron i *and its neighbours in the array* towards $\boldsymbol{x}$; rotate the synaptic vector of all other neurons slightly away from $\boldsymbol{x}$

step 4: return to 1

The neuron that was already the one most responsive to the signal $\boldsymbol{x}$ will be made even more so, together with its neighbours; the other neurons are made less responsive to $\boldsymbol{x}$. In biology, the above is achieved via Hebbian-type learning rules, and by having short-range excitatory synapses which ensure that neighbouring neurons tend to be simultaneously active, and team up in the synaptic adaptation.

We note that in the above formulation the normalization of synaptic vectors and input vectors was introduced purely in order to retain the connection with the biological picture of firing neurons, via expressions like (5.14). For the purpose of computation and learning in synthetic systems, on the other hand, we can move away from the firing of neurons and work directly in terms of the $\{\boldsymbol{m}_i\}$ only. Henceforth we will define $\boldsymbol{m}_i$ simply as the signal in input space to which neuron i is tuned; we forget about how this is actually realized, and also ignore the issue of normalization.

Visualization of the learning process: fishing nets

The above formulation of self-organizing maps (SOMs) in terms of the $\{\boldsymbol{m}_i\}$ has brought us (deliberately) very close to the VQ and SVQ algorithms. However, there is an important difference, which is the insistence that the various code-book vectors $\boldsymbol{m}_i$ are no longer interchangeable (in VQ and SVQ we only cared about the overall distribution of code-book vectors in input space): now each $\boldsymbol{m}_i$ is associated with a specific location $\boldsymbol{r}_i$ in an array, with the condition that those (i, j) which belong to nearby locations $\{\boldsymbol{r}_i, \boldsymbol{r}_j\}$ in the array must have code-book vectors $\{\boldsymbol{m}_i, \boldsymbol{m}_j\}$ which are very similar. Hence, simply drawing the code-book vectors in input space as we did for VQ and SVQ is no longer adequate, because it will not tell us about the topological features of the state.

In the case of SOMs the standard visual representation of a state $\{\boldsymbol{m}_i\}$ is the following:

- Draw each $\boldsymbol{m}_i$ as a point (or knot) in input space (as in VQ and SVQ)
- Connect with line segments all those points (i, j) which correspond to neighbours in the array of the $\{\boldsymbol{r}_i\}$

We then end up with a graphical representation of the synaptic structure of a network in the form of a fishing net, with the positions of the knots representing the signals in the world to which the neurons

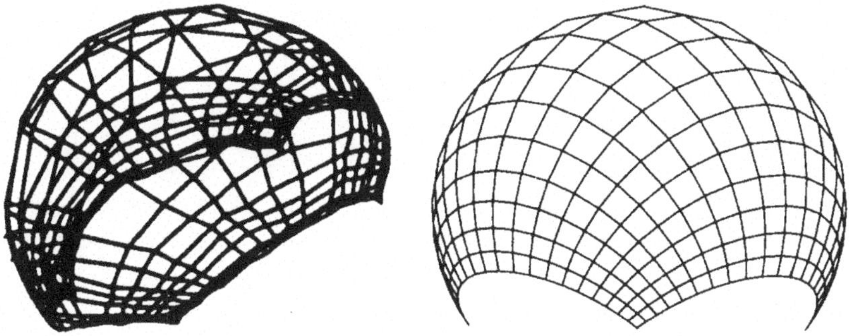

Figure 5.15 Graphical representation of the state of a SOM in the form of a fishing net. Here $\boldsymbol{r}_i \in [0,1]^2$ (i.e. the neurons live in a square 2-dimensional array) and $\boldsymbol{x} \in \mathbb{R}^3$, with $|\boldsymbol{x}| = 1$ (i.e. the data live on the surface of a sphere). The positions of the knots represent the signals $\boldsymbol{m}_i$ to which the neurons are tuned, and the cords connect the knots of neighbouring neurons in the array. Left: equilibrium result of the numerical simulation of a particular version on the SOM algorithm. Right: corresponding theoretical prediction.

are tuned and with the cords indicating neighbourship, see Figures 5.15 and 5.16. The three objectives of map formation set out at the beginning of this section thereby translate into the following desired properties of the graph:

(1) all knots in the graph are separated;

(2) all cords of the graph are similarly stretched;

(3) there are no regions with overlapping pieces of graph.

Note that this representation is in practice useful only for one- or two-dimensional arrays, that is, when creating one- or two-dimensional internal representations.

The SOM algorithm and its properties

The SOM algorithm is an abstract realization of the processes underlying the creation of topologically correct internal representations in the higher brain regions of humans and animals. It is defined in terms of code-book vectors $\boldsymbol{m}_i$, which represent the specific signals in data space to which neurons are tuned. It aims to create a topologically correct internal representation of potentially non-linear low-dimensional structure hidden in possibly high-dimensional data.

Each neuron is located in a physical array, the dimension of which will become the dimension of the internal map to be created; the vector $\boldsymbol{r}_i$ indicates the location of neuron i. We define a neighbourhood function h_{ij} as

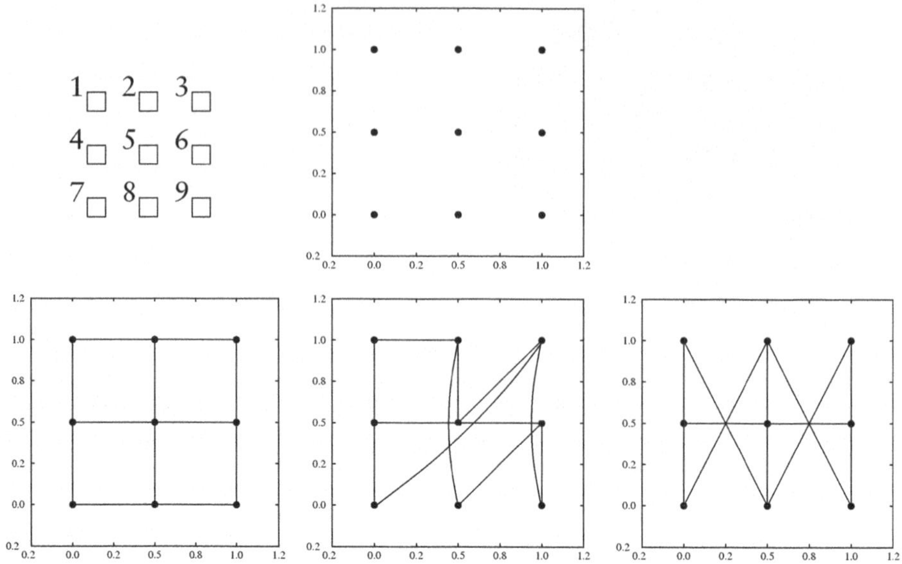

Figure 5.16 Example of the fishing net representation of the state of a SOM system. Upper left: the arrangement of 9 neurons in a physical array (defining the $\{\boldsymbol{r}_i\}$, and hence the notion of neighbours). Upper middle: the positioning of the nine code-book vectors $\boldsymbol{m}_i$ in data space, corresponding to the state $\{\boldsymbol{m}_1 = (0, 1), \boldsymbol{m}_2 = (\frac{1}{2}, 1), \boldsymbol{m}_3 = (1, 1), \boldsymbol{m}_4 = (0, \frac{1}{2}), \boldsymbol{m}_5 = (\frac{1}{2}, \frac{1}{2}), \boldsymbol{m}_6 = (1, \frac{1}{2}), \boldsymbol{m}_7 = (0, 0), \boldsymbol{m}_8 = (\frac{1}{2}, 0), \boldsymbol{m}_9 = (1, 0)\}$. Bottom left: the fishing net graph corresponding to this state. Bottom middle: the fishing net graph corresponding to the state obtained by exchanging code-book vectors $\boldsymbol{m}_3$ and $\boldsymbol{m}_8$. Bottom right: the fishing net graph corresponding to the state obtained by exchanging code-book vectors $\boldsymbol{m}_2$ and $\boldsymbol{m}_8$. Note that all cases give rise to exactly the same distribution of code-book vectors, so that the incorrect topology of the last two states can indeed only be inferred from the fishing net graph.

follows:

$$h_{ij} = h\left(\frac{|\boldsymbol{r}_i - \boldsymbol{r}_j|}{\sigma}\right), \quad \sigma > 0 \tag{5.15}$$

in which $h(z)$ is a monotonically decreasing function, with $h(0) = 1$, $h(\infty) = 0$, and with a width of order 1. For example:

$$h(z) = e^{-(1/2)\,z^2}: \quad h_{ij} = e^{-(\boldsymbol{r}_i - \boldsymbol{r}_j)^2/2\sigma^2}$$

$$h(z) = \theta(1 - z): \quad h_{ij} = \begin{cases} 1, & \text{if } |\boldsymbol{r}_i - \boldsymbol{r}_j| < \sigma \\ 0, & \text{if } |\boldsymbol{r}_i - \boldsymbol{r}_j| > \sigma \end{cases}$$

in which $\theta(z)$ is the step function ($\theta(z > 0) = 1, \theta(z < 0) = 0$). The SOM algorithm can now be defined as follows. First we initialize the N code-book vectors $\boldsymbol{m}_i \in \mathbb{R}^n$ randomly. Then we iterate the following stochastic process:

step 1: pick a data point $\boldsymbol{x}$ at random, according to the probability density $p(\boldsymbol{x})$

step 2: find the Voronoi cell containing $\boldsymbol{x}$, that is, find i such that $|\boldsymbol{x}-\boldsymbol{m}_i| < |\boldsymbol{x}-\boldsymbol{m}_j|$ for all $j \neq i$

step 3: move *all* $\boldsymbol{m}_j$ towards $\boldsymbol{x}$: $\boldsymbol{m}_j \to \boldsymbol{m}_j + \eta(\boldsymbol{x}-\boldsymbol{m}_j)F_j(\boldsymbol{x}, \{\boldsymbol{m}(\ell)\})$, where $F_j(\cdots) = h_{ij}$

step 4: return to 1

The learning rate $0 < \eta \ll 1$ controls, as always, the overall magnitude of the changes.

The SOM algorithm can be seen to have the following general properties:

1. All code-book vectors are moved towards $\boldsymbol{x}$ at every iteration step, but those which are closest to the code-book vector in whose Voronoi cell the data point is, or in other words the neuron which is triggered most, are moved the most.
2. Unless we reduce η during the process, the code-book vectors will continue to move stochastically, although the *density* of code-book vectors in any given region should become stationary.
3. The properties of the $\{h_{ij}\}$ guarantee that neighbouring neurons team up, and develop similar code-book vectors.
4. SOM has one more parameter than VQ. This extra parameter, σ, defines a characteristic distance in the original physical array of the neurons: code-book vectors with $|\boldsymbol{r}_i - \boldsymbol{r}_j| < \sigma$ will be the ones to feel one another's influence.
5. $\lim_{\sigma\to 0}$ SOM = VQ (the proof is trivial). Hence we can see the SOM as VQ plus enforced spatial continuity.

We observe that the SOM is again of the general form (5.4), hence we can apply our results on time-dependent learning rates also to the SOM. The relation between the three processes discussed so far is

$$\lim_{\beta\to\infty} \text{SVQ} = \text{VQ} = \lim_{\sigma\to 0} \text{SOM}$$

It will be clear that the determination of the right value for σ is delicate. If σ is too small, the system will behave like VQ, and the correct topology will not emerge, or be correct only locally. If σ is too large, all neurons will drag one another along, and all code-book vectors will become identical; see also the simulation examples below. The new parameter σ

also introduces boundary effects. Since neurons drag along one another's code-book vectors, those neurons which are at the boundary of the array will feel an effective force dragging their code-book vectors towards the inner region of the array, simply because there are no neurons pulling from the outside. This shows itself in a tendency for the boundaries of the fishing net to keep a certain σ-dependent distance from the boundaries of the data region. In practice one therefore chooses a time-dependent σ, similar to the time-dependent learning rate, that is,

$$\eta(t) = \frac{\eta(0)}{1 + t/\tau_\eta}, \qquad \sigma(t) = \frac{\sigma(0)}{1 + t/\tau_\sigma}$$

Applications of the SOM include sensor fusion (in robotics), data visualization and data-base mining (finding hidden low-dimensional regularities in messy or high-dimensional data), data preprocessing, medical diagnostics (finding causal relationships in medical data), etc.

Examples of SOM in action

Figures 5.17 and 5.18 illustrate the functioning of the SOM algorithm for a number of simple examples with $n = 2$ (i.e. where one has data points $\boldsymbol{x} = (x_1, x_2)$ in a plane) and a 10×10 array of neurons (i.e. a population of 100 code-book vectors), but for different choices of the distance parameter σ and of the time-dependence of the learning rate. Figure 5.17 illustrates the need for having a sufficiently large range σ, in order to capture the correct topology of the data, but also the σ-dependent boundary effects. In Figure 5.18 we vary the reduction speed of the learning rate, showing that suboptimal stationary states may result when the learning rate goes to zero too quickly.

5.5 Exercises

Exercise 5.1. (Soft SOM.) Define an alternative algorithm SOM2 in the following way. Each neuron is located in a physical array whose dimension determines that of the internal map to be created; the vector $\boldsymbol{r}_i$ indicates the location of neuron i. Define a neighbourhood function $h_{ij} = h(|\boldsymbol{r}_i - \boldsymbol{r}_j|/\sigma)$ as in the standard SOM. First we initialize the N code-book vectors $\boldsymbol{m}_i \in \mathbb{R}^n$ randomly. Then we iterate the following stochastic process:

step 1: pick a data point $\boldsymbol{x}$ at random, according to probability density $p(\boldsymbol{x})$

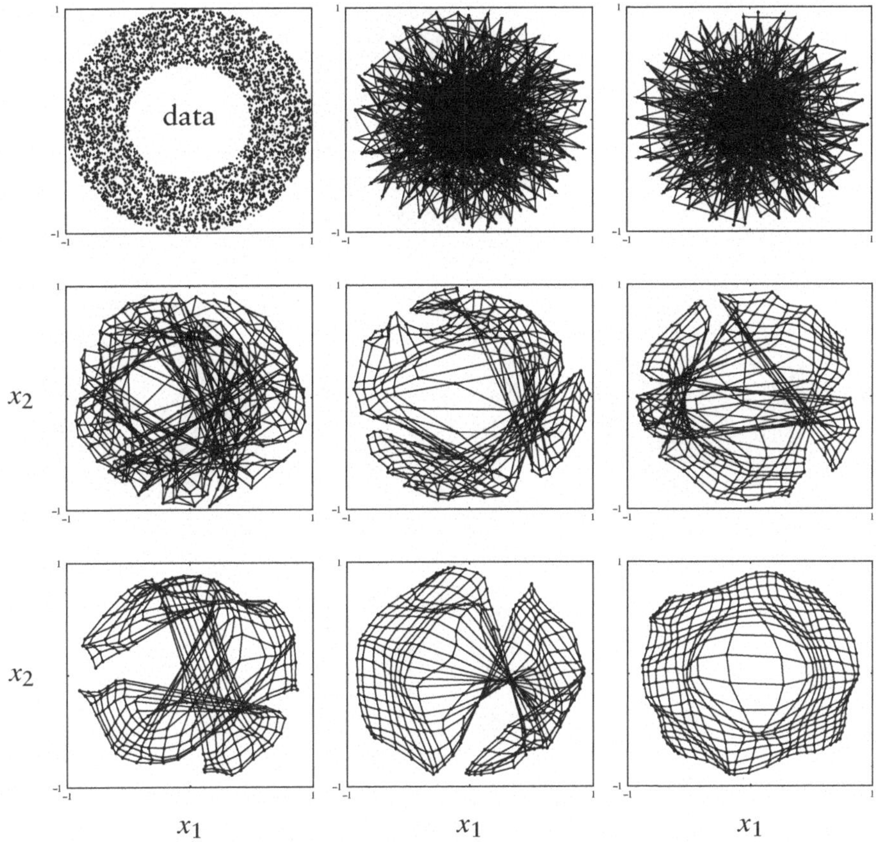

Figure 5.17 Numerical simulation of a SOM, with $n = 2$, $\eta = 0.5$, and $N = 100$. Top left graph: data distribution $p(\boldsymbol{x})$, uniform over the strip $\frac{1}{2} < |\boldsymbol{x}| < 1$. Other eight graphs: system state after 20,000 iteration steps, for different values of the range parameter σ ($\sigma \in \{0.1, 0.3, 0.5, 0.7, 0.9, 1.1, 1.3, 1.5\}$, from top middle to bottom right). One clearly observes the two effects of losing the correct topology for σ too small, with only local correctness for intermediate σ, and of the code-book vectors of boundary neurons keeping a σ-dependent distance from the data boundary.

step 2: move *all* $\boldsymbol{m}_i$ according to: $\boldsymbol{m}_i \rightarrow \boldsymbol{m}_i + \eta(\boldsymbol{x} - \boldsymbol{m}_i)F_i[\boldsymbol{x}, \{\boldsymbol{m}(\ell)\}]$, where

$$F_i(\boldsymbol{x}, \{\boldsymbol{m}(\ell)\}) = h_{ij^\star}, \quad \text{with } j^\star = \text{argmin}_j \sum_\ell h_{j\ell}(\boldsymbol{x} - \boldsymbol{m}_\ell)^2$$

step 3: return to 1

Discuss the difference(s) between this new SOM2 algorithm and the standard SOM. Next define a 'soft' version SSOM2 of the above algorithm, by replacing the SOM2 definition of $F_i[\boldsymbol{x}, \{\boldsymbol{m}_\ell\}]$ with the

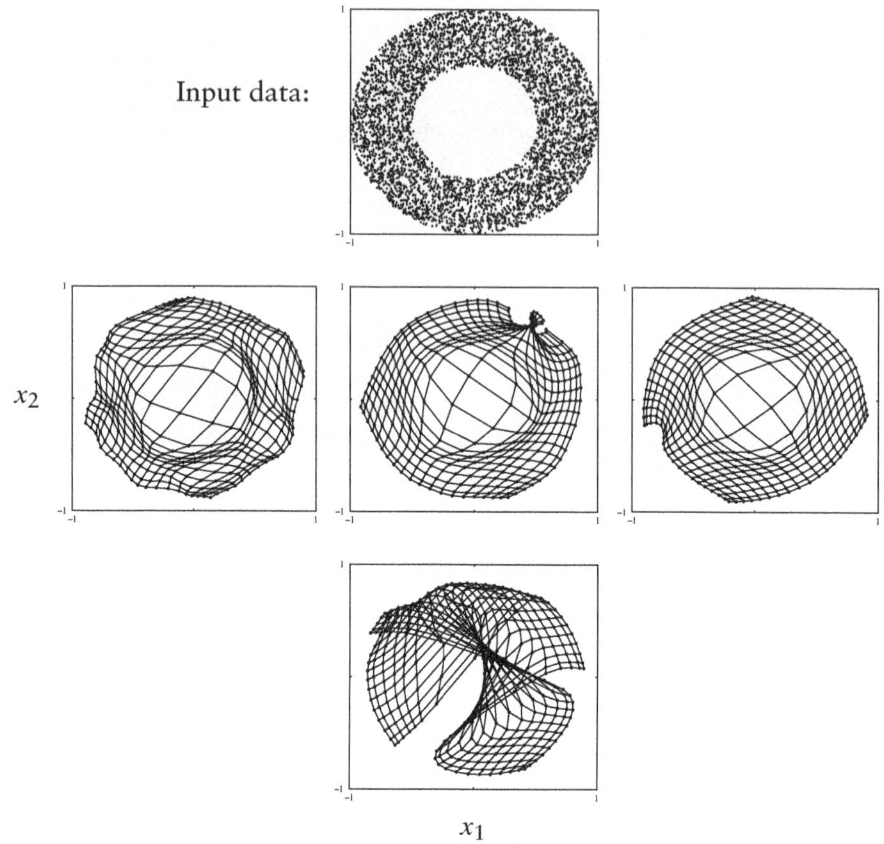

Figure 5.18 Example: numerical simulation of a SOM, with $n = 2$, $\sigma = 1.5$, $\eta(0) = 0.5$, and $N = 100$. Top graph: data distribution $p(\boldsymbol{x})$, uniform over the strip $\frac{1}{2} < |\boldsymbol{x}| < 1$. Other eight graphs: system state after 20,000 iteration steps, for different choices of the time-dependence of the learning rate η. Second row left: $\eta = 0.5$ (constant). Second row, middle: $\eta(t) = \eta(0)/[1 + t/\tau]$, with $\tau = 10$. Second row, right: $\eta(t) = \eta(0)/[1 + t^2/\tau^2]$, with $\tau = 10$. Bottom: $\eta(t) = \eta(0)\exp[-t/\tau]$, with $\tau = 10$. One clearly observes that the system can get stuck in a suboptimal state, where the topology is only locally correct.

following:

$$F_i(\boldsymbol{x}, \{\boldsymbol{m}(\ell)\}) = \sum_j h_{ij} \frac{e^{-\beta \sum_k h_{jk}(\boldsymbol{x}-\boldsymbol{m}_k)^2}}{\sum_\ell e^{-\beta \sum_k h_{\ell k}(\boldsymbol{x}-\boldsymbol{m}_k)^2}}$$

Show that $\lim_{\beta \to \infty}$ SSOM2 = SOM2, and that $\lim_{\sigma \to 0}$ SSOM2 = SVQ.

Exercise 5.2. (Lyapunov functions and interpretation of SSOM2 and SOM2.) Consider the SSOM2 algorithm defined in the previous exercise. Consider small learning rates in the usual manner, such that in the $\eta \to 0$

limit SSOM2 reduces to the following deterministic equation

$$\frac{\mathrm{d}}{\mathrm{d}t}\boldsymbol{m}_i = \langle (\boldsymbol{x} - \boldsymbol{m}_i) F_i(\boldsymbol{x}, \{\boldsymbol{m}\}) \rangle$$

Show that for $F_i(\boldsymbol{x}, \{\boldsymbol{m}\}) = F_i^{\mathrm{SSOM2}}(\boldsymbol{x}, \{\boldsymbol{m}\})$, this deterministic equation describes a gradient descent dynamics for an error measure $E[\{\boldsymbol{m}\}]$, given (unlike the case of SVQ) by the sum of the Kullback–Leibler distance between the data distribution $p(\boldsymbol{x})$ and a distribution $q(\boldsymbol{x}|\{\boldsymbol{m}\})$ parametrized by the set $\{\boldsymbol{m}\}$ of code-book vectors, and an extra term which does not involve the data distribution. Find $q(\boldsymbol{x}|\{\boldsymbol{m}\})$. What does your result imply for the interpretation of the SOM2 algorithm?

6 Bayesian techniques in supervised learning

In this chapter, we discuss the Bayesian approach to supervised learning from examples. Its introduction in the 1990s has been a very welcome development, in that it contributed significantly to converting artificial neural computation, especially learning in multilayer networks, from a collection of interesting but ad hoc algorithms ('invent a rule, play with parameters, draw performance graphs, and hope for the best') to a sound, well grounded, and systematic scientific procedure. It also contributed to the area becoming more mathematical in nature.

6.1 Preliminaries and introduction

Supervised learning from examples

Let us first set the scene and define our terminology. In supervised learning from examples we are confronted with a task, defined by a collection of questions $\boldsymbol{\xi}^{\mu}$, drawn randomly from some set $\Omega \subseteq \mathbb{R}^N$ (with probabilities, or probability density, $p(\boldsymbol{\xi})$), with corresponding answers t_{μ}:

$$\text{the task:} \quad \begin{array}{ll} \text{questions:} & \{\boldsymbol{\xi}^1, \ldots, \boldsymbol{\xi}^p\}, \;\; \boldsymbol{\xi}^{\mu} \in \Omega \subseteq \mathbb{R}^N \\ \text{answers:} & \{t_1, \ldots, t_p\}, \;\; t_{\mu} \in \mathbb{R} \end{array}$$

This task, assumed to have been generated by a teacher, is to be learned by a student (the neural network). The student executes a parametrized operation $S\colon \mathbb{R}^N \to \mathbb{R}$, where $S(\boldsymbol{\xi}) = f(\boldsymbol{\xi}; \boldsymbol{w})$. The parameters $\boldsymbol{w}$ determine the details of the operation, and thus represent the 'program'; in multilayer neural networks they would be the synaptic weights and the neuronal thresholds.[11] If the outputs (or targets) are binary, for example, $t_{\mu} \in \{0, 1\}$ or $t_{\mu} \in \{-1, 1\}$, we would call the task *binary classification*. If the outputs can truly take values from a continuous set, we would speak about *regression*.

[11] In order not to deviate from established notation in literature we now write input vectors as $\boldsymbol{\xi}$ rather than $\boldsymbol{x}$, and adjustable parameters as $\boldsymbol{w}$ rather than $\boldsymbol{J}$.

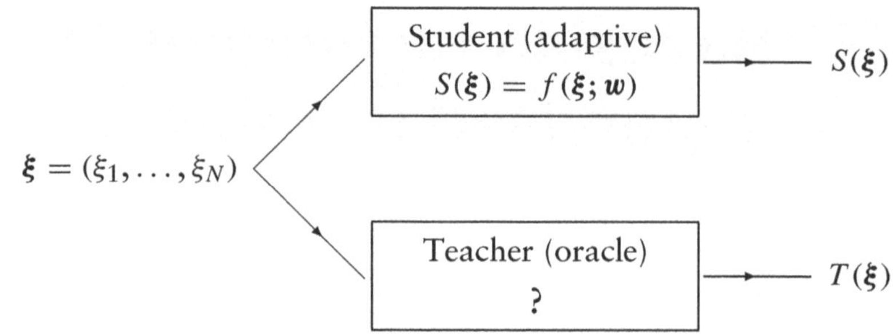

Figure 6.1 The teacher–student scenario of online supervised learning. The student can be any type of parametrized operation (not necessarily neural or neural-inspired).

It is assumed that the data (or answers) were not assigned randomly by the teacher—otherwise there would be no point in learning—but that they were generated according to some function $T: \mathbb{R}^N \to \mathbb{R}$. The student has no direct information on the function T (the teacher is a black box, or oracle), but has to infer T from the p input–output pairs $(\boldsymbol{\xi}^\mu, t_\mu)$; this is the objective of the learning process. See figure 6.1. The problem faced by the student is made more difficult by the fact—which is rather common in the real world—that the data are not perfect, that is, the teacher can make mistakes, or is subject to noise. If for simplicity we assume that the inaccuracy or noise is independent for the different outputs, that is, that the teacher is sloppy rather than using a consistently wrong rule, we have:

$$\begin{array}{ll} \text{binary classification:} & \text{Prob}[t_\mu = T(\boldsymbol{\xi}^\mu)] = 1 - \epsilon, \quad 0 \leq \epsilon \leq 1 \\ \text{regression:} & t_\mu = T(\boldsymbol{\xi}^\mu) + z_\mu, \\ & z_\mu \in \mathbb{R} \text{ drawn randomly from } P(z) \end{array} \tag{6.1}$$

In the case of binary classification, the parameter ϵ measures the amount of noise in the data, with $\epsilon = 0$ corresponding to perfect data. In the case of regression we may without loss of generality assume that $\langle z \rangle = \int \mathrm{d}z\, z P(z) = 0$; a nonzero average would be equivalent to a structural modification of the underlying rule T, and could be absorbed into its definition. Hence the amount of noise in the data is here measured by the variance of $P(z)$, with perfect data given by $P(z) = \delta(z)$ (see Appendix F for details of the δ-distribution).

Due to the possibility of data noise and the difference between our finite sample $\{\boldsymbol{\xi}^1, \ldots, \boldsymbol{\xi}^p\}$ and the full set of possible questions Ω, there are several performance measures one could define. Here we concentrate on two: the *training error* E_t (measuring how well the student reproduces the given answers t_μ), and the *generalization error* E_g (measuring how well the student has learned the underlying rule T):

$$E_t = \frac{1}{p}\sum_{\mu=1}^{p} \mathcal{E}(t_\mu, S(\boldsymbol{\xi}^\mu)) \qquad E_g = \int_\Omega \mathrm{d}\boldsymbol{\xi}\, p(\boldsymbol{\xi})\mathcal{E}(T(\boldsymbol{\xi}), S(\boldsymbol{\xi}))$$

where $\mathcal{E}(t, s)$ is some, as yet unspecified, measure of the difference between t and s, such as $\mathcal{E}(t, s) = |t - s|^\gamma$ (with $\gamma > 0$). Given the dependence of the student's operation on the parameters $\boldsymbol{w}$, via $S(\boldsymbol{\xi}) = f(\boldsymbol{\xi}; \boldsymbol{w})$, this becomes

$$E_t(\boldsymbol{w}) = \frac{1}{p}\sum_{\mu=1}^{p} \mathcal{E}(t_\mu, f(\boldsymbol{\xi}^\mu; \boldsymbol{w})) \qquad E_g(\boldsymbol{w}) = \int_\Omega \mathrm{d}\boldsymbol{\xi}\, p(\boldsymbol{\xi})\mathcal{E}(T(\boldsymbol{\xi}), f(\boldsymbol{\xi}; \boldsymbol{w})) \tag{6.2}$$

There are three important observations to make at this stage:

- The above two error measures $E_t(\boldsymbol{w})$ and $E_g(\boldsymbol{w})$ differ in two aspects: (i) E_t is an average only over the p available questions $\{\boldsymbol{\xi}^1, \ldots, \boldsymbol{\xi}^p\}$, whereas E_g involves *all* questions in Ω. (ii) E_t checks performance relative to the noisy answers $\{t_\mu\}$ given, whereas E_g checks performance relative to the correct underlying rule T. However, for E_g the alternative definition which measures the error relative to the noisy rule can also be found in the literature, and then this second distinction disappears.
- The real objective of learning is to minimize $E_g(\boldsymbol{w})$, via suitable modification of the parameters $\boldsymbol{w}$, since we ultimately wish to use our system for predicting the answers to novel questions, rather than just parrot the answers to those of the training stage.
- In the learning process, however, we have no access to $E_g(\boldsymbol{w})$, since we know neither the full set Ω nor the true rule T; we only have the data $\{(\boldsymbol{\xi}^1, t_1), \ldots, (\boldsymbol{\xi}^p, t_p)\}$.

Many of the obstacles and problems in neural network learning in the past (i.e. before, say, 1990) had their origin in the fact that one wished to minimize one object (E_g), but one could only measure the other (E_t), and one tried to get away—out of necessity, it seemed—with pretending that the differences between the two were not too important.

Conventional network types

Let us next briefly review the most common types of neural network $S(\boldsymbol{\xi}) = f(\boldsymbol{\xi}; \boldsymbol{w})$ which are used in practice for the above purpose. We first consider regression tasks, where the outputs are supposed to be continuous:

- Single layer neural networks (perceptrons):

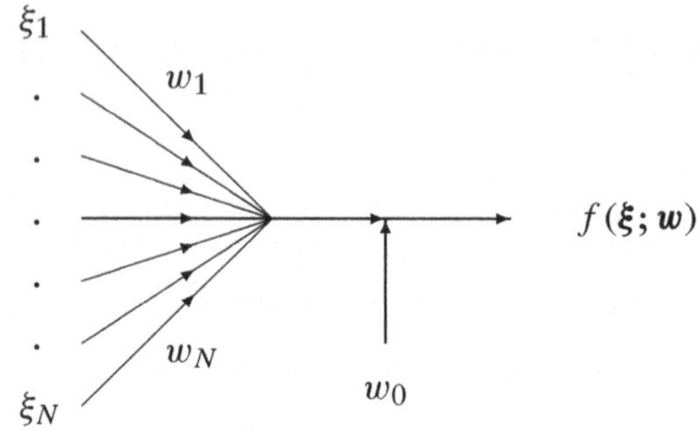

Their output is of the form

$$f(\boldsymbol{\xi}, \boldsymbol{w}) = g(\boldsymbol{w} \cdot \boldsymbol{\xi} + w_0) \tag{6.3}$$

with $g(z)$ a monotonically increasing sigmoidal function, which saturates for $z \to \pm\infty$. Perceptrons are basically single neurons, carrying out a (soft) linear separation in the space Ω of the input vectors $\boldsymbol{\xi}$, $S(\boldsymbol{\xi}) = g(\boldsymbol{w} \cdot \boldsymbol{\xi} + w_0)$. The modifiable parameters (i.e. the 'program') are the synaptic weights $(w_1, \ldots, w_N)$ and the threshold w_0.
- Multilayer neural networks (or multilayer perceptrons, MLPs):

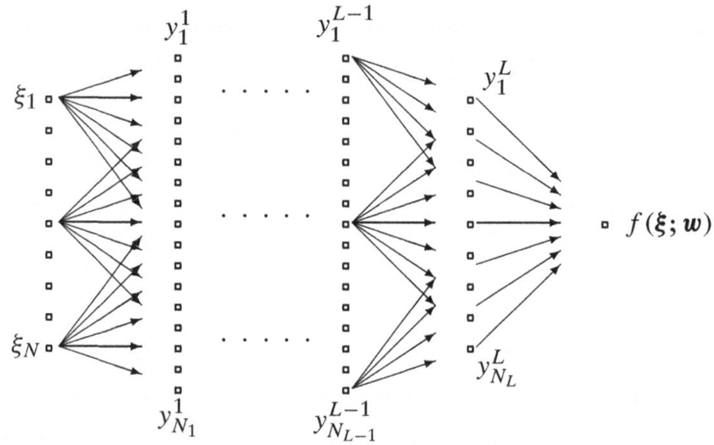

These are feed-forward processing networks of neurons of the type described above (soft linear separators), with monotonically increasing and saturating sigmoidal functions $g(z)$. The overall output

$$f(\boldsymbol{\xi}; \boldsymbol{w}) = g\left(\sum_{j=1}^{N_L} w_j^L y_j^L(\boldsymbol{\xi}) + w_0^L\right) \tag{6.4}$$

is calculated iteratively from the outputs of the preceding layers, according to

$$y_i^1 = \sum_{j=1}^{N} g(w_{ij}^0 \xi_j + w_0^0) \qquad y_i^{\ell+1} = \sum_{j=1}^{N_\ell} g(w_{ij}^\ell y_j^\ell + w_0^\ell) \quad 1 \leq \ell < L \tag{6.5}$$

and the modifiable parameters (i.e. the program) are the synaptic weights and thresholds of all L layers, that is, $\boldsymbol{w} = \{w_{ij}^\ell, w_i^L, w_0^\ell\}$. Given a sufficient number of layers and units within each layer (dependent on the problem to be solved), these networks have been proven to be universal approximators: any sufficiently well-behaved continuous function $f: \mathbb{R}^N \to \mathbb{R}$ can be approximated to arbitrary accuracy by MLPs. We will not discuss the precise conditions or the proof here.

- Radial basis function (RBF) networks:

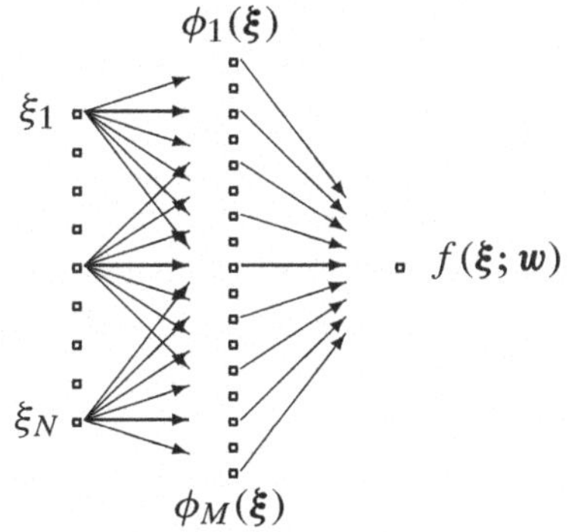

The overall output is now a linear combination of a predefined set of functions $\{\phi_i\}$ of the input signals,

$$f(\boldsymbol{\xi}; \boldsymbol{w}) = \sum_{i=1}^{M} w_i \phi_i(\boldsymbol{\xi}) + w_0 \tag{6.6}$$

The motivation behind the construction of these networks is also the principle underlying the previous multilayer networks: one converts a problem that is not linearly separable into one that is. In the previous network the final neuron does the linear separation, and the preceding L layers do the preprocessing. In radial basis function (RBF) networks one chooses specific functions $\phi_i(\boldsymbol{\xi})$ (the 'radial basis functions') for the preprocessing. These are allowed to depend only on the distance $|\boldsymbol{\xi} - \boldsymbol{m}_i|$ between the input vector and a code-book vector $\boldsymbol{m}_i$,

$$\phi_i(\boldsymbol{\xi}) = \phi(|\boldsymbol{\xi} - \boldsymbol{m}_i|) \tag{6.7}$$

For the remaining scalar function ϕ several choices have been proposed; which one to pick is crucial for performance, but unfortunately highly dependent on the problem at hand.[12] Popular choices are:

$$\text{localized basis functions:} \quad \begin{aligned} &\phi(u) = e^{-u^2/2\sigma^2} \\ &\phi(u) = (u^2+\sigma^2)^{-\alpha} \quad (\alpha > 0) \end{aligned}$$

$$\text{non-localized basis functions:} \quad \begin{aligned} &\phi(u) = u \\ &\phi(u) = (u^2+\sigma^2)^{\beta} \quad (0 < \beta < 1) \end{aligned}$$

The modifiable parameters are the weights $\boldsymbol{w}$, though sometimes one also allows the code-book vectors $\boldsymbol{m}_i$ to adapt. Note, finally, that in RBF networks the output does not undergo a non-linear sigmoidal operation, and hence depends linearly on the parameters $\boldsymbol{w}$.

Model complexity and overfitting

Systems such as those discussed above have been used (and are still being used) as student networks $S(\boldsymbol{\xi}) = f(\boldsymbol{\xi}; \boldsymbol{w})$ in the sense of Figure 6.1. The strategy for finding the best parameters $\boldsymbol{w}$ was in the early stages of neural computation based on performing gradient descent on the surface defined by the training error $E_t(\boldsymbol{w})$ as given in (6.2), with a quadratic error measure $\mathcal{E}(t,s) = \frac{1}{2}(t-s)^2$:

$$\frac{\mathrm{d}}{\mathrm{d}t}\boldsymbol{w} = -\eta \nabla_{\boldsymbol{w}} E_t(\boldsymbol{w}) \qquad E_t(\boldsymbol{w}) = \frac{1}{2p}\sum_{\mu=1}^{p}[t_\mu - f(\boldsymbol{\xi}^\mu; \boldsymbol{w})]^2 \tag{6.8}$$

with a learning rate $\eta > 0$. The objective is to find $\boldsymbol{w}^\star$ such that $\min_{\boldsymbol{w}} E_t(\boldsymbol{w}) = E_t(\boldsymbol{w}^\star)$; the above process would at least be guaranteed to lead us to a local minimum of $E_t(\boldsymbol{w})$, since

$$\frac{\mathrm{d}}{\mathrm{d}t}E_t(\boldsymbol{w}) = \nabla_{\boldsymbol{w}} E_t(\boldsymbol{w}) \cdot \frac{\mathrm{d}}{\mathrm{d}t}\boldsymbol{w} = -\eta\,(\nabla_{\boldsymbol{w}} E_t(\boldsymbol{w}))^2 \leq 0$$

$$\frac{\mathrm{d}}{\mathrm{d}t}\boldsymbol{w} = 0 \iff \nabla_{\boldsymbol{w}} E_t(\boldsymbol{w}) = 0$$

---

[12] This illustrates how in RBF networks the learning problem is, in a way, simply swept under the carpet. For how do we now choose the function $\phi(u)$, the code-book vectors $\boldsymbol{x}_i$, or the number M? And under which conditions can we be sure that the ad hoc restriction to RBF units does not render the problem unlearnable? At least in image processing, however, one can set up a rigorous framework, and show that all non-pathological images can be decomposed in terms of a bundle of local expansions (derivatives of Gaussian functions), which can in turn be constructed by adding and subtracting Gaussian functions of the type (6.7).

One problem with this approach has been clear from the beginning: one can end in a local rather than a global minimum. A second problem was appreciated only some 10 years later: gradient descent is not the optimal local process to find minima on an error surface (see the chapter on information geometry in Part III of this book). Here we concentrate on a third problem, called inappropriate model complexity, or 'overfitting'.

This problem is best explained using a very simple example. Suppose we have a task $T: \mathbb{R} \to \mathbb{R}$ defined by a teacher who calculates some function $g(x)$. The student $S: \mathbb{R} \to \mathbb{R}$ tries to emulate the teacher by some parametrized function $f(x; \boldsymbol{w})$, for which we choose a finite polynomial, that is, a truncated Taylor expansion:

$$f(x; \boldsymbol{w}) = w_0 + w_1 x + \cdots + w_M x^M \quad \text{or} \quad f(x; \boldsymbol{w}) = \boldsymbol{w} \cdot \boldsymbol{\Phi}(x), \quad \phi_\ell(x) = x^\ell \tag{6.9}$$

Learning means adapting $\boldsymbol{w} = (w_0, \ldots, w_M)$. The data consist of examples of p inputs x_μ and corresponding outputs t_μ (with $p \geq M + 1$). However, the teacher is not perfect—there is a noise source in the data generation—so $t_\mu = g(x_\mu) + z_\mu$ where the z_μ are drawn independently according to a zero-average distribution $P(z)$. The training error is given by

$$E_t(\boldsymbol{w}) = \frac{1}{2p} \sum_{\mu=1}^{p} [t_\mu - \boldsymbol{w} \cdot \boldsymbol{\Phi}(x_\mu)]^2$$

Gradient descent learning then boils down to

$$\begin{aligned} \frac{p}{\eta} \frac{\mathrm{d}}{\mathrm{d}t} w_i &= \sum_{\mu=1}^{p} [t_\mu - \boldsymbol{w} \cdot \boldsymbol{\Phi}(x_\mu)] \phi_i(x_\mu) \\ &= \sum_{\mu=1}^{p} t_\mu \phi_i(x_\mu) - \sum_{j=0}^{M} \left[\sum_{\mu=1}^{p} \phi_i(x_\mu) \phi_j(x_\mu) \right] w_j \end{aligned}$$

This can be written as $p\eta^{-1}(\mathrm{d}\boldsymbol{w}/\mathrm{d}t) = \boldsymbol{u} - \boldsymbol{A}\boldsymbol{w}$, with $u_i = \sum_{\mu=1}^{p} t_\mu (x_\mu)^i$ and $A_{ij} = \sum_{\mu=1}^{p} (x_\mu)^{i+j}$, with solution (provided the matrix $\boldsymbol{A}$ is invertible)

$$\boldsymbol{w}(t) = \boldsymbol{A}^{-1}\boldsymbol{u} + e^{-(\eta t/p)\boldsymbol{A}} [\boldsymbol{w}(0) - \boldsymbol{A}^{-1}\boldsymbol{u}]$$

The final outcome of the learning process is the weight vector $\boldsymbol{w}^\star = \boldsymbol{w}(\infty) = \boldsymbol{A}^{-1}\boldsymbol{u}$. Insertion into (6.9) gives the associated function extracted by the student from the data. In Figure 6.2 we show the result for the example $g(x) = \frac{1}{2} + \sin(2\pi x)$, with $0 \leq x \leq 1$. For small M (e.g. $M = 1$ in the figure), the complexity of the student is insufficient for reducing either training or generalization error. Increasing the complexity of the student, that is, M, initially improves both; see, for example, the case $M = 3$ in the

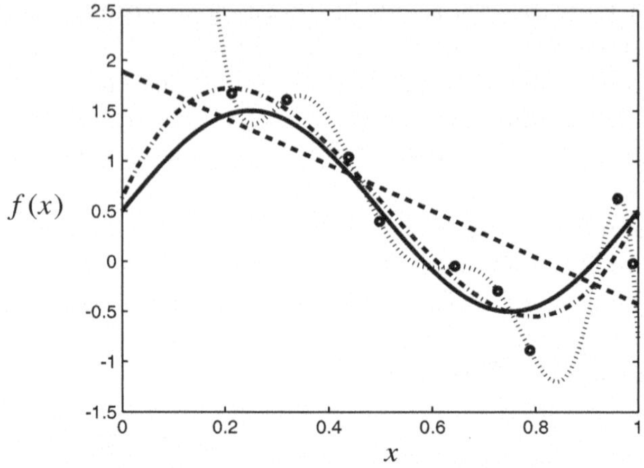

Figure 6.2 Example of a simple learning process where a system learns via gradient descent on a quadratic error measure to approximate a function $g(x) = \frac{1}{2} + \sin(2\pi x)$ (solid line) by an Mth-order polynomial $f(x; \mathbf{w}) = w_0 + w_1 x + \cdots + w_M x^M$, on the basis of nine noisy sample points of this function (circles). The resulting polynomials are shown for $M = 1$ (dashed), $M = 3$ (dot-dashed), and $M = 9$ (dotted).

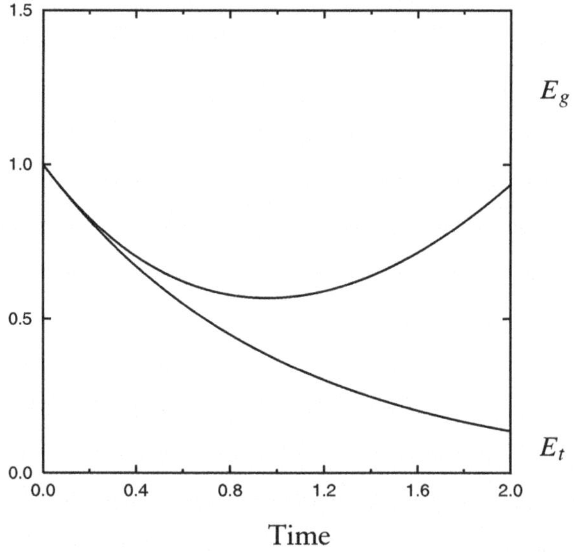

Figure 6.3 Evolution of training and generalization errors during a learning process defined as gradient descent on an error surface, with noisy data, in the regime where the student is too complex and starts overfitting, that is, reproducing also the noise in the data.

figure. However, for large M the system increasingly succeeds in reducing the training error by reproducing exactly the locations of the data points *including the noise*, with the side-effect of a deterioration of generalization; see the case $M = 9$ in the figure. Plotting the values of E_t and E_g as functions of time for a student with excessive complexity (M too large) would lead to the behaviour illustrated in Figure 6.3.

Two commonly used solutions to the overfitting problem are cross-validation and regularization. In *cross-validation*, the idea is to split the p available data points into two subsets: a training set $\{(\boldsymbol{\xi}^1, t_1), \ldots, (\boldsymbol{\xi}^k, t_k)\}$ and a validation set $\{(\boldsymbol{\xi}^{k+1}, t_{k+1}), \ldots, (\boldsymbol{\xi}^p, t_p)\}$. One then uses the training set for learning, and the validation set to estimate the generalization error:

$$E_t(\boldsymbol{w}) = \frac{1}{k}\sum_{\mu=1}^{k} \mathcal{E}(t_\mu, f(\boldsymbol{\xi}^\mu; \boldsymbol{w})) \qquad E_g(\boldsymbol{w}) \approx \frac{1}{p-k}\sum_{\mu=k+1}^{p} \mathcal{E}(t_\mu, f(\boldsymbol{\xi}^\mu; \boldsymbol{w})) \tag{6.10}$$

This latter estimate can be used in two possible ways:

(a) *Controlling model complexity (or: finding optimal complexity).* In terms of the example of Figure 6.2: start learning by minimizing the training error E_t with a small value of M, measure the estimate of the generalization error in (6.10), and repeat this procedure for increased values of M until E_g is seen to increase.

(b) *Controlling learning times (or 'early stopping').* As suggested by Figures 6.2 and 6.3, in this approach we minimize the training error E_t with a large value of M (a complex student) but monitor the estimate of the generalization error in (6.10) as a function of time. We then terminate learning as soon as E_g is seen to increase.

It should be emphasized that in both cases the value of E_g that one ends up with is still a *biased* estimate of the true generalization error. This is because both procedures actually try to minimize E_g, by choosing either M or the early stopping time, and so make it atypically small.

Note also that in (a), in order to reduce fluctuations in the estimate of E_g for any given M, one often considers several splits of the data into training and validation sets. A standard way of doing this is c-fold cross-validation: split the data into c equal-sized chunks, then leave out each chunk in turn as a validation set and use the rest of the data as the training set. This means running the training procedure c times, training each time on a fraction $(c-1)/c$ of the data. For each run one estimates E_g from the validation set as in (6.10) and then averages the c results to get the overall estimate of E_g for the given M. The extreme version of this with $c = p$, where the training algorithm is run p times and only one data point is left out each time, is also called leave-one-out cross-validation.

The method of *regularization* is based on the assumption that both the function to be learned and the basis functions of the student are in principle smooth, and that any observed irregularity and discontinuity of data must have been due to noise. Since the only way for the student to reproduce irregular or discontinuous functions is by having large and possibly diverging components of the parameter vector $\boldsymbol{w}$, regularization tries to prevent

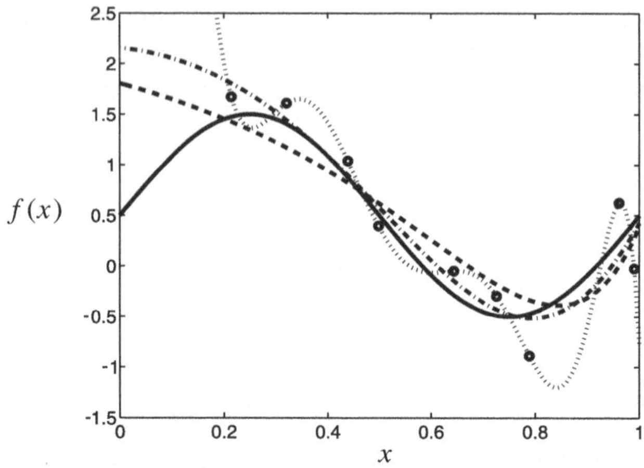

Figure 6.4 Regularization with a quadratic penalty term, as in equation (6.11), for the example of Figure 6.2. Solid line: the function to be learned. Circles: nine noisy sample points of this function. Dotted line: approximation by a 9th-order polynomial, without regularization. Other lines: similar, but with regularization coefficient $\lambda = 0.001$ (dot-dashed) and $\lambda = 0.1$ (dashed), respectively. The $\lambda = 0.001$ curve improves generalization compared to the un-regularized one, that is, it resembles the true function more closely. However, for $\lambda = 0.1$ we observe over-regularization: the approximation becomes too smooth.

$\boldsymbol{w}$ from becoming too large by adding a suitable penalty term to the function to be minimized, such as:

$$\frac{\mathrm{d}}{\mathrm{d}t}\boldsymbol{w} = -\eta\nabla_{\boldsymbol{w}}\left[E_t(\boldsymbol{w}) + \frac{1}{2}\lambda\boldsymbol{w}^2\right] \qquad E_t(\boldsymbol{w}) = \frac{1}{p}\sum_{\mu=1}^{p}\mathcal{E}(t_\mu, f(\boldsymbol{\xi}^\mu;\boldsymbol{w})) \tag{6.11}$$

Neither cross-validation nor regularization are ideal. In the first case we waste data and CPU time which could have been used for learning. In the second we must tune or guess the form of the penalty term and its coefficient λ; see also Figure 6.4. In either case we cannot be sure that we arrive at the lowest possible generalization error. The origin of the problem is clear: we continue to minimize an object which we can easily measure (E_t). This differs from the object which we would really like to minimize (E_g), but which we cannot measure.

6.2 Bayesian learning of network weights

Ideas, definitions, and benefits

The Bayesian approach deals in a systematic way with the general problem of learning in neural networks and other parametrized information processing systems of the general form $S(\boldsymbol{\xi}) = f(\boldsymbol{\xi};\boldsymbol{w}) + \text{noise}$, given the observation of generally noisy data $D = \{(\boldsymbol{\xi}^1, t_1), \ldots, (\boldsymbol{\xi}^p, t_p)\}$. In its simplest form, that is, for a given model, it is based on the following three ideas:

- Consider not just a single parameter vector $\boldsymbol{w}$, but an *ensemble* of parameter vectors, characterized by a probability distribution $p(\boldsymbol{w})$ which evolves during learning.
- Assume that the data D were generated by a system of the form $S(\boldsymbol{\xi}) = f(\boldsymbol{\xi};\boldsymbol{w})+\text{noise}$. Try to calculate the probability $p(\boldsymbol{w}|D)$ of the parameter vectors, given the data.
- Use the general Bayesian relation $P(A|B)P(B) = P(B|A)P(A)$ to express the desired object $p(\boldsymbol{w}|D)$ in terms of $p(D|\boldsymbol{w})$; the latter can be calculated quite easily.

Learning is regarded as a process during which the arrival of data reduces our uncertainty about the 'right' parameter vector $\boldsymbol{w}$ from a *prior distribution* $p(\boldsymbol{w})$, reflecting prior knowledge or prejudices about the problem, to a *posterior distribution* $p(\boldsymbol{w}|D)$ that reflects both prior assumptions and the evidence provided by the data. Note that we can combine the general statistical relations $p(D|\boldsymbol{w})p(\boldsymbol{w}) = p(\boldsymbol{w}|D)P(D)$ and $p(D) = \int \mathrm{d}\boldsymbol{w}\, p(\boldsymbol{w}, D)$ to obtain

$$p(\boldsymbol{w}|D) = \frac{p(D|\boldsymbol{w})p(\boldsymbol{w})}{\int \mathrm{d}\boldsymbol{w}' p(\boldsymbol{w}')p(D|\boldsymbol{w}')} \tag{6.12}$$

This is the core identity.

Putting the above ideas into practice, Bayesian learning works as follows:

Stage 1: definitions. Define (i) the parametrized model, assumed responsible for the data, (ii) the prior distribution $p(\boldsymbol{w})$ of its parameters, and (iii) the data $D = \{(\boldsymbol{\xi}^1, t_1), \ldots, (\boldsymbol{\xi}^p, t_p)\}$.

Stage 2: model translation. Convert the model definition into a standard probabilistic form, that is, specify the likelihood of finding output t upon presentation of input $\boldsymbol{\xi}$, given the parameters $\boldsymbol{w}$:

$$\text{model definition in standard form:} \quad p(t|\boldsymbol{\xi}, \boldsymbol{w}) \tag{6.13}$$

Stage 3: the posterior distribution. Calculate the *data* likelihood $p(D|\boldsymbol{w}) = \prod_{\mu=1}^{p} p(t_\mu|\boldsymbol{\xi}^\mu, \boldsymbol{w})$, as a function of the parameters $\boldsymbol{w}$. From this, together with identity (6.12), follows the desired posterior parameter distribution

$$p(\boldsymbol{w}|D) = \frac{p(\boldsymbol{w}) \prod_{\mu=1}^{p} p(t_\mu|\boldsymbol{\xi}^\mu, \boldsymbol{w})}{\int \mathrm{d}\boldsymbol{w}' p(\boldsymbol{w}') \prod_{\mu=1}^{p} p(t_\mu|\boldsymbol{\xi}^\mu, \boldsymbol{w}')} \tag{6.14}$$

Stage 4: prediction. The residual uncertainty in the parameters $\boldsymbol{w}$ generates uncertainty in subsequent data prediction. Prediction of the output t corresponding to a new input $\boldsymbol{\xi}$, given our observation of the data D and our choice of model, thus takes the probabilistic form:

$$p(t|\boldsymbol{\xi}, D) = \int d\boldsymbol{w}\; p(t|\boldsymbol{\xi}, \boldsymbol{w})p(\boldsymbol{w}|D) \qquad (6.15)$$

This concludes the description of Bayesian learning for a single model: the problem has in principle been reduced to doing integrals, although how one evaluates these efficiently is quite another matter. Before we move on to the remainder of this section, which deals with implementation and understanding, and with the generalization of the ideas to model selection, two comments on the expression for $p(D|\boldsymbol{w})$ in Stage 3 are in order. (i) The fact that we have a product of terms for the individual data points implies the assumption that the data are *independently and identically distributed* (i.i.d.) for a given $\boldsymbol{w}$. In other words, there is nothing special about any particular data point; as a counter-example one could think of the noise level depending on μ. Also, different data points are not correlated with each other, as could happen if data arrive, for example, in batches, with each batch having a persistent bias towards low or high values. (ii) Strictly speaking, $P(D|\boldsymbol{w})$ as written is the probability of the *outputs* $t_1, \ldots, t_p$ given $\boldsymbol{w}$ *and* the inputs $\boldsymbol{\xi}^1, \ldots, \boldsymbol{\xi}^p$. The *joint* probability of outputs and inputs given $\boldsymbol{w}$ would be $\prod_{\mu=1}^{p} p(t_\mu|\boldsymbol{\xi}^\mu, \boldsymbol{w})p(\boldsymbol{\xi}^\mu)$ if we make the reasonable assumption that the input distribution is not influenced by $\boldsymbol{w}$. Since the extra factor $\prod_{\mu=1}^{p} p(\boldsymbol{\xi}^\mu)$ is independent of $\boldsymbol{w}$, it cancels from identities such as (6.12) and would not change any of the results.

The Bayesian approach to learning has become very popular within a relatively short period of time. The reason for this can be appreciated by simply listing some of its main appeals and benefits, to be derived below:

- It provides an interpretation of regularizers and their associated parameters.
- It provides an interpretation of single-point error measures.
- There is no need for cross-validation, so all data can be used for learning.
- It allows for the selection of the optimal complexity within a given model class, and for the selection of the optimal model class from a given set of candidates.
- It provides not only predictions, but also specific estimates of our confidence in these predictions, that is, error bars.
- Traditional learning via gradient descent training error minimization, with regularization, is recovered as a particular approximation within the Bayesian framework.

Let us gain intuition on how in the Bayesian picture the arrival of data is converted into probabilistic statements about model parameters, by working out the steps (6.13, 6.14) for some simple examples. We will write inputs as $\xi \in \mathbb{R}$ or $\boldsymbol{\xi} \in \mathbb{R}^N$, adjustable parameters as $w \in \mathbb{R}$ or $\boldsymbol{w} \in \mathbb{R}^M$, outputs as $t \in \mathbb{R}$, and data as $D = \{(\boldsymbol{\xi}^1, t_1), \ldots, (\boldsymbol{\xi}^p, t_p)\}$.

Example 1. Our first example describes a deterministic model with one real-valued input and one real-valued output. Stage one in the process is the definition of model, prior parameter distribution[13] and data, for which we take:

$$t(\xi) = \tanh(w\xi) \qquad p(w) = (2\pi)^{-1/2} e^{-w^2/2} \qquad D = \{(1, -\tfrac{1}{2})\}$$

(one data point). Next we convert the model into the standard probabilistic form[14] (6.13):

$$p(t|\xi, w) = \delta(t - \tanh(w\xi))$$

We can now calculate the posterior distribution (6.14):

$$\begin{aligned} p(w|D) &= \frac{p(w)p(t_1|\xi^1, w)}{\int \mathrm{d}w'\, p(w')p(t_1|\xi^1, w')} = \frac{\delta(-(1/2) - \tanh(w))e^{-w^2/2}}{\int \mathrm{d}w'\, \delta(-(1/2) - \tanh(w'))e^{-w'^2/2}} \\ &= \delta(w - \operatorname{artanh}(-\tfrac{1}{2})) = \delta(w + \ln\sqrt{3}) \end{aligned} \tag{6.16}$$

Here we have used the two identities $\delta(f(w)) = |f'(f^{-1}(0))|^{-1}\delta(w - f^{-1}(0))$ (see Appendix F) and $\operatorname{artanh}(z) = \frac{1}{2}\ln((1+z)/(1-z))$.

Before we had observed any data our uncertainty about the parameter w was described by the Gaussian prior $p(w)$. The arrival of the data point $(1, -\frac{1}{2})$ induced a collapse of this prior to the δ-distributed posterior $p(w|D) = \delta(w + \ln\sqrt{3})$, without any uncertainty. This is illustrated in Figure 6.5 (left).

Example 2. Let us now make matters slightly more interesting and replace the one-parameter function of the first example by a two-parameter function:

$$t(\xi) = \tanh(w_0 + w_1\xi) \qquad p(\boldsymbol{w}) = (2\pi)^{-1} e^{-\boldsymbol{w}^2/2} \qquad D = \{(1, -\tfrac{1}{2})\}$$

---

[13] Note that for any fixed choice of average and variance, the Gaussian distribution is the maximum entropy (i.e. maximum uncertainty) distribution for real-valued random variables. See Part III of this book, dealing with applications of information theory.

[14] See Appendix F on distributions for the definition and properties of the distribution $\delta(z)$.

The standard probabilistic form becomes

$$p(t|\xi, \boldsymbol{w}) = \delta(t - \tanh(w_0 + w_1\xi))$$

The posterior distribution becomes:

$$\begin{aligned} p(\boldsymbol{w}|D) &= \frac{p(\boldsymbol{w})p(t_1|\xi^1, \boldsymbol{w})}{\int \mathrm{d}\boldsymbol{w}'\, p(\boldsymbol{w}')p(t_1|\xi^1, \boldsymbol{w}')} \\ &= \frac{\delta(-(1/2) - \tanh(w_0 + w_1))e^{-\boldsymbol{w}^2/2}}{\int \mathrm{d}\boldsymbol{w}'\, \delta(-(1/2) - \tanh(w_0' + w_1'))e^{-\boldsymbol{w}'^2/2}} \\ &= \frac{\delta(w_0 + w_1 + \mathrm{artanh}(1/2))e^{-\boldsymbol{w}^2/2}}{\int \mathrm{d}\boldsymbol{w}'\, \delta(w_0' + w_1' + \mathrm{artanh}(1/2))e^{-\boldsymbol{w}'^2/2}} \\ &= \frac{\delta(w_0 + w_1 + \ln\sqrt{3})e^{-\boldsymbol{w}^2/2}}{\int \mathrm{d}\boldsymbol{w}'\, \delta(w_0' + w_1' + \ln\sqrt{3})e^{-\boldsymbol{w}'^2/2}} \end{aligned} \tag{6.17}$$

using the same identities as in (6.16). Note that the posterior (6.17) is nonzero only along the line $w_0 + w_1 = -\ln\sqrt{3}$ in the parameter plane, and that along this line it is maximal for the choice $w_0 = w_1 = -\frac{1}{2}\ln\sqrt{3}$. This latter result simply follows from calculating the minimum of $\boldsymbol{w}^2$ along the line $w_0 + w_1 = -\ln\sqrt{3}$, and is illustrated in Figure 6.5 (right).

Before we observed any data our uncertainty about the parameters $\boldsymbol{w} = (w_0, w_1)$ was described by the Gaussian prior $p(\boldsymbol{w})$. The arrival of the data point $(1, -\frac{1}{2})$ induced a collapse of this prior to an infinitely narrow distribution along the line $w_0 + w_1 = -\ln\sqrt{3}$, that is, a 'slice' of the

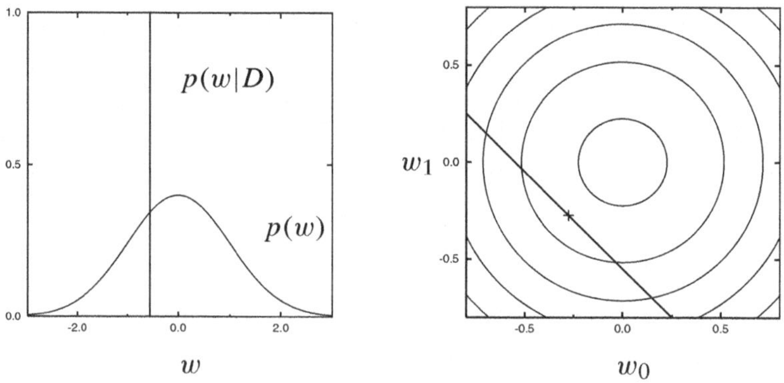

Figure 6.5 Left: reduction of parameter uncertainty due to arrival of data in Example 1, from a Gaussian prior distribution $p(w)$ to a δ-peaked posterior distribution $p(w|D)$. Right: reduction of parameter uncertainty in Example 2, from a Gaussian prior distribution $p(w_0, w_1)$ (contour lines) to a posterior distribution $p(w_0, w_1|D)$ with support only along the line $w_0 + w_1 = -\ln\sqrt{3}$ (with its maximum at the point indicated by + in the figure).

two-dimensional Gaussian prior in the parameter plane. The most likely parameter vector is $w_0 = w_1 = -\frac{1}{2}\ln\sqrt{3}$, but we note that in (6.17) we also have exact quantitative information regarding the uncertainty in (w_0, w_1).

Note, finally, that in contrast to the above two simple examples we will generally have to allow for data generating models that incorporate noise, in order to retain a nonzero probability for having generated the—generally noisy—observed data.

The link between Bayesian learning and traditional learning

At first sight it appears that Bayesian learning is quite remote from traditional gradient descent learning on an error surface, possibly with regularization, as in

$$\frac{\mathrm{d}}{\mathrm{d}t}\boldsymbol{w} = -\eta\nabla_{\boldsymbol{w}}[E_t(\boldsymbol{w}) + \lambda E_w(\boldsymbol{w})] \qquad E_t(\boldsymbol{w}) = \frac{1}{p}\sum_{\mu=1}^{p}\mathcal{E}(t_\mu - f(\boldsymbol{\xi}^\mu; \boldsymbol{w})) \quad (6.18)$$

in which $\mathcal{E}(u)$ represents a single-point error measure, the function $E_w(\boldsymbol{w})$ represents a regularizer, and with $\boldsymbol{w} \in \mathbb{R}^M$. To reveal the link between the two points of view we must turn to (6.14), which we write as

$$\ln p^{-1}(\boldsymbol{w}|D) = -\ln p(\boldsymbol{w}) - \sum_{\mu=1}^{p}\ln p(t_\mu|\boldsymbol{\xi}^\mu, \boldsymbol{w}) + \ln\int \mathrm{d}\boldsymbol{w}'\, p(\boldsymbol{w}')\prod_{\mu=1}^{p} p(t_\mu|\boldsymbol{\xi}^\mu, \boldsymbol{w}')$$

Finding the *most probable* parameter vector $\boldsymbol{w}_{\mathrm{MP}}$, given the data D, is equivalent to minimizing $\ln p^{-1}(\boldsymbol{w}|D)$, that is, to minimizing the quantity $S(\boldsymbol{w}, D)$:

$$S(\boldsymbol{w}, D) = -\ln p(\boldsymbol{w}) - \sum_{\mu=1}^{p}\ln p(t_\mu|\boldsymbol{\xi}^\mu, \boldsymbol{w}) \quad (6.19)$$

Let us work out this expression for the following simple and natural class of data-generating models: $t = f(\boldsymbol{\xi}; \boldsymbol{w}) + z$,

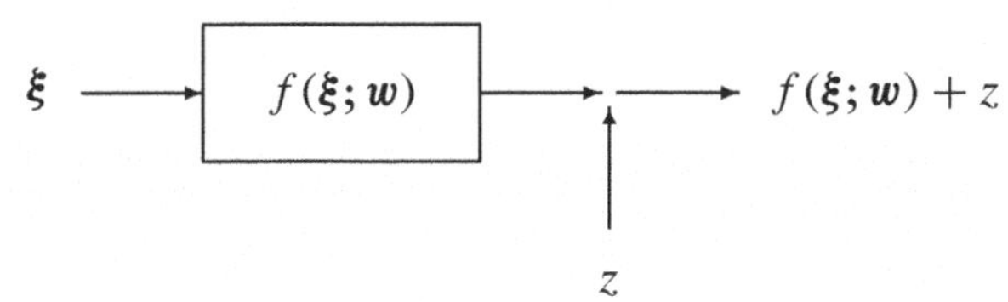

Here f denotes some parametrized function, as performed, for example, by the standard neural networks (MLP, RBF) that are traditionally used in gradient descent learning of the type (6.18). Additive noise in the data is represented by z, a zero-average random number. If this noise variable is distributed according to $P(z)$, one has

$$p(t|\boldsymbol{\xi};\boldsymbol{w}) = P(t - f(\boldsymbol{\xi};\boldsymbol{w})) \tag{6.20}$$

Now the function (6.19), whose minimum gives the most probable parameters, reduces to

$$\frac{1}{p}S(\boldsymbol{w},D) = -\frac{1}{p}\sum_{\mu=1}^{p}\ln P(t_\mu - f(\boldsymbol{\xi}^\mu;\boldsymbol{w})) - \frac{1}{p}\ln p(\boldsymbol{w})$$

Comparison with expression (6.18) reveals the following:

- Learning by finding the minimum on a training error surface, with regularizer, as in (6.18), is equivalent to finding the *most probable* parameter vector $\boldsymbol{w}_{\rm MP}$. This is also called the Maximum A Posteriori Probability (MAP) procedure.
- Choosing a specific single-point error measure $\mathcal{E}(u)$ in (6.18) means making the following assumption on the data noise statistics: $P(z) \sim e^{-\mathcal{E}(z)}$.
- Choosing a specific regularizer $\lambda E_w(\boldsymbol{w})$ in (6.18) means deciding on the following specific prior distribution for the parameters $\boldsymbol{w}$: $p(\boldsymbol{w}) \sim e^{-p\lambda E_w(\boldsymbol{w})}$.

Our previously ad hoc choices of error measure and regularizer are now replaced by direct interpretations, and hence guides for how to make appropriate choices. We also learn *en passant* that the regularizer strength must scale with the number of examples as $\lambda \sim p^{-1}$.

For example, learning by minimization of the simplest (quadratic) training error measure $\mathcal{E}(u) = \frac{1}{2}u^2$ and quadratic regularizer, viz.

$$\frac{\mathrm{d}}{\mathrm{d}t}\boldsymbol{w} = -\eta\nabla_{\boldsymbol{w}}\left\{\frac{1}{2p}\sum_{\mu=1}^{p}[t_\mu - f(\boldsymbol{\xi}^\mu;\boldsymbol{w})]^2 + \frac{1}{2}\lambda\boldsymbol{w}^2\right\} \tag{6.21}$$

is now recognized as fully equivalent to finding the most probable parameter vector $\boldsymbol{w}_{\rm MP}$ for the following type of model:

$$p(t|\boldsymbol{\xi};\boldsymbol{w}) = \left(\frac{\beta}{2\pi}\right)^{1/2} e^{-\beta[t-f(\boldsymbol{\xi};\boldsymbol{w})]^2/2} \qquad p(\boldsymbol{w}) = \left(\frac{\alpha}{2\pi}\right)^{M/2} e^{-\alpha\boldsymbol{w}^2/2} \tag{6.22}$$

For this choice the function (6.19) simplifies, up to an irrelevant constant, to:

$$\begin{aligned} S(\boldsymbol{w}, D) &= \frac{\beta}{2}\sum_{\mu=1}^{p}[t_\mu - f(\boldsymbol{\xi}^\mu; \boldsymbol{w})]^2 + \frac{\alpha}{2}\boldsymbol{w}^2 \\ &= \beta p\left\{\frac{1}{2p}\sum_{\mu=1}^{p}[t_\mu - f(\boldsymbol{\xi}^\mu; \boldsymbol{w})]^2 + \frac{1}{2}\frac{\alpha}{\beta p}\boldsymbol{w}^2\right\} \end{aligned} \tag{6.23}$$

This is indeed proportional to the function being optimized in (6.21) if we identify $\lambda = \alpha/\beta p$. We thus need no longer guess the value of λ, but can relate it to our assumptions about the prior and the noise level

$$\lambda = \frac{\alpha}{\beta p} \qquad \alpha = \frac{1}{\langle w_i^2\rangle_{\text{prior}}} \qquad \beta = \frac{1}{\langle t^2\rangle_{\text{noise}} - \langle t\rangle_{\text{noise}}^2}$$

Quantities such as α or β in (6.22), which are not themselves adjustable parameters in the sense of $\boldsymbol{w}$, but are more global parameters which reflect prior knowledge of the problem and influence the learning process are called *hyperparameters*.

Approximation of the posterior parameter distribution

If we were to only calculate the most probable parameter vector $\boldsymbol{w}_{\text{MP}}$ we would gain only interpretations compared to old-fashioned training error minimization. The power of the Bayesian techniques is that they also provide information on the reliability of a learning outcome. This information is embodied in the full posterior distribution $p(\boldsymbol{w}|D)$, which can be written in terms of (6.19) as

$$p(\boldsymbol{w}|D) = \frac{e^{-S(\boldsymbol{w},D)}}{\int \mathrm{d}\boldsymbol{w}'\, e^{-S(\boldsymbol{w}',D)}} \tag{6.24}$$

In those cases where $S(\boldsymbol{w}, D)$ has only a single relevant local (and thus also global) minimum $\boldsymbol{w}_{\text{MP}}$, the reliability of the learning outcome is mainly coded in the local curvature (i.e. the 'width') of $S(\boldsymbol{w}, D)$ around $\boldsymbol{w}_{\text{MP}}$. We now expand $S(\boldsymbol{w}, D)$ in the vicinity of $\boldsymbol{w}_{\text{MP}}$:

$$S(\boldsymbol{w}, D) = S(\boldsymbol{w}_{\text{MP}}, D) + \tfrac{1}{2}(\boldsymbol{w} - \boldsymbol{w}_{\text{MP}}) \cdot \boldsymbol{A}(\boldsymbol{w} - \boldsymbol{w}_{\text{MP}}) + \mathcal{O}(|\boldsymbol{w} - \boldsymbol{w}_{\text{MP}}|^3) \tag{6.25}$$

$$A_{ij} = \left.\frac{\partial^2 S}{\partial w_i \partial w_j}\right|_{\boldsymbol{w}_{\text{MP}}} \tag{6.26}$$

Here A is called the Hessian matrix of S at the point w_{MP}; linear terms are absent in (6.25) due to w_{MP} being a minimum. Truncation of the expansion (6.25) after the quadratic term leads to a Gaussian approximation of the posterior $p(w|D)$:

$$S(w, D) \to \tilde{S}(w, D) = S(w_{\mathrm{MP}}, D) + \tfrac{1}{2}(w - w_{\mathrm{MP}}) \cdot A(w - w_{\mathrm{MP}}) \qquad (6.27)$$

$$p(w|D) \to \tilde{p}(w|D) = \left[\frac{\det A}{(2\pi)^M}\right]^{1/2} e^{-(w-w_{\mathrm{MP}})\cdot A(w-w_{\mathrm{MP}})/2} \qquad (6.28)$$

Average, variance and covariance matrix of the approximated posterior distribution $\tilde{p}(w|D)$ are given by the following identities (see Appendix D) involving the inverse of the Hessian (6.26), with the notation $\langle f(w)\rangle = \int \mathrm{d}w\, f(w)\tilde{p}(w|D)$:

$$\langle w\rangle = w_{\mathrm{MP}} \qquad \langle w_i w_j\rangle - \langle w_i\rangle\langle w_j\rangle = (A^{-1})_{ij} \qquad (6.29)$$

6.3 Predictions with error bars: real-valued functions

Learning and predicting the action of continuous real-valued functions from (noisy) data examples is called *regression*. As we have seen in the previous section, a trained network is within the Bayesian framework described by the posterior distribution $p(w|D)$ for the system parameters, as given by (6.14). Prediction then proceeds via formula (6.15), which can also be written in terms of the function $S(w, D)$ from (6.19) as

$$p(t|\xi, D) = \int \mathrm{d}w\, p(t|\xi, w)p(w|D) \qquad p(w|D) = \frac{e^{-S(w,D)}}{\int \mathrm{d}w'\, e^{-S(w',D)}} \qquad (6.30)$$

This formally defines the statistics of the output to be associated with input ξ; $p(t|\xi)$ is also called the predictive distribution.

Mean and variance for Gaussian output noise and Gaussian priors

We now work out output average and variance of (6.30) for the simplest class of systems (6.22), that is, a parametrized function $f(\xi; w)$ with additive zero-average Gaussian data noise:

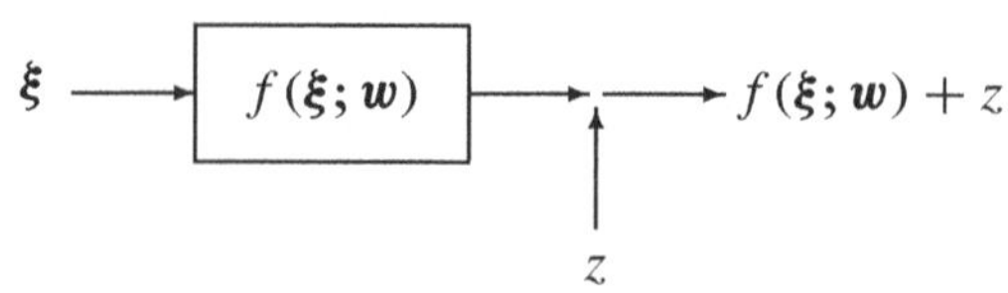

The moments $\langle t \rangle = \int \mathrm{d}t\, t\, p(t|\boldsymbol{\xi}, D)$ and $\langle t^2 \rangle = \int \mathrm{d}t\, t^2\, p(t|\boldsymbol{\xi}, D)$ become, if we transform the integration variable by putting $t = f(\boldsymbol{\xi}; \boldsymbol{w}) + z/\sqrt{\beta}$:

$$\langle t \rangle = \left(\frac{\beta}{2\pi}\right)^{1/2} \int \mathrm{d}t\, t \int \mathrm{d}\boldsymbol{w}\, e^{-\beta[t - f(\boldsymbol{\xi};\boldsymbol{w})]^2/2} p(\boldsymbol{w}|D) \tag{6.31}$$

$$= \int \mathrm{d}\boldsymbol{w} \int \frac{\mathrm{d}z}{\sqrt{2\pi}} e^{-z^2/2} [f(\boldsymbol{\xi}; \boldsymbol{w}) + z/\sqrt{\beta}] p(\boldsymbol{w}|D)$$

$$= \int \mathrm{d}\boldsymbol{w}\, f(\boldsymbol{\xi}; \boldsymbol{w}) p(\boldsymbol{w}|D) \tag{6.32}$$

$$\langle t^2 \rangle = \left(\frac{\beta}{2\pi}\right)^{1/2} \int \mathrm{d}t\, t^2 \int \mathrm{d}\boldsymbol{w}\, e^{-\beta[t - f(\boldsymbol{\xi};\boldsymbol{w})]^2/2} p(\boldsymbol{w}|D)$$

$$= \int \mathrm{d}\boldsymbol{w} \int \frac{\mathrm{d}z}{\sqrt{2\pi}} e^{-z^2/2} [f(\boldsymbol{\xi}; \boldsymbol{w}) + z/\sqrt{\beta}]^2 p(\boldsymbol{w}|D)$$

$$= \frac{1}{\beta} + \int \mathrm{d}\boldsymbol{w}\, f^2(\boldsymbol{\xi}; \boldsymbol{w}) p(\boldsymbol{w}|D) \tag{6.33}$$

The prediction variance $\sigma^2 = \langle t^2 \rangle - \langle t \rangle^2$ now follows as

$$\sigma^2 = \frac{1}{\beta} + \underbrace{\int \mathrm{d}\boldsymbol{w}\, f^2(\boldsymbol{\xi}; \boldsymbol{w}) p(\boldsymbol{w}|D) - \left[\int \mathrm{d}\boldsymbol{w}\, f(\boldsymbol{\xi}; \boldsymbol{w}) p(\boldsymbol{w}|D)\right]^2}_{\text{variance due to uncertainty about system parameters}} \tag{6.34}$$

The first term, β^{-1}, represents the intrinsic uncertainty in the data generation model; the remainder in (6.34) reflects our uncertainty about the right parameters after having learned the data. The Bayesian predicted output $t^\star(\boldsymbol{\xi})$ for the input $\boldsymbol{\xi}$, and its associated error margin $\Delta t^\star(\boldsymbol{\xi})$, are now defined as $\langle t \rangle$ and σ, respectively[15]:

$$t^\star(\boldsymbol{\xi}) = \int \mathrm{d}\boldsymbol{w}\, f(\boldsymbol{\xi}; \boldsymbol{w}) p(\boldsymbol{w}|D) \tag{6.35}$$

$$[\Delta t^\star(\boldsymbol{\xi})]^2 = \frac{1}{\beta} + \int \mathrm{d}\boldsymbol{w}\, f^2(\boldsymbol{\xi}; \boldsymbol{w}) p(\boldsymbol{w}|D) - \left[\int \mathrm{d}\boldsymbol{w}\, f(\boldsymbol{\xi}; \boldsymbol{w}) p(\boldsymbol{w}|D)\right]^2 \tag{6.36}$$

---

[15] Note: $t^\star(\boldsymbol{\xi})$ need not be identical to $f(\boldsymbol{\xi}; \boldsymbol{w}_{\mathrm{MP}})$, where $\boldsymbol{w}_{\mathrm{MP}}$ denotes the most probable parameters.

We note briefly that the above results for $\langle t\rangle$ and $\langle t^2\rangle$ can also be derived by writing

$$\langle t^n\rangle = \int \mathrm{d}\boldsymbol{w}\, p(\boldsymbol{w}|D) \int \mathrm{d}t\, t^n\, p(t|\boldsymbol{\xi},\boldsymbol{w})$$

Because $p(t|\boldsymbol{\xi},\boldsymbol{w})$ is a Gaussian distribution with mean $f(\boldsymbol{\xi};\boldsymbol{w})$ and variance $1/\beta$, the integral—or average—over t gives $f(\boldsymbol{\xi};\boldsymbol{w})$ for $n=1$ and $f^2(\boldsymbol{\xi};\boldsymbol{w})+1/\beta$ for $n=2$, respectively. This leads directly to (6.32, 6.33).

We assume in the following that the prior on $\boldsymbol{w}$ is Gaussian. The function $S(\boldsymbol{w},D)$ is then given by (6.23) and $p(\boldsymbol{w}|D)$ has the form

$$p(\boldsymbol{w}|D) = \frac{e^{-S(\boldsymbol{w},D)}}{\int \mathrm{d}\boldsymbol{w}'\, e^{-S(\boldsymbol{w}',D)}} \qquad S(\boldsymbol{w},D) = \frac{\beta}{2}\sum_{\mu=1}^{p}[t_\mu - f(\boldsymbol{\xi}^\mu;\boldsymbol{w})]^2 + \frac{\alpha}{2}\boldsymbol{w}^2$$

In the pair (6.35, 6.36) we now have proper predictions *with error bars*.

Simplification for approximated posterior distribution

The above exact result (6.35, 6.36) can be simplified using the approximated posterior distribution $\tilde{p}(\boldsymbol{w}|D)$ of (6.28). To get the (approximate) predicted outputs and error bars, we need the averages $\langle f^n(\boldsymbol{\xi};\boldsymbol{w})\rangle$ taken over $\tilde{p}(\boldsymbol{w}|D)$, a Gaussian distribution with mean $\langle\boldsymbol{w}\rangle = \boldsymbol{w}_{\mathrm{MP}}$ and, from (6.29), covariance matrix $\boldsymbol{A}^{-1}$. We isolate the mean by writing $\boldsymbol{w} = \boldsymbol{w}_{\mathrm{MP}} + \boldsymbol{u}$, so that $\boldsymbol{u}$ is a Gaussian random vector with zero mean and covariance matrix $\langle u_i u_j\rangle = (\boldsymbol{A}^{-1})_{ij}$. Even so, we cannot in general evaluate the averages $\langle f^n(\boldsymbol{\xi};\boldsymbol{w}_{\mathrm{MP}}+\boldsymbol{u})\rangle$ exactly. We therefore make one further and final approximation: if the width of the distribution of $\boldsymbol{u}$ is small, that is, if $\boldsymbol{A}$ is large, then we can expand

$$f(\boldsymbol{\xi};\boldsymbol{w}_{\mathrm{MP}}+\boldsymbol{u}) = f(\boldsymbol{\xi};\boldsymbol{w}_{\mathrm{MP}}) + \boldsymbol{u}\cdot\boldsymbol{x}(\boldsymbol{\xi}) + \tfrac{1}{2}\boldsymbol{u}\cdot\boldsymbol{B}(\boldsymbol{\xi})\boldsymbol{u} + \mathcal{O}(\boldsymbol{u}^3) \qquad (6.37)$$

where $x_i(\boldsymbol{\xi}) = \partial f(\boldsymbol{\xi};\boldsymbol{w})/\partial w_i|_{\boldsymbol{w}_{\mathrm{MP}}}$ and $B_{ij}(\boldsymbol{\xi}) = \partial^2 f(\boldsymbol{\xi};\boldsymbol{w})/\partial w_i\partial w_j|_{\boldsymbol{w}_{\mathrm{MP}}}$. We now systematically neglect all terms of order $\boldsymbol{u}^3$ and higher. The average over the zero-mean Gaussian vector $\boldsymbol{u}$ kills the third-order terms anyway, so the first terms that we are genuinely neglecting are those of order $\boldsymbol{u}^4$, whose averages would scale[16] as $\boldsymbol{A}^{-2}$. We thus get

$$\begin{aligned} t^\star(\boldsymbol{\xi}) &= \langle f(\boldsymbol{\xi};\boldsymbol{w}_{\mathrm{MP}}+\boldsymbol{u})\rangle \\ &= f(\boldsymbol{\xi};\boldsymbol{w}_{\mathrm{MP}}) + \langle\boldsymbol{u}\rangle\cdot\boldsymbol{x}(\boldsymbol{\xi}) + \frac{1}{2}\sum_{ij} B_{ij}(\boldsymbol{\xi})\langle u_i u_j\rangle + \mathcal{O}(\boldsymbol{A}^{-2}) \\ &= f(\boldsymbol{\xi};\boldsymbol{w}_{\mathrm{MP}}) + \tfrac{1}{2}\mathrm{tr}[\boldsymbol{B}(\boldsymbol{\xi})\boldsymbol{A}^{-1}] + \mathcal{O}(\boldsymbol{A}^{-2}) \end{aligned} \qquad (6.38)$$

16 We symbolically write $\boldsymbol{A}^{-2}$ here to refer to terms which are quadratic or of higher order in the elements of the matrix $\boldsymbol{A}^{-1}$.

where the trace of a matrix is defined as usual, $\mathrm{tr}\,\boldsymbol{C} = \sum_i C_{ii}$. For the calculation of the error bars, squaring (6.37) and retaining only terms up to quadratic order in $\boldsymbol{u}$ gives

$$\begin{aligned} f^2(\boldsymbol{\xi}; \boldsymbol{w}_{\mathrm{MP}} + \boldsymbol{u}) &= [f(\boldsymbol{\xi}; \boldsymbol{w}_{\mathrm{MP}}) + \boldsymbol{u} \cdot \boldsymbol{x}(\boldsymbol{\xi}) + \tfrac{1}{2}\boldsymbol{u} \cdot \boldsymbol{B}(\boldsymbol{\xi})\boldsymbol{u}]^2 + \mathcal{O}(\boldsymbol{u}^3) \\ &= f^2(\boldsymbol{\xi}; \boldsymbol{w}_{\mathrm{MP}}) + 2f(\boldsymbol{\xi}; \boldsymbol{w}_{\mathrm{MP}})\boldsymbol{u} \cdot \boldsymbol{x}(\boldsymbol{\xi}) \\ &\quad + f(\boldsymbol{\xi}; \boldsymbol{w}_{\mathrm{MP}})\boldsymbol{u} \cdot \boldsymbol{B}(\boldsymbol{\xi})\boldsymbol{u} + [\boldsymbol{u} \cdot \boldsymbol{x}(\boldsymbol{\xi})]^2 + \mathcal{O}(\boldsymbol{u}^3) \end{aligned}$$

Averaging over $\boldsymbol{u}$ then leads to

$$\begin{aligned} \langle f^2(\boldsymbol{\xi}; \boldsymbol{w}_{\mathrm{MP}} + \boldsymbol{u})\rangle &= f^2(\boldsymbol{\xi}; \boldsymbol{w}_{\mathrm{MP}}) + f(\boldsymbol{\xi}; \boldsymbol{w}_{\mathrm{MP}})\mathrm{tr}[\boldsymbol{B}(\boldsymbol{\xi})\boldsymbol{A}^{-1}] \\ &\quad + \boldsymbol{x}(\boldsymbol{\xi}) \cdot \boldsymbol{A}^{-1}\boldsymbol{x}(\boldsymbol{\xi}) + \mathcal{O}(\boldsymbol{A}^{-2}) \end{aligned}$$

For the error bars (6.36) we need the difference between this and $[t^\star(\boldsymbol{\xi})]^2$. The latter is, from (6.38),

$$[t^\star(\boldsymbol{\xi})]^2 = f^2(\boldsymbol{\xi}; \boldsymbol{w}_{\mathrm{MP}}) + f(\boldsymbol{\xi}; \boldsymbol{w}_{\mathrm{MP}})\mathrm{tr}[\boldsymbol{B}(\boldsymbol{\xi})\boldsymbol{A}^{-1}] + \mathcal{O}(\boldsymbol{A}^{-2}) \tag{6.39}$$

and so the approximate error bars follow as

$$\begin{aligned} [\Delta t^\star(\boldsymbol{\xi})]^2 &= \frac{1}{\beta} + \langle f^2(\boldsymbol{\xi}; \boldsymbol{w}_{\mathrm{MP}} + \boldsymbol{u})\rangle - \langle f(\boldsymbol{\xi}; \boldsymbol{w}_{\mathrm{MP}} + \boldsymbol{u})\rangle^2 \\ &= \frac{1}{\beta} + \boldsymbol{x}(\boldsymbol{\xi}) \cdot \boldsymbol{A}^{-1}\boldsymbol{x}(\boldsymbol{\xi}) + \mathcal{O}(\boldsymbol{A}^{-2}) \end{aligned} \tag{6.40}$$

For expressions (6.38, 6.40) to be accurate[17] and useful—given our earlier assumptions of Gaussian additive data noise and a Gaussian prior—we need $p(\boldsymbol{w}|D)$ to be (i) approximately Gaussian, and (ii) sufficiently narrow. The latter condition means, in view of (6.29), that (the elements of) $\boldsymbol{A}^{-1}$ can indeed be treated as small.

Models for which the above truncation is exact

In order to appreciate the nature of the approximations one would arrive at by simply neglecting the $\mathcal{O}(\boldsymbol{A}^{-2})$ terms in (6.38, 6.40), it is instructive to determine the conditions under which they become exact. Given Gaussian data output noise and a Gaussian prior

$$p(\boldsymbol{w}) = \left(\frac{\alpha}{2\pi}\right)^{M/2} e^{-\alpha \boldsymbol{w}^2/2}$$

[17] In many textbooks one finds that the second term in $t^\star(\boldsymbol{\xi})$ is also neglected; this is equivalent to retaining only the first two terms in the expansion (6.37).

the approximation (6.28) is exact only if $S(\boldsymbol{w}, D)$ (6.19) depends quadratically on $\boldsymbol{w}$, that is, if $f(\boldsymbol{\xi}; \boldsymbol{w})$ depends linearly on $\boldsymbol{w}$,

$$p(t|\boldsymbol{\xi}; \boldsymbol{w}) = \left(\frac{\beta}{2\pi}\right)^{1/2} e^{-\beta[t-f(\boldsymbol{\xi};\boldsymbol{w})]^2/2}, \quad f(\boldsymbol{\xi}; \boldsymbol{w}) = \sum_{i=1}^{M} w_i \phi_i(\boldsymbol{\xi}) \tag{6.41}$$

Here $\{\phi_i(\boldsymbol{\xi})\}$ is a set of in principle arbitrary functions; RBF networks constitute a concrete example. Because of the linear dependence of $f(\boldsymbol{\xi}; \boldsymbol{w})$ on $\boldsymbol{w}$, models of the form (6.41) are also known as generalized linear models. For them, also (6.37) is exact when truncated after the term linear in z, so $\boldsymbol{B}(\boldsymbol{\xi}) = 0$ and the $\mathcal{O}(\boldsymbol{A}^{-2})$ terms in (6.38, 6.40) are absent. Furthermore, since $S(\boldsymbol{w}, D)$ is now truly quadratic, we can calculate $\boldsymbol{x}(\boldsymbol{\xi})$ and $\boldsymbol{w}_{\text{MP}}$ explicitly. We define $\boldsymbol{\Phi}(\boldsymbol{\xi}) = (\phi_1(\boldsymbol{\xi}), \ldots, \phi_M(\boldsymbol{\xi}))$, and get

$$\begin{aligned} S(\boldsymbol{w}, D) &= \frac{1}{2}\beta \sum_{\mu=1}^{p} [t_\mu - \boldsymbol{w} \cdot \boldsymbol{\Phi}(\boldsymbol{\xi}^\mu)]^2 + \frac{1}{2}\alpha \boldsymbol{w}^2 \\ &= \frac{1}{2}\beta \sum_{\mu=1}^{p} t_\mu^2 - \beta \boldsymbol{w} \cdot \sum_{\mu=1}^{p} t_\mu \boldsymbol{\Phi}(\boldsymbol{\xi}^\mu) + \frac{1}{2}\boldsymbol{w} \cdot \boldsymbol{A}\boldsymbol{w} \end{aligned} \tag{6.42}$$

$$A_{ij} = \alpha \delta_{ij} + \beta \sum_{\mu=1}^{p} \phi_i(\boldsymbol{\xi}^\mu) \phi_j(\boldsymbol{\xi}^\mu) \tag{6.43}$$

Since the Hessian matrix $\boldsymbol{A}$ is positive definite (provided $\alpha > 0$), the surface $S(\boldsymbol{w}, D)$ is convex and has a unique minimum, which is calculated simply by putting $\partial S(\boldsymbol{w}, D)/\partial w_i = 0$ for all i. This reveals $\boldsymbol{A}\boldsymbol{w}_{\text{MP}} = \beta \sum_{\mu=1}^{p} t_\mu \boldsymbol{\Phi}(\boldsymbol{\xi}^\mu)$, or

$$\boldsymbol{w}_{\text{MP}} = \beta \boldsymbol{A}^{-1} \sum_{\mu=1}^{p} t_\mu \boldsymbol{\Phi}(\boldsymbol{\xi}^\mu) \tag{6.44}$$

One also has, from (6.37), $x_i(\boldsymbol{\xi}) = \phi_i(\boldsymbol{\xi})$. Insertion into (6.38, 6.40) then gives, for models of the form (6.41), the fully exact result

$$t^\star(\boldsymbol{\xi}) = \beta \boldsymbol{\Phi}(\boldsymbol{\xi}) \cdot \boldsymbol{A}^{-1} \sum_{\mu=1}^{p} t_\mu \boldsymbol{\Phi}(\boldsymbol{\xi}^\mu), \qquad [\Delta t^\star(\boldsymbol{\xi})]^2 = \frac{1}{\beta} + \boldsymbol{\Phi}(\boldsymbol{\xi}) \cdot \boldsymbol{A}^{-1} \boldsymbol{\Phi}(\boldsymbol{\xi}) \tag{6.45}$$

Estimation of hyperparameters

The predictions and error margins in (6.38, 6.40) and (6.45) obviously depend on the choices made for the hyperparameters α and β. We will discuss a proper procedure for this later. A simpler and sometimes quicker

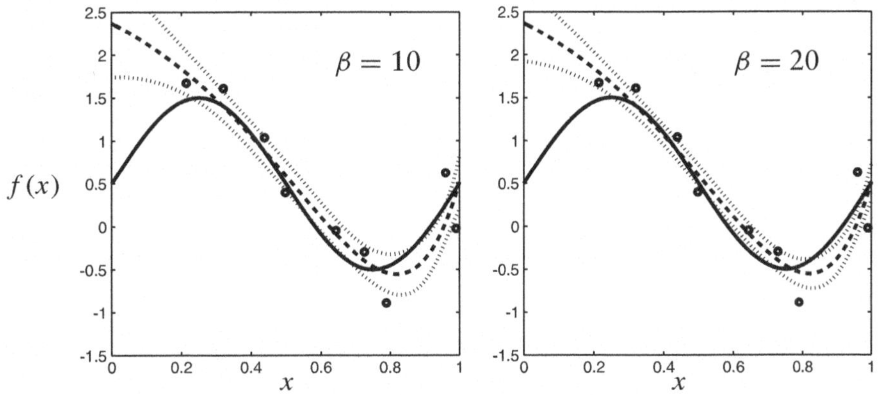

Figure 6.6 Bayesian prediction on the basis of a 9th-order polynomial with assumed Gaussian data noise of variance β^{-1}, and a Gaussian prior of variance $\alpha^{-1} = (0.005\beta)^{-1}$. Solid line: the target function $g(x) = \frac{1}{2} + \sin(2\pi x)$ to be learned. Circles: nine noisy sample points of this function. Dashed line: predicted function $t^\star(x)$ after learning. Dotted lines: $t^\star(x) \pm \Delta t^\star(x)$, where $\Delta t^\star(x)$ denotes the Bayesian prediction uncertainty. Note: the actual noise variance corresponds to $\beta = 12$.

method for estimating α and β is the following. Provided the number of data points p is not too small, it makes sense to require that the trained system will *on average* (i) predict correctly the outputs for the data points used in training, and (ii) make errors on these training data whose magnitude is of the order of the uncertainty it associates with its own predictions:

$$\frac{1}{p}\sum_{\mu=1}^{p}[t_\mu - t^\star(\boldsymbol{\xi}^\mu)] = 0 \qquad \frac{1}{p}\sum_{\mu=1}^{p}\{[t_\mu - t^\star(\boldsymbol{\xi}^\mu)]^2 - [\Delta t^\star(\boldsymbol{\xi}^\mu)]^2\} = 0 \tag{6.46}$$

These two equations can be used to determine α and β.

Example 1. Let us illustrate the above procedures using the example problem of (6.9), which involves a parametrized function of the form (6.41), with a quadratic regularizer term $\frac{1}{2}\lambda \boldsymbol{w}^2$. The non-Bayesian solution to this simple problem—that is, minimize the training error plus regularizer—is easily calculated and found to be

$$t^\star(x) = \sum_{ij}\phi_i(x)(\boldsymbol{B}^{-1})_{ij}\sum_{\mu} t_\mu \phi_j(x_\mu), \qquad B_{ij} = \lambda p \delta_{ij} + \sum_{\mu=1}^{p}\phi_i(x_\mu)\phi_j(x_\mu) \tag{6.47}$$

The Bayesian answer (6.45), assuming Gaussian output noise and a Gaussian prior, would be exactly the same[18] as (6.47), with $\lambda = \alpha/\beta p$ and $\boldsymbol{A} = \beta \boldsymbol{B}$, but it would also equip this answer with the following error estimate:

$$\Delta t^\star(x) = \beta^{-1/2} \sqrt{1 + \sum_{ij=0}^{M} \phi_i(x)(\boldsymbol{B}^{-1})_{ij}\phi_j(x)} \tag{6.48}$$

The result is shown in Figure 6.6 for $\alpha/\beta = 0.005$, $\phi_\ell(x) = x^\ell$ for $0 \leq \ell < M = 9$, and $\beta \in \{10, 20\}$. The actual value of the variance of the noise on the training outputs in this example, which is unknown to the network, corresponds to $\beta = 12$. As expected, we see again in the above graphs that it will be very important to have a tool with which to calculate the hyperparameters α and β.

Example 2. Our second example is also a simple linear system as in (6.41), but now the input vectors are two-dimensional, and we will focus on finding the hyperparameters via the conditions (6.46):

$$p(t|\boldsymbol{\xi}; \boldsymbol{w}) = \left(\frac{\beta}{2\pi}\right)^{1/2} e^{-\beta[t - f(\boldsymbol{\xi};\boldsymbol{w})]^2/2}, \quad f(\boldsymbol{\xi}; \boldsymbol{w}) = \boldsymbol{w} \cdot \boldsymbol{\xi} \tag{6.49}$$

with $\boldsymbol{\xi}, \boldsymbol{w} \in \mathbb{R}^2$, and prior

$$p(\boldsymbol{w}) = \frac{\alpha}{2\pi} e^{-\alpha \boldsymbol{w}^2/2}$$

In the notation of (6.41) we here have $\phi_i(\boldsymbol{\xi}) = \xi_i$ and $M = N = 2$. The data points to be learned from, four in number, are taken to be the following:

$$(\boldsymbol{\xi}^1, t_1) = ((1,0), \tfrac{3}{4}) \qquad (\boldsymbol{\xi}^2, t_2) = ((0,1), \tfrac{1}{4})$$
$$(\boldsymbol{\xi}^3, t_3) = ((-1,0), -\tfrac{1}{4}) \qquad (\boldsymbol{\xi}^4, t_4) = ((0,-1), -\tfrac{3}{4})$$

For this choice of data the matrix $\boldsymbol{A}$ (6.43) becomes

$$\begin{aligned} \boldsymbol{A} &= \alpha \begin{pmatrix} 1 & 0 \\ 0 & 1 \end{pmatrix} + \beta \left\{ \begin{pmatrix} 1 & 0 \\ 0 & 0 \end{pmatrix} + \begin{pmatrix} 0 & 0 \\ 0 & 1 \end{pmatrix} + \begin{pmatrix} 1 & 0 \\ 0 & 0 \end{pmatrix} + \begin{pmatrix} 0 & 0 \\ 0 & 1 \end{pmatrix} \right\} \\ &= (\alpha + 2\beta)\mathbf{1} \end{aligned}$$

[18] This is, of course, a direct consequence of our choice of a simple linear example.

Its inversion is trivial, and hence the predictions and error bars (6.45) can be worked out explicitly. Using $\boldsymbol{A}^{-1} = (\alpha + 2\beta)^{-1}\mathbf{1}$ and $\sum_{\mu=1}^{4} t_\mu \boldsymbol{\xi}^\mu = (1, 1)$ one arrives at

$$t^\star(\boldsymbol{\xi}) = \frac{\beta(\xi_1 + \xi_2)}{\alpha + 2\beta} \qquad [\Delta t^\star(\boldsymbol{\xi})]^2 = \beta^{-1} + \frac{\xi_1^2 + \xi_2^2}{\alpha + 2\beta} \tag{6.50}$$

In order to work out the relations (6.46) for the present example we next calculate the system's output predictions for the four data points:

$$t^\star(\boldsymbol{\xi}^1) = t^\star(\boldsymbol{\xi}^2) = \frac{\beta}{\alpha + 2\beta} \qquad t^\star(\boldsymbol{\xi}^3) = t^\star(\boldsymbol{\xi}^4) = \frac{-\beta}{\alpha + 2\beta}$$

$$\Delta t^\star(\boldsymbol{\xi}^1) = \Delta t^\star(\boldsymbol{\xi}^2) = \Delta t^\star(\boldsymbol{\xi}^3) = \Delta t^\star(\boldsymbol{\xi}^4) = \sqrt{\frac{\alpha + 3\beta}{\beta(\alpha + 2\beta)}}$$

Since also $\sum_{\mu=1}^{4} t_\mu = 0$, the first condition of (6.46) now reduces to the trivial identity $0 = 0$. The second condition of (6.46), however, gives us

$$\begin{aligned}\frac{\alpha + 3\beta}{\beta(\alpha + 2\beta)} &= \frac{1}{4}\Bigg[\left(\frac{3}{4} - \frac{\beta}{\alpha + 2\beta}\right)^2 + \left(\frac{1}{4} - \frac{\beta}{\alpha + 2\beta}\right)^2 \\ &\quad + \left(-\frac{1}{4} + \frac{\beta}{\alpha + 2\beta}\right)^2 + \left(-\frac{3}{4} + \frac{\beta}{\alpha + 2\beta}\right)^2\Bigg] \\ &= \frac{1}{32}\left[\left(\frac{3\alpha + 2\beta}{\alpha + 2\beta}\right)^2 + \left(\frac{\alpha - 2\beta}{\alpha + 2\beta}\right)^2\right]\end{aligned}$$

Working out this expression and putting $\alpha = \lambda\beta p = 4\lambda\beta$ leads to

$$\beta = 24\frac{1 + (10/3)\lambda + (8/3)\lambda^2}{1 + 4\lambda + 20\lambda^2} \tag{6.51}$$

We thus have only one free hyperparameter left. Putting $\alpha \to 0$ (since $p = 4$ and we have just two adjustable parameters there should in principle be little need for regularization via a prior) gives, via (6.51), the prescription $\beta = 24$, and hence the final predictions

$$t^\star(\boldsymbol{\xi}) = \tfrac{1}{2}(\xi_1 + \xi_2) \qquad \Delta t^\star(\boldsymbol{\xi}) = \tfrac{1}{4}\sqrt{\tfrac{1}{3}(2 + \xi_1^2 + \xi_2^2)} \tag{6.52}$$

This result is indeed perfectly consistent with the statistics of the training data:

	actual data	$t^\star(\boldsymbol{\xi}^\mu) \pm \Delta t^\star(\boldsymbol{\xi}^\mu)$
t_1:	$3/4$	$1/2 \pm 1/4$
t_2:	$1/4$	$1/2 \pm 1/4$
t_3:	$-1/4$	$-1/2 \pm 1/4$
t_4:	$-3/4$	$-1/2 \pm 1/4$

From (6.50), the model is also seen to take the sensible decision to assign increasing error bars when predictions are requested on input vectors which are further away from the origin (around which the training data are located).

6.4 Predictions with error bars: binary classification

Predicting binary classifications on the basis of (noisy) data examples proceeds in a way similar to regression. A trained network is in the Bayesian picture given by the posterior distribution $p(\boldsymbol{w}|D)$ (6.14) for the system parameters, and prediction is again based on (6.15):

$$p(t|\boldsymbol{\xi}, D) = \int \mathrm{d}\boldsymbol{w}\; p(t|\boldsymbol{\xi}, \boldsymbol{w})p(\boldsymbol{w}|D)$$

$$p(\boldsymbol{w}|D) = \frac{p(\boldsymbol{w})\prod_{\mu=1}^{p} p(t_\mu|\boldsymbol{\xi}^\mu, \boldsymbol{w})}{\int \mathrm{d}\boldsymbol{w}'\; p(\boldsymbol{w}')\prod_{\mu=1}^{p} p(t_\mu|\boldsymbol{\xi}^\mu, \boldsymbol{w}')} \tag{6.53}$$

The only difference with regression is that, in view of the requirement to extract binary outputs from continuous parametrized functions, the output noise can never be Gaussian.

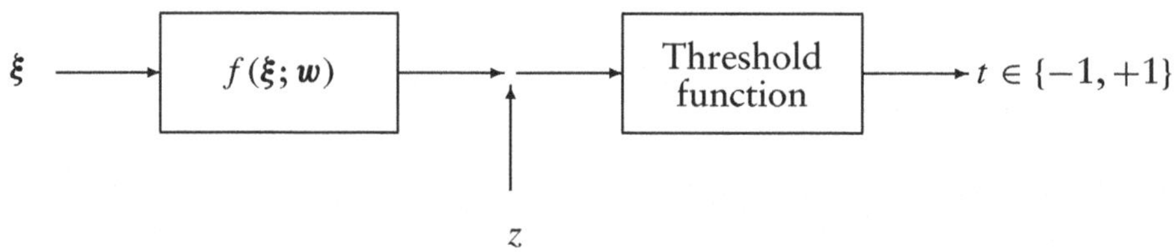

Without output noise we could define the deterministic binary operation $t(\boldsymbol{\xi}) = \mathrm{sgn}(f(\boldsymbol{\xi};\boldsymbol{w}))$, with the usual sign function. Adding noise implies allowing (occasionally) for the output $t = -1$ even when $f(\boldsymbol{\xi};\boldsymbol{w}) > 0$ and for $t = 1$ even when $f(\boldsymbol{\xi};\boldsymbol{w}) < 0$. So $p(1|\boldsymbol{\xi},\boldsymbol{w})$ must be a monotonically increasing function of $f(\xi; \boldsymbol{w})$, such that $p(1|\xi, \boldsymbol{w}) \to 0$ when $f(\xi; \boldsymbol{w}) \to -\infty$ and $p(1|\xi, \boldsymbol{w}) \to 1$ when[19] $f(\xi; \boldsymbol{w}) \to \infty$. A common choice is:

$$
\begin{aligned}
p(1|\xi, \boldsymbol{w}) &= \tfrac{1}{2} + \tfrac{1}{2}\tanh(f(\xi; \boldsymbol{w})) \\
p(-1|\xi, \boldsymbol{w}) &= \tfrac{1}{2} - \tfrac{1}{2}\tanh(f(\xi; \boldsymbol{w}))
\end{aligned}
\tag{6.54}
$$

Decision boundary and measure of uncertainty

Our objective is to classify new inputs ξ into one of two categories. Hence learning from data is here equivalent to deciding on the decision boundary in input space, and to quantify the uncertainty of this decision. If we simply combine (6.53, 6.54) we arrive at (with $t = \pm 1$)

$$p(t|\xi, D) = \tfrac{1}{2} + \tfrac{1}{2}t\, I(\xi, D) \tag{6.55}$$

$$I(\xi, D) = \frac{\int \mathrm{d}\boldsymbol{w}\, \tanh(f(\xi; \boldsymbol{w}))p(\boldsymbol{w}) \prod_{\mu=1}^{p} p(t_\mu|\xi^\mu, \boldsymbol{w})}{\int \mathrm{d}\boldsymbol{w}\, p(\boldsymbol{w}) \prod_{\mu=1}^{p} p(t_\mu|\xi^\mu, \boldsymbol{w})} \tag{6.56}$$

We classify $t^\star(\xi) = 1$ if $p(1|\xi, D) > p(-1|\xi, D)$, and $t^\star(\xi) = -1$ if $p(1|\xi, D) < p(-1|\xi, D)$. Hence the decision boundary in ξ-space is defined by $I(\xi, D) = 0$. Our uncertainty is measured by

$$\Delta t^\star(\xi) = \text{Prob[incorrect classification]} = \begin{cases} p(1|\xi, D), & \text{when } t^\star(\xi) = -1 \\ p(-1|\xi, D), & \text{when } t^\star(\xi) = 1 \end{cases}$$

Using the definition (6.56) these statements can be summarized as

$$t^\star(\xi) = \operatorname{sgn}(I(\xi, D)) \qquad \Delta t^\star(\xi) = \tfrac{1}{2} - \tfrac{1}{2}|I(\xi, D)| \tag{6.57}$$

At the decision boundary $I(\xi, D) = 0$ we have $\Delta t^\star(\xi) = \frac{1}{2}$, that is, a misclassification probability equivalent to random guessing, as it should be.

[19] An implicit requirement is that the selected parametrized function $f(\xi; \boldsymbol{w})$ can actually be made to approach $\pm\infty$ by suitably boosting the parameters $\boldsymbol{w}$. This, however, can always be achieved. For example, if we initially have a bounded function $g(\xi; \boldsymbol{w})$, we can add an extra adjustable parameter w_0 and define $f(x; \boldsymbol{w}) = w_0 g(\xi; \boldsymbol{w})$.

Example. Let us consider a simple task involving the binary classification of two-dimensional vectors, with a linear parametrized function and a Gaussian prior:

$$\boldsymbol{\xi}, \boldsymbol{w} \in \mathbb{R}^2 \qquad f(\boldsymbol{\xi}; \boldsymbol{w}) = \boldsymbol{w} \cdot \boldsymbol{\xi} \qquad p(\boldsymbol{w}) = \frac{\alpha}{2\pi} e^{-\alpha \boldsymbol{w}^2/2} \tag{6.58}$$

and with the following two data points

$$D = \{((0, -1), 1),\ ((0, 1), -1)\} \tag{6.59}$$

Working out the key function $I(\boldsymbol{\xi}, D)$ of (6.56) for this example gives

$$I(\boldsymbol{\xi}, D) = \frac{\int \mathrm{d}\boldsymbol{w}\, \tanh(\boldsymbol{w} \cdot \boldsymbol{\xi}) e^{-\alpha \boldsymbol{w}^2/2} \prod_{\mu=1}^{2} p(t_\mu | \boldsymbol{\xi}^\mu, \boldsymbol{w})}{\int \mathrm{d}\boldsymbol{w}\, e^{-\alpha \boldsymbol{w}^2/2} \prod_{\mu=1}^{2} p(t_\mu | \boldsymbol{\xi}^\mu, \boldsymbol{w})}$$

$$= \frac{\int \mathrm{d}\boldsymbol{w}\, \tanh(w_1\xi_1 + w_2\xi_2) e^{-\alpha \boldsymbol{w}^2/2} [1 - \tanh(w_2)]^2}{\int \mathrm{d}\boldsymbol{w}\, e^{-\alpha \boldsymbol{w}^2/2} [1 - \tanh(w_2)]^2} \tag{6.60}$$

The decision boundary in input space is found to be given by the line $\xi_2 = 0$: if we substitute this into (6.60) we indeed find $I((\xi_1, 0), D) = 0$. Verification of the behaviour of (6.60) for $\xi_2 \to \pm\infty$ further shows that $I(\boldsymbol{\xi}, D) > 0$ (and hence $t^\star(\boldsymbol{\xi}) = 1$) for $\xi_2 < 0$, and $I(\boldsymbol{\xi}, D) < 0$ (and hence $t^\star(\boldsymbol{\xi}) = -1$) for $\xi_2 > 0$.

The more interesting and less trivial results concern the dependence of the error measure $\Delta t^\star(\boldsymbol{\xi})$ in (6.57) on $\boldsymbol{\xi}$. In Figure 6.7 (left panel) we show a contour plot of the misclassification probability $\Delta t^\star(\boldsymbol{\xi})$ in the input plane, for $\alpha = 1$. The model (6.58) assumes for any given $\boldsymbol{w}$ a linear separation, plus data noise, along a line perpendicular to $\boldsymbol{w}$. Clearly, the further away from the data points, the larger the possible impact of an uncertainty in the direction of this linear boundary, and this is seen to be reflected in the contours of $\Delta t^\star(\boldsymbol{\xi})$.

We continue with the example model (6.58), but now we add one more data point, namely $(\boldsymbol{\xi}^3, t_3) = ((1, \frac{1}{2}), -1)$ and study its effect on the decision boundary and the misclassification probability:

$$D = \{((0, -1), 1), ((0, 1), -1), ((1, \tfrac{1}{2}), -1)\} \tag{6.61}$$

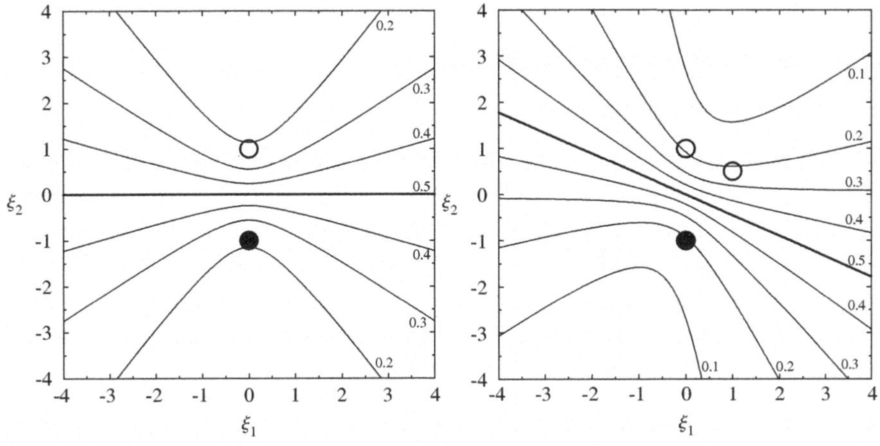

Figure 6.7 Bayesian binary classification of two-dimensional input vectors $\boldsymbol{\xi} = (\xi_1, \xi_2)$, using linear classifiers with non-Gaussian data noise and a Gaussian prior on $\boldsymbol{w}$ of variance $\alpha^{-1} = 1$. Thick solid line: the decision boundary, where $p(1|\boldsymbol{\xi}, D) = p(-1|\boldsymbol{\xi}, D) = \frac{1}{2}$; here the prediction uncertainty $\Delta t^\star(\boldsymbol{\xi}) = \frac{1}{2}$ is maximal. Below this line all points are classified as $t^\star(\boldsymbol{\xi}) = 1$, above it as $t^\star(\boldsymbol{\xi}) = -1$. Circles: data points $\boldsymbol{\xi}^\mu$ (filled: $t_\mu = 1$, open: $t_\mu = -1$). Thin continuous curves: contour lines of the error probability $\Delta t^\star(\boldsymbol{\xi})$. Left panel: $p = 2$. Right panel: $p = 3$, that is, one further data point has been added to those of the left panel; see the main text for details.

Working out $I(\boldsymbol{\xi}, D)$ of (6.56) now gives

$$
\begin{aligned}
I(\boldsymbol{\xi}, D) \\
&= \frac{\int \mathrm{d}\boldsymbol{w}\ \tanh(\boldsymbol{w}\cdot\boldsymbol{\xi}) e^{-\alpha \boldsymbol{w}^2/2} \prod_{\mu=1}^{3} p(t_\mu|\boldsymbol{\xi}^\mu, \boldsymbol{w})}{\int \mathrm{d}\boldsymbol{w}\ e^{-\alpha \boldsymbol{w}^2/2} \prod_{\mu=1}^{3} p(t_\mu|\boldsymbol{\xi}^\mu, \boldsymbol{w})} \\
&= \frac{\int \mathrm{d}\boldsymbol{w} \tanh(w_1\xi_1 + w_2\xi_2) e^{-\alpha \boldsymbol{w}^2/2}[1 - \tanh(w_2)]^2[1 - \tanh(w_1 + w_2/2)]}{\int \mathrm{d}\boldsymbol{w}\ e^{-\alpha \boldsymbol{w}^2/2}[1 - \tanh(w_2)]^2[1 - \tanh(w_1 + w_2/2)]}
\end{aligned}
$$

The decision boundary is now no longer given by $\xi_2 = 0$; the balance of evidence has changed. In Figure 6.7 (right panel) we show a contour plot of the misclassification probability $\Delta t^\star(\boldsymbol{\xi})$ in the input plane for the new situation. Compared to the previous $p = 2$ case we observe both a change in the location of the decision boundary (which also is no longer a straight line, though numerically it is very close to one) and an overall reduction of the misclassification probability. Note that, had the new data point been less compatible with the first two, one could also have found an *increase* in the misclassification probability.

6.5 Bayesian model selection

Bayesian model comparison

In the formalism described so far one chooses beforehand a model assumed responsible for having generated the data, followed by an analysis of the likelihood of parameters for this model. This picture can be generalized to include multiple candidate models. Instead of working with the joint distribution $p(D, \boldsymbol{w})$ of data and model parameters, we must switch to the joint distribution $p(D, \boldsymbol{w}, H)$ to find data D, model H, and parameters[20] $\boldsymbol{w}$ for model H. The generalized picture then becomes

- Consider an *ensemble* of models H with associated parameter vectors $\boldsymbol{w}$, characterized by a probability distribution $p(H, \boldsymbol{w})$ which evolves during learning.
- Assume that the data D were generated by a system of a form contained in our ensemble of models. Calculate the likelihood $p(\boldsymbol{w}, H|D)$ of models and their parameters, given the data.
- Express the desired objects $p(\boldsymbol{w}|D, H)$ in terms of $p(D|\boldsymbol{w}, H)$ (as before) and $p(H|D)$ in terms of $p(D|H)$, where $p(D|H) = \int \mathrm{d}\boldsymbol{w}\, p(D|\boldsymbol{w}, H) \times p(\boldsymbol{w}|H)$.

Learning is a process during which the arrival of data reduces our uncertainty about the 'right' model H and its 'right' parameters $\boldsymbol{w}$ from the *prior distributions* $p(H)$ and $p(\boldsymbol{w}|H)$ to the *posterior distributions* $p(H|D)$ and $p(\boldsymbol{w}|D, H)$. Note that

$$p(\boldsymbol{w}|D, H) = \frac{p(D|\boldsymbol{w}, H)p(\boldsymbol{w}|H)}{\int \mathrm{d}\boldsymbol{w}'\, p(\boldsymbol{w}'|H)p(D|\boldsymbol{w}', H)} \tag{6.62}$$

$$p(H|D) = \frac{p(D|H)p(H)}{\sum_{H'} p(D|H')p(H')} \tag{6.63}$$

Generalized Bayesian learning, with multiple models, now works like this:

Stage 1: definitions. Define (i) the parametrized models H, assumed responsible for the data, (ii) the prior distribution $p(H)$ for these models, (iii) the prior distributions $p(\boldsymbol{w}|H)$ of their parameters, and (iv) the data $D = \{(\boldsymbol{\xi}^1, t_1), \ldots, (\boldsymbol{\xi}^p, t_p)\}$.

Stage 2: model translation. Convert the model definition into a standard probabilistic form: specify the likelihood of finding output t on

[20] Note that different models will generally have parameter vectors $\boldsymbol{w}$ with different dimensionality.

presentation of input $\boldsymbol{\xi}$, given model H and parameters $\boldsymbol{w}$:

$$\text{model definition in standard form} \quad p(t|\boldsymbol{\xi}, \boldsymbol{w}, H) \tag{6.64}$$

Stage 3: the posterior distribution. Calculate the *data* likelihood, given model H and model parameters $\boldsymbol{w}$,

$$p(D|\boldsymbol{w}, H) = \prod_{\mu=1}^{p} p(t_\mu|\boldsymbol{\xi}^\mu, \boldsymbol{w}, H)$$

From this follow the desired posterior parameter and model distributions

$$p(\boldsymbol{w}|D, H) = \frac{p(\boldsymbol{w}|H)\prod_{\mu=1}^{p} p(t_\mu|\boldsymbol{\xi}^\mu, \boldsymbol{w}, H)}{\int \mathrm{d}\boldsymbol{w}'\, p(\boldsymbol{w}'|H)\prod_{\mu=1}^{p} p(t_\mu|\boldsymbol{\xi}^\mu, \boldsymbol{w}', H)} \tag{6.65}$$

$$p(H|D) = \frac{p(H)\int \mathrm{d}\boldsymbol{w}\, \prod_{\mu=1}^{p} p(t_\mu|\boldsymbol{\xi}^\mu, \boldsymbol{w}, H)p(\boldsymbol{w}|H)}{\sum_{H'} p(H')\int \mathrm{d}\boldsymbol{w}\, \prod_{\mu=1}^{p} p(t_\mu|\boldsymbol{\xi}^\mu, \boldsymbol{w}, H')p(\boldsymbol{w}|H')} \tag{6.66}$$

Stage 4: prediction. The residual uncertainty in the choice of model H and parameters $\boldsymbol{w}$ generates the uncertainty in predictions. Prediction of the output t corresponding to input $\boldsymbol{\xi}$, given our observation of the data D and our choice of model set, takes the probabilistic form:

$$p(t|\boldsymbol{\xi}, D) = \sum_H p(H|D)\int \mathrm{d}\boldsymbol{w}\, p(t|\boldsymbol{\xi}, \boldsymbol{w}, H)p(\boldsymbol{w}|D, H) \tag{6.67}$$

As an alternative to Stage 4, which describes the final output statistics as a weighted average over all models under consideration, one could also simply select the most probable model $H^\star$, defined as $p(H^\star|D) = \max_H p(H|D)$. This boils down to finding

$$\max_H[p(H)p(D|H)] = \max_H\left[p(H)\int \mathrm{d}\boldsymbol{w}\, \prod_{\mu=1}^{p} p(t_\mu|\boldsymbol{\xi}^\mu, \boldsymbol{w}, H)p(\boldsymbol{w}|H)\right] \tag{6.68}$$

or, equivalently, can be done by comparing models pairwise via the ratios

$$\frac{p(H|D)}{p(H'|D)} = \frac{p(D|H)}{p(D|H')}\frac{p(H)}{p(H')} \tag{6.69}$$

This can then be followed by the ordinary Bayesian parameter analysis for a *single* model $H^\star$, as described in the previous sections.

Application to hyperparameter selection

We note that the above reasoning can also be applied to the hyperparameter selection problem, as systems which differ in the choice of hyperparameters (rather than in architecture) can be regarded as different candidate models in the sense above. For instance, to describe the family of systems (6.22)

$$p(t|\boldsymbol{\xi}, \boldsymbol{w}, \beta) = \left(\frac{\beta}{2\pi}\right)^{1/2} e^{-\beta[t-f(\boldsymbol{\xi};\boldsymbol{w})]^2/2} \qquad p(\boldsymbol{w}|\alpha) = \left(\frac{\alpha}{2\pi}\right)^{M/2} e^{-\alpha \boldsymbol{w}^2/2} \tag{6.70}$$

with two hyperparameters (α, β), we can simply make the replacement $H \to (\alpha, \beta)$ in our above formulae. The specific form of (6.70), for which, for instance $p(t|\boldsymbol{\xi}, \boldsymbol{w}, \alpha, \beta)$ is independent of α, and $p(\boldsymbol{w}|\alpha, \beta)$ is independent of β, also generates slight simplifications:

- Consider an *ensemble* of models of the form (6.70), characterized by a probability distribution $p(\alpha, \beta, \boldsymbol{w})$ which evolves during learning.
- Assume that the data D were generated by a system of the form (6.70). Calculate the likelihood $p(\boldsymbol{w}, \alpha, \beta|D)$ of its parameters and hyperparameters, given the data.
- Express the desired objects $p(\boldsymbol{w}|D, \alpha, \beta)$ in terms of $p(D|\boldsymbol{w}, \alpha, \beta)$, and $p(\alpha, \beta|D)$ in terms of $p(D|\alpha, \beta)$, where $p(D|\alpha, \beta) = \int \mathrm{d}\boldsymbol{w} \times p(D|\boldsymbol{w}, \beta) p(\boldsymbol{w}|\alpha)$.

Learning is a process during which the arrival of data reduces our uncertainty about the hyperparameters (α, β) and the parameters $\boldsymbol{w}$ from the *prior distributions* $p(\alpha, \beta)$ and $p(\boldsymbol{w}|\alpha, \beta)$ to the *posterior distributions* $p(\alpha, \beta|D)$ and $p(\boldsymbol{w}|D, \alpha, \beta)$, according to

$$p(\boldsymbol{w}|D, \alpha, \beta) = \frac{p(D|\boldsymbol{w}, \beta) p(\boldsymbol{w}|\alpha)}{\int \mathrm{d}\boldsymbol{w}' \; p(D|\boldsymbol{w}', \beta) p(\boldsymbol{w}'|\alpha)} \tag{6.71}$$

$$p(\alpha, \beta|D) = \frac{p(D|\alpha, \beta) p(\alpha, \beta)}{\int \mathrm{d}\alpha' \mathrm{d}\beta' \; p(D|\alpha', \beta') p(\alpha', \beta')} \tag{6.72}$$

Generalized Bayesian learning, including learning of hyperparameters, now works like this:

Stage 1: definitions. Define (i) the function $f(\boldsymbol{\xi}; \boldsymbol{w})$ in the parametrized model (6.70), (ii) the prior distribution $p(\alpha, \beta)$ for its hyperparameters, and (iii) the data $D = \{(\boldsymbol{\xi}^1, t_1), \ldots, (\boldsymbol{\xi}^p, t_p)\}$.

Stage 2: the posterior distribution. Calculate the *data* likelihood, given (α, β) and $\boldsymbol{w}$:

$$p(D|\boldsymbol{w}, \beta) = \prod_{\mu=1}^{p} p(t_\mu|\boldsymbol{\xi}^\mu, \boldsymbol{w}, \beta)$$

From this follow the desired posterior distributions

$$p(\boldsymbol{w}|D, \alpha, \beta) = \frac{e^{-\alpha \boldsymbol{w}^2/2 - \beta \sum_{\mu=1}^{p} [t_\mu - f(\boldsymbol{\xi}^\mu; \boldsymbol{w})]^2/2}}{\int \mathrm{d}\boldsymbol{w}'\, e^{-\alpha \boldsymbol{w}'^2/2 - \beta \sum_{\mu=1}^{p} [t_\mu - f(\boldsymbol{\xi}^\mu; \boldsymbol{w}')]^2/2}} \tag{6.73}$$

$$p(\alpha, \beta|D) = \frac{p(\alpha, \beta)\sqrt{\alpha^M \beta^p} \int \mathrm{d}\boldsymbol{w}\, e^{-\alpha \boldsymbol{w}^2/2 - \beta \sum_{\mu=1}^{p} [t_\mu - f(\boldsymbol{\xi}^\mu; \boldsymbol{w})]^2/2}}{\int \mathrm{d}\alpha' \mathrm{d}\beta'\, p(\alpha', \beta')\sqrt{\alpha'^M \beta'^p} \int \mathrm{d}\boldsymbol{w}\, e^{-\alpha' \boldsymbol{w}^2/2 - \beta' \sum_{\mu=1}^{p} [t_\mu - f(\boldsymbol{\xi}^\mu; \boldsymbol{w})]^2/2}} \tag{6.74}$$

Stage 3: prediction. Prediction of the output t corresponding to a new input $\boldsymbol{\xi}$, given our observation of the data D and our choice of model family (6.70), takes the probabilistic form:

$$p(t|\boldsymbol{\xi}, D) = \int \mathrm{d}\alpha \mathrm{d}\beta\, p(\alpha, \beta|D) \left[\frac{\alpha^M \beta}{(2\pi)^{M+1}}\right]^{1/2} \times \int \mathrm{d}\boldsymbol{w}\, p(\boldsymbol{w}|D, \alpha, \beta) e^{-\alpha \boldsymbol{w}^2/2 - \beta[t - f(\boldsymbol{\xi}; \boldsymbol{w})]^2/2} \tag{6.75}$$

Again the learning problem has in principle been reduced to calculating integrals. However, one will now have to think about how to choose the hyperparameter prior $p(\alpha, \beta)$.

Model selection—Occam's razor

The Bayesian model comparison procedure, followed by model selection according to (6.68) or (6.69), will automatically lead to the selection of the simplest possible model $H^\star$ which can account for the data D, subject to prejudices embodied in the prior $p(H)$. This desirable action is referred to as implementing 'Occam's razor'.[21] To see how it comes about we return to (6.69), and remove the effect of prejudice by putting $p(H) = p(H')$ for

[21] After a monk, William of Occam, who is claimed to have first proposed the general philosophical principle that one should always select the *simplest* possible explanation for an observed phenomenon.

all models $\{H, H'\}$ under consideration. This gives

$$\frac{p(H|D)}{p(H'|D)} = \frac{p(D|H)}{p(D|H')} \tag{6.76}$$

To simplify the argument we will take the collection of possible data sets D to be discrete and countable. Let us compare the following three models:

$$\begin{array}{llll} \text{model } H_1: & p(D|H_1) = 0 & & \\ \text{model } H_2: & p(D|H_2) > 0 & p(D'|H_2) = 0 & \text{for all } D' \neq D \\ \text{model } H_3: & p(D|H_3) > 0 & p(D'|H_3) > 0 & \text{for some } D' \neq D \end{array}$$

Model 1 cannot explain the data D. Models 2 and 3 can explain the data, but 3 is more complex than 2 because it can explain, by a suitable choice of parameters, a greater variety of possible data other than D. Hence Model 2 is the *simplest* model which can account for data D. Insertion into (6.76) reveals

$$\frac{p(H_1|D)}{p(H_2|D)} = \frac{p(H_1|D)}{p(H_3|D)} = 0 \qquad \frac{p(H_2|D)}{p(H_3|D)} = \frac{p(D|H_2)}{p(D|H_3)} \tag{6.77}$$

One now always has $\sum_{D'} p(D'|H) = 1$ because conditional distributions are normalized, for any model H. From this it follows for the above examples that $p(D|H_2) = 1 - \sum_{D' \neq D} p(D'|H_2) = 1$ and $p(D|H_3) = 1 - \sum_{D' \neq D} p(D'|H_3) < 1$. Hence we find in (6.77) that $p(H_2|D) > p(H_3|D) > p(H_1|D)$, and that the Bayesian procedure instructs us to select Model 2.

Example. We close with a simple example, to illustrate the action of Occam's razor. The task is to learn a binary classification of the inputs $\xi \in \{0, 1\}$ to the targets $t \in \{-1, 1\}$. There are four such classifications possible, that is, four possible data sets with $p = 2$:

$$\begin{array}{ll} D_A = \{(0,1),(1,-1)\} & D_B = \{(0,-1),(1,-1)\} \\ D_C = \{(0,1),(1,1)\} & D_D = \{(0,-1),(1,1)\} \end{array}$$

Given one of these data sets, we have to choose between two deterministic parametrized candidate models H_1 and H_2, without initial prejudice, that is,

$p(H_1) = p(H_2) = \frac{1}{2}$:

$$H_1: \quad t(\xi) = \text{sgn}(w_1) \tag{6.78}$$

$$H_2: \quad t(\xi) = \text{sgn}(w_1 + w_2\xi) \tag{6.79}$$

with $\boldsymbol{w} = (w_1, w_2) \in \mathbb{R}^2$. As a prior parameter distribution we take $p(\boldsymbol{w}) = (2\pi)^{-1}e^{-\boldsymbol{w}^2/2}$. Clearly Model 2 is more complex than 1. We will select our model by working out the ratio (6.69). This requires calculating $p(D|H_1) = \int \text{d}w_1\, p(w_1)p(D|w_1, H_1)$ and $p(D|H_2) = \int \text{d}\boldsymbol{w} \times p(\boldsymbol{w})p(D|\boldsymbol{w}, H_2)$.

First consider model H_1. Here we have $t(\xi) = 1$ for all ξ if $w_1 > 0$, and $t(\xi) = -1$ for all ξ if $w_1 < 0$. Hence we simply find

$$p(D_A|w_1, H_1) = p(D_D|w_1, H_1) = 0$$

$$p(D_B|w_1, H_1) = \theta(-w_1) \qquad p(D_C|w_1, H_1) = \theta(w_1)$$

with θ being the step function, $\theta(z) = 1$ for $z > 0$, $\theta(z) = 0$ for $z < 0$. This gives

$$\begin{aligned} p(D_A|H_1) &= 0 \\ p(D_B|H_1) &= \int_{-\infty}^{0} \text{d}w_1\, p(w_1) = \frac{1}{2} \\ p(D_C|H_1) &= \int_{0}^{\infty} \text{d}w_1\, p(w_1) = \frac{1}{2} \\ p(D_D|H_1) &= 0 \end{aligned} \tag{6.80}$$

Next we turn to the two-parameter model H_2. Here we have $t(0) = \text{sgn}(w_1)$ and $t(1) = \text{sgn}(w_1 + w_2)$. Hence we find

$$p(D_A|\boldsymbol{w}, H_2) = \theta(w_1)\theta(-(w_1 + w_2))$$

$$p(D_B|\boldsymbol{w}, H_2) = \theta(-w_1)\theta(-(w_1 + w_2))$$

$$p(D_C|\boldsymbol{w}, H_2) = \theta(w_1)\theta(w_1 + w_2)$$

$$p(D_D|\boldsymbol{w}, H_2) = \theta(-w_1)\theta(w_1 + w_2)$$

With the shorthand $\chi = (2\pi)^{-1}\int_0^\infty dw_1 e^{-w_1^2/2}\int_{w_1}^\infty dw_2\, e^{-w_2^2/2} > 0$ and using the symmetries of the prior $p(\boldsymbol{w})$, this leads to:

$$p(D_A|H_2) = \int_0^\infty dw_1 \int_{-\infty}^{-w_1} dw_2\, p(\boldsymbol{w}) = \chi \tag{6.81}$$

$$p(D_B|H_2) = \int_{-\infty}^0 dw_1 \int_{-\infty}^{-w_1} dw_2\, p(\boldsymbol{w}) = \int_0^\infty dw_1 \int_{-\infty}^{w_1} dw_2\, p(\boldsymbol{w}) = \frac{1}{2} - \chi \tag{6.82}$$

$$p(D_C|H_2) = \int_0^\infty dw_1 \int_{-w_1}^{\infty} dw_2\, p(\boldsymbol{w}) = \frac{1}{2} - \chi \tag{6.83}$$

$$p(D_D|H_2) = \int_{-\infty}^0 dw_1 \int_{-w_1}^{\infty} dw_2\, p(\boldsymbol{w}) = \int_0^\infty dw_1 \int_{w_1}^{\infty} dw_2\, p(\boldsymbol{w}) = \chi \tag{6.84}$$

Finally we combine the results (6.80) and (6.81–6.84) into the following picture:

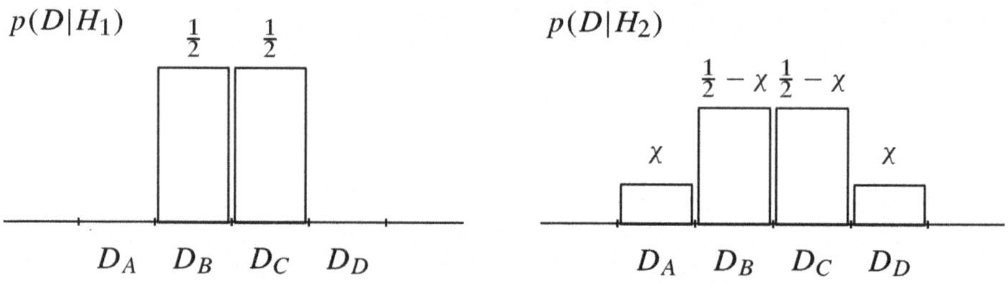

It follows from (6.69) that

$$\frac{p(H_1|D_A)}{p(H_2|D_A)} = \frac{p(H_1|D_D)}{p(H_2|D_D)} = 0 \qquad \frac{p(H_1|D_B)}{p(H_2|D_B)} = \frac{p(H_1|D_C)}{p(H_2|D_C)} = \frac{1/2}{1/2-\chi} > 1$$

We conclude that when observing data D_A or D_D we must select model H_2, which is the only candidate model to explain these data, but that when observing data D_B or D_C we must select model H_1: both models can explain these data, but H_1 wins simply because it is the simpler explanation.

6.6 Practicalities: measuring curvature

When learning by gradient descent on the surface $S(\boldsymbol{w}, D)$, (6.19), and using simple expressions such as (6.40) to assign error bars to neural network predictions, one needs to know the curvature matrix $\boldsymbol{A}$ as given in (6.26) at the minimum $\boldsymbol{w}_{\text{MP}}$ of $S(\boldsymbol{w}, D)$. In principle this matrix can be calculated directly from the model definitions, but for many-parameter and/or multilayer networks this is difficult. Here we discuss an alternative, based on the idea that the degree of curvature around the minimum will have a direct effect on the gradient descent dynamics at the minimum when such dynamics is equipped with additive noise. As a result the curvature matrix can be extracted from a measurement of the fluctuations.

Let us assume we have arrived by gradient descent at the minimum $\boldsymbol{w}_{\text{MP}}$ of $S(\boldsymbol{w}, D)$. We now replace the (discretized) gradient descent dynamics by the following noisy version:

$$w_i(t+\epsilon) = w_i(t) - \epsilon\,\frac{\partial S(\boldsymbol{w}, D)}{\partial w_i} + \sqrt{2\epsilon}\;\eta_i(t) \tag{6.85}$$

where the $\eta_i(t)$ are independently distributed zero-average Gaussian random variables, with $\langle \eta_i^2(t) \rangle = 1$, and with $0 < \epsilon \ll 1$. The parameter dynamics is now a stochastic process. Let us define averages and covariances of this process as

$$\overline{w}_i(t) = \langle w_i(t) \rangle \qquad C_{ij}(t) = \langle [w_i(t) - \overline{w}_i(t)][w_j(t) - \overline{w}_j(t)] \rangle \tag{6.86}$$

Their dynamics follow directly from (6.85):

$$\begin{aligned}
\overline{w}_i(t+\epsilon) &= \overline{w}_i(t) - \epsilon \left\langle \frac{\partial S(\boldsymbol{w}, D)}{\partial w_i} \right\rangle \\
C_{ij}(t+\epsilon) &= \langle w_i(t+\epsilon) w_j(t+\epsilon) \rangle - \overline{w}_i(t+\epsilon)\overline{w}_j(t+\epsilon) \\
&= \left\langle \left[w_i(t) - \epsilon\,\frac{\partial S(\boldsymbol{w}, D)}{\partial w_i} \right] \left[w_j(t) - \epsilon\,\frac{\partial S(\boldsymbol{w}, D)}{\partial w_j} \right] \right\rangle \\
&\quad + 2\epsilon\,\delta_{ij} - \overline{w}_i(t+\epsilon)\overline{w}_j(t+\epsilon) \\
&= C_{ij}(t) + \epsilon \left\{ 2\delta_{ij} - \left\langle w_i(t) \frac{\partial S(\boldsymbol{w}, D)}{\partial w_j} \right\rangle + \overline{w}_i(t) \left\langle \frac{\partial S(\boldsymbol{w}, D)}{\partial w_j} \right\rangle \right. \\
&\quad \left. - \left\langle w_j(t) \frac{\partial S(\boldsymbol{w}, D)}{\partial w_i} \right\rangle + \overline{w}_j(t) \left\langle \frac{\partial S(\boldsymbol{w}, D)}{\partial w_i} \right\rangle \right\} + \mathcal{O}(\epsilon^2)
\end{aligned}$$

Since $\epsilon \ll 1$, the system can only make infinitesimal excursions $\boldsymbol{w} = \boldsymbol{w}_{\text{MP}} + \mathcal{O}(\sqrt{\epsilon})$ away from the minimum $\boldsymbol{w}_{\text{MP}}$, hence we may safely replace $S(\boldsymbol{w}, D)$

by the quadratic approximation (6.25)

$$S(\boldsymbol{w}, D) = S(\boldsymbol{w}_{\mathrm{MP}}, D) + \tfrac{1}{2}(\boldsymbol{w} - \boldsymbol{w}_{\mathrm{MP}}) \cdot \boldsymbol{A}(\boldsymbol{w} - \boldsymbol{w}_{\mathrm{MP}}) + \mathcal{O}(\epsilon^{3/2})$$

This implies that

$$\frac{\partial S(\boldsymbol{w}, D)}{\partial w_i} = \sum_j A_{ij}(w_j - w_{\mathrm{MP},j}) + \mathcal{O}(\epsilon^{3/2})$$

Thus:

$$\overline{\boldsymbol{w}}(t+\epsilon) = \overline{\boldsymbol{w}}(t) - \epsilon\, \boldsymbol{A}(\overline{\boldsymbol{w}} - \boldsymbol{w}_{\mathrm{MP}}) + \mathcal{O}(\epsilon^{3/2})$$

$$\begin{aligned} C_{ij}(t+\epsilon) = C_{ij}(t) + \epsilon \Bigg\{ & 2\delta_{ij} - \Big\langle w_i(t) \sum_k A_{jk}(w_k(t) - w_{\mathrm{MP},k}) \Big\rangle \\ & + \overline{w}_i(t) \sum_k A_{jk}(\overline{w}_k - w_{\mathrm{MP},k}) - \Big\langle w_j(t) \sum_k A_{ik}(w_k(t) - w_{\mathrm{MP},k}) \Big\rangle \\ & + \overline{w}_j(t) \sum_k A_{ik}(\overline{w}_k - w_{\mathrm{MP},k}) \Bigg\} + \mathcal{O}(\epsilon^{3/2}) \end{aligned}$$

We now arrive at the simple result (using the symmetry of both $\boldsymbol{A}$ and $\boldsymbol{C}$):

$$\boldsymbol{C}(t+\epsilon) = \boldsymbol{C}(t) + \epsilon[2\mathbf{1} - \boldsymbol{C}\boldsymbol{A} - \boldsymbol{A}\boldsymbol{C}] + \mathcal{O}(\epsilon^{3/2}) \tag{6.87}$$

One can show that, provided $\epsilon \ll 1$ (more specifically: provided $\epsilon < 2/a_i$ for all eigenvalues a_i of the matrix $\boldsymbol{A}$), the leading order of (6.87) will evolve towards the stationary state $\boldsymbol{C} = \boldsymbol{A}^{-1} + \mathcal{O}(\sqrt{\epsilon})$, and the vector $\overline{\boldsymbol{w}}$ will evolve towards $\boldsymbol{w}_{\mathrm{MP}}$. Hence the desired curvature matrix $\boldsymbol{A}$ can be measured in equilibrium, by choosing ϵ sufficiently small, according to

$$\epsilon \to 0: \quad \boldsymbol{A} = \boldsymbol{C}^{-1} \qquad C_{ij} = \lim_{t\to\infty} \langle [w_i - w_{\mathrm{MP},i}][w_j - w_{\mathrm{MP},j}] \rangle \tag{6.88}$$

6.7 Exercises

Exercise 6.1. (Reduction of uncertainty due to data.) For Example 1 in Section 6.2, consider the more general case where the outputs are corrupted by additive Gaussian noise, which corresponds to $p(t|\xi, w) = (\beta/2\pi)^{1/2} \exp[-\beta(t - \tanh(w\xi))^2/2]$. The normalization of the posterior $p(w|D) \sim p(w)p(t_1|\xi^1, w)$ is not easy to work out, but for getting the shape of $p(w|D)$ this is unimportant. Plot the unnormalized $p(w|D)$ for a range of values of β and try to get an intuitive understanding of the effects of β. In particular, for large β you should see a very peaked posterior—why, and how does this relate to the case covered in the notes? Also consider the opposite limit of small β—how does the posterior peak move as β decreases and why, and what happens for $\beta \to 0$?

Exercise 6.2. (Reduction of uncertainty due to data.) Consider, similarly, the generalization of the next Example 2 to noisy outputs. Make contour plots of the unnormalized posterior, and study the effect of β. Also consider what happens if a second training example (ξ^2, t_2) is added to D, and play with the values of ξ^2 and t_2. For generic values (with $|t_2| < 1$) you should see the posterior becoming concentrated on a point in the (w_1, w_2)-plane as $\beta \to \infty$. What happens for $\xi^2 = 1$, $t_2 \neq -\frac{1}{2}$, and why is this case special?

Exercise 6.3. (Bayesian regression.) Explore Bayesian regression with generalized linear models, as defined by (6.41), for inputs in one dimension, that is, for $x \in \mathbb{R}$. Choose, for example, a sample of input points x_μ, either regularly spaced or random. Define corresponding training outputs t_μ by adding noise to some target function which you choose. Choose a set of basis functions ϕ_i—powers of x are a natural choice to start with—and hyperparameters α and β. Then evaluate the prediction and error bars (6.45). Play with: α, β, the size of the training set, the complexity of the target function (e.g. try polynomials of various order), the complexity of the model used for learning (e.g. by varying the number of basis functions, which corresponds to fitting polynomials of different orders) and the level of noise on the training outputs. Compare also with the case of RBFs, for example, with $\phi_i(x) = \exp[-(x - r_i)^2/2\ell^2]$ where the r_i are the centres of the RBF and ℓ is their width.

Exercise 6.4. (Bayesian regression.) Continuing with the case of generalized linear models of the previous exercise, consider the probability of the data D given the model specified by α and β, $p(D|\alpha, \beta) = \int \mathrm{d}\boldsymbol{w}\, p(D|\boldsymbol{w}, \beta)p(\boldsymbol{w}|\alpha)$. The integral over $\boldsymbol{w}$ can be done explicitly because it is Gaussian; you should find

$$2 \ln p(D|\alpha, \beta) = M \ln \alpha + p \ln(\beta/2\pi) - \beta \sum_\mu t_\mu^2 - \ln \det(\boldsymbol{A}) + \boldsymbol{c} \cdot \boldsymbol{A}^{-1}\boldsymbol{c}$$

with $\boldsymbol{A}$ defined in (6.43) and $\boldsymbol{c} = \beta \sum_\mu t_\mu \boldsymbol{\Phi}(\boldsymbol{\xi}^\mu) = \boldsymbol{A}\boldsymbol{w}_{\mathrm{MP}}$. All sums over μ run from 1 to p as usual. Verify that for $p = 0$, where all these sums are 0, this expression reduces to $p(D|\alpha, \beta) = 1$, and explain from the definition of $p(D|\alpha, \beta)$ why this result must hold quite generally.

Exercise 6.5. (Bayesian regression.) Consider a linear neural network which produces an output $t \in \mathbb{R}$ for every input vector (or question) $\boldsymbol{\xi} \in \mathbb{R}^N$, subject to output noise whose strength is measured by $\sigma > 0$, such that

$$p(t|\boldsymbol{\xi}, \boldsymbol{w}) = \sigma^{-1} W\Big(\frac{t - \boldsymbol{w} \cdot \boldsymbol{\xi}}{\sigma}\Big) \qquad \int \mathrm{d}z\, z^2 W(z) = 1, \quad W(z) = W(-z)$$

for some noise distribution $W(z)$. The data used in training consist of p pairs of questions and corresponding answers: $D = \{(\boldsymbol{\xi}^1, t_1), \ldots, (\boldsymbol{\xi}^p, t_p)\}$, with all $t_\mu \in \{-1, 1\}$. Choose the Gaussian prior $p(\boldsymbol{w}) = (\alpha/2\pi)^{N/2} e^{-\alpha \boldsymbol{w}^2/2}$, and consider data sets with orthogonal and normalized input vectors: $\boldsymbol{\xi}^\mu \cdot \boldsymbol{\xi}^\nu = \delta_{\mu\nu}$. Show that

$$\langle w_i \rangle_D = K_1 \sum_\mu t_\mu \xi_i^\mu$$

$$\langle w_i w_j \rangle_D = \frac{1}{\alpha}\delta_{ij} + K_2 \sum_\mu \xi_i^\mu \xi_j^\mu + K_1^2 \sum_{\mu \neq \nu} t_\mu \xi_i^\mu \xi_j^\nu t_\nu$$

where

$$K_n = \frac{\int \mathrm{d}z\, (1 + \sigma z)^n\, e^{-\alpha(1+\sigma z)^2/2}\, W(z)}{\int \mathrm{d}z\, e^{-\alpha(1+\sigma z)^2/2}\, W(z)}$$

Hint: in doing $\boldsymbol{w}$ integrations it might be helpful to use input vectors as basis vectors, by putting $\boldsymbol{w} = \sum_{\mu=1}^p u_\mu t_\mu \boldsymbol{\xi}^\mu + \boldsymbol{v}$, with $\boldsymbol{v} \cdot \boldsymbol{\xi}^\mu = 0$ for all μ. Calculate the prediction $t^\star(\boldsymbol{\xi})$ and its uncertainty $\Delta t^\star(\boldsymbol{\xi})$ for the case of *Gaussian* output noise: $W_g(z) = (2\pi)^{-1/2} e^{-z^2/2}$. Also calculate the prediction $t^\star(\boldsymbol{\xi})$ and its uncertainty $\Delta t^\star(\boldsymbol{\xi})$ for the case of *binary* output noise: $W_b(z) = \frac{1}{2}\delta(z - 1) + \frac{1}{2}\delta(z + 1)$.

Exercise 6.6. (Bayesian hyperparameter selection.) Apply the result of Exercise 6.4 to the problem of selecting the best values of the hyperparameters α and β. Ignoring the hyperprior factor $p(\alpha, \beta)$ in (6.72), we need to maximize $p(D|\alpha, \beta)$, or equivalently $2 \ln p(D|\alpha, \beta)$. Show that the extremum condition for α is

$$0 = 2\frac{\partial \ln p(D|\alpha, \beta)}{\partial \alpha} = \frac{M}{\alpha} - \mathrm{tr}\, \boldsymbol{A}^{-1} - \boldsymbol{c} \cdot \boldsymbol{A}^{-2} \boldsymbol{c}$$

Hint: You will need the identities $(\partial/\partial\alpha) \ln \det(\alpha\mathbf{1} + \boldsymbol{M}) = \mathrm{tr}(\alpha\mathbf{1} + \boldsymbol{M})^{-1}$ and $(\partial/\partial\alpha)(\alpha\mathbf{1} + \boldsymbol{M})^{-1} = -(\alpha\mathbf{1} + \boldsymbol{M})^{-2}$, which hold for symmetric matrices $\boldsymbol{M}$.

Using the properties of the Gaussian posterior, show that this extremum condition can be written in the intuitively appealing form $\langle \boldsymbol{w}^2 \rangle_{p(\boldsymbol{w})} = \langle \boldsymbol{w}^2 \rangle_{p(\boldsymbol{w}|D)}$: the mean-squared length of $\boldsymbol{w}$ must be the same over the prior and the posterior. Also try to derive the extremum condition for β. This is somewhat easier if you first rewrite $2 \ln p(D|\alpha, \beta)$ in terms of β and

$\lambda = \alpha/p\beta$; the vanishing of the λ-derivative gives you back the condition on α found above.

Exercise 6.7. (Bayesian model selection) For the model selection example at the end of Section 6.5, show that $\chi = 1/8$. This can be seen as follows: in the (w_1, w_2)-plane, sketch the integration domain which defines χ. Then exploit the fact that the integrand $p(\boldsymbol{w}) = (2\pi)^{-1} \exp[-\frac{1}{2}(w_1^2 + w_2^2)]$ is isotropic, with integral across the whole plane equal to unity. Alternatively, transform the integral defining χ to polar coordinates in the (w_1, w_2)-plane.

Exercise 6.8. (Bayesian model selection) Consider linear neural networks H that produce outputs $t \in \mathbb{R}$ for every input vector $\boldsymbol{\xi} \in \mathbb{R}^N$, subject to Gaussian output noise, and with the usual Gaussian priors for their weights. The data used in training consist of p pairs of questions and corresponding answers: $D = \{(\boldsymbol{\xi}^1, t_1), \ldots, (\boldsymbol{\xi}^p, t_p)\}$. Choose $N = 2$ and compare two models H_1 and H_2 of this type, both with $\alpha = 1$ but with different hyperparameters β:

$$H_1: \quad p(t|\boldsymbol{\xi}, \boldsymbol{w}) = \left(\frac{\beta_1}{2\pi}\right)^{1/2} e^{-\beta_1(t-\boldsymbol{w}\cdot\boldsymbol{\xi})^2/2} \qquad p(\boldsymbol{w}) = (2\pi)^{-N/2} e^{-\boldsymbol{w}^2/2}$$

$$H_2: \quad p(t|\boldsymbol{\xi}, \boldsymbol{w}) = \left(\frac{\beta_2}{2\pi}\right)^{1/2} e^{-\beta_2(t-\boldsymbol{w}\cdot\boldsymbol{\xi})^2/2} \qquad p(\boldsymbol{w}) = (2\pi)^{-N/2} e^{-\boldsymbol{w}^2/2}$$

Assume the a priori odds to be unbiased, that is, $P(H_1) = P(H_2)$. Evaluate the ratio $P(H_1|D)/P(H_2|D)$ for the data $D = \{((1,0),1),\ ((0,1),-2)\}$, and find the most likely model for these data if $\beta_1 = 2/3$ and $\beta_2 = 1$. Hint: study the properties of the function $f(x) = x\exp(-Kx)$ for $x > 0$.

7 Gaussian processes

We return in this chapter to the general Bayesian formalism for a single model. So far we have worked out everything in terms of the posterior distribution $p(\boldsymbol{w}|D)$ of the model parameters $\boldsymbol{w}$, given the data D; to get predictions, we need to integrate over this distribution. Often the model parameters $\boldsymbol{w}$ are not easy to interpret, so knowing their distribution is in itself not particularly desirable. Also, it is not easy to see exactly what prior assumptions on the input–output relation are implicit in choosing, for example, a Gaussian prior on $\boldsymbol{w}$. One may therefore ask oneself whether it is possible to eliminate the parameters $\boldsymbol{w}$ and such model-specific details as network architectures from the formalism, and recast everything directly in terms of the relation between inputs and outputs that we are really concerned with. We show in this chapter that the answer is yes. In fact, it will turn out that for a large class of models such an approach leads to easily interpretable priors, and simple explicit predictions and error bars.

7.1 The underlying idea

From model parameter statistics to input–output statistics

We begin by showing that the predictive distribution $p(t|\boldsymbol{\xi}, D)$ for the output t corresponding to some test input $\boldsymbol{\xi}$ can be written as a ratio of prior probabilities. The data are, as before, given by pairs of example inputs $\boldsymbol{\xi}^\mu$ with corresponding noisy outputs t_μ:

$$D = \{(\boldsymbol{\xi}^1, t_1), \ldots, (\boldsymbol{\xi}^p, t_p)\}$$

Writing this out in full, the predictive distribution $p(t|\boldsymbol{\xi}, D) = \int d\boldsymbol{w}\; p(t|\boldsymbol{\xi}, \boldsymbol{w})p(\boldsymbol{w}|D)$ becomes

$$p(t|\boldsymbol{\xi}, \boldsymbol{\xi}^1, \ldots, \boldsymbol{\xi}^p, t_1, \ldots, t_p) = \int d\boldsymbol{w}\; p(t|\boldsymbol{\xi}, \boldsymbol{w})p(\boldsymbol{w}|\boldsymbol{\xi}^1, \ldots, \boldsymbol{\xi}^p, t_1, \ldots, t_p) \tag{7.1}$$

Using the core identity (6.14) for the posterior distribution $p(\boldsymbol{w}|D) = p(\boldsymbol{w}|\boldsymbol{\xi}^1, \ldots, \boldsymbol{\xi}^p, t_1, \ldots, t_p)$ gives

$$p(t|\boldsymbol{\xi}, \boldsymbol{\xi}^1, \ldots, \boldsymbol{\xi}^p, t_1, \ldots, t_p) = \frac{\int d\boldsymbol{w}\; p(t|\boldsymbol{\xi}, \boldsymbol{w})\; p(\boldsymbol{w}) \prod_{\mu=1}^p p(t_\mu|\boldsymbol{\xi}^\mu, \boldsymbol{w})}{\int d\boldsymbol{w}\; p(\boldsymbol{w}) \prod_{\mu=1}^p p(t_\mu|\boldsymbol{\xi}^\mu, \boldsymbol{w})}$$

The expression in the denominator is recognized as

$$p(t_1,\ldots,t_p|\boldsymbol{\xi}^1,\ldots,\boldsymbol{\xi}^p) = \int \mathrm{d}\boldsymbol{w}\; p(\boldsymbol{w}) \prod_{\mu=1}^{p} p(t_\mu|\boldsymbol{\xi}^\mu,\boldsymbol{w}) \tag{7.2}$$

that is, the joint probability of the training outputs $t_1,\ldots,t_p$ given the training inputs $\boldsymbol{\xi}^1,\ldots,\boldsymbol{\xi}^p$, under the prior $p(\boldsymbol{w})$. The numerator has a similar form except that the test input and output are included. We thus arrive at the simple and transparent expression

$$p(t|\boldsymbol{\xi},\boldsymbol{\xi}^1,\ldots,\boldsymbol{\xi}^p,t_1\ldots,t_p) = \frac{p(t,t_1,\ldots,t_p|\boldsymbol{\xi},\boldsymbol{\xi}^1,\ldots,\boldsymbol{\xi}^p)}{p(t_1,\ldots,t_p|\boldsymbol{\xi}^1,\ldots,\boldsymbol{\xi}^p)} \tag{7.3}$$

This is of course just Bayes' theorem: conditioned overall on $\boldsymbol{\xi},\boldsymbol{\xi}^1,\ldots,\boldsymbol{\xi}^p$, the conditional probability of t given $t_1,\ldots,t_p$ equals the joint probability of t and $t_1,\ldots,t_p$, divided by the probability of $t_1,\ldots,t_p$. To get (7.3) one then only needs to realize that the latter probability is independent of $\boldsymbol{\xi}$. This is clear intuitively, or can be shown formally by integrating over t:

$$\begin{aligned}
p(t_1,\ldots,t_p|\boldsymbol{\xi},\boldsymbol{\xi}^1,\ldots,\boldsymbol{\xi}^p) &= \int \mathrm{d}t\; p(t,t_1,\ldots,t_p|\boldsymbol{\xi},\boldsymbol{\xi}^1,\ldots,\boldsymbol{\xi}^p) \\
&= \int \mathrm{d}t \int \mathrm{d}\boldsymbol{w}\; p(t|\boldsymbol{\xi},\boldsymbol{w})\left(\prod_{\mu=1}^{p} p(t_\mu|\boldsymbol{\xi}^\mu,\boldsymbol{w})\right)p(\boldsymbol{w}) \\
&= \int \mathrm{d}\boldsymbol{w}\left(\prod_{\mu=1}^{p} p(t_\mu|\boldsymbol{\xi}^\mu,\boldsymbol{w})\right)p(\boldsymbol{w}) \\
&= p(t_1,\ldots,t_p|\boldsymbol{\xi}^1,\ldots,\boldsymbol{\xi}^p)
\end{aligned} \tag{7.4}$$

Here we have used the normalization of $p(t|\boldsymbol{\xi},\boldsymbol{w})$ to do the t-integral.

The summary so far is that knowledge of joint output probabilities of the type $p(t_1,\ldots,t_p|\boldsymbol{\xi}^1,\ldots,\boldsymbol{\xi}^p)$—for arbitary p, $\{\boldsymbol{\xi}^1,\ldots,\boldsymbol{\xi}^p\}$ and $\{t_1,\ldots,t_p\}$—is enough to let us make predictions within a Bayesian framework. Gaussian processes are a simple way of specifying these probabilities without needing to refer to the prior over weights as in (7.2). Before we define them, it is useful to separate off the effects of the noise on the data. We do this by writing $t_\mu = y_\mu + z_\mu$, where $y_\mu = f(\boldsymbol{\xi}^\mu,\boldsymbol{w})$ is the 'clean' output corresponding to $\boldsymbol{\xi}^\mu$ and z_μ is the noise, distributed according to some zero-mean distribution $P(z)$. We can then write (see Appendix F for information on the δ-distribution)

$$p(t_\mu|\boldsymbol{\xi}^\mu,\boldsymbol{w}) = \int \mathrm{d}y_\mu\; p(t_\mu|y_\mu)\delta(y_\mu - f(\boldsymbol{\xi}^\mu,\boldsymbol{w})) \tag{7.5}$$

Here the conditional probability of the noisy output given the clean one is $p(t_\mu|y_\mu) = P(t_\mu - y_\mu)$ and is, as indicated by the notation, independent of $\boldsymbol{\xi}^\mu$ and $\boldsymbol{w}$. Inserting these identities, one for each of $\mu = 1,\ldots,p$, into (7.2)

we have

$$
\begin{aligned}
p(t_1,\ldots,t_p|\boldsymbol{\xi}^1,\ldots,\boldsymbol{\xi}^p) &= \int \left(\prod_{\mu=1}^{p} \mathrm{d}y_\mu\, p(t_\mu|y_\mu)\right) \\
&\quad \times \int \mathrm{d}\boldsymbol{w} \prod_{\mu=1}^{p} \delta(y_\mu - f(\boldsymbol{\xi}^\mu, \boldsymbol{w}))\; p(\boldsymbol{w}) \\
&= \int \left(\prod_{\mu=1}^{p} \mathrm{d}y_\mu\, p(t_\mu|y_\mu)\right) p(y_1,\ldots,y_p|\boldsymbol{\xi}^1,\ldots,\boldsymbol{\xi}^p)
\end{aligned} \tag{7.6}
$$

As could have been expected, this expresses the joint prior distribution of the noisy t_μ in terms of the joint prior distribution of the clean outputs y_μ,

$$
p(y_1,\ldots,y_p|\boldsymbol{\xi}^1,\ldots,\boldsymbol{\xi}^p) = \int \mathrm{d}\boldsymbol{w} \prod_{\mu=1}^{p} \delta(y_\mu - f(\boldsymbol{\xi}^\mu, \boldsymbol{w}))\; p(\boldsymbol{w}) \tag{7.7}
$$

by adding independent noise to each y_μ.

Definition of Gaussian processes

The defining property of a Gaussian process is now that the distribution (7.7) is a multivariate *Gaussian distribution*, for any p and any choice of the inputs $\{\boldsymbol{\xi}^1,\ldots,\boldsymbol{\xi}^p\}$. Note that this definition refers to the *prior* distribution of the y_μ, so Gaussian processes are one way of specifying our prior knowledge about a problem; the noise distribution can be chosen independently. The joint distribution of the $\{y_1,\ldots,y_p\}$ is fully specified by its means and covariances. Let us work out how these will depend on the inputs $\{\boldsymbol{\xi}^1,\ldots,\boldsymbol{\xi}^p\}$. If we denote averages over the distribution (7.7) by $\langle\cdots\rangle$, we have for the means

$$
\begin{aligned}
\langle y_\mu\rangle &= \int \left(\prod_{\rho=1}^{p} \mathrm{d}y_\rho\right) y_\mu\, p(y_1,\ldots,y_p|\boldsymbol{\xi}^1,\ldots,\boldsymbol{\xi}^p) \\
&= \int \mathrm{d}y_\mu\; y_\mu\, p(y_\mu|\boldsymbol{\xi}^1,\ldots,\boldsymbol{\xi}^p) \\
&= \int \mathrm{d}y_\mu\; y_\mu\, p(y_\mu|\boldsymbol{\xi}^\mu)
\end{aligned}
$$

This shows that $\langle y_\mu\rangle$ is dependent only on $\boldsymbol{\xi}^\mu$ and can be written as some function $a(\boldsymbol{\xi}^\mu)$ which defines the input-dependence of the mean of the Gaussian process. In deriving this result we have used the fact that the distribution of y_μ is independent of all the inputs $\boldsymbol{\xi}^1,\ldots,\boldsymbol{\xi}^p$ except for $\boldsymbol{\xi}^\mu$. This follows in a manner analogous to (7.4), by integrating (7.7) over all the y_ρ with $\rho \neq \mu$. Similarly, the average of a product $y_\mu y_\nu$,

$$\begin{aligned}\langle y_\mu y_\nu \rangle &= \int \left(\prod_{\rho=1}^{p} \mathrm{d}y_\rho \right) y_\mu y_\nu \, p(y_1, \ldots, y_p | \boldsymbol{\xi}^1, \ldots, \boldsymbol{\xi}^p) \\ &= \int \mathrm{d}y_\mu \mathrm{d}y_\nu \; y_\mu y_\nu \, p(y_\mu, y_\nu | \boldsymbol{\xi}^1, \ldots, \boldsymbol{\xi}^p) \\ &= \int \mathrm{d}y_\mu \mathrm{d}y_\nu \; y_\mu y_\nu \, p(y_\mu, y_\nu | \boldsymbol{\xi}^\mu, \boldsymbol{\xi}^\nu)\end{aligned}$$

depends only on $\boldsymbol{\xi}^\mu$ and $\boldsymbol{\xi}^\nu$. The same is therefore also true of the covariance $\langle y_\mu y_\nu \rangle - \langle y_\mu \rangle \langle y_\nu \rangle$, so we can write the latter as a function $C(\boldsymbol{\xi}^\mu, \boldsymbol{\xi}^\nu)$. This is known as the *covariance function* of a Gaussian process. Overall, a Gaussian process is thus fully specified by the mean function $a(\boldsymbol{\xi})$ and the covariance function $C(\boldsymbol{\xi}, \boldsymbol{\xi}')$. It is common to work with zero-mean Gaussian processes (i.e. $a(\boldsymbol{\xi}) = 0$), for which only the covariance function needs to be specified.

7.2 Examples of networks reducing to Gaussian processes

Before considering the general implications of using Gaussian process priors, we discuss two example scenarios which naturally lead to Gaussian processes. Both have a Gaussian prior on the model parameters $\boldsymbol{w}$ and the clean outputs are, as before, given in terms of some deterministic function $f(\boldsymbol{\xi}; \boldsymbol{w})$ parametrized by $\boldsymbol{w}$:

$$y_\mu = f(\boldsymbol{\xi}^\mu, \boldsymbol{w}) \qquad p(\boldsymbol{w}) = \left(\frac{\alpha}{2\pi} \right)^{M/2} e^{-\alpha \boldsymbol{w}^2/2} \tag{7.8}$$

Radial basis function networks

RBF (radial basis function) networks with Gaussian priors are members of the class (7.8), with f of the form $f(\boldsymbol{w}; \boldsymbol{\xi}) = \boldsymbol{w} \cdot \boldsymbol{\Phi}(\boldsymbol{\xi})$. Here $\boldsymbol{w} \in \mathbb{R}^M$ and $\boldsymbol{\Phi}(\boldsymbol{\xi})$ is a vector of M functions $\phi_i(\boldsymbol{\xi})$. It turns out that we do not in fact need to put RBF-type restrictions on the ϕ_i, so our discussion here will apply to all generalized linear models.

The joint distribution (7.7) can be worked out formally by using a Fourier representation of the δ-functions (see Exercise 7.1). However, it is easier to note that the components w_i of the parameter vector $\boldsymbol{w}$ have a prior distribution (7.8) with means and covariances

$$\langle w_i \rangle = 0 \qquad \langle w_i w_j \rangle = \alpha^{-1} \delta_{ij} \tag{7.9}$$

Now writing the y_μ explicitly,

$$y_\mu = \boldsymbol{w} \cdot \boldsymbol{\Phi}(\boldsymbol{\xi}^\mu) = \sum_{i=1}^{M} w_i \phi_i(\boldsymbol{\xi}^\mu) \tag{7.10}$$

we see that each is a linear combination of the w_i, with coefficients $\phi_i(\boldsymbol{\xi}^\mu)$ depending on the corresponding inputs (which we can regard as fixed, since we are considering the distribution of the y_μ *given* the $\boldsymbol{\xi}^\mu$). Since any set of linear combinations of Gaussian random variables is again a set of jointly Gaussian variables (see Appendix D), it follows directly that RBF networks with Gaussian priors define Gaussian processes. The means and covariances of the joint distribution of the y_μ are, using (7.9),

$$\langle y_\mu \rangle = \sum_{i=1}^{M} \langle w_i \rangle \phi_i(\boldsymbol{\xi}^\mu) = 0$$

$$\langle y_\mu y_\nu \rangle = \sum_{i,j=1}^{M} \langle w_i w_j \rangle \phi_i(\boldsymbol{\xi}^\mu) \phi_j(\boldsymbol{\xi}^\nu)$$

$$= \alpha^{-1} \sum_{i=1}^{M} \phi_i(\boldsymbol{\xi}^\mu) \phi_i(\boldsymbol{\xi}^\nu) = \alpha^{-1} \boldsymbol{\Phi}(\boldsymbol{\xi}^\mu) \cdot \boldsymbol{\Phi}(\boldsymbol{\xi}^\nu)$$

This shows that the covariance function of the Gaussian process prior defined by RBF networks with Gaussian parameter priors has zero mean and covariance function

$$C(\boldsymbol{\xi}, \boldsymbol{\xi}') = \alpha^{-1} \boldsymbol{\Phi}(\boldsymbol{\xi}) \cdot \boldsymbol{\Phi}(\boldsymbol{\xi}') \tag{7.11}$$

Linear-output two-layer perceptrons

Let us next turn to a less trivial model example, still of the form (7.8), which is also found to reduce to a Gaussian process in a specific limit. We take a two-layer network with sigmoidal transfer functions $g(u)$ in the hidden layer (of size L) and a linear output neuron, that is, $f(\boldsymbol{\xi}; \boldsymbol{w}, \boldsymbol{J}) = \sum_{i=1}^{L} w_i\, g(\sum_{j=1}^{N} J_{ij} \xi_j)$. The prior distributions over the parameters $\boldsymbol{w}$ and $\boldsymbol{J}$ are assumed to be Gaussian, and independent of each other:

$$p(\boldsymbol{w}) = \left(\frac{\alpha_w L}{2\pi}\right)^{L/2} e^{-\alpha_w L \boldsymbol{w}^2/2} \qquad p(\boldsymbol{J}) = \left(\frac{\alpha_J}{2\pi}\right)^{NL/2} e^{-\alpha_J \sum_{i=1}^{L} \boldsymbol{j}_i^2/2} \tag{7.12}$$

Here we have organized the input-to-hidden layer weights $\{J_{ij}\}$ into L vectors $\boldsymbol{j}_i$ of dimension N each, $\boldsymbol{j}_i = (J_{i1}, J_{i2}, \ldots, J_{iN})$; this allows us to write the overall output as

$$f(\boldsymbol{\xi}; \boldsymbol{w}, \boldsymbol{J}) = \sum_{i=1}^{L} w_i\, g(\boldsymbol{j}_i \cdot \boldsymbol{\xi})$$

The width of the prior for the L hidden-to-output weights $\{w_i\}$ has been rescaled by a factor $1/\sqrt{L}$, in order to find a well-defined limit $L \to \infty$ (corresponding to an infinitely large hidden layer) later. This prior has two hyperparameters: α_w and α_J.

Before we start the calculation, let us get some intuition why a Gaussian process might result from these assumptions for $L \to \infty$. The $\boldsymbol{j}_i$ are independent of each other under the Gaussian prior (7.12). So for a given $\boldsymbol{\xi}$, the outputs $g(\boldsymbol{j}_i \cdot \boldsymbol{\xi})$ of the hidden units are independently distributed, and the same is true of the weighted outputs $w_i g(\boldsymbol{j}_i \cdot \boldsymbol{\xi})$ because the w_i are likewise independent of each other under the prior. The overall output $f(\boldsymbol{\xi}; \boldsymbol{w}, \boldsymbol{J})$ is just the sum of these L weighted outputs. As such, we expect it to acquire a Gaussian distribution for $L \to \infty$, on the basis of the central limit theorem, and it is not too surprising that this argument generalizes to joint distributions of outputs for different $\boldsymbol{\xi}^\mu$.

To calculate the prior distribution (7.7) of a set of outputs $y_1, \ldots, y_p$ explicitly, we replace each δ-function by its Fourier representation (see Appendix F),

$$\delta(y_\mu - f(\boldsymbol{\xi}^\mu; \boldsymbol{w}, \boldsymbol{J})) = \int \frac{\mathrm{d}k_\mu}{2\pi} e^{-\mathrm{i}k_\mu [y_\mu - f(\boldsymbol{\xi}^\mu; \boldsymbol{w}, \boldsymbol{J})]}$$

$$= \int \frac{\mathrm{d}k_\mu}{2\pi} e^{-\mathrm{i}k_\mu y_\mu + \mathrm{i}k_\mu \sum_{i=1}^{L} w_i g(\boldsymbol{j}_i \cdot \boldsymbol{\xi}^\mu)} \tag{7.13}$$

to get (with $\mu, \nu = 1, \ldots, p$ and $i = 1, \ldots, L$ throughout)

$$p(y_1, \ldots, y_p | \boldsymbol{\xi}^1, \ldots, \boldsymbol{\xi}^p) = \int \mathrm{d}\boldsymbol{w}\, \mathrm{d}\boldsymbol{J}\, p(\boldsymbol{w}) p(\boldsymbol{J}) \prod_\mu \frac{\mathrm{d}k_\mu}{2\pi}$$

$$e^{-\mathrm{i}\sum_\mu k_\mu [y_\mu - \sum_i w_i g(\boldsymbol{j}_i \cdot \boldsymbol{\xi}^\mu)]} \tag{7.14}$$

As expected (see Appendix D), this is just the Fourier transform of the characteristic function of the $y_\mu = \sum_i w_i g(\boldsymbol{j}_i \cdot \boldsymbol{\xi}^\mu)$,

$$\phi(\boldsymbol{k}) = \left\langle e^{\mathrm{i}\sum_\mu k_\mu y_\mu} \right\rangle = \int \mathrm{d}\boldsymbol{w}\, \mathrm{d}\boldsymbol{J} e^{\mathrm{i}\sum_\mu k_\mu \sum_i w_i g(\boldsymbol{j}_i \cdot \boldsymbol{\xi}^\mu)}\, p(\boldsymbol{w}) p(\boldsymbol{J}) \tag{7.15}$$

The integral over the Gaussian prior on $\boldsymbol{w}$ is easily done (see Appendix D):

$$\phi(\boldsymbol{k}) = \int \mathrm{d}\boldsymbol{J} e^{-\sum_i \left[\sum_\mu k_\mu g(\boldsymbol{j}_i \cdot \boldsymbol{\xi}^\mu)\right]^2 / 2\alpha_w L}\, p(\boldsymbol{J}) \tag{7.16}$$

Inserting $p(\boldsymbol{J}) = \prod_{i=1}^{L} \rho(\boldsymbol{j}_i)$ with $\rho(\boldsymbol{j}_i) = (\alpha_J / 2\pi)^{1/2} e^{-\alpha_J \boldsymbol{j}_i^2/2}$, one sees that this integral factorizes into L integrals over the individual $\boldsymbol{j}_i$, each one giving the same contribution:

$$\phi(\boldsymbol{k}) = \left\{ \int \mathrm{d}\boldsymbol{j}\, e^{-[\sum_\mu k_\mu g(\boldsymbol{j}\cdot\boldsymbol{\xi}^\mu)]^2/2\alpha_w L}\, \rho(\boldsymbol{j}) \right\}^L \tag{7.17}$$

For large L the exponent is small and we can expand the exponential and then use that $[1 + a/L + \mathcal{O}(1/L^2)]^L \to \exp(a)$ for $L \to \infty$, yielding

$$\begin{aligned}
\phi(\boldsymbol{k}) &= \left\{ \int \mathrm{d}\boldsymbol{j} \left(1 - \frac{1}{2\alpha_w L} \left[\sum_\mu k_\mu g(\boldsymbol{j}\cdot\boldsymbol{\xi}^\mu) \right]^2 + \mathcal{O}(L^{-2}) \right) \rho(\boldsymbol{j}) \right\}^L \\
&\to \exp\left(-\frac{1}{2\alpha_w} \int \mathrm{d}\boldsymbol{j} \left[\sum_\mu k_\mu g(\boldsymbol{j}\cdot\boldsymbol{\xi}^\mu) \right]^2 \rho(\boldsymbol{j}) \right) \\
&= \exp\left(-\frac{1}{2} \sum_{\mu\nu} k_\mu k_\nu D_{\mu\nu} \right)
\end{aligned} \tag{7.18}$$

with

$$D_{\mu\nu} = \frac{1}{\alpha_w} \int \mathrm{d}\boldsymbol{j}\; g(\boldsymbol{j}\cdot\boldsymbol{\xi}^\mu) g(\boldsymbol{j}\cdot\boldsymbol{\xi}^\nu)\; \rho(\boldsymbol{j}) \tag{7.19}$$

The form of the characteristic function (7.18) tells us that the distribution of the y_μ is Gaussian with zero means and with covariances $\langle y_\mu y_\nu \rangle = D_{\mu\nu}$ (see Appendix D). Formally, this follows by carrying out the Gaussian integral in (7.14):

$$\begin{aligned}
p(y_1, \ldots, y_p | \boldsymbol{\xi}^1, \ldots, \boldsymbol{\xi}^p) &= \int \prod_\mu \frac{\mathrm{d}k_\mu}{2\pi} e^{-\mathrm{i}\sum_\mu k_\mu y_\mu} \phi(\boldsymbol{k}) \\
&= \int \prod_\mu \frac{\mathrm{d}k_\mu}{2\pi} e^{-\mathrm{i}\sum_\mu k_\mu y_\mu - \sum_{\mu\nu} k_\mu k_\nu D_{\mu\nu}/2} \\
&= [(2\pi)^p \det \boldsymbol{D}]^{-1/2} e^{-\sum_{\mu\nu} y_\mu y_\nu (\boldsymbol{D}^{-1})_{\mu\nu}/2}
\end{aligned} \tag{7.20}$$

In summary, we have shown that linear-output MLPs with Gaussian weight priors correspond, in the limit of an infinitely large hidden layer, to Gaussian processes with zero mean. The covariance function can be read off from (7.19):

$$C(\boldsymbol{\xi}, \boldsymbol{\xi}') = \frac{1}{\alpha_w} \int \mathrm{d}\boldsymbol{j}\, g(\boldsymbol{j}\cdot\boldsymbol{\xi}) g(\boldsymbol{j}\cdot\boldsymbol{\xi}') \rho(\boldsymbol{j}) \tag{7.21}$$

In the derivation above, an alternative argument for the step from (7.16) to (7.18) would have been as follows. Because of the independence of the $\boldsymbol{j}_i$, the exponent in (7.16) is an average of L independent and identically distributed random terms. For $L \to \infty$, this average must approach the mean of any one of these terms over its distribution, giving (7.18).

Working out the covariance matrix (7.21) of this example is hard for arbitrary $g(u)$. However, for data vectors $\boldsymbol{\xi}$ close to the origin (alternatively: for large values of the hyperparameter α_J, which force $\boldsymbol{j}$ to be small) we may expand typical choices such as $g(u) = \tanh(u)$ as $g(u) = u + \mathcal{O}(u^3)$ and find

$$\begin{aligned} C(\boldsymbol{\xi}, \boldsymbol{\xi}') &= \frac{1}{\alpha_w} \int d\boldsymbol{j}\,(\boldsymbol{j}\cdot\boldsymbol{\xi})(\boldsymbol{j}\cdot\boldsymbol{\xi}')p(\boldsymbol{j}) + \mathcal{O}(|\boldsymbol{\xi}||\boldsymbol{\xi}'|^3, |\boldsymbol{\xi}|^3|\boldsymbol{\xi}'|) \\ &= \frac{\boldsymbol{\xi}\cdot\boldsymbol{\xi}'}{\alpha_w\alpha_J} + \mathcal{O}(|\boldsymbol{\xi}||\boldsymbol{\xi}'|^3, |\boldsymbol{\xi}|^3|\boldsymbol{\xi}'|) \end{aligned} \tag{7.22}$$

Truncation after the first term is obviously exact only for $g(u) = u$. In this case our MLP degenerates into a simple linear function of the inputs, and accordingly (7.22) is of the same form as the RBF result (7.11) with the choice $\boldsymbol{\Phi}(\boldsymbol{\xi}) = \boldsymbol{\xi}$.

7.3 The 'priors over functions' point of view

So far we have shown how some of the models we are already familiar with actually lead to Gaussian process priors once we eliminate the model parameters $\boldsymbol{w}$. It would also be useful to have some intuitive understanding of the meaning of a Gaussian process in cases where we only have the mean and covariance functions $a(\boldsymbol{\xi})$ and $C(\boldsymbol{\xi}, \boldsymbol{\xi}')$ but no parametrization of the input–output relation $f(\boldsymbol{\xi})$ in terms of an underlying $\boldsymbol{w}$.

This is achieved by regarding the Gaussian process as a prior over *functions*. To see how this works, consider a simple case, where the inputs $\boldsymbol{\xi}$ come from a discrete set $\boldsymbol{\xi}_1, \ldots \boldsymbol{\xi}_K$. This is not as exceptional a scenario as it may appear: in practice, even real-valued inputs are known only to some finite accuracy, so that we are effectively dealing with a discrete set of possible input values on a (normally finely spaced) grid. Now, with there being only K different inputs, a function $f(\boldsymbol{\xi})$ can equivalently be thought of as the K-dimensional vector $(f(\boldsymbol{\xi}_1), \ldots, f(\boldsymbol{\xi}_K))$. A prior over functions is then just a probability distribution over K-dimensional vectors, an object we are quite familiar with. We have a Gaussian process prior if this distribution is a K-dimensional Gaussian distribution, with means $\langle f(\boldsymbol{\xi}_\alpha)\rangle = a(\boldsymbol{\xi}_\alpha)$ and covariances $\langle f(\boldsymbol{\xi}_\alpha) f(\boldsymbol{\xi}_\beta)\rangle - \langle f(\boldsymbol{\xi}_\alpha)\rangle\langle f(\boldsymbol{\xi}_\beta)\rangle = C(\boldsymbol{\xi}_\alpha, \boldsymbol{\xi}_\beta)$ (where $\alpha, \beta = 1, \ldots, K$).

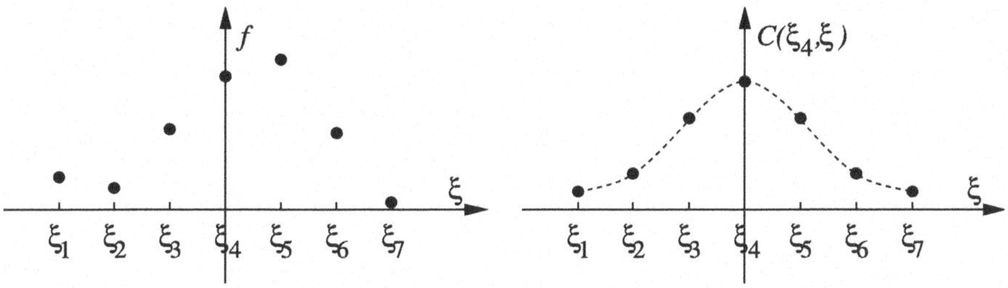

Figure 7.1 Left: sketch of a sample 'function' from a Gaussian process prior, for the case of discrete one-dimensional inputs. Right: The associated values of the covariance function $C(\xi_4, \xi)$ with the function value $f(\xi_4)$ at point ξ_4.

A pictorial representation of this view is shown in Figure 7.1 for a one-dimensional input space and $K = 7$. A 'function' drawn at random from a Gaussian process prior is just a list of seven numbers $f(\xi_1), \ldots, f(\xi_7)$. Considering for simplicity the zero-mean case, we can now see the intuitive meaning of the covariance function. $C(\xi_4, \xi_4)$, for example, is the variance of $f(\xi_4)$ under the prior: a typical function will have $f(\xi_4)$ of order $\pm[C(\xi_4, \xi_4)]^{1/2}$. $C(\xi_4, \xi_5)$, on the other hand, gives us the covariance of the function values at ξ_4 and ξ_5. If this is similar to $C(\xi_4, \xi_4)$ and $C(\xi_5, \xi_5)$—assuming for simplicity that these are the same—then these function values are strongly correlated: typical functions from the prior will change little between ξ_4 and ξ_5. If $C(\xi_4, \xi_5)$ is small, on the other hand, then the function typically changes significantly. Generalizing this argument, we could imagine plotting $C(\xi_4, \xi)$ as a function of ξ (see Figure 7.1); in the present case there are only seven values of this. Then the range of ξ where $C(\xi_4, \xi)$ is close to $C(\xi_4, \xi_4)$ tells us where functions from the prior will be roughly constant and equal to their value at ξ_4; their values outside this range will be almost uncorrelated with that at ξ_4.

7.4 Stationary covariance functions

To reinforce the intuition gained in the last section and introduce a useful class of covariance functions, let us work out explicitly the covariance function (7.11) of RBF networks, for the example of Gaussian basis functions of width σ, that is, $\phi_i(\boldsymbol{\xi}) = (2\pi\sigma^2)^{-N/2} \exp[-\frac{1}{2}(\boldsymbol{\xi} - \boldsymbol{x}_i)^2/\sigma^2]$. This gives the following covariance function:

$$C(\boldsymbol{\xi}, \boldsymbol{\xi}') = \frac{1}{\alpha(2\pi\sigma^2)^N} \sum_{i=1}^{M} e^{-[(\boldsymbol{\xi}-\boldsymbol{x}_i)^2 + (\boldsymbol{\xi}'-\boldsymbol{x}_i)^2]/2\sigma^2}$$

We now imagine having a very large number $M \to \infty$ of basis functions which become distributed uniformly over $\mathbb{R}^N$ in this limit, and we rescale our hyperparameter α accordingly as $\alpha = \tilde{\alpha}/\Delta_M$. Here Δ_M denotes a small volume element in $\mathbb{R}^N$ such that $\lim_{M\to\infty} \sum_{i=1}^{M} \Delta_M f(\boldsymbol{x}_i) = \int \mathrm{d}\boldsymbol{x}\, f(\boldsymbol{x})$ for any sufficiently 'nice' function f. We then find

$$\begin{aligned}\lim_{M\to\infty} C(\boldsymbol{\xi},\boldsymbol{\xi}') &= \frac{1}{\tilde{\alpha}(2\pi\sigma^2)^N} \int \mathrm{d}\boldsymbol{x}\, e^{-[(\boldsymbol{\xi}-\boldsymbol{x})^2+(\boldsymbol{\xi}'-\boldsymbol{x})^2]/2\sigma^2} \\ &= \frac{e^{-[\boldsymbol{\xi}^2+(\boldsymbol{\xi}')^2]/2\sigma^2}}{\tilde{\alpha}(2\pi\sigma^2)^N} \int \mathrm{d}\boldsymbol{x}\, e^{-[\boldsymbol{x}^2-\boldsymbol{x}\cdot(\boldsymbol{\xi}+\boldsymbol{\xi}')]/\sigma^2} \\ &= \frac{e^{-(\boldsymbol{\xi}-\boldsymbol{\xi}')^2/4\sigma^2}}{\tilde{\alpha}(4\pi\sigma^2)^{N/2}} \end{aligned} \tag{7.23}$$

This is an example of a *stationary* covariance function: $C(\boldsymbol{\xi},\boldsymbol{\xi}')$ depends only on $\boldsymbol{\xi} - \boldsymbol{\xi}'$, that is, on the distance vector between the points $\boldsymbol{\xi}$ and $\boldsymbol{\xi}'$ but not otherwise on their actual location. In fact, the covariance function (7.23) has the further property that it depends only the modulus $|\boldsymbol{\xi}-\boldsymbol{\xi}'|$, that is, on the distance between the two points. Here the covariance structure is fully isotropic in input space (i.e. invariant under arbitrary translations and/or rotations applied jointly to $\boldsymbol{\xi}$ and $\boldsymbol{\xi}'$). Within this subclass of isotropic stationary covariance functions, the only remaining freedom is in the choice of the function $c(\cdot)$ in $C(\boldsymbol{\xi},\boldsymbol{\xi}') = c(|\boldsymbol{\xi} - \boldsymbol{\xi}'|)$. Even so, however, we can get quite a range of different Gaussian process priors. Figure 7.2 shows examples of functions on the unit square $\boldsymbol{\xi},\boldsymbol{\xi}' \in [0,1]^2$, sampled from

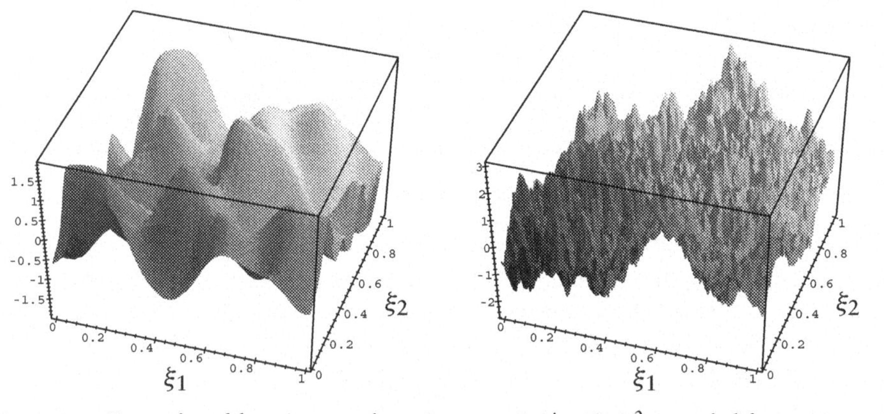

Figure 7.2 Examples of functions on the unit square $\boldsymbol{\xi},\boldsymbol{\xi}' \in [0,1]^2$, sampled from zero-mean Gaussian process priors with stationary covariance functions. Left: $C(\boldsymbol{\xi},\boldsymbol{\xi}') = K_0 e^{-|\boldsymbol{\xi}-\boldsymbol{\xi}'|^2/2\sigma^2}$, with $K_0 = 10$ and $\sigma = 0.1$. Right: $C(\boldsymbol{\xi},\boldsymbol{\xi}') = K_0 e^{-|\boldsymbol{\xi}-\boldsymbol{\xi}'|/\sigma}$, with $K_0 = 10$ and $\sigma = 0.1$.

Gaussian process priors with the following covariance functions:

$$\text{Squared exponential (SE):} \quad C(\boldsymbol{\xi},\boldsymbol{\xi}') = K_0 e^{-|\boldsymbol{\xi}-\boldsymbol{\xi}'|^2/2\sigma^2}$$

$$\text{Ornstein–Uhlenbeck (OU):} \quad C(\boldsymbol{\xi},\boldsymbol{\xi}') = K_0 e^{-|\boldsymbol{\xi}-\boldsymbol{\xi}'|/\sigma}$$

(the SE covariance function is essentially the one derived above for RBFs, except that we have replaced $4\sigma^2 \to 2\sigma^2$ to match standard conventions in the literature). In both cases the values for the constants were chosen as $K_0 = 10$, $\sigma = 0.1$. From the intuition developed in the previous section, we deduce that the typical values of functions from these priors will be of order $K_0^{1/2} = \sqrt{10}$, and this is consistent with the examples in the figure. The parameter σ tells us in both cases over which typical distance $|\boldsymbol{\xi}-\boldsymbol{\xi}'|$ the covariance function is roughly constant before decaying to zero. Correspondingly, the functions sampled from these priors are roughly constant over regions of this size.

There is a further qualitative difference between the two cases: clearly the function on the right of Figure 7.2 is 'rough' whereas the one on the left is rather smooth. This arises from the different behaviour of the two covariance functions for $\boldsymbol{\xi}' \to \boldsymbol{\xi}$. Writing $\boldsymbol{\xi}'-\boldsymbol{\xi} = \boldsymbol{\epsilon}$, with $|\boldsymbol{\epsilon}| \ll 1$, we have for our two examples:

$$e^{-(1/2)|\boldsymbol{\xi}-\boldsymbol{\xi}'|^2/\sigma^2} = 1 - \frac{\boldsymbol{\epsilon}^2}{2\sigma^2} + \mathcal{O}(|\boldsymbol{\epsilon}|^4) \qquad e^{-|\boldsymbol{\xi}-\boldsymbol{\xi}'|/\sigma} = 1 - \frac{|\boldsymbol{\epsilon}|}{\sigma} + \mathcal{O}(|\boldsymbol{\epsilon}|^2)$$

Hence the OU covariance function indeed describes much faster decorrelation of outputs for small differences in the inputs. More generally, one can show that the differentiability of $C(\boldsymbol{\xi},\boldsymbol{\xi}')$ at the point $\boldsymbol{\xi}' = \boldsymbol{\xi}$ determines how many smooth derivatives functions from the corresponding Gaussian process priors will have. The OU covariance function is not differentiable at $\boldsymbol{\xi}' = \boldsymbol{\xi}$, due to the appearance of the $|\boldsymbol{\epsilon}|$ in the expansion above; this leads to rough sample functions which are continuous but not differentiable. The SE or RBF covariance function, on the other hand, is infinitely often differentiable at $\boldsymbol{\xi}' = \boldsymbol{\xi}$. The corresponding sample functions can then also be shown to have this property, consistent with the smooth appearance of the left part of Figure 7.2.

One can construct intermediate priors where the sample functions have derivatives up to some finite order: for example, for one-dimensional inputs, $C(\xi,\xi') = c(|\xi-\xi'|)$, $c(u) = (1+u/\sigma)\exp(-u/\sigma)$ produces sample functions that are once but not twice differentiable. Note that not all functions $c(u)$ lead to valid Gaussian process priors though: one has to ensure that all covariance matrices $C(\boldsymbol{\xi}^\mu,\boldsymbol{\xi}^\nu)$ $(\mu,\nu = 1,\ldots,p)$ of p outputs corresponding to p inputs $\boldsymbol{\xi}^1,\ldots,\boldsymbol{\xi}^p$ are positive (or at least non-negative) definite. For stationary covariance functions, one can show that the criterion for this is that the Fourier transform of $C(\boldsymbol{\xi}, \boldsymbol{\xi}')$ with respect to $\boldsymbol{\xi}' - \boldsymbol{\xi}$ is everywhere non-negative.

7.5 Learning and prediction with Gaussian processes

Having clarified the definition and meaning of Gaussian process priors, we now proceed to discuss how they are put to work for learning and prediction. Recall the definition: a prior is a Gaussian process if the joint distribution (7.7) of the clean outputs $y_1, \ldots, y_p$ is Gaussian, for any p and any set of inputs $\boldsymbol{\xi}^1, \ldots, \boldsymbol{\xi}^p$. The means and covariances of this distribution are $a(\boldsymbol{\xi}^\mu)$ and $C(\boldsymbol{\xi}^\mu, \boldsymbol{\xi}^\nu)$, where $a(\boldsymbol{\xi})$ is the mean function of the Gaussian process and $C(\boldsymbol{\xi}, \boldsymbol{\xi}')$ its covariance function. We mostly restrict ourselves to the much more commonly used zero-mean case and only briefly indicate the appropriate generalizations. The reason for this is that using Gaussian process priors with nonzero mean only makes sense if—unusually—we have quite specific prior information about the problem to be learned. Consistent with this, all the specific examples discussed above (e.g. RBF and MLP) indeed gave zero-mean Gaussian processes.

As we have stressed, the definition of a Gaussian process prior is independent of that of the noise model, that is, of the distribution $P(z)$ of the noise variables z_μ which relate noisy and clean outputs via $t_\mu = y_\mu + z_\mu$. We assume in this section that the z_μ are Gaussian with variance $1/\beta$, $P(z) = (\beta/2\pi)^{1/2} \exp(-\beta z^2/2)$. The advantage of this choice is that, with the y_μ and z_μ being Gaussian, also the $t_\mu = y_\mu + z_\mu$ are Gaussian. This can be formally derived from (7.6)—see Exercises 7.2 and 7.3. We therefore only need to work out their means and covariances

$$\langle t_\mu \rangle = \langle y_\mu \rangle + \langle z_\mu \rangle \; = \; 0 + 0 \; = \; 0 \tag{7.24}$$

$$\begin{aligned} \langle t_\mu t_\nu \rangle = \langle (y_\mu + z_\mu)(y_\nu + z_\nu) \rangle \; &= \; \langle y_\mu y_\nu \rangle + \langle y_\mu \rangle \langle z_\nu \rangle + \langle z_\mu \rangle \langle y_\nu \rangle + \langle z_\mu z_\nu \rangle \\ = C(\boldsymbol{\xi}^\mu, \boldsymbol{\xi}^\nu) + \beta^{-1} \delta_{\mu\nu} \; &\equiv \; K_{\mu\nu} \end{aligned} \tag{7.25}$$

Here we have used the fact that the noise variables z_μ are independent of the clean outputs y_μ and of each other; the last equality defines the $p \times p$ matrix $\boldsymbol{K}$.

We now want to predict the output t corresponding to a test input $\boldsymbol{\xi}$, given the data set $D = \{(\boldsymbol{\xi}^1, t_1), \ldots, (\boldsymbol{\xi}^p, t_p)\}$. The distribution of t is given by (7.3). One can formally work out the ratio of the two probability distributions involved, both of which are Gaussian (see Exercise 7.4). It is easier, however, to use general relations for the properties of conditional Gaussian distributions: given the $\boldsymbol{\xi}, \boldsymbol{\xi}^1, \ldots, \boldsymbol{\xi}^p$, the predictive distribution (7.3) is the conditional distribution of t given $t_1, \ldots, t_p$. The joint distribution of these $p+1$ variables is, from (7.24) and (7.25), a zero mean Gaussian with covariances ($\mu, \nu = 1, \ldots, p$):

$$\langle t_\mu t_\nu \rangle = K_{\mu\nu} \tag{7.26}$$

$$\langle t_\mu t \rangle = C(\boldsymbol{\xi}^\mu, \boldsymbol{\xi}) \equiv k_\mu(\boldsymbol{\xi}) \tag{7.27}$$

$$\langle t^2 \rangle = C(\boldsymbol{\xi}, \boldsymbol{\xi}) + 1/\beta \tag{7.28}$$

The second equality defines the vector $\boldsymbol{k}(\boldsymbol{\xi})$. From (D.22) in Appendix D we can thus write down directly that the predictive distribution of t is Gaussian with mean

$$t^\star(\boldsymbol{\xi}) = \langle t \rangle_{\{t_1,\ldots,t_p\}} = \sum_{\mu\nu} k_\mu(\boldsymbol{\xi})(\boldsymbol{K}^{-1})_{\mu\nu} t_\nu = \boldsymbol{k}(\boldsymbol{\xi}) \cdot \boldsymbol{K}^{-1}\boldsymbol{t} \tag{7.29}$$

and variance

$$\begin{aligned}
[\Delta t^\star(\boldsymbol{\xi})]^2 &= \langle t^2 \rangle_{\{t_1,\ldots,t_p\}} - \langle t \rangle^2_{\{t_1,\ldots,t_p\}} \\
&= \beta^{-1} + C(\boldsymbol{\xi}, \boldsymbol{\xi}) - \sum_{\mu\nu} k_\mu(\boldsymbol{\xi})(\boldsymbol{K}^{-1})_{\mu\nu} k_\nu(\boldsymbol{\xi}) \\
&= \beta^{-1} + C(\boldsymbol{\xi}, \boldsymbol{\xi}) - \boldsymbol{k}(\boldsymbol{\xi}) \cdot \boldsymbol{K}^{-1}\boldsymbol{k}(\boldsymbol{\xi})
\end{aligned} \tag{7.30}$$

In these expressions, the subscript on $\langle \cdots \rangle_{\{t_1,\ldots,t_p\}}$ indicates the conditioning on $t_1, \ldots, t_p$. We see that prediction with Gaussian process is a good deal simpler than using, for example, MLPs: there is no iterative learning procedure, and equations (7.29, 7.30) give explicit expressions for the prediction $t^\star(\boldsymbol{\xi})$ and the associated error bar $\Delta t^\star(\boldsymbol{\xi})$. The computational effort is reduced to the inversion of the symmetric and positive definite $p \times p$ matrix $\boldsymbol{K}$; this only needs to be done once, even if we want to make predictions at a number of test inputs. That such simplifications occur is all the more striking given the fact that Gaussian processes can capture the properties of functions that would otherwise be described with an *infinite* number of parameters $\boldsymbol{w}$—recall our discussion of MLPs with infinite hidden layers and RBF networks with infinitely many basis functions.

To generalize the above results to nonzero mean Gaussian processes, it is sufficient to note that we can reduce everything back to the case of zero-mean variables by replacing $t_\mu \to t_\mu - a(\boldsymbol{\xi}^\mu)$ and $y_\mu \to y_\mu - a(\boldsymbol{\xi}^\mu)$. This leaves the error bar (7.30) unaffected, but gives for the prediction

$$t^\star(\boldsymbol{\xi}) = a(\boldsymbol{\xi}) + \sum_{\mu\nu} k_\mu(\boldsymbol{\xi})(\boldsymbol{K}^{-1})_{\mu\nu}[t_\nu - a(\boldsymbol{\xi}^\nu)]$$

as the generalization of (7.29).

We conclude by briefly commenting on the problem of evaluating the matrix inverse $\boldsymbol{K}^{-1}$. The CPU time for a matrix inversion scales with the matrix size p as $\mathcal{O}(p^3)$, which for large datasets quickly becomes prohibitive. The search for efficient algorithms to overcome this problem is an active area of research. We mention here only one basic idea which is helpful for online learning, where data points arrive sequentially. Rather than inverting the matrix $\boldsymbol{K}$ afresh every time, one can build it up iteratively. Denote the analogue of the matrix $\boldsymbol{K}$ for the enlarged set of training inputs $\boldsymbol{\xi}^1, \ldots, \boldsymbol{\xi}^{p+1}$ by $\boldsymbol{K}^+$. Then $\boldsymbol{K}^+$ has the block form

$$\boldsymbol{K}^+ = \begin{pmatrix} & \boldsymbol{K} & & k_1 \\ & & & k_2 \\ & & & \vdots \\ & & & k_p \\ k_1 & k_2 & \cdots & \alpha \end{pmatrix}$$

where $\alpha \equiv K^+_{p+1,p+1} = C(\boldsymbol{\xi}^{p+1}, \boldsymbol{\xi}^{p+1}) + 1/\beta$ and we have abbreviated $\boldsymbol{k}(\boldsymbol{\xi}^{p+1})$ to $\boldsymbol{k}$. The result (E.6) from Appendix E for inverses of block matrices then shows that the inverse of $\boldsymbol{K}^+$ has the form

$$(\boldsymbol{K}^+)^{-1} = \begin{pmatrix} & \boldsymbol{K}^{-1} - b\boldsymbol{v}\boldsymbol{v}^{\mathrm{T}} & & v_1 \\ & & & v_2 \\ & & & \vdots \\ & & & v_p \\ v_1 & v_2 & \cdots & 1/b \end{pmatrix}$$

$$\boldsymbol{v} = -\frac{1}{b}\boldsymbol{K}^{-1}\boldsymbol{k} \qquad b = \alpha - \boldsymbol{k}^{\mathrm{T}}\boldsymbol{K}^{-1}\boldsymbol{k}$$

If we know the inverse $\boldsymbol{K}^{-1}$ already, we can therefore calculate the inverse $(\boldsymbol{K}^+)^{-1}$ of the enlarged matrix $\boldsymbol{K}^+$ quite efficiently, in $\mathcal{O}(p^2)$ operations.

7.6 Exercises

Exercise 7.1. (RBF networks and Gaussian processes.) Show that RBFs with Gaussian weight priors generate Gaussian processes. Start from (7.8) and apply the Fourier transform method illustrated in (7.13) to derive explicitly the joint distribution $p(y_1, \ldots, y_p|\boldsymbol{\xi}^1, \ldots, \boldsymbol{\xi}^p)$. You should find that this is a zero-mean Gaussian with covariances $C(\boldsymbol{\xi}^\mu, \boldsymbol{\xi}^\nu)$, where $C(\boldsymbol{\xi}, \boldsymbol{\xi}')$ is the covariance function (7.11). Make sure you understand how this proves that we have a Gaussian process prior.

Exercise 7.2. (GPs with Gaussian noise.) Prove explicitly the statement before (7.24): for a Gaussian process prior combined with Gaussian noise, the *noisy* outputs $t_1, \ldots, t_p$ are jointly Gaussian distributed. Do this by using equation (7.6), inserting $p(t_\mu|y_\mu) = (\beta/2\pi)^{1/2} \exp[-\frac{1}{2}\beta(t_\mu - y_\mu)^2]$ for Gaussian noise together with the Gaussian form of $p(y_1, \ldots, y_p|\boldsymbol{\xi}^1, \ldots, \boldsymbol{\xi}^p)$, and performing the Gaussian integrals over the y_μ. To get to a Gaussian distribution for the t_μ with covariance matrix $K_{\mu\nu}$ needs a bit of shuffling around of the matrix inverses and determinants.

Exercise 7.3. (GPs with Gaussian noise.) Surprisingly, the last exercise is easier if you first introduce an extra Fourier transform to represent the Gaussian noise distributions, by writing $p(t_\mu|y_\mu) = (2\pi)^{-1} \int dk_\mu \exp[ik_\mu(t_\mu - y_\mu) - \frac{1}{2}k_\mu^2/\beta]$. If you then do the integrals over the y_μ, followed by those over the k_μ, you should get the desired Gaussian form of the distribution of the t_μ rather more easily.

Exercise 7.4. (The predictive output distribution.) For the case of a Gaussian process prior and Gaussian output noise, derive the predictive distribution for a new output t corresponding to input $\boldsymbol{\xi}$ by explicitly evaluating the ratio (7.3). Exploit the fact that the numerator and the denominator are Gaussian distributions; see also Appendix D. You should find that t has a Gaussian distribution with mean (7.29) and variance (7.30).

Exercise 7.5. (GP prediction for RBF networks.) In (7.29, 7.30) we worked out the general formulas for the prediction and error bars in Gaussian process regression. We know also that RBFs with Gaussian weight priors define Gaussian processes. So (7.29, 7.30), when applied to the RBF case, should agree with (6.45) from the previous chapter. Verify that this is indeed the case. Suggested route: Define the matrix $\boldsymbol{\Psi}$ by $\Psi_{\mu i} = \phi_i(\boldsymbol{\xi}^\mu)$. Show that $\boldsymbol{K} = \beta^{-1}\mathbf{1} + \alpha^{-1}\boldsymbol{\Psi}\boldsymbol{\Psi}^\dagger$, where $(\boldsymbol{\Psi}^\dagger)_{ij} = (\boldsymbol{\Psi})_{ji}$, and therefore that (7.29) can be written as $t^*(\boldsymbol{\xi}) = \alpha^{-1}\boldsymbol{\Phi}(\boldsymbol{\xi}) \cdot \boldsymbol{\Psi}^\dagger[\beta^{-1}\mathbf{1} + \alpha^{-1}\boldsymbol{\Psi}\boldsymbol{\Psi}^\dagger]^{-1}\boldsymbol{t}$. For (6.45), on the other hand, show that $\boldsymbol{A} = \alpha\mathbf{1} + \beta\boldsymbol{\Psi}^\dagger\boldsymbol{\Psi}$ and hence $t^*(\boldsymbol{\xi}) = \beta\boldsymbol{\Phi}(\boldsymbol{\xi}) \cdot [\alpha\mathbf{1} + \beta\boldsymbol{\Psi}^\dagger\boldsymbol{\Psi}]^{-1}\boldsymbol{\Psi}^\dagger\boldsymbol{t}$. Now use, for example, the Woodbury formula from Appendix E to show that these two expressions for $t^*(\boldsymbol{\xi})$ give the same result. Proceed similarly for the error bar.

8 Support vector machines for binary classification

Support vector machines (SVMs) carry out binary classifications. They involve a preprocessing stage which aims to transform data sets that are not linearly separable into ones that are. First, however, we will have to return to the properties of linearly separable problems, for reasons which will become clear. The preprocessing will be introduced afterwards.

8.1 Optimal separating plane for linearly separable tasks

Linear separations and stability parameters

Consider a linearly separable binary classification task, with a set of data of the usual form $D = \{(\boldsymbol{\xi}^1, t_1), \ldots, (\boldsymbol{\xi}^p, t_p)\}$, where $\boldsymbol{\xi}^\mu \in \mathbb{R}^N$ and $t_\mu \in \{-1, 1\}$. If this problem is linearly separable, we know that

$$\exists \boldsymbol{w} \in \mathbb{R}^N, w_0 \in \mathbb{R}: \quad t_\mu = \mathrm{sgn}(\boldsymbol{w} \cdot \boldsymbol{\xi}^\mu + w_0) \quad \text{for all } (\boldsymbol{\xi}^\mu, t_\mu) \in D \tag{8.1}$$

We even have algorithms which are guaranteed to converge towards a solution $(\boldsymbol{w}, w_0)$ (a 'separating plane') of the type (8.1), for example, the so-called perceptron or AdaTron rules. However, it is clear that in general there are an infinite number of separating planes $(\boldsymbol{w}, w_0)$ that meet the requirements (8.1). See, for example, Figure 8.1 (left panel) for the case $N = 2$; here a separating plane is any line separating all points $\boldsymbol{\xi}^\mu$ with $t_\mu = 1$ (marked $+$) from those with $t_\mu = -1$ (marked $\times$).

A natural question to ask is whether one can quantify the quality of the various solutions of (8.1). This can be done on the basis of generalization performance: a good plane $(\boldsymbol{w}, w_0)$ is one which where possible keeps a safe distance from the data points, so that detrimental effects of noise (which might change the locations of these points slightly) are minimal. Hence we wish to measure not only whether points are correctly classified by a candidate separating plane, but also the *distance* of such a plane to the data points. Both are given by the so-called *stability parameters* γ_μ, one for every data point:

$$\gamma_\mu(\boldsymbol{w}, w_0) = t_\mu(\boldsymbol{w} \cdot \boldsymbol{\xi}^\mu + w_0)/|\boldsymbol{w}| \tag{8.2}$$

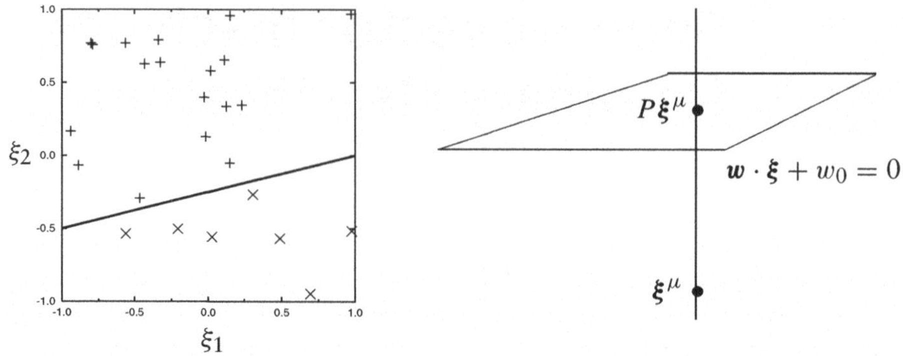

Figure 8.1 Left: illustration of a linearly separable task for $(N = 2)$-dimensional inputs. A linear separation is here performed by any line $\boldsymbol{w}\cdot\boldsymbol{\xi}+w_0 = 0$ that separates all points $\boldsymbol{\xi}^\mu$ with $t_\mu = 1$ (marked +) from those with $t_\mu = -1$ (marked $\times$). Note that there will generally be infinitely many such lines. Right: measuring separation quality on the basis of the distance of data points $\boldsymbol{\xi}^\mu$ from the separating plane as calculated via projection; see the main text.

These stability parameters have the following properties:

- The plane $(\boldsymbol{w}, w_0)$ correctly classifies point $\boldsymbol{\xi}^\mu$ if and only if $\gamma_\mu(\boldsymbol{w}, w_0) > 0$.
- The distance of the plane $(\boldsymbol{w}, w_0)$ to point $\boldsymbol{\xi}^\mu$ is $|\gamma_\mu(\boldsymbol{w}, w_0)|$.

The first property is immediately obvious from (8.1). Demonstrating the second property requires only simple geometry. We first construct a parametrization of the line in $\mathbb{R}^N$ which goes through $\boldsymbol{\xi}^\mu$ and is orthogonal to our plane (see Figure 8.1, right panel): $\boldsymbol{\xi}(\rho) = \boldsymbol{\xi}^\mu + \rho\boldsymbol{w}$ ($\rho \in \mathbb{R}$). Insertion into the plane's equation $\boldsymbol{w}\cdot\boldsymbol{\xi}+w_0 = 0$ gives the solution $\rho = -(\boldsymbol{w}\cdot\boldsymbol{\xi}^\mu+w_0)/\boldsymbol{w}^2$. Hence the projection $P\boldsymbol{\xi}^\mu$ of $\boldsymbol{\xi}^\mu$ onto the plane $(\boldsymbol{w}, w_0)$ is given by

$$P\boldsymbol{\xi}^\mu = \boldsymbol{\xi}^\mu - \boldsymbol{w}\left(\frac{\boldsymbol{w}\cdot\boldsymbol{\xi}^\mu + w_0}{\boldsymbol{w}^2}\right)$$

Thus the desired distance $|\boldsymbol{\xi}^\mu - P\boldsymbol{\xi}^\mu|$ indeed equals

$$|\boldsymbol{\xi}^\mu - P\boldsymbol{\xi}^\mu| = \left|\boldsymbol{w}\left(\frac{\boldsymbol{w}\cdot\boldsymbol{\xi}^\mu + w_0}{\boldsymbol{w}^2}\right)\right| = |\gamma_\mu(\boldsymbol{w}, w_0)|$$

as claimed, using that $|t_\mu| = 1$ for all μ. As a consequence of the properties of the stability parameters we may now sharpen our requirements of a separating plane:

$$\begin{array}{l}\text{all data points separated correctly and}\\ \text{all data points at distance} \geq \kappa \text{ from}\\ \quad\text{the plane}\end{array} \iff \gamma_\mu(\boldsymbol{w}, w_0) \geq \kappa > 0 \quad \forall\mu$$

There will be an upper limit to the values of the distance $\kappa > 0$ which are compatible with correct separation, since clearly 2κ cannot be larger than the minimum distance[22] between data points $\boldsymbol{\xi}^\mu$ with $t_\mu = 1$ and data points $\boldsymbol{\xi}^\nu$ with $t_\nu = -1$. However, if we choose a value of κ such that a solution $(\boldsymbol{w}, w_0)$ of (8.1) exists, then there is an algorithm which is guaranteed to achieve the objective. This is a straightforward generalization of the classic perceptron learning rule, which is indeed recovered for $\kappa \to 0$:

(1) draw at random a $\mu \in \{1, \ldots, p\}$;

(2) calculate $\gamma_\mu(\boldsymbol{w}, w_0)$ as given in (8.2);

(3) if $\gamma_\mu(\boldsymbol{w}, w_0) < \kappa$, modify parameters: $\boldsymbol{w} \to \boldsymbol{w} + t_\mu \boldsymbol{\xi}^\mu$, $w_0 \to w_0 + t_\mu$;

(4) return to 1.

The generalized perceptron convergence theorem, which was proved by E. Gardner, states that if $\exists \boldsymbol{w}^\star \in \mathbb{R}^N, w_0^\star \in \mathbb{R}: \gamma_\mu(\boldsymbol{w}^\star, w_0^\star) > \kappa$ for all $\mu \in \{1, \ldots, p\}$, then the above algorithm will converge towards a solution $(\boldsymbol{w}, w_0)$ with $\gamma_\mu(\boldsymbol{w}, w_0) \geq \kappa$ in a finite number of iteration steps.

The proof will not be given here. For $w_0 = 0$ it is a simple generalization of the original perceptron convergence proof. For $w_0 \neq 0$, however, the situation is more complicated; the reason is that the threshold w_0 does not occur in the denominator of the stability parameters (8.2), so that it cannot simply be absorbed into the classic proof by adding a 'dummy' extra component $\xi_0^\mu = 1$ to all input vectors $\boldsymbol{\xi}^\mu$.

Figure 8.2 illustrates perceptron learning with stability for a perceptron having $N = 500$ input nodes. A set of $p = 750$ input patterns $\boldsymbol{\xi}^\mu$, with zero-mean unit-variance Gaussian random components ξ_i^μ, half of them classified as $t_\mu = 1$, the other half as $t_\mu = -1$, is generated and the perceptron is trained to separate them according to their classification, with stability $\kappa = 0.125$. The figure shows the projections of the input patterns onto a two-dimensional space spanned by the weight vector $\boldsymbol{w}$ and a fixed random vector orthogonal to $\boldsymbol{w}$ as learning proceeds. Before learning, no structure is visible in this projection. After 30 complete sweeps through the pattern set, the system has picked up the direction in which linear separation is possible but misclassifications still occur. After 60 sweeps the number of outright misclassifications is down to 4, but the desired stability has not yet been reached for several more of the correctly classified patterns.

[22] We assume implicitly here and in the following that the data set does contain points from both classes; otherwise the separation task is clearly trivial.

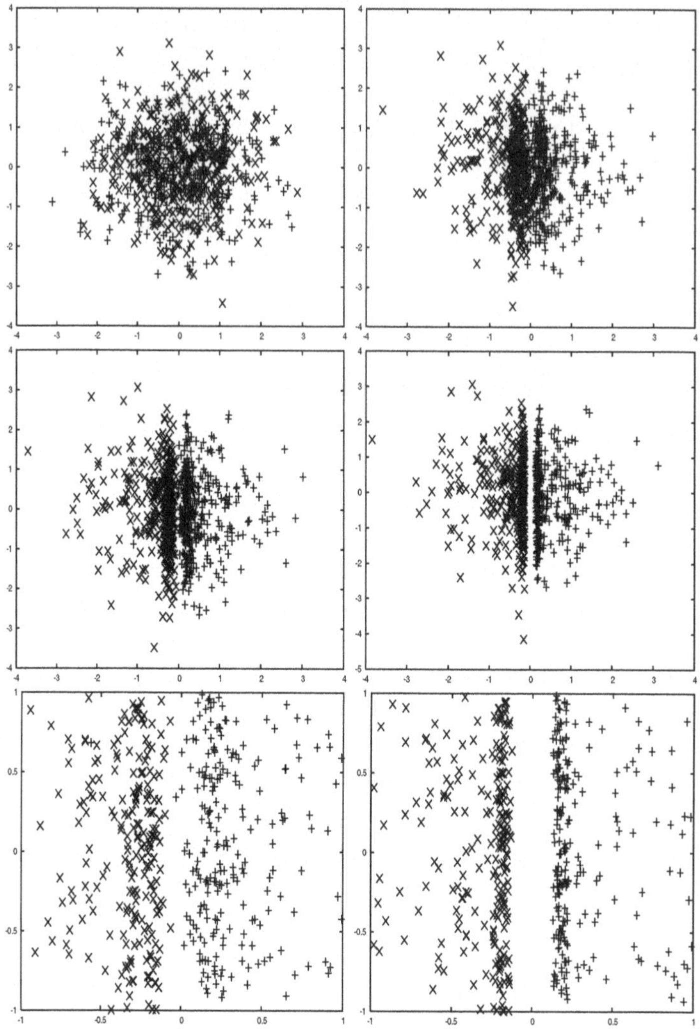

Figure 8.2 Illustration of perceptron learning with stability as described in the main text. Before learning (upper left panel) the perceptron misclassifies approximately 50% of the patterns; no structure is visible in the projection onto a plane spanned by the weight vector and a random vector orthogonal to it. The following panels (upper right, middle left) show the situation after 30 and 60 complete learning sweeps through the pattern set, while the middle right panel depicts the situation when linear separation with the desired stability is completed after 358 sweeps. The lower two panels show enlarged central regions of the two middle ones above them.

The optimal separating plane

We are now in a position to define the optimal separating plane $(\boldsymbol{w}^\star, w_0^\star)$ as the one having the largest κ. Equivalently, the *smallest* of the $\{\gamma_\mu(\boldsymbol{w}, w_0)\}$ (i.e. the stability parameter of the data point which is most in danger of being misclassified when data are subject to noise) should be as large as possible:

$$\text{Optimal separating plane } (\boldsymbol{w}^\star, w_0^\star) = \arg\max_{(\boldsymbol{w},w_0)} [\min_\mu \gamma_\mu(\boldsymbol{w}, w_0)] \tag{8.3}$$

Note that:

- If the problem is linearly separable, then definition (8.3) will produce a separating plane with the largest distance to the closest data point. If the problem is not linearly separable, definition (8.3) will produce a plane which does not separate the data (since that is impossible), but for which the largest distance from the plane among misclassified points is minimal.
- By construction, there must be at least two μ such that $\gamma_\mu(\boldsymbol{w}^\star, w_0^\star) = \min_\rho \gamma_\rho(\boldsymbol{w}^\star, w_0^\star)$ for the optimal separating plane (8.3) (see, for example, Figure 8.1 and Figure 8.4).

Finding the optimal plane has now been reduced to a well-defined optimization problem (8.3). The only remaining issue is that its solution $(\boldsymbol{w}^\star, w_0^\star)$ is still not unique, since there remains the trivial degree of freedom relating to overall scaling: if we multiply $(\boldsymbol{w}, w_0) \to (\rho\boldsymbol{w}, \rho w_0)$ with $\rho > 0$ we simply get the same plane. To eliminate this freedom we nail down ρ by insisting that

$$\min_\mu t_\mu(\boldsymbol{w} \cdot \boldsymbol{\xi}^\mu + w_0) = 1$$

which, given the assumption of linear separability, is always possible. This implies that $\min_\mu \gamma_\mu(\boldsymbol{w}, w_0) = 1/|\boldsymbol{w}|$, and that

$$\max_{(\boldsymbol{w},w_0)} [\min_\mu \gamma_\mu(\boldsymbol{w}, w_0)] = 1/\min_{(\boldsymbol{w},w_0)} |\boldsymbol{w}|$$

Hence we have now converted the initial optimization problem (8.3) into

$$\text{find: } \min_{(\boldsymbol{w},w_0)} \tfrac{1}{2}\boldsymbol{w}^2 \quad \text{subject to} \quad t_\mu(\boldsymbol{w} \cdot \boldsymbol{\xi}^\mu + w_0) \geq 1 \;\; \forall\mu \tag{8.4}$$

8.2 Representation in terms of support vectors

Background: optimization theory

The optimization problem (8.4) is of the following general form. If we set $\boldsymbol{x} = (\boldsymbol{w}, w_0)$ and define

$$f(\boldsymbol{x}) \equiv f(\boldsymbol{w}, w_0) = \tfrac{1}{2}\boldsymbol{w}^2 \qquad c_\mu(\boldsymbol{x}) = t_\mu(\boldsymbol{w} \cdot \boldsymbol{\xi}^\mu + w_0) - 1 \tag{8.5}$$

we have

$$\text{find:} \quad \min_{x} f(x) \quad \text{subject to } c_\mu(x) \geq 0 \;\; \forall \mu \tag{8.6}$$

A direct (say numerical) attack on this problem may be possible for small N, but becomes difficult for large N. This issue becomes even more severe after the preprocessing considered below, where the dimensionality of the vector $\boldsymbol{w}$ can be much larger than N (and in fact effectively infinite). It is therefore useful to transform our problem to a version written in terms of Lagrange multipliers; there are only p of those, one for each of the constraints. To achieve this transformation, we need a little background on optimization problems with inequality constraints of the type (8.6). We assume that the functions f and c_μ are all 'nice', that is, at least have smooth first derivatives.

Suppose we have found a local minimum $\boldsymbol{x}$ of (8.6). (We dispense with the superscript '$*$' for optimal quantities in the following when no confusion can arise.) Then the value of f at a nearby point $\boldsymbol{x} + \boldsymbol{\Delta}$ is $f(\boldsymbol{x} + \boldsymbol{\Delta}) = f(\boldsymbol{x}) + \boldsymbol{\Delta} \cdot \boldsymbol{g}$ for small $\boldsymbol{\Delta}$, where $\boldsymbol{g} = \nabla f(\boldsymbol{x})$. In an unconstrained problem, this gives us the familiar condition $\boldsymbol{g} = 0$ for a minimum; otherwise we could reduce the value of f by choosing $\boldsymbol{\Delta}$ along $-\boldsymbol{g}$. For a constrained problem we can argue similarly, but have to consider that not all changes $\boldsymbol{\Delta}$ are necessarily feasible, that is, compatible with the constraints $c_\mu \geq 0$. Constraints with $c_\mu(\boldsymbol{x}) > 0$ are called inactive at $\boldsymbol{x}$ because they do not restrict $\boldsymbol{\Delta}$: for small enough $\boldsymbol{\Delta}$, we will still have $c_\mu(\boldsymbol{x} + \boldsymbol{\Delta}) > 0$. We can therefore focus on the set of active constraints, $A = \{\mu | c_\mu(\boldsymbol{x}) = 0\}$. For every $\mu \in A$, $c_\mu(\boldsymbol{x} + \boldsymbol{\Delta}) = c_\mu(\boldsymbol{x}) + \boldsymbol{\Delta} \cdot \boldsymbol{a}_\mu = \boldsymbol{\Delta} \cdot \boldsymbol{a}_\mu$ for small $\boldsymbol{\Delta}$, where $\boldsymbol{a}_\mu = \nabla c_\mu(\boldsymbol{x})$. Thus, a small enough change $\boldsymbol{\Delta}$ is feasible if $\boldsymbol{\Delta} \cdot \boldsymbol{a}_\mu \geq 0$ for all $\mu \in A$. At a local minimum we must not have any such $\boldsymbol{\Delta}$ which simultaneously reduces the value of f, that is, which has $\boldsymbol{\Delta} \cdot \boldsymbol{g} < 0$. This is the case exactly if we can write $\boldsymbol{g} = \sum_{\mu \in A} \lambda_\mu \boldsymbol{a}_\mu$ with $\lambda_\mu \geq 0$, a result known as Farkas' lemma. One direction of the proof is easy: if indeed $\boldsymbol{g} = \sum_{\mu \in A} \lambda_\mu \boldsymbol{a}_\mu$, then $\boldsymbol{\Delta} \cdot \boldsymbol{g} = \sum_{\mu \in A} \lambda_\mu \boldsymbol{\Delta} \cdot \boldsymbol{a}_\mu \geq 0$ for any feasible $\boldsymbol{\Delta}$, since $\lambda_\mu \geq 0$ and $\boldsymbol{\Delta} \cdot \boldsymbol{a}_\mu \geq 0$. The reverse direction can be seen geometrically. The set of vectors $\{\boldsymbol{v} = \sum_{\mu \in A} \lambda_\mu \boldsymbol{a}_\mu | \lambda_\mu \geq 0 \, \forall \mu\}$ is a *cone*. If $\boldsymbol{g}$ is not contained in this cone, there is a hyperplane which separates $\boldsymbol{g}$ and the cone. By choosing $\boldsymbol{\Delta}$ proportional to the normal vector of this plane, we can thus ensure that $\boldsymbol{\Delta} \cdot \boldsymbol{g} < 0$ while simultaneously $\boldsymbol{\Delta} \cdot \boldsymbol{v} > 0$ for all $\boldsymbol{v}$ in the cone (and thus in particular for all $\boldsymbol{a}_\mu$), so that $\boldsymbol{\Delta}$ is a feasible step which reduces f.

So far, we have established that at a local minimum $\boldsymbol{x}$ of the optimization problem (8.6) we must have $\nabla f(\boldsymbol{x}) = \sum_{\mu \in A} \lambda_\mu \nabla c_\mu(\boldsymbol{x})$ with $\lambda_\mu \geq 0$. We can extend the sum to include also the inactive constraints if we require the associated λ_μ to be zero. This condition can be written as $\lambda_\mu c_\mu(\boldsymbol{x}) = 0$ since $c_\mu(\boldsymbol{x}) > 0$ for inactive constraints, and then in fact applies to all μ because for active constraints $c_\mu(\boldsymbol{x})$ itself is zero. Altogether, a local minimum $\boldsymbol{x}$ of (8.6) together with the associated λ_μ must satisfy

$$\nabla f(\boldsymbol{x}) - \sum_\mu \lambda_\mu \nabla c_\mu(\boldsymbol{x}) = 0 \text{ and}$$

$$c_\mu(\boldsymbol{x}) \geq 0, \quad \lambda_\mu \geq 0, \quad \lambda_\mu c_\mu(\boldsymbol{x}) = 0 \;\; \forall \mu \tag{8.7}$$

with the sum now running over all constraints, $\mu = 1, \ldots, p$. The conditions (8.7) are known as the Karush–Kuhn–Tucker (KKT) conditions; the λ_μ are called Lagrange multipliers. They are familiar from the solution of optimization problems with equality constraints $c_\mu(\boldsymbol{x}) = 0$, where conditions similar to (8.7) apply but the λ_μ can be both positive and negative. Also as in the case of equality constraints, one notes that the first condition in (8.7) can be written as $\nabla_{\boldsymbol{x}} L(\boldsymbol{x}, \boldsymbol{\lambda}) = 0$, where $\boldsymbol{\lambda} = (\lambda_1, \ldots, \lambda_p)$ and the function

$$L(\boldsymbol{x}, \boldsymbol{\lambda}) = f(\boldsymbol{x}) - \sum_\mu \lambda_\mu c_\mu(\boldsymbol{x}) \tag{8.8}$$

is known as the Lagrangian.

The Wolfe dual

Based on the KKT conditions we can further transform the optimization problem into a *maximization* problem. This is possible if—as it turns out to be in our case—the Lagrangian is *convex* in $\boldsymbol{x}$ for any fixed $\boldsymbol{\lambda}$ with $\lambda_\mu \geq 0$ for all μ; we write the latter condition as $\boldsymbol{\lambda} \geq \boldsymbol{0}$ for short. The condition for a function $F(\boldsymbol{x})$ to be convex (see Appendix G) is that, for arbitrary $\boldsymbol{x}$ and $\boldsymbol{x}'$,

$$F((1-\theta)\boldsymbol{x} + \theta \boldsymbol{x}') \leq (1-\theta)F(\boldsymbol{x}) + \theta F(\boldsymbol{x}') \quad \text{for } 0 < \theta < 1 \tag{8.9}$$

As Figure 8.3 illustrates, a convex function thus always curves upward rather than downward. From this it also follows that it lies above any tangent: (8.9) can be written as $F(\boldsymbol{x} + \theta(\boldsymbol{x}' - \boldsymbol{x})) - F(\boldsymbol{x}) \leq \theta[F(\boldsymbol{x}') - F(\boldsymbol{x})]$. Dividing by θ and taking $\theta \to 0$ thus gives $(\boldsymbol{x}' - \boldsymbol{x}) \cdot \nabla F(\boldsymbol{x}) \leq F(\boldsymbol{x}') - F(\boldsymbol{x})$ or

$$F(\boldsymbol{x}') \geq F(\boldsymbol{x}) + (\boldsymbol{x}' - \boldsymbol{x}) \cdot \nabla F(\boldsymbol{x}) \tag{8.10}$$

which means that $F(\boldsymbol{x}')$ is above the tangent plane at the point $\boldsymbol{x}$ (see Figure 8.3).

Under the assumption of a convex Lagrangian, the Wolfe dual can now be stated as follows. A local *minimum* $\boldsymbol{x}$ of our original optimization problem (8.6) together with the associated Lagrange multipliers $\boldsymbol{\lambda}$ also solves the

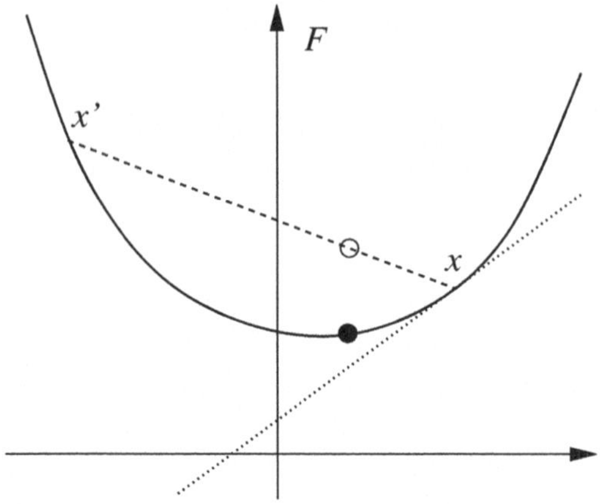

Figure 8.3 Illustration of convexity for a function $F(x)$. The convexity criterion (8.9) says that the linear interpolation (dashed line) between two function values, $(1-\theta)F(x)+\theta F(x')$ must always lie above the function value $F((1-\theta)x+\theta x')$ at the corresponding argument; an example is shown by the open and filled circles. Alternatively, from (8.10), the function must lie above any tangent to it, as illustrated here for the tangent at x (dotted line).

following *maximization* problem:

$$\text{find:} \quad \max_{\boldsymbol{x},\boldsymbol{\lambda}} L(\boldsymbol{x},\boldsymbol{\lambda}) \quad \text{subject to } \nabla_{\boldsymbol{x}} L(\boldsymbol{x},\boldsymbol{\lambda}) = 0, \;\; \boldsymbol{\lambda} \geq 0 \tag{8.11}$$

To prove this statement, assume that $\boldsymbol{x}^*$ is a local minimum of (8.6); together with the corresponding Lagrange multipliers $\boldsymbol{\lambda}^*$ it therefore obeys (8.7). Now consider any other point $\boldsymbol{x}$, $\boldsymbol{\lambda}$ which obeys the constraints in (8.11), that is, $\nabla_{\boldsymbol{x}} L(\boldsymbol{x},\boldsymbol{\lambda}) = 0$ and $\boldsymbol{\lambda} \geq 0$. Then

$$\begin{aligned}
L(\boldsymbol{x}^*,\boldsymbol{\lambda}^*) &= f(\boldsymbol{x}^*) - \sum_\mu \lambda^*_\mu c_\mu(\boldsymbol{x}^*) \\
&= f(\boldsymbol{x}^*) && \text{(KKT conditions)} \\
&\geq f(\boldsymbol{x}^*) - \sum_\mu \lambda_\mu c_\mu(\boldsymbol{x}^*) && (\lambda_\mu \geq 0,\ c_\mu(\boldsymbol{x}^*) \geq 0) \\
&= L(\boldsymbol{x}^*,\boldsymbol{\lambda}) \\
&\geq L(\boldsymbol{x},\boldsymbol{\lambda}) + (\boldsymbol{x}^* - \boldsymbol{x}) \cdot \nabla_{\boldsymbol{x}} L(\boldsymbol{x},\boldsymbol{\lambda}) && \text{(convexity of } L\text{, (8.10))} \\
&= L(\boldsymbol{x},\boldsymbol{\lambda}) && (\nabla_{\boldsymbol{x}} L(\boldsymbol{x},\boldsymbol{\lambda}) = 0)
\end{aligned} \tag{8.12}$$

This shows that $\boldsymbol{x}^*$, $\boldsymbol{\lambda}^*$ solves the maximization problem (8.11). The first step in the proof shows in addition that the maximal value of L equals the minimum value of f, that is, $f(\boldsymbol{x}^*)$. In fact, convexity of L implies that all local minima of (8.6) are also global minima and have the same value of f.

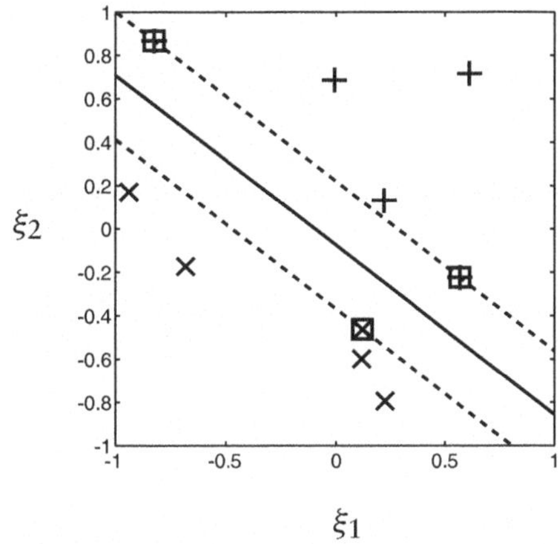

Figure 8.4 Illustration of SVM classification of $(N = 2)$-dimensional inputs (ξ_1, ξ_2). Points with $t_\mu = 1$ and $t_\mu = -1$ are marked by $+$ and $\times$, respectively. The solid line is the optimal separating plane (which in two dimensions becomes a line). The dashed lines correspond to $\boldsymbol{w} \cdot \boldsymbol{\xi} + w_0 = \pm 1$, respectively. The support vectors, marked by $\square$, lie on these lines as they must; they have the minimal distance from the separating plane.

Application to SVMs

We now apply these tools to our SVM optimization problem (8.4). The Lagrangian is, from (8.5),

$$L = \frac{1}{2}\boldsymbol{w}^2 - \sum_\mu \lambda_\mu [t_\mu(\boldsymbol{w} \cdot \boldsymbol{\xi}^\mu + w_0) - 1] \tag{8.13}$$

The first part $\nabla_{\boldsymbol{x}} L = 0$ of the KKT conditions (8.7) becomes $\nabla_{\boldsymbol{w}} L = 0$ and $\partial L / \partial w_0 = 0$, that is,

$$\boldsymbol{w} = \sum_\mu \lambda_\mu t_\mu \boldsymbol{\xi}^\mu \qquad \sum_\mu \lambda_\mu t_\mu = 0 \tag{8.14}$$

This needs to be solved together with $c_\mu = t_\mu(\boldsymbol{w} \cdot \boldsymbol{\xi}^\mu + w_0) - 1 \geq 0$, $\lambda_\mu \geq 0$ and $\lambda_\mu c_\mu = 0$ for all μ. From (8.14) we see that the optimal $\boldsymbol{w}$ is a superposition of those input vectors $\boldsymbol{\xi}^\mu$ with $\lambda_\mu > 0$. These are called the *support vectors* and we denote the relevant set of data point indices by $S = \{\mu | \lambda_\mu > 0\}$. Note that from the KKT condition $\lambda_\mu c_\mu = 0$, we have $c_\mu = 0$ for all $\mu \in S$ so that the support vector set S is a subset of the set A of active constraints. The two sets differ only in those exceptional μ for which the constraint is active ($c_\mu = 0$) but which nevertheless have $\lambda_\mu = 0$. Geometrically, the situation is as follows (see Figure 8.4):

- All support vectors have the minimal distance from the separating plane, since the distance for pattern μ equals $\gamma_\mu = t_\mu(\boldsymbol{w} \cdot \boldsymbol{\xi}^\mu + w_0)/|\boldsymbol{w}|$ and $c_\mu = 0$

is equivalent to $t_\mu(\boldsymbol{w}\cdot\boldsymbol{\xi}^\mu+w_0)=1$, hence $\gamma_\mu=1/|\boldsymbol{w}|$. There can be non-support vectors at the same, minimal, distance from the separating plane; these are the exceptional $\boldsymbol{\xi}^\mu$ with $\mu\in A$ but $\mu\notin S$.

- Only support vectors occur in the construction of the optimal separating plane. All other inputs, having at least the minimal distance from the separating plane, are classified correctly once the support vectors are.

Once we know the set of support vectors, we can in fact write down explicit expressions for $\boldsymbol{w}$ and w_0. We will need the following (symmetric and non-negative definite) $|S|\times|S|$ matrix $\boldsymbol{C}$:

$$C_{\mu\nu}=t_\mu t_\nu(\boldsymbol{\xi}^\mu\cdot\boldsymbol{\xi}^\nu)\quad\text{for }\mu,\nu\in S \tag{8.15}$$

Using the expression for $\boldsymbol{w}$ from (8.14), the condition that $c_\mu=0$ for all $\mu\in S$ can be written as

$$t_\mu\left[\sum_{\nu\in S}\lambda_\nu t_\nu(\boldsymbol{\xi}^\mu\cdot\boldsymbol{\xi}^\nu)+w_0\right]=1 \tag{8.16}$$

and this system of linear equations is solved by

$$\lambda_\mu=\sum_{\nu\in S}(\boldsymbol{C}^{-1})_{\mu\nu}(1-w_0t_\nu)\quad\text{for }\mu\in S \tag{8.17}$$

Inserting into the second part of (8.14) then gives us the threshold w_0 as

$$w_0=\frac{\sum_{\mu\nu\in S}t_\mu(\boldsymbol{C}^{-1})_{\mu\nu}}{\sum_{\mu\nu\in S}t_\mu(\boldsymbol{C}^{-1})_{\mu\nu}t_\nu} \tag{8.18}$$

Note that the last two identities also hold if instead of the set of support vectors $\mu\in S$ we consider the larger active set $\mu\in A$, and a correspondingly enlarged matrix $\boldsymbol{C}$. This is because we only exploited the support vector assumption through the condition $c_\mu=0$, which also holds for $\mu\in A$.

If we already know the optimal normal vector $\boldsymbol{w}$ of the hyperplane, we can of course deduce w_0 by a simpler method than (8.18). Consider any support vector $\boldsymbol{\xi}^\mu$. This has $c_\mu=0$ and hence (using $t_\mu^2=1$) $\boldsymbol{w}\cdot\boldsymbol{\xi}^\mu+w_0=t_\mu$. Thus

$$w_0=t_\mu-\boldsymbol{w}\cdot\boldsymbol{\xi}^\mu\quad\text{for any }\mu\in S \tag{8.19}$$

Alternatively, adding two identities of this type for two support vectors (μ,ν) with opposite outputs, that is, $t_\mu=-t_\nu$, we could write $w_0=-\frac{1}{2}\boldsymbol{w}\cdot(\boldsymbol{\xi}^\mu+\boldsymbol{\xi}^\nu)$.

Next we consider the Wolfe dual form of the SVM optimization problem; the Lagrangian (8.13) is clearly convex in $(\boldsymbol{w},w_0)$ (see Exercise 8.1).

From (8.11), we need to maximize this Lagrangian over w_0, $\boldsymbol{w}$, and $\boldsymbol{\lambda}$, subject to the conditions (8.14) and $\boldsymbol{\lambda} \geq \mathbf{0}$. But the expression for $\boldsymbol{w}$ in (8.14) in fact lets us eliminate $\boldsymbol{w}$ directly, and the second part of (8.14) also removes the term involving w_0, giving

$$
\begin{aligned}
L &= \frac{1}{2}\Big(\sum_\mu \lambda_\mu t_\mu \boldsymbol{\xi}^\mu\Big)^2 - \sum_\mu \lambda_\mu t_\mu \Big(\sum_\nu \lambda_\nu t_\nu \boldsymbol{\xi}^\nu\Big)\cdot\boldsymbol{\xi}^\mu - \sum_\mu \lambda_\mu t_\mu w_0 + \sum_\mu \lambda_\mu \\
&= -\frac{1}{2}\sum_{\mu\nu} \lambda_\mu \lambda_\nu t_\mu t_\nu \boldsymbol{\xi}^\mu \cdot \boldsymbol{\xi}^\nu + \sum_\mu \lambda_\mu
\end{aligned}
$$

Our Wolfe dual therefore becomes

$$
\text{find:} \quad \begin{aligned}
&\max_{\boldsymbol{\lambda}} \Big(-\frac{1}{2}\sum_{\mu\nu} \lambda_\mu \lambda_\nu t_\mu t_\nu \boldsymbol{\xi}^\mu \cdot \boldsymbol{\xi}^\nu + \sum_\mu \lambda_\mu \Big) \\
&\text{subject to } \sum_\mu \lambda_\mu t_\mu = 0, \quad \boldsymbol{\lambda} \geq \mathbf{0}
\end{aligned} \tag{8.20}
$$

This achieves our original aim of having an optimization problem containing only the p Lagrange multipliers λ_μ, independently of the dimension of the space in which $\boldsymbol{w}$ 'lives' (which so far is identical to the input space dimension N but can be much larger after preprocessing as shown below).

A simple example

Let us assume, for simplicity, that the input vectors in our data set D are orthogonal and normalized, that is, $\boldsymbol{\xi}^\mu \cdot \boldsymbol{\xi}^\nu = \delta_{\mu\nu}$ (which implies also that $p \leq N$). In this case the function to be maximized in the Wolfe dual (8.20) becomes simply $-\frac{1}{2}\sum_\mu \lambda_\mu^2 + \sum_\mu \lambda_\mu$, a sum of p identical terms. If we ignore the inequality constraints in (8.20) for now and take the equality constraint into account via a Lagrange multiplier a, we get as the necessary condition for a maximum

$$
\frac{\partial}{\partial \lambda_\nu} \sum_\mu \Big(-\frac{1}{2}\lambda_\mu^2 + \lambda_\mu - a\lambda_\mu t_\mu \Big) = 0
$$

and hence $\lambda_\nu = 1 - a t_\nu$. Inserting into the constraint $\sum_\mu \lambda_\mu t_\mu = 0$ gives $\sum_\mu (t_\mu - a) = 0$, that is,

$$
\lambda_\mu = 1 - a t_\mu \qquad a = \frac{1}{p}\sum_\mu t_\mu
$$

If there are training outputs from both classes as assumed, then $-1 < a < 1$ and so $\lambda_\mu > 0$. Our solution thus automatically satisfies the inequality constraints of the Wolfe dual and is therefore the optimal solution. Because of the very simple structure of our example, all inputs are support vectors. To find w_0, we can apply (8.19), $\boldsymbol{w} = \sum_\nu \lambda_\nu t_\nu \boldsymbol{\xi}^\nu$ and $\boldsymbol{\xi}^\mu \cdot \boldsymbol{\xi}^\nu = \delta_{\mu\nu}$ to get

$$w_0 = t_\mu - \boldsymbol{w} \cdot \boldsymbol{\xi}^\mu = t_\mu - t_\mu \lambda_\mu = t_\mu[1 - (1 - a t_\mu)] = a$$

Our final solution for the separating hyperplane is therefore

$$\boldsymbol{w} = \sum_\mu (t_\mu - w_0)\boldsymbol{\xi}^\mu \qquad w_0 = \frac{1}{p}\sum_\mu t_\mu$$

This is also known as the 'biased Hebb rule'. The corresponding stability parameters $\gamma_\mu = |\boldsymbol{w}|^{-1}$ are all equal since $\mu \in S$ for all μ, and explicitly given by

$$\gamma_\mu = \left[\sum_\mu (t_\mu - w_0)^2\right]^{-1/2} = [p - 2pw_0^2 + pw_0^2]^{-1/2} = [p(1 - w_0^2)]^{-1/2}$$

For the sake of illustration, let us show how to retrieve this solution from (8.17, 8.18), in their versions extended to all $\mu \in A$. In the present example $C_{\mu\nu} = \delta_{\mu\nu}$, so that (8.17) becomes $\lambda_\mu = 1 - w_0 t_\mu$ for all $\mu \in A$. Equation (8.18) for w_0 also simplifies to

$$w_0 = \frac{1}{|A|}\sum_{\mu \in A} t_\mu$$

which implies in particular $-1 \le w_0 \le 1$. To show that this is the same solution as before, it remains to establish that *all* μ are in A. This is easily shown by contradiction. Any $\mu \notin A$ would have, by definition, $c_\mu > 0$ and thus $\lambda_\mu = 0$ from the KKT conditions (8.7). But then $c_\mu = t_\mu(\boldsymbol{w} \cdot \boldsymbol{\xi}^\mu + w_0) - 1 = t_\mu(t_\mu \lambda_\mu + w_0) - 1 = t_\mu w_0 - 1$, which clearly cannot be positive for $-1 \le w_0 \le 1$ and $t_\mu = \pm 1$.

The above example was chosen for ease of calculation. It is atypical in the sense that all training inputs turned out to be support vectors. In many applications on real-world data, it turns out that the SVM solution is *sparse*, that is, only a small fraction of the λ_μ are nonzero. This is obviously a desirable feature; it means, for example, that evaluating predictions on new data points (see (8.25)) can be relatively fast even for large data sets.

8.3 Preprocessing and SVM kernels

Preprocessing

Let us now turn to problems which are not linearly separable, but could possibly be made so via suitable preprocessing. This implies that we will no longer view the $\boldsymbol{\xi}$ as the input vectors, but regard them as the outcome of some preprocessing of true input vectors $\boldsymbol{x} \in \mathbb{R}^N$, according to $\boldsymbol{\xi} = \boldsymbol{\Phi}(\boldsymbol{x}) \in \mathbb{R}^M$. Here $\boldsymbol{\Phi}(\boldsymbol{x}) = (\phi_1(\boldsymbol{x}), \ldots, \phi_M(\boldsymbol{x}))$ and usually $M > N$, so that the preprocessing maps the data into a higher-dimensional space where one expects linear separation to be easier to achieve. If we write the overall action of our classification machine as $\mathcal{S}(\boldsymbol{x}) \in \{-1, 1\}$ we thus have

$$\mathcal{S}(\boldsymbol{x}) = \text{sgn}(\boldsymbol{w} \cdot \boldsymbol{\Phi}(\boldsymbol{x}) + w_0) \tag{8.21}$$

The set of preprocessing operations $\phi_i(\boldsymbol{x})$ is typically chosen to contain non-linear functions (otherwise there would be no point in preprocessing), such as

$$\phi_i(\boldsymbol{x}) = x_i \quad \text{for } i = 1, \ldots, N$$

$$\phi_{N+i}(\boldsymbol{x}) = x_i^2 \quad \text{for } i = 1, \ldots, N$$

$$\phi_{2N+1}(\boldsymbol{x}) = x_1 x_2 \qquad \phi_{2N+2}(\boldsymbol{x}) = x_1 x_3 \qquad \phi_{2N+3}(\boldsymbol{x}) = x_2 x_3 \text{ etc.}$$

Our previous results regarding the optimal separating plane can now be applied directly by making the replacement $\boldsymbol{\xi}^\mu \to \boldsymbol{\Phi}(\boldsymbol{x}^\mu)$ everywhere, leading to the following representations of the optimal $\boldsymbol{w}$ and w_0

$$\boldsymbol{w} = \sum_\mu \lambda_\mu t_\mu \boldsymbol{\Phi}(\boldsymbol{x}^\mu) \tag{8.22}$$

$$\begin{aligned} w_0 &= t_\mu - \boldsymbol{w} \cdot \boldsymbol{\Phi}(\boldsymbol{x}^\mu) \\ &= t_\mu - \sum_\nu \lambda_\nu t_\nu \boldsymbol{\Phi}(\boldsymbol{x}^\mu) \cdot \boldsymbol{\Phi}(\boldsymbol{x}^\nu) \quad \text{for any } \mu \in S \end{aligned} \tag{8.23}$$

The support vectors are now those $\boldsymbol{x}^\mu$ for which $\lambda_\mu > 0$, and the $\{\lambda_\mu\}$ are determined by solving the Wolfe dual,

$$\text{find:} \quad \begin{aligned} &\max_{\boldsymbol{\lambda}} \left[-\frac{1}{2} \sum_{\mu\nu} \lambda_\mu \lambda_\nu t_\mu t_\nu \boldsymbol{\Phi}(\boldsymbol{x}^\mu) \cdot \boldsymbol{\Phi}(\boldsymbol{x}^\nu) + \sum_\mu \lambda_\mu \right] \\ &\text{subject to } \sum_\mu \lambda_\mu t_\mu = 0, \quad \boldsymbol{\lambda} \geq 0 \end{aligned} \tag{8.24}$$

Insertion of the above expressions (8.22, 8.23) into the machine's operation rule (8.21) gives the final classification recipe

$$\mathcal{S}(\boldsymbol{x}) = \mathrm{sgn}\left(\sum_{\mu} \lambda_\mu t_\mu \boldsymbol{\Phi}(\boldsymbol{x}^\mu) \cdot \boldsymbol{\Phi}(\boldsymbol{x}) + w_0\right) \tag{8.25}$$

The decision boundary in input space of our machine is then defined as the set of all $\boldsymbol{x} \in \mathbb{R}^N$ for which $\mathcal{S}(\boldsymbol{x}) = 0$.

At this stage one makes the important observation that neither in (8.25), nor in the result for w_0 in (8.23), nor in the equations (8.24) from which to extract $\boldsymbol{\lambda}$, is any 'bare' occurrence of the preprocessing functions $\phi_i(\boldsymbol{x})$ retained. Instead we consistently encounter only the dot product

$$K(\boldsymbol{x}, \boldsymbol{y}) = \boldsymbol{\Phi}(\boldsymbol{x}) \cdot \boldsymbol{\Phi}(\boldsymbol{y}) = \sum_{i=1}^{M} \phi_i(\boldsymbol{x})\phi_i(\boldsymbol{y}) \tag{8.26}$$

We therefore never need to refer to or construct the $\boldsymbol{\Phi}(\boldsymbol{x})$ explicitly, and can work exclusively with $K(\boldsymbol{x}, \boldsymbol{y})$, which is called the SVM kernel.

SVM kernels—properties and examples

We have seen above how a choice of preprocessing via $\boldsymbol{\Phi}(\boldsymbol{x})$ leads to a specific SVM kernel (8.26). Conversely, it turns out that 'most' positive definite and symmetric kernels $K(\boldsymbol{x}, \boldsymbol{y})$ can be written in the form (8.26). The specific conditions for this are given in Mercer's theorem, which we will not prove here: a symmetric kernel $K(\boldsymbol{x}, \boldsymbol{y})$ has an expansion of the form

$$K(\boldsymbol{x}, \boldsymbol{y}) = \sum_{i=1}^{\infty} \phi_i(\boldsymbol{x})\phi_i(\boldsymbol{y}) \tag{8.27}$$

in the function space $L^2(\mathbb{R}^N)$ if and only if

$$0 < \int \mathrm{d}\boldsymbol{x}\mathrm{d}\boldsymbol{y}\, g(\boldsymbol{x})K(\boldsymbol{x}, \boldsymbol{y})g(\boldsymbol{y}) < \infty \quad \text{for all functions } g \in L^2(\mathbb{R}^N)$$

The first inequality here is clearly analogous to the requirement of positive definiteness for a matrix. Mercer's theorem shows that in general, by choosing a kernel directly rather than constructing it from (8.26), we are effectively using an *infinite* number M of preprocessing functions $\phi_i(\boldsymbol{x})$. The recognition of the crucial role of the kernel thus allows us to treat sets of preprocessing functions which could not be tackled by working directly in the space of hyperplane weight vectors $\boldsymbol{w}$. It should also be noted that the decomposition (8.27) is not unique; for example, making a second copy of each function $\phi_i(\boldsymbol{x})$ and rescaling both copies by $1/\sqrt{2}$ would lead to the same kernel.

To see the link between kernels and preprocessing functions more explicitly, we consider some examples.

- Kernels generating *preprocessing via polynomials*:

$$K(\boldsymbol{x}, \boldsymbol{y}) = (1 + \boldsymbol{x} \cdot \boldsymbol{y})^d$$

Expansion of this type of kernel gives:

$$\begin{aligned} K(\boldsymbol{x}, \boldsymbol{y}) &= 1 + d(\boldsymbol{x} \cdot \boldsymbol{y}) + \frac{1}{2}d(d-1)(\boldsymbol{x} \cdot \boldsymbol{y})^2 \\ &\quad + \frac{1}{6}d(d-1)(d-2)(\boldsymbol{x} \cdot \boldsymbol{y})^3 + \cdots \\ &= 1 + d\sum_i x_i y_i + \frac{1}{2}d(d-1)\sum_{ij}(x_i x_j)(y_i y_j) \\ &\quad + \frac{1}{6}d(d-1)(d-2)\sum_{ijk}(x_i x_j x_k)(y_i y_j y_k) + \cdots \end{aligned}$$

This expression is indeed seen to be of the form (8.27), with polynomial preprocessing functions. The expansion truncates if d is chosen to be a positive integer; otherwise one has effectively $M = \infty$.

- Kernels generating *preprocessing via radial basis functions*:

$$K(\boldsymbol{x}, \boldsymbol{y}) = K(|\boldsymbol{x} - \boldsymbol{y}|)$$

Let us consider positive definite kernels of the form $K(\boldsymbol{x} - \boldsymbol{y})$, such that the Fourier transform $\hat{K}(\boldsymbol{k})$ of the function $K(\boldsymbol{z})$ exists:

$$\hat{K}(\boldsymbol{k}) = \int \mathrm{d}\boldsymbol{x}\, e^{\mathrm{i}\boldsymbol{k}\cdot\boldsymbol{x}} K(\boldsymbol{x}) \qquad K(\boldsymbol{x}) = \int \frac{\mathrm{d}\boldsymbol{k}}{(2\pi)^N} e^{-\mathrm{i}\boldsymbol{k}\cdot\boldsymbol{x}} \hat{K}(\boldsymbol{k})$$

The symmetry of the kernel $K(\boldsymbol{x}, \boldsymbol{y}) = K(\boldsymbol{y}, \boldsymbol{x})$ implies $K(\boldsymbol{x}) = K(-\boldsymbol{x})$ and thus also $\hat{K}(\boldsymbol{k}) = \hat{K}(-\boldsymbol{k})$. We can also argue that $\hat{K}(\boldsymbol{k}) \geq 0$ for all $\boldsymbol{k} \in \mathbb{R}^N$. This follows from working out

$$\int \mathrm{d}\boldsymbol{y}\, K(\boldsymbol{x}, \boldsymbol{y}) e^{\mathrm{i}\boldsymbol{k}\cdot\boldsymbol{y}} = \int \mathrm{d}\boldsymbol{y}\, K(\boldsymbol{x} - \boldsymbol{y}) e^{\mathrm{i}\boldsymbol{k}\cdot\boldsymbol{y}} = \hat{K}(\boldsymbol{k}) e^{\mathrm{i}\boldsymbol{k}\cdot\boldsymbol{x}}$$

Thus the $\hat{K}(\boldsymbol{k})$ are seen to be eigenvalues of the positive definite kernel K, and therefore themselves positive. To construct a set of preprocessing functions generating the kernel $\boldsymbol{K}$, define

$$\phi_z(\boldsymbol{x}) = L(\boldsymbol{x} - z) \qquad L(\boldsymbol{x}) = \int \frac{\mathrm{d}\boldsymbol{k}}{(2\pi)^N} e^{-\mathrm{i}\boldsymbol{k}\cdot\boldsymbol{x}} \sqrt{\hat{K}(\boldsymbol{k})}$$

We work out the product

$$\begin{aligned}
\int \mathrm{d}z\, \phi_z(\boldsymbol{x})\phi_z(\boldsymbol{y}) &= \int \frac{\mathrm{d}\boldsymbol{u}\mathrm{d}\boldsymbol{v}}{(2\pi)^{2N}} \sqrt{\hat{K}(\boldsymbol{u})\hat{K}(\boldsymbol{v})} \int \mathrm{d}z\, e^{-\mathrm{i}\boldsymbol{u}\cdot(\boldsymbol{x}-z)-\mathrm{i}\boldsymbol{v}\cdot(\boldsymbol{y}-z)} \\
&= \int \frac{\mathrm{d}\boldsymbol{u}\mathrm{d}\boldsymbol{v}}{(2\pi)^{2N}} \sqrt{\hat{K}(\boldsymbol{u})\hat{K}(\boldsymbol{v})}\, e^{-\mathrm{i}\boldsymbol{u}\cdot\boldsymbol{x}-\mathrm{i}\boldsymbol{v}\cdot\boldsymbol{y}} \int \mathrm{d}z\, e^{\mathrm{i}z\cdot(\boldsymbol{u}+\boldsymbol{v})} \\
&= \int \frac{\mathrm{d}\boldsymbol{u}}{(2\pi)^N} \hat{K}(\boldsymbol{u}) e^{-\mathrm{i}\boldsymbol{u}\cdot(\boldsymbol{x}-\boldsymbol{y})} = K(\boldsymbol{x} - \boldsymbol{y})
\end{aligned}$$

(making use of the identity $(2\pi)^{-N} \int \mathrm{d}z\, e^{\mathrm{i}z\cdot(\boldsymbol{u}+\boldsymbol{v})} = \delta(\boldsymbol{u} + \boldsymbol{v})$, see also Appendix F). We can therefore view the kernel K as generated by preprocessing functions $\phi_z(\boldsymbol{x})$, with the 'locations' z of these functions uniformly spread across $\mathbb{R}^N$.

If, in addition, $K(\boldsymbol{x})$ has the isotropic form $K(|\boldsymbol{x}|)$, then also $\hat{K}(\boldsymbol{k}) = \hat{K}(|\boldsymbol{k}|)$ and $L(\boldsymbol{x}) = L(|\boldsymbol{x}|)$, so that $\phi_z(\boldsymbol{x}) = L(|\boldsymbol{x} - z|)$ and we have preprocessing by radial basis functions.

- Kernels generating *preprocessing via sigmoidal neurons*:

$$K(\boldsymbol{x}, \boldsymbol{y}) = g(\boldsymbol{x} \cdot \boldsymbol{y})$$

Here we choose $g(u)$ to be a sigmoidal function, such as $g(u) = \tanh(au + b)$ with constants $a, b \in \mathbb{R}$. It turns out that this kernel cannot always be written in the form (8.27). Nevertheless, simply from equation (8.25)—with $\boldsymbol{\Phi}(\boldsymbol{x})\cdot\boldsymbol{\Phi}(\boldsymbol{y})$ replaced by $K(\boldsymbol{x}, \boldsymbol{y})$—it is clear that we effectively have preprocessing via a 'hidden' layer of sigmoidal neurons:

$$S(\boldsymbol{x}) = \mathrm{sgn}\Big(\sum_\mu \lambda_\mu t_\mu g(\boldsymbol{x}^\mu \cdot \boldsymbol{x}) + w_0\Big)$$

The number of support vectors then corresponds to the number of hidden neurons in the neural network, and the input-to-hidden weights are given by the support vectors $\boldsymbol{\xi}^\mu$ themselves.

A toy example

We close this section with an example of the application of SVMs to a binary classification task which is not linearly separable. We generated a data set D with $p = 30$ and with data points $\boldsymbol{\xi}^\mu \in \mathbb{R}^2$; around half of

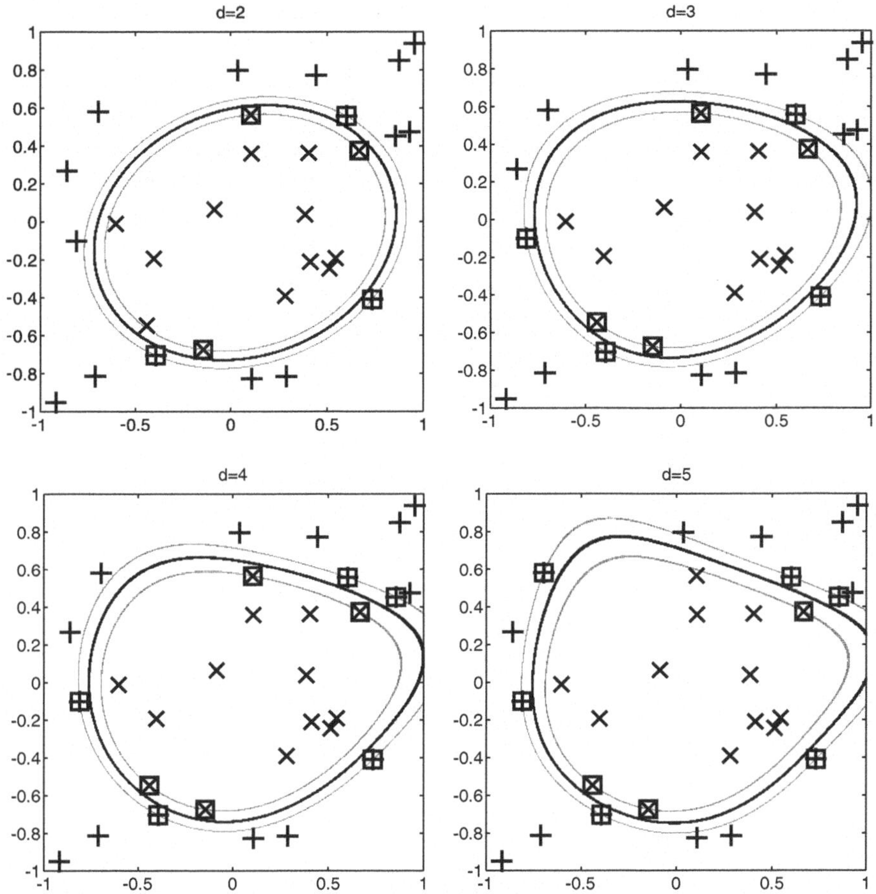

Figure 8.5 Binary classification of $p = 30$ training examples, with two-dimensional input vectors $\boldsymbol{x}^\mu = (x_1^\mu, x_2^\mu)$. The data points further from the origin have $t_\mu = 1$ (marked by $+$), the others have $t_\mu = -1$ (crosses). The data are clearly not linearly separable. Classification is by an SVM with kernel $K(\boldsymbol{x}, \boldsymbol{y}) = (1 + \boldsymbol{x} \cdot \boldsymbol{y})^d$. From top left to bottom right: $d = 2, 3, 4, 5$. The thick lines represent the decision boundaries. The support vectors of the solution are marked in each case by $\square$. They lie on the curves $\boldsymbol{w} \cdot \boldsymbol{\Phi}(\boldsymbol{x}) + w_0 = \pm 1$ (thin lines) as they must.

these points—those located further from the origin—have $t_\mu = 1$, the other half have $t_\mu = -1$. We tried to separate the two classes with an SVM using the polynomial kernel $K(\boldsymbol{x}, \boldsymbol{y}) = (1 + \boldsymbol{x} \cdot \boldsymbol{y})^d$ and solved the Wolfe dual (8.24) numerically. Figure 8.5 shows the resulting decision boundaries, together with the training examples, for different values of the parameter $d = 2, 3, 4, 5$. Note that for the kernel used here, the parameter d controls the number M of underlying preprocessing functions. As d (and thus the complexity of the SVM) is increased, we observe decision boundaries with increasingly detailed class separation.

There are clearly open issues here on how to control overfitting in SVMs, and how to predict, for example, misclassification probabilities. Progress can be made by integrating SVMs into a Bayesian framework; it then turns out, for example, that the SVM kernel corresponds essentially to the covariance function of an underlying Gaussian process prior. We also have not discussed how to extend the SVM method to noisy data. It turns out that this can be done relatively simply, and in fact only ends up adding the additional constraint $\lambda_\mu \leq C$ to the Wolfe dual (8.24); see Exercise 8.5. Here C is a parameter that broadly defines the penalty for misclassified examples, or more precisely those that violate the condition $t_\mu(\boldsymbol{w}\cdot\boldsymbol{\xi}^\mu + w_0) \geq 1$; the limit $C \to \infty$ then recovers the 'hard' SVM classification discussed throughout this chapter.

8.4 Exercises

Exercise 8.1. (Completion of proof.) Prove that the Lagrangian (8.13) for the SVM optimization problem is convex in $(\boldsymbol{w}, w_0)$.

Exercise 8.2. (Binary classification with SVMs.) An SVM produces a binary output $t \in \{-1, 1\}$ for every input vector (or question) $\boldsymbol{\xi} \in \mathbb{R}^N$. The system is parametrized by a weight vector $\boldsymbol{w} \in \mathbb{R}^N$ and a threshold w_0, such that

$$t(\boldsymbol{\xi}) = \text{sgn}(\boldsymbol{w}\cdot\boldsymbol{\xi} + w_0)$$

The data used in training the SVM consists of a set of questions and corresponding answers: $D = \{(\boldsymbol{\xi}^1, t_1), \ldots, (\boldsymbol{\xi}^p, t_p)\}$, where $\boldsymbol{\xi}^\mu \in \mathbb{R}^N$ and $t_\mu \in \{-1, 1\}$, and with $p \leq N$. Show that, for the case where $\boldsymbol{\xi}^\mu\cdot\boldsymbol{\xi}^\nu = a_\mu^2\delta_{\mu\nu}$ (with $a_\mu \in \mathbb{R}$) the SVM solution (the optimal separating plane) is given by

$$\boldsymbol{w} = \sum_{\mu=1}^{p} \frac{1}{a_\mu^2}(t_\mu - w_0)\boldsymbol{\xi}^\mu \qquad w_0 = \frac{\sum_{\mu=1}^{p} t_\mu/a_\mu^2}{\sum_{\mu=1}^{p} 1/a_\mu^2}$$

Exercise 8.3. (Support vectors versus active constraints.) Consider binary classification of two-dimensional inputs $\boldsymbol{\xi}$, and in particular a data set D consisting of $p = 2$ examples, with $\boldsymbol{\xi}^1 = (0, 1)$, $t_1 = 1$ and $\boldsymbol{\xi}^2 = (1, 0)$, $t_2 = -1$. For an SVM without preprocessing, use the equality constraint in the Wolfe dual (8.20) to show that the latter reduces to maximizing $2\lambda_1 - \lambda_1^2$ over $\lambda_1 \geq 0$. Hence show that both training inputs are SVs, with $\lambda_1 = \lambda_2 = 1$, and that the optimal weight vector and offset are $\boldsymbol{w} = (-1, 1)$ and $w_0 = 0$. Sketch the position of the training points, of the optimal separating plane and the minimal-distance planes either side of it, as in Figure 8.4.

Now consider adding a third data point to D, with $\boldsymbol{\xi}^3 = (-1, 0)$ and $t_3 = 1$. Use the equality constraint to show that the Wolfe dual reduces to maximization of $1 - (\lambda_1 - 1)^2/2 - (\lambda_1 + 2\lambda_3 - 1)^2/2$ over $\lambda_1, \lambda_3 \geq 0$. Hence show that the optimal values are $\lambda_1 = 1$, $\lambda_3 = 0$, and that the optimal $\boldsymbol{w}$ and w_0 are as before. Add the third data point to your earlier diagram: you should see that it has the minimal distance from the separating hyperplane. It thus corresponds to an active constraint. Nevertheless, its Lagrange multiplier λ_3 vanishes, so it is not an SV.

Exercise 8.4. (Preprocessing with Gaussian RBFs.) A very common choice for preprocessing with RBFs is the Gaussian kernel $K(\boldsymbol{x}, \boldsymbol{y}) = \exp(-|\boldsymbol{x} - \boldsymbol{y}|^2/2\sigma^2)$. This exercise shows that the width parameter σ controls the complexity of the SVM classifier: for large σ, one essentially retrieves the linear kernel $K_{\text{lin}}(\boldsymbol{x}, \boldsymbol{y}) = \boldsymbol{x} \cdot \boldsymbol{y}$, which corresponds to SVM classification without preprocessing. For $\sigma \to 0$, on the other hand, the SVM classifier can fit arbitrary data sets, and as a consequence may overfit and generalize poorly.

Consider the case of large σ first. In the objective function of the Wolfe dual (8.24), expand $K(\boldsymbol{x}^\mu, \boldsymbol{x}^\nu) = \exp(-(\boldsymbol{x}^\mu - \boldsymbol{x}^\nu)^2/2\sigma^2)$ to linear order in $1/\sigma^2$, discarding quadratic and higher order terms in $1/\sigma^2$. Taking into account the equality constraint $\sum_\mu \lambda_\mu t_\mu = 0$, rearrange the dual objective function into the form $\sigma^2(\sum_\mu \tilde{\lambda}_\mu - \frac{1}{2}\sum_{\mu\nu} \tilde{\lambda}_\mu \tilde{\lambda}_\nu t_\mu t_\nu \boldsymbol{x}^\mu \cdot \boldsymbol{x}^\nu)$, with $\tilde{\lambda}_\mu = \lambda_\mu/\sigma^2$. Thus the rescaled Lagrange multipliers $\tilde{\lambda}_\mu$ will be the same as for SVM classification with a linear kernel. Show further that the decision function (8.25) can be written as $\mathcal{S}(\boldsymbol{x}) = \tilde{\boldsymbol{w}} \cdot \boldsymbol{x} + \tilde{w}_0$ with $\tilde{\boldsymbol{w}} = \sum_\mu \tilde{\lambda}_\mu t_\mu \boldsymbol{x}^\mu$; this is again of the same form as for a linear kernel. Give an expression for $\tilde{w}_0$. How would you show that the optimal value of $\tilde{w}_0$ is the same as the optimal value of w_0 for classification with a linear kernel? (Hint: use that $\mathcal{S}(\boldsymbol{x}^\mu) = t_\mu$ for SVs $\boldsymbol{x}^\mu$.)

In the opposite limit $\sigma \to 0$, and excluding the pathological case where two input vectors $\boldsymbol{x}^\mu$ coincide, show that the dual objective becomes $\sum_\mu (\lambda_\mu - \lambda_\mu^2/2)$. Hence show that at optimality all $\lambda_\mu = 1$. This means that all training inputs are SVs, and that all training points are correctly classified whatever the training outputs t_μ. Write down the decision function (8.25) and show that for $\sigma \to 0$ it vanishes if $\boldsymbol{x}$ is not contained in the training set. Would you expect the resulting classifier to generalize well?

Exercise 8.5. (Soft SVM classification.) Here one allows violations of the margin constraint by writing $t_\mu(\boldsymbol{w} \cdot \boldsymbol{\xi}^\mu + w_0) \geq 1 - \eta_\mu$. The $\eta_\mu \geq 0$ are slack variables and measure by how much the constraint is violated. To prevent large violations, one adds a term $C \sum_\mu \eta_\mu$ to the objective function $\boldsymbol{w}^2/2$. The coefficient C determines how strongly violations of the margin constraint—and the resulting misclassifications, if $\eta_\mu > 1$—are penalized; $C \to \infty$ recovers hard SVM classification.

The Lagrangian for this problem is

$$L = \frac{1}{2}\boldsymbol{w}^2 + C\sum_{\mu} \eta_\mu - \sum_{\mu} \lambda_\mu [t_\mu(\boldsymbol{w} \cdot \boldsymbol{\xi}^\mu + w_0) - 1 + \eta_\mu] - \sum_{\mu} \beta_\mu \eta_\mu$$

The 'primal' variables, denoted $\boldsymbol{x}$ in Section 8.2, are $\boldsymbol{w}$, w_0, and $\{\eta_\mu\}$, while the Lagrange multipliers are the λ_μ and β_μ. The latter serve to enforce the constraint $\eta_\mu \geq 0$.

Derive the Wolfe dual of this soft SVM optimization problem, following the same steps as in the derivation of (8.20). You should find that the dual objective is the same as in (8.20), but that the constraints are now $\lambda_\mu \geq 0$, $\beta_\mu \geq 0$, $\lambda_\mu - C + \beta_\mu = 0$ (for all μ), and $\sum_\mu \lambda_\mu t_\mu = 0$. Eliminate the β_μ from the constraints to show that the only difference to hard SVM classification is that the λ_μ must now be in the range $0 \leq \lambda_\mu \leq C$.

9 Notes and suggestions for further reading

In Chapter 5 we dealt with some unsupervised learning techniques, namely vector quantization and self-organized maps. The books by Kohonen [26] and by Ritter *et al.* [27] are good sources of further information on these; much of the early work on self-organizing maps was done in particular by Amari [28] and Kohonen [29]. We saw for vector quantization that this can be thought as learning a probability distribution from data. This point of view is rather powerful, and in fact lets one integrate unsupervised learning with Bayesian techniques: different probability models for the data can be given prior probabilities and these are combined with likelihood factors to determine how likely a given model is once the data have arrived. A survey of this approach has recently been given by Ghahramani [30]. The probability models one might consider here can be a good deal more complicated than the Gaussian mixture distributions which we recognized at the root of vector quantization. To model time series data, for example, where each data point corresponds to a segment of the series over some time interval, one needs to account properly for temporal correlations; so-called hidden Markov models, also described briefly in the review [30], are often used for this purpose. Alternatively each data point could consist of answers to a set of questions—for example 'is the grass wet?', 'is the neighbour's sprinkler switched on?' and 'has it rained recently?'—and we might have to model how these facts are related to each other. It is then often useful to constrain the possible ways in which dependencies between the facts can arise. Such constraints can be represented compactly in so-called graphical models; see, for example, [31–33]. The parameters to be learned then quantify those dependencies that are allowed by the graph. Sometimes prior knowledge is not sufficient to determine the graph structure completely, and the latter then needs to be learnt as well. There is much ongoing research in this area of learning in graphical models.

The self-organizing map is a particular instance of a model which assumes some underlying low-dimensional structure in the data. It can be generalized to a so-called generative topographic mapping [34] which has the advantage of a natural interpretation as a probabilistic data model. The roots of such dimensionality-reduction techniques go back at least to principal components analysis (e.g. see [35]), which finds the linear subspace across which the data have maximal variance. How one best finds non-linear low-dimensional structure in data remains of significant interest, and many different approaches have been and continue to be proposed.

The Bayesian techniques for regression and classification described in Chapter 6 have a very long history in statistics, with a correspondingly large amount of literature which we will not attempt to review here; see, for example, the books by Bishop [35] and by Ripley [36]. Papers by MacKay [37–40] contributed significantly to the recognition of the value of these tools within the neural networks community. By now they are entirely mainstream, with hundreds of papers on Bayesian learning methods published every year. For numerical approaches to Bayesian inference, the book by Neal [41] has become a standard reference; a recent and very comprehensive treatment of Bayesian learning within the framework of information theory is [42].

The history of Gaussian processes also goes a long way back, at least to the 1960s, as described, for example, in the review article [43]; the latter also contains a very illuminating explanation of the various ways in which Gaussian processes can be understood. Key early papers that brought the methodology to the attention of neural networks researchers were [44,45]; a more recent and rather more technical overview is given in [46]. This reference also covers applications of Gaussian process prior to other problems such as classification, which we have not discussed in this book.

Support vector machines were proposed by Vapnik and co-workers, and the books [47,48] provide useful and comprehensive background material; a more recent overview is [49]. As explained in these references, the original motivation for SVMs came from the worst-case analysis of learning. This approach is known variously as computational or statistical learning theory, or probably approximately correct (PAC) learning; see, for example, [50–53]. The distinction to the statistical mechanics analysis of learning presented in this book is that one tries to remove assumptions on, for example, the distribution of training inputs. One then derives bounds on quantities such as the generalization error which hold with probability close to one even for the worst input distribution. Following work by McAllester [54], this approach has recently also been merged with concepts from Bayesian learning, and much research continues to be done in this direction.

Finally, the idea underlying the preprocessing in SVMs, that is, the replacement of dot products by kernels to allow for non-linearities, has seen fruitful application in many other problem domains. The development of such 'kernel methods' remains a very active area; recent overviews can be found in [55,56].

Part III Information theory and neural networks

Neural networks are information processing systems, so it is hardly a surprise that, if we aim to quantify the operation of neural networks or to systematically design appropriate architectures and learning rules, we can use many of the tools that have already been developed for the more conventional information processing systems in engineering and computer science. Information theory is a very elegant, well founded and rigorous framework to quantify information and information processing. It is remarkable that this framework was to a large extent the sole project of Claude Shannon, who more or less launched information theory with a publication in 1948, building on work he did during the war on radar communication and on fruitful suggestions and preparatory work of others.

In this part of the book we first explain and derive the basic ideas and mathematical tools of conventional information theory, such as entropy, conditional entropy, and mutual information. We include the relevant proofs, wherever possible. This is then followed by an exposé of various different applications of information theory to inference problems in general, and to the derivation and optimization of learning rules for neural information processing systems in particular. These applications include layered networks (e.g. unsupervised learning on the basis of information preservation criteria), recurrent networks (e.g. learning input–output relationships in so-called Boltzmann machines), but also more fundamental issues such as learning via 'natural gradient descent'. The latter generalizes the more conventional gradient descent and gives us the opportunity to explore the basics of information geometry.

10 Measuring information

Measuring information at first sight appears to be a somewhat vague and strange concept. Although especially those of us who are reasonably familiar with using computers will be used to thinking about information content (in terms of *bits*), we will find out that measuring information is not simply counting the number of bits in a data file but involves, somewhat surprisingly, concepts from probability. Therefore we will start with an introduction aimed at developing some intuition for what the relevant issues are and why probablities enter the game. We also play with a number of simple examples before diving into formal definitions and proofs.

One best thinks about information in a down-to-earth manner, in terms of messages communicated between a sender and a receiver. Before meaningful communication can take place, sender and receiver need to agree on the format of these messages. This could be lines of text, numbers, bleeps representing morse-code, smoke-signals, electric pulses, etc. We write the set of possible messages, agreed upon by sender and receiver, as

$$A = \{a_1, a_2, \ldots\} \quad \text{with } |A| \text{ elements} \tag{10.1}$$

Consider the example of a horse race, with five competitors. Sending a message to reveal the outcome of the race just means sending the number of the winning horse, so the set of possible messages is $A = \{1, 2, 3, 4, 5\}$, with $|A| = 5$. Another example: sending a message consisting of a single word with up to three ordinary characters from the alphabet. Here $A = \{a, b, \ldots, z, aa, ab, ac, \ldots, aaa, aab, aac, \ldots, zzz\}$, with $|A| = 26 + 26^2 + 26^3 = 18{,}278$. The set A could also have an infinite number of elements. If we put no a priori limit on the number of bleeps used in a telegraphic message, the set A, being the set of all such possible telegraphic messages, will be infinitely large. Now suppose I am sent a message $a \in A$: I receive a card with something written on it, or I am told the number of the winning horse in a race. How much information have I received? Is it at all possible to give a sensible unambiguous meaning to such a question?

10.1 Brute force: counting messages

Information content based on naive enumeration

The first approach we can take is to label all elements in A with binary numbers (strings of bits). Let us, for simplicity, assume that the number of possible messages is some integer power of two, that is, $|A| = 2^n$ and so $A = \{a_1, \ldots, a_{2^n}\}$:

message:	$n -$ *bit string*:	*corresponding number*:
a_1	$0\ldots000$	0
a_2	$0\ldots001$	1
a_3	$0\ldots010$	2
a_4	$0\ldots011$	3
$\vdots$	$\vdots$	$\vdots$
a_{2^n}	$1\ldots111$	$2^n - 1$

The correspondence between the elements of A and the integer numbers $\{0, 1, \ldots, 2^n - 1\}$ is one-to-one; in other words:

n bits are *sufficient* to uniquely describe each $a \in A$

n bits are *necessary* to uniquely describe each $a \in A$

It appears that a measure of the amount of information communicated by a message can be obtained by simply counting the number of bits n needed to specify the label. In terms of the number of elements $|A| = 2^n$ in the set A this gives the tentative expression

$$\text{information content of a single message } a \in A = \log_2|A| \qquad (10.2)$$

This simple result has a nice self-consistency property, which any candidate definition of information content must have. Consider the example of having two sets of messages A and B:

$$A = \{a_1, a_2, \ldots\} \quad \text{with } |A| \text{ elements}$$
$$B = \{b_1, b_2, \ldots\} \quad \text{with } |B| \text{ elements}$$

Now imagine that the message being communicated is a pair of variables (a, b), with $a \in A$ and $b \in B$ (like giving both the name of a winning horse and the current price of your favourite CD). If the two individual variables a and b are completely independent we must require the information content of the pair (a, b) to be the sum of the two individual information contents of a and b, giving the value $\log_2|A| + \log_2|B|$. On the other hand we can also apply the above method of labelling messages with bit-strings to the set C of all pairs (a, b):

$$C = \{(a, b)|\ a \in A,\ b \in B\}$$
$$C = \{c_1, c_2, \ldots\} \quad \text{with } |C| = |A||B| \text{ elements}$$

The information content in the latter case would come out as $\log_2|C|$. We see that the two outcomes are indeed identical, since $\log_2|C| = \log_2|A| + \log_2|B|$.

Problems with naive enumeration

However, this cannot be the end of the story. There are several ways to show that the above definition of information content, although correct in the case where we just communicate one single message a from a specified set A, is not sufficiently powerful to deal with all relevant situations. First, let us go back to the example of communicating a message pair (a, b), where we assumed independence of a and b (without as yet specifying precisely what this means) and subsequently found

$$a \text{ and } b \text{ independent:} \quad \text{information in message pair } (a,b) = \log_2|A| + \log_2|B|$$

Alternatively we can choose messages which are clearly related. To consider an extreme choice: suppose a represents the number of a winning horse and b the name of its jockey. In this case knowledge of a implies knowledge of b, and vice versa. We gain nothing by knowing both, so in this case

$$a \text{ and } b \text{ strongly dependent:} \quad \text{information in message pair } (a,b) = \log_2|A|$$

In general one will have a situation in between, with messages relating to data which are correlated to some degree, for example, with $a \in A$ representing the name of the winning horse and $b \in B$ representing its age (assuming old horses to have on average a reduced chance of winning). Such situations can only be dealt with properly by using probability theory.

Another way to see how probabilities come in is to compare the simple situation of a single set of messages $a \in A$, where we found

$$A = \{a_1, a_2, a_3, \ldots\} \quad \text{information in message } a \in A = \log_2|A|$$

with the situation we get when one of the messages, say a_1, never occurs, giving

$$\begin{aligned} A' = \{a_2, a_3, \ldots\} \quad \text{information in message } a \in A' &= \log_2|A'| \\ &= \log_2(|A| - 1) \end{aligned}$$

So far no problem. However, what happens if we have a situation in between, where element a_1 does occur but rather infrequently? If a_1 can be expected to occur on average only once every 1,000,000,000 times (e.g. a_1 happens to be the name of a racing horse with three legs), we would be inclined to say that the information content of a message $a \in A$ is closer to $\log_2(|A|-1)$ (corresponding to a_1 simply being absent) than to $\log_2|A|$. Again we need statistical tools to deal with real-world situations, where not all messages are equally likely to occur.

The solution of these problems lies in realizing that communicating information is equivalent to *reducing uncertainty*. Before we actually open the envelope and read the message inside, as far as we know the envelope could contain any of the messages of the set A. By reading the message, however, our uncertainty is reduced to zero. In the case of the combined message (a, b) where we have already been told what a is, it is clear that our reduction in uncertainty on hearing the value of b is less in the case where a and b are strongly correlated than in the case where they are independent. Similarly, knowing that in a race with two horses the four-legged horse has won (at the expense of the three-legged one) does not reduce our uncertainty about the outcome very much, whereas it does in the case of two equally fast contenders.

10.2 Exploiting message likelihood differences via coding

Bit-count reduction due to coding

We will now demonstrate that the average information content of messages from a message set A can indeed be less than $\log_2|A|$, as soon as not all messages are equally likely to occur, by looking at various methods of coding these messages. We will give formal and precise definitions later, but for now it will be sufficient to define binary coding of messages simply as associating with each message $a \in A$ a unique string of binary numbers (the 'codewords'). We have already played with an example of this procedure; we will now call the bit-string associated with each element its codeword, and the full table linking messages to their codewords simply a 'code':

$$\begin{array}{cc} \textit{message:} & \textit{code word:} \\ a_1 & 0\ldots000 \\ a_2 & 0\ldots001 \\ a_3 & 0\ldots010 \\ a_4 & 0\ldots011 \\ \vdots & \vdots \\ a_{2^n} & 1\ldots111 \end{array}$$

This particular code, where the elements of the set A are enumerated and where the codeword of each element is simply the binary representation of its rank in the list is called an 'enumerative code'. All codewords are of the same length. Clearly, enumerative coding can be used only if $|A|$ is finite.

The key idea now is to realize that one is not forced to use a set of codewords which are all of the same length. In the case where some messages will occur more frequently then others, it might make sense to use *shorter* codewords for frequent messages, and to accept longer codewords for the infrequent messages. For instance, in Morse code the number of symbols used for infrequent characters such as Q (represented by '−− · −') is deliberately chosen larger than that of frequent characters, such as E (represented by ' · '). The fact that this alternative way of coding can indeed *on average* reduce the number of bits needed for communicating messages which are not all equally frequent is easily demonstrated via explicit construction. Let us enumerate the messages in a given finite set A as $A = \{a_1, a_2, \ldots\}$ and let us write the probability that message a occurs as $p(a)$; if all messages are equally likely then $p(a) = |A|^{-1}$ for all a. Finally, the length of the binary codeword used for element a (the number of bits) will be denoted by $\ell(a)$. Note that for enumerative codes all $\ell(a)$ are the same, by construction. For example:

$$A = \{a_1, a_2, a_3, a_4\} \qquad p(a_1) = \tfrac{1}{2} \quad p(a_2) = \tfrac{1}{4} \quad p(a_3) = \tfrac{1}{8} \quad p(a_4) = \tfrac{1}{8}$$

Let us now compare the performance of enumerative coding to that of an alternative coding recipe, a so-called 'prefix code', where the lengths of the codewords are adapted to the probabilities of occurrence of the four messages:

message:	*enumerative code*:		*prefix code*:	
a_1	00	$\ell(a_1) = 2$	1	$\ell(a_1) = 1$
a_2	01	$\ell(a_2) = 2$	01	$\ell(a_2) = 2$
a_3	10	$\ell(a_3) = 2$	001	$\ell(a_3) = 3$
a_4	11	$\ell(a_4) = 2$	000	$\ell(a_4) = 3$

The name prefix code indicates that it is constructed in such a way that no codeword occurs as the prefix of another codeword. Since codewords are no longer guaranteed to have a uniform length, this property is needed in order to ensure that the receiver knows when one codeword ends and the next codeword begins. In the present example we can always be sure that a codeword ends precisely when we either receive a '1' or when we receive the third '0' in a row.

Clearly, if we communicate just one individual message it could be that we use more bits in the prefix code ($a_3 \to 001$, $a_4 \to 000$) than in the enumerative code ($a_3 \to 10$, $a_4 \to 11$) to do so. However, if we calculate the *average number of bits* used, then the picture is interestingly different. If we send m messages $\{a(1), a(2), \ldots, a(m)\}$, where the message $a(t)$ communicated at 'time' t is at each instance drawn at random from A according to the above probabilities, then the average number of bits is by definition

$$\text{average number of bits} = \frac{1}{m}\sum_{t=1}^{m} \ell(a(t))$$

We can now define the code length L as the average number of bits used in the limit $m \to \infty$, that is, $L = \lim_{m\to\infty} m^{-1}\sum_{t=1}^{m} \ell(a(t))$. Since all individual messages $a(t)$ have been drawn at random from the set A, with the specified probabilities, we can use the property that in the limit $m \to \infty$ any average over m independent trials becomes an average over the underlying probability distribution (this is in fact one way of defining probabilities), so:

$$\text{code length:} \quad L = \lim_{m\to\infty} \frac{1}{m}\sum_{t=1}^{m} \ell(a(t)) = \sum_{i=1}^{4} p(a_i)\ell(a_i)$$

which for the present example gives:

$$\text{enumerative code:} \quad L = \tfrac{1}{2}\times 2 + \tfrac{1}{4}\times 2 + \tfrac{1}{8}\times 2 + \tfrac{1}{8}\times 2 = 2 \text{ bits}$$

$$\text{prefix code:} \quad L = \tfrac{1}{2}\times 1 + \tfrac{1}{4}\times 2 + \tfrac{1}{8}\times 3 + \tfrac{1}{8}\times 3 = 1.75 \text{ bits}$$

We see explicitly in this example that the *average* information content of messages must be smaller than $\log_2|A| = 2$, since simply by coding messages cleverly one can on average communicate the messages $a \in A$ using less than two bits each.

One can easily generalize the construction of the above simple version of a prefix-code to message sets A of arbitrary size. First we order the messages $a \in A$ according to decreasing probability of occurrence, that is,

$$A = \{a_1, a_2, \ldots, a_n\} \quad p(a_1) \geq p(a_2) \geq \cdots \geq p(a_n)$$

We now assign to each element $a \in A$ a binary codeword $C(a) \in \bigcup_{K\geq 1}\{0,1\}^K$ (the latter set is the union of all binary strings with one or more symbols) in the following manner:

message:	*prefix code*:	
a_1	1	$\ell(a_1) = 1$
a_2	01	$\ell(a_2) = 2$
a_3	001	$\ell(a_3) = 3$
$\vdots$	$\vdots$	$\vdots$
a_{n-1}	00...01	$\ell(a_{n-1}) = n-1$
a_n	00...00	$\ell(a_n) = n-1$

The idea is simple. For $i < n$ we take $i-1$ zeros, followed by a one. For $i = n$ we choose $n-1$ zeros. Note that the code is again of the prefix type: no codeword occurs as the prefix of another codeword, so the receiver always knows when one message ends and the next message begins: a message terminates either when one occurs, or when $n-1$ zeros have occurred in a row. In a formula, which is more suitable for further analysis, we would write:

$$i < n: \quad C(a_i) = \overbrace{00\ldots01}^{i-1 \text{ times}} \quad \ell(a_i) = i$$

$$i = n: \quad C(a_n) = \underbrace{00\ldots00}_{n-1 \text{ times}} \quad \ell(a_n) = n-1$$

An alternative way of viewing this particular code, and a simple way to decode a message received, is obtained by interpreting the bits in each codeword as representing successive answers in a decision tree. The following tree gives the codeword $C(a)$ for each given message a:

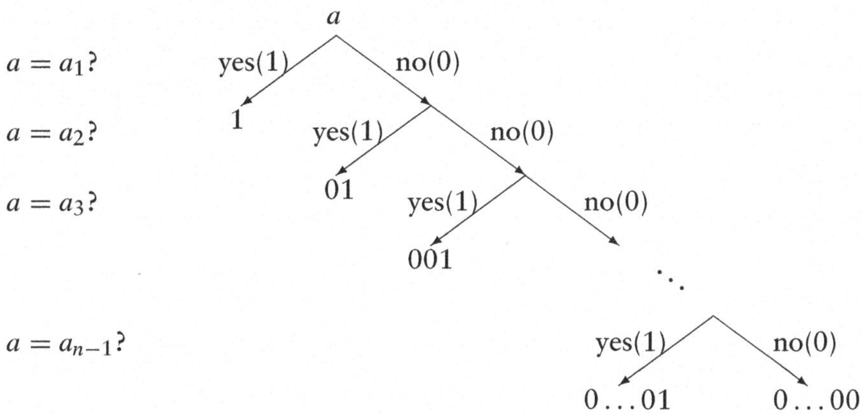

Conversely, the following tree gives the message a for each given codeword $C(a)$:

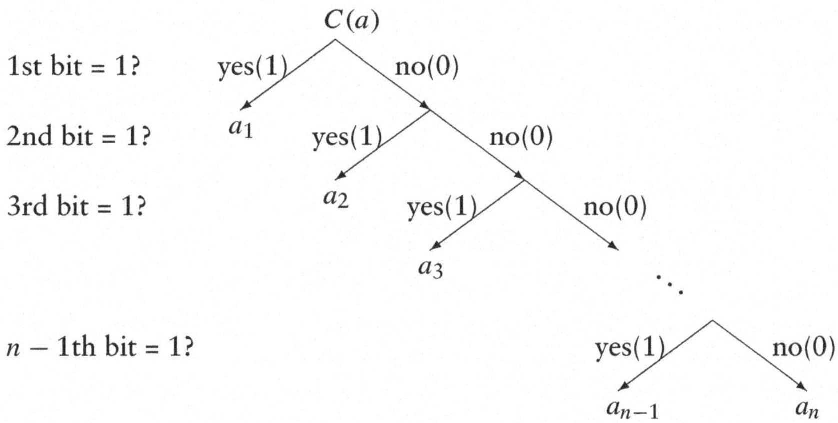

We can now very easily calculate the code length L, that is, the average number of bits needed to communicate a message, for arbitrary ordered message sets $A = \{a_1, a_2, \cdots\}$ with occurrence probabilities $p(a_1) \geq p(a_2) \geq p(a_3) \geq \ldots$. Let us for now restrict ourselves to finite message sets, so $|A| < \infty$:

$$L = \sum_{k\geq 1} p(a_k)\ell(a_k) = \begin{cases} \sum_{k=1}^{|A|} p(a_k)k - p(a_{|A|}) & \text{(prefix code)} \\ \log_2|A| & \text{(enumerative code)} \end{cases} \tag{10.3}$$

The value given for the code length L of the enumerative code, as before, refers to the case where $|A|$ is some integer power of 2. If this is not true, its code length will be given by the smallest integer following $\log_2|A|$. Note also that, while the enumerative code can only be used for finite message sets, that is, $|A| < \infty$, the prefix code has no such restriction.

Let us now turn to a couple of examples to illustrate the above ideas. To simplify the notation we shall put $|A| = n$. The calculations involve some simple mathematical tools which can be found in Appendix C.

Example 1. The first example is a message set A in which all messages are equally likely to occur:

$$A = \{a_1, \ldots, a_n\} \qquad p(a_k) = 1/n$$

Working out the expression in (10.3) for the prefix code gives:

$$L_{\text{pref}} = \frac{1}{n}\sum_{k=1}^{n} k - \frac{1}{n} = \frac{1}{2}(n+1) - \frac{1}{n}$$

For message sets with size equal to some power of two, for simplicity of comparison with the enumerative code, this gives the following results:

n	2	4	8	16	32	$\cdots$	$n \to \infty$
L_{enu}	1	2	3	4	5	$\cdots$	$\sim\log_2 n$
L_{pref}	1	$2\frac{1}{4}$	$4\frac{3}{8}$	$8\frac{7}{16}$	$16\frac{15}{32}$	$\cdots$	$\sim\frac{1}{2}n$

It is clear that for this example the prefix code is definitely less efficient, which could have been expected since the prefix code is based on exploiting likelihood differences. In the present example there are no such differences; each message is equally likely to occur.

Example 2. As a second example we will choose a message set A in which the messages are not equally likely to occur, but the likelihood differences are not yet too large. Specifically it is assumed that the $p(a_k)$ decrease *linearly* with message index k:

$$A = \{a_1, \ldots, a_n\} \qquad p(a_k) = \frac{2}{n}\left(1 - \frac{k}{n+1}\right)$$

The elements of the set A are ordered according to decreasing probability of occurrence; that is, the message probabilities obey $p(a_1) \geq p(a_2) \geq \cdots \geq p(a_n)$, and they decrease linearly, from $p(a_1) = 2/(n+1)$ to $p(a_n) = 2/n(n+1)$, such that $\sum_{k=1}^{n} p(a_k) = 1$.

Working out the expression in (10.3) for the prefix code now gives

$$L_{\mathrm{pref}} = \frac{2}{n}\sum_{k=1}^{n}\left(1 - \frac{k}{n+1}\right)k - \frac{2}{n(n+1)}$$
$$= \frac{1}{3}n + \frac{2}{3} - \frac{2}{n(n+1)}$$

For message sets with size equal to some power of two this gives the following results:

n	2	4	8	16	$\cdots$	$n \to \infty$
L_{enu}	1	2	3	4	$\cdots$	$\sim\log_2 n$
L_{pref}	1	$1\frac{9}{10}$	$3\frac{11}{36}$	$5\frac{405}{409}$	$\cdots$	$\sim\frac{1}{3}n$

Again the prefix code is generally less efficient, although to a somewhat lesser extent. Apparently for the prefix code to beat the enumerative code the likelihood differences to be exploited need to be significantly larger.

Example 3. As a third example we will inspect a message set $A = \{a_1, \ldots, a_n\}$ in which the message probabilities decrease exponentially:

$$A = \{a_1, \ldots, a_n\} \qquad p(a_k) = \frac{1}{B_n} e^{-\lambda k} \quad (\lambda > 0)$$

in which the constant B_n follows from the normalization requirement (using the tools in Appendix A to deal with the summations):

$$B_n = \sum_{k=1}^{n} e^{-\lambda k} = e^{-\lambda}\frac{1 - e^{-n\lambda}}{1 - e^{-\lambda}} = \frac{1 - e^{-\lambda n}}{e^{\lambda} - 1}$$

Working out expression (10.3), using the result for B_n, now leads to

$$L_{\text{pref}} = \frac{1}{B_n}\sum_{k=1}^{n} e^{-\lambda k}k - \frac{e^{-\lambda n}}{B_n}$$
$$= \frac{1}{1-e^{-\lambda}} - \frac{n+e^{\lambda}-1}{e^{\lambda n}-1} \sim \frac{1}{1-e^{-\lambda}} - ne^{-\lambda n} \quad \text{as } n \to \infty$$

Here we see a dramatic difference between enumerative coding and our prefix code. At the same time this demonstrates convincingly that for message sets where the messages are not all equally likely the appropriate measure of information content *cannot be* $\log_2 n$. Even in the limit of an infinite number of messages, $n \to \infty$, we can still communicate them by using on average only a finite number of bits:

$$\lim_{n\to\infty} L_{\text{pref}} = \frac{1}{1-e^{-\lambda}}$$

The dependence on λ of this result is consistent with the picture sketched so far. For $\lambda \to 0$, where the messages again tend to become equally likely, we indeed find that the average number of bits needed diverges, $\lim_{n\to\infty} L_{\text{pref}} = \infty$. For $\lambda \to \infty$, where $p(a_1) \to 1$ and $p(a_k) \to 0$ for $k > 1$ so that just one message will be communicated, we find that $\lim_{n\to\infty} L_{\text{pref}} = 1$: we just communicate a single bit for messages with zero information content.

Figure 10.1 compares enumerative with prefix codes for different message statistics. Note that for the exponential decay, the prefix code is superior to the enumerative code only for $n > \mathcal{O}(10^3)$. The location of the crossing point depends of course on the value of λ. For the power-law statistics $p(a_k) \sim k^{-\alpha}$ to give a finite value L_{pref} in the $n \to \infty$-limit one requires $\alpha > 2$.

10.3 Proposal for a measure of information

We have seen, by investigating examples of message sets and coding schemes, that the information content of messages must be dependent on the probabilities of the various messages that *can* occur in a given setting. However, we have not given the precise recipe yet to express the information content in terms of these probabilities. The hypothesis emerging from our investigations is that the measure of information should indeed depend on these probabilities and *only* on these probabilities.

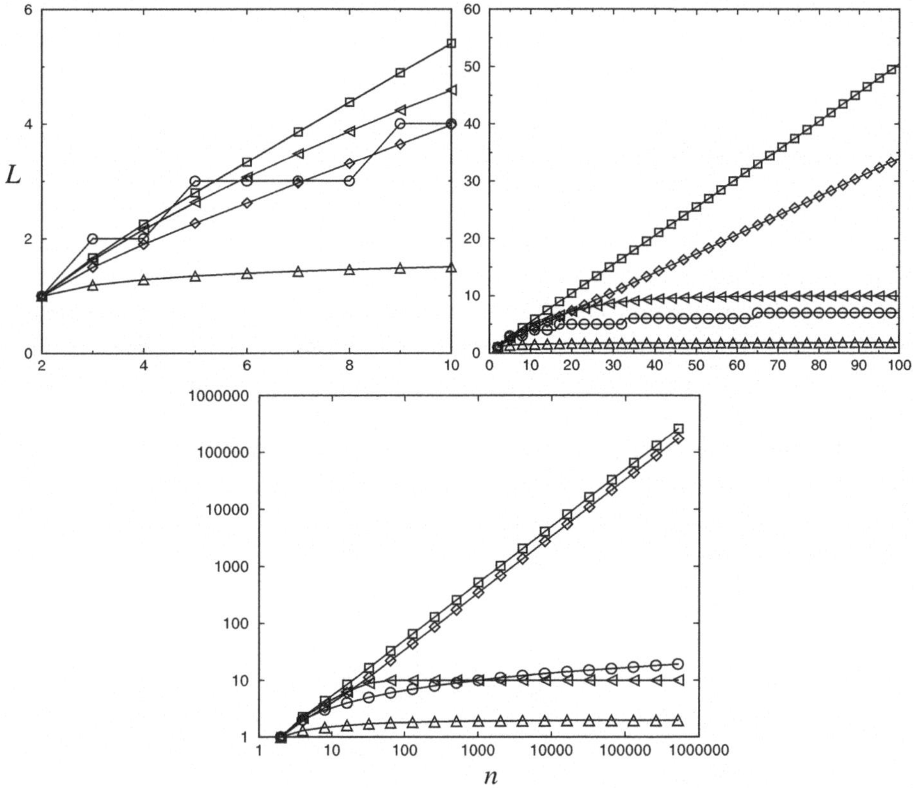

Figure 10.1 Codelengths L of enumerative code (circles) and prefix codes for 4 different message statistics, as functions of $|A| = n$. (i) $p(a_k) = \text{const.}$ as in Example 1 (squares), (ii) $p(a_k)$ linearly decreasing as in Example 2 (diamonds), (iii) $p(a_k)$ decreasing exponentially as in Example 3, with $z = e^{-\lambda} = 0.9$ (left pointing triangles), and (iv) $p(a_k) \sim k^{-\alpha}$ for $\alpha = 2.5$ (triangles). The three panels cover the regions of small, intermediate, and large n, respectively. The lines connecting the markers are just guides to the eye.

A sensible, unique and—as shown in the following chapter—workable measure of the information content of a set A of messages in terms of codes is then obtained by defining information content as the *average number of bits* needed to communicate the messages from set A when using the *optimal*, that is, shortest possible, code. The examples above have shown that this optimal code will be different for different message sets. Needless to say it is anything but straightforward to infer from this definition the resulting expression for the measure of information in terms of the set of probabilities $\{p(a_k)\}$ involved; the bulk of Chapter 11 will be devoted to its derivation. Here we only quote the result, and briefly explore its properties for the examples that we inspected above.

Proposition. The information content of a set $A = \{a_1, a_2, \ldots, a_n\}$ of messages, occurring with probabilities $p(a_k)$, is given by the *entropy*

$H = H[p]$

$$H[p] = -\sum_{k=1}^{n} p(a_k) \log_2 p(a_k) \tag{10.4}$$

associated with the probabilities.

This is Shannon's celebrated source coding theorem. Entropy as defined by equation (10.4) is one of the key concepts of information theory. We shall establish its relation to optimal codes in Chapter 11. Thereafter, in Chapter 12, we go on to explore its properties along with those of a number of useful related concepts, and finally in Chapters 13 and 14 we apply these concepts to problems in statistical inference and neural networks, respectively.

For the remainder of this introduction, however, we will restrict ourselves to briefly showing what (10.4) predicts as the value for the entropy of the specific examples we discussed earlier.

Our first example had uniform message probabilities: $p(a_k) = 1/n$ for $k = 1, \ldots, n$. Here we get

$$H = -\sum_{k=1}^{n} \frac{1}{n} \log_2 \frac{1}{n} = \log_2 n \tag{10.5}$$

which is precisely the length of the enumerative code.

Our second example was the message set with linearly decreasing probabilities, $p(a_k) = (2/n)(1 - (k/n+1))$. In this case the entropy is

$$H = -\frac{2}{n} \sum_{k=1}^{n} \left(1 - \frac{k}{n+1}\right) \log_2 \left[\frac{2}{n}\left(1 - \frac{k}{n+1}\right)\right] \tag{10.6}$$

Asymptotically, that is, for $n \gg 1$, we can replace the sum in this expression by an integral, by putting $x_k = k/(n+1)$ and $\Delta x_k = 1/(n+1) \to \mathrm{d}x$; with $\log_2 z = \ln z / \ln 2$ one gets for $n \gg 1$:

$$\begin{aligned} H &\simeq -2 \int_0^1 \mathrm{d}x\, (1-x) \left[1 - \log_2 n + \frac{1}{\ln 2} \ln(1-x)\right] \\ &= -1 + \log_2 n + \frac{1}{2 \ln 2} \sim \log_2 n \quad \text{as } n \to \infty \end{aligned}$$

For our third example, with message probabilities decreasing exponentially, that is, $p(a_k) = e^{-\lambda k}/B_n$, one finds

$$H = -\frac{1}{B_n} \sum_{k=1}^{n} e^{-\lambda k} \left[\log_2 \left(\frac{1}{B_n}\right) - \frac{\lambda k}{\ln 2}\right]$$

Asymptotically this gives:

$$H = -\log_2(e^{\lambda} - 1) + \frac{\lambda}{\ln 2}\frac{e^{\lambda}}{e^{\lambda} - 1} \qquad \text{as } n \to \infty$$

This result is shown in Figure 10.2, together with the limit $n \to \infty$ of the code length of the simple prefix code, $L_{\text{pref}} = 1/(1 - e^{-\lambda})$, for comparison. We observe that always $L_{\text{pref}} \geq H$ (as it should). The two graphs appear to

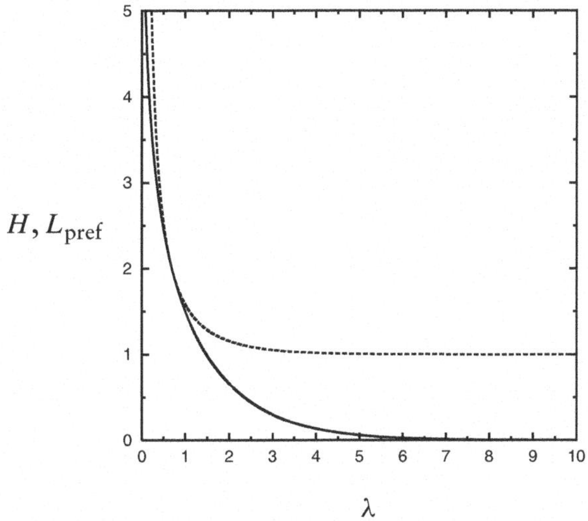

Figure 10.2 Code length L_{pref} of simple prefix code (dashed curve) versus information content H (solid curve) of infinitely large message set (i.e. $n = \infty$) with exponentially decaying message probabilities $p(a_\ell) \sim e^{-\lambda\ell}$, as a function of the decay rate λ.

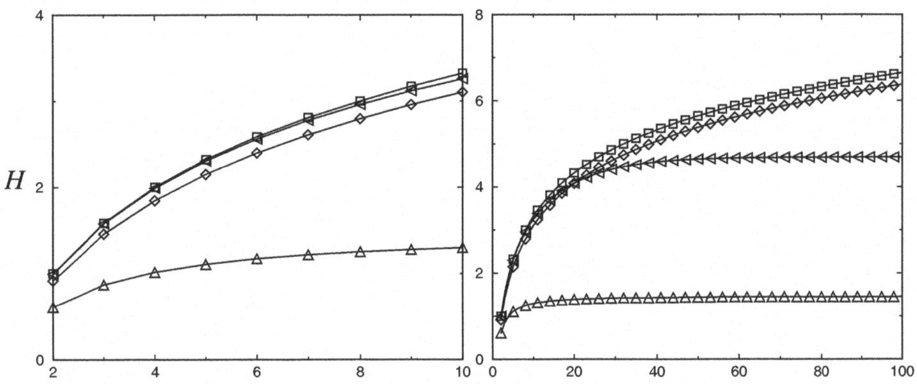

Figure 10.3 Shannon entropies for four different message statistics, as functions of $|A| = n$. (i) $p(a_k) = \text{const.}$ as in Example 1 (squares), (ii) $p(a_k)$ linearly decreasing as in Example 2 (diamonds), (iii) $p(a_k)$ decreasing exponentially as in Example 3, with $z = e^{-\lambda} = 0.9$ (left pointing triangles), and (iv) $p(a_k) \sim k^{-\alpha}$ for $\alpha = 2.5$ (triangles). The two panels cover the regimes of small and intermediate n, respectively. The lines are only guides to the eye.

touch at $\lambda = \ln 2 = 0.693\ldots$, which is indeed true since

$$\lambda = \ln 2: \quad L_{\text{pref}} = \frac{1}{1-1/2} = 2 \qquad H = -\log_2(2-1) + \frac{\ln 2}{\ln 2}\frac{2}{2-1} = 2$$

This shows that the prefix code is optimal for $\lambda = \ln 2$.

Finally, Figure 10.3 compares the values of Shannon's entropy (10.4) for four different types of message statistics (the examples studied earlier), as functions of the size n of the message sets.

11 Identification of entropy as an information measure

In this chapter, we will use coding theory to prove that the entropy does indeed represent the information content of a set of messages generated according to a set of prescribed probabilities. We will first do this by showing that the average number of bits used per message is equal to the entropy H, if we use the optimal code to represent the possible values of the messages (i.e. the one with the smallest average length of codewords). Thereafter, we shall also present the main line of reasoning of Shannon's elegant original proof, which is based on a few basic assumption about properties of a sensible measure of information, and does not refer to optimal codes.

11.1 Coding theory and the Kraft inequality

For simplicity we will restrict ourselves to binary codes, that is, to those that use only symbols from the set $\{0, 1\}$. Generalization of the theory to families of codes which employ a larger alphabet of symbols is straightforward.

Definitions

To get our vocabulary in place, we begin with a number of definitions about codes and their properties:

- A binary code $C : A \to \bigcup_{L\geq 1}\{0,1\}^L$ is a mapping from the set A of all messages to the set of all binary strings of nonzero length. It associates a codeword $C(x) \in \bigcup_{L\geq 1}\{0,1\}^L$ to each message $x \in A$.
- A non-singular binary code C is a binary code with the property that if $x, x' \in A$, with $x \neq x'$, then $C(x) \neq C(x')$. Different messages are always given different codewords, so each individual codeword is uniquely decodable.
- The length $\ell(x)$ of codeword $C(x)$ is defined as the number of symbols in the string $C(x)$, that is, $\ell(x) = \ell$ if and only if $C(x) \in \{0,1\}^\ell$.
- The code-length $L[C]$ of a binary code C is the average length of its codewords: $L[C] = \sum_{x\in A} p(x)\ell(x)$.
- A prefix code is a non-singular binary code C with the property that no codeword $C(x)$ is the prefix of another codeword $C(x')$, where $x, x' \in A$ and $x \neq x'$.

- The extension $C^\star : A^n \to \bigcup_{L\geq 1}\{0,1\}^L$ of a binary code $C : A \to \bigcup_{L\geq 1}\{0,1\}^L$ is a mapping from the set A^n of all groups $(x_1,\ldots,x_n)$ of n messages to the set of all binary strings of nonzero length. The codeword $C^\star(x_1,\ldots,x_n)$ which $C^\star$ assigns to a group of n messages $(x_1,\ldots,x_n) \in A^n$ is defined simply as the concatenation of the codewords $C(x_i)$ of the n individual messages: $C^\star(x_1,x_2,\ldots,x_n) = C(x_1)C(x_2),\ldots,C(x_n)$.
- A uniquely decodable binary code C is one with the property that its extension $C^\star$ is non-singular for any n. Note that this also implies that C must be a prefix code.

Note that the definition of the extended code $C^\star$ precisely covers the situation where one sends several codewords $C(x)$, one after the other. $C^\star$ being non-singular then means that (i) the original code C is non-singular (so the individual codewords $C(x)$ are uniquely decodable), and in addition (ii) the receiver of a string of codewords $C(x)$ can always tell when one codeword ends and the next codeword begins.

To give an example, let $A = \{x_1, x_2, x_3\}$, and

$$C(x_1) = 00, \qquad C(x_2) = 01, \qquad C(x_3) = 1$$

Then:

$$\begin{aligned} C^\star(x_1,x_1) &= 0000 \\ C^\star(x_1,x_2) &= 0001 \\ C^\star(x_1,x_3) &= 001 \\ C^\star(x_2,x_1) &= 0100 \\ &\vdots \\ C^\star(x_1,x_2,x_3) &= 00011 \\ &\vdots \end{aligned}$$

After these preliminaries, we are in a position to state in informal terms how entropy H will be established as the proper measure of information.

First, it is clear that a proper measure of information ought to constitute a lower bound for the length $L[C]$ of *any* (binary) code C: $H \leq L[C]$. In fact it is suggested to define the measure of information precisely as the length of the optimal code, given the statistics of the message set. Our next steps then will be (i) to prove the so-called Kraft inequality, which states that every binary prefix code C satisfies $\sum_{x\in A}\left(\frac{1}{2}\right)^{\ell(x)} \leq 1$, (ii) to show that $H \leq L[C]$ for *any* prefix code, and (iii) that, given a message set A with probability assignment $p(x)$ for $x \in A$, there exists a prefix code which satisfies $L[C] < H + 1$, finally (iv) to argue that the 'extra bit' in the last inequality can be avoided on a per-message basis by using optimal codes for large groups of messages.

The Kraft inequality

We now turn to the first step in our line of reasoning—the Kraft inequality for codeword lengths $\{\ell(x)\}$—and first prove that it will hold for any prefix code, and conversely that, if a set of proposed codeword lengths $\{\ell(x)\}$ satisfies the Kraft inequality, then there always exists a prefix code C with precisely these codeword lengths $\{\ell(x)\}$.

Proposition 1 (Kraft inequality). Let A denote a message set. Any prefix code C characterized by a set of codeword lengths $\{\ell(x); x \in A\}$ satisfies the Kraft inequality

$$\sum_{x \in A} \left(\frac{1}{2}\right)^{\ell(x)} \leq 1 \tag{11.1}$$

Proof:

- In order to prove this inequality, we first build a tree representation of all possible binary strings, in the following way:

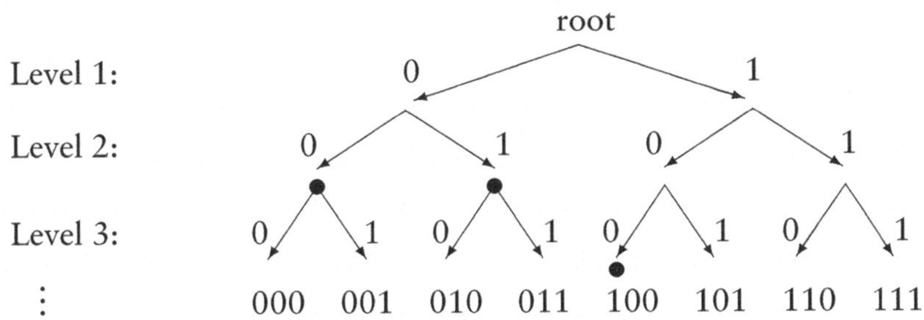

  This tree extends downward towards infinity. To each branch point in this tree we associate a binary string, which simply represents all bits one runs into if one follows the directed path (see arrows) from the root to that particular branch point. For example, at level 1 in the tree we find the branch points 0 and 1; at level 2 in the tree we have 00, 01, 10, and 11; at level 3 in the tree one finds 000, 001, 010, 011, 100, 101, 110, and 111, and so on.
- At level n, the binary stings associated with the nodes are (from left to right) just the *binary* (base-2) *representations* of the numbers $0, 1, \ldots, 2^n - 1$.
- Those strings that actually occur among the codewords of a prefix code C under consideration are marked with a • (in the example above, the codewords occurring up to length 3 are 00, 01, and 100).
- Since C is a prefix code we know that, once a branch point is selected to correspond to a codeword (marked by a •), there can be no other codeword further down along the sub-tree rooted in that particular branch point.

- Weights are associated with the branch points of the tree as follows. Start with weight 1 at the root. The two nodes at level 1 each carry weight $\frac{1}{2}$, the four nodes at level 2 each carry weight $\frac{1}{4}$, and so on, that is, the 2^k nodes at level k each carry weight 2^{-k}. This construction ensures that, irrespective of the level k, (i) the total weight of all 2^k nodes at that level adds up to 1, (ii) the total weight of the complete set of descendants of a node at level $\ell < k$ (containing $2^{k-\ell}$ elements) is $2^{-\ell}$, that is, the weight of the originating node.
- Now, at each level $n \geq 1$ one can divide the set of nodes into *three* disjoint groups: (i) nodes that are blocked and may not be used for codewords, because they are descendants of a node that has been used as a codeword $C(x)$ at a level $\ell = \ell(x) < n$; by construction their total weight adds up to $2^{-\ell(x)}$, (ii) nodes that are used as codewords at the level n in question, and (iii) nodes that are unused (and may or may not represent the first n bits of further codewords of length $m > n$).
- Labelling the nodes at level n by their associated bitstrings $\boldsymbol{c}_n \in \{0,1\}^n$, and recalling that the weight $w(\boldsymbol{c}_n)$ of a node associated with $\boldsymbol{c}_n$ (at level n) is $w(\boldsymbol{c}_n) = 2^{-n}$, we thus have for all $n \geq 1$:

$$\begin{aligned}\sum_{\boldsymbol{c}_n} w(\boldsymbol{c}_n) &= \sum_{\boldsymbol{c}_n;\text{ blocked}} \left(\frac{1}{2}\right)^n + \sum_{\boldsymbol{c}_n;\text{ used}} \left(\frac{1}{2}\right)^n + \sum_{\boldsymbol{c}_n;\text{ unused}} \left(\frac{1}{2}\right)^n \\ &= \sum_{x\in A;\ \ell(x)<n} \left(\frac{1}{2}\right)^{\ell(x)} + \sum_{x\in A;\ \ell(x)=n} \left(\frac{1}{2}\right)^{\ell(x)} + \sum_{\boldsymbol{c}_n;\text{ unused}} \left(\frac{1}{2}\right)^n \\ &= 1\end{aligned}$$

By omitting the weights of the unused nodes from the sum we thus get

$$\forall n \geq 1: \qquad \sum_{x\in A;\ \ell(x)\leq n} \left(\frac{1}{2}\right)^{\ell(x)} \leq 1$$

From this result immediately follows, by taking the limit $n \to \infty$:

$$\sum_{x\in A} \left(\frac{1}{2}\right)^{\ell(x)} \leq 1$$

which completes our proof. □

Conversely, we have the additional

Proposition 2. If a set of codeword lengths $\{\ell(x)\}$ satisfies the Kraft inequality (11.1), then there exists a corresponding prefix code that has the $\{\ell(x)\}$ as codeword lengths.

Proof. This is proven by explicit construction of a code.

- We first order the codeword lengths—writing $\ell_i = \ell(x_i)$—according to increasing length:

$$\ell_1 \le \ell_2 \le \ell_3 \le \cdots$$

Codewords are then constructed in terms of the binary tree introduced above (and reproduced below) as follows:

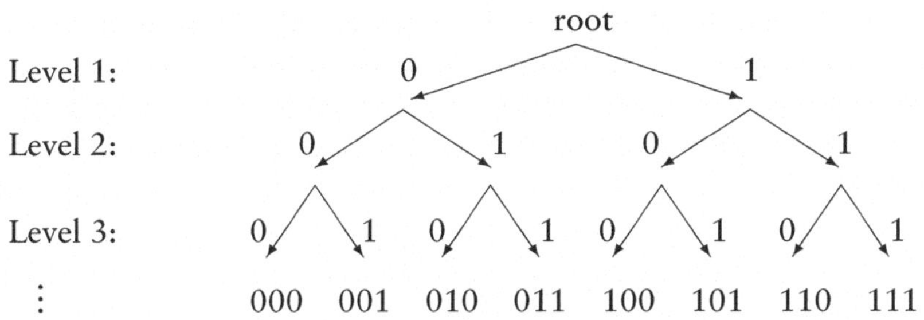

Choose for the first codeword C_1 the leftmost branch point at level ℓ_1 in the tree. That is

$$C_1 = 00\ldots0 \ (\ell_1 \text{ zeros})$$

Then iterate:
– If $\ell_{i+1} = \ell_i$ $\quad C_{i+1}$ is branch point to the right of C_i.
– If $\ell_{i+1} > \ell_i$ $\quad C_{i+1}$ is leftmost available[23] node at level ℓ_{i+1}.
– $i \to i+1$

- There is a concise algebraic representation of this iterative scheme in terms of arithmetic in base-2 representation, viz.

$$C_1 = 0$$
$$C_{i+1} = 2^{(\ell_{i+1}-\ell_i)} \times (C_i + 1), \quad i \ge 1$$

where it is understood that the binary representation of C_i uses ℓ_i bits—allowing as many leading zeros as necessary to achieve this, if $C_i < 2^{\ell_i}-1$, and indicating failure of the construction if $C_i > 2^{\ell_i} - 1$.

- This construction could only fail if we find ourselves having allocated a codeword to the rightmost node at some level n at a stage where there are still further codeword lengths waiting to get a codeword. In terms of the categorization of the codewords at level n this means that they are all either *blocked* (by codewords assigned at levels higher up in the tree) or

[23] Note that a branch point is available if it is not a descendant of a codeword used earlier and therefore blocked.

used, and no unused ones are left (hence *all* nodes further down the tree would be blocked), so

$$\sum_{i:\ \ell_i \le n} \left(\frac{1}{2}\right)^{\ell_i} = 1$$

However, in this situation we *must* have allocated all codeword lengths ℓ_i to codewords C_i, since otherwise the Kraft inequality would have been violated. This completes our proof. □

In order to develop further intuition for the above formal results, let us turn to a number of explicit examples. We will illustrate the construction of prefix codes, described in the previous proof, from a given set of desired codeword lengths, focusing on the crucial role of the Kraft inequality.

Example 1. We first choose the set of codeword lengths $\{\ell_i\} = \{1, 2, 3, 3\}$. This set saturates the Kraft inequality, since

$$\sum_{i=1}^{4} \left(\frac{1}{2}\right)^{\ell_i} = \frac{1}{2} + \left(\frac{1}{2}\right)^2 + 2\left(\frac{1}{2}\right)^3 = 1$$

The construction recipe for the corresponding code gives:

construction:	result:
$C_1 = 0$	0
$C_2 = 2 \times (C_1 + 1) = 2$	10
$C_3 = 2 \times (C_2 + 1) = 6$	110
$C_4 = C_3 + 1 = 7$	111

This is indeed a prefix code, with the required codeword lengths. The fact that a codeword consisting entirely of 1s appears as the last entry indicates that the rightmost node at level 3 has been reached, so that all nodes further down the tree are blocked, or equivalently that the Kraft inequality is saturated as an equality.

Example 2. Next we choose the set $\{\ell_i\} = \{2, 2, 3, 3, 4, 4\}$. This set also satisfies the Kraft inequality:

$$\sum_{i=1}^{6} \left(\frac{1}{2}\right)^{\ell_i} = 2\left[\left(\frac{1}{2}\right)^2 + \left(\frac{1}{2}\right)^3 + \left(\frac{1}{2}\right)^4\right] = \frac{7}{8}$$

The construction recipe for the corresponding code gives:

construction:	result:
$C_1 = 0$	00
$C_2 = C_1 + 1 = 1$	01
$C_3 = 2 \times (C_2 + 1) = 4$	100
$C_4 = C_3 + 1 = 5$	101
$C_5 = 2 \times (C_4 + 1) = 12$	1100
$C_6 = C_5 + 1 = 13$	1101

This is again a prefix code, with the required codeword lengths.

Example 3. Our third example illustrates how the construction fails when the Kraft inequality is not satisfied. Let us choose the set $\{\ell_i\} = \{1, 2, 2, 2\}$. This set violates the Kraft inequality:

$$\sum_{i=1}^{4} \left(\frac{1}{2}\right)^{\ell_i} = \frac{1}{2} + 3\left(\frac{1}{2}\right)^2 = \frac{5}{4} > 1$$

Now our construction recipe generates the code:

construction:	result:
$C_1 = 0$	0
$C_2 = 2 \times (C_1 + 1) = 2$	10
$C_3 = C_2 + 1 = 3$	11
$C_4 = C_3 + 1 = 4$	(≡100, not a 2-bit string!)

We see that a prefix code with codeword lengths $\{\ell_i\}$ that violates the Kraft inequality cannot be constructed. Once C_3 is found, the rightmost node at level 2 has been reached (C_3 consists only of 1s); the tentative C_4 constructed via the algebraic iteration scheme does not allow a 2-bit representation as required. Another way to see the failure of the construction is to note that C_2 is a prefix of the tentatively constructed C_4.

11.2 Entropy and optimal coding

Bounds for optimal codes

We will now prove two important theorems. The first one states that no uniquely decodable code C will allow us to communicate messages $x \in A$

in such a way that the average number of bits used is less than the entropy: $L[C] \geq H[p]$, an inequality which we had argued should be satisfied by any sensible measure of information. The second theorem, on the other hand, states that for every message set A with prescribed probabilities $p(x)$ for the occurrence of $x \in A$ there exists a uniquely decodable code that comes very close to this bound: $L[C] < H[p] + 1$. Note that every uniquely decodable code must be a prefix code.

Proposition 3. Every prefix code C to encode messages $x \in A$ obeys $L[C] \geq H[p]$, with equality if and only if $\ell(x) = \log_2[1/p(x)]$ for each $x \in A$.

Proof. Subtract the two sides of the inequality to be established:

$$
\begin{aligned}
L[C] - H[p] &= \sum_{x\in A} p(x)[\ell(x) + \log_2 p(x)] = \sum_{x\in A} p(x)\log_2\left(\frac{p(x)}{(1/2)^{\ell(x)}}\right) \\
&\geq \left(\sum_{x\in A} p(x)\right)\log_2\left(\frac{\sum_{x\in A} p(x)}{\sum_{x\in A}(1/2)^{\ell(x)}}\right) \\
&= -\log_2\left(\sum_{x\in A}\left(\frac{1}{2}\right)^{\ell(x)}\right) \geq 0
\end{aligned}
$$

Here the first inequality follows from an inequality related to convexity, which we prove in Appendix G, the so-called the log–sum inequality (LSI). The second inequality follows from the Kraft inequality (KI). Full equality is obtained only if both the LSI and the Kraft inequality simultaneously reduce to equalities, so:

$$
\text{LSI: } \exists\lambda > 0: \quad p(x) = \lambda\left(\frac{1}{2}\right)^{\ell(x)}, \qquad \text{KI: } \sum_{x\in A}\left(\frac{1}{2}\right)^{\ell(x)} = 1
$$

Combination of these two conditions gives $\lambda = 1$, so indeed $p(x) = \left(\frac{1}{2}\right)^{\ell(x)}$ for each $x \in A$. Equivalently: $\ell(x) = \log_2[1/p(x)]$ for each $x \in A$. This completes the proof. □

Proposition 4. For every message set A with prescribed probabilities $p(x)$ for the occurrence of the messages $x \in A$ there exists a prefix code C with the property $L[C] < H[p] + 1$.

Proof. The proof is based on the explicit construction of a code with the stated properties. It is clear from the previous theorem that efficient codes are those which approach the relation $\ell(x) = \log_2[1/p(x)]$. However, since each $\ell(x)$ must be an integer the ideal situation is not always achievable.

Thus we attempt to get as close to achieving this condition as possible within the integers by choosing

$$\ell(x) = \text{ceil}\,[\log_2(1/p(x))]$$

where we define

$$\text{ceil}[z] = \min\{n \in \mathbb{N} \mid n \geq z\} \;\Rightarrow\; z \leq \text{ceil}[z] < z + 1$$

These lengths obey the Kraft inquality, since

$$\begin{aligned}\sum_{x \in A}\left(\frac{1}{2}\right)^{\ell(x)} &= \sum_{x \in A}\left(\frac{1}{2}\right)^{\text{ceil}\,[\log_2(1/p(x))]} \\ &\leq \sum_{x \in A}\left(\frac{1}{2}\right)^{\log_2(1/p(x))} \\ &= \sum_{x \in A} 2^{\log_2 p(x)} = \sum_{x \in A} p(x) = 1\end{aligned}$$

Here we used $\text{ceil}[z] \geq z$. Proposition 2 now guarantees that there exists a prefix code with the codeword lengths $\ell(x) = \text{ceil}\,[\log_2(1/p(x))]$; it even provides a construction. This code will then have the following code-length:

$$\begin{aligned}L[C] &= \sum_{x \in A} p(x)\text{ceil}\,[\log_2(1/p(x))] \\ &< \sum_{x \in A} p(x)[\log_2(1/p(x)) + 1] = H[p] + 1\end{aligned}$$

where $\text{ceil}[z] < z + 1$ was used. This completes our proof. □

At this point it is appropriate to summarize our present knowledge about the relation between codes and entropy in a compact way. If we define the optimal code (or most efficient code) for a given ensemble of messages (described by the message set A and the message probabilities $\{p(x), x \in A\}$) as that uniquely decodable code C which has the smallest codelength $L[C]$, we get the following proposition.

Proposition 5. The optimal code C to encode messages for a given ensemble of messages (described by $A, \{p(x), x \in A\}$) uses an average number $L[C]$ of bits per message which obeys

$$H[p] \leq L[C] < H[p] + 1 \tag{11.2}$$

Proof. This theorem follows directly from the previous two propositions; note once more that uniquely decodable codes are always of the prefix type. □

Killing the final bit

One notes that the '+1' contribution on the right-hand side of (11.2) is purely due to the fact that the ideal values $\ell(x) = \log_2(1/p(x))$ cannot always be realized in practice, but have to be rounded off to the nearest integer. Equation (11.2) is thus in itself adequate proof that the average information content of messages $x \in A$ generated with probabilities $\{p(x)\}$ is indeed the entropy $H[p]$ given in (10.4).

In what follows, we briefly demonstrate that the extra bit by which the optimal code may exceed the entropy of an information source can in a certain sense be eliminated. This is obviously not just a challenge of purely academic interest but would be very useful for any high throughput communication system.

The key observation to achieve this elimination of the final bit is based on the fact that nowhere in the line of reasoning leading to (11.2) did we in any essential way make use of the fact that the messages to be encoded were single-component messages.

Thus to eliminate the final bit, one would use codes which are optimized in such a way as to encode groups of n messages, *independently* generated from a message set A with probabilities $\{p(x)\}$. That is, denoting by $\boldsymbol{x} = (x_1, x_2, \ldots, x_n)$ with $x_i \in A$ the n-component messages, generated with probabilities $p_n(\boldsymbol{x}) = \prod_{i=1}^n p(x_i)$, and by C_n the optimal uniquely decodable code used to encode these messages, we know that the inequality (11.2) of the previous proposition generalizes as follows.

Proposition 6. The optimal code C_n to encode messages for a given ensemble of n-component messages generated from A, with $p_n(\boldsymbol{x}) = \prod_{i=1}^n p(x_i)$ uses an average number $L[C_n]$ of bits per n-component message which obeys

$$H[p_n] \leq L[C_n] < H[p_n] + 1 \tag{11.3}$$

Using the fact that $H[p_n] = nH[p]$, since the n messages are drawn independently, we thus find that the number of bits of code used on average *per message* satisfies

$$H[p] \leq n^{-1}L[C_n] < H[p] + n^{-1} \tag{11.4}$$

which can be as close to $H[p]$—the average information per message generated according to the prescribed probabilities—as desired, if coding is optimized for large groups of messages.

The various practicalities of the approach to coding via coding of message sets are themselves of some intrinsic interest, leading to the notion of *typical* and *atypical* message sets and and the idea of using enumerative codes to code these message sets separately, granting an additional bit for the information to which group a message belongs. However, we shall not deal with these issues here and refer instead to the specialized literature for further details.

11.3 Shannon's original proof

Let us finally give a brief outline of Shannon's elegant original proof that entropy $H[p]$ is the proper measure of information of an ensemble of messages generated according to a set of prescribed probabilities $p_i = p(a_i)$, with $a_i \in A$.

The proof is based on three assumptions about properties which a good measure of information should have, thus rendering Shannon's approach to information axiomatic.

1. $H[p] = H(\{p_i\})$ should be continuous in the probabilities p_i.
2. For uniform probabilities $p_i = 1/n$, $i = 1, \ldots, n$, the information

$$H\left(\frac{1}{n}, \ldots, \frac{1}{n}\right) \equiv F(n) \tag{11.5}$$

   is a monotonically increasing function of n (i.e. of the number of possibilities to choose from).
3. Information is additive. More specifically: if a message set can be grouped and messages can accordingly be identified by first identifying the group to which they belong, and then by identifying which member of a group they are, these pieces of information must add up. Formally, if p_j denotes the probability of a message to belong to group j and $p_{i|j}$ denotes the conditional probability that it is the ith member of the group, given that the group is j, then

$$H(\{p_{ij}\}) = H(\{p_{i|j}\, p_j\}) = H(\{p_j\}) + \sum_j p_j H(\{p_{i|j}\}) \tag{11.6}$$

   Thus the total amount of information equals the information about group membership plus the weighted average over the groups of the information concerning choice within groups.

Since one can always decompose a choice of s^m equally likely possibilities into a series of m choices of s equally likely possibilities, one has according to assumption 3:

$$F(s^m) = mF(s)$$

for the function F, which is the measure of information for uniform probabilities as introduced in assumption 2. This functional relation is seen to be satisfied by

$$F(x) = k \ln x,$$

for some $k > 0$, and since the relation is supposed to hold for *all* integers s and m, one can show that this choice is unique (up to the prefactor k).

Similarly, given a set of n equally likely messages which is decomposed into groups containing n_j equally likely messages ($n = \sum_j n_j$), so that the probabilities $p_j = n_j/n$ of belonging to the various groups are rational, one can use assumption 3 and the definition of F to write

$$F(n) = H(\{p_j\}) + \sum_j p_j F(n_j)$$

For the form (11.3) of F obtained above we find

$$H(\{p_j\}) = F(n) - \sum_j p_j F(n_j) = -k \sum_j p_j \ln(n_j/n) = -k \sum_j p_j \ln p_j \tag{11.7}$$

as the expression for the information in case of *rational* probabilities. By the continuity assumption, the same expression must hold for any choice of *real* p_j. This completes Shannon's original proof that entropy is the proper measure of information. The constant k appearing here obviously only affects the unit in which it is measured. The standard choice is $k = 1/\ln 2$, corresponding to information being measured in bits.

It is very satisfactory to observe that the earlier proof involving the optimal code did not involve any of the above axioms, and that, conversely, Shannon's proof does not involve coding. The two proofs are thus quite distinct, yet both confirm the validity of the central result that (10.4) represents the correct information measure.

12 Building blocks of Shannon's information theory

In this chapter, we explore properties of entropy and of related measures of information theory, which will be useful for later applications of the framework. The chapter has the character of a compilation of key results (and proofs); it may thus also be taken as a reference.

We will find it useful to formulate the results in terms of the concept of random variables X characterizing information sources. A random variable X is specified by the set A of values x that the random variable X can assume, and a probability assignment $\{p(x); x \in A\}$. Instead of writing $H[p]$ for the entropy—thereby emphasizing the dependence of information on probabilities—we shall thus often write $H(X)$, thereby indicating both the range of values that X can assume *and* the probability assignments.

We begin by developing the framework for discrete random variables, in which case probabilities are assigned to individual elements of A. Continuous random variables will be treated later on. Elementary concepts of probability theory in as much as they are needed for what follows are gathered in Appendix A.

12.1 Entropy

The entropy $H(X)$ of a discrete random variable X, measured in *bits*, is defined as follows:

$$H(X) = -\sum_{x \in A} p(x) \log_2 p(x) \tag{12.1}$$

We assume that $p(x) > 0$ for all $x \in A$, which can always be arranged via the definition of A, unless stated otherwise (in the latter cases we define $0 \log_2 0 = \lim_{\epsilon \downarrow 0} \epsilon \log_2 \epsilon = 0$). As demonstrated in the previous chapter, the entropy represents the average information content of messages x from the set A with the specified probabilities $p(x)$ of occurrence.

General properties

Property 1. $H(X) \geq 0$, with equality if and only if x is a constant.

Proof. Use the property $p(x) \leq 1$ for all $x \in A$:

$$H(X) = \sum_{x \in A} p(x) \log_2 \left[\frac{1}{p(x)} \right] \geq \sum_{x \in A} p(x) \log_2 1 = 0 \tag{12.2}$$

Equality implies that $p(x) = 1$ $(\forall x \in A)$. Since also $\sum_{x \in A} p(x) = 1$, this forces x to be a constant. Conversely, if x is a constant then the equality indeed holds. □

Property 2. $H(X) \leq \log_2 |A|$, with equality if and only if $p(x) = |A|^{-1}$ for all $x \in A$.

Proof. Define auxiliary probabilities $q(x) = |A|^{-1}$, and use the log-sum inequality (G.5) (to be referred to as LSI in what follows):

$$\begin{aligned} \log_2 |A| - H(X) &= \sum_{x \in A} p(x) [\log_2 p(x) + \log_2 |A|] \\ &= \sum_{x \in A} p(x) \log_2 \left[\frac{p(x)}{q(x)} \right] \geq \left[\sum_{x \in A} p(x) \right] \log_2 \left[\frac{\sum_{x \in A} p(x)}{\sum_{x \in A} q(x)} \right] = 0 \end{aligned}$$

Equality holds if and only if it holds in the log-sum inquality, so $(\exists \lambda > 0)$: $p(x) = \lambda q(x)$. Since $\sum_{x \in A} p(x) = \sum_{x \in A} q(x) = 1$ the constant λ must be 1, so $p(x) = |A|^{-1}$ for all $x \in A$. □

Property 3. $H(F(X)) \leq H(X)$, with equality if and only if F is invertible.

Proof. Define the new random variable $Y = F(X)$ with $y \in A_Y$, with non-overlapping domains $D_y = \{x \in A \mid F(x) = y\}$ which obey $\cup_{y \in A_Y} D_y = A$, and associated probabilities

$$\hat{p}(y) = \sum_{x \in D_y} p(x) \qquad \sum_{y \in A_Y} \hat{p}(y) = \sum_{y \in A_Y} \sum_{x \in D_y} p(x) = \sum_{x \in A} p(x) = 1$$

Now work out the difference between the two entropies:

$$
\begin{aligned}
H(F(X)) - H(X) &= -\sum_{y\in A_Y} \hat{p}(y)\log_2 \hat{p}(y) + \sum_{x\in A} p(x)\log_2 p(x) \\
&= -\sum_{y\in A_Y} \Big[\hat{p}(y)\log_2 \hat{p}(y) - \sum_{x\in D_y} p(x)\log_2 p(x)\Big] \\
&= -\sum_{y\in A_Y}\sum_{x\in D_y} p(x)\log_2\left[\frac{\sum_{x'\in D_y} p(x')}{p(x)}\right] \\
&= -\sum_{y\in A_Y}\sum_{x\in D_y} p(x)\log_2\left[1 + \frac{1}{p(x)}\sum_{x'(\neq x)\in D_y} p(x')\right] \leq 0
\end{aligned}
$$

Note that equality implies that *each* of the terms $\sum_{x'(\neq x)\in D_y} p(x')$ vanishes, which happens if and only if $(\forall y \in A_Y)$: $|D_y| = 1$. This is precisely the condition for invertibility of the operation F. □

Examples

Example 1. Let us see how these three properties surface in the calculation of the entropy for specific choices of random variables. We first inspect the simplest non-trivial discrete random variables x, the ones which can take only two values: $A = \{0, 1\}$, with $p(1) = p$ and $p(0) = 1 - p$ (with $p \in [0, 1]$). Here we obtain from: (12.1):

$$H(X) = -p\log_2 p - (1-p)\log_2(1-p) \tag{12.3}$$

This expression has the following properties (note: $\log_2 z = \ln z/\ln 2$):

(i) $H(X)_p = H(X)_{1-p}$ for all $p \in [0, 1]$.

(ii) $H(X)_{p=0} = H(X)_{p=1} = 0$, $H(X)_{p=1/2} = 1$.

(iii) $\mathrm{d}H(X)/\mathrm{d}p > 0$ for $p \in [0, \frac{1}{2})$, $\mathrm{d}H(X)/\mathrm{d}p < 0$ for $p \in (\frac{1}{2}, 1]$, with $\mathrm{d}H(X)/\mathrm{d}p = 0$ for $p = \frac{1}{2}$. This follows immediately from:

$$
\begin{aligned}
\frac{\mathrm{d}}{\mathrm{d}p}H(X) &= -\frac{1}{\ln 2}\frac{\mathrm{d}}{\mathrm{d}p}[p\ln p + (1-p)\ln(1-p)] = \frac{1}{\ln 2}\ln\left(\frac{1-p}{p}\right) \\
&= \log_2(p^{-1} - 1)
\end{aligned}
$$

These properties have straightforward explanations in terms of information content: (i) states that the information content is invariant under $0 \leftrightarrow 1$ (alternative coding), (ii) + (iii) state that the information content is maximal for uniform probabilities $p(1) = p(0)$ and decreases monotonically with increasing probability differences, until it vanishes at $p \in \{0, 1\}$ (where x reduces to a constant). Figure 12.1 shows the dependence of $H(X)$ on p in a graph.

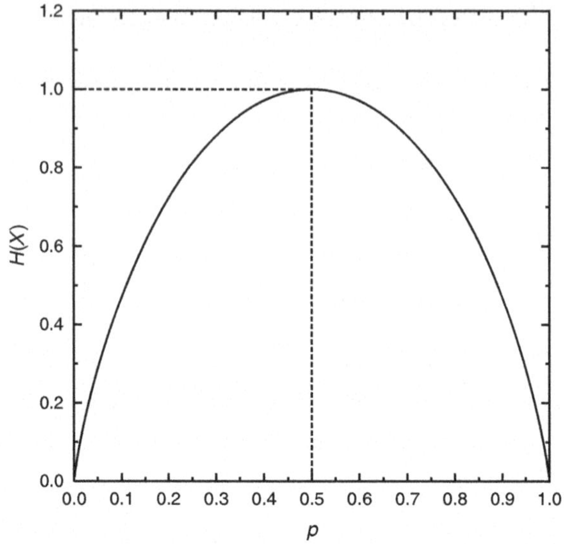

Figure 12.1 Entropy $H(X)$ for a binary random variable $x \in \{0, 1\}$, with probabilities $p(1) = p$ and $p(0) = 1 - p$, as a function of p. See equation (12.3). The maximum value $H(X) = 1$ for the entropy (i.e. for the information content) is obtained for $p = \frac{1}{2}$ (indicated by dashed lines).

Example 2. Our second example concerns the information content of messages conveying events in a casino, where a coin is thrown until the first head (h) occurs, as opposed to tails (t) only. The random variable M represents the number of times the coin is thrown (i.e. the number of throws needed for the first head to show up), so $A = \{1, 2, 3, \dots\}$ with $|A| = \infty$. The probabilities $p(m)$, $m \in A$ are obtained by inspection of the various scenarios:

$$\begin{aligned} p(1) &= \text{Prob(h)} &&= \tfrac{1}{2} \\ p(2) &= \text{Prob(th)} &&= \tfrac{1}{2} \cdot \tfrac{1}{2} \\ p(3) &= \text{Prob(tth)} &&= \tfrac{1}{2} \cdot \tfrac{1}{2} \cdot \tfrac{1}{2} \\ &\vdots && \vdots \\ p(m) &= \text{Prob(t\dots th)} &&= \left(\tfrac{1}{2}\right)^m \end{aligned}$$

With the help of the simple tools in Appendix C to deal with the summation, the entropy (12.1) now comes out as

$$\begin{aligned} H(M) &= -\sum_{m=1}^{\infty} \left(\frac{1}{2}\right)^m \log_2 \left(\frac{1}{2}\right)^m = \sum_{m=1}^{\infty} m \left(\frac{1}{2}\right)^m = \lim_{z \to 1/2} z \frac{\mathrm{d}}{\mathrm{d}z} \sum_{m=0}^{\infty} z^m \\ &= \lim_{z \to 1/2} z \frac{\mathrm{d}}{\mathrm{d}z} \frac{1}{1-z} = \lim_{z \to 1/2} \frac{z}{(1-z)^2} = 2 \text{ bits} \end{aligned}$$

On average such messages therefore convey just two bits of information. Note that for this example the prefix code is optimal:

$$C(m) = \underbrace{00\ldots0}_{m-1 \text{ times}}1 \quad \ell(m) = m: \qquad L = \sum_{m\geq 1} p(m)\ell(m) = \sum_{m\geq 1} m\left(\frac{1}{2}\right)^m = H$$

Example 3. Our third example is an illustration of how the information content of a random variable is reduced if it undergoes a non-invertible operation. Let us choose the event set $A = \{0, 1, 2, 3, 4, 5, 6, 7\}$ and the following operation: $F(x) = \cos(\pi x)$. Equivalently (at least for the present event set): $F(x) = 1$ for x even, $F(x) = -1$ for x odd. This example is quite typical of real-world communication via imperfect channels, such as poor telephone lines. Here the only information delivered at the receiving end of the communication channel is whether the original message variable x was even or odd. The new random variable $Y = F(X)$ has the following set of possible values and associated probabilities:

$$y \in A_Y = \{-1, 1\} \qquad \begin{aligned} \hat{p}(-1) &= p(1) + p(3) + p(5) + p(7) \\ \hat{p}(1) &= p(0) + p(2) + p(4) + p(6) \end{aligned} \tag{12.4}$$

The information content of the two types of messages, before and after the operation F, is given, respectively, by

$$\begin{aligned} H(X) &= -\sum_{x\in A} p(x)\log_2 p(x) \\ H(F(X)) &= -\hat{p}(-1)\log_2 \hat{p}(-1) - \hat{p}(1)\log_2 \hat{p}(1) \end{aligned} \tag{12.5}$$

The outcome of the information reduction $\Delta H = H(F(X)) - H(X)$ due to the non-invertible operation (the poor communication medium) will thus depend on the choice made for the probabilities $p(x)$.

In the simplest case where all messages x are equally likely, that is, where $p(x) = \frac{1}{8}$ for all $x \in A$, we obtain $\hat{p}(-1) = \hat{p}(1) = \frac{1}{2}$ which results in

$$\begin{aligned} &H(X) = \log_2|A| = 3 \text{ bits} \\ &H((F(X)) = \log_2|A_Y| = 1 \text{ bits} \qquad \Delta H = -2 \text{ bits} \end{aligned}$$

Only one-third of the original information content survives the operation F. Alternatively we could inspect a situation where the events in A have different probabilities of occurrence. Let us choose the following probabilities:

x	0	1	2	3	4	5	6	7
$p(x)$	$\frac{1}{2}$	$\frac{1}{4}$	$\frac{1}{8}$	$\frac{1}{16}$	$\frac{1}{32}$	$\frac{1}{64}$	$\frac{1}{128}$	$\frac{1}{128}$

According to (12.4) we now have $\hat{p}(-1) = \frac{43}{128}$ and $\hat{p}(1) = \frac{85}{128}$, so that we find for the two entropies (12.5):

$$H(X) = 1\frac{63}{64} \approx 1.984 \text{ bits}$$

$$H(F(X)) = -\frac{43}{128}\log_2\left(\frac{43}{128}\right) - \frac{85}{128}\log_2\left(\frac{85}{128}\right) \approx 0.921 \text{ bits}$$

so

$$\Delta H \approx -1.063 \text{ bits}$$

Here about one half of the original information content survives the operation F. This example illustrates that for a given type of message deterioration (i.e. for a given operation F, which could also involve a probabilistic element) the information loss is dependent on the various probabilities of occurrence of the individual messages.

12.2 Joint and conditional entropy

The joint entropy $H(X, Y)$ of a pair of discrete random variables (X, Y), measured in *bits*, is defined as follows:

$$H(X, Y) = -\sum_{(x,y)\in A} p(x, y)\log_2 p(x, y) \tag{12.6}$$

where $A = A_X \otimes A_Y$. The joint entropy represents the average information content of messages (x, y) from the set A with the specified probabilities of occurrence $p(x, y)$. As before: $0 \leq H(X, Y) \leq \log_2|A|$, with zero occurring only when (x, y) is constant, and $\log_2|A|$ occurring only when $p(x, y) = |A|^{-1}$. The proofs of these statements are identical to those for $H(X)$. Generalization of the definition of joint entropy to messages consisting of n random variables $H(X_1, \ldots, X_n)$ is also straightforward.

The conditional entropy $H(Y|X)$ of a pair of discrete random variables $(x, y) \in A$, measured in bits, is defined as follows:

$$\begin{aligned} H(Y|X) &= -\sum_{(x,y)\in A} p(x, y)\log_2 p(y|x) \\ &= \sum_{x\in A_X} p(x)\left[-\sum_{y\in A_Y} p(y|x)\log_2 p(y|x)\right] \end{aligned} \tag{12.7}$$

The conditional entropy represents the average information content of message component y of a combined message (x, y) from the set A, given that one knows the other component x already. Generalization of the definition of conditional entropy to messages consisting of more than two random variables, giving objects such as $H(X, Y|Z)$, is again straightforward.

General properties

Property 1. The entropy $H(X,Y)$ of a pair of random variables (X,Y), with $(x,y) \in A = A_X \otimes A_Y \subseteq \mathbb{R}^2$ satisfies: $H(X,Y) \leq H(X) + H(Y)$, with equality if and only if X and Y are independent.

Proof. Subtract the two sides of the proposed inequality and use the definitions of the marginal distributions, $p(x) = \sum_{y\in A_Y} p(x,y)$ and $p(y) = \sum_{x\in A_X} p(x,y)$:

$$\begin{aligned}
H(X,Y) - H(X) - H(Y) &= -\sum_{x\in A_X}\sum_{y\in A_Y} p(x,y)\log_2 p(x,y) \\
&\quad + \sum_{x\in A_X} p(x)\log_2 p(x) \\
&\quad + \sum_{y\in A_Y} p(y)\log_2 p(y) \\
&= \sum_{x\in A_X}\sum_{y\in A_Y} p(x,y)\log_2\left[\frac{p(x)p(y)}{p(x,y)}\right]
\end{aligned}$$

We now use the LSI (G.5) and obtain:

$$\begin{aligned}
&H(X,Y) - H(X) - H(Y) \\
&\leq \left[\sum_{x\in A_X}\sum_{y\in A_Y} p(x,y)\right]\log_2\left[\frac{\sum_{x\in A_X}\sum_{y\in A_Y} p(x)p(y)}{\sum_{x\in A_X}\sum_{y\in A_Y} p(x,y)}\right] = 0
\end{aligned}$$

Equality is obtained if and only if $(\exists\lambda > 0)$: $p(x,y) = \lambda p(x)p(y)$ for all $(x,y) \in A$. We can then sum over all $(x,y) \in A$ and obtain $\lambda = 1$. We conclude that equality holds if and only if the two random variables X and Y are independent. □

Property 2. $H(Y|X) \geq 0$, with equality if and only if there exists a function F such that $y = F(x)$ for all (x,y) with $p(x,y) > 0$.

Proof. Using

$$p(y|x) = \frac{p(x,y)}{p(x)} = \frac{p(x,y)}{\sum_{y'\in A_Y} p(x,y')} = \frac{p(x,y)}{p(x,y) + \sum_{y'(\neq y)\in A_Y} p(x,y')} \leq 1$$

one obtains

$$H(Y|X) = \sum_{(x,y)\in A} p(x,y)\log_2\left[\frac{1}{p(y|x)}\right] \geq \sum_{(x,y)\in A} p(x,y)\log_2 1 = 0$$

Equality requires $p(x,y) = p(x)$ for all $(x,y) \in A$, or $\sum_{y'(\neq y)\in A_Y} p(x,y') = 0$. In other words: there can for each $x \in A_X$ be just a single $y \in A_Y$ for which $p(x,y) \neq 0$. This means that y can be written as a function of x for all allowed pairs (x,y). □

Property 3. $H(F(X)|X) = 0$.

Proof. This identity is included in the proof of Property 2. □

Property 4. $H(X|F(X)) \geq 0$, with equality if and only if F is invertible.

Proof. We simply apply Property 1 to the random variables X and $Y = F(X)$, according to which $H(X|Y) \geq 0$, with equality if and only if there exists a function G such that $x = G(y) = G(F(x))$ for all x with $p(x) > 0$, which requires F to be invertible. □

Property 5. $H(Y|X) \leq H(Y)$, with equality if and only if x and y are statistically independent.

Proof. Upon evaluating the difference $H(Y) - H(Y|X)$ and using the LSI (G.5) one obtains:

$$\begin{aligned}
H(Y) - H(Y|X) &= \sum_{(x,y)\in A} p(x,y)\log_2 p(y|x) - \sum_{y\in A_Y} p(y)\log_2 p(y) \\
&= \sum_{(x,y)\in A} p(x,y)\log_2 \left[\frac{p(x,y)}{p(x)p(y)}\right] \\
&\geq \left[\sum_{(x,y)\in A} p(x,y)\right]\log_2 \left[\frac{\sum_{(x,y)\in A} p(x,y)}{\sum_{(x,y)\in A} p(x)p(y)}\right] = 0
\end{aligned}$$

Equality holds if and only if it holds in the log–sum inequality, so $(\exists\lambda > 0)$: $p(x,y) = \lambda p(x)p(y)$. Since $\sum_{(x,y)\in A} p(x,y) = \sum_{(x,y)\in A} p(x)$ $p(y) = 1$ the constant λ must be 1, so $p(x,y) = p(x)p(y)$ for all $(x,y) \in A$. □

Property 6 (Chain rule).[24] $H(X,Y) = H(X) + H(Y|X)$.

Proof. Simply use $p(x,y) = p(y|x)p(x)$:

$$\begin{aligned}
H(X,Y) &= -\sum_{(x,y)\in A} p(x,y)\log_2 p(x,y) = -\sum_{(x,y)\in A} p(x,y)\log_2[p(y|x)p(x)] \\
&= -\sum_{(x,y)\in A} p(x,y)\log_2 p(y|x) - \sum_{(x,y)\in A} p(x,y)\log_2 p(x) \\
&= H(Y|X) - \sum_{x\in A_X} p(x)\log_2 p(x) \\
&= H(Y|X) + H(X)
\end{aligned}$$

which completes the proof. □

[24] Note that this identity was part of the set of assumptions (viz. the additivity property 3) required for any good measure of information, in Shannon's proof of the source coding theorem. No wonder therefore that we recover it as a property of the (joint) entropy.

Property 7. $H(X,Y) \geq H(X)$, with equality if and only if there exists a function F such that $y = F(x)$ for all (x,y) with $p(x,y) > 0$.

Proof. The result follows by combination of Properties 2 and 6. □

Property 8 (Conditioned chain rule). $H(X,Y|Z) = H(X|Z) + H(Y|X,Z)$.

Proof. This result follows from the identity

$$p(x,y|z) = \frac{p(x,y,z)}{p(x,z)}\frac{p(x,z)}{p(z)} = p(y|x,z)p(x|z),$$

from which one infers

$$\begin{aligned} H(X,Y|Z) &= -\sum_{(x,y,z)\in A} p(x,y,z)\log_2 p(x,y|z) \\ &= -\sum_{(x,y,z)\in A} p(x,y,z)\log_2 [p(y|x,z)p(x|z)] \\ &= H(Y|X,Z) + H(X|Z) \end{aligned}$$

□

Examples

Example 1. Our first example serves to illustrate the above properties, and to demonstrate that in general $H(Y|X) \neq H(X|Y)$. We consider the stochastic variables X and Y with $A_X = A_Y = \{1,2,3,4\}$ (and $A = A_X \otimes A_Y$), and with joint probabilities $p(x,y)$ as given in the following table:

$y \backslash x$	1	2	3	4
1	$\frac{1}{8}$	$\frac{1}{16}$	$\frac{1}{32}$	$\frac{1}{32}$
2	$\frac{1}{16}$	$\frac{1}{8}$	$\frac{1}{32}$	$\frac{1}{32}$
3	$\frac{1}{16}$	$\frac{1}{16}$	$\frac{1}{16}$	$\frac{1}{16}$
4	$\frac{1}{4}$	0	0	0

The marginal probabilities $p(x) = \sum_{y\in A_Y} p(x,y)$ and $p(y) = \sum_{x\in A_X} p(x,y)$ follow as:

x	1	2	3	4
$p(x)$	$\frac{1}{2}$	$\frac{1}{4}$	$\frac{1}{8}$	$\frac{1}{8}$

y	1	2	3	4
$p(y)$	$\frac{1}{4}$	$\frac{1}{4}$	$\frac{1}{4}$	$\frac{1}{4}$

If we simply insert the appropriate probabilities in the various definitions, we obtain for the individual entropies $H(X)$ and $H(Y)$ and for the joint entropy $H(X,Y)$ the following results:

$$H(X) = -\sum_{x\in A_X} p(x)\log_2 p(x) = 1\frac{3}{4} \text{ bits}$$

$$H(Y) = -\sum_{y\in A_Y} p(y)\log_2 p(y) = 2 \text{ bits}$$

$$H(X,Y) = -\sum_{(x,y)\in A} p(x,y)\log_2 p(x,y) = 3\frac{3}{8} \text{ bits}$$

After careful bookkeeping (summing over all nonzero entries in the table of the joint probabilities) we obtain the conditional entropies $H(Y|X)$ and $H(X|Y)$:

$$H(X|Y) = -\sum_{(x,y)\in A} p(x,y)\log_2 p(x|y) = 1\frac{3}{8} \text{ bits}$$

$$H(Y|X) = -\sum_{(x,y)\in A} p(x,y)\log_2 p(y|x) = 1\frac{5}{8} \text{ bits}$$

Thus the average amount of extra information contained in x if we already know y need not be identical to the average amount of extra information conveyed by y if we already know x. There is no symmetry in that sense.The present example obeys the following inequalities and equalities:

$$0 < H(Y|X) < H(Y) < H(X,Y)$$
$$0 < H(X|Y) < H(X) < H(X,Y)$$
$$H(X,Y) = H(X) + H(Y|X)$$
$$H(X,Y) = H(Y) + H(X|Y)$$
$$H(X) - H(X|Y) = H(Y) - H(Y|X)$$

The first four lines indeed confirm the general properties derived earlier in this section. The bottom line points at a property to be built upon in the subsequent section.

Example 2. Our second and trivial example is the one with a non-invertible operation we inspected earlier (Example 3 of the previous section), $F(x) = \cos(\pi x)$ with $A_X = \{0, 1, 2, 3, 4, 5, 6, 7\}$. We introduce the variable $Y = F(X)$, with $A_Y = \{-1, 1\}$. The joint probability distribution $p(x, y)$ now becomes

$$p(x, y) = p(x)\delta_{y,F(x)}$$

with $\delta_{nm} = 1$ if and only if $n = m$ and zero otherwise. Here we obtain the following expressions for joint and conditional entropies:

$$\begin{aligned}
H(X,Y) &= -\sum_{(x,y)\in A_X\otimes A_Y} p(x,y)\log_2 p(x,y) \\
&= -\sum_{x\in A_X} p(x)\log_2 p(x) = H(X) \\
H(X|Y) &= -\sum_{(x,y)\in A_X\otimes A_Y} p(x,y)\log_2 p(x|y) \\
&= \sum_{(x,y)\in A_X\otimes A_Y} p(x,y)[\log_2 p(y) - \log_2 p(x,y)] \\
&= H(X,Y) - H(Y) = H(X) - H(Y) \\
H(Y|X) &= -\sum_{(x,y)\in A_X\otimes A_Y} p(x,y)\log_2 p(y|x) \\
&= \sum_{(x,y)\in A_X\otimes A_Y} p(x,y)[\log_2 p(x) - \log_2 p(x,y)] \\
&= H(X,Y) - H(X) = 0
\end{aligned}$$

Such results make perfect sense. The additional information conveyed by learning the value of $y = F(x)$ is zero if we know x already, so $H(Y|X) = 0$. In contrast, learning the precise value of x does convey additional information if previously we knew only $y = F(x)$ (i.e. whether x is even or odd).

12.3 Relative entropy and mutual information

The relative entropy $D(p||q)$, measured in bits, of two discrete random variables X and X' with $A_X = A_{X'} = A$ described by probability distributions $p(x)$ and $q(x)$, respectively, is defined as

$$D(p||q) = \sum_{x\in A} p(x)\log_2 \left[\frac{p(x)}{q(x)}\right] \tag{12.8}$$

with the usual convention $0\log_2 0 = \lim_{\epsilon\downarrow 0} \epsilon\log_2 \epsilon = 0$. The relative entropy is alternatively often called cross-entropy, or 'Kullback–Leibler distance', a term which has to be used with some care since $D(p||q)$ cannot play the role of a true distance as $D(p||q) \neq D(q||p)$ in general. As we will demonstrate shortly it does, however, have the nice property that $D(p||q) \geq 0$ for any pair of distributions p and q, with equality if and only if $p(x) = q(x)$ for all $x \in A$.

It is only natural to introduce also a measure which is similar to the relative entropy but symmetric in the two probability distributions $p(x)$ and $q(x)$:

$$J(p||q) = D(p||q) + D(q||p) \tag{12.9}$$

which is called Jeffreys' divergence. Its properties of course follow trivially from those of the relative entropy.

An important object, especially in the context of neural networks as we will see, is the so-called mutual information $I(X, Y)$ of a pair of random variables X and Y, with values $(x, y) \in A$, defined as

$$I(X, Y) = \sum_{(x,y)\in A} p(x, y)\log_2\left[\frac{p(x, y)}{p(x)p(y)}\right] \tag{12.10}$$

Note that $I(X, Y) = I(Y, X)$ and that for independent variables X and Y one would find $I(X, Y) = 0$.

Similarly one can define the conditional mutual information $I(X, Y|Z)$ involving three random variables as

$$I(X, Y|Z) = \sum_{(x,y,z)\in A} p(x, y, z)\log_2\left[\frac{p(x, y|z)}{p(x|z)p(y|z)}\right] \tag{12.11}$$

This conditional mutual information is also symmetric in its first arguments, $I(X, Y|Z) = I(Y, X|Z)$ and for conditionally independent variables X and Y, for which $p(x, y|z) = p(x|z)p(y|z)$, one finds $I(X, Y|Z) = 0$.

General properties

Property 1. $D(p||q) \geq 0$ for any pair of distributions p and q, with equality if and only if $p(x) = q(x)$ for all $x \in A$.

Proof. Use the LSI (G.5) and the normalization $\sum_x p(x) = \sum_x q(x) = 1$:

$$D(p||q) = \sum_{x\in A} p(x)\log_2\left[\frac{p(x)}{q(x)}\right] \geq \left[\sum_{x\in A} p(x)\right]\log_2\left[\frac{\sum_{x\in A} p(x)}{\sum_{x\in A} q(x)}\right] = 0$$

Equality holds if and only if it holds in the LSI, so if $(\exists\lambda > 0)$: $q(x) = \lambda p(x)$ for all $x \in A$. Normalization of p and q subsequently dictates that $\lambda = 1$. □

Property 2. $I(X,Y) \geq 0$ for any pair of random variables with values $(x,y) \in A$, with equality if and only if X and Y are independent.

Proof. Note that $I(X,Y) = D(\{p(x,y)\}||\{p(x)p(y)\})$ and use Property 1. □

Property 3. $I(X,Y) = H(X) - H(X|Y)$

Proof. Substitute $p(x,y) = p(x|y)p(y)$ in the definition of $I(X,Y)$:

$$I(X,Y) = \sum_{(x,y)\in A} p(x,y)\log_2\left[\frac{p(x,y)}{p(x)p(y)}\right]$$

$$= \sum_{(x,y)\in A} p(x,y)\log_2\left[\frac{p(x|y)}{p(x)}\right] = H(X) - H(X|Y)$$ □

Note that from $I(X,Y) = I(Y,X)$ it immediately follows that also $I(X,Y) = H(Y) - H(Y|X)$ (see Example 1 in the previous section). Note further that Property 3 allows us to attach a clear meaning to mutual information: $I(X,Y)$ is seen to be the average amount of information in messages x minus the residual average information that is left after we have learned about y. Since the reduction was entirely due to the revelation of y we find that $I(X,Y)$ is the average amount of information that y reveals about x, and vice versa (the 'vice-versa' simply follows from $I(X,Y) = I(Y,X)$). This interpretation follows alternatively from the following statement:

Property 4. $I(X,Y) = H(X) + H(Y) - H(X,Y)$

Proof. Use the chain rule $H(X,Y) = H(Y) + H(X|Y)$ (Property 6) of Section 12.2 in combination with Property 3 above:

$$I(X,Y) = H(X) - H(X|Y)$$

$$= H(X) - [H(X,Y) - H(Y)] = H(X) + H(Y) - H(X,Y)$$

□

Property 5. $I(X,F(X)) \leq H(X)$, with equality if and only if F is invertible.

Proof. Combine Property 3 with Property 4 of Section 12.2:

$$I(X,F(X)) - H(X) = -H(X|F(X)) \leq 0$$

with equality only if F is invertible. □

In particular we find that $I(X,X) = H(X)$, that is, the average amount of information that x conveys about x is simply the average amount of information in x (as it should).

Property 6. $I(X, Y|Z) \geq 0$, with equality if and only if $p(x, y|z) = p(x|z)p(y|z)$ for all $(x, y, z) \in A$ (i.e. if x and y are conditionally independent).

Proof. Write

$$I(X, Y|Z) = \sum_{(x,y,z)\in A} p(x, y, z)\log_2 \left[\frac{p(x, y|z)}{p(x|z)p(y|z)}\right]$$
$$= \sum_{(x,y,z)\in A} p(x, y, z)\log_2 \left[\frac{p(x, y, z)}{p(x|z)p(y|z)p(z)}\right]$$

and use the LSI (G.5) to conclude

$$I(X, Y|Z) \geq \left[\sum_{(x,y,z)\in A} p(x, y, z)\right]\log_2 \left[\frac{\sum_{(x,y,z)\in A} p(x, y, z)}{\sum_{(x,y,z)\in A} p(x|z)p(y|z)p(z)}\right] = 0$$

Equality holds only when it holds in the LSI, which requires that $(\exists\lambda > 0)$: $p(x, y|z) = \lambda p(x|z)p(y|z)$ for all $(x, y, z) \in A$. Normalization forces the constant λ to be one. So indeed $p(x, y|z) = p(x|z)p(y|z)$ for all $(x, y, z) \in A$. □

Property 7 (Data processing inequality). If three random variables X, Y, Z with values $(x, y, z) \in A$ are related by a Markov chain $X \to Y \to Z$, that is, $p(x, y, z) = p(z|y)p(y|x)p(x)$, then $I(X, Y) \geq I(X, Z)$.

Proof. Show that $I(X, Y) - I(X, Z) = I(X, Y|Z)$:

$$I(X, Y) - I(X, Z) = \sum_{(x,y,z)\in A} p(x, y, z)\log_2 \left[\frac{p(x, y)p(x)p(z)}{p(x)p(y)p(x, z)}\right]$$
$$= \sum_{(x,y,z)\in A} p(x, y, z)\log_2 \left[\frac{p(x, y)}{p(x|z)p(y)}\right] = I(X, Y|Z)$$

where in the last step the Markov property was used in the form $p(x, y, z) = p(y, z)p(x, y)/p(y)$ which entails $p(x, y)/p(y) = p(x, y|z)/p(y|z)$ The assertion then follows from Property 6 (which states that $I(X, Y|Z) \geq 0$). □

The data processing inequality shows explicitly that no processing of the random variable y (converting it into a new random variable z), whether deterministic or probabilistic, can increase the information that it contains about the random variable x. This obviously makes sense.

Examples

Example 1. As usual we try to facilitate the digestion of all this via explicit examples. Let us first illustrate the relative entropy by considering the simplest non-trivial discrete variables X and X' with values in $A = \{0, 1\}$. We compare two probability distributions, $p(x)$ and $q(x)$, where

$$p(0) = 1 - \rho \quad p(1) = \rho \qquad q(0) = 1 - \sigma \quad q(1) = \sigma$$

with $0 \leq \rho, \sigma \leq 1$. Inserting the above probabilities into the definition (12.8) we obtain the following expressions for the relative entropies $D(p||q)$ and $D(q||p)$:

$$D(p||q) = (1 - \rho)\log_2[(1 - \rho)/(1 - \sigma)] + \rho \log_2(\rho/\sigma)$$
$$D(q||p) = (1 - \sigma)\log_2[(1 - \sigma)/(1 - \rho)] + \sigma \log_2(\sigma/\rho)$$

We can find the minimum of, for instance, $D(p||q)$ by calculating its derivative with respect to the parameter σ for a given value of ρ:

$$\frac{\partial}{\partial \sigma} D(p||q) = \frac{1}{\ln 2} \frac{\sigma - \rho}{\sigma(1 - \sigma)}$$

from which it can be concluded that the (unique) minimum is obtained at $\sigma = \rho$, giving $D(p||p) = 0$ (as it should).

The asymmetry in the definition of $D(p||q)$ is clearly seen by working out the difference

$$D(p||q) - D(q||p) = (2 - \rho - \sigma)\log_2 \left(\frac{1 - \sigma}{1 - \rho}\right) + (\rho + \sigma)\log_2 \left(\frac{\rho}{\sigma}\right)$$

which is nonzero except for $\rho = \sigma$.

Example 2. Our second example serves to illustrate that in general $I(X, Y) \neq I(X, Y|Z)$, and that there is even no inequality to order the two. Consider the triple (X, Y, Z) of stochastic variables with $A_X = A_Y = A_Z = \{0, 1\}$ (so $A = \{0, 1\}^3$), and with joint probabilities $p(x, y, z)$ as given in the following table:

(x, y, z)	$(0,0,0)$	$(1,0,0)$	$(0,1,0)$	$(1,1,0)$	$(0,0,1)$	$(1,0,1)$	$(0,1,1)$	$(1,1,1)$
$p(x, y, z)$	1/4	0	0	1/4	0	1/4	1/4	0

By summing over one of the random variables we obtain from these the marginal probabilities $p(x, y) = \sum_{z \in A_Z} p(x, y, z)$, $p(y, z) = \sum_{x \in A_X} p(x, y, z)$ and $p(x, z) = \sum_{y \in A_Y} p(x, y, z)$, which for this example all come out to be the same:

$$p(x,y) = p(x,z) = p(y,z) = \tfrac{1}{4} \quad \text{for all } (x,y,z) \in A$$

The marginal probabilities $p(x) = \sum_{y \in A_Y} p(x,y)$, $p(y) = \sum_{z \in A_Z} p(y,z)$ and $p(z) = \sum_{y \in A_Y} p(y,z)$ are similarly identical:

$$p(x) = p(y) = p(z) = \tfrac{1}{2} \quad \text{for all } (x,y,z) \in A$$

If we calculate for the present example the mutual information $I(X,Y)$ (12.10) and the conditional mutual information $I(X,Y|Z)$ (12.11) we find:

$$I(X,Y) = \sum_{(x,y) \in A_X \otimes A_Y} p(x,y) \log_2 \left[\frac{p(x,y)}{p(x)p(y)} \right] = \frac{1}{4} \sum_{(x,y) \in A_X \otimes A_Y} \log_2 1 = 0$$

$$\begin{aligned} I(X,Y|Z) &= \sum_{(x,y,z) \in A} p(x,y,z) \log_2 \left[\frac{p(x,y|z)}{p(x|z)p(y|z)} \right] \\ &= \sum_{(x,y,z) \in A} p(x,y,z) \log_2 \left[\frac{p(x,y,z)p(z)}{p(x,z)p(y,z)} \right] = \log_2 2 = 1 \end{aligned}$$

At first sight it seems somewhat strange to find simultaneously $I(X,Y|Z) > 0$ and $I(X,Y) = 0$. Apparently y reveals nothing about x if we do not take z into account, but y does reveal something about x when in addition z is known. The explanation is as follows. If we inspect the probability distributions $p(x,y)$, $p(x)$, and $p(y)$ we see that X and Y are independent, so $I(X,Y) = 0$ (as it should). However, if z is known the situation changes considerably. From the table of $p(x,y,z)$ we infer the following. If $z = 1$ we know that $(x,y) \in \{(0,1),(1,0)\}$, so that knowing one means knowing the other. If $z = 0$ we know that $(x,y) \in \{(0,0),(1,1)\}$, and we have a similar situation. This explains why $I(X,Y|Z) > 0$.

Now we will show that the opposite situation can occur as well, with $I(X,Y) > 0$ and $I(X,Y|Z) = 0$. We change the table of the joint probabilities in the following way:

(x,y,z)	$(0,0,0)$	$(1,0,0)$	$(0,1,0)$	$(1,1,0)$	$(0,0,1)$	$(1,0,1)$	$(0,1,1)$	$(1,1,1)$
$p(x,y,z)$	0	1/2	0	0	0	0	1/2	0

By summing over one of the random variables we obtain from these the marginal probabilities $p(x,y) = \sum_{z \in A_Z} p(x,y,z)$, $p(y,z) = \sum_{x \in A_X} p(x,y,z)$

and $p(x,z) = \sum_{y \in A_Y} p(x,y,z)$:

(x,y)	$(0,0)$	$(1,0)$	$(0,1)$	$(1,1)$
$p(x,y)$	0	1/2	1/2	0

(y,z)	$(0,0)$	$(1,0)$	$(0,1)$	$(1,1)$
$p(y,z)$	1/2	0	0	1/2

(x,z)	$(0,0)$	$(1,0)$	$(0,1)$	$(1,1)$
$p(x,z)$	0	1/2	1/2	0

The marginal probabilities $p(x) = \sum_{y \in A_Y} p(x,y)$, $p(y) = \sum_{z \in A_Z} p(y,z)$ and $p(z) = \sum_{y \in A_Y} p(y,z)$ again come out the same:

$$p(x) = p(y) = p(z) = \tfrac{1}{2} \quad \text{for all } (x,y,z) \in A$$

If we now calculate the mutual information $I(X,Y)$ (12.10) and the conditional mutual information $I(X,Y|Z)$ we find:

$$I(X,Y) = \sum_{(x,y) \in A_X \otimes A_Y} p(x,y) \log_2 \left[\frac{p(x,y)}{p(x)p(y)} \right] = \log_2 \left[\frac{1/2}{(1/2)^2} \right] = 1$$

$$\begin{aligned} I(X,Y|Z) &= \sum_{(x,y,z) \in A} p(x,y,z) \log_2 \left[\frac{p(x,y|z)}{p(x|z)p(y|z)} \right] \\ &= \sum_{(x,y,z) \in A} p(x,y,z) \log_2 \left[\frac{p(x,y,z)p(z)}{p(x,z)p(y,z)} \right] = 0 \end{aligned}$$

Now the situation is reversed: y reveals information about x if we do not take z into account, but fails to do so when in addition z is known. The explanation is as follows. If we inspect the probability distributions $p(x,y)$, $p(x)$, and $p(y)$ we see that x and y are not independent, so $I(X,Y) > 0$ (as it should). However, if z is known the situation changes. If $z = 1$ it immediately follows that $(x,y) = (0,1)$: we know everything already, and knowing x adds nothing to what we know about y. If $z = 0$ it follows that $(x,y) = (1,0)$: knowing x does not increase our knowledge of y. This explains why $I(X,Y|Z) = 0$.

12.4 Information measures for continuous random variables

So far we have restricted ourselves to discrete random variables. In the case where the variables are continuous we have to be somewhat careful, since not all properties of our information-theoretic quantities as established for discrete random variables survive the transition to continuous ones.

Differential entropy

Let us consider a discrete random variable X which can assume the values $x_k = k\delta x$ (for a given spacing δx), with $k = 0, \pm 1, \pm 2, \ldots$, so $A = \{\ldots, -3\delta x, -2\delta x, -\delta x, 0, \delta x, 2\delta x, 3\delta x, \ldots\}$. Let $\hat{p}(x_k)$ be the associated probabilities. Eventually we will consider the limit $\delta x \to 0$ which will turn x into a continuous random variable. As long as δx remains finite, however, the theory as developed so far applies, and we obtain

$$H(X) = -\sum_{k=-\infty}^{\infty} \hat{p}(x_k)\log_2 \hat{p}(x_k) \qquad \sum_{k=-\infty}^{\infty} \hat{p}(x_k) = 1 \tag{12.12}$$

In order to pave the way for the continuum limit we now define a probability *density* $p(x_k) = \hat{p}(x_k)/\delta x$. Transformation of (12.12) into an expression involving this density gives

$$H(X) = -\sum_{k=-\infty}^{\infty} \delta x \; p(x_k)\log_2 p(x_k) - \log_2 \delta x \qquad \sum_{k=-\infty}^{\infty} \delta x \; p(x_k) = 1$$

Note that

$$\lim_{\delta x \to 0} \sum_{k=-\infty}^{\infty} \delta x \; p(x_k)\log_2 p(x_k) = \int \mathrm{d}x \; p(x)\log_2 p(x)$$

$$\lim_{\delta x \to 0} \sum_{k=-\infty}^{\infty} \delta x \; p(x_k) = \int \mathrm{d}x \; p(x) = 1$$

provided these integrals exist. However, we observe that we cannot define the entropy of a continuous random variable simply as the continuum limit $\delta x \to 0$ of the entropy of an underlying discrete random variable, since $\lim_{\delta x \to 0} \log_2(1/\delta x) = \infty$. The natural adaptation of the discrete definition of the entropy to the case of a continuous random variable described by the probability density $p(x)$, with $\int \mathrm{d}x \; p(x) = 1$, appears to be restricting ourselves to what is left after we eliminate the offending term $\log_2(1/\delta x)$ from the discrete expression, giving:

$$\tilde{H}(X) = -\int \mathrm{d}x \; p(x)\log_2 p(x) \tag{12.13}$$

which is called the *differential entropy*. Since in order to arrive at (12.13) we have subtracted a positive term from a discrete entropy $H(X)$, we may no longer assume that $\tilde{H}(X) \geq 0$. Yet, since what has been subtracted is simply a constant which does not depend on the shape of the probability density $p(x)$, the differential entropy still has the property that it measures information content. But this is now in a relative rather than an absolute sense, like a thermometer with correctly spaced marks but without an indication of where the zero is.

Example 1. Let us calculate the differential entropy for a block-shaped probability density, with $A = [a - \frac{1}{2}b, a + \frac{1}{2}b]$:

$$p(x) = \begin{cases} b^{-1}, & \text{for } a - \frac{1}{2}b \leq x \leq a + \frac{1}{2}b \\ 0, & \text{elsewhere} \end{cases}$$

For the differential entropy we find:

$$\tilde{H}(X) = -\frac{1}{b}\int_{a-b/2}^{a+b/2} \mathrm{d}x \, \log_2(1/b) = \log_2(b)$$

The result is negative for $b < 1$ (narrow distributions $p(x)$). We conclude that the differential entropy can indeed have negative values, even for simple and well-behaved probability densities. We also observe that for continuous random variables with uniform probabilities the familiar rule $\tilde{H}(X) = \log_2|A|$ again holds, where $|A|$ is now defined as the size of the interval of allowed values for x.

Generalization to multivariate densities is straightforward. Let us consider $\boldsymbol{x} \in \mathbb{R}^N$, with the set A centered at $(a_1, \ldots, a_N)$, that is, $A = [a_1 - \frac{1}{2}b_1, a_1 + \frac{1}{2}b_1] \otimes \cdots \otimes [a_N - \frac{1}{2}b_N, a_N + \frac{1}{2}b_N]$:

$$p(\boldsymbol{x}) = \begin{cases} \prod_{i=1}^{N} b_i^{-1}, & \text{for } a_i - \dfrac{1}{2}b_i \leq x_i \leq a_i + \dfrac{1}{2}b_i, \quad i = 1, \ldots, N \\ 0, & \text{elsewhere} \end{cases}$$

For the differential entropy we now find:

$$\tilde{H}(X_1, \ldots, X_N) = -\left(\prod_{i=1}^{N} b_i^{-1}\right)\int_A \mathrm{d}\boldsymbol{x} \, \log_2 \prod_{i=1}^{N} b_i^{-1} = \log_2 \prod_{i=1}^{N} b_i = \sum_{i=1}^{N} \log_2 b_i$$

The result is negative for $\prod_{i=1}^{N} b_i < 1$ (sharply concentrated distributions). Again we find $\tilde{H}(X_1, \ldots, X_N) = \log_2|A|$, where $|A|$ is now defined as the volume of the region of allowed values for $\boldsymbol{x}$.

Example 2. Our second example is a probability density with a Gaussian shape (see also Appendix D):

$$p(x) = \frac{e^{-(x-\mu)^2/2\sigma^2}}{\sigma\sqrt{2\pi}} \qquad A = (-\infty, \infty) \tag{12.14}$$

Here the differential entropy is found to be

$$\begin{aligned}\tilde{H}(X) &= -\int \frac{\mathrm{d}x}{\sigma\sqrt{2\pi}}\, e^{-(x-\mu)^2/2\sigma^2} \log_2\left[\frac{e^{-(x-\mu)^2/2\sigma^2}}{\sigma\sqrt{2\pi}}\right] \\ &= \int \frac{\mathrm{d}x\,(x-\mu)^2}{2\sigma^3\sqrt{2\pi}\ln 2}\, e^{-(x-\mu)^2/2\sigma^2} + \log_2(\sigma\sqrt{2\pi}) = \frac{1}{2\ln 2}[1 + \ln(2\pi\sigma^2)]\end{aligned}$$

We find a negative differential entropy for sufficiently small width σ of the probability density, and an infinite differential entropy for $\sigma \to \infty$.

There is one special property of Gaussian probability densities to be mentioned here, namely that they are the ones that maximize differential entropy subject to the constraints of prescribed mean and variance. This statement is of deep significance in connection with statistical inference, as will be explained later in Chapter 13. It provides the second reason for the importance of Gaussian probability densities in probability theory and statistics, in addition to the key role they play in the central limit theorem.

Multivariate Gaussian distributions, where $\boldsymbol{x} \in \mathbb{R}^N$, pose no fundamental problems, although the calculations are slightly more involved. The fundamental properties one always uses are normalization and the expression for the second order moments (see Appendix D):

$$p(\boldsymbol{x}) = \frac{e^{-(1/2)(\boldsymbol{x}-\langle\boldsymbol{x}\rangle)\cdot\boldsymbol{A}(\boldsymbol{x}-\langle\boldsymbol{x}\rangle)}}{(2\pi)^{N/2}\det^{-1/2}\boldsymbol{A}} \qquad (\boldsymbol{A}^{-1})_{ij} = \langle(x_i - \langle x_i\rangle)(x_j - \langle x_j\rangle)\rangle \tag{12.15}$$

Let us denote the (real and positive) eigenvalues of the (symmetric) covariance matrix $\boldsymbol{A}^{-1}$ as $\{c_i\}$. Inserting (12.15) into the definition (12.13) of the differential entropy and explicitly working out the $\log_2 p(\boldsymbol{x})$ in that expression gives:

$$\begin{aligned}\tilde{H}(X_1,\ldots,X_N) &= -\int \mathrm{d}\boldsymbol{x}\, p(\boldsymbol{x})\log_2 p(\boldsymbol{x}) \\ &= \frac{1}{2\ln 2}\int \mathrm{d}\boldsymbol{x}\, p(\boldsymbol{x})(\boldsymbol{x} - \langle\boldsymbol{x}\rangle)\cdot\boldsymbol{A}(\boldsymbol{x} - \langle\boldsymbol{x}\rangle) \\ &\quad + \log_2[(2\pi)^{N/2}\det^{-1/2}\boldsymbol{A}] \\ &= \frac{1}{2\ln 2}\sum_{ij=1}^{N} A_{ij}\langle(x_i - \langle x_i\rangle)(x_j - \langle x_j\rangle)\rangle \\ &\quad + \log_2[(2\pi)^{N/2}\det^{-1/2}\boldsymbol{A}]\end{aligned}$$

Thus, using (12.15) and $\det^{-1}\boldsymbol{A} = \det \boldsymbol{A}^{-1} = \prod_i c_i$, we finally obtain

$$\tilde{H}(X_1,\ldots,X_N) = \frac{1}{2\ln 2}\sum_{i=1}^{N}[1+\ln(2\pi c_i)] \tag{12.16}$$

The simplest type of covariance matrix is a diagonal one, describing independent variables $\{x_i\}$: $\langle(x_i-\langle x_i\rangle)(x_j-\langle x_j\rangle)\rangle = \sigma_i^2\delta_{ij}$, and $A_{ij} = \sigma_i^{-2}\delta_{ij}$ (with the variances σ_i of the individual variables x_i). Here the differential entropy reduces to the sum of the differential entropies of the N individual x_i, as it should:

$$\tilde{H}(X_1,\ldots,X_N) = \frac{1}{2\ln 2}\sum_{i=1}^{N}[1+\ln(2\pi\sigma_i^2)] = \sum_{i=1}^{N}\tilde{H}(X_i)$$

Differential mutual information

Let us next consider two discrete random variables X and Y, which can assume the values $x_k = k\delta x$ (for a given spacing δx), with $k = 0, \pm 1, \pm 2, \ldots$, and $y_\ell = \ell\delta y$ (for a given spacing δy), with $\ell = 0, \pm 1, \pm 2, \ldots$, respectively. The associated joint probabilities are $\hat{p}(x_k, y_\ell)$, with marginal probabilities $\hat{p}(x_k) = \sum_{\ell=-\infty}^{\infty}\hat{p}(x_k, y_\ell)$ and $\hat{p}(y_\ell) = \sum_{k=-\infty}^{\infty}\hat{p}(x_k, y_\ell)$. As long as both δx and δy remain finite, the theory for discrete random variables applies, and we obtain

$$I(X,Y) = \sum_{k,\ell=-\infty}^{\infty}\hat{p}(x_k, y_\ell)\log_2\left[\frac{\hat{p}(x_k, y_\ell)}{\hat{p}(x_k)\hat{p}(y_\ell)}\right], \qquad \sum_{k,\ell=-\infty}^{\infty}\hat{p}(x_k, y_\ell) = 1 \tag{12.17}$$

As in the section dealing with the differential entropy, we now define joint and marginal probability *densities* $p(x_k, y_\ell) = \hat{p}(x_k, y_\ell)/\delta x\delta y$, as well as $p(x_k) = \sum_{\ell=-\infty}^{\infty}\hat{p}(x_k, y_\ell)/\delta x$ and $p(y_\ell) = \sum_{k=-\infty}^{\infty}\hat{p}(x_k, y_\ell)/\delta y$. Here the transformation of (12.17) into an expression involving only densities does not generate diverging terms; the spacing parameters δx and δy cancel in the argument of the logarithm and we find

$$I(X,Y) = \sum_{k,\ell=-\infty}^{\infty}\delta x\delta y p(x_k, y_\ell)\log_2\left[\frac{p(x_k, y_\ell)}{p(x_k)p(y_\ell)}\right], \qquad \sum_{k,\ell=-\infty}^{\infty}\delta x\delta y p(x_k, y_\ell) = 1$$

We can now simply define the mutual information of two continuous random variables as the continuum limit $\delta x \to 0$, $\delta y \to 0$ of the mutual information of a pair of underlying discrete random variables, that is, as

$$\tilde{I}(X,Y) = \int \mathrm{d}x\mathrm{d}y\, p(x,y)\log_2\left[\frac{p(x,y)}{p(x)p(y)}\right] \tag{12.18}$$

provided this integral exists. $\tilde{I}(X, Y)$ is called the *differential mutual information*. Since the differential mutual information can be obtained by taking a limit of a discrete expression for mutual information, we are now guaranteed that $\tilde{I}(X, Y) \geq 0$.

Examples

Example 1. Let us work out the mutual information of two (possibly correlated) Gaussian variables x and y with zero averages (for simplicity), that is, $\langle x \rangle = \langle y \rangle = 0$, and with variances $\langle x^2 \rangle = \sigma_x^2$ and $\langle y^2 \rangle = \sigma_y^2$:

$$p(x, y) = \frac{\exp\left[-(1/2) \begin{pmatrix} x \\ y \end{pmatrix} \cdot \boldsymbol{A} \begin{pmatrix} x \\ y \end{pmatrix} \right]}{2\pi \det^{-1/2} \boldsymbol{A}}, \quad \boldsymbol{A}^{-1} = \begin{pmatrix} \sigma_x^2 & \langle xy \rangle \\ \langle xy \rangle & \sigma_y^2 \end{pmatrix}$$

with the marginal probability densities

$$p(x) = \frac{e^{-x^2/2\sigma_x^2}}{\sigma_x \sqrt{2\pi}} \qquad p(y) = \frac{e^{-y^2/2\sigma_x^2}}{\sigma_y \sqrt{2\pi}}$$

For the differential mutual information we now find:

$$\begin{aligned} \tilde{I}(X, Y) &= \frac{1}{2 \ln 2} \int \mathrm{d}x\mathrm{d}y \; p(x, y) \left[\frac{x^2}{\sigma_x^2} + \frac{y^2}{\sigma_y^2} - \begin{pmatrix} x \\ y \end{pmatrix} \cdot \boldsymbol{A} \begin{pmatrix} x \\ y \end{pmatrix} \right] \\ &\quad + \log_2(\sigma_x \sigma_y \sqrt{\det \boldsymbol{A}}) \\ &= \frac{1}{2 \ln 2} \left(2 - \sum_{i,j=1}^{2} A_{ij}^{-1} A_{ji} \right) + \log_2(\sigma_x \sigma_y \sqrt{\det \boldsymbol{A}}) \\ &= \log_2(\sigma_x \sigma_y \sqrt{\det \boldsymbol{A}}) \\ &= -\frac{1}{2 \ln 2} \ln \left(1 - \frac{\langle xy \rangle^2}{\sigma_x^2 \sigma_y^2} \right) \end{aligned} \tag{12.19}$$

Example 2. Our second example is a pair of random variables (X, Y) which are only allowed to take values from within the square $A_X \otimes A_Y$, where $A_X = A_Y = [-1, 1]$, with joint probability density:

$$\begin{aligned} (x, y) \notin [-1, 1]^2 &: \quad p(x, y) = 0 \\ (x, y) \in [-1, 1]^2 &: \quad p(x, y) = \frac{k + \theta(xy)}{2(2k + 1)} \end{aligned}$$

The parameter $k \geq 0$ controls the degree of dependence of the two variables. For $k \to \infty$ the two random variables become statistically independent; for $k = 0$ we find a strong coupling, since x and y are forced to have the same sign. The marginal probability densities are obtained by integration:

$$x, y \in [-1, 1]: \quad p(x) = \int_{-1}^{1} \mathrm{d}y \frac{k + \theta(xy)}{2(2k+1)} = \frac{1}{2}$$

$$p(y) = \int_{-1}^{1} \mathrm{d}x \, \frac{k + \theta(xy)}{2(2k+1)} = \frac{1}{2}$$

The differential mutual information can be calculated easily:

$$\tilde{I}(X, Y) = \int_{-1}^{1} \mathrm{d}x\mathrm{d}y \, \frac{k + \theta(xy)}{2(2k+1)} \log_2 \left[\frac{2[k + \theta(xy)]}{2k+1}\right]$$
$$= \frac{k+1}{2k+1} \log_2 \left(\frac{2k+2}{2k+1}\right) + \frac{k}{2k+1} \log_2 \left(\frac{2k}{2k+1}\right)$$

This result makes sense. For $k \to 0$ we get $\tilde{I}(X, Y) \to 1$; here the two variables are forced to have identical sign, so they do indeed convey exactly one bit of information about one another. For $k \to \infty$ we get $\tilde{I}(X, Y) \to 0$ because the two variables are independent.

Example 3. As a third and final example we will calculate the differential mutual information of two (possibly correlated) Gaussian variables which are themselves vectors, rather than scalars: $\boldsymbol{x} \in \mathbb{R}^N$ and $\boldsymbol{y} \in \mathbb{R}^M$ with zero averages (for simplicity), $\langle \boldsymbol{x} \rangle = \langle \boldsymbol{y} \rangle = 0$. The joint probability distribution for the pair $(\boldsymbol{x}, \boldsymbol{y})$ must then be

$$p(\boldsymbol{x}, \boldsymbol{y}) = \frac{\exp\left[-(1/2)\begin{pmatrix}\boldsymbol{x}\\ \boldsymbol{y}\end{pmatrix} \cdot \boldsymbol{A}\begin{pmatrix}\boldsymbol{x}\\ \boldsymbol{y}\end{pmatrix}\right]}{(2\pi)^{(N+M)/2} \det^{-1/2} \boldsymbol{A}}, \qquad \boldsymbol{A}^{-1} = \begin{pmatrix} \boldsymbol{C}^{xx} & \boldsymbol{C}^{xy} \\ \boldsymbol{C}^{yx} & \boldsymbol{C}^{yy} \end{pmatrix}$$

with the matrices:

$$C_{ij}^{xx} = \langle x_i x_j \rangle, \qquad C_{ij}^{xy} = \langle x_i y_j \rangle, \qquad C_{ij}^{yx} = \langle y_i x_j \rangle, \qquad C_{ij}^{yy} = \langle y_i y_j \rangle$$

and with the marginal densities

$$p(\boldsymbol{x}) = \frac{e^{-\boldsymbol{x}\cdot(\boldsymbol{C}^{xx})^{-1}\boldsymbol{x}/2}}{(2\pi)^{N/2} \det^{1/2} \boldsymbol{C}^{xx}}, \qquad p(\boldsymbol{y}) = \frac{e^{-\boldsymbol{y}\cdot(\boldsymbol{C}^{yy})^{-1}\boldsymbol{y}/2}}{(2\pi)^{M/2} \det^{1/2} \boldsymbol{C}^{yy}}$$

For the differential mutual information we find:

$$\begin{aligned}
\tilde{I}(X,Y) &= \int \mathrm{d}\boldsymbol{x}\mathrm{d}\boldsymbol{y}\, p(\boldsymbol{x},\boldsymbol{y})\log_2\left[\frac{p(\boldsymbol{x},\boldsymbol{y})}{p(\boldsymbol{x})p(\boldsymbol{y})}\right] \\
&= \frac{1}{2\ln 2}\int \mathrm{d}\boldsymbol{x}\mathrm{d}\boldsymbol{y}\, p(\boldsymbol{x},\boldsymbol{y})\left[\boldsymbol{x}\cdot(\boldsymbol{C}^{xx})^{-1}\boldsymbol{x} + \boldsymbol{y}\cdot(\boldsymbol{C}^{yy})^{-1}\boldsymbol{y}\right. \\
&\quad \left. - \begin{pmatrix}\boldsymbol{x}\\ \boldsymbol{y}\end{pmatrix}\cdot \boldsymbol{A}\begin{pmatrix}\boldsymbol{x}\\ \boldsymbol{y}\end{pmatrix}\right] + \frac{1}{2}\log_2[\det \boldsymbol{C}^{yy}\det \boldsymbol{C}^{xx}\det \boldsymbol{A}] \\
&= \frac{1}{2\ln 2}\left[\sum_{ij=1}^{N} C_{ij}^{xx}(\boldsymbol{C}^{xx})^{-1}_{ji} + \sum_{ij=1}^{M} C_{ij}^{yy}(\boldsymbol{C}^{yy})^{-1}_{ji} - \sum_{ij=1}^{N+M} A_{ij}A^{-1}_{ij}\right] \\
&\quad + \frac{1}{2}\log_2[\det \boldsymbol{C}^{yy}\det \boldsymbol{C}^{xx}\det \boldsymbol{A}] \\
&= \frac{1}{2}\log_2[\det \boldsymbol{C}^{yy}\det \boldsymbol{C}^{xx}\det \boldsymbol{A}]
\end{aligned}$$

Equivalently:

$$\begin{aligned}
\tilde{I}(X,Y) &= -\frac{1}{2}\log_2\det\left[\begin{pmatrix}(\boldsymbol{C}^{xx})^{-1} & 0\\ 0^{\dagger} & (\boldsymbol{C}^{yy})^{-1}\end{pmatrix}\begin{pmatrix}\boldsymbol{C}^{xx} & \boldsymbol{C}^{xy}\\ \boldsymbol{C}^{yx} & \boldsymbol{C}^{yy}\end{pmatrix}\right] \\
&= -\frac{1}{2}\log_2\det\begin{pmatrix}\boldsymbol{1} & (\boldsymbol{C}^{xx})^{-1}\boldsymbol{C}^{xy}\\ (\boldsymbol{C}^{yy})^{-1}\boldsymbol{C}^{yx} & \boldsymbol{1}\end{pmatrix} \qquad (12.20)
\end{aligned}$$

in which $\boldsymbol{1}$ denotes the identity matrix, 0 is an $N \times M$ matrix containing only zeros, and $0^{\dagger}$ is its transpose. Note that the previous result (12.19) can be recovered as a special case from (12.20) since for $N = M = 1$ we obtain $\boldsymbol{1} = 1$, $\boldsymbol{C}^{xx} = \langle x^2\rangle$, $\boldsymbol{C}^{yy} = \langle y^2\rangle$ and $\boldsymbol{C}^{xy} = \boldsymbol{C}^{yx} = \langle xy\rangle$.

12.5 Exercises

Exercise 12.1. (Entropy.) Consider the pair of stochastic variables (X, Y), defined by $A_X = A_Y = \{-1, 1\}$, and by the joint probabilities $p(x, y) = K\, e^{\beta xy}$. Compute the normalization constant K, the marginal distributions $p(x)$ and $p(y)$, the entropies $H(X)$, $H(Y)$, and the joint entropy $H(X, Y)$. Verify the inequalities $0 \leq H(X,Y) \leq H(X)+H(Y)$. Determine the value(s) of β for which $H(X, Y)$ is minimal. Determine the value(s) of β for which $H(X, Y)$ is maximal. Explain why for the present example $H(X, Y)$ can never be zero.

Exercise 12.2. (Conditional entropy and mutual information.) For the pair of random variables introduced in the previous exercise, compute the conditional information $H(X|Y)$ and the mutual information $I(X,Y)$, and verify the identity $I(X,Y) = H(X) - H(X|Y)$. Investigate the behaviour of the results as functions of the parameter β. Interpret your findings.

Exercise 12.3. (Entropy reduction by non-invertible transformations.) Define the stochastic variable X, taking values from the set $A_X = \{\mathtt{a}, \mathtt{b}, \mathtt{c}, \ldots, \mathtt{z}\}$ (the 26 lower-case letters of the alphabet), with the probabilities $p(x) = 1/26$ for all $x \in A_x$. Calculate $H(X)$, $H(F(X))$, and $I(X, F(X))$, and verify the two statements $I(X, F(X)) = H(F(X))$ and $H(F(X)) \leq H(X)$ for the 'broken typewriter' operation

$$F(x) = x \quad \text{for } x \in \{\mathtt{a}, \mathtt{b}, \mathtt{c}, \ldots, \mathtt{q}\}$$
$$F(x) = \mathtt{z} \quad \text{for } x \in \{\mathtt{r}, \mathtt{s}, \ldots, \mathtt{z}\}$$

Exercise 12.4. (Differential entropy.) Given a continuous random variable X with $A = \mathbb{R}^+$, that is, $x \geq 0$, compute the differential entropy for an exponential probability density of the form $p(x) = x_0^{-1} e^{-x/x_0}$, and investigate its dependence on x_0. What is the meaning of x_0, apart from it acting as a normalization constant? Compare the behaviour of $\tilde{H}(X)$ with what we derived for the Gaussian case.

Exercise 12.5. (Differential mutual information.) Consider the following stochastic processes (i.e. time dependent random variables) X_t and Z_t, all assumed to be real valued, which produce an output process Y_t via $Y_t = X_t + \sigma Z_t$. Let X_t be defined as a so-called *auto-regressive process*: that is, it is assumed that

$$x_t = \sqrt{a} x_{t-1} + \sqrt{1-a} \xi_t$$

in which $0 < a < 1$ is a fixed parameter, and z_t and ξ_t are realizations of independent Gaussian random variables of zero mean and unit variance. Assuming that X_0 is a zero mean and unit variance Gaussian, one finds that X_t and Y_t are Gaussians as well, although no longer independent for different t. Processes of this type are sometimes used to mimic statistical properties of financial time series. For this setup, show that X_t is a zero-mean and unit-variance Gaussian at all t, while Y_t is a zero-mean Gaussian of variance $1 + \sigma^2$. Compute correlations of the form $C_k = \langle y_t x_{t-k} \rangle$ and use these results to obtain the differential mutual information $\tilde{I}(Y_t, X_{t-k})$, which quantifies the amount of information that X_{t-k} reveals about the output process at a later time t.

Exercise 12.6. (Differential mutual information.) Repeat the analysis of the previous exercise for the case that the output process is defined as a superposition of many input processes, $Y_t = \sum_{i=1}^{N} \alpha_i X_{i,t} + \sigma Z_t$, and assume independent auto-regressive processes for each of the inputs,

$$x_{i,t} = \sqrt{a_i} x_{i,t-1} + \sqrt{1 - a_i} \xi_{i,t}$$

In particular, it will be interesting to investigate the dependence of the differential mutual information $\tilde{I}(Y_t, X_{i,t-k})$ on the so-called load-factors α_i and on the set $\{a_i\}$ of coefficients describing the auto-regressive processes. The results obtained are relevant for assessing the relative importance of the $X_{i,t-k}$ in determining the output Y_t.

13 Information theory and statistical inference

This chapter deals with applications of information theoretic concepts to problems of statistical inference, namely density estimation for a random variable X which is *not completely specified*, in the sense that the full set of probabilities $\{p(x); x \in A\}$ or, in the case of a continuous random variable, the probability density function are unknown. We shall consider two fundamentally different cases.

(i) In the first case, incomplete information about probabilities is available in the form of a finite number of *observations*, that is, independent realizations x_i of X that are generated according to the underlying unknown probability density function p. The task is to estimate p by approximating it as closely as possible within a parametrized family $\{p_{\boldsymbol{\lambda}}; \boldsymbol{\lambda} \in \Lambda\}$ of functions, using the available information. The classical method in this context is Maximum Likelihood (ML) estimation; this approach and its relation to minimizing a Kullback–Leibler distance are discussed in Section 13.1.

(ii) In the second case, it is assumed that information about probabilities is available in the form of the values of averages $\langle f_\alpha(x) \rangle$ for a family $\{f_\alpha\}$ of functions of X; these could, but need not, include moments $\mu_n = \langle x^n \rangle$ of x. The task is once more to estimate p solely on the basis of the available information, that is, the set of known averages. The method of choice here is the Maximum Entropy (MaxEnt) principle for density estimation, which is also deeply rooted in information theory and is discussed in Section 13.2.

13.1 Maximum likelihood estimation

Let us first discuss ML estimation of a probability density function on the basis of finitely many independent observations of a random variable X.[25] We shall denote by

$$D = \{x_i;\ i = 1, \ldots, N\}$$

the set of available data, that is, N independent realizations or observations of X.

[25] Throughout this section, we shall use the language appropriate for continuous random variables; however, all identities we are going to derive have obvious analogues for discrete random variables.

Principal relations

Maximum Likelihood estimation attempts to approximate an unknown probability density p from which the data set (13.1) is supposedly sampled within a parametrized family of probability density functions, denoted by

$$\{p_\lambda;\ \lambda \in \Lambda\}, \qquad \Lambda \subseteq \mathbb{R}^n \tag{13.1}$$

The starting point of the ML method is to write down the joint probability density of the data, assuming that the set was sampled from a member p_λ of the family. This is also called the likelihood of the data D for a given λ,

$$p(D|\lambda) = \prod_{i=1}^{N} p_\lambda(x_i) = \exp\left[\sum_{i=1}^{N} \ln p_\lambda(x_i)\right] \equiv \exp[\mathcal{L}(\lambda|D)] \tag{13.2}$$

ML estimation proposes to find the *maximum* of the likelihood w.r.t. the parameter $\lambda \in \Lambda$ and use the maximizing λ as the parameter that provides the best approximation to the unknown density p within the family. Using the monotonicity of the exponential function, one observes that finding the maximum of $p(D|\lambda)$ is equivalent to finding the maximum of the so-called log-likelihood

$$L(\lambda|D) = \frac{1}{N}\mathcal{L}(\lambda|D) = \frac{1}{N}\sum_{i=1}^{N} \ln p_\lambda(x_i) \tag{13.3}$$

Clearly, this task is unaffected by adding a constant (i.e. a quantity independent of λ) to the log-likelihood. By taking this constant to be the so-called *empirical entropy*

$$H_N[p] = -\frac{1}{N}\sum_{i=1}^{N} \ln p(x_i)$$

associated with the (unknown) probability density p, one immediately establishes a straightforward link between ML estimation and information theory, since we now find:

$$L(\lambda|D) = -\frac{1}{N}\sum_{i=1}^{N} \ln\left[\frac{p(x_i)}{p_\lambda(x_i)}\right] - H_N[p] \tag{13.4}$$

Maximizing the (log-) likelihood of the data over the family $\{p_\lambda\}$ is seen to be equivalent to *minimizing*

$$D_N(p\|p_\lambda) = \frac{1}{N}\sum_{i=1}^{N} \ln\left[\frac{p(x_i)}{p_\lambda(x_i)}\right] \tag{13.5}$$

with respect to λ. Up to a factor ln 2, this quantity is nothing but an *empirical approximation* of the Kullback–Leibler distance $D(p\|p_\lambda)$ between the unknown density p and the parametrized density $p_{\boldsymbol{\lambda}}$. Indeed, by the law of large numbers, it is expected that $D_N(p\|p_{\boldsymbol{\lambda}})$ will (up to the factor ln 2) converge to the Kullback–Leibler distance $D(p\|p_{\boldsymbol{\lambda}})$ as the size N of the data set D becomes large,

$$D_N(p\|p_{\boldsymbol{\lambda}}) \to \int \mathrm{d}x\, p(x) \ln\left[\frac{p(x)}{p_{\boldsymbol{\lambda}}(x)}\right] = \ln 2\, D(p\|p_{\boldsymbol{\lambda}}), \quad \text{as } N = |D| \to \infty \tag{13.6}$$

The convergence referred to in (13.6) is a *convergence in probability*, meaning that $\lim_{N\to\infty} \text{Prob}[|D_N(p\|p_{\boldsymbol{\lambda}}) - \ln 2\, D(p\|p_{\boldsymbol{\lambda}})| > \varepsilon] = 0$ for all $\varepsilon > 0$.

To summarize, ML estimation attempts to approximate the unknown probability density function p as closely as possible by a member of the family $p_{\boldsymbol{\lambda}}$, using the empirical approximation $D_N(p\|p_{\boldsymbol{\lambda}})$ to the Kullback–Leibler distance as a distance measure. See also our earlier discussion of the interpretation of the SVQ algorithm for small learning rates.

Algorithms

Having established the above fundamental relations, let us briefly mention two algorithms that allow one to improve systematically estimates of the parameters $\boldsymbol{\lambda}$ for minimizing (13.5). We will not go into details here, as neural network related algorithms following similar ideas are described and analysed at some length elsewhere in this book.

A first possibility that comes to mind is iterative gradient descent improvement of parameters, viz.

$$\boldsymbol{\lambda}(t+\epsilon) = \boldsymbol{\lambda}(t) - \epsilon \nabla_{\boldsymbol{\lambda}} D_N(p\|p_{\boldsymbol{\lambda}}) \tag{13.7}$$

For sufficiently small learning rate ϵ this process is guaranteed to reduce $D_N(p\|p_{\boldsymbol{\lambda}})$. Indeed, taking the limit $\epsilon \to 0$ we obtain

$$\frac{\mathrm{d}}{\mathrm{d}t}\boldsymbol{\lambda} = -\nabla_{\boldsymbol{\lambda}} D_N(p\|p_{\boldsymbol{\lambda}})$$

and thus

$$\frac{\mathrm{d}}{\mathrm{d}t} D_N(p\|p_{\boldsymbol{\lambda}}) = \nabla_{\boldsymbol{\lambda}} D_N(p\|p_{\boldsymbol{\lambda}}) \cdot \frac{\mathrm{d}}{\mathrm{d}t}\boldsymbol{\lambda} = -[\nabla_{\boldsymbol{\lambda}} D_N(p\|p_{\boldsymbol{\lambda}})]^2 \le 0$$

This process is of the batch learning type, as it uses the complete data set D for each iterative improvement. *Asymptotically*, the algorithm is expected to converge as (13.6) states that $D_N(p\|p_{\boldsymbol{\lambda}})$ converges to a multiple of the Kullback–Leibler distance, which is bounded from below. Without going into any detail, a note of caution may be appropriate at this point, however: for finite N, due to the fact that the convergence (13.6) is defined in a probabilistic sense, boundedness of $D_N(p\|p_{\boldsymbol{\lambda}})$ and hence also convergence of the algorithm are not *guaranteed.*

An alternative approach that goes under the name of stochastic approximation consists in updating parameters sequentially as the data points x_i come in, according to

$$\boldsymbol{\lambda}_{i+1} = \boldsymbol{\lambda}_i - \epsilon \nabla_{\boldsymbol{\lambda}} \ln\left[\frac{p(x_i)}{p_{\boldsymbol{\lambda}}(x_i)}\right] = \boldsymbol{\lambda}_i + \frac{\epsilon}{p_{\boldsymbol{\lambda}}(x_i)} \nabla_{\boldsymbol{\lambda}} p_{\boldsymbol{\lambda}}(x_i) \qquad (13.8)$$

Following the line of reasoning described in, for example, Section 2.3, one may also formulate a continuous-time limit of stochastic approximation. This presupposes that an infinite sequence of data points x_i can be generated, and in the continuous-time limit it does in fact amount to a gradient descent algorithm on the Kullback–Leibler distance proper. Filling in the details of this argument is left as an exercise to the reader.

13.2 The maximum entropy principle

We are now going to discuss the problem of density estimation for the case where information about probabilities is incomplete in the sense that information is available only in the form of the values of averages $\langle f_\alpha(x)\rangle$ for some family $\{f_\alpha\}$ of functions of x. These could, but need not, include the moments $\mu_n = \langle x^n\rangle$ of X. The task is to estimate the true density p on the basis of these averages. The method of choice here is the MaxEnt principle for density estimation. It is worth noting that, whereas ML estimation as discussed in the previous section was invented in the 1920s, that is, long before the advent of information theory in the late 1940s, the MaxEnt principle for density estimation to be discussed here makes explicit reference to concepts and heuristics underlying information theory. We will formulate the solution to the problem first for discrete random variables, and deal with the continuous case thereafter.

Discrete random variables

The solution to the problem formulated above, as proposed by Jaynes in the 1950s, is based on the observation that the entropy associated with a random variable X,

$$H(X) = -\sum_{x\in A} p(x)\log_2 p(x) \qquad (13.9)$$

describes the average uncertainty about actual outcomes of observations of X, and thus is a measure of our ignorance about X. According to Jaynes, a consequence of that observation is that the *best estimate* of a set of probabilities $\{p(x);\ x \in A\}$, compatible with the available information is given by an assignment of probabilities which maximizes the entropy, that is, our ignorance about X, subject *only* to the constraints coming from the available information. One thereby expects to prevent inappropriate implicit assumptions about X, involving properties that we have in fact no knowledge of, from sneaking into the probability assignment that is being made. Jaynes' MaxEnt prescription thus provides a *systematic method of being maximally unbiased* in a probability estimate, subject to constraints given in the form of a set of averages.

In order to formulate the solution in detail, we return to the convention of making the dependence of the entropy on the distribution p explicit by using the notation $H[p]$. Moreover, it will be convenient to write the entropy in terms of *natural* rather than digital logarithms. With the shorthand $k = 1/\ln 2$ we may put

$$H[p] = -k \sum_{x \in A} p(x) \ln p(x) \tag{13.10}$$

The problem to be solved can now formally be stated as follows. Let X be a random variable, with the set A of possible realizations given. It is assumed that the only information available about the probabilities $\{p(x);\ x \in A\}$ is given in terms of a set of averages

$$\langle f_\alpha(x) \rangle = \sum_{x \in A} p(x) f_\alpha(x) = \bar{f}_\alpha, \quad f_\alpha \in \mathcal{M} \tag{13.11}$$

with $\mathcal{M} = \{f_\alpha\}$ denoting a given family of functions. This family will *always* have to include the function $f_0(x) \equiv 1$, whose average gives the normalization constraint

$$\langle f_0(x) \rangle = \sum_{x \in A} p(x) = 1 \tag{13.12}$$

which must always hold. Other functions may, but need not be included in $\mathcal{M}$. Let p^* denote the best estimate of the probability distribution compatible with (13.11). Then p^* is found according to the following MaxEnt principle:

$$H[p^*] = \max_p \{H[p]\} \quad \text{subject to } \langle f_\alpha(x) \rangle = \bar{f}_\alpha,\ f_\alpha \in \mathcal{M} \tag{13.13}$$

or, equivalently

$$p^* = \underset{p}{\text{argmax}} \{H[p]\} \quad \text{subject to } \langle f_\alpha(x) \rangle = \bar{f}_\alpha,\ f_\alpha \in \mathcal{M} \tag{13.14}$$

The MaxEnt principle requires us to find the maximum of a function subject to a set of constraints on its variables $\{p(x);\ x \in A\}$. Such a problem is solved by the method of Lagrange parameters (see also Chapter 8). We first explain the method using two examples and then proceed to the general case.

Example 1. Let us first assume that nothing is known about X. Thus the only constraint on p is that it should be normalized. So one has to solve

$$p^* = \underset{p}{\operatorname{argmax}}\{H[p]\} \quad \text{subject to} \sum_{x \in A} p(x) = 1 \tag{13.15}$$

This is done by introducing a Lagrange parameter, conveniently written as $k\lambda_0$, and solving an unconstrained maximization problem for

$$H_{\lambda_0}[p] = H[p] + k\lambda_0\Big(\sum_{x \in A} p(x) - 1\Big) \tag{13.16}$$

Thus p^* is found by solving

$$\frac{\partial H_{\lambda_0}[p]}{\partial p(x)} = -k \ln p(x) - k + k\lambda_0 = 0, \quad \forall x \in A$$
$$\frac{\partial H_{\lambda_0}[p]}{\partial \lambda_0} = k\Big(\sum_{x \in A} p(x) - 1\Big) = 0$$

The first set of equations require

$$p(x) = \exp(\lambda_0 - 1) = \text{const.} \tag{13.17}$$

The second imposes the normalization constraint, and entails

$$p^*(x) = \exp(\lambda_0 - 1) = |A|^{-1} \tag{13.18}$$

which fixes the proper value of the Lagrange parameter λ_0. Since the entropy $H[p]$ is strictly *concave*, in the sense that for all $0 < r < 1$:

$$H[rp_1 + (1-r)p_2] \geq rH[p_1] + (1-r)H[p_2]$$

with equality if and only if $p_1 = p_2$, and since moreover the probabilities satisfying the constraints form a convex set, the unique stationary point found can only be a maximum. Note that the entropy attains its maximum possible value

$$H[p^*] = H_{\lambda_0}[p^*] = k \ln|A| = \log_2|A| \tag{13.19}$$

This is a very reasonable result as our ignorance about X is complete: nothing apart from the normalization constraint is known.

Example 2. Here we take the average of X to be known, and given by μ_1. This constitutes a second constraint, over and above the one of normalization. In this case one has to solve

$$p^* = \underset{p}{\operatorname{argmax}}\{H[p]\} \quad \text{subject to} \sum_{x\in A} p(x) = 1 \text{ and } \sum_{x\in A} p(x)x = \mu_1 \tag{13.20}$$

With the help of Lagrange multipliers as above, this translates into an unconstrained maximization problem for

$$H_{\lambda_0,\lambda_1}[p] = H[p] + k\lambda_0\Big(\sum_{x\in A} p(x) - 1\Big) + k\lambda_1\Big(\sum_{x\in A} p(x)x - \mu_1\Big) \tag{13.21}$$

The maximizing distribution is found by solving

$$\frac{\partial H_{\lambda_0,\lambda_1}[p]}{\partial p(x)} = -k \ln p(x) - k + k\lambda_0 + k\lambda_1 x = 0\,, \quad \forall x \in A$$

$$\frac{\partial H_{\lambda_0,\lambda_1}[p]}{\partial \lambda_0} = k\Big(\sum_{x\in A} p(x) - 1\Big) = 0$$

$$\frac{\partial H_{\lambda_0,\lambda_1}[p]}{\partial \lambda_1} = k\Big(\sum_{x\in A} p(x)x - \mu_1\Big) = 0$$

The solution can be written as

$$p^*(x) = \exp(\lambda_0 - 1 + \lambda_1 x) = \frac{1}{Z}\exp(\lambda_1 x) \tag{13.22}$$

with

$$Z = Z(\lambda_1) = \exp(1 - \lambda_0) = \sum_{x\in A} \exp(\lambda_1 x) \tag{13.23}$$

to enforce the normalization constraint, and with λ_1 chosen such as to solve the following equation (required by the constraint of the given mean):

$$\mu_1 = \frac{\partial}{\partial \lambda_1} \ln Z = \sum_{x\in A} p^*(x)x \tag{13.24}$$

The general case

We are now able to formulate the solution to the general case (13.13). By following and expanding the line of reasoning from the two examples above, and using $f_0 \equiv 1$ and the corresponding Lagrangian multiplier λ_0 to deal with the normalization constraint, one finds immediately that the best estimate for the distribution p is of the form

$$p^*(x) = \exp\Big(\lambda_0 - 1 + \sum_{\alpha\neq 0} \lambda_\alpha f_\alpha(x)\Big) = \frac{1}{Z}\exp\Big(\sum_{\alpha\neq 0} \lambda_\alpha f_\alpha(x)\Big) \tag{13.25}$$

Here the factor

$$Z = \exp(1 - \lambda_0) = Z(\{\lambda_{\alpha(\neq 0)}\}) = \sum_{x \in A} \exp\Big(\sum_{\alpha \neq 0} \lambda_\alpha f_\alpha(x)\Big) \tag{13.26}$$

is introduced in order to satisfy the normalization constraint. The parameters $\{\lambda_{\alpha(\neq 0)}\}$ are chosen to solve the following system of equations that describe the impact of the non-trivial constraints:

$$\bar{f}_\alpha = \frac{\partial}{\partial \lambda_\alpha} \ln Z(\{\lambda_{\alpha(\neq 0)}\}) = \sum_{x \in A} p^*(x) f_\alpha(x), \quad \alpha \neq 0 \tag{13.27}$$

In the general case, as before, the concavity of $H[p]$ in combination with the fact that the set of constraints is formulated in terms of averages, that is, linear functionals of p, guarantee that the MaxEnt solution of the density estimation problem is unique, as long as the set of constraints is kept finite.

At this point it is appropriate to point out one of the salient features of the MaxEnt approach, namely that it gives rise to an *exponential family* of distributions. Let us in particular also draw the attention to the fact that the stationary Gibbs–Boltzmann distributions which form the central object of study in equilibrium statistical mechanics (see Part V) are precisely of the form obtainable from a MaxEnt principle. In the context of statistical mechanics, the only non-trivial information available about a system is typically that it has some average energy

$$\bar{E} = \sum_{x \in A} p(x) E(x)$$

with $E(x)$ denoting the energy of the system as a function of the state variable X. The Gibbs–Boltzmann distribution in that case takes the form

$$p(x) = Z^{-1} \, e^{-\beta E(x)}$$

with the Lagrangian multiplier λ_E associated with the constraint of average energy written as $\lambda_E = -\beta$, and $\beta = 1/T$ denoting inverse temperature. The normalization constant Z is in statistical mechanics referred to as a *partition function*. It is quite remarkable that a 'subjective' problem such as that of density estimation appears to be so closely related to fundamental levels of description in the world of physics.

Continuous random variables

In the case of a continuous real-valued random variable X, the MaxEnt argument proceeds along the by now familiar lines, except that one here determines the best estimate of a probability density function by maximizing the *differential entropy*

$$\tilde{H}[p] = -k \int_A \mathrm{d}x\, p(x) \ln p(x) \qquad (13.28)$$

subject to whatever constraints are known about the system. The only procedural change involved is that *functional derivatives* with respect to the $p(x)$ take the role of partial derivatives. In the cases considered here, functional derivatives are evaluated according to rules completely analogous to those for partial derivatives (including product rules, chain rule etc.).

In the case of a continuous version of the previous Example 2, one would look for the unconstrained maximum of

$$\tilde{H}_{\lambda_0,\lambda_1}[p] = \tilde{H}[p] + k\lambda_0\left(\int_A \mathrm{d}x\, p(x) - 1\right) + k\lambda_1\left(\int_A \mathrm{d}x\, p(x)x - \mu_1\right) \qquad (13.29)$$

by solving

$$\frac{\delta \tilde{H}_{\lambda_0,\lambda_1}[p]}{\delta p(x)} = -k \ln p(x) - k + k\lambda_0 + k\lambda_1 x = 0, \quad \forall x \in A$$

$$\frac{\partial \tilde{H}_{\lambda_0,\lambda_1}[p]}{\partial \lambda_0} = k\left(\int_A \mathrm{d}x\, p(x) - 1\right) = 0$$

$$\frac{\partial H_{\lambda_0,\lambda_1}[p]}{\partial \lambda_1} = k\left(\int_A \mathrm{d}x\, p(x)x - \mu_1\right) = 0$$

Note that these expressions are *formally* identical to the corresponding equations in the discrete case. The solution can be written as

$$p^*(x) = \frac{1}{Z} \exp(\lambda_1 x) \qquad (13.30)$$

with now

$$Z = Z(\lambda_1) = \int_A \mathrm{d}x\, \exp(\lambda_1 x) = \exp(1 - \lambda_0) \qquad (13.31)$$

to enforce the normalization constraint, and with λ_1 chosen such as to solve

$$\mu_1 = \frac{\partial}{\partial \lambda_1} \ln Z = \int_A \mathrm{d}x\, p^*(x)x \qquad (13.32)$$

as required by the constraint of the given mean.

Example 3. Of particular relevance to the continuous case is another example, where both the first moment $\mu_1 = \langle x \rangle$ and the second moment

$\mu_2 = \langle x^2 \rangle$ of a real random variable X, with $A = \mathbb{R}$, are known. The best estimate for the probability density p in this case is found by determining the unconstrained maximum of

$$\tilde{H}_{\lambda_0,\lambda_1,\lambda_2}[p] = \tilde{H}[p] + k\lambda_0\left(\int \mathrm{d}x\ p(x) - 1\right) + k\lambda_1\left(\int \mathrm{d}x\ p(x)x - \mu_1\right) + k\lambda_2\left(\int \mathrm{d}x\ p(x)x^2 - \mu_2\right)$$

in which integrals extend over $\mathbb{R}$. Following the established procedures, one finds a solution of the form

$$p^*(x) = \frac{1}{Z}e^{\lambda_1 x + \lambda_2 x^2} \tag{13.33}$$

For this solution to make sense, that is, be properly normalizable, we must obviously have $\lambda_2 < 0$. A minute of reflection then shows that the solution can be rewritten in the form

$$p^*(x) = \frac{1}{Z}\ e^{-(x-\hat{\lambda}_1)^2/2\hat{\lambda}_2}$$

with $\hat{\lambda}_2 = -\frac{1}{2}\lambda_2$ and $\lambda_1 = \hat{\lambda}_1/\hat{\lambda}_2$, and where Z is an appropriately redefined normalization constant. The reader will immediately realize that this is nothing but a Gaussian probability density function, and read off that

$$\hat{\lambda}_1 = \mu_1, \qquad \hat{\lambda}_2 = \sigma^2 = \mu_2 - \mu_1^2, \text{ and } Z = \sqrt{2\pi\sigma^2}$$

Thus the Gaussian probability density, apart from its key role in the central limit theorem describing the asymptotic distribution of sums of independent random variables (of zero mean), enjoys a privileged role also as a maximally unbiased estimator of a probability density function, subject to the constraints of given first and second moments, or equivalently of given mean and variance.

13.3 Exercises

Exercise 13.1. (Stochastic approximation.) Show that the continuous time limit of the stochastic approximation algorithm (13.8) amounts to a gradient descent algorithm for the Kullback–Leibler distance proper, and is therefore guaranteed to converge, although of course not necessarily to a global minimum.

Exercise 13.2. (MaxEnt inference for continuous random variables.) Supply detailed reasoning for the steps leading to the solution of the general case of MaxEnt estimation for discrete random variables discussed in Section 13.2, at the level of detail as given in Examples 1 and 2.

Exercise 13.3. (MaxEnt inference for continuous random variables.) We are given a continuous random variable X with event set $A = [-1, 1] \subseteq \mathbb{R}$, of which the mean is known to be zero: $\mu_1 = \langle x \rangle = 0$. What is the best estimate for the probability density function $p(x)$ on A? Use your result to compute the best estimate for $\mu_2 = \langle x^2 \rangle$.

Exercise 13.4. (MaxEnt inference for continuous random variables.) We are given a continuous random variable X with event set $A = \mathbb{R}$, of which the mean is known to be zero: $\mu_1 = \langle x \rangle = 0$, and where also the expectation of the function $F(X) = X^2$ is known to be $\mu_2 = \langle x^2 \rangle$. What the best estimate for the probability distribution function $p(x)$ on A? Use your result to compute the best estimate for the fluctuations in the quantity F, that is, of $\langle F(x)^2 \rangle - \langle F(x) \rangle^2$. Hint: convince yourself of the fact that the sign of one of the Lagrange multipliers (which one?) must be negative, in order for the equations to make sense. You will need properties of Gaussian integrals, which you can find in Appendix D.

Exercise 13.5. (MaxEnt and value constraints.) Show that a constraint of the form $p(x_0) = p_0$ for some $x_0 \in A$ and $p_0 > 0$ can also be handled within the framework of the general MaxEnt procedures described in this chapter, as such a constraint can be written as an average of a function. Which function? Discuss the discrete and continuous cases separately. Work out the case where $A = \{-1, 0, 1\}$, and where $p(1) = \rho$ is given as the constraint.

14 Applications to neural networks

The main contribution of information theory to the field of information processing in natural or artificial neural networks is that it provides exact performance measures. This allows us to compare the performance of different models or algorithms in a rigorous way. It also lets us develop learning rules based on the maximization of these information-theoretic performance measures, which are no longer ad hoc and also apply in unsupervised scenarios. The examples we will discuss here are the Boltzmann machine learning rule for recurrent layered neural networks and various types of learning rules (e.g. maximum information preservation) for layered networks. In addition we will touch on the topic of learning by *natural* gradient descent, based on thinking in terms of distances between probability distributions (i.e. information geometry).

14.1 Supervised learning: Boltzmann machines

One of the earliest and most elegant applications of information theory in neural networks is the so-called Boltzmann machine learning rule. It gives a recipe for training symmetric recurrent layered neural networks to perform a given input–output operation.

Definitions and general properties

Let us start with the architecture of the Boltzmann machine. We imagine a network composed of $N + K + M$ binary neurons $s_i \in \{-1, 1\}$ that has been partitioned into an input layer (of N neurons), a so-called hidden layer (of K neurons), and an output layer (of M neurons); see Figure 14.1. To simplify subsequent notation we denote the states of the neurons in these three layers by the vectors $\boldsymbol{x} \in \{-1, 1\}^N$, $\boldsymbol{\sigma} \in \{-1, 1\}^K$, and $\boldsymbol{y} \in \{-1, 1\}^M$, respectively, and the combined state of all three layers by

$$\boldsymbol{s} = (\boldsymbol{x}, \boldsymbol{\sigma}, \boldsymbol{y}) \in \{-1, 1\}^{N+K+M} \tag{14.1}$$

The connectivity of the network is described by a symmetric interaction matrix $\{J_{ij}\}$, with $i, j \in \{1, \ldots, M + N + K\}$. It is assumed to have the

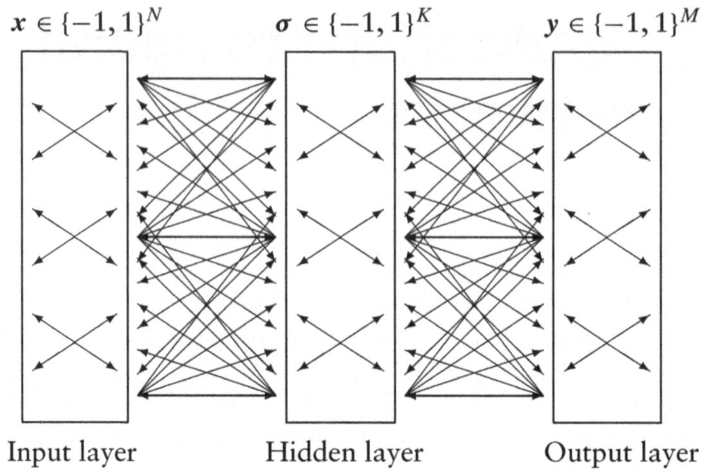

Figure 14.1 Architecture of the Boltzmann machine, with arrows indicating potential synaptic interactions. All interactions present are required to be symmetric, $J_{ij} = J_{ji}$, and self-interactions J_{ii} are absent. Direct synaptic interactions between input- and output layer are also allowed, but have not been drawn in order not to mess up the picture.

following properties:

$$J_{ii} = 0 \quad \text{for all } i, \qquad J_{ij} = J_{ji} \quad \text{for all } (i, j) \tag{14.2}$$

An absent interaction simply corresponds to $J_{ij} = 0$. Due to the symmetry requirement $J_{ij} = J_{ji}$ the network is recurrent, potentially involving interactions within all three layers as well as between them, but it need not be fully recurrent (the interaction matrix could be sparse). We will assume as a minimum requirement the presence of nonzero interactions between the input layer and the hidden layer, and between the hidden layer and the output layer, in order to guarantee that input signals can at least reach the output side.

Next we specify the dynamics of the neuron states. These (binary) states evolve in time in a stochastic manner; however, we have the freedom to allow only a subset $S \subseteq \{1, \ldots, N + K + M\}$ of neurons to actually change their states, while the others remain fixed. At each time step we perform:

1. Choose a neuron i to be updated, at random from the set

$$S \subseteq \{1, \ldots, N + K + M\}$$

2. Calculate its local field (or postsynaptic potential):

$$h_i(s) = \sum_j J_{ij} s_j + \vartheta_i$$

3. Change its state with probability

$$\text{Prob}[s_i \to -s_i] = \tfrac{1}{2}[1 - \tanh(\beta s_i h_i(\boldsymbol{\sigma}))]$$

The parameter ϑ_i determine the firing thresholds of the neurons, as always, and the parameter β controls the degree of randomness in the dynamics. For $\beta = 0$ the dynamics just assigns random values to the states of the updated neurons. For $\beta \to \infty$, on the other hand, the candidate neurons align their states strictly to the sign of the local fields: $s_i \to 1$ if $h_i(\mathbf{s}) > 0$, $s_i \to -1$ if $h_i(\mathbf{s}) < 0$. We observe that this form of stochastic dynamics has been introduced before in Chapter 1. It is nothing but recipe (1.34), with the function $g(x)$ as given by (1.32) and with $\beta = T^{-1}$. Since the dynamics is stochastic we can only talk about the probability $p_t(\mathbf{s})$ to find the system in a certain state $\mathbf{s}$ at a certain time t.

A very important aspect of the specific form of the dynamics chosen above (in combination with the constraints on the synaptic interaction matrix) is the fact that one can write down an exact expression for the asymptotic stationary state of the system, and even prove that it is unique. Here we simply quote the result, leaving the proof to subsequent chapters (viz. 20.1 and 20.2), where the issue of stationary distributions of stochastic dynamics will be dealt with in more detail.

Proposition. The unique stationary probability distribution of the neuronal dynamics formulated above is

$$p_\infty(\mathbf{s}) = \frac{1}{Z} e^{-\beta H(\mathbf{s})} \qquad H(\mathbf{s}) = -\frac{1}{2}\sum_{ij} J_{ij} s_i s_j - \sum_i s_i \vartheta_i \tag{14.3}$$

in which Z is a normalization constant, which depends on the choice made for the set S of neurons that are allowed to change state.

The energy function $H(\mathbf{s})$ appearing in (14.3) is nothing but the Lyapunov function (3.11) of the noiseless version of the present (sequential) dynamics, as introduced in Chapter 3.

The important property of the present dynamics and the postulated stationary distribution (14.3) is that the distribution and the transition rates satisfy the so-called *detailed balance* condition, namely that $\forall i \in S$:

$$p_\infty(s_1, \ldots, s_i, \ldots)\text{Prob}[s_i \to -s_i] = p_\infty(s_1, \ldots, -s_i, \ldots)\text{Prob}[-s_i \to s_i] \tag{14.4}$$

This states that for each neuron $i \in S$ the number of transitions $s_i \to -s_i$ will on average equal the number of transitions $-s_i \to s_i$. This property is established for the Gibbs–Boltzmann distribution (14.3) in Section 20.2.

In general (14.4) is sufficient although not necessary for a candidate distribution $p_\infty(s)$ to be stationary.

Using the above proposition, we can proceed to give exact expressions for equilibrium state probabilities under various different operation conditions. The differences between the various choices to be made for the set S of 'free' neurons (defining different modes of operation for the Boltzmann machine) only affect the normalization factor Z in (14.3), for instance:

(A) States of *all* neurons free to evolve:

$$p_\infty^{\mathrm{A}}(\boldsymbol{x}, \boldsymbol{\sigma}, \boldsymbol{y}) = \frac{1}{Z}\, e^{-\beta H(\boldsymbol{x},\boldsymbol{\sigma},\boldsymbol{y})} \tag{14.5}$$

with

$$Z = \sum_{\boldsymbol{x}\boldsymbol{\sigma}\boldsymbol{y}} e^{-\beta H(\boldsymbol{x},\boldsymbol{\sigma},\boldsymbol{y})} \tag{14.6}$$

(B) States of *hidden & output* neurons free to evolve:

$$p_\infty^{\mathrm{B}}(\boldsymbol{x}, \boldsymbol{\sigma}, \boldsymbol{y}) = p_\infty(\boldsymbol{\sigma}, \boldsymbol{y}|\boldsymbol{x})\, p(\boldsymbol{x}) \tag{14.7}$$

with

$$p_\infty(\boldsymbol{\sigma}, \boldsymbol{y}|\boldsymbol{x}) = \frac{1}{Z(\boldsymbol{x})}\, e^{-\beta H(\boldsymbol{x},\boldsymbol{\sigma},\boldsymbol{y})}, \quad Z(\boldsymbol{x}) = \sum_{\boldsymbol{\sigma}\boldsymbol{y}} e^{-\beta H(\boldsymbol{x},\boldsymbol{\sigma},\boldsymbol{y})} \tag{14.8}$$

(C) States of *hidden* neurons free to evolve:

$$p_\infty^{\mathrm{C}}(\boldsymbol{x}, \boldsymbol{\sigma}, \boldsymbol{y}) = p_\infty(\boldsymbol{\sigma}|\boldsymbol{x}, \boldsymbol{y})\, p(\boldsymbol{x}, \boldsymbol{y}) \tag{14.9}$$

with

$$p_\infty(\boldsymbol{\sigma}|\boldsymbol{x}, \boldsymbol{y}) = \frac{1}{Z(\boldsymbol{x}, \boldsymbol{y})}\, e^{-\beta H(\boldsymbol{x},\boldsymbol{\sigma},\boldsymbol{y})}, \quad Z(\boldsymbol{x}, \boldsymbol{y}) = \sum_{\boldsymbol{\sigma}} e^{-\beta H(\boldsymbol{x},\boldsymbol{\sigma},\boldsymbol{y})} \tag{14.10}$$

Derivation of the learning rule

We are now in a position to define the aim of the learning process. The task is to learn a prescribed target joint input–output probability distribution $q(\boldsymbol{x}, \boldsymbol{y})$. The system has accomplished this when $p_\infty(\boldsymbol{x}, \boldsymbol{y})$ (the equilibrium input–output probability distribution of the network) equals the target distribution $q(\boldsymbol{x}, \boldsymbol{y})$. An information-theoretic measure is used to quantify the 'distance' between $q(\boldsymbol{x}, \boldsymbol{y})$ and $p_\infty(\boldsymbol{x}, \boldsymbol{y})$. This is the relative entropy, or Kullback–Leibler distance (12.8):

$$D(q \| p_\infty) = \sum_{\boldsymbol{x}\boldsymbol{y}} q(\boldsymbol{x}, \boldsymbol{y}) \log_2 \left[\frac{q(\boldsymbol{x}, \boldsymbol{y})}{p_\infty(\boldsymbol{x}, \boldsymbol{y})} \right] \tag{14.11}$$

We know that $D(q \| p_\infty)$ is minimal (and equal to zero) only when $p_\infty(\boldsymbol{x}, \boldsymbol{y})$ and $q(\boldsymbol{x}, \boldsymbol{y})$ are identical. We now aim to minimize $D(q \| p_\infty)$ by changing the network parameters (the synaptic interactions J_{ij} and the thresholds ϑ_i) via a gradient descent learning rule:

$$\Delta J_{ij} = -\epsilon \frac{\partial D(q \| p_\infty)}{\partial J_{ij}} \qquad \Delta \vartheta_i = -\epsilon \frac{\partial D(q \| p_\infty)}{\partial \vartheta_i}, \quad 0 < \epsilon \ll 1 \tag{14.12}$$

which guarantees that

$$\begin{aligned} \Delta D(q \| p_\infty) &= \sum_{ij} \frac{\partial D(q \| p_\infty)}{\partial J_{ij}} \Delta J_{ij} + \sum_i \frac{\partial D(q \| p_\infty)}{\partial \vartheta_i} \Delta \vartheta_i + \mathcal{O}(\epsilon^2) \\ &= -\epsilon \left\{ \sum_{ij} \left[\frac{\partial D(q \| p_\infty)}{\partial J_{ij}} \right]^2 + \sum_i \left[\frac{\partial D(q \| p_\infty)}{\partial \vartheta_i} \right]^2 \right\} + \mathcal{O}(\epsilon^2) \end{aligned}$$

For sufficiently small modification sizes ϵ the 'distance' $D(q \| p_\infty)$ decreases monotonically until a stationary state is reached (which could, but need not correspond to $D(q \| p_\infty) = 0$). For any parameter λ in our system, whether synaptic interaction or threshold, we get:

$$\frac{\partial}{\partial \lambda} D(q \| p_\infty) = -\frac{1}{\ln 2} \sum_{\boldsymbol{x}\boldsymbol{y}} q(\boldsymbol{x}, \boldsymbol{y}) \frac{\partial}{\partial \lambda} \ln p_\infty(\boldsymbol{x}, \boldsymbol{y}) \tag{14.13}$$

The details of the subsequent calculation will now depend on the network operation mode (A, B, or C, see above) for which we want to minimize $D(q \| p_\infty)$ (i.e. the choice made for the set S), since this mode was seen to determine $p_\infty(\boldsymbol{x}, \boldsymbol{y})$. We will first analyse the case where all neurons evolve freely (mode A) and then turn to the case where the input neurons are always prescribed and only the hidden and output neurons are free to evolve (mode B). Both cases will lead to similar results.

- *Operation with all neurons freely evolving*
  Here the relevant expression with which to calculate $p_\infty(\boldsymbol{x}, \boldsymbol{y})$ is equation (14.5), which gives

$$p_\infty(\boldsymbol{x}, \boldsymbol{y}) = \sum_{\boldsymbol{\sigma}} p_\infty(\boldsymbol{x}, \boldsymbol{\sigma}, \boldsymbol{y}) = \frac{\sum_{\boldsymbol{\sigma}} e^{-\beta H(\boldsymbol{x}, \boldsymbol{\sigma}, \boldsymbol{y})}}{Z} = \frac{Z(\boldsymbol{x}, \boldsymbol{y})}{Z}$$

where (14.10) was used as an abbreviation for the nominator. Derivatives of the type (14.13) are found to be

$$\begin{aligned}
\frac{\partial}{\partial\lambda}D(q\|p_\infty) &= -\frac{1}{\ln 2}\sum_{xy} q(x,y)\frac{\partial}{\partial\lambda}[\ln Z(x,y) - \ln Z] \\
&= \frac{\beta}{\ln 2}\sum_{xy} q(x,y)\Bigg[\sum_{\sigma} p_\infty(\sigma|x,y)\frac{\partial H(x,\sigma,y)}{\partial\lambda} \\
&\quad - \sum_{x'\sigma'y'} p_\infty(x',\sigma',y')\frac{\partial H(x',\sigma',y')}{\partial\lambda}\Bigg] \\
&= \frac{\beta}{\ln 2}\Bigg[\sum_{x\sigma y} p_\infty^{\mathrm{C}}(x,\sigma,y)\frac{\partial}{\partial\lambda}H(x,\sigma,y) \\
&\quad - \sum_{x\sigma y} p_\infty^{\mathrm{A}}(x,\sigma,y)\frac{\partial}{\partial\lambda}H(x,\sigma,y)\Bigg] \\
&= \frac{\beta}{\ln 2}\left[\left\langle\frac{\partial}{\partial\lambda}H(x,\sigma,y)\right\rangle_+ - \left\langle\frac{\partial}{\partial\lambda}H(x,\sigma,y)\right\rangle_-\right]
\end{aligned} \tag{14.14}$$

Here averages indicated with '+' are those where the system is only allowed to change the states of hidden neurons, in mode C, the case described by (14.9). The states of the input and output neurons are imposed on the system, with statistics given by the task distribution $q(x,y)$:

$$\begin{aligned}
\langle f(x,\sigma,y)\rangle_+ &= \sum_{x\sigma y} f(x,\sigma,y)p_\infty^{\mathrm{C}}(x,\sigma,y) \\
&= \sum_{x\sigma y} f(x,\sigma,y)p_\infty(\sigma|x,y)q(x,y)
\end{aligned} \tag{14.15}$$

Averages indicated with '–' are those where the system evolves freely in mode A, as described by (14.5):

$$\langle f(x,\sigma,y)\rangle_- = \sum_{x\sigma y} f(x,\sigma,y)p_\infty^{\mathrm{A}}(x,\sigma,y) \tag{14.16}$$

What remains is to calculate the derivatives of $H(x,\sigma,y)$, and use (14.14) to evaluate (14.12):

$$\frac{\partial}{\partial J_{ij}}H(s) = -s_i s_j \qquad \frac{\partial}{\partial\vartheta_i}H(s) = -s_i \tag{14.17}$$

Hence

$$\frac{\partial}{\partial J_{ij}} D(q\|p_\infty) = -\frac{\beta}{\ln 2}(\langle s_i s_j\rangle_+ - \langle s_i s_j\rangle_-)$$
$$\frac{\partial}{\partial \vartheta_i} D(q\|p_\infty) = -\frac{\beta}{\ln 2}(\langle s_i\rangle_+ - \langle s_i\rangle_-)$$

entailing the update rules

$$\Delta J_{ij} = \frac{\epsilon\beta}{\ln 2}(\langle s_i s_j\rangle_+ - \langle s_i s_j\rangle_-) \quad \Delta\vartheta_i = \frac{\epsilon\beta}{\ln 2}(\langle s_i\rangle_+ - \langle s_i\rangle_-) \tag{14.18}$$

Each individual modification step, to be carried out repeatedly, thus involves:

(*i*) Operate the neuronal dynamics with input and output neuron states $(\boldsymbol{x}, \boldsymbol{y})$ fixed until equilibrium is reached, and measure the averages $\langle s_i s_j\rangle_+$ and $\langle s_i\rangle_+$; repeat this for many combinations of $(\boldsymbol{x}, \boldsymbol{y})$ generated according to the desired joint distribution $q(\boldsymbol{x}, \boldsymbol{y})$.

(*ii*) Operate the neuronal dynamics with all neurons evolving freely until equilibrium is reached, and measure the averages $\langle s_i s_j\rangle_-$ and $\langle s_i\rangle_-$.

(*iii*) Insert the results of (*i*, *ii*) into (14.18) and execute the rule (14.18).

- *Operation with hidden and output neurons freely evolving*
Now we consider the situation where the states of the input neurons are prescribed, with statistics given by $p(\boldsymbol{x}) = q(\boldsymbol{x}) = \sum_{\boldsymbol{y}} q(\boldsymbol{x}, \boldsymbol{y})$. The task to be solved by the network is to implement a distribution of outputs $\boldsymbol{y}$ conditioned on prescribed inputs $\boldsymbol{x}$. Thus the relevant expression with which to calculate $p_\infty(\boldsymbol{x}, \boldsymbol{y})$ is equation (14.7), which gives

$$p_\infty(\boldsymbol{x}, \boldsymbol{y}) = \sum_{\boldsymbol{\sigma}} p_\infty(\boldsymbol{x}, \boldsymbol{\sigma}, \boldsymbol{y}) = \sum_{\boldsymbol{\sigma}} p_\infty(\boldsymbol{\sigma}, \boldsymbol{y}|\boldsymbol{x}) q(\boldsymbol{x}) = q(\boldsymbol{x})\frac{Z(\boldsymbol{x}, \boldsymbol{y})}{Z(\boldsymbol{x})}$$

in which (14.8) and (14.10) were used to express $\sum_{\boldsymbol{\sigma}} p_\infty(\boldsymbol{\sigma}, \boldsymbol{y}|\boldsymbol{x})$. Derivatives of the type (14.13) follow as

$$\frac{\partial}{\partial\lambda} D(q\|p_\infty) = -\frac{1}{\ln 2}\sum_{\boldsymbol{x}\boldsymbol{y}} q(\boldsymbol{x}, \boldsymbol{y})\frac{\partial}{\partial\lambda}[\ln Z(\boldsymbol{x}, \boldsymbol{y}) - \ln Z(\boldsymbol{x})]$$
$$= \frac{\beta}{\ln 2}\sum_{\boldsymbol{x}\boldsymbol{y}} q(\boldsymbol{x}, \boldsymbol{y})\Bigg[\sum_{\boldsymbol{\sigma}} p_\infty(\boldsymbol{\sigma}|\boldsymbol{x}, \boldsymbol{y})\frac{\partial H(\boldsymbol{x}, \boldsymbol{\sigma}, \boldsymbol{y})}{\partial\lambda}$$
$$- \sum_{\boldsymbol{\sigma}'\boldsymbol{y}'} p_\infty(\boldsymbol{\sigma}', \boldsymbol{y}'|\boldsymbol{x})\frac{\partial H(\boldsymbol{x}, \boldsymbol{\sigma}', \boldsymbol{y}')}{\partial\lambda}\Bigg]$$

$$\frac{\partial}{\partial\lambda}D(q\|p_\infty) = \frac{\beta}{\ln 2}\Bigg[\sum_{x\sigma y} p_\infty^{\mathrm{C}}(\boldsymbol{x},\boldsymbol{\sigma},\boldsymbol{y})\frac{\partial}{\partial\lambda}H(\boldsymbol{x},\boldsymbol{\sigma},\boldsymbol{y})$$
$$- \sum_{x\sigma y} p_\infty^{\mathrm{B}}(\boldsymbol{x},\boldsymbol{\sigma},\boldsymbol{y})\frac{\partial}{\partial\lambda}H(\boldsymbol{x},\boldsymbol{\sigma},\boldsymbol{y})\Bigg]$$
$$= \frac{\beta}{\ln 2}\left[\left\langle\frac{\partial}{\partial\lambda}H(\boldsymbol{x},\boldsymbol{\sigma},\boldsymbol{y})\right\rangle_+ - \left\langle\frac{\partial}{\partial\lambda}H(\boldsymbol{x},\boldsymbol{\sigma},\boldsymbol{y})\right\rangle_-\right] \tag{14.19}$$

Averages indicated with '+' are again those where the system is only allowed to change the states of hidden neurons, in mode A, the case described by (14.9). The states of the input and output neurons are imposed on the system, with statistics given by the task distribution $q(\boldsymbol{x}, \boldsymbol{y})$:

$$\langle f(\boldsymbol{x},\boldsymbol{\sigma},\boldsymbol{y})\rangle_+ = \sum_{x\sigma y} f(\boldsymbol{x},\boldsymbol{\sigma},\boldsymbol{y})p_\infty^{\mathrm{C}}(\boldsymbol{x},\boldsymbol{\sigma},\boldsymbol{y})$$
$$= \sum_{x\sigma y} f(\boldsymbol{x},\boldsymbol{\sigma},\boldsymbol{y})p_\infty(\boldsymbol{\sigma}|\boldsymbol{x},\boldsymbol{y})q(\boldsymbol{x},\boldsymbol{y}) \tag{14.20}$$

Averages indicated with '–', however, now describe a system where only hidden and output neurons evolve freely in mode B, as described by (14.7), with the states of the input neurons as before imposed on the system, with probabilities $q(\boldsymbol{x}) = \sum_{\boldsymbol{y}} q(\boldsymbol{x}, \boldsymbol{y})$:

$$\langle f(\boldsymbol{x},\boldsymbol{\sigma},\boldsymbol{y})\rangle_- = \sum_{x\sigma y} f(\boldsymbol{x},\boldsymbol{\sigma},\boldsymbol{y})p_\infty^{\mathrm{B}}(\boldsymbol{x},\boldsymbol{\sigma},\boldsymbol{y})$$
$$= \sum_{x\sigma y} f(\boldsymbol{x},\boldsymbol{\sigma},\boldsymbol{y})p_\infty(\boldsymbol{\sigma},\boldsymbol{y}|\boldsymbol{x})q(\boldsymbol{x}) \tag{14.21}$$

Note that the derivatives of $H(\boldsymbol{x},\boldsymbol{\sigma},\boldsymbol{y})$ are still given by (14.17). Using (14.19), which differs from (14.14) only in the definition of the average (14.21), our learning rule (14.12) indeed acquires the same form as the previous one:

$$\Delta J_{ij} = \frac{\epsilon\beta}{\ln 2}(\langle s_i s_j\rangle_+ - \langle s_i s_j\rangle_-) \qquad \Delta\vartheta_i = \frac{\epsilon\beta}{\ln 2}(\langle s_i\rangle_+ - \langle s_i\rangle_-) \tag{14.22}$$

Each modification step, to be carried out repeatedly, now involves:

(*i*) Operate the neuronal dynamics with input and output neuron states $(\boldsymbol{x}, \boldsymbol{y})$ fixed until equilibrium is reached, and measure the averages $\langle s_i s_j\rangle_+$ and $\langle s_i\rangle_+$; repeat this for many combinations of $(\boldsymbol{x}, \boldsymbol{y})$ generated according to the desired joint distribution $q(\boldsymbol{x}, \boldsymbol{y})$.

(*ii*) Operate the neuronal dynamics with all hidden and output neurons evolving freely until equilibrium is reached, and measure the averages $\langle s_i s_j \rangle_-$ and $\langle s_i \rangle_-$; repeat this for many input configurations $\boldsymbol{x}$ generated according to the desired distribution $q(\boldsymbol{x}) = \sum_{\boldsymbol{y}} q(\boldsymbol{x}, \boldsymbol{y})$.

(*iii*) Insert the results of (*i*, *ii*) into (14.18) and execute the rule (14.18).

The advantages of the Boltzmann machine learning rule are that it aims to optimize a well-defined and sensible performance measure, and that it can deal in a clean way with probabilistic data (which is the more natural situation in real-world information processing). The disadvantage is that it is usually very slow; each infinitesimal parameter modification already requires equilibration of a recurrent stochastic system, which can obviously take a lot of CPU time.

14.2 Maximum information preservation

As a second class of applications of information theory we will discuss unsupervised learning in layered neural systems. For simplicity we will consider linear neurons only. The techniques and strategies that we will discuss can also be used and followed in the more general case of arbitrary (not necessarily linear) neuronal transfer functions; this we will demonstrate in a subsequent section. In contrast to most of the previous settings, our present neurons will have to adapt their synaptic interactions and carry out meaningful information processing tasks on some input signal $\boldsymbol{x} \in \mathbb{R}^N$ according to unsupervised rules, that is, there is no task signal available which can be used as a reference or target.

Linear neurons with Gaussian output noise

Imagine a single linear neuron y: $\mathbb{R}^N \to \mathbb{R}$, the output $y(\boldsymbol{x})$ of which is corrupted by a Gaussian noise source ξ in the following way:

$$y(\boldsymbol{x}) = \sum_{i=1}^{N} w_i x_i + \xi \qquad p(\xi) = \frac{e^{-\xi^2/2\sigma^2}}{\sigma\sqrt{2\pi}} \tag{14.23}$$

with synaptic weights $\{w_i\}$ (the system's adjustable parameters). The strength of the noise is measured by $\sigma^2 = \langle \xi^2 \rangle$. We assume the input signals to obey $\langle x_i \rangle = 0$, and to be statistically independent of the noise source ξ. We also assume the uncorrupted signal $z(\boldsymbol{x}) = \sum_{i=1}^{N} w_i x_i$ to have a Gaussian probability distribution; this is true for any N if the inputs x_i are themselves Gaussian distributed random variables, and it is true for $N \to \infty$ if the inputs x_i are independent (under some weak conditions on the parameters $\{w_i\}$, see Appendix B). As a result we can now be sure that the pair (y, z) is described by a Gaussian joint probability distribution. The setup is depicted schematically in the following figure:

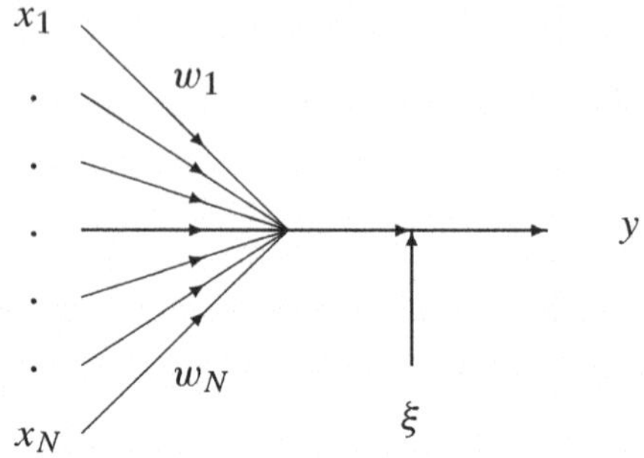

Since we have no reference (or teacher) signal to compare the output of our neuron with, the application of learning rules for updating the parameters $\{w_i\}$ which are based on error reduction is ruled out; there is no such thing as an error. This situation is quite common in the primary stages of (biological or artificial) sensory information processing, where one does not yet know how the incoming information should be used, but one still wants to extract the maximum amount of information from the available data. Alternatively, one can view the present problem as that of data compression: try to concentrate as much information as is possible about the input vectors $\boldsymbol{x} \in \mathbb{R}^N$ into a single variable $y(\boldsymbol{x}) \in \mathbb{R}$.

Here we apply the principle of Maximum Information Preservation (InfoMax): we try to maximize the differential mutual information (12.10) between the corrupted signal $y(\boldsymbol{x})$ and the uncorrupted signal $z(\boldsymbol{x})$, that is, we maximize the amount of information that $y(\boldsymbol{x})$ reveals about $z(\boldsymbol{x})$. Since the relevant variables have a Gaussian joint probability distribution, and since $\langle z(\boldsymbol{x})\rangle = \sum_{i=1}^N w_i \langle x_i\rangle = 0$ and $\langle y(\boldsymbol{x})\rangle = \langle z(\boldsymbol{x})\rangle + \langle \xi\rangle = 0$, we can express the differential mutual information $\tilde{I}(Y, Z)$ in terms of the second-order moments (see (12.19)):

$$\langle z^2\rangle = \sum_{ij} w_i w_j \langle x_i x_j\rangle$$

$$\langle yz\rangle = \left\langle \left(\sum_i w_i x_i\right)\left(\sum_j w_j x_j + \xi\right)\right\rangle = \sum_{ij} w_i w_j \langle x_i x_j\rangle$$

$$\begin{aligned}\langle y^2\rangle &= \left\langle \left(\sum_i w_i x_i + \xi\right)\left(\sum_j w_j x_j + \xi\right)\right\rangle = \sum_{ij} w_i w_j \langle x_i x_j\rangle + \langle \xi^2\rangle \\ &= \sum_{ij} w_i w_j \langle x_i x_j\rangle + \sigma^2\end{aligned}$$

Substitution of these values into $\tilde{I}(Y,Z)$ as defined in (12.19) gives:

$$\tilde{I}(Y,Z) = -\frac{1}{2}\log_2\left(1 - \frac{\langle yz\rangle^2}{\langle y^2\rangle\langle z^2\rangle}\right)$$

$$= -\frac{1}{2}\log_2\left(1 - \frac{\sum_{ij} w_i w_j \langle x_i x_j\rangle}{\sum_{ij} w_i w_j \langle x_i x_j\rangle + \sigma^2}\right)$$

$$= \frac{1}{2}\log_2\left(1 + \frac{\sum_{ij} w_i w_j \langle x_i x_j\rangle}{\sigma^2}\right) \qquad (14.24)$$

We conclude that we can make this expression (14.24) for the differential information as large as we like, simply by boosting all synapses according to $w_i \to \lambda w_i$, which would give

$$\tilde{I}(Y,Z) \to \frac{1}{2}\log_2\left(1 + \lambda^2\sigma^{-2}\sum_{ij} w_i w_j \langle x_i x_j\rangle\right)$$

Note that $\sum_{ij} w_i w_j \langle x_i x_j\rangle = \langle(\sum_i w_i x_i)^2\rangle \geq 0$. In the present setup, the differential mutual information apparently has no upper bound. This makes sense: since the output is simply the sum of a signal term (with strength partly controlled by the synaptic weights) and a noise term (of constant strength), the signal/noise ratio can be improved to an arbitrary extent by simply increasing the strength of the signal via a boost of all the weights.

Linear neurons with Gaussian input noise

Imagine next a single linear neuron $y\colon \mathbb{R}^N \to \mathbb{R}$ of which not the output, but rather the inputs $\{x_i\}$ are corrupted with mutually independent Gaussian noise sources $\{\xi_i\}$, in the following way:

$$y(\boldsymbol{x}) = \sum_{i=1}^{N} w_i(x_i + \xi_i) \qquad p(\xi_i) = \frac{e^{-\xi_i^2/2\sigma_i^2}}{\sigma_i\sqrt{2\pi}} \qquad (14.25)$$

with synaptic weights $\{w_i\}$. The strengths of the N noise sources ξ_i are measured by $\sigma_i^2 = \langle\xi_i^2\rangle$. As before, we assume that the input signals obey $\langle x_i\rangle = 0$ and are statistically independent of the noise sources, and that the uncorrupted signal $z(\boldsymbol{x}) = \sum_{i=1}^{N} w_i x_i$ has a Gaussian probability distribution. We can now again be sure that the pair (y,z) is described by a Gaussian joint probability distribution with $\langle y(\boldsymbol{x})\rangle = \langle z(\boldsymbol{x})\rangle = 0$. The figure below gives a schematic representation of this new situation:

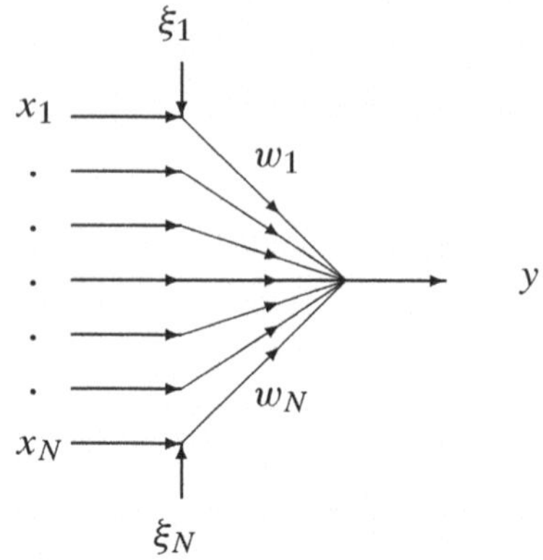

Here the second-order moments are given by

$$\langle z^2 \rangle = \sum_{ij} w_i w_j \langle x_i x_j \rangle$$

$$\langle yz \rangle = \left\langle \left(\sum_i w_i x_i \right) \left(\sum_j w_j (x_j + \xi_j) \right) \right\rangle = \sum_{ij} w_i w_j \langle x_i x_j \rangle$$

$$\langle y^2 \rangle = \left\langle \left(\sum_i w_i (x_i + \xi_i) \right) \left(\sum_j w_j (x_j + \xi_j) \right) \right\rangle$$
$$= \sum_{ij} w_i w_j \langle x_i x_j \rangle + \sum_i w_i^2 \sigma_i^2$$

Substitution into the differential mutual information $\tilde{I}(Y, Z)$ of (12.19) gives:

$$\tilde{I}(Y, Z) = -\frac{1}{2} \log_2 \left(1 - \frac{\langle yz \rangle^2}{\langle y^2 \rangle \langle z^2 \rangle} \right)$$
$$= \frac{1}{2} \log_2 \left(1 + \frac{\sum_{ij} w_i w_j \langle x_i x_j \rangle}{\sum_i w_i^2 \sigma_i^2} \right) \qquad (14.26)$$

Now we find ourselves in a completely different situation. Note that, with $v_i = w_i \sigma_i$:

$$\max_{\boldsymbol{w} \in \mathbb{R}^N} \left\{ \frac{\sum_{ij} w_i w_j \langle x_i x_j \rangle}{\sum_i w_i^2 \sigma_i^2} \right\} = \max_{\boldsymbol{v} \in \mathbb{R}^N} \left\{ \frac{\sum_{ij} v_i \langle (x_i/\sigma_i)(x_j/\sigma_j) \rangle v_j}{\sum_i v_i^2} \right\}$$
$$= \Lambda < \infty$$

where Λ is the largest eigenvalue of the (non-negative) matrix with entries

$$L_{ij} = \sigma_i^{-1} \langle x_i x_j \rangle \sigma_j^{-1}$$

The maximum differential mutual information between uncorrupted and corrupted signal is obtained when the vector $\boldsymbol{v}$ is chosen to be an eigenvector of the matrix $\{L_{ij}\}$, with eigenvalue Λ. In terms of $\boldsymbol{w}$ this means

$$\boldsymbol{w}^{\text{opt}} = \text{solution of} \quad \sum_{j=1}^{N} \langle x_i x_j \rangle w_j = \Lambda \sigma_i^2 w_i \quad \text{with largest } \Lambda \qquad (14.27)$$

Expression (14.26) for the differential information is no longer affected by a simple boost of all synapses. This would simply increase both the signal and the noise, without any net effect on the signal/noise ratio. Interestingly, in the case where the input noise levels are uniform, $\sigma_i = \sigma$, equation (14.27) shows that the optimal weight vector picks out the 'principal component' of the uncorrupted input vectors x, that is, the direction in which the distribution of x has the largest variance.

Let us finally choose the simplest scenario within the settings of our present example, where the input signals x_i are mutually independent so that $\langle x_i x_j \rangle = S_i^2 \delta_{ij}$. The matrix elements L_{ij} then become $L_{ij} = (S_i^2/\sigma_i^2)\delta_{ij}$. The largest eigenvalue is

$$\Lambda = \max_i \{S_i^2/\sigma_i^2\}$$

Let us denote the set of all channels i with the largest signal/noise ratio by $S = \{i | S_i/\sigma_i = \sqrt{\Lambda}\}$. The optimal synaptic weights $\boldsymbol{w}$ are now those where the system 'tunes' into these particular input channels: $w_i^{\text{opt}} = 0$ for $i \notin S$, $w_i^{\text{opt}} \neq 0$ for $i \in S$. If there is precisely one input channel with the largest signal/noise ratio, then the optimal network will only be connected to this single channel.

14.3 Neuronal specialization

In the first case that we studied in this section, a single neuron with Gaussian output noise, a simple boost of all synaptic weights allowed the neuron to obtain any desired value of the differential mutual information between the uncorrupted and corrupted signals. However, in practice this would usually not have been an option: in the real world one tends to have constraints on the possible values of the weights, which forbid unlimited boosting. Here we will inspect such cases in the context of a population of M linear neurons $y_i\colon \mathbb{R}^N \to \mathbb{R}$ $(i = 1, \ldots, M)$, the outputs $y_i(\boldsymbol{x})$ of which are once more corrupted by Gaussian noise sources ξ_i:

$$y_i(\boldsymbol{x}) = \sum_{j=1}^{N} w_{ij}x_j + \xi_i \qquad p(\xi_i) = \frac{e^{-\xi_i^2/2\sigma_i^2}}{\sigma_i\sqrt{2\pi}} \tag{14.28}$$

with the synaptic weights $\{w_{ij}\}$.

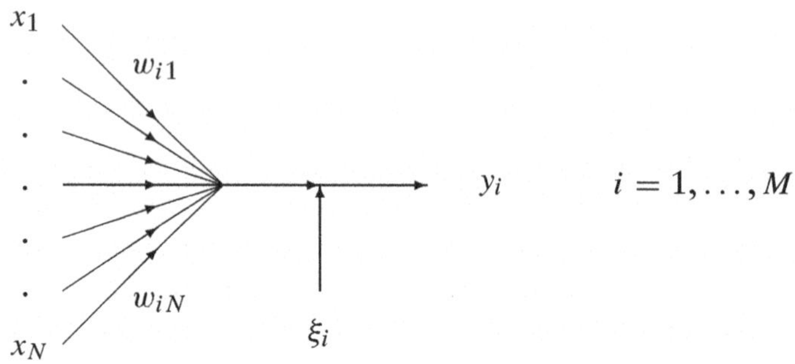

The strengths of the noise channels are given by $\sigma_i^2 = \langle \xi_i^2 \rangle$. We assume the input signals to obey $\langle x_i \rangle = 0$ and to be statistically independent of the noise sources, and we take the uncorrupted signals $z_i(\boldsymbol{x}) = \sum_{j=1}^{N} w_{ij}x_j$ to have a Gaussian joint probability distribution. So we can once more be sure that the pair $(\boldsymbol{y}, \boldsymbol{z})$ is described by a Gaussian joint probability distribution, where $\boldsymbol{y} = (y_1, \ldots, y_M)$ and $\boldsymbol{z} = (z_1, \ldots, z_M)$, with $\langle \boldsymbol{y} \rangle = \langle \boldsymbol{z} \rangle = 0$, so that the mutual information between the uncorrupted signals $\boldsymbol{z}$ and the corrupted signals $\boldsymbol{y}$ is given by equation (12.20). The various covariance matrices are now

$$C_{ij}^{zz} = \langle z_i z_j \rangle = \sum_{kl} w_{ik}w_{jl}\langle x_k x_l \rangle$$

$$C_{ij}^{yz} = C_{ij}^{zy} = \langle y_i z_j \rangle = \sum_{kl} w_{ik}w_{jl}\langle x_k x_l \rangle$$

$$C_{ij}^{yy} = \langle y_i y_j \rangle = \sum_{kl} w_{ik}w_{jl}\langle x_k x_l \rangle + \sigma_i^2\delta_{ij}$$

Only two different matrices appear, for which we use the shorthands $C_{ij} = C_{ij}^{zz}$ and $D_{ij} = \sigma_i^2\delta_{ij}$. We can then write equation (12.20) in the form

$$\tilde{I}(\boldsymbol{Y}, \boldsymbol{Z}) = -\frac{1}{2}\log_2 \det\begin{pmatrix} \boldsymbol{1} & (\boldsymbol{C}+\boldsymbol{D})^{-1}\boldsymbol{C} \\ \boldsymbol{1} & \boldsymbol{1} \end{pmatrix} \tag{14.29}$$

where $\boldsymbol{1}$ denotes the $M \times M$ identity matrix.

From this point onwards we will restrict ourselves for simplicity to the simple situation where the input signals x_i are statistically independent, so $\langle x_i x_j \rangle = S_i^2 \delta_{ij}$, where the different noise signals are of uniform strength, so $\sigma_i^2 = \sigma^2$, and where there are just two neurons, $M = 2$. We also assume for simplicity that all input variances S_i^2 are different (so that in subsequent calculations we will have no degenerate eigenspaces). We define

$$\begin{aligned}\epsilon_1 &= \sigma^{-2} \sum_{k=1}^{N} w_{1k}^2 S_k^2 \\ \epsilon_2 &= \sigma^{-2} \sum_{k=1}^{N} w_{2k}^2 S_k^2 \\ \epsilon_{12} &= \sigma^{-2} \sum_{k=1}^{N} w_{1k} w_{2k} S_k^2\end{aligned} \tag{14.30}$$

The matrix $(\boldsymbol{C} + \boldsymbol{D})^{-1}\boldsymbol{C}$ in (14.29) can now be written as

$$\begin{aligned}(\boldsymbol{C} + \boldsymbol{D})^{-1}[\boldsymbol{C} + \boldsymbol{D} - \boldsymbol{D}] &= \mathbf{1} - (\boldsymbol{C} + \boldsymbol{D})^{-1}\boldsymbol{D} \\ &= \mathbf{1} - (\mathbf{1} + \boldsymbol{D}^{-1}\boldsymbol{C})^{-1} = \mathbf{1} - \begin{pmatrix} 1 + \epsilon_1 & \epsilon_{12} \\ \epsilon_{12} & 1 + \epsilon_2 \end{pmatrix}^{-1}\end{aligned}$$

Furthermore, we can use the general rule (which can be verified directly for $M = 2$) that:

$$\det \begin{pmatrix} \mathbf{1} & \mathbf{1} - \boldsymbol{K} \\ \mathbf{1} & \mathbf{1} \end{pmatrix} = \det \boldsymbol{K}$$

which gives us:

$$\begin{aligned}\tilde{I}(\boldsymbol{Y}, \boldsymbol{Z}) &= \frac{1}{2} \log_2 \det \begin{pmatrix} 1 + \epsilon_1 & \epsilon_{12} \\ \epsilon_{12} & 1 + \epsilon_2 \end{pmatrix} \\ &= \frac{1}{2} \log_2 (1 + \epsilon_1 + \epsilon_2 + \epsilon_1\epsilon_2 - \epsilon_{12}^2)\end{aligned} \tag{14.31}$$

We are interested in finding out which is the optimal choice for the weights in the specific case where the latter are prevented, via a constraint, from growing unboundedly. For this constraint we choose the so-called spherical one:

$$\sum_{k=1}^{N} w_{1k}^2 = \sum_{k=1}^{N} w_{2k}^2 = 1 \tag{14.32}$$

We will inspect various regime for the noise level σ, and, depending on this noise level, we will observe completely different optimal weight arrangements.

High noise levels, $\sigma \gg 1$

Since each term in (14.30) is of order $\mathcal{O}(\sigma^{-2})$ the terms which are quadratic in the epsilons are now negligible compared to the ones that are linear in the epsilons. Thus we get, using $\ln(1+x) = x + \mathcal{O}(x^2)$:

$$\begin{aligned}\tilde{I}(\boldsymbol{Y},\boldsymbol{Z}) &= \frac{1}{2\ln 2}\ln(1+\epsilon_1+\epsilon_2+\mathcal{O}(\sigma^{-4})) \\ &= \frac{1}{2\sigma^2\ln 2}\sum_{k=1}^{N} S_k^2(w_{1k}^2+w_{2k}^2)+\mathcal{O}(\sigma^{-4})\end{aligned}$$

We may now calculate the maximum of the leading term in this expression under the constraints (14.32) using Lagrange multipliers, which gives the following equations for the extrema:

$$\frac{\partial\tilde{I}}{\partial w_{1k}} = \gamma_1 w_{1k} \qquad \frac{\partial\tilde{I}}{\partial w_{2k}} = \gamma_2 w_{2k} \qquad \sum_{k=1}^{N} w_{1k}^2 = \sum_{k=1}^{N} w_{2k}^2 = 1$$

(in which γ_1 and γ_2 are the Lagrange multipliers). Working out the derivatives to the leading order in σ gives:

$$S_k^2 w_{1k} = \gamma_1\sigma^2\ln 2\ w_{1k} \qquad S_k^2 w_{2k} = \gamma_2\sigma^2\ln 2\ w_{2k}$$

Since all S_k were assumed to be different, the only solutions are those where both weight vectors $\{w_{1k}\}$ and $\{w_{2k}\}$ have just one nonzero component: $(\exists i_1)(\forall k \neq i_1)$: $w_{1k} = 0$, and $(\exists i_2)(\forall k \neq i_2)$: $w_{2k} = 0$. The nonzero components must then obey (via the normalization constraint): $w_{1i_1}^2 = w_{2i_2}^2 = 1$. The corresponding value for the leading order of the differential mutual information is

$$\tilde{I}(\boldsymbol{Y},\boldsymbol{Z}) = \frac{S_{i_1}^2 + S_{i_2}^2}{2\sigma^2\ln 2}$$

Its maximum is obtained when both nonzero weight components are those coupled to the strongest input signal: $i_1 = i_2 = i^\star$, where $i^\star$ is defined via $\max_i S_i^2 = S_{i^\star}^2$. This shows that for high noise levels we make the best use of our available hardware if we force our neurons to team up and both tune into the strongest input channel.

Low noise levels, $\sigma \ll 1$

Since all epsilons are of order $\mathcal{O}(\sigma^{-2})$, in this case the dominant terms in (14.31) are those which are quadratic in the epsilons:

$$\tilde{I}(\boldsymbol{Y}, \boldsymbol{Z}) = \frac{1}{2}\log_2(\epsilon_1\epsilon_2 - \epsilon_{12}^2 + \mathcal{O}(\sigma^{-2}))$$
$$= \frac{1}{2}\log_2\left[\frac{1}{\sigma^4}\left(\sum_{k=1}^{N} w_{1k}^2 S_k^2\right)\left(\sum_{k=1}^{N} w_{2k}^2 S_k^2\right) - \frac{1}{\sigma^4}\left(\sum_{k=1}^{N} w_{1k}w_{2k}S_k^2\right)^2 + \mathcal{O}(\sigma^{-2})\right]$$

We now have to calculate the maximum of the leading term in the argument of the logarithm, under the constraints (14.32), using Lagrange multipliers, which gives the following equations:

$$2S_k^2\left[w_{1k}\left(\sum_{k=1}^{N} w_{2k}^2 S_k^2\right) - w_{2k}\left(\sum_{k=1}^{N} w_{1k}w_{2k}S_k^2\right)\right] = \gamma_1 w_{1k} \qquad (14.33)$$

$$2S_k^2\left[w_{2k}\left(\sum_{k=1}^{N} w_{1k}^2 S_k^2\right) - w_{1k}\left(\sum_{k=1}^{N} w_{1k}w_{2k}S_k^2\right)\right] = \gamma_2 w_{2k} \qquad (14.34)$$

As before, these equations are to be solved for each k, in combination with the constraint equation (14.32). We now put

$$\tilde{\epsilon}_1 = \sum_{k=1}^{N} w_{1k}^2 S_k^2 \qquad \tilde{\epsilon}_2 = \sum_{k=1}^{N} w_{2k}^2 S_k^2 \qquad \tilde{\epsilon}_{12} = \sum_{k=1}^{N} w_{1k}w_{2k}S_k^2$$

so that equations (14.33, 14.34) acquire the following compact form

$$\begin{pmatrix} 2S_k^2\tilde{\epsilon}_2 - \gamma_1 & -2S_k^2\tilde{\epsilon}_{12} \\ -2S_k^2\tilde{\epsilon}_{12} & 2S_k^2\tilde{\epsilon}_1 - \gamma_2 \end{pmatrix}\begin{pmatrix} w_{1k} \\ w_{2k} \end{pmatrix} = 0$$

so

$$\forall k\colon \quad (w_{1k}, w_{2k}) = 0 \quad \text{or} \quad \left(S_k^2\tilde{\epsilon}_2 - \frac{1}{2}\gamma_1\right)\left(S_k^2\tilde{\epsilon}_1 - \frac{1}{2}\gamma_2\right) = S_k^4\tilde{\epsilon}_{12}^2$$

Since all S_k are assumed to be different, and since the second equation, when solved for S_k^2, can have at most two solutions, we are forced to conclude that each weight vector can have at most *two* nonzero-components, with identical indices: $(\exists i_1, i_2)(\forall k \neq i_1, i_2)$: $w_{1k} = w_{2k} = 0$. Normalization subsequently dictates that $w_{1i_1}^2 + w_{1i_2}^2 = w_{2i_1}^2 + w_{2i_2}^2 = 1$. The corresponding value for the leading order of the differential mutual information is now

$$i_1 = i_2: \quad \tilde{I}(\boldsymbol{Y}, \boldsymbol{Z}) = \frac{1}{2}\log_2[\mathcal{O}(\sigma^{-2})]$$

$$\begin{aligned} i_1 \neq i_2: \quad \tilde{I}(\boldsymbol{Y}, \boldsymbol{Z}) &= \frac{1}{2}\log_2\Bigg[\frac{1}{\sigma^4}(w_{1i_1}^2 S_{i_1}^2 + w_{1i_2}^2 S_{i_2}^2)(w_{2i_1}^2 S_{i_1}^2 + w_{2i_2}^2 S_{i_2}^2) \\ &\quad - \frac{1}{\sigma^4}(w_{1i_1} w_{2i_1} S_{i_1}^2 + w_{1i_2} w_{2i_2} S_{i_2}^2)^2 + \mathcal{O}(\sigma^{-2})\Bigg] \\ &= \frac{1}{2}\log_2\left[\frac{1}{\sigma^4} S_{i_1}^2 S_{i_2}^2 (w_{1i_1} w_{2i_2} - w_{1i_2} w_{2i_1})^2 + \mathcal{O}(\sigma^{-2})\right] \end{aligned}$$

Clearly the maximum of $\tilde{I}(\boldsymbol{Y}, \boldsymbol{Z})$ is obtained for $i_1 \neq i_2$. To work out the last maximization step we use once more the spherical constraints, and write

$$w_{1i_1} = \cos\phi_1 \qquad w_{1i_2} = \sin\phi_1 \qquad w_{2i_1} = \cos\phi_2 \qquad w_{2i_2} = \sin\phi_2$$

giving

$$\begin{aligned} \tilde{I}(\boldsymbol{Y}, \boldsymbol{Z}) &= \frac{1}{2}\log_2\left(\frac{1}{\sigma^4} S_{i_1}^2 S_{i_2}^2 (\cos\phi_1 \sin\phi_2 - \sin\phi_1 \cos\phi_2)^2 + \mathcal{O}(\sigma^{-2})\right) \\ &= \frac{1}{2}\log_2\left(\frac{1}{\sigma^4} S_{i_1}^2 S_{i_2}^2 \sin^2(\phi_1 - \phi_2) + \mathcal{O}(\sigma^{-2})\right) \end{aligned}$$

The maximum of this expression is found for $\phi_1 = \phi_2 + (n + \frac{1}{2})\pi$, where

$$\begin{aligned} \begin{pmatrix} w_{1i_1} \\ w_{1i_2} \end{pmatrix} \cdot \begin{pmatrix} w_{2i_1} \\ w_{2i_2} \end{pmatrix} &= \begin{pmatrix} \cos\left(\phi_2 + \dfrac{\pi}{2} + n\pi\right) \\ \sin\left(\phi_2 + \dfrac{\pi}{2} + n\pi\right) \end{pmatrix} \cdot \begin{pmatrix} \cos\phi_2 \\ \sin\phi_2 \end{pmatrix} \\ &= \begin{pmatrix} (-1)^{n+1}\sin\phi_2 \\ (-1)^n \cos\phi_2 \end{pmatrix} \cdot \begin{pmatrix} \cos\phi_2 \\ \sin\phi_2 \end{pmatrix} = 0 \end{aligned}$$

We conclude that the optimal nonzero weight vectors of our two neurons (with two nonzero components each) are mutually orthogonal, and we get the resulting value

$$\tilde{I}(\boldsymbol{Y},\boldsymbol{Z}) = \frac{1}{2}\log_2\left(\frac{1}{\sigma^4}S_{i_1}^2 S_{i_2}^2 + \mathcal{O}(\sigma^{-2})\right)$$

This is maximal if the two input channels i_1 and i_2 tuned into by our weight vectors are chosen to be the *strongest* two (note that we are not allowed to choose $i_1 = i_2$ here), so

$$S_{\max}^2 = S_{i_1}^2 > S_{i_2}^2 > \cdots \quad \text{or} \quad S_{\max}^2 = S_{i_2}^2 > S_{i_1}^2 > \cdots$$

Thus, for low noise levels the best strategy is no longer for our two neurons to team up, but rather to let them specialize and form an orthogonal basis in the space of the two strongest non-identical channels.

The transition to specialization

So far we have just checked the two extreme cases of very high and very low noise levels. The results obtained hint at the existence of a transition, at some critical noise level, where specialization sets in. To simplify notation we arrange the input channels in such a way that

$$S_1 > S_2 > S_3 > \cdots$$

Knowing that the optimum configurations in both extreme cases $\sigma \to 0$ and $\sigma \to \infty$ exhibit at most two nonzero weight components for each neuron (connected to the strongest two input signals), we are now led to inspecting the behaviour at intermediate noise levels by putting

$$(w_{11}, w_{12}) = (\cos\phi_1, \sin\phi_1) \qquad (w_{21}, w_{22}) = (\cos\phi_2, \sin\phi_2)$$

In terms of the angles (ϕ_1, ϕ_2) maximizing the differential mutual information (14.31) amounts to maximizing

$$L = \sigma^4(\epsilon_1 + \epsilon_2 + \epsilon_1\epsilon_2 - \epsilon_{12}^2)$$

With $\epsilon_i = (S_1^2\cos^2\phi_i + S_2^2\sin^2\phi_i)/\sigma^2$ for $i = 1, 2$, and $\epsilon_{12} = (S_1^2\cos\phi_1\cos\phi_2 + S_2^2\sin\phi_1\sin\phi_2)/\sigma^2$ this gives

$$\begin{aligned} L &= \sigma^2[2S_2^2 + (S_1^2 - S_2^2)(\cos^2\phi_1 + \cos^2\phi_2)] + S_1^2 S_2^2 \sin^2(\phi_1 - \phi_2) \\ &= \sigma^2\left[S_1^2 + S_2^2 + \frac{1}{2}(S_1^2 - S_2^2)(\cos(2\phi_1) + \cos(2\phi_2))\right] \\ &\quad + \frac{1}{2}S_1^2 S_2^2 - \frac{1}{2}S_1^2 S_2^2\cos(2\phi_1 - 2\phi_2) \end{aligned} \tag{14.35}$$

The weight constraints (14.32) have now been built-in, so that extremization of (14.35) reduces to simply putting two derivatives to zero:

$$\begin{aligned} \partial L/\partial\phi_1 = 0: &\quad \sigma^2(S_1^2 - S_2^2)\sin(2\phi_1) = S_1^2 S_2^2 \sin(2\phi_1 - 2\phi_2) \\ \partial L/\partial\phi_2 = 0: &\quad \sigma^2(S_1^2 - S_2^2)\sin(2\phi_2) = -S_1^2 S_2^2 \sin(2\phi_1 - 2\phi_2) \end{aligned} \tag{14.36}$$

Addition of the two equations in (14.36) shows that (14.36) can be replaced by the equivalent set

$$\begin{aligned} \sin(2\phi_1) &= -\sin(2\phi_2) \\ \sigma^2(S_1^2 - S_2^2)\sin(2\phi_1) &= S_1^2 S_2^2 \sin(2\phi_1 - 2\phi_2) \end{aligned} \tag{14.37}$$

This latter set (14.37) admits two types of solutions (modulo irrelevant multiples of 2π), namely

$$\begin{aligned} 2\phi_2 = -2\phi_1: &\quad \sigma^2(S_1^2 - S_2^2)\sin(2\phi_1) = S_1^2 S_2^2 \sin(4\phi_1) \\ &\quad \sin(2\phi_1)[\sigma^2(S_1^2 - S_2^2) - 2S_1^2 S_2^2 \cos(2\phi_1)] = 0 \\ &\quad 2\phi_1 \in \{0, \pi\} \quad \text{or} \quad \cos(2\phi_1) = \tfrac{1}{2}\sigma^2(S_1^2 - S_2^2)/S_1^2 S_2^2 \\ 2\phi_2 = 2\phi_1 + \pi: &\quad \sin(2\phi_1) = 0 \quad \text{so} \quad 2\phi_1 \in \{0, \pi\} \end{aligned}$$

We can now simply list the various extrema with their corresponding value for the quantity L we wish to maximize. First we have the simplest ones, $2\phi_1 \in \{0, \pi\}$ with $2\phi_2 = -2\phi_1$, where both neurons tune into the same channel:

$\cos(2\phi_1)$	$\sin(2\phi_1)$	$\cos(2\phi_2)$	$\sin(2\phi_2)$	(w_{11}, w_{12})	(w_{21}, w_{22})	L
1	0	1	0	$(\pm 1, 0)$	$(\pm 1, 0)$	$2\sigma^2 S_1^2$
-1	0	-1	0	$(0, \pm 1)$	$(0, \pm 1)$	$2\sigma^2 S_2^2$

(14.38)

Then we have alternative extrema, $2\phi_1 \in \{0, \pi\}$ with $2\phi_2 = 2\phi_1 + \pi$, where each neuron tunes into a single but different input channel:

$\cos(2\phi_1)$	$\sin(2\phi_1)$	$\cos(2\phi_2)$	$\sin(2\phi_2)$	(w_{11}, w_{12})	(w_{21}, w_{22})	L
1	0	-1	0	$(\pm 1, 0)$	$(0, \pm 1)$	$\sigma^2(S_1^2 + S_2^2) + S_1^2 S_2^2$
-1	0	1	0	$(0, \pm 1)$	$(\pm 1, 0)$	$\sigma^2(S_1^2 + S_2^2) + S_1^2 S_2^2$

(14.39)

Finally there is a third non-trivial solution type, where each neuron tunes into a specific combination of the two strongest channels:

$$\cos(2\phi_2) = \cos(2\phi_1) \qquad \sin(2\phi_2) = -\sin(2\phi_1)$$
$$\cos(2\phi_1) = \frac{\sigma^2(S_1^2 - S_2^2)}{2S_1^2 S_2^2} \tag{14.40}$$

$$L = \sigma^2(S_1^2 + S_2^2) + S_1^2 S_2^2 + \frac{\sigma^4(S_1^2 - S_2^2)^2}{4S_1^2 S_2^2} \tag{14.41}$$

The solution (14.40) can only exist for small noise levels (since $\cos(2\phi_i) \leq 1$):

$$\sigma \leq \sigma_c = \left(\frac{2S_1^2 S_2^2}{S_1^2 - S_2^2}\right)^{1/2} \tag{14.42}$$

Since the solution (14.40) obeys $\phi_2 = -\phi_1 + n\pi$, we can directly calculate the angle between the weight vectors (w_{11}, w_{12}) and (w_{21}, w_{22}) of our two neurons:

$$\begin{pmatrix} w_{11} \\ w_{12} \end{pmatrix} \cdot \begin{pmatrix} w_{21} \\ w_{22} \end{pmatrix} = \cos\phi_1 \cos(n\pi - \phi_1) + \sin\phi_1 \sin(n\pi - \phi_1)$$
$$= (-1)^n(\cos^2\phi_1 - \sin^2\phi_1) = (-1)^n \cos(2\phi_1) = (-1)^n \sigma^2/\sigma_c^2$$

Here we have used (14.40) and (14.42). This expression shows that the solution (14.40) starts off at $\sigma = \sigma_c$ as two (anti-)parallel weight vectors (as in (14.38)), followed by a continuous 'unfolding' of the two weight vectors as the noise decreases further, until they form a perfect orthogonal basis for $\sigma = 0$. Comparison of (14.41) with (14.39) immediately shows that the solution (14.40), provided it exists, has a larger value for L. Finally we check the condition for the solution (14.40) to give the maximum mutual information (i.e. for L in (14.41) to be also larger than $2\sigma^2 S_1^2$):

$$\sigma^2(S_1^2 + S_2^2) + S_1^2 S_2^2 + \frac{\sigma^4(S_1^2 - S_2^2)^2}{4S_1^2 S_2^2} > 2\sigma^2 S_1^2$$

or

$$\sigma^4 - 2\sigma^2\left(\frac{2S_1^2 S_2^2}{S_1^2 - S_2^2}\right) + \left(\frac{2S_1^2 S_2^2}{S_1^2 - S_2^2}\right)^2 > 0$$

Since this condition is identical to $(\sigma^2 - \sigma_c^2)^2 > 0$, see (14.42), we conclude that as soon as the solution (14.40) exists it will give the maximum mutual information.

If the solution (14.40) does not exist, that is, when $\sigma > \sigma_c$, we have to find the maximum of L by comparing the values (14.38) and (14.39) of the alternative extrema. The condition $\sigma > \sigma_c$ is then found to translate into the statement that the value in (14.38) is largest. In conclusion, all this implies that the optimal weight arrangement indeed shows a specialization transition at the critical noise level given in (14.42). For $\sigma > \sigma_c$ both neurons operate identical rules; for $\sigma < \sigma_c$ the two neurons specialize and start to operate different rules. This example illustrates how heuristic strategies, like doing detailed data fitting only in cases where there is not much noise in the data, can be rigorously quantified with information-theoretic tools. Here the theory tells us exactly when to specialize and when not to.

14.4 Detection of coherent features

We now turn to a different problem. Imagine having two types of input channels, $\{x_i^a\}$ and $\{x_i^b\}$, each corrupted by independent Gaussian noise sources $\{\xi_i^a\}$ and $\{\xi_i^b\}$, and each feeding into a linear neuron, y_a: $\mathbb{R}^N \to \mathbb{R}$ and y_b: $\mathbb{R}^N \to \mathbb{R}$, respectively:

$$y_a(\boldsymbol{x}^a) = \sum_{i=1}^{N} w_i^a(x_i^a + \xi_i^a) \qquad p(\xi_i^a) = \frac{e^{-(\xi_i^a)^2/2\sigma^2}}{\sigma\sqrt{2\pi}}$$

$$y_b(\boldsymbol{x}^b) = \sum_{i=1}^{N} w_i^b(x_i^b + \xi_i^b) \qquad p(\xi_i^b) = \frac{e^{-(\xi_i^b)^2/2\sigma^2}}{\sigma\sqrt{2\pi}}$$

with the two types of synaptic weights $\{w_i^a\}$ and $\{w_i^b\}$. The uniform strength of the $2N$ noise sources $\xi_i^{a,b}$ is measured by $\sigma^2 = \langle(\xi_i^{a,b})^2\rangle$. Note that $\langle\xi_i^a\xi_j^b\rangle = 0$. The situation is depicted below:

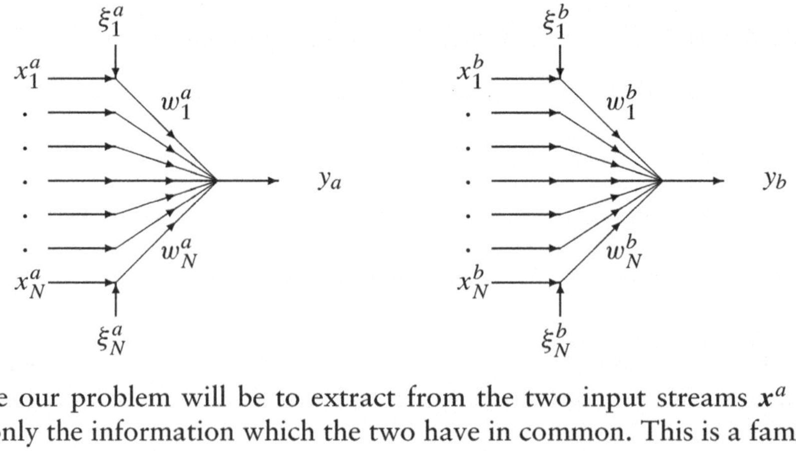

Here our problem will be to extract from the two input streams $\boldsymbol{x}^a$ and $\boldsymbol{x}^b$ only the information which the two have in common. This is a familiar problem in sensory information processing in biology, where various sensory systems each provide only partial and often messy information. The total information stream is integrated or filtered in such a way that only those underlying regularities that are coherent across the various sensory systems are retained. Examples are the merging of visual images to produce stereo vision, the integration of the signals from various sensors that measure muscle stretch in order to build a correct internal representation of the position of the limbs, etc. In order to study such situations, let us assume here a simple scenario. Here the original uncorrupted input signals are related in a deterministic way, for instance via an orthogonal transformation, that is, by a rotation or rotation–reflection in $\mathbb{R}^N$:

$$\boldsymbol{x}^b = \boldsymbol{U}\boldsymbol{x}^a \qquad \boldsymbol{U}\boldsymbol{U}^\dagger = \boldsymbol{U}^\dagger\boldsymbol{U} = \mathbf{1}$$

with $(\boldsymbol{U}^\dagger)_{ij} = U_{ji}$ and with $\mathbf{1}_{ij} = \delta_{ij}$. The appropriate strategy here is to maximize the differential mutual information between the two neuron outputs y_a and y_b, since this quantity is precisely generated by the information that is coherent across the two input streams.

As before we assume that all input signals obey $\langle x_i^{a,b}\rangle = 0$ and are statistically independent of the noise sources, and that the uncorrupted signals $z_a(\boldsymbol{x}_a) = \sum_{i=1}^N w_i^a x_i^a$ and $z_b(\boldsymbol{x}_b) = \sum_{i=1}^N w_i^b x_i^b$ have a Gaussian joint probability distribution; the same must then be true for the pair (y_a, y_b). We write the two weight vectors as $\boldsymbol{w}^a = (w_1^a, \ldots, w_N^a)$ and $\boldsymbol{w}^b = (w_1^b, \ldots, w_N^b)$, and define the covariance matrix $\boldsymbol{C}$ with elements $C_{ij} = \langle x_i^a x_j^a\rangle$. The second-order moments are given by

$$\begin{aligned}
\langle y_a^2\rangle &= \sum_{ij} w_i^a w_j^a (\langle x_i^a x_j^a\rangle + \langle \xi_i^a \xi_j^a\rangle) = \boldsymbol{w}^a \cdot (\boldsymbol{C} + \sigma^2\mathbf{1})\boldsymbol{w}^a \\
\langle y_a y_b\rangle &= \sum_{ij} w_i^a w_j^b \langle x_i^a x_j^b\rangle = \sum_{ijk} w_i^a w_j^b U_{jk} \langle x_i^a x_k^a\rangle = \boldsymbol{w}^a \cdot \boldsymbol{C}\boldsymbol{U}^\dagger \boldsymbol{w}^b \\
\langle y_b^2\rangle &= \sum_{ij} w_i^b w_j^b (\langle x_i^b x_j^b\rangle + \langle \xi_i^b \xi_j^b\rangle) = \sum_{ijkl} w_i^b w_j^b U_{ik} U_{jl} \langle x_k^a x_l^a\rangle + \sigma^2(\boldsymbol{w}^b)^2 \\
&= \boldsymbol{w}^b \cdot \boldsymbol{U}(\boldsymbol{C} + \sigma^2\mathbf{1})\boldsymbol{U}^\dagger \boldsymbol{w}^b
\end{aligned}$$

Substitution into $\tilde{I}(Y, Z)$ as given by (12.19) leads to

$$\tilde{I}(Y_a, Y_b) = -\frac{1}{2}\log_2\left(1 - \frac{(\boldsymbol{w}^a \cdot \boldsymbol{C}\boldsymbol{U}^\dagger \boldsymbol{w}^b)^2}{[\boldsymbol{w}^a \cdot (\boldsymbol{C} + \sigma^2\mathbf{1})\boldsymbol{w}^a][\boldsymbol{w}^b \cdot \boldsymbol{U}(\boldsymbol{C} + \sigma^2\mathbf{1})\boldsymbol{U}^\dagger \boldsymbol{w}^b]}\right) \tag{14.43}$$

We now try to maximize (14.43), which is seen to be equivalent to maximizing the fraction in the argument of the logarithm in (14.43). This fraction is greatly simplified by the symmetrizing transformation $\boldsymbol{w} = \boldsymbol{w}^a$, $\boldsymbol{v} = \boldsymbol{U}^\dagger \boldsymbol{w}^b$ (so $\boldsymbol{w}^b = \boldsymbol{U}\boldsymbol{v}$), which reduces our problem to the calculation of

$$L = \max_{\boldsymbol{w},\boldsymbol{v}\in\mathbb{R}^N} \left\{ \frac{(\boldsymbol{w}\cdot\boldsymbol{C}\boldsymbol{v})^2}{[\boldsymbol{w}\cdot(\boldsymbol{C}+\sigma^2\mathbf{1})\boldsymbol{w}][\boldsymbol{v}\cdot(\boldsymbol{C}+\sigma^2\mathbf{1})\boldsymbol{v}]} \right\}$$

Extremization by putting the various derivatives $\partial L/\partial w_i$ and $\partial L/\partial v_i$ to zero gives the following two vector equations:

$$[\boldsymbol{w}\cdot(\boldsymbol{C}+\sigma^2\mathbf{1})\boldsymbol{w}]\boldsymbol{C}\boldsymbol{v} = (\boldsymbol{w}\cdot\boldsymbol{C}\boldsymbol{v})(\boldsymbol{C}+\sigma^2\mathbf{1})\boldsymbol{w}$$

$$[\boldsymbol{v}\cdot(\boldsymbol{C}+\sigma^2\mathbf{1})\boldsymbol{v}]\boldsymbol{C}\boldsymbol{w} = (\boldsymbol{v}\cdot\boldsymbol{C}\boldsymbol{w})(\boldsymbol{C}+\sigma^2\mathbf{1})\boldsymbol{v}$$

which can be transformed into

$$\boldsymbol{v} = \Lambda_1(\mathbf{1}+\sigma^2\boldsymbol{C}^{-1})\boldsymbol{w} \qquad \boldsymbol{w} = \Lambda_2(\mathbf{1}+\sigma^2\boldsymbol{C}^{-1})\boldsymbol{v} \tag{14.44}$$

with

$$\Lambda_1 = \frac{\boldsymbol{w}\cdot\boldsymbol{C}\boldsymbol{v}}{\boldsymbol{w}\cdot(\boldsymbol{C}+\sigma^2\mathbf{1})\boldsymbol{w}} \qquad \Lambda_2 = \frac{\boldsymbol{v}\cdot\boldsymbol{C}\boldsymbol{w}}{\boldsymbol{v}\cdot(\boldsymbol{C}+\sigma^2\mathbf{1})\boldsymbol{v}} \tag{14.45}$$

giving $L = \Lambda_1\Lambda_2$. Combining the two equations in (14.44) gives the eigenvalue problem

$$\boldsymbol{w} = L(\mathbf{1}+\sigma^2\boldsymbol{C}^{-1})^2\boldsymbol{w}$$

the solutions of which are just the eigenvectors of the covariance matrix $\boldsymbol{C}$. If we denote the corresponding eigenvalues by λ, we arrive at:

$$\boldsymbol{C}\boldsymbol{w}_\lambda = \lambda\boldsymbol{w}_\lambda \qquad \boldsymbol{C}\boldsymbol{v}_\lambda = \lambda\boldsymbol{v}_\lambda \qquad L = \left(\frac{\lambda}{\lambda+\sigma^2}\right)^2$$

Since $\boldsymbol{C}$ is a covariance matrix it cannot have negative eigenvalues, so that the maximum in (14.43) is obtained if we choose for λ the largest eigenvalue $\lambda_{\max}$ of $\boldsymbol{C}$:

$$\max \tilde{I}(Y_a, Y_b) = -\frac{1}{2}\log_2\left[1 - \frac{\lambda_{\max}^2}{(\lambda_{\max}+\sigma^2)^2}\right] \tag{14.46}$$

In the simplest case where the $\lambda_{\max}$ is not degenerate, the associated eigenspace is simply spanned by one corresponding eigenvector $\boldsymbol{w}_{\lambda_{\max}}$.

The optimal weight configuration for which the maximum (14.46) is achieved is, in terms of the original variables:

$$\boldsymbol{w}^a_{\rm opt} = k_a \boldsymbol{w}_{\lambda_{\max}} \qquad \boldsymbol{w}^b_{\rm opt} = k_b \boldsymbol{U}\boldsymbol{w}_{\lambda_{\max}} \tag{14.47}$$

with k_a and k_b arbitrary constants, and where we may always choose $|\boldsymbol{w}_{\lambda_{\max}}| = 1$. By inserting into the original operation rules of the two neurons, and using $\boldsymbol{x}^b = \boldsymbol{U}\boldsymbol{x}^a$, one observes that in this optimal setup the system operates a rule in which, apart from an overall constant, the signal terms of the two neuron outputs have become identical:

$$y_a(\boldsymbol{x}^a) = k_a \boldsymbol{w}_{\lambda_{\max}} \cdot \boldsymbol{x}^a + k_a \boldsymbol{w}_{\lambda_{\max}} \cdot \boldsymbol{\xi}^a$$

$$y_b(\boldsymbol{x}^b) = k_b(\boldsymbol{U}\boldsymbol{w}_{\lambda_{\max}}) \cdot \boldsymbol{x}^b + k_b(\boldsymbol{U}\boldsymbol{w}_{\lambda_{\max}}) \cdot \boldsymbol{\xi}^b$$

$$= k_b \boldsymbol{w}_{\lambda_{\max}} \cdot \boldsymbol{x}^a + k_b \boldsymbol{w}_{\lambda_{\max}} \cdot \boldsymbol{U}^{\dagger}\boldsymbol{\xi}^b$$

There is an additional bonus. If we now go back and, for the present example, work out our previous result (14.27) for the weight arrangements of our two neurons that each maximize the mutual information between their corrupted and uncorrupted signals, we find exactly the same result (14.47). Thus, the weight configuration that maximizes the mutual information between y_a and y_b will maximize at the same time the amount of information about the uncorrupted signals that reach the output! What is nice about this feature is that the latter is a quantity that one can never observe at the output side of the system, whereas $\tilde{I}(y_a, y_b)$ only involves the statistics of the output signals and can thus be maximized; for instance by a simple stochastic search procedure, using available information only.

14.5 The effect of non-linearities

Finally we will here give the justification of a previous remark that the analysis performed for various arrangements involving linear neurons of the type $y(\boldsymbol{x}) = \sum_{i=1}^{N} w_i x_i$, possibly corrupted by noise sources, carry over directly to the more general case of neurons with arbitrary (usually non-linear) invertible transfer functions: $y(\boldsymbol{x}) = f\big(\sum_{i=1}^{N} w_i x_i\big)$. The reason for this is that the differential mutual information, on which our analysis was built, is not sensitive to invertible transformations. Note that the following result is essentially the case where the data processing inequality (viz. Property 7 in Section 12.3) becomes an equality, but now applied to real-valued random variables; the variables (Z, Y, U) below would correspond to (X, Y, Z) in Section 12.3.

Proposition. If two random variables $u \in A \subseteq \mathbb{R}$ and $y \in \mathbb{R}$ are related by a continuously differentiable and invertible transformation $f\colon \mathbb{R} \to A$, that is, $u = f(y)$, and z is an arbitrary third random variable, then

$$\tilde{I}(U, Z) = \tilde{I}(Y, Z) \tag{14.48}$$

Proof. First we construct the joint distribution $p(u, z)$ from the original distribution $p(y, z)$, using the δ-distribution (see Appendix F), and the marginal distribution $p(u)$:

$$p(u, z) = \int \mathrm{d}y\, p(u|y, z)p(y, z) = \int \mathrm{d}y\, \delta(u - f(y))p(y, z)$$

$$p(u) = \int \mathrm{d}z\, p(u, z) = \int \mathrm{d}y\, \delta(u - f(y)) \int \mathrm{d}z\, p(y, z)$$

$$= \int \mathrm{d}y\, \delta(u - f(y))p(y)$$

The differential mutual information for the pair (u, z) then becomes

$$\tilde{I}(U, Z) = \int \mathrm{d}u\mathrm{d}z\, p(u, z) \log_2 \left[\frac{p(u, z)}{p(u)p(z)}\right]$$

$$= \int \mathrm{d}u\mathrm{d}y\mathrm{d}z\, p(y, z)\delta(u - f(y)) \log_2 \left[\frac{\int \mathrm{d}y'\, \delta(u - f(y'))p(y', z)}{p(z) \int \mathrm{d}y'\, \delta(u - f(y'))p(y')}\right]$$

$$= \int \mathrm{d}y\mathrm{d}z\, p(y, z) \log_2 \left[\frac{\int \mathrm{d}y'\, \delta(f(y) - f(y'))p(y', z)}{p(z) \int \mathrm{d}y'\, \delta(f(y) - f(y'))p(y')}\right]$$

Now we may use identity (F.8) of Appendix F, which gives

$$\tilde{I}(U, Z) = \int \mathrm{d}y\mathrm{d}z\, p(y, z) \log_2 \left[\frac{\int \mathrm{d}y'\, \delta(y - y')p(y', z)}{p(z) \int \mathrm{d}y'\, \delta(y - y')p(y')}\right]$$

$$= \int \mathrm{d}y\mathrm{d}z\, p(y, z) \log_2 \left[\frac{p(y, z)}{p(z)p(y)}\right] = \tilde{I}(Y, Z)$$

This completes the proof. □

Application of this result to the two random variables under consideration allows us to write more generally:

$$F, G \text{ invertible:} \quad \tilde{I}(F(Y), G(Z)) = \tilde{I}(Y, Z) \tag{14.49}$$

Similarly we can prove that such statements are true for random variables which are themselves vectors rather than scalars. This shows that all of our previous statements on linear neurons apply also to neurons with arbitrary non-linear (but invertible) transfer functions.

14.6 Introduction to Amari's information geometry

In this final section we will briefly touch on the area of information geometry and its applications to information processing in neural networks. We consider the general scenario of a neural network whose operation is parametrized by a vector $\boldsymbol{\theta} \in \mathbb{R}^L$. This vector represents both weights and thresholds; we follow with this notation the convention in the information geometry community. The input–output characteristics are described by a conditional probability distribution $p_{\boldsymbol{\theta}}(\boldsymbol{x}_{\text{out}}|\boldsymbol{x}_{\text{in}})$, in which $\boldsymbol{x}_{\text{in}} \in \mathbb{R}^N$ and $\boldsymbol{x}_{\text{out}} \in \mathbb{R}^M$ denote input and output vectors, respectively. The performance of this network on a given input $\boldsymbol{x}_{\text{in}}$, leading to a corresponding network response $\boldsymbol{x}_{\text{out}}$, is assumed to be measured by some error measure $\mathcal{E}(\boldsymbol{x}_{\text{in}}, \boldsymbol{x}_{\text{out}})$. If the probability of an input $\boldsymbol{x}_{\text{in}}$ to be encountered is defined as $p(\boldsymbol{x}_{\text{in}})$, the global error made by a network with parameters $\boldsymbol{\theta}$ is given by

$$E(\boldsymbol{\theta}) = \sum_{\boldsymbol{x}_{\text{in}}} \sum_{\boldsymbol{x}_{\text{out}}} \mathcal{E}(\boldsymbol{x}_{\text{in}}, \boldsymbol{x}_{\text{out}}) p_{\boldsymbol{\theta}}(\boldsymbol{x}_{\text{out}}|\boldsymbol{x}_{\text{in}}) p(\boldsymbol{x}_{\text{in}}) \tag{14.50}$$

We next abbreviate $\boldsymbol{x} = (\boldsymbol{x}_{\text{in}}, \boldsymbol{x}_{\text{out}}) \in A = \mathbb{R}^{N+M}$ and we define $p_{\boldsymbol{\theta}}(\boldsymbol{x}) = p_{\boldsymbol{\theta}}(\boldsymbol{x}_{\text{out}}|\boldsymbol{x}_{\text{in}}) p(\boldsymbol{x}_{\text{in}})$, which now combines both the parametrized properties of the network and the likelihood of input data:

$$E(\boldsymbol{\theta}) = \sum_{\boldsymbol{x} \in A} p_{\boldsymbol{\theta}}(\boldsymbol{x}) \mathcal{E}(\boldsymbol{x}) \tag{14.51}$$

This setup is as yet sufficiently general to cover the majority of neural learning scenarios, although not all. The goal of learning is to find an efficient iterative recipe for modifying the parameters $\boldsymbol{\theta}$ in order to minimize the global error $E(\boldsymbol{\theta})$ as quickly as possible.

Drawbacks of ordinary gradient descent

The most commonly used dynamical rule for the parameters $\boldsymbol{\theta}$ to systematically minimize the error in (14.51) is the celebrated gradient descent procedure:

$$\frac{\mathrm{d}}{\mathrm{d}t}\boldsymbol{\theta} = -\eta \nabla_{\boldsymbol{\theta}} E(\boldsymbol{\theta})$$

In spite of the fact that this appears to be a sensible choice (choosing the steepest direction in order to get to the nearest valley), and that it ensures

$$\frac{\mathrm{d}}{\mathrm{d}t}E = \nabla_{\boldsymbol{\theta}} E(\boldsymbol{\theta}) \cdot \frac{\mathrm{d}}{\mathrm{d}t}\boldsymbol{\theta} = -\eta\,[\nabla_{\boldsymbol{\theta}} E(\boldsymbol{\theta})]^2 \leq 0 \tag{14.52}$$

it is in fact generally far from optimal, and the source of the plateau-phases of slow convergence that haunt learning rules such as error back-propagation; see, for example, Figure 2.9.

In order to appreciate what might be missing, we first note that one can insert an arbitrary positive definite (even parameter dependent) $L \times L$ matrix $\boldsymbol{M}(\boldsymbol{\theta})$ in front of the gradient, without losing the key property of the gradient descent rule that it leads to a consistent reduction of the error measure (14.51):

$$\frac{\mathrm{d}}{\mathrm{d}t}\boldsymbol{\theta} = -\eta \boldsymbol{M}(\boldsymbol{\theta})\nabla_{\boldsymbol{\theta}} E(\boldsymbol{\theta}): \quad \frac{\mathrm{d}}{\mathrm{d}t}E = -\eta[\nabla_{\boldsymbol{\theta}} E(\boldsymbol{\theta}) \cdot \boldsymbol{M}(\boldsymbol{\theta})\nabla E(\boldsymbol{\theta})] \leq 0 \tag{14.53}$$

The conventional gradient descent algorithm just corresponds to the simplest choice $\boldsymbol{M}(\boldsymbol{\theta}) = \mathbf{1}$. One can easily convince oneself by experimentation with such matrices that $\boldsymbol{M}(\boldsymbol{\theta}) = \mathbf{1}$ is usually not optimal. For example: in error back-propagation one finds that using different learning rates for different network layers, dependent on the fan-in of these layers, speeds up convergence; this is an example of inserting a simple (diagonal) type of positive definite matrix. We are thus automatically led to the following question: which is the optimal choice for $\boldsymbol{M}(\boldsymbol{\theta})$?

Seen from a different perspective, we have to realize that the way in which we choose to parametrize the action of our network is (at least from a mathematical point of view) rather arbitrary. For example, instead of a parameter component $\theta_i \in \mathbb{R}$ one could have also inserted θ_i^5, or any other monotonic function of θ_i, without affecting the range of possible operations $p_{\boldsymbol{\theta}}(\boldsymbol{x})$ that the resulting network could perform. More generally, the space of possible operations of the form $p_{\boldsymbol{\theta}}(\boldsymbol{x})$ is invariant under arbitrary invertible transformations $f\colon \mathbb{R}^L \to \mathbb{R}^L$ of the parameter vector $\boldsymbol{\theta}$; mathematically, there is no preferred choice for f.

Yet, the gradient descent learning rule is highly sensitive to such parameter transformations. Just consider two equivalent choices of parameters $\boldsymbol{\theta} \in \mathbb{R}^L$ and $\boldsymbol{\xi} \in \mathbb{R}^L$, which are related by an invertible transformation: $\boldsymbol{\theta} = f(\boldsymbol{\xi})$. A gradient descent dynamics derived in the language of $\boldsymbol{\xi}$, when written explicitly in components, gives:

$$\frac{\mathrm{d}}{\mathrm{d}t}\xi_i = -\eta\frac{\partial}{\partial \xi_i}E(f(\boldsymbol{\xi})) = -\eta\sum_{j=1}^{L}\frac{\partial \theta_j}{\partial \xi_i}\frac{\partial E(\boldsymbol{\theta})}{\partial \theta_j}$$

If we now work out what this implies for the evolution of the alternative parameters $\boldsymbol{\theta}$ we find:

$$\frac{\mathrm{d}}{\mathrm{d}t}\theta_i = \sum_{j=1}^{N} \frac{\partial \theta_i}{\partial \xi_j} \frac{\mathrm{d}}{\mathrm{d}t}\xi_j = -\eta \sum_{jk=1}^{L} \frac{\partial \theta_i}{\partial \xi_j} \frac{\partial \theta_k}{\partial \xi_j} \frac{\partial E(\boldsymbol{\theta})}{\partial \theta_k}$$

Thus

$$\frac{\mathrm{d}}{\mathrm{d}t}\boldsymbol{\theta} = -\eta \boldsymbol{M}(\boldsymbol{\theta}) \nabla_{\boldsymbol{\theta}} E(\boldsymbol{\theta}) \qquad M_{ik}(\boldsymbol{\theta}) = \sum_{j} \frac{\partial \theta_i}{\partial \xi_j} \frac{\partial \theta_k}{\partial \xi_j}$$

The matrix $\boldsymbol{M}(\boldsymbol{\theta})$ is positive definite, so we are still guaranteed that $\mathrm{d}E/\mathrm{d}t \leq 0$. However, we recover a gradient descent equation in terms of the parameters $\boldsymbol{\theta}$ only if $M_{ik}(\boldsymbol{\theta}) = \delta_{ik}$, which in general will not be the case. We conclude that the error evolution that we obtain is strongly dependent on how we choose to parametrize our network in the first place. We are thus automatically led to ask: which is the optimal choice of (alternative) parametrization?

Derivation of gradient descent

In order to understand better the properties of the gradient descent rule, with a view to ultimately replacing it, let us first see how it can be derived from an extremization procedure. We try to extremize $E(\boldsymbol{\theta} + \Delta\boldsymbol{\theta})$ by variation of $\Delta\boldsymbol{\theta}$, subject to the constraint that the magnitude of the change $\boldsymbol{\theta}$ is fixed: $|\Delta\boldsymbol{\theta}| = \Delta$. The solution (extremization of a given function under a constraint) is easily obtained with the method of Lagrange, which tells us that we have to solve the following equations:

$$\frac{\partial E(\boldsymbol{\theta} + \Delta\boldsymbol{\theta})}{\partial(\Delta\theta_i)} = \lambda \frac{\partial}{\partial(\Delta\theta_i)} (\Delta\boldsymbol{\theta})^2 = 2\lambda \Delta\theta_i \qquad (\Delta\boldsymbol{\theta})^2 = \Delta^2$$

We can eliminate λ by taking the inner product with $\Delta\boldsymbol{\theta}$ on both sides of the above equation, giving $\lambda = \frac{1}{2}\Delta^{-2}[\Delta\boldsymbol{\theta} \cdot \nabla E(\boldsymbol{\theta})] + \mathcal{O}(\Delta^0)$. For small changes, that is, $\Delta\boldsymbol{\theta} = \mathrm{d}t(\mathrm{d}\boldsymbol{\theta}/\mathrm{d}t) + \mathcal{O}(\mathrm{d}t^2)$ with $0 < \mathrm{d}t \ll 1$, we then find

$$\nabla E(\boldsymbol{\theta}) = \left[\frac{(\mathrm{d}\boldsymbol{\theta}/\mathrm{d}t) \cdot \nabla E(\boldsymbol{\theta})}{(\mathrm{d}\boldsymbol{\theta}/\mathrm{d}t)^2}\right] \frac{\mathrm{d}}{\mathrm{d}t}\boldsymbol{\theta} + \mathcal{O}(\mathrm{d}t)$$

Taking the limit $\mathrm{d}t \to 0$ finally gives

$$\frac{\mathrm{d}}{\mathrm{d}t}\boldsymbol{\theta} = -\eta \nabla E(\boldsymbol{\theta}) \qquad \eta = \frac{(\mathrm{d}\boldsymbol{\theta}/\mathrm{d}t)^2}{(\mathrm{d}\boldsymbol{\theta}/\mathrm{d}t) \cdot [-\nabla E(\boldsymbol{\theta})]}$$

Note that the right equation can be dropped, as it simply follows from the left one by taking the inner product with $\mathrm{d}\boldsymbol{\theta}/\mathrm{d}t$. We have thereby recovered the ordinary gradient descent rule.

Derivation of natural gradient descent

We now repeat the above exercise of extremizing $E(\boldsymbol{\theta}+\Delta\boldsymbol{\theta})$ w.r.t. variations of $\Delta\boldsymbol{\theta}$, subject to the constraint that the magnitude of the change of $\boldsymbol{\theta}$ is fixed. Now, however, the magnitude of the the change is not given in terms of the Euclidean distance but rather in terms of a more general distance measure as described in Appendix H. This distance is defined in terms of a local metric via

$$d^2(\boldsymbol{\theta},\boldsymbol{\theta}+\Delta\boldsymbol{\theta}) = \sum_{ij} \Delta\theta_i g_{ij}(\boldsymbol{\theta})\Delta\theta_j + \mathcal{O}(\Delta^3)$$

and the constraint is $d^2(\boldsymbol{\theta},\boldsymbol{\theta}+\Delta\boldsymbol{\theta}) = \Delta^2$ with $0 \leq \Delta \ll 1$. The solution of this constrained extremization problem is again obtained with the method of Lagrange multipliers:

$$\frac{\partial E(\boldsymbol{\theta}+\Delta\boldsymbol{\theta})}{\partial(\Delta\theta_i)} = \lambda\frac{\partial}{\partial(\Delta\theta_i)}d^2(\boldsymbol{\theta},\boldsymbol{\theta}+\Delta\boldsymbol{\theta}) = 2\lambda\left[\sum_j g_{ij}(\boldsymbol{\theta})\Delta\theta_j \;+\; \mathcal{O}(\Delta^2)\right]$$

$$d^2(\boldsymbol{\theta},\boldsymbol{\theta}+\Delta\boldsymbol{\theta}) = \Delta^2$$

As before we eliminate λ by taking the inner product with $\Delta\boldsymbol{\theta}$ on both sides of the above equation, giving $\lambda = \frac{1}{2}\Delta^{-2}[\Delta\boldsymbol{\theta}\cdot\nabla E(\boldsymbol{\theta})] + \mathcal{O}(\Delta^0)$. We next consider small changes only, that is, we write $\Delta\boldsymbol{\theta} = \mathrm{d}t(\mathrm{d}\boldsymbol{\theta}/\mathrm{d}t) + \mathcal{O}(\mathrm{d}t^2)$ with $0 < \mathrm{d}t \ll 1$. Consequently the constraint equation becomes $\Delta^2 = \mathrm{d}t^2[(\mathrm{d}\boldsymbol{\theta}/\mathrm{d}t)\cdot \boldsymbol{g}(\boldsymbol{\theta})(\mathrm{d}\boldsymbol{\theta}/\mathrm{d}t)] + \mathcal{O}(\mathrm{d}t^3)$, and

$$\nabla E(\boldsymbol{\theta}) = \left[\frac{(\mathrm{d}\boldsymbol{\theta}/\mathrm{d}t)\cdot\nabla E(\boldsymbol{\theta})}{(\mathrm{d}\boldsymbol{\theta}/\mathrm{d}t)\cdot\boldsymbol{g}(\boldsymbol{\theta})(\mathrm{d}\boldsymbol{\theta}/\mathrm{d}t)}\right]\boldsymbol{g}(\boldsymbol{\theta})\frac{\mathrm{d}}{\mathrm{d}t}\boldsymbol{\theta} + \mathcal{O}(\mathrm{d}t)$$

Taking the limit $\mathrm{d}t \to 0$ produces

$$\frac{\mathrm{d}}{\mathrm{d}t}\boldsymbol{\theta} = -\eta\boldsymbol{g}^{-1}(\boldsymbol{\theta})\nabla E(\boldsymbol{\theta}) \qquad \eta = \frac{(\mathrm{d}\boldsymbol{\theta}/\mathrm{d}t)\cdot\boldsymbol{g}(\boldsymbol{\theta})(\mathrm{d}\boldsymbol{\theta}/\mathrm{d}t)}{(\mathrm{d}\boldsymbol{\theta}/\mathrm{d}t)\cdot[-\nabla E(\boldsymbol{\theta})]}$$

As before the right equation is redundant, as it follows from the left one by taking the inner product with $\boldsymbol{g}(\boldsymbol{\theta})(\mathrm{d}\boldsymbol{\theta}/\mathrm{d}t)$. We have thereby derived the so-called *natural* gradient descent rule:

$$\frac{\mathrm{d}}{\mathrm{d}t}\boldsymbol{\theta} = -\eta\, \boldsymbol{g}^{-1}(\boldsymbol{\theta})\nabla E(\boldsymbol{\theta}) \tag{14.54}$$

Only in the special case where our metric is Euclidean, that is, $\boldsymbol{g}(\boldsymbol{\theta}) = \mathbf{1}$ for all $\boldsymbol{\theta}$, will natural gradient descent be identical to ordinary gradient descent. Note that we can now also interpret the meaning of inserting a positive definite matrix into the ordinary gradient descent rule, as in (14.53), and identify the optimal choice for such a matrix according to (14.54): the optimal choice is to select $\boldsymbol{M}(\boldsymbol{\theta})$ in (14.53) as the inverse of the metric $\boldsymbol{g}(\boldsymbol{\theta})$. This choice thus depends crucially on the choice we make for the distance $d(\boldsymbol{\theta},\boldsymbol{\theta}')$ in parameter space.

What remains is to choose the appropriate metric in parameter space. Our aim is to base this choice on the premise that the natural distance between two parameter vectors $\boldsymbol{\theta}$ and $\boldsymbol{\theta}'$ should be determined by the extent to which the corresponding networks, encoded in the two distributions $p_{\boldsymbol{\theta}}(\boldsymbol{x})$ and $p_{\boldsymbol{\theta}'}(\boldsymbol{x})$, are similar. The more different these two distributions, the larger should be the natural distance between $\boldsymbol{\theta}$ and $\boldsymbol{\theta}'$.

Expansion of the Kullback–Leibler distance

One object that measures the distance between two probability distributions is, as we have seen earlier, the Kullback–Leibler distance:

$$D(p_{\boldsymbol{\theta}}\|p_{\boldsymbol{\theta}'}) = \sum_{\boldsymbol{x}\in A} p_{\boldsymbol{\theta}}(\boldsymbol{x}) \ln\left[\frac{p_{\boldsymbol{\theta}}(\boldsymbol{x})}{p_{\boldsymbol{\theta}'}(\boldsymbol{x})}\right] \tag{14.55}$$

(where we have replaced $\log_2 \to \ln$ in order to eliminate the irrelevant prefactor $\ln 2$ which would otherwise be generated in subsequent calculations). This expression can itself not serve as our distance $d(\boldsymbol{\theta},\boldsymbol{\theta}')$, since it violates $d(\boldsymbol{\theta},\boldsymbol{\theta}') = d(\boldsymbol{\theta}',\boldsymbol{\theta})$. However, locally it turns out to give a well-behaved distance measure in the sense of (H.3). To see this we put $\boldsymbol{\theta}' = \boldsymbol{\theta} + \Delta\boldsymbol{\theta}$, with $|\Delta\boldsymbol{\theta}| \ll 1$, and expand (14.55) in powers of $\Delta\boldsymbol{\theta}$. This gives

$$\begin{aligned} D(p_{\boldsymbol{\theta}}\|p_{\boldsymbol{\theta}+\Delta\boldsymbol{\theta}}) &= \sum_{\boldsymbol{x}\in A} p_{\boldsymbol{\theta}}(\boldsymbol{x})[\ln p_{\boldsymbol{\theta}}(\boldsymbol{x}) - \ln p_{\boldsymbol{\theta}+\Delta\boldsymbol{\theta}}(\boldsymbol{x})] \\ &= \sum_{ij} \Delta\theta_i g_{ij}(\boldsymbol{\theta})\Delta\theta_j + \mathcal{O}(|\Delta\boldsymbol{\theta}|^3) \end{aligned}$$

with the metric

$$g_{ij}(\boldsymbol{\theta}) = \frac{1}{2}\sum_{\boldsymbol{x}\in A} p_{\boldsymbol{\theta}}(\boldsymbol{x}) \left(\frac{\partial \ln p_{\boldsymbol{\theta}}(\boldsymbol{x})}{\partial\theta_i}\right)\left(\frac{\partial \ln p_{\boldsymbol{\theta}}(\boldsymbol{x})}{\partial\theta_j}\right) \tag{14.56}$$

The key observation needed to obtain this result is that, when writing the expansion of the distance as

$$D(p_{\boldsymbol{\theta}}\|p_{\boldsymbol{\theta}+\Delta\boldsymbol{\theta}}) = -\sum_{\boldsymbol{x}\in A} p_{\boldsymbol{\theta}}(\boldsymbol{x})\ln(1+\epsilon)$$

with

$$\begin{aligned}\epsilon &= \frac{p_{\boldsymbol{\theta}+\Delta\boldsymbol{\theta}}(x) - p_{\boldsymbol{\theta}}(x)}{p_{\boldsymbol{\theta}}(x)} \\ &= \sum_i \frac{\Delta\theta_i}{p_{\boldsymbol{\theta}}(\boldsymbol{x})}\frac{\partial}{\partial\theta_i}p_{\boldsymbol{\theta}}(\boldsymbol{x}) + \frac{1}{2}\sum_{ij}\frac{\Delta\theta_i\Delta\theta_j}{p_{\boldsymbol{\theta}}(\boldsymbol{x})}\frac{\partial^2}{\partial\theta_i\partial\theta_j}p_{\boldsymbol{\theta}}(\boldsymbol{x}) + \cdots\end{aligned}$$

the first order in ϵ in the expansion of the logarithm vanishes due to normalization of the distribution $p_{\boldsymbol{\theta}}$.

Up to the factor 1/2, the matrix in (14.56) is called the Fisher Information matrix. It plays an important role in measuring the average amount of information that can be extracted from a single observation $\boldsymbol{x}$ about the values of the parameters $\boldsymbol{\theta}$ of a parametrized distribution $p_{\boldsymbol{\theta}}(\boldsymbol{x})$. The metric (14.56) satisfies all our requirements. It generates a general definition of a distance $d(\boldsymbol{\theta},\boldsymbol{\theta}')$ via the route described in Appendix H. This is based on the shortest path connecting $\boldsymbol{\theta}$ and $\boldsymbol{\theta}'$, given by a geodesic.

Invariance of natural gradient descent under re-parametrization

Due to the fact that the distance $d(\boldsymbol{\theta},\boldsymbol{\theta}')$ generated by the metric (14.56) is based on measuring the mismatch between two probability distributions (rather than on properties of the underlying parametrization), one finds that the corresponding natural gradient descent equation is *invariant* under parametrization changes, in contrast to the ordinary gradient descent rule. The proof of this important statement is elementary. Just consider two equivalent choices of parameters, $\boldsymbol{\theta} \in \mathbb{R}^L$ and $\boldsymbol{\xi} \in \mathbb{R}^L$, which are related by an invertible transformation $f\colon \mathbb{R}^L \to \mathbb{R}^L$:

$$\boldsymbol{\theta} = f(\boldsymbol{\xi}) \qquad p_{\boldsymbol{\xi}}(\boldsymbol{x}) = \hat{p}_{\boldsymbol{\theta}}(\boldsymbol{x}) \qquad E(\boldsymbol{\xi}) = \hat{E}(\boldsymbol{\theta}) \qquad g_{ij}(\boldsymbol{\xi}) = \hat{g}_{ij}(\boldsymbol{\theta})$$

The metric $g_{ij}(\boldsymbol{\xi})$ as given by (14.56), derived in the language of $\boldsymbol{\xi}$, can be related to the metric $\hat{g}_{ij}(\boldsymbol{\theta})$, derived in the language of $\boldsymbol{\theta}$, in the following way:

$$\begin{aligned}g_{ij}(\boldsymbol{\xi}) &= \sum_{\boldsymbol{x}\in A} p_{\boldsymbol{\xi}}(\boldsymbol{x})\,\frac{\partial \ln p_{\boldsymbol{\xi}}(\boldsymbol{x})}{\partial\xi_i}\frac{\partial \ln p_{\boldsymbol{\xi}}(\boldsymbol{x})}{\partial\xi_j} \\ &= \sum_{\boldsymbol{x}\in A}\hat{p}_{\boldsymbol{\theta}}(\boldsymbol{x})\sum_{kl}\frac{\partial\theta_k}{\partial\xi_i}\frac{\partial \ln \hat{p}_{\boldsymbol{\theta}}(\boldsymbol{x})}{\partial\theta_k}\frac{\partial\theta_l}{\partial\xi_j}\frac{\partial \ln \hat{p}_{\boldsymbol{\theta}}(\boldsymbol{x})}{\partial\theta_l} = \sum_{kl} K_{ij,kl}(\boldsymbol{\theta})\hat{g}_{kl}(\boldsymbol{\theta})\end{aligned}$$

with

$$K_{ij,kl}(\boldsymbol{\theta}) = \frac{\partial \theta_k}{\partial \xi_i} \frac{\partial \theta_l}{\partial \xi_j}$$

We can now use this relation to derive the dynamical equation which the parameters $\boldsymbol{\theta}$ will obey, given that the evolution of the parameters $\boldsymbol{\xi}$ is defined by natural gradient descent (14.54) with the metric $\boldsymbol{g}(\boldsymbol{\xi})$, written as

$$\sum_j g_{ij}(\boldsymbol{\xi}) \frac{\mathrm{d}}{\mathrm{d}t} \xi_j + \eta \frac{\partial}{\partial \xi_i} E(\boldsymbol{\xi}) = 0$$

Using the above transformation for the metric and partial derivatives this gives

$$\sum_{jkl} K_{ij,kl}(\boldsymbol{\theta}) \hat{g}_{kl}(\boldsymbol{\theta}) \frac{\mathrm{d}}{\mathrm{d}t} \xi_j + \eta \sum_k \frac{\partial \theta_k}{\partial \xi_i} \frac{\partial}{\partial \theta_k} \hat{E}(\boldsymbol{\theta}) = 0$$

which can be rewritten as

$$\sum_k \frac{\partial \theta_k}{\partial \xi_i} \left[\sum_{jl} \frac{\partial \theta_l}{\partial \xi_j} \hat{g}_{kl}(\boldsymbol{\theta}) \frac{\mathrm{d}}{\mathrm{d}t} \xi_j + \eta \frac{\partial}{\partial \theta_k} \hat{E}(\boldsymbol{\theta}) \right] = 0$$

Since the matrix with entries $J_{ki}(\boldsymbol{\theta}) = \partial \theta_k / \partial \xi_i$ is just the Jacobian of the invertible transformation f, and therefore itself invertible, it immediately follows that

$$\sum_l \hat{g}_{kl}(\boldsymbol{\theta}) \sum_j \frac{\partial \theta_l}{\partial \xi_j} \frac{\mathrm{d}}{\mathrm{d}t} \xi_j + \eta \frac{\partial}{\partial \theta_k} \hat{E}(\boldsymbol{\theta}) = 0$$

or

$$\sum_l \hat{g}_{kl}(\boldsymbol{\theta}) \frac{\mathrm{d}}{\mathrm{d}t} \theta_l + \eta \frac{\partial}{\partial \theta_k} \hat{E}(\boldsymbol{\theta}) = 0$$

This is again the natural gradient descent equation, but now expressed in the language of $\boldsymbol{\theta}$. Thus, whatever parametrization one chooses for the network, if one uses the natural gradient descent rule with the metric (14.56) one always generates exactly the same dynamics.

It can be shown that, apart from an irrelevant prefactor, the metric (14.56) is the unique proper metric in a space of parametrized probability distributions, although the proof is not trivial and will not be given in the present book. Here we have only provided intuitive evidence for this statement, by showing that it is locally equivalent to the Kullback–Leibler distance (which is indeed a measure of the mismatch between distributions, independent of parametrization), and by showing that the corresponding natural gradient descent dynamics is invariant under re-parametrizations.

In practice, explicit calculation of the inverse of the matrix (14.56) will usually not be possible, and thus exact execution of the natural gradient descent rule out of the question. However, at least one knows what the optimal rule is, so that improving upon gradient descent can be done in a systematic way, via approximation of the inverse of (14.56), rather than in an ad hoc manner. There are many ways in which an inverse can be approximated. If $\boldsymbol{g}(\boldsymbol{\theta})$ is close to the unity matrix $\mathbf{1}$, for instance, one could use the expansion $\boldsymbol{g}^{-1}(\boldsymbol{\theta}) = \sum_{n\geq 0}[\mathbf{1} - \boldsymbol{g}(\boldsymbol{\theta})]^n$. An alternative is to manipulate general identities for symmetric matrices such as

$$g_{ij}^{-1} = \frac{\int \mathrm{d}\boldsymbol{y}\, y_i y_j\, e^{-(1/2)\boldsymbol{y}\cdot\boldsymbol{g}\boldsymbol{y}}}{\int \mathrm{d}\boldsymbol{y}\, e^{-(1/2)\boldsymbol{y}\cdot\boldsymbol{g}\boldsymbol{y}}}$$

14.7 Simple applications of information geometry

Let us finally illustrate the application of the above ideas in neural information processing systems with two simple examples.

Example 1: a single neuron without systematic input. Our first example represents the simplest possible scenario of a binary neuron, without systematic input or weights, but with only a threshold θ. It receives input only from a noise source ξ, that is,

$$x_{\text{out}} = \text{sgn}(\xi - \theta)$$

We assume that it is being trained to permanently generate the output $x_{\text{out}} = 1$ via adaptation of its threshold θ. This obviously requires lowering the threshold to $\theta = -\infty$. We denote by $w(\xi)$ (with $\xi \in \mathbb{R}$) the probability density of the noise source, and take this distribution to be symmetric: $w(\xi) = w(-\xi)$ for all $\xi \in \mathbb{R}$. We also define $W(u) = 2\int_0^u \mathrm{d}\xi\, w(\xi)$. Our assumptions entail $-1 \leq W(u) \leq 1$.

We now first have to establish contact with the formalism of the present chapter. Since there are no systematic inputs, we simply have $p_\theta(x) = \text{Prob}[x_{\text{out}} = x]$, giving

$$p_\theta(1) = \text{Prob}[x_{\text{out}} = 1] = \int_\theta^\infty \mathrm{d}\xi\, w(\xi) = \frac{1}{2}[1 - W(\theta)]$$

and thus

$$p_\theta(x) = \tfrac{1}{2}[1 - xW(\theta)]$$

The error measure $\mathcal{E}(x)$ is required to signal the occurrence of the wrong output value $x = -1$, so $\mathcal{E}(x) = \delta_{x,-1}$. Recalling the definition of the global error $E(\theta) = \sum_x p_\theta(x)\mathcal{E}(x)$, one obtains

$$E(\theta) = \tfrac{1}{2}[1 + W(\theta)] \tag{14.57}$$

Ordinary gradient descent learning would give for this example:

$$\left.\frac{\mathrm{d}}{\mathrm{d}t}\theta\right|_{\mathrm{GD}} = -\eta\frac{\partial}{\partial\theta}E(\theta) = -\frac{1}{2}\eta\frac{\partial}{\partial\theta}W(\theta) = -\eta w(\theta)$$

Let us now compare this to the recipe prescribed by natural gradient descent. The present example has only a single adjustable parameter, viz. θ, so the Fisher matrix (14.56) reduces to a (time-dependent) scalar (a 1×1 matrix) $g(\theta)$:

$$g(\theta) = \sum_{x=\pm 1} p_\theta(x)\left[\frac{\partial}{\partial\theta}\ln[1 - xW(\theta)]\right]^2 = \sum_{x=\pm 1} p_\theta(x)\frac{4w^2(\theta)}{[1 - xW(\theta)]^2}$$

$$= 2w^2(\theta)\left(\frac{1}{1 - W(\theta)} + \frac{1}{1 + W(\theta)}\right) = \frac{4w^2(\theta)}{1 - W^2(\theta)}$$

Natural gradient descent thus reduces to:

$$\left.\frac{\mathrm{d}}{\mathrm{d}t}\theta\right|_{\mathrm{NGD}} = -\eta\frac{1 - W^2(\theta)}{4w(\theta)}$$

Let us now make a specific choice for the noise distribution to push the present analysis further, viz. $w(\xi) = \frac{1}{2}[1 - \tanh^2(\xi)]$, so $W(\theta) = \int_0^\theta \mathrm{d}\xi\ [1 - \tanh^2(\xi)] = \tanh(\theta)$. This results in

$$\left.\frac{\mathrm{d}}{\mathrm{d}t}\theta\right|_{\mathrm{GD}} = -\frac{1}{2}\eta[1 - \tanh^2(\theta)] \qquad \left.\frac{\mathrm{d}}{\mathrm{d}t}\theta\right|_{\mathrm{NGD}} = -\frac{1}{2}\eta$$

It is clear that the threshold θ decreases more slowly in the case of gradient descent learning than for natural gradient descent learning, especially as $|\theta| \to \infty$. The superiority of the natural gradient learning algorithm can be exhibited in a more striking fashion, if we translate the laws for the evolution of θ into equations involving the global error $E(\theta)$ only, using the simple relation $E(\theta) = \frac{1}{2}[1 + \tanh\theta]$:

$$\frac{\mathrm{d}}{\mathrm{d}t}E\bigg|_{\mathrm{GD}} = -4\eta E^2(1-E)^2 \qquad \frac{\mathrm{d}}{\mathrm{d}t}E\bigg|_{\mathrm{NGD}} = -\eta E(1-E)$$

In both cases the error decreases monotonically to zero. Asymptotically, that is, for $t \to \infty$, we can thus expand these equations in powers of E. The asymptotic form of these equations at small E and their solution are then given by

$$\frac{\mathrm{d}}{\mathrm{d}t}E\bigg|_{\mathrm{GD}} = -4\eta E^2 + \cdots \quad \text{with solution} \quad E \sim \frac{1}{4\eta t} \quad (t \to \infty)$$

$$\frac{\mathrm{d}}{\mathrm{d}t}E\bigg|_{\mathrm{NGD}} = -\eta E + \cdots \quad \text{with solution} \quad E \sim e^{-\eta t} \quad (t \to \infty)$$

This clearly illustrates the potential of natural gradient descent.

Example 2: a single neuron with inputs. Our second example is a noisy binary neuron with nonzero inputs and weights, but without a threshold,

$$x_{\mathrm{out}} = \mathrm{sgn}\left(\sum_{i=1}^{L}\theta_i x_i^{\mathrm{in}} + \xi\right) \qquad \boldsymbol{x}_{\mathrm{in}} = (x_1^{\mathrm{in}}, \ldots, x_L^{\mathrm{in}}) \in \{-1,1\}^L$$

which is being trained to execute some operation $\sigma\colon \{-1,1\}^L \to \{-1,1\}$ via adaptation of the weight vector $\boldsymbol{\theta} \in \mathrm{I\!R}^L$. As before, we assume that the noise source $\xi \in \mathrm{I\!R}$ has a symmetric probability density $w(\xi)$, so $w(\xi) = w(-\xi)$ for all $\xi \in \mathrm{I\!R}$, and we define $W(u) = 2\int_0^u \mathrm{d}\xi\, w(\xi)$. Thus

$$p_{\boldsymbol{\theta}}(x_{\mathrm{out}}|\boldsymbol{x}_{\mathrm{in}}) = \tfrac{1}{2}[1 + x_{\mathrm{out}}W(\boldsymbol{\theta}\cdot\boldsymbol{x}_{\mathrm{in}})] \qquad p_{\boldsymbol{\theta}}(\boldsymbol{x}_{\mathrm{in}}, x_{\mathrm{out}}) = p_{\boldsymbol{\theta}}(x_{\mathrm{out}}|\boldsymbol{x}_{\mathrm{in}})p(\boldsymbol{x}_{\mathrm{in}})$$

The error measure $\mathcal{E}(\boldsymbol{x}_{\mathrm{in}}, x_{\mathrm{out}})$ is now required to signal the occurrence of $x_{\mathrm{out}} \neq \sigma(\boldsymbol{x}_{\mathrm{in}})$, giving $\mathcal{E}(\boldsymbol{x}_{\mathrm{in}}, x_{\mathrm{out}}) = \frac{1}{2}[1 - x_{\mathrm{out}}\sigma(\boldsymbol{x}_{\mathrm{in}})]$. The global error (14.50) is then seen to become

$$\begin{aligned} E(\boldsymbol{\theta}) &= \frac{1}{4}\sum_{\boldsymbol{x}_{\mathrm{in}}} p(\boldsymbol{x}_{\mathrm{in}}) \sum_{x_{\mathrm{out}}} [1 + x_{\mathrm{out}}W(\boldsymbol{\theta}\cdot\boldsymbol{x}_{\mathrm{in}})][1 - x_{\mathrm{out}}\sigma(\boldsymbol{x}_{\mathrm{in}})] \\ &= \frac{1}{2} - \frac{1}{2}\sum_{\boldsymbol{x}_{\mathrm{in}}} p(\boldsymbol{x}_{\mathrm{in}})\sigma(\boldsymbol{x}_{\mathrm{in}})W(\boldsymbol{\theta}\cdot\boldsymbol{x}_{\mathrm{in}}) \end{aligned} \qquad (14.58)$$

and the metric (14.56) is evaluated as follows:

$$\begin{aligned}
g_{ij}(\boldsymbol{\theta}) &= \sum_{\boldsymbol{x}_{\text{in}}}\sum_{x_{\text{out}}} p(\boldsymbol{x}_{\text{in}})p_{\boldsymbol{\theta}}(x_{\text{out}}|\boldsymbol{x}_{\text{in}})\left(\frac{\partial \ln p_{\boldsymbol{\theta}}(x_{\text{out}}|\boldsymbol{x}_{\text{in}})}{\partial\theta_i}\right)\left(\frac{\partial \ln p_{\boldsymbol{\theta}}(x_{\text{out}}|\boldsymbol{x}_{\text{in}})}{\partial\theta_j}\right) \\
&= \sum_{\boldsymbol{x}_{\text{in}}}\sum_{x_{\text{out}}} \frac{p(\boldsymbol{x}_{\text{in}})}{p_{\boldsymbol{\theta}}(x_{\text{out}}|\boldsymbol{x}_{\text{in}})}[x_i^{\text{in}}x_{\text{out}}w(\boldsymbol{\theta}\cdot\boldsymbol{x}_{\text{in}})][x_j^{\text{in}}x_{\text{out}}w(\boldsymbol{\theta}\cdot\boldsymbol{x}_{\text{in}})] \\
&= \sum_{\boldsymbol{x}_{\text{in}}} p(\boldsymbol{x}_{\text{in}})x_i^{\text{in}}x_j^{\text{in}}w^2(\boldsymbol{\theta}\cdot\boldsymbol{x}_{\text{in}})\left(\frac{2}{1+W(\boldsymbol{\theta}\cdot\boldsymbol{x}_{\text{in}})}+\frac{2}{1-W(\boldsymbol{\theta}\cdot\boldsymbol{x}_{\text{in}})}\right) \\
&= \sum_{\boldsymbol{x}_{\text{in}}} p(\boldsymbol{x}_{\text{in}})x_i^{\text{in}}x_j^{\text{in}}\frac{w^2(\boldsymbol{\theta}\cdot\boldsymbol{x}_{\text{in}})}{(1/4)[1-W^2(\boldsymbol{\theta}\cdot\boldsymbol{x}_{\text{in}})]} \qquad (14.59)
\end{aligned}$$

If we now choose the same noise distribution as in the first example, that is, $w(\xi) = \frac{1}{2}[1-\tanh^2(\xi)]$, giving $W(\theta) = \tanh(\theta)$, and in addition assume uniformly distributed input vectors $\boldsymbol{x}_{\text{in}} \in \{-1,1\}^L$, we find the following transparent expressions:

$$E(\boldsymbol{\theta}) = \tfrac{1}{2}[1-\langle\sigma(\boldsymbol{x})\tanh(\boldsymbol{\theta}\cdot\boldsymbol{x})\rangle] \qquad g_{ij}(\boldsymbol{\theta}) = \delta_{ij} - \langle x_i x_j \tanh^2(\boldsymbol{\theta}\cdot\boldsymbol{x})\rangle \qquad (14.60)$$

with the shorthand $\langle(\cdots)\rangle = 2^{-L}\sum_{\boldsymbol{x}\in\{-1,1\}^L}(\cdots)$. Gradient descent and natural gradient descent would now generate the following learning dynamics,

$$\left.\frac{\mathrm{d}}{\mathrm{d}t}\theta_i\right|_{\text{GD}} = \frac{\eta}{2}\langle x_i\sigma(\boldsymbol{x})[1-\tanh^2(\boldsymbol{\theta}\cdot\boldsymbol{x})]\rangle$$

and

$$\left.\frac{\mathrm{d}}{\mathrm{d}t}\theta_i\right|_{\text{NGD}} = \frac{\eta}{2}\sum_j g_{ij}^{-1}(\boldsymbol{\theta})\langle x_j\sigma(\boldsymbol{x})[1-\tanh^2(\boldsymbol{\theta}\cdot\boldsymbol{x})]\rangle$$

respectively.

In general one cannot easily invert the matrix in (14.60) analytically. For small values of L it can, however, be done. Let us work out the case $L = 2$ (two inputs) as an explicit example. We assume that the task σ is realizable, that is, there exists a vector $\boldsymbol{B} \in \mathbb{R}^2$ such that $\sigma(\boldsymbol{x}) = \text{sgn}(B_1x_1 + B_2x_2)$. Defining $\sigma_\pm = \text{sgn}(B_1 \pm B_2)$ and $\theta_\pm = \theta_1 \pm \theta_2$ we obtain

$$E(\theta_1,\theta_2) = \tfrac{1}{2}[1-\tfrac{1}{2}\sigma_+\tanh(\theta_+)-\tfrac{1}{2}\sigma_-\tanh(\theta_-)] \qquad (14.61)$$

$$\begin{aligned}
\boldsymbol{g}(\boldsymbol{\theta}) &= \frac{1}{2}[1-\tanh^2(\theta_+)]\begin{pmatrix}1 & 1\\ 1 & 1\end{pmatrix} \\
&\quad + \frac{1}{2}[1-\tanh^2(\theta_-)]\begin{pmatrix}1 & -1\\ -1 & 1\end{pmatrix} \qquad (14.62)
\end{aligned}$$

One can easily convince oneself that the relevant inverse is

$$\boldsymbol{g}^{-1}(\boldsymbol{\theta}) = \frac{1}{2[1 - \tanh^2(\theta_+)]}\begin{pmatrix} 1 & 1 \\ 1 & 1 \end{pmatrix} + \frac{1}{2[1 - \tanh^2(\theta_-)]}\begin{pmatrix} 1 & -1 \\ -1 & 1 \end{pmatrix}$$

We now obtain the following learning rules:

$$\left.\frac{\mathrm{d}}{\mathrm{d}t}\boldsymbol{\theta}\right|_{\mathrm{GD}} = \frac{1}{4}\eta\sigma_+[1 - \tanh^2(\theta_+)]\begin{pmatrix} 1 \\ 1 \end{pmatrix} + \frac{1}{4}\eta\sigma_-[1 - \tanh^2(\theta_-)]\begin{pmatrix} 1 \\ -1 \end{pmatrix}$$

$$\left.\frac{\mathrm{d}}{\mathrm{d}t}\boldsymbol{\theta}\right|_{\mathrm{NGD}} = \frac{1}{4}\eta\sigma_+\begin{pmatrix} 1 \\ 1 \end{pmatrix} + \frac{1}{4}\eta\sigma_-\begin{pmatrix} 1 \\ -1 \end{pmatrix}$$

In terms of $\theta_\pm$ these expressions simplify to

$$\left.\frac{\mathrm{d}}{\mathrm{d}t}\theta_\pm\right|_{\mathrm{GD}} = \frac{1}{2}\eta\sigma_\pm[1 - \tanh^2(\theta_\pm)] \qquad \left.\frac{\mathrm{d}}{\mathrm{d}t}\theta_\pm\right|_{\mathrm{NGD}} = \frac{1}{2}\eta\sigma_\pm$$

Clearly the gradient descent rule will show a saturation slowing down as $|\theta_\pm| \to \infty$, which is absent, or rather compensated for automatically, in the case of natural gradient descent learning. If $\boldsymbol{\theta}(t = 0) = 0$, we find in both cases $\theta_\pm(t) = \sigma_\pm\phi(t)$, with $\phi(0) = 0$ and

$$E = \frac{1}{2}[1 - \tanh(\phi)] \qquad \left.\frac{\mathrm{d}}{\mathrm{d}t}\phi\right|_{\mathrm{GD}} = \frac{1}{2}\eta[1 - \tanh^2(\phi)] \qquad \left.\frac{\mathrm{d}}{\mathrm{d}t}\phi\right|_{\mathrm{NGD}} = \frac{1}{2}\eta$$

As with the previous example, we can convert our equations directly into equations for the error E, which in fact turn out to be identical to those of the previous example:

$$\left.\frac{\mathrm{d}}{\mathrm{d}t}E\right|_{\mathrm{GD}} = -4\eta E^2(1 - E)^2 \qquad \left.\frac{\mathrm{d}}{\mathrm{d}t}E\right|_{\mathrm{NGD}} = -\eta E(1 - E)$$

We find a significant convergence speed-up with, asymptotically,

$$E|_{\mathrm{GD}} \sim \frac{1}{4\eta t} \qquad E|_{\mathrm{NGD}} \sim e^{-\eta t} \quad (t \to \infty)$$

showing once more the superiority of natural gradient descent over simple gradient descent learning.

14.8 Exercises

Exercise 14.1. (Coupled oscillator Boltzmann machines.) In a coupled oscillator version of the Boltzmann machine the states of the N input, L hidden, and M output oscillators are all *continuous* variables, and are denoted by $\boldsymbol{x} \in [-\pi,\pi]^N$, $\boldsymbol{\sigma} \in [-\pi,\pi]^L$, and $\boldsymbol{y} \in [-\pi,\pi]^M$, respectively. The combined state vector is written as $\boldsymbol{s} = (\boldsymbol{x},\boldsymbol{\sigma},\boldsymbol{y})$. During free relaxation of all oscillators, equilibrium averages of observables $f(\boldsymbol{s})$ are given by $\langle f\rangle_- = \int_{-\pi}^{\pi}\cdots\int_{-\pi}^{\pi} \mathrm{d}\boldsymbol{s}\, p_-(\boldsymbol{s})f(\boldsymbol{s})$, with

$$p_-(\boldsymbol{x},\boldsymbol{\sigma},\boldsymbol{y}) = Z^{-1}e^{-\beta E(\boldsymbol{x},\boldsymbol{\sigma},\boldsymbol{y})}$$

with the normalization constant Z given by $Z = \int_{-\pi}^{\pi}\cdots\int_{-\pi}^{\pi} \mathrm{d}\boldsymbol{x}\mathrm{d}\boldsymbol{\sigma}\mathrm{d}\boldsymbol{y} \times e^{-\beta E(\boldsymbol{x},\boldsymbol{\sigma},\boldsymbol{y})}$. During so-called clamped relaxation, where the state vectors $\boldsymbol{x}$ and $\boldsymbol{y}$ are controlled externally to have the joint probability density $q(\boldsymbol{x},\boldsymbol{y})$, equilibrium averages of observables $f(\boldsymbol{s})$ are given by $\langle f\rangle_+ = \int_{-\pi}^{\pi}\cdots\int_{-\pi}^{\pi} \mathrm{d}\boldsymbol{s}\, p_+(\boldsymbol{s})f(\boldsymbol{s})$, with

$$p_+(\boldsymbol{x},\boldsymbol{\sigma},\boldsymbol{y}) = q(\boldsymbol{x},\boldsymbol{y})p_+(\boldsymbol{\sigma}|\boldsymbol{x},\boldsymbol{y}) \qquad p_+(\boldsymbol{\sigma}|\boldsymbol{x},\boldsymbol{y}) = \frac{e^{-\beta E(\boldsymbol{x},\boldsymbol{\sigma},\boldsymbol{y})}}{Z(\boldsymbol{x},\boldsymbol{y})}$$

where $Z(\boldsymbol{x},\boldsymbol{y}) = \int_{-\pi}^{\pi}\cdots\int_{-\pi}^{\pi} \mathrm{d}\boldsymbol{\sigma}\, e^{-\beta E(\boldsymbol{x},\boldsymbol{\sigma},\boldsymbol{y})}$. Explain which quantity the Boltzmann machine learning for continuous neural variables aims to minimize, in terms of the above probability densities, and what is being achieved by this minimization. Consider the case where $E(\boldsymbol{s}) = -\frac{1}{2}\sum_{ij} w_{ij}\cos(s_i - s_j) - \sum_i \theta_i \cos(s_i)$, with $w_{ij} = w_{ji}$ for all (i,j). Derive the Boltzmann machine learning rule for updating the system parameters $\{w_{ij},\theta_i\}$ in the coupled oscillator Boltzmann machine.

Exercise 14.2. (Maximum information preservation.) Consider a linear neuron whose inputs are corrupted by Gaussian noise sources ξ_i, which are mutually independent and statistically independent of the input variables $\boldsymbol{x}$:

$$y(\boldsymbol{x}) = \sum_{i=1}^{N} w_i(x_i + \xi_i) \qquad p(\xi_i) = \frac{1}{\sigma\sqrt{2\pi}}\, e^{-\xi_i^2/2\sigma^2}$$

Assume that $\langle x_i\rangle = 0$ ($\forall i$), and that the noise-free part $z(\boldsymbol{x}) = \sum_{i=1}^{N} w_i x_i$ of the output y has a Gaussian probability distribution. This is a special case of the situation discussed in Section 14.2, in which now the noise sources are identically distributed. Imagine that one tries to maximize the differential mutual information of the uncorrupted input signal $z(\boldsymbol{x})$ and the output $y(\boldsymbol{x})$ for the system by modification of the weights $\{w_i\}$, according to a gradient ascent procedure,

$$\frac{\mathrm{d}}{\mathrm{d}t}w_i = \eta\frac{\partial}{\partial w_i}\tilde{I}(Y,Z)$$

Show that the gradient ascent has N fixed points, each of them corresponding to an eigenvector of the correlation matrix $\boldsymbol{C}$ of inputs with elements $C_{ij} = \langle x_i x_j \rangle$, and hence that the optimal weight vector identified in Equation 14.2 indeed corresponds to a fixed point of this gradient ascent procedure.

Exercise 14.3. (Natural gradient descent.) Compare gradient descent and natural gradient descent algorithms for Maximum Likelihood parameter estimation. Given N observations x_i of a random variable X, one attempts to estimate parameters $\boldsymbol{\theta}$ of a probability density $p_{\boldsymbol{\theta}}(x)$ so as to minimize

$$E(\boldsymbol{\theta}) = \frac{1}{N}\sum_{i=1}^{N}\ln\left[\frac{p(x_i)}{p_{\boldsymbol{\theta}}(x_i)}\right] \simeq \int \mathrm{d}x\, p(x)\ln\left[\frac{p(x)}{p_{\boldsymbol{\theta}}(x)}\right]$$

where p is the unknown probability density of X. We assumed that N is sufficiently large for the above integral approximation above to apply. Investigate this, assuming that the unknown distribution $p(x)$ is Gaussian:

$$p(x) = \frac{\exp[-(x-\mu)^2/2\sigma^2]}{\sigma\sqrt{2\pi}}$$

and that one attempts to approximate it using the Gaussian family

$$p_{\boldsymbol{\theta}}(x) = \frac{\exp[-(x-\theta_1)^2/2\theta_2^2]}{\theta_2\sqrt{2\pi}}$$

Write down the gradient descent equations for this problem, and show that $(\theta_1,\theta_2) = (\mu,\sigma)$ is a stable fixed point of the dynamics. Determine the asymptotic convergence rates. Compute the Fisher-Information matrix for this problem, and use it to formulate the natural gradient dynamics. Show that natural gradient dynamics also converges to the fixed point $(\theta_1,\theta_2) = (\mu,\sigma)$, and that the asymptotic convergence rate is *independent* of the parameters μ and σ of the unknown distribution, unlike in the case of simple gradient descent.

15 Notes and suggestions for further reading

Information theory in its modern formulation has come upon us mainly through the seminal work of Claude Shannon [57–59] which, in turn, builds on earlier work of Nyquist [60] and Hartley [61] on problems related to transmission of information. The proposal to quantify information in terms of the logarithm of the size of a message set in case of equally likely messages appears in fact to have been made first by Hartley, but its generalization to ensembles of messages that are not equally likely—using *entropy* as the appropriate measure—was achieved only in 1948, independently by Shannon [57, 58] and Wiener [62, 63].

Shannon was in fact concerned with the *entire* process of communication of information, from the information source, and a transmitter used to transform messages into a form suitable for transmission, over some (noisy) channel which defines the medium used to transmit signals, via a receiver inverting the operations of the transmitter in order to reconstruct the message from the transmitted signal, to the final destination of the message. The operations of transmitter and receiver involve some form of encoding and decoding. The characterization of the channel as noisy implies that errors will be introduced into the signal stream on its way from transmitter to receiver. A key issue in such a process is then how information can reliably be transmitted over noisy channels, using appropriate coding, and at which rate. It was Shannon's deep and original insight that the entropy of the information source would be the important limiting factor for the rate of transmission of information over a (noisy) channel.

In this book we have not dealt with issues related specifically to transmission of information and channel capacity. A number of excellent monographs dedicated to information theory can be consulted on these and related topics; references [42, 59, 64–66] can be considered as classics, old and new, and are particularly recommended.

Our discussion has had a somewhat different focus, namely the application of entropy and related concepts to problems in statistical inference and neural information processing systems. In the context of statistical inference, we looked at parameter estimation using the maximum likelihood (ML) method and at the maximum entropy (MaxEnt) method for density estimation. While ML estimation as a tool of statistical inference

[67] precedes the advent of information theory by several decades, the MaxEnt method for density estimation, pioneered by Jaynes in the 1950s [68–70], makes explicit reference to concepts and intuitions underlying Shannon's measure of information. Boltzmann-machine learning for recurrent stochastic networks, one of the paradigmatic examples of the use of information theoretic tools for the design of algorithms, was introduced by Ackley and co-workers [71, 72]. It is discussed at some length also in the book by Hertz *et al.* [23], which is still one of the most comprehensive sources on the theory of neural computation. Hertz, Krogh, and Palmer also deal with issues of information preservation and feature detection in feedforward networks; on these topics a more recent book by Deco and Obradovic [73] also provides a wealth of information. Natural gradient descent learning was introduced by Amari [74]. For more on the formal theory of information geometry, which is based on identifying the Fisher information matrix as the object that defines a natural Riemannian metric in spaces of probability distributions, see also [75].

As comprehensive sources for the probability theory used in this book, the monographs by Feller [76,77], Gardiner [78], and van Kampen [79] are highly recommended. For further general background material on statistical inference the reader may wish to consult Vapnik's lucid book [48] and for details and proofs the earlier volume [80].

Part IV Macroscopic analysis of dynamics

Statistical mechanics deals with large systems of interacting microscopic elements. Its strategy is to move away from solving models of such systems at the microscopic level, trying instead to use the microscopic laws to calculate laws describing the behaviour of suitably chosen *macroscopic* observables. This may seem hopeless: if we cannot solve the microscopic laws, what makes us think we can find their macroscopic consequences? It turns out that if we consider large systems, things become easier: the macroscopic laws are then usually deterministic and simple, even though the microscopic ones are stochastic and complex. Macroscopic observables normally present a kind of average behaviour of the microscopic ones: the more elements we average over, the smaller the fluctuations of the average. In the limit of an infinitely large system the fluctuations vanish, and the averages evolve deterministically. The toolbox of statistical mechanics consists of methods and tricks to perform this reduction from the microscopic to a macroscopic level, which are based on clever ways of doing the bookkeeping of probabilities. The experience and intuition built up in over a century tells us what to expect (e.g. phase transitions), and serves as a guide in choosing the macroscopic observables and in seeing the difference between relevant and irrelevant mathematical subtleties.

We apply statistical mechanics to two aspects of neural networks. We begin with network *operation*; here the microscopic dynamical variables are the states of the neurons, with the synaptic weights remaining fixed. The networks we consider will be recurrent, which means that there are feedback loops between the neurons. We will study their ability to function as associative memories. By an appropriate choice of synaptic weights, we can ensure that the neural firing patterns, starting from an appropriate initial state, will converge towards one of a number of patterns that we wish to store. We will not be interested in knowing the states of the individual neurons (just as, in a bucket of water, we would not want to know the positions of all the molecules) but instead in quantities like the overlap of the actual network state with the various stored patterns. The latter will be our macroscopic variables. In our second application of statistical mechanics we consider *learning* processes, where the synaptic weights change. For recurrent networks this is quite complicated, because one needs to analyse how the dynamics of the neurons reacts to the changes in the synapses. We therefore restrict ourselves to learning in feed-forward networks, where all connections between neurons are uni-directional, leading from some input neurons to one or several output neurons. These networks can be thought of as implementing a mapping from inputs to outputs, and learning (i.e. changing the synaptic weights) becomes the process of adapting the parameters of this mapping by a student network such that it approximates a certain target mapping (the teacher). Here our macroscopic observables will be the quality of this approximation, as measured by generalization and training errors.

16 Network operation: macroscopic dynamics

In non-equilibrium statistical mechanics one aims to derive from the laws of the underlying microscopic system $\boldsymbol{x}$, and solve, dynamical equations for a suitable small set of macroscopic quantities $\boldsymbol{\Omega}(\boldsymbol{x}) = (\Omega_1(\boldsymbol{x}), \ldots, \Omega_n(\boldsymbol{x}))$. In principle this can be done in two ways. The first route (clockwise in the diagram), which is normally too complicated, would consist of solving the microscopic stochastic equations directly. From the solution one then calculates the values of the macroscopic quantities. The second route (anti-clockwise) consists of first calculating from the microscopic stochastic laws a dynamical equation for the macroscopic probability distribution $P_t(\boldsymbol{\Omega})$, which then has to be solved. If applicable, this is the easiest and preferred approach. In many cases one finds, as a further simplification, that the macroscopic dynamics becomes deterministic for $N \to \infty$.

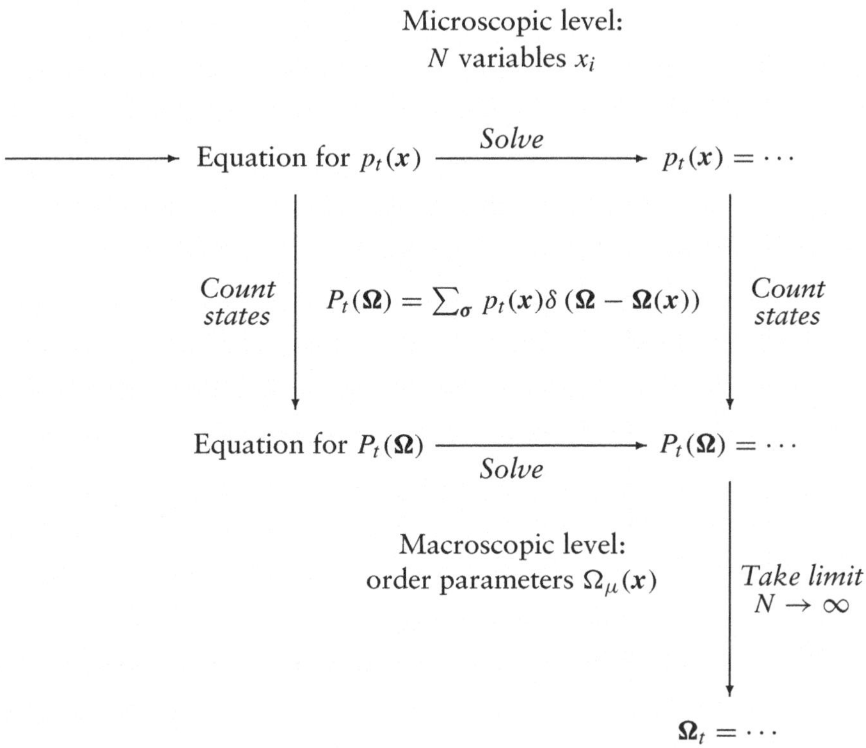

It turns out that, for such programmes to work in analysing the neuron dynamics in recurrent neural networks (where $\boldsymbol{x}$ will represent the neuronal firing states), the interaction matrix must have a suitable structure. A common feature of many solvable statistical mechanical models for neural networks is separability of the interaction matrix, which naturally leads to a convenient description in terms of macroscopic order parameters. When the interaction matrix is symmetric, we will see that relatively simple behaviour results. Such systems obey what in Part V we will call detailed balance. They always reach an equilibrium state at long times, which can be analysed using equilibrium statistical mechanics. For non-symmetric interactions, on the other hand, detailed balance is absent and dynamical studies are the only option available; here the behaviour at long times can be much more complicated, exhibiting, for example, limit cycles.

16.1 Microscopic dynamics in probabilistic form

We define in this section the models of stochastic neuronal dynamics that we will consider; mathematically these will be described by Markov chains.

We choose to work with the stochastic binary units (1.29) as defined in Part I, so we model our network as a set of N recurrently connected neurons which are either firing (on) or quiet (off), and we describe the state of each neuron by a binary variable $\sigma_i = \pm 1$ (with $\sigma_i = 1$ meaning firing and $\sigma_i = -1$ not firing, and with $i = 1, \ldots, N$). Given the values of the N postsynaptic potentials h_i at time t, the probability to find any given microscopic state $\boldsymbol{\sigma}(t + \Delta t) = (\sigma_1(t + \Delta t), \ldots, \sigma_N(t + \Delta t))$ at the next time step $t + \Delta t$ now depends on whether neurons are updated in parallel or sequentially, and is given by either (1.33) or (1.34), respectively. For the neuronal noise distribution we will choose $P(z) = \frac{1}{2}[1 - \tanh^2(z)]$, for reasons which will become clear in Part V, so that the non-linear function $g(z)$ will be given by (1.32). We also abbreviate the inverse noise level as $\beta = T^{-1} \in [0, \infty)$. Insertion of (1.32) into (1.33) and (1.34), and using $\tanh(\sigma z) = \sigma \tanh(z)$ for $\sigma \in \{-1, 1\}$, then allows us to write the microscopic dynamics in the following form

$$\text{parallel:} \quad \text{Prob}\,[\boldsymbol{\sigma}(t + \Delta t)] = \prod_{i=1}^{N} \left[\frac{1}{2} + \frac{1}{2}\sigma_i(t + \Delta t) \tanh(\beta h_i(\boldsymbol{\sigma}(t)))\right] \tag{16.1}$$

$$\text{sequential:} \quad \begin{cases} \text{choose } i \text{ randomly from } \{1, \ldots, N\} \\ \text{Prob}\,[\sigma_i(t + \Delta t)] = \frac{1}{2} + \frac{1}{2}\sigma_i(t + \Delta t) \tanh(\beta h_i(\boldsymbol{\sigma}(t))) \end{cases} \tag{16.2}$$

with

$$h_i(\boldsymbol{\sigma}) = \sum_{j=1}^{N} J_{ij}\sigma_j + \vartheta_i \tag{16.3}$$

The J_{ij} are the synaptic weights, which in physics are called the 'interaction strengths' or 'couplings'; the binary variables $\sigma_i \in \{-1, 1\}$ would in physics be called 'Ising spins'. The term ϑ_i represents the effects of the firing threshold or an external input to neuron i. For $\beta \to \infty$ (i.e. $T \to 0$) we remove the noise, and the neurons will respond deterministically to their local fields (if indeed they are updated): they fire at the next time step if their individual field is positive, and are silent otherwise. For $\beta = 0$ (i.e. $T \to \infty$) noise dominates, and the neurons fire randomly, independently of the values of the local fields. We will find later that, for systems with symmetric synapses, the parameter T is identical to the temperature in equilibrium statistical mechanics.

Note that the microscopic laws (16.1, 16.2) can be rewritten in a number of ways, for example via

$$\frac{1}{2}[1 + \sigma\tanh(\beta h)] = \frac{e^{\beta\sigma h}}{2\cosh(\beta h)} = \frac{1}{1 + e^{-2\beta\sigma h}} \tag{16.4}$$

where we have used the identities $\tanh(\sigma z) = \sigma\tanh(z)$ for $\sigma \in \{-1, 1\}$, and $1 + \tanh(z) = 1 + (e^z - e^{-z})/(e^z + e^{-z}) = e^z/\cosh(z)$. We now set out to write the above two versions of the stochastic dynamics fully in terms of the (evolving) microscopic state probabilities

$$p_t(\boldsymbol{\sigma}) \equiv \mathrm{Prob}[\boldsymbol{\sigma}(t) = \boldsymbol{\sigma}] \tag{16.5}$$

Parallel dynamics

For parallel dynamics it is natural to simply choose the elementary time unit to be $\Delta t = 1$. We first use identity (16.4) to rewrite equation (16.1) in terms of the state probabilities $p_t(\boldsymbol{\sigma})$ as

$$p_{t+1}(\boldsymbol{\sigma}) = \prod_{i=1}^{N} \frac{1}{2}[1 + \sigma_i \tanh(\beta h_i(\boldsymbol{\sigma}(t)))] = \prod_{i=1}^{N} \frac{e^{\beta\sigma_i h_i(\boldsymbol{\sigma}(t))}}{2\cosh(\beta h_i(\boldsymbol{\sigma}(t)))}$$

If, instead of the precise microscopic state $\boldsymbol{\sigma}(t)$, the probability distribution $p_t(\boldsymbol{\sigma}')$ over all possible values $\boldsymbol{\sigma}'$ of $\boldsymbol{\sigma}(t)$ is given, the above expression generalizes to the corresponding average over $\boldsymbol{\sigma}'$:

$$p_{t+1}(\boldsymbol{\sigma}) = \sum_{\boldsymbol{\sigma}'} W(\boldsymbol{\sigma}, \boldsymbol{\sigma}') p_t(\boldsymbol{\sigma}') \tag{16.6}$$

with

$$W(\boldsymbol{\sigma},\boldsymbol{\sigma}')=\prod_{i=1}^{N}\frac{e^{\beta\sigma_i h_i(\boldsymbol{\sigma}')}}{2\cosh[\beta h_i(\boldsymbol{\sigma}')]} \tag{16.7}$$

The dynamics described by (16.6) is called a Markov chain. It tells us how the probability $p_t(\boldsymbol{\sigma})$ of finding the network in state $\boldsymbol{\sigma}$ evolves in time; crucially, the probabilities at time $t+1$ depend only on those at time t, but *not on those at earlier times*. $W(\boldsymbol{\sigma},\boldsymbol{\sigma}')$ is the probability of making a transition from state $\boldsymbol{\sigma}'$ to state $\boldsymbol{\sigma}$ in a single iteration; it is called the transition probability. Because probabilities are non-negative, and because the total probability of making a transition to *any* state $\boldsymbol{\sigma}$ is one, $W(\boldsymbol{\sigma},\boldsymbol{\sigma}')$ obeys

$$W(\boldsymbol{\sigma},\boldsymbol{\sigma}')\in[0,1] \qquad \sum_{\boldsymbol{\sigma}}W(\boldsymbol{\sigma},\boldsymbol{\sigma}')=1 \tag{16.8}$$

If we think of $p_t(\boldsymbol{\sigma})$ as a 2^N-dimensional vector (indexed by the possible states $\boldsymbol{\sigma}$ of the network), then (16.6) has a simple interpretation: the vector p_{t+1} is simply the product of the $2^N\times 2^N$ 'transition matrix' W with the vector p_t.

Sequential dynamics

In the case of sequential dynamics the stochasticity of the dynamics is both in the stochastic update of the chosen neuron and in the choice of site i to be updated; the latter is drawn randomly from the set $\{1,\ldots,N\}$ of all sites. The microscopic equations (16.2) can again be transformed into an equation describing the evolution of the microscopic state probability $p_t(\boldsymbol{\sigma})$. First, if both $\boldsymbol{\sigma}(t)$ and the site i to be updated are given, we find

$$p_{t+\Delta t}(\boldsymbol{\sigma})=\frac{1}{2}[1+\sigma_i\tanh(\beta h_i(\boldsymbol{\sigma}(t)))]\prod_{j\neq i}\delta_{\sigma_j,\sigma_j(t)}$$

The product of the Kronecker deltas simply says that the states of all neurons $j\neq i$ remain unchanged. After averaging this expression over the random site i we obtain

$$p_{t+\Delta t}(\boldsymbol{\sigma})=\frac{1}{N}\sum_{i=1}^{N}\left\{\frac{1}{2}[1+\sigma_i\tanh(\beta h_i(\boldsymbol{\sigma}(t)))]\prod_{j\neq i}\delta_{\sigma_j,\sigma_j(t)}\right\}$$

If, instead of $\boldsymbol{\sigma}(t)$, only the probability distribution $p_t(\boldsymbol{\sigma})$ is given, this expression is again to be averaged over the possible states at time t:

$$p_{t+\Delta t}(\boldsymbol{\sigma}) = \sum_{\boldsymbol{\sigma}'} W(\boldsymbol{\sigma}, \boldsymbol{\sigma}') p_t(\boldsymbol{\sigma}') \tag{16.9}$$

where now

$$W(\boldsymbol{\sigma}, \boldsymbol{\sigma}') = \frac{1}{N} \sum_{i=1}^{N} \left\{ \frac{1}{2}[1 + \sigma_i \tanh(\beta h_i(\boldsymbol{\sigma}'))] \prod_{j \neq i} \delta_{\sigma_j, \sigma_j'} \right\} \tag{16.10}$$

Equation (16.9) describes the Markov chain corresponding to the sequential process (16.2). The relevant transition matrix can be written in a simpler form, as follows. If we look at the ith term in the sum (16.10), which corresponds to neuron i being picked for an update, we see that the transition probability is nonzero only in two cases: either $\boldsymbol{\sigma}$ and $\boldsymbol{\sigma}'$ are equal ($\boldsymbol{\sigma}' = \boldsymbol{\sigma}$), or they differ solely in the state of neuron i. We can write the latter occurrence as $\boldsymbol{\sigma}' = F_i \boldsymbol{\sigma}$, where F_i is the ith spin-flip operator:

$$F_i \boldsymbol{\sigma} = (\sigma_1, \ldots, \sigma_{i-1}, -\sigma_i, \sigma_{i+1}, \ldots, \sigma_N)$$

Together with the obvious definition of Kronecker deltas for the occurrence of equality of the two states $\boldsymbol{\sigma}$ and $\boldsymbol{\sigma}'$, $\delta_{\boldsymbol{\sigma}, \boldsymbol{\sigma}'} = \prod_{i=1}^{N} \delta_{\sigma_i, \sigma_i'}$, we can therefore write

$$\begin{aligned} W(\boldsymbol{\sigma}, \boldsymbol{\sigma}') = \frac{1}{N} \sum_{i=1}^{N} \bigg\{ & \frac{1}{2}[1 + \sigma_i' \tanh(\beta h_i(\boldsymbol{\sigma}'))] \delta_{\boldsymbol{\sigma}, \boldsymbol{\sigma}'} \\ & + \frac{1}{2}[1 - \sigma_i' \tanh(\beta h_i(\boldsymbol{\sigma}'))] \delta_{F_i \boldsymbol{\sigma}, \boldsymbol{\sigma}'} \bigg\} \end{aligned} \tag{16.11}$$

If we also define

$$w_i(\boldsymbol{\sigma}') = \frac{1}{2}[1 - \sigma_i' \tanh(\beta h_i(\boldsymbol{\sigma}'))] = \frac{e^{-\beta \sigma_i' h_i(\boldsymbol{\sigma}')}}{2 \cosh(\beta h_i(\boldsymbol{\sigma}'))} \tag{16.12}$$

which is the probability of neuron i being in state $\sigma_i = -\sigma_i'$ at time $t + \Delta t$ if it was in the opposite state σ_i' at time t (i.e. the probability of the corresponding spin i to 'flip', when going from time t to time $t + \Delta t$), we see that we can write the transition matrix in yet another form:

$$W(\boldsymbol{\sigma}, \boldsymbol{\sigma}') = \delta_{\boldsymbol{\sigma}, \boldsymbol{\sigma}'} + \frac{1}{N} \sum_{i=1}^{N} [w_i(\boldsymbol{\sigma}') \delta_{F_i \boldsymbol{\sigma}, \boldsymbol{\sigma}'} - w_i(\boldsymbol{\sigma}') \delta_{\boldsymbol{\sigma}, \boldsymbol{\sigma}'}] \tag{16.13}$$

Using expression (16.13) we are able to rewrite the Markov chain (16.9) as a so-called master equation

$$p_{t+\Delta t}(\boldsymbol{\sigma}) - p_t(\boldsymbol{\sigma}) = \frac{1}{N}\sum_{i=1}^{N}[w_i(F_i\boldsymbol{\sigma})p_t(F_i\boldsymbol{\sigma}) - w_i(\boldsymbol{\sigma})p_t(\boldsymbol{\sigma})] \tag{16.14}$$

From discrete to continuous times for sequential dynamics

Equation (16.13) shows that, for sequential updating, the probability of any one neuron σ_i changing state in any given time step is very small (of order $1/N$) if N is large. That is, $\mathcal{O}(N)$ microscopic steps would have to be accumulated before we will be able to detect changes in the probabilities of the states. In order to find characteristic timescales in the dynamics which are of order $\mathcal{O}(1)$ even for $N \to \infty$, we will therefore have to choose our time units appropriately.

Let us first proceed in an intuitive way. In order to observe changes at a finite rate when $N \to \infty$, we ensure that the time increment Δt for a single sequential update has duration N^{-1}. Now, on average, in one unit of time each neuron will be selected for updating once, so that with this new definition one indeed ought to find observable changes on timescales of order N^0, even for large N. Choosing $\Delta t = N^{-1}$ implies that instead of (16.14) we now have

$$p_{t+1/N}(\boldsymbol{\sigma}) - p_t(\boldsymbol{\sigma}) = \frac{1}{N}\sum_{i=1}^{N}[w_i(F_i\boldsymbol{\sigma})p_t(F_i\boldsymbol{\sigma}) - w_i(\boldsymbol{\sigma})p_t(\boldsymbol{\sigma})]$$

With the approximation

$$p_{t+1/N}(\boldsymbol{\sigma}) - p_t(\boldsymbol{\sigma}) \approx \frac{1}{N}\frac{\mathrm{d}}{\mathrm{d}t}p_t(\boldsymbol{\sigma}) \tag{16.15}$$

we then obtain a master equation with the desired properties, in continuous time:

$$\frac{\mathrm{d}}{\mathrm{d}t}p_t(\boldsymbol{\sigma}) = \sum_{i=1}^{N}[w_i(F_i\boldsymbol{\sigma})p_t(F_i\boldsymbol{\sigma}) - w_i(\boldsymbol{\sigma})p_t(\boldsymbol{\sigma})] \tag{16.16}$$

The quantities $w_i(\boldsymbol{\sigma})$, defined in (16.12), have now come to play the role of *transition rates*: in any short interval $\mathrm{d}t$ of rescaled time, the probability for neuron i to change state (or spin i to flip) is $w_i(\boldsymbol{\sigma})\mathrm{d}t$. The two terms in the square brackets in (16.16) have a simple interpretation: the first one tells us that we can get to state $\boldsymbol{\sigma}$ by starting in state $F_i\boldsymbol{\sigma}$ and flipping spin i; this process increases the probability of being in state $\boldsymbol{\sigma}$ and therefore has a positive sign. The second term tells us that we can also leave state $\boldsymbol{\sigma}$

and go to state $F_i\boldsymbol{\sigma}$ by flipping spin i; this reduces $p_t(\boldsymbol{\sigma})$ and therefore has a negative sign.

We have obtained (16.16) by using the approximation (16.15). One can show that this approximation becomes exact in the limit $N \to \infty$. An elegant and more precise alternative route towards the desired continuous time formulation is to construct a modified sequential update process, which is exactly described by (16.16), for any value of N, and then to show that this becomes identical to the original sequential dynamics for $N \to \infty$. For the modified process, we let the times t at which the state of the network is updated (which in our intuitive derivation were fixed to $t = 0, 1/N, 2/N, \ldots$) be chosen stochastically. Our new Markov process, with state probabilities $\hat{p}_t(\boldsymbol{\sigma})$, will then be described by

$$\hat{p}_t(\boldsymbol{\sigma}) = \sum_{m\geq 0} \pi_m(t) p_m(\boldsymbol{\sigma}) = \sum_{m\geq 0} \pi_m(t) \sum_{\boldsymbol{\sigma}'} W^m(\boldsymbol{\sigma},\boldsymbol{\sigma}') p_0(\boldsymbol{\sigma}')$$

Here t is again a continuous time variable (now even for finite N), W^m is the m-fold product of the transition matrix W with itself, and $\pi_m(t)$ specifies the probability that up to time $t \in \mathbb{R}$ exactly m discrete updates have taken place. To be specific, let us assume that the probability for an update to occur within an infinitesimal time interval $\mathrm{d}t$ is given by $\mathrm{d}t/\bar{\tau}$. We choose $\bar{\tau} = 1/N$ so that on average we get again one neuron update in a time interval of duration $1/N$, as in the previous intuitive approach. The time intervals τ between individual neuron updates can then be shown to have an exponential probability distribution:

$$P(\tau) = \bar{\tau}^{-1} e^{-\tau/\bar{\tau}}$$

One then also finds that at any given t the probabilities $\pi_m(t)$ (with $m \in \{0, 1, 2, \ldots\}$) are given by a Poisson distribution with mean $t/\bar{\tau}$:

$$\pi_m(t) = \frac{1}{m!}\left(\frac{t}{\bar{\tau}}\right)^m e^{-t/\bar{\tau}} \tag{16.17}$$

which has the convenient properties

$$\frac{\mathrm{d}}{\mathrm{d}t}\pi_{m\geq 1}(t) = \frac{1}{\bar{\tau}}[\pi_{m-1}(t) - \pi_m(t)] \qquad \frac{\mathrm{d}}{\mathrm{d}t}\pi_0(t) = -\frac{1}{\bar{\tau}}\pi_0(t)$$

This allows us to write for the temporal derivative of $\hat{p}_t(\boldsymbol{\sigma})$:

$$\begin{aligned}\bar{\tau}\frac{\mathrm{d}}{\mathrm{d}t}\hat{p}_t(\boldsymbol{\sigma}) &= \sum_{m\geq 1} \pi_{m-1}(t) \sum_{\boldsymbol{\sigma}'} W^m(\boldsymbol{\sigma},\boldsymbol{\sigma}') p_0(\boldsymbol{\sigma}') - \sum_{m\geq 0} \pi_m(t) \\ &\quad \times \sum_{\boldsymbol{\sigma}'} W^m(\boldsymbol{\sigma},\boldsymbol{\sigma}') p_0(\boldsymbol{\sigma}') = \left[\sum_{\boldsymbol{\sigma}'} W(\boldsymbol{\sigma},\boldsymbol{\sigma}')\hat{p}_t(\boldsymbol{\sigma}')\right] - \hat{p}_t(\boldsymbol{\sigma})\end{aligned}$$

Using $\bar{\tau} = 1/N$ and the form of the transition matrix (16.13), this then gives us exactly the master equation (16.16). The proof that this master equation also describes our original sequential update process for $N \to \infty$ is completed with the observation that for fixed t the standard deviation of the fluctuations of the number of updates m (as given by the Poisson distribution $\pi_m(t)$) around its mean value Nt equals $\sqrt{m} = \sqrt{Nt}$. This means that the fluctuations of m/N around its mean value t are $\sqrt{t/N}$. For $N \to \infty$ we therefore have $m/N = t$ with probability one, and the original and modified sequential update processes indeed become identical.

Terminology

In order to simplify our tapping into the existing reservoir of statistical mechanical techniques, we have *en passant* already started to use quite a bit of terminology from physics, and from statistical mechanics in particular. For ease of reference we now summarize in a 'dictionary' table the neural versus the statistical mechanics names for some of the more common objects and variables that we will have to deal with:

Neural networks		Statistical mechanics
Neuron on (firing)/off (quiet)	$\sigma_i = \pm 1$	Spin up/down
Change of neuron state on $\leftrightarrow$ off	$\sigma_i = +1 \leftrightarrow -1$	Spin flip up $\leftrightarrow$ down
Synaptic weight	J_{ij}	Interaction strength
External input, negative threshold	ϑ_i	External field
Postsynaptic potential	h_i	Local field
Noise parameter	$\beta = 1/T$	Inverse temperature
Set of all possible network states	$\{\sigma\}$	Phase space

16.2 Sequential dynamics

In this section we begin to look at macroscopic dynamics proper. In particular, we show how for sequential dynamics one can calculate from the microscopic stochastic evolution equations (at the level of individual neurons) differential equations for the probability distribution of suitably defined macroscopic state variables. For mathematical convenience our starting point will be the continuous-time master equation (16.16), rather than the discrete version (16.13). We will consider several classes of models, with and without detailed balance (see Part V), and show how the macroscopic equations can be used to illuminate and understand the dynamics of neural network operation.

A toy model

Let us first illustrate the basic ideas behind our methods with the help of a simple toy model:

$$J_{ij} = \frac{J}{N}\eta_i \xi_j \qquad \vartheta_i = 0 \tag{16.18}$$

The variables η_i and ξ_i are arbitrary, but may not depend on N. We observe that for $\eta_i = \xi_i \in \{-1, 1\}$ (random) and $J > 0$ this is just the Hopfield model (3.18) with only one stored pattern, apart from the presence in (16.18) of additional self-interactions J_{ii}. The local fields become $h_i(\boldsymbol{\sigma}) = J\eta_i m(\boldsymbol{\sigma})$ with $m(\boldsymbol{\sigma}) = N^{-1}\sum_k \xi_k \sigma_k$. Since they depend on the microscopic state $\boldsymbol{\sigma}$ only through the value of m, the latter quantity is a natural candidate observable for a macroscopic level of description. The probability of finding the value $m(\boldsymbol{\sigma}) = m$ at time t is given by (see also the discussion on page 416)

$$\mathcal{P}_t(m) = \sum_{\boldsymbol{\sigma}} p_t(\boldsymbol{\sigma})\delta(m - m(\boldsymbol{\sigma})) \tag{16.19}$$

Its time derivative is obtained by inserting (16.16):

$$\frac{\partial}{\partial t}\mathcal{P}_t(m) = \sum_i \sum_{\boldsymbol{\sigma}} \delta(m - m(\boldsymbol{\sigma}))[w_i(F_i\boldsymbol{\sigma})p_t(F_i\boldsymbol{\sigma}) - w_i(\boldsymbol{\sigma})p_t(\boldsymbol{\sigma})]$$

Note that on the left-hand side we now write the time-derivative as $\partial/\partial t$, to make clear that this derivative is taken at fixed m. We can simplify this expression by relabelling the summation variable $\boldsymbol{\sigma} \to F_i\boldsymbol{\sigma}$ in the first term; this gives

$$\frac{\partial}{\partial t}\mathcal{P}_t(m) = \sum_i \sum_{\boldsymbol{\sigma}} w_i(\boldsymbol{\sigma})p_t(\boldsymbol{\sigma})[\delta(m - m(F_i\boldsymbol{\sigma})) - \delta(m - m(\boldsymbol{\sigma}))]$$

From the simple relation $m(F_i\boldsymbol{\sigma}) = m(\boldsymbol{\sigma}) - 2\sigma_i\xi_i/N$ it follows that the arguments of the two δ-functions differ only by an $\mathcal{O}(1/N)$ term, so we can make a Taylor expansion of the right-hand side:

$$\frac{\partial}{\partial t}\mathcal{P}_t(m) = \sum_i \sum_{\boldsymbol{\sigma}} w_i(\boldsymbol{\sigma})p_t(\boldsymbol{\sigma})\left[\left(\frac{2}{N}\sigma_i\xi_i\right)\frac{\partial}{\partial m}\delta(m - m(\boldsymbol{\sigma})) + \mathcal{O}(N^{-2})\right]$$

The m-derivative can be pulled in front of the sum; none of the other terms depend on m, and upon reordering the i-dependent terms we are left with

$$\frac{\partial}{\partial t}\mathcal{P}_t(m) = \frac{\partial}{\partial m}\left[\sum_{\boldsymbol{\sigma}} p_t(\boldsymbol{\sigma})\delta(m - m(\boldsymbol{\sigma}))\frac{2}{N}\sum_i \xi_i\sigma_i w_i(\boldsymbol{\sigma})\right] + \mathcal{O}(N^{-1})$$

Inserting the expression (16.12) for the transition rates and the local fields gives

$$\frac{\partial}{\partial t}\mathcal{P}_t(m) = -\frac{\partial}{\partial m}\left\{\sum_{\boldsymbol{\sigma}} p_t(\boldsymbol{\sigma})\delta(m - m(\boldsymbol{\sigma})) \times \left[\frac{1}{N}\sum_{i=1}^{N} \xi_i \tanh(\beta h_i(\boldsymbol{\sigma})) - m(\boldsymbol{\sigma})\right]\right\} + \mathcal{O}(N^{-1}) \tag{16.20}$$

So far everything is rather general. In fact, it looks like we have not yet gained much: the evolution equation for $\mathcal{P}_t(m)$ still involves the unknown microscopic probability distribution $p_t(\boldsymbol{\sigma})$. The key simplification which allows us to eliminate $p_t(\boldsymbol{\sigma})$ is that, for the model at hand, the local fields $h_i(\boldsymbol{\sigma}) = \eta_i J m(\boldsymbol{\sigma})$ depend on the state $\boldsymbol{\sigma}$ *only* through the value of our parameter $m(\boldsymbol{\sigma})$. The δ-function in (16.20) furthermore constrains $m(\boldsymbol{\sigma})$ to equal m, which is simply a number and no longer a function of $\boldsymbol{\sigma}$. We can therefore now carry out the sum over states $\boldsymbol{\sigma}$ and get

$$\frac{\partial}{\partial t}\mathcal{P}_t(m) = -\frac{\partial}{\partial m}\left\{\mathcal{P}_t(m)\left[\frac{1}{N}\sum_{i=1}^{N} \xi_i \tanh(\eta_i \beta J m) - m\right]\right\} + \mathcal{O}(N^{-1}) \tag{16.21}$$

In the thermodynamic limit $N \to \infty$ only the first term survives and we have a *closed* equation for the macroscopic probability distribution $\mathcal{P}_t(m)$:

$$\frac{\partial}{\partial t}\mathcal{P}_t(m) = -\frac{\partial}{\partial m}[\mathcal{P}_t(m)F(m)] \tag{16.22}$$

with

$$F(m) = \lim_{N\to\infty}\frac{1}{N}\sum_{i=1}^{N} \xi_i \tanh(\eta_i \beta J m) - m \tag{16.23}$$

Equation (16.22) is called a *Liouville equation*. As shown in Appendix F, its solution, for any function $F(m)$, is the probability density

$$\mathcal{P}_t(m) = \int \mathrm{d}m_0\, \mathcal{P}_0(m_0)\, \delta(m - m^*(t; m_0))$$

where $m^*(t; m_0)$ denotes the solution of the differential equation

$$\frac{\mathrm{d}}{\mathrm{d}t}m^* = F(m^*) \quad \text{for the initial condition} \quad m^*(0) = m_0 \tag{16.24}$$

Our solution $\mathcal{P}_t(m)$ describes deterministic evolution; the only uncertainty in the value of m is due to uncertainty in initial conditions. If at $t = 0$ the quantity m is known exactly, we see that this will remain the case for finite timescales, with the value of m evolving in time according to (16.24). Note that for $\eta_i = \xi_i$, we thereby also recover the macroscopic laws for the Hopfield model with a single pattern.[26] In that particular case, the function $F(m)$ controlling the time evolution (16.24) of m becomes $F(m) = \tanh(\beta Jm) - m$, and we obtain

$$\frac{\mathrm{d}}{\mathrm{d}t}m = \tanh(\beta Jm) - m \tag{16.25}$$

For $t \to \infty$, m will therefore converge to a point where $\tanh(\beta Jm) - m = 0$, that is, $m = \tanh(\beta Jm)$. In Part V we will find that the solutions of this equation provide a macroscopic characterization of *thermodynamic equilibrium* for these models. The detailed balance condition for a stochastic dynamics to converge to equilibrium will be discussed in depth in Section 20.2.

In our derivation of (16.21), it may seem strange that we have made a Taylor expansion of a δ-function, which is not exactly a smooth object. That this is valid can be confirmed by a a slightly more elaborate derivation using so-called test functions; see also Appendix F. Let $G(m)$ be such a test function (smooth, that is, with continuous derivatives of any order, and nonzero only within a bounded interval). The average of such a test function over $\mathcal{P}_t$ is given by

$$\langle G \rangle_t = \int \mathrm{d}m\, G(m)\mathcal{P}_t(m) = \sum_{\sigma} G(m(\sigma))p_t(\sigma) \tag{16.26}$$

One can now go through exactly the same calculation as above to work out the time-derivative of this average; because $G(m)$ is assumed smooth, the Taylor expansion is now unproblematic. One finds (with $G' \equiv \mathrm{d}G/\mathrm{d}m$):

$$\frac{\mathrm{d}}{\mathrm{d}t}\langle G \rangle_t = \int \mathrm{d}m\, \mathcal{P}_t(m) \left[\frac{1}{N} \sum_{i=1}^{N} \xi_i \tanh(\eta_i \beta Jm) - m \right] G'(m) + \mathcal{O}(N^{-1}) \tag{16.27}$$

[26] Inclusion or exclusion of the weak self-interactions J_{ii} in (16.18) is seen to make no difference to the derivation of our macroscopic laws, for $N \to \infty$.

Using (16.26) on the left-hand side, and integrating by parts on the right-hand side, gives us

$$\int \mathrm{d}m \, \frac{\partial}{\partial t} \mathcal{P}_t(m) G(m)$$
$$= -\int \mathrm{d}m \, \frac{\partial}{\partial m} \left\{ \mathcal{P}_t(m) \left[\frac{1}{N} \sum_{i=1}^{N} \xi_i \tanh(\eta_i \beta J m) - m \right] \right\} G(m) + \mathcal{O}(N^{-1})$$

Since this identity holds for *any* test function $G(m)$, the previous result (16.21) inevitably follows.

The general formalism

Let us now allow for less trivial choices of the interaction matrix and try to calculate the evolution in time of a given set of macroscopic state variables $\mathbf{\Omega}(\boldsymbol{\sigma}) \equiv (\Omega_1(\boldsymbol{\sigma}), \ldots, \Omega_n(\boldsymbol{\sigma}))$ in the thermodynamic limit $N \to \infty$. At this stage there are no restrictions yet on the form or the number n of these state variables; such conditions, however, arise naturally if we require the evolution of the variables $\mathbf{\Omega}$ to obey a closed set of deterministic laws, as we will show below. The ensemble probability of finding the system in macroscopic state $\mathbf{\Omega}$ is given by:

$$\mathcal{P}_t(\mathbf{\Omega}) = \sum_{\boldsymbol{\sigma}} p_t(\boldsymbol{\sigma}) \delta(\mathbf{\Omega} - \mathbf{\Omega}(\boldsymbol{\sigma}))$$

The time derivative of this distribution is obtained by inserting (16.16). If in those parts of the resulting expression which contain the spin-flip operators F_i we subsequently relabel the summation index $\boldsymbol{\sigma} \to F_i \boldsymbol{\sigma}$, we arrive at

$$\frac{\partial}{\partial t} \mathcal{P}_t(\mathbf{\Omega}) = \sum_i \sum_{\boldsymbol{\sigma}} p_t(\boldsymbol{\sigma}) w_i(\boldsymbol{\sigma}) [\delta(\mathbf{\Omega} - \mathbf{\Omega}(F_i \boldsymbol{\sigma})) - \delta(\mathbf{\Omega} - \mathbf{\Omega}(\boldsymbol{\sigma}))]$$

Writing $\Omega_\mu(F_i \boldsymbol{\sigma}) = \Omega_\mu(\boldsymbol{\sigma}) + \Delta_{i\mu}(\boldsymbol{\sigma})$ and making a Taylor expansion in powers of $\{\Delta_{i\mu}(\boldsymbol{\sigma})\}$, we finally obtain the so-called Kramers–Moyal expansion:

$$\frac{\partial}{\partial t} \mathcal{P}_t(\mathbf{\Omega}) = \sum_{\ell \geq 1} \frac{(-1)^\ell}{\ell!} \sum_{\mu_1=1}^{n} \cdots \sum_{\mu_\ell=1}^{n} \frac{\partial^\ell}{\partial \Omega_{\mu_1} \cdots \partial \Omega_{\mu_\ell}} [\mathcal{P}_t(\mathbf{\Omega}) F^{(\ell)}_{\mu_1 \cdots \mu_\ell}(\mathbf{\Omega}; t)] , \tag{16.28}$$

with

$$F^{(\ell)}_{\mu_1 \cdots \mu_\ell}(\mathbf{\Omega}; t) = \left\langle \sum_{j=1}^{N} w_j(\boldsymbol{\sigma}) \Delta_{j\mu_1}(\boldsymbol{\sigma}) \cdots \Delta_{j\mu_\ell}(\boldsymbol{\sigma}) \right\rangle_{\mathbf{\Omega}; t}$$

defined in terms of the conditional (or sub-shell) averages $\langle\cdots\rangle_{\mathbf{\Omega};t}$,

$$\langle\cdots\rangle_{\mathbf{\Omega};t} = \frac{\sum_{\sigma} p_t(\boldsymbol{\sigma})\,(\cdots)\,\delta(\mathbf{\Omega}-\mathbf{\Omega}(\boldsymbol{\sigma}))}{\sum_{\sigma} p_t(\boldsymbol{\sigma})\delta(\mathbf{\Omega}-\mathbf{\Omega}(\boldsymbol{\sigma}))}$$

As in the previous toy model, expansion (16.28) is to be interpreted in a *distributional* sense, that is, only to be used in expressions of the form $\int d\mathbf{\Omega}\,\mathcal{P}_t(\mathbf{\Omega})G(\mathbf{\Omega})$ with sufficiently smooth functions $G(\mathbf{\Omega})$, so that all derivatives are well-defined and finite. Furthermore, (16.28) will only make sense if the 'discrete derivatives' $\Delta_{j\mu}(\boldsymbol{\sigma})$, which measure the sensitivity of our macroscopic quantities to single spin flips, are sufficiently small. This is to be expected for suitably defined macroscopic state variable in the limit of large system sizes. Indeed, whereas for finite N *any* state variable $\Omega_\mu(\boldsymbol{\sigma})$ can only assume a finite number of possible values, we may in the limit $N \to \infty$ expect to find smooth probability distributions for macroscopic quantities which depend sufficiently homogeneously on a sufficiently large number of microscopic variables. The probability distribution of state variables $\Omega_\mu(\boldsymbol{\sigma})$ which only depend on a *small* number of neurons, however, will *not* become smooth, whatever the system size.

The first ($\ell = 1$) term in the series (16.28) is called the flow term. Retaining only this term leads us to a Liouville equation which describes deterministic flow in $\mathbf{\Omega}$ space, driven by the flow field $\boldsymbol{F}^{(1)}$, as in the toy model. Including the second ($\ell = 2$) term as well leads us to a Fokker–Planck equation, which in addition to the flow also describes diffusion of the macroscopic probability density $\mathcal{P}_t(\mathbf{\Omega})$, generated by the diffusion matrix $\{F^{(2)}_{\mu\nu}\}$. Note, however, that in general (16.28) need not necessarily constitute a systematic expansion in terms of some small parameter.

According to (16.28) a sufficient condition for the observables $\mathbf{\Omega}(\boldsymbol{\sigma})$ to evolve in time deterministically, in the limit $N \to \infty$, is:

$$\lim_{N\to\infty} \sum_{\ell\geq 2} \frac{1}{\ell!} \sum_{\mu_1=1}^{n} \cdots \sum_{\mu_\ell=1}^{n} \sum_{j=1}^{N} \langle|\Delta_{j\mu_1}(\boldsymbol{\sigma})\cdots\Delta_{j\mu_\ell}(\boldsymbol{\sigma})|\rangle_{\mathbf{\Omega};t} = 0 \qquad (16.29)$$

since in that case for $N \to \infty$ only the $\ell = 1$ term in expansion (16.28) is retained. Note that the distributional interpretation of the Kramers–Moyal expansion has been used to obtain the condition (16.29). It ensures that in evaluating time derivatives of $\langle G(\mathbf{\Omega})\rangle_t$ for sufficiently smooth $G(\mathbf{\Omega})$ in terms of the expansion (16.28), the partial derivatives $\partial/\partial\Omega_\mu$ appearing in the expansion can be made to apply to the function $G(\mathbf{\Omega})$ *alone*, via integration by parts; since the latter are (uniformly) bounded by assumption, the partial derivatives need not be included in the condition (16.29). Note also that the bound $|w_j(\boldsymbol{\sigma})| < 1$ has been used.

In the simplest instance where the state variables $\Omega_\mu(\boldsymbol{\sigma})$ scale similarly in the sense that all derivatives $\Delta_{j\mu}(\boldsymbol{\sigma})$ are of the same order in the system size N (i.e. there is a monotonic function $\tilde{\Delta}_N$ such that $\Delta_{j\mu}(\boldsymbol{\sigma}) = \mathcal{O}(\tilde{\Delta}_N)$ for all j and μ), the above criterion becomes:

$$\lim_{N\to\infty} n\tilde{\Delta}_N\sqrt{N} = 0 \tag{16.30}$$

If for a given set of macroscopic quantities the condition (16.29) is satisfied, we can for large N describe the evolution of the macroscopic probability density by the Liouville equation:

$$\frac{\partial}{\partial t}\mathcal{P}_t(\boldsymbol{\Omega}) = -\sum_{\mu=1}^{n} \frac{\partial}{\partial \Omega_\mu}[\mathcal{P}_t(\boldsymbol{\Omega})F_\mu^{(1)}(\boldsymbol{\Omega};t)]$$

the solution of which describes deterministic flow:

$$\mathcal{P}_t(\boldsymbol{\Omega}) = \int \mathrm{d}\boldsymbol{\Omega}_0\, \mathcal{P}_0(\boldsymbol{\Omega}_0)\delta(\boldsymbol{\Omega} - \boldsymbol{\Omega}^*(t;\boldsymbol{\Omega}_0))$$

$$\frac{\mathrm{d}}{\mathrm{d}t}\boldsymbol{\Omega}^*(t;\boldsymbol{\Omega}_0) = \boldsymbol{F}^{(1)}(\boldsymbol{\Omega}^*(t;\boldsymbol{\Omega}_0);t) \qquad \boldsymbol{\Omega}^*(0;\boldsymbol{\Omega}_0) = \boldsymbol{\Omega}_0 \tag{16.31}$$

In taking the limit $N \to \infty$, however, we have to keep in mind that the resulting deterministic theory is obtained by taking this limit for *finite* t. According to (16.28), the $\ell > 1$ terms do come into play for sufficiently large times t; for $N \to \infty$, however, these times diverge by virtue of (16.29).

Equation (16.31) will in general not be autonomous; tracing back the origin of the explicit time dependence in the right-hand side of (16.31) one finds that in order to calculate $\boldsymbol{F}^{(1)}$ one needs to know the microscopic probability density $p_t(\boldsymbol{\sigma})$. This, in turn, requires solving the master equation (16.16), which is exactly what one would like to avoid. However, there are elegant ways of avoiding this pitfall. We will discuss two constructions that allow for the elimination of the explicit time dependence in the right-hand side of (16.31) and thereby turn the state variables $\boldsymbol{\Omega}$ and their dynamic equations (16.31) into an autonomous level of description.

The first way out is to choose the macroscopic state variables $\boldsymbol{\omega}$ in such a way that there is no explicit time dependence in the flow field $\boldsymbol{F}^{(1)}(\boldsymbol{\Omega};t)$ (if possible). According to the definition of the flow field, this implies making sure that there exists a vector field $\boldsymbol{\Phi}(\boldsymbol{\Omega})$ such that

$$\lim_{N\to\infty} \sum_{j=1}^{N} w_j(\boldsymbol{\sigma})\boldsymbol{\Delta}_j(\boldsymbol{\sigma}) = \boldsymbol{\Phi}(\boldsymbol{\Omega}(\boldsymbol{\sigma})) \tag{16.32}$$

(with $\boldsymbol{\Delta}_j \equiv (\Delta_{j1}, \ldots, \Delta_{jn})$) in which case the time dependence of $\boldsymbol{F}^{(1)}$ drops out, and the macroscopic state vector evolves in time according to:

$$\frac{\mathrm{d}}{\mathrm{d}t}\boldsymbol{\Omega} = \boldsymbol{\Phi}(\boldsymbol{\Omega})$$

This is the situation which we encountered earlier in our toy model. The advantage is that no restrictions need to be imposed on the initial microscopic configuration; the disadvantage is that for the method to apply, a suitable separable structure of the interaction matrix is required. If, for instance, the macroscopic state variables Ω_μ depend linearly on the microscopic state variables $\boldsymbol{\sigma}$, that is, $\boldsymbol{\Omega}(\boldsymbol{\sigma}) = N^{-1}\sum_{j=1}^{N} \boldsymbol{\omega}_j \sigma_j$, then we obtain with the transition rates (16.12):

$$\lim_{N\to\infty} \sum_{j=1}^{N} w_j(\boldsymbol{\sigma})\boldsymbol{\Delta}_j(\boldsymbol{\sigma}) = \lim_{N\to\infty} \frac{1}{N} \sum_{j=1}^{N} \boldsymbol{\omega}_j \tanh(\beta h_j(\boldsymbol{\sigma})) - \boldsymbol{\Omega}$$

In this case it turns out that the only further condition necessary for (16.32) to hold is that all local fields h_k must (to leading order in N) depend on the microscopic state $\boldsymbol{\sigma}$ only through the values of the macroscopic state variables $\boldsymbol{\Omega}$. Since the local fields depend linearly on $\boldsymbol{\sigma}$ this, in turn, implies that the interaction matrix must be separable.

If it is not possible to find a set of macroscopic state variables that satisfies both conditions (16.29, 16.32), additional assumptions or restrictions are needed. One natural assumption that allows us to close the hierarchy of dynamical equations and obtain an autonomous flow for the state variables $\boldsymbol{\Omega}$ is to assume equi-partitioning of probability in the $\boldsymbol{\Omega}$-subshells of the ensemble, which allows us to make the replacement:

$$\boldsymbol{F}^{(1)}(\boldsymbol{\Omega}; t) \quad \to \quad \boldsymbol{F}^{\text{equi}}(\boldsymbol{\Omega}) = \frac{\sum_{\boldsymbol{\sigma}} \delta(\boldsymbol{\Omega} - \boldsymbol{\Omega}(\boldsymbol{\sigma})) \sum_j w_j(\boldsymbol{\sigma})\boldsymbol{\Delta}_j(\boldsymbol{\sigma})}{\sum_{\boldsymbol{\sigma}} \delta(\boldsymbol{\Omega} - \boldsymbol{\Omega}(\boldsymbol{\sigma}))}$$

Whether or not the above way of closing the set of equations is allowed will depend on the extent to which the relevant stochastic vector $\sum_{j=1}^{N} w_j(\boldsymbol{\sigma})\boldsymbol{\Delta}_j(\boldsymbol{\sigma})$ is homogeneous within the $\boldsymbol{\Omega}$-subshells of the ensemble. At $t = 0$ there is no problem, since one can always *choose* the initial microscopic distribution $p_0(\boldsymbol{\sigma})$ to obey equi-partitioning. In the case of extremely diluted networks this situation is subsequently maintained by assuring that, due to the extreme dilution, no correlations can build up in finite time. The advantage of extreme dilution is that less strict requirements on the structure of the interaction matrix are involved. The disadvantage is that the required sparseness of the interactions compared to the system size does not correspond to biological reality.

Next we will show how the above formalism can be applied to networks for which the matrix of interactions J_{ij} has a separable form; this includes most symmetric and non-symmetric Hebbian-type attractor models. We will restrict ourselves to models with $\vartheta_i = 0$; the introduction of nonzero thresholds is straightforward and does not pose new problems.

Separable models: description at the level of sublattice magnetizations

Let us consider the following class of models, in which the interaction matrix have the form

$$J_{ij} = \frac{1}{N} Q(\boldsymbol{\xi}_i, \boldsymbol{\xi}_j) \qquad \boldsymbol{\xi}_i = (\xi_i^1, \ldots, \xi_i^p) \tag{16.33}$$

The components ξ_i^μ are assumed to be drawn from a finite discrete set Λ which contains n_Λ elements; again the variables ξ_i^μ are not allowed to depend on N. As usual in these models they represent the information or patterns to be stored or processed. The Hopfield model, for instance, corresponds to choosing $Q(\boldsymbol{x}, \boldsymbol{y}) = \boldsymbol{x} \cdot \boldsymbol{y}$ and $\Lambda = \{-1, 1\}$. One can now introduce a partition of the system $\{1, \ldots, N\}$ into n_Λ^p so-called sublattices $I_{\boldsymbol{\eta}}$:

$$I_{\boldsymbol{\eta}} = \{i \mid \boldsymbol{\xi}_i = \boldsymbol{\eta}\} \qquad \{1, \ldots, N\} = \bigcup_{\boldsymbol{\eta}} I_{\boldsymbol{\eta}} \qquad \boldsymbol{\eta} = (\eta^1, \ldots, \eta^p) \in \Lambda^p$$

The number of spins in sublattice $I_{\boldsymbol{\eta}}$ will be denoted by $|I_{\boldsymbol{\eta}}|$ and is assumed to be large. If we choose as our macroscopic state variables the average firing rates (or 'magnetizations') within these sublattices, we are able to express the fields h_k solely in terms of macroscopic quantities:

$$m_{\boldsymbol{\eta}}(\boldsymbol{\sigma}) = \frac{1}{|I_{\boldsymbol{\eta}}|} \sum_{i \in I_{\boldsymbol{\eta}}} \sigma_i \qquad h_k(\boldsymbol{\sigma}) = \sum_{\boldsymbol{\eta}} p_{\boldsymbol{\eta}} Q(\boldsymbol{\xi}_k, \boldsymbol{\eta}) m_{\boldsymbol{\eta}} \tag{16.34}$$

with the relative sublattice sizes $p_{\boldsymbol{\eta}} = |I_{\boldsymbol{\eta}}|/N$. If all $p_{\boldsymbol{\eta}}$ are of the same order in N (which, for example, is the case if the vectors $\boldsymbol{\xi}_i$ have been drawn at random from the set Λ^p) we may write $\Delta_{j\boldsymbol{\eta}} = \mathcal{O}(n_\Lambda^p N^{-1})$ and use (16.30). The evolution in time of our sublattice magnetizations is then found to be deterministic in the thermodynamic limit if

$$\lim_{N \to \infty} \frac{p}{\ln N} = 0$$

Furthermore, condition (16.32) is seen to hold, since

$$\sum_{j=1}^{N} w_j(\boldsymbol{\sigma}) \Delta_{j\boldsymbol{\eta}}(\boldsymbol{\sigma}) = \tanh\left(\beta \sum_{\boldsymbol{\eta}'} p_{\boldsymbol{\eta}'} Q(\boldsymbol{\eta}, \boldsymbol{\eta}') m_{\boldsymbol{\eta}'}\right) - m_{\boldsymbol{\eta}}$$

We may conclude that the evolution in time of the sublattice magnetizations is governed by the following autonomous set of differential equations:

$$\frac{\mathrm{d}}{\mathrm{d}t}m_\eta = \tanh\left(\beta\sum_{\eta'} p_{\eta'}Q(\eta,\eta')m_{\eta'}\right) - m_\eta \tag{16.35}$$

The above procedure does not require symmetry of the interaction matrix. In the symmetric case $Q(x,y) = Q(y,x)$ the system will approach equilibrium; if the kernel $Q(.,.)$ is positive definite this can be shown, for instance, by inspection of the Lyapunov function $\mathcal{L}[\{m_\eta\}]$:

$$\mathcal{L}[\{m_\eta\}] = \frac{1}{2}\sum_{\eta\eta'} p_\eta m_\eta Q(\eta,\eta')m_{\eta'}p_{\eta'} - \frac{1}{\beta}\sum_{\eta} p_\eta \ln\cosh\left(\beta\sum_{\eta'} Q(\eta,\eta')m_{\eta'}p_{\eta'}\right)$$

which is bounded from below, and which obeys:

$$\frac{\mathrm{d}}{\mathrm{d}t}\mathcal{L} = -\sum_{\eta\eta'}\left(p_\eta\frac{\mathrm{d}}{\mathrm{d}t}m_\eta\right)Q(\eta,\eta')\left(p_{\eta'}\frac{\mathrm{d}}{\mathrm{d}t}m_{\eta'}\right) \leq 0 \tag{16.36}$$

Note that from the sublattice magnetizations one can also quite easily calculate the overlaps of the network state with the various stored patterns. These overlaps can be written as averages over the n_Λ^p sublattice magnetizations via:

$$m_\mu(\boldsymbol{\sigma}) = \frac{1}{N}\sum_{i=1}^{N}\xi_i^\mu\sigma_i = \sum_\eta p_\eta \eta^\mu m_\eta \tag{16.37}$$

Whether or not, in turn, there exists an *autonomous* set of laws at the level of overlaps depends on the form of the kernel $Q(.,.)$.

Simple examples of relevant models of the type (16.33), the dynamics of which is for large N described by equation (16.35), are for instance the ones where one applies a non-linear operation Φ to the standard Hopfield interactions:

$$Q(\boldsymbol{x},\boldsymbol{y}) = \Phi(\boldsymbol{x}\cdot\boldsymbol{y}): \quad J_{ij} = \frac{1}{N}\Phi\left(\sum_{\mu=1}^{p}\xi_i^\mu\xi_j^\mu\right)$$

with $\Phi(0) = 0$ and $\Phi'(x) \geq 0$. This non-linearity could result from, for example, a clipping procedure,

$$\Phi(x) = \begin{cases} -K, & \text{for } x \leq -K \\ x, & \text{for } -K < x < K \\ K, & \text{for } x \geq K \end{cases}$$

or from retaining only the *sign* of the original interactions (21.2):

$$\Phi(x) = \text{sgn}(x)$$

It turns out that the effect of introducing such non-linearities is of a quantitative nature only, giving rise to little more than a re-scaling of critical noise levels and storage capacities. We will not go into full details here, but illustrate this statement with a simple example, by working out our equations for $p = 2$ (i.e. a network with two stored patterns) and randomly drawn pattern bits $\xi^\mu \in \{-1, 1\}$, where there are only four sublattices, and where $p_\eta = \frac{1}{4}$ for all $\boldsymbol{\eta}$. Using $\Phi(0) = 0$ and $\Phi(-x) = -\Phi(x)$, as is the case for the above examples, we obtain:

$$\frac{\mathrm{d}}{\mathrm{d}t} m_\eta = \tanh\left(\frac{1}{4}\beta\Phi(2)(m_\eta - m_{-\eta})\right) - m_\eta \qquad (16.38)$$

This demonstrates that the choice made for the non-linearity $\Phi(x)$ shows up only as a re-scaling of the noise level as measured by β, at least for the simple case $p = 2$. From (16.38) we further obtain $(\mathrm{d}/\mathrm{d}t)(m_\eta + m_{-\eta}) = -(m_\eta + m_{-\eta})$. This shows that the system decays exponentially towards a macroscopic state where, according to (16.37), all sublattices contribute equally to the overlaps in pairs: $m_\eta = -m_{-\eta}$ for all $\boldsymbol{\eta}$. If at $t = 0$ this is already the case, we simply find decoupled equations of the form (16.25) for each of the four observables m_η.

Separable models: description at the level of overlaps

A more general version of the toy model (16.18), which still allows for a description of the dynamics in terms of macroscopic overlap parameters, and does not require the intricacies of the sublattice description discussed above, is obtained by choosing

$$J_{ij} = \frac{1}{N}\sum_{\mu\nu=1}^{p} \xi_i^\mu A_{\mu\nu} \xi_j^\nu \qquad \boldsymbol{\xi}_i = (\xi_i^1, \ldots, \xi_i^p) \qquad (16.39)$$

We will see that now the components ξ_i^μ need not be drawn from a finite discrete set,[27] as long as they do not depend on N. The Hopfield model corresponds to the choice $A_{\mu\nu} = \delta_{\mu\nu}$ and $\xi_i^\mu \in \{-1, 1\}$. The fields h_k can now be written in terms of the overlap order parameters m_μ:

$$m_\mu(\boldsymbol{\sigma}) = \frac{1}{N}\sum_{i=1}^{N} \xi_i^\mu \sigma_i \qquad h_k(\boldsymbol{\sigma}) = \boldsymbol{\xi}_k \cdot \boldsymbol{A}\boldsymbol{m}(\boldsymbol{\sigma}) \qquad \boldsymbol{m} = (m_1, \ldots, m_p) \tag{16.40}$$

Since now $\Delta_{i\mu}(\boldsymbol{\sigma}) = m_\mu(F_i\boldsymbol{\sigma}) - m_\mu(\boldsymbol{\sigma}) = \mathcal{O}(N^{-1})$, we see that condition (16.30) is met as soon as we choose the number p of patterns such that $\lim_{N\to\infty} p/\sqrt{N} = 0$. In the thermodynamic limit, we can then be sure that the evolution in time of the overlap vector $\boldsymbol{m}$ will be governed by an autonomous set of differential equations. If the vectors $\boldsymbol{\xi}_k$ are drawn at random according to some distribution $\rho(\boldsymbol{\xi})$ these dynamical laws become, by analogy with (16.24):

$$\frac{\mathrm{d}}{\mathrm{d}t}\boldsymbol{m} = \langle \boldsymbol{\xi} \tanh(\beta\boldsymbol{\xi} \cdot \boldsymbol{A}\boldsymbol{m})\rangle_{\boldsymbol{\xi}} - \boldsymbol{m} \qquad \langle f(\boldsymbol{\xi})\rangle_{\boldsymbol{\xi}} = \int \mathrm{d}\boldsymbol{\xi}\ \rho(\boldsymbol{\xi}) f(\boldsymbol{\xi}) \tag{16.41}$$

Again symmetry of the interaction matrix is not required. For specific non-symmetric choices for the matrix $\boldsymbol{A}$ stable limit cycle solutions of (16.41) can be found, while in the symmetric case $A_{\mu\nu} = A_{\nu\mu}$ the system will approach equilibrium.[28]

Figure 16.1 shows in the m_1, m_2-plane the result of solving the macroscopic laws (16.41) numerically for $p = 2$, randomly drawn pattern bits $\xi_i^\mu \in \{-1, 1\}$, and two specific choices of the matrix $\boldsymbol{A}$. The first choice (upper row) corresponds to the Hopfield model; as the noise level T increases (i.e. β decreases) the amplitudes of the four attractors (corresponding to the two patterns $\boldsymbol{\xi}^\mu$ and their mirror images $-\boldsymbol{\xi}^\mu$) continuously decrease, until at the critical noise level $T_c = 1$ they merge into the trivial attractor $\boldsymbol{m} = (0, 0)$. The second choice corresponds to a non-symmetric model, that is, one without detailed balance. At the macroscopic level of description and on finite timescales the system clearly does not approach equilibrium. Macroscopic order now manifests itself in the form of a limit cycle, provided the noise level T is below the critical value $T_c = 1$ where this limit cycle is destroyed. To what extent the laws (16.41) are in agreement with the result of performing the actual numerical simulations in finite systems is illustrated in Figure 16.2.

[27] Continuous $\{\xi_i^\mu\}$ can in fact be accommodated in the earlier sublattice formalism, but then require the introduction of functional order parameters.

[28] The Lyapunov function (16.36) for positive definite matrices $\boldsymbol{A}$ now becomes $\mathcal{L}[\{m_\mu\}] = \frac{1}{2}\boldsymbol{m} \cdot \boldsymbol{A}\boldsymbol{m} - \beta^{-1}\langle \ln\cosh(\beta\boldsymbol{\xi} \cdot \boldsymbol{A}\boldsymbol{m})\rangle_{\boldsymbol{\xi}}$.

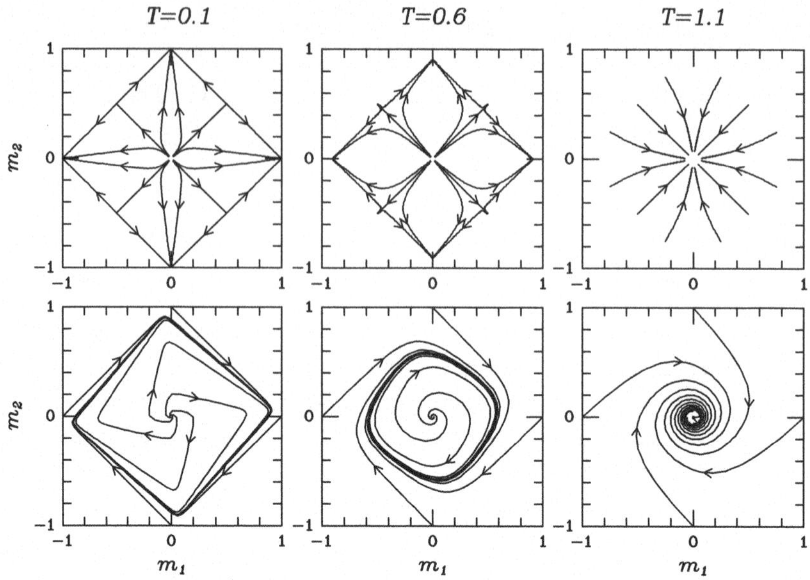

Figure 16.1 Flow diagrams obtained by numerically solving the deterministic overlap equations (16.41) for $p = 2$. Upper row: $A_{\mu\nu} = \delta_{\mu\nu}$ (the Hopfield model); lower row: $\boldsymbol{A} = \begin{pmatrix} 1 & 1 \\ -1 & 1 \end{pmatrix}$. The noise level T is related to the parameter β via $\beta = T^{-1}$. For both models the critical noise level is given by $\beta_c = T_c^{-1} = 1$.

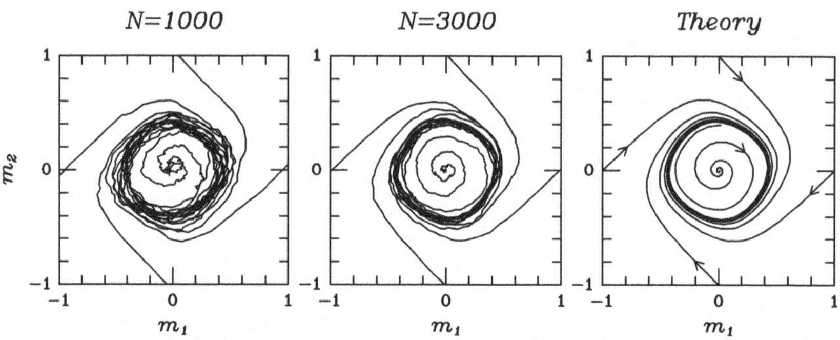

Figure 16.2 Comparison between simulation results for finite systems ($N = 1000$ and $N = 3000$) and the analytical prediction for the evolution of the order parameters (m_1, m_2) from the macroscopic flow equations; here $p = 2$, $T = \beta^{-1} = 0.8$, and $\boldsymbol{A} = \begin{pmatrix} 1 & 1 \\ -1 & 1 \end{pmatrix}$.

As a second simple application of the flow equation (16.41) we turn to the relaxation times associated with the attractors of the Hopfield model, corresponding to the choice $A_{\mu\nu} = \delta_{\mu\nu}$. Expanding (16.41) near a stable fixed point $\boldsymbol{m}^*$, that is, putting $\boldsymbol{m} = \boldsymbol{m}^* + \boldsymbol{x}$ with $|\boldsymbol{x}| \ll 1$, gives the linearized equation

$$\frac{\mathrm{d}}{\mathrm{d}t} x_\mu = \left[\beta \sum_\nu \langle \xi_\mu \xi_\nu [1 - \tanh^2(\beta \boldsymbol{\xi} \cdot \boldsymbol{m}^*)] \rangle_{\boldsymbol{\xi}} - \delta_{\mu\nu}\right] x_\nu + \mathcal{O}(\boldsymbol{x}^2) \qquad (16.42)$$

The Jacobian of (16.41), which here determines the linearized equation (16.42), turns out to be *minus* the (symmetric) curvature matrix $\boldsymbol{D}$ which in Section 21.1 will play a central role in the stability analysis of the phases of the Hopfield model. This matrix has entries

$$D_{\mu\nu} = \delta_{\mu\nu} - \beta\langle\xi_\mu\xi_\nu[1 - \tanh^2(\beta\boldsymbol{\xi}\cdot\boldsymbol{m}^*)]\rangle_{\boldsymbol{\xi}}$$

The form of (16.42), that is, $\mathrm{d}\boldsymbol{x}/\mathrm{d}t = -\boldsymbol{D}\boldsymbol{x} + \mathcal{O}(\boldsymbol{x}^2)$, shows that the asymptotic relaxation towards any stable attractor is generally exponential, with a characteristic time τ given by the inverse of the smallest eigenvalue of the $p \times p$ matrix $\boldsymbol{D}$. If, in particular, for the fixed point $\boldsymbol{m}^*$ we substitute an n-mixture state (which is a solution of the form $\boldsymbol{m}^\star = m_n(1,\ldots,1,0,\ldots,0)$, with n-components equal to m_n and all others zero), and subsequently transform (16.42) to the basis where the corresponding curvature matrix $\boldsymbol{D}^{(n)}$ is diagonal, $\boldsymbol{x} \to \tilde{\boldsymbol{x}}$, we obtain

$$\tilde{x}_\lambda(t) = \tilde{x}_\lambda(0)\, e^{-tD_\lambda^{(n)}}$$

where the $D_\lambda^{(n)}$ are the eigenvalues of $\boldsymbol{D}^{(n)}$. It follows that $\tau^{-1} = \min_\lambda D_\lambda^{(n)}$. We will calculate this quantity explicitly in Section 21.1; here we simply show the results[29] of this calculation in Figure 16.3. The relaxation time for the n-mixture attractors is seen to increase monotonically with the degree of mixing n, for any temperature. This implies that the mixtures with smaller values of n are more stable than those with larger n.

For each value of n, there is also seen to be a critical value of the noise level T where the corresponding relaxation time diverges, indicating loss of stability for that particular mixture state $\boldsymbol{m}^\star$. Each of these critical values will later be shown to correspond to a transition where the associated macroscopic state $\boldsymbol{m}^*$ ceases to define a local minimum of the so-called free energy surface. At these points the Jacobian develops a zero eigenvalue, the relaxation time diverges, and the long-time behaviour is no longer obtained from the linearized equation. This gives rise to so-called critical slowing down, that is, power law relaxation as opposed to exponential relaxation. For instance, at the critical temperature $T_c = 1$ we find by expanding (16.41):

$$\frac{\mathrm{d}}{\mathrm{d}t}m_\mu = m_\mu\left(\frac{2}{3}m_\mu^2 - \boldsymbol{m}^2\right) + \mathcal{O}(\boldsymbol{m}^5)$$

One can show that this gives rise to a relaxation towards the trivial macroscopic fixed point $\boldsymbol{m} = 0$, of the form $\boldsymbol{m} \sim t^{-1/2}$.

---

[29] Note that we show only results for odd values of n; it will be shown in Section 21.1 that mixture states with even values of n are always unstable solutions of our macroscopic laws.

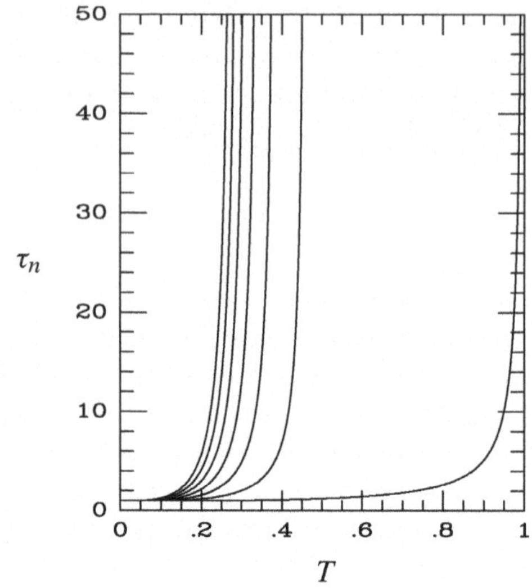

Figure 16.3 Asymptotic relaxation times τ_n describing relaxation towards the n-mixture states $\boldsymbol{m}^\star = m_n(1, \ldots, 1, 0, \ldots, 0)$ of the Hopfield model, as functions of the noise level T. From bottom to top: $n = 1, 3, 5, 7, 9, 11, 13$.

Looking back at the results of this section, we finally note that if one is willing to pay the price of restricting oneself to the more limited class of models (16.39) (as opposed to the more general class (16.33)) and to the more global level of description in terms of p overlap parameters m_μ (as opposed to the n_Λ^p sublattice magnetizations m_η), then there are two rewards from an operational point of view. First, there are no restrictions on the stored quantities ξ_i^μ (for instance, they are allowed to be real-valued). Second, the number p of patterns stored can be much larger for the deterministic autonomous dynamical laws to hold; we only require $p \ll \sqrt{N}$ instead of $p \ll \ln N$.

16.3 Parallel dynamics

We now turn to the case of parallel dynamics, that is, the discrete-time stochastic microscopic laws (16.6). The evolution of the macroscopic probability distribution will now be described by discrete mappings, instead of differential equations.

The toy model

Let us first see what happens to our toy model (16.18) if we switch from sequential to parallel dynamics. As before we try to describe the dynamics at the macroscopic level of the quantity $m(\boldsymbol{\sigma}) = N^{-1} \sum_k \xi_k \sigma_k$. The evolution of the macroscopic probability distribution $\mathcal{P}_t(m)$ is obtained without difficulty by combining (16.6) with the definition (16.19):

$$\mathcal{P}_{t+1}(m) = \sum_{\sigma\sigma'} \delta(m - m(\boldsymbol{\sigma}))W(\boldsymbol{\sigma},\boldsymbol{\sigma}')p_t(\boldsymbol{\sigma}')$$
$$= \int \mathrm{d}m' \, \tilde{W}_t(m,m')\mathcal{P}_t(m') \qquad (16.43)$$

with

$$\tilde{W}_t(m,m') = \frac{\sum_{\sigma\sigma'} \delta(m - m(\boldsymbol{\sigma}))\delta(m' - m(\boldsymbol{\sigma}'))W(\boldsymbol{\sigma},\boldsymbol{\sigma}')p_t(\boldsymbol{\sigma}')}{\sum_{\sigma'} \delta(m' - m(\boldsymbol{\sigma}'))p_t(\boldsymbol{\sigma}')}$$

We next insert the expression (16.7) for the transition probabilities and the local fields. Due to the fact that the fields depend on the microscopic state $\boldsymbol{\sigma}$ only through $m(\boldsymbol{\sigma})$, the microscopic distribution $p_t(\boldsymbol{\sigma})$ drops out of the above expression for the kernel $\tilde{W}_t$ which thereby loses its explicit time-dependence, $\tilde{W}_t(m,m') \to \tilde{W}(m,m')$:

$$\tilde{W}(m,m') = e^{-\sum_i \ln\cosh(\beta J m' \eta_i)}\langle \delta(m - m(\boldsymbol{\sigma}))e^{\beta J m' \sum_i \eta_i \sigma_i}\rangle_{\sigma}$$

with $\langle \cdots \rangle_\sigma = 2^{-N}\sum_\sigma \cdots$. Inserting the integral representation for the δ-function (see Appendix F) allows us to perform the spin average, giving

$$\tilde{W}(m,m') = \frac{\beta N}{2\pi}\int \mathrm{d}k \, e^{N\Psi(m,m',k)}$$

$$\Psi(m,m',k) = \mathrm{i}\beta k m + \langle \ln\cosh\beta(J\eta m' - \mathrm{i}k\xi)\rangle_{\eta,\xi} - \langle \ln\cosh\beta(J\eta m')\rangle_\eta$$

where $\langle f(\eta)\rangle_\eta = N^{-1}\sum_i f(\eta_i)$. Since the kernel $\tilde{W}(m,m')$ is normalized by construction, that is, $\int \mathrm{d}m \, \tilde{W}(m,m') = 1$, we find that for $N \to \infty$ the expectation value with respect to $\tilde{W}(m,m')$ of any sufficiently smooth function $f(m)$ will be determined only by the value $m^*(m')$ of m in the relevant saddle point[30] of Ψ:

$$\int \mathrm{d}m \, f(m)\tilde{W}(m,m') = \frac{\int \mathrm{d}m \, \mathrm{d}k \, f(m) \, e^{N\Psi(m,m',k)}}{\int \mathrm{d}m \, \mathrm{d}k \, e^{N\Psi(m,m',k)}} \to f(m^*(m')) \quad (N \to \infty)$$

Variation of Ψ with respect to k and m gives the two saddle point equations:

$$m = \langle \xi \tanh\beta(J\eta m' - \xi k)\rangle_{\eta,\xi} \qquad k = 0$$

[30] The reason for this is that, for any given m', all values of the integration variables (m, k) other than that where Ψ is maximal will give vanishing contributions to the integral for $N \to \infty$, at least compared to that generated around the maximum of Ψ. For a more detailed discussion of this and more general so-called saddle point integrals we refer to Appendix I.

We may now conclude that $\lim_{N\to\infty} \tilde{W}(m,m') = \delta(m - m^*(m'))$ with $m^*(m') = \langle \xi \tanh(\beta J \eta m')\rangle_{\eta,\xi}$, and that the macroscopic equation (16.43) becomes:

$$\mathcal{P}_{t+1}(m) = \int dm'\ \delta(m - \langle \xi \tanh(\beta J \eta m')\rangle_{\eta,\xi})\mathcal{P}_t(m') \quad (N \to \infty)$$

This relation, of course, describes deterministic evolution. If at $t = 0$ we know m exactly, this will remain so for finite timescales, and m will evolve according to a discrete version of the flow equation (16.24) for sequential dynamics:

$$m_{t+1} = \langle \xi \tanh(\beta J \eta m_t)\rangle_{\eta,\xi} \tag{16.44}$$

The general formalism

We now attempt once more to generalize the above approach to less trivial classes of models. As for the sequential case we will find in the limit $N \to \infty$ closed deterministic evolution equations for more general sets of intensive macroscopic state variables $\mathbf{\Omega}(\boldsymbol{\sigma}) = (\Omega_1(\boldsymbol{\sigma}), \ldots, \Omega_n(\boldsymbol{\sigma}))$, provided the local alignment fields (16.3) depend on the microscopic state $\boldsymbol{\sigma}$ only through the values of $\mathbf{\Omega}(\boldsymbol{\sigma})$ in the limit of infinitely large networks, and if the number n of state variables required for this to be true is not too large.

The evolution of the ensemble probability of finding the system in macroscopic state $\mathbf{\Omega}$,

$$\mathcal{P}_t(\mathbf{\Omega}) = \sum_{\boldsymbol{\sigma}} p_t(\boldsymbol{\sigma})\delta(\mathbf{\Omega} - \mathbf{\Omega}(\boldsymbol{\sigma}))$$

is obtained by combining the Markov chain (16.6) with the definition of the transition probabilities (16.7) and the local fields (16.3):

$$\mathcal{P}_{t+1}(\mathbf{\Omega}) = \int \mathrm{d}\mathbf{\Omega}'\ \tilde{W}_t(\mathbf{\Omega}, \mathbf{\Omega}')\mathcal{P}_t(\mathbf{\Omega}') \tag{16.45}$$

with

$$\begin{aligned}\tilde{W}_t(\mathbf{\Omega}, \mathbf{\Omega}') &= \frac{\sum_{\boldsymbol{\sigma}\boldsymbol{\sigma}'} \delta(\mathbf{\Omega} - \mathbf{\Omega}(\boldsymbol{\sigma}))\delta(\mathbf{\Omega}' - \mathbf{\Omega}(\boldsymbol{\sigma}'))W(\boldsymbol{\sigma}, \boldsymbol{\sigma}')p_t(\boldsymbol{\sigma}')}{\sum_{\boldsymbol{\sigma}'} \delta(\mathbf{\Omega}' - \mathbf{\Omega}(\boldsymbol{\sigma}'))p_t(\boldsymbol{\sigma}')} \\ &= \Big\langle \delta(\mathbf{\Omega} - \mathbf{\Omega}(\boldsymbol{\sigma}))\Big\langle e^{\sum_i [\beta\sigma_i h_i(\boldsymbol{\sigma}') - \ln\cosh(\beta h_i(\boldsymbol{\sigma}'))]}\Big\rangle_{\mathbf{\Omega}';t}\Big\rangle_{\boldsymbol{\sigma}}\end{aligned} \tag{16.46}$$

with an ordinary homogeneous spin-average $\langle \cdots \rangle_{\boldsymbol{\sigma}} = 2^{-N}\sum_{\boldsymbol{\sigma}}(\cdots)$, and with the sub-shell (or conditional) spin-average, defined as before as

$$\langle f(\boldsymbol{\sigma})\rangle_{\mathbf{\Omega};t} = \frac{\sum_{\boldsymbol{\sigma}} f(\boldsymbol{\sigma})\delta(\mathbf{\Omega} - \mathbf{\Omega}(\boldsymbol{\sigma}))p_t(\boldsymbol{\sigma})}{\sum_{\boldsymbol{\sigma}} \delta(\mathbf{\Omega} - \mathbf{\Omega}(\boldsymbol{\sigma}))p_t(\boldsymbol{\sigma})}$$

It is clear from (16.46) that in order to find autonomous macroscopic equations, that is, for the unknown microscopic distribution $p_t(\boldsymbol{\sigma})$ to drop out, the local alignment fields must depend on the microscopic state $\boldsymbol{\sigma}$ only through the macroscopic quantities $\boldsymbol{\Omega}(\boldsymbol{\sigma})$:

$$h_i(\boldsymbol{\sigma}) = h_i(\boldsymbol{\Omega}(\boldsymbol{\sigma}))$$

In this case $\tilde{W}_t$ loses its explicit time-dependence, $\tilde{W}_t(\boldsymbol{\Omega}, \boldsymbol{\Omega}') \to \tilde{W}(\boldsymbol{\Omega}, \boldsymbol{\Omega}')$. Inserting integral representations for the δ-functions then leads to:

$$\tilde{W}(\boldsymbol{\Omega}, \boldsymbol{\Omega}') = \left(\frac{\beta N}{2\pi}\right)^n \int \mathrm{d}\boldsymbol{K}\, e^{N\Psi(\boldsymbol{\Omega},\boldsymbol{\Omega}',\boldsymbol{K})}$$

$$\Psi = \mathrm{i}\beta \boldsymbol{K}\cdot\boldsymbol{\Omega} + \frac{1}{N}\ln\left\langle e^{\beta[\sum_i \sigma_i h_i(\boldsymbol{\Omega}') - \mathrm{i}N\boldsymbol{K}\cdot\boldsymbol{\Omega}(\boldsymbol{\sigma})]}\right\rangle_{\boldsymbol{\sigma}} - \frac{1}{N}\sum_i \ln\cosh(\beta h_i(\boldsymbol{\Omega}'))$$

Using the normalization relation $\int \mathrm{d}\boldsymbol{\Omega}\ \tilde{W}(\boldsymbol{\Omega}, \boldsymbol{\Omega}') = 1$, we can write expectation values with respect to $\tilde{W}(\boldsymbol{\Omega}, \boldsymbol{\Omega}')$ of macroscopic quantities $f(\boldsymbol{\Omega})$ as

$$\int \mathrm{d}\boldsymbol{\Omega}\ f(\boldsymbol{\Omega})\tilde{W}(\boldsymbol{\Omega}, \boldsymbol{\Omega}') = \frac{\int \mathrm{d}\boldsymbol{\Omega}\,\mathrm{d}\boldsymbol{K}\ f(\boldsymbol{\Omega})\, e^{N\Psi(\boldsymbol{\Omega},\boldsymbol{\Omega}',\boldsymbol{K})}}{\int \mathrm{d}\boldsymbol{\Omega}\,\mathrm{d}\boldsymbol{K}\, e^{N\Psi(\boldsymbol{\Omega},\boldsymbol{\Omega}',\boldsymbol{K})}} \tag{16.47}$$

This type of integral, involving an exponential dependence on N, can again for $N \to \infty$ be evaluated using the saddle point (or 'steepest descent') method; see Appendix I. For this to apply in determining the leading order in N of the average (16.47), we encounter at this stage a restriction on the number n of our macroscopic quantities, since n determines the dimension of the integrations concerned. This restriction can be found by expanding Ψ around its maximum Ψ^*. After defining $\boldsymbol{x} = (\boldsymbol{\Omega}, \boldsymbol{K})$, of dimension $2n$, and after translating the location of the maximum to the origin, one has

$$\Psi(\boldsymbol{x}) = \Psi^* - \frac{1}{2}\sum_{\mu\nu} x_\mu x_\nu A_{\mu\nu} + \sum_{\mu\nu\rho} x_\mu x_\nu x_\rho B_{\mu\nu\rho} + \mathcal{O}(\boldsymbol{x}^4)$$

Because after the translation Ψ is maximal at $\boldsymbol{x} = 0$, we know that $\nabla_{\boldsymbol{x}}\Psi|_{\boldsymbol{x}=0} = 0$, so there are no linear terms in this Taylor expansion. Hence

$$\begin{aligned}\int \mathrm{d}\boldsymbol{x}\, e^{N\Psi(\boldsymbol{x})} &= e^{N\Psi^*}\int \mathrm{d}\boldsymbol{x}\, e^{-N\boldsymbol{x}\cdot\boldsymbol{A}\boldsymbol{x}/2 + N\sum_{\mu\nu\rho} x_\mu x_\nu x_\rho B_{\mu\nu\rho} + \mathcal{O}(N\boldsymbol{x}^4)}\\ &= e^{N\Psi^*} N^{-n}\int \mathrm{d}\boldsymbol{y}\, e^{-\boldsymbol{y}\cdot\boldsymbol{A}\boldsymbol{y}/2}[1 + \mathcal{O}(n^2/N)]\end{aligned}$$

and therefore

$$\frac{1}{N}\ln\int \mathrm{d}\boldsymbol{x}\, e^{N\Psi(\boldsymbol{x})} = \Psi^* + \frac{n}{N}\ln\left(\frac{2\pi}{N}\right) - \frac{1}{2N}\sum_{\mu=1}^{2n}\ln(a_\mu) + \mathcal{O}(n^2/N^2)$$

where $\{a_\mu\}$ are the (positive) eigenvalues of the curvature matrix $\boldsymbol{A}$ at the minimum of Ψ. Since, by definition, these eigenvalues scale with the dimension n as $a_\mu \sim n$ at the most, we find the sufficient condition

$$\lim_{N\to\infty}(n\ln n)/N = 0: \quad \lim_{N\to\infty}\int \mathrm{d}\boldsymbol{\Omega}\, f(\boldsymbol{\Omega})\tilde{W}(\boldsymbol{\Omega},\boldsymbol{\Omega}') = f(\boldsymbol{\Omega}^*(\boldsymbol{\Omega}'))$$

where $\boldsymbol{\Omega}^*(\boldsymbol{\Omega}')$ denotes the value of $\boldsymbol{\Omega}$ in the saddle point where Ψ is minimized. Variation of Ψ with respect to $\boldsymbol{\Omega}$ and $\boldsymbol{K}$ gives us the following saddle point equations:

$$\boldsymbol{\Omega} = \frac{\left\langle \boldsymbol{\Omega}(\boldsymbol{\sigma})\, e^{\beta[\sum_i \sigma_i h_i(\boldsymbol{\Omega}') - \mathrm{i}N\boldsymbol{K}\cdot\boldsymbol{\Omega}(\boldsymbol{\sigma})]}\right\rangle_{\boldsymbol{\sigma}}}{\left\langle e^{\beta[\sum_i \sigma_i h_i(\boldsymbol{\Omega}') - \mathrm{i}N\boldsymbol{K}\cdot\boldsymbol{\Omega}(\boldsymbol{\sigma})]}\right\rangle_{\boldsymbol{\sigma}}}, \qquad \boldsymbol{K} = 0$$

We may now conclude that $\lim_{N\to\infty}\tilde{W}(\boldsymbol{\Omega},\boldsymbol{\Omega}') = \delta(\boldsymbol{\Omega} - \boldsymbol{\Omega}^*(\boldsymbol{\Omega}'))$, with

$$\boldsymbol{\Omega}^*(\boldsymbol{\Omega}') = \frac{\left\langle \boldsymbol{\Omega}(\boldsymbol{\sigma})\, e^{\beta\sum_i \sigma_i h_i(\boldsymbol{\Omega}')}\right\rangle_{\boldsymbol{\sigma}}}{\left\langle e^{\beta\sum_i \sigma_i h_i(\boldsymbol{\Omega}')}\right\rangle_{\boldsymbol{\sigma}}}$$

and that for $N \to \infty$ the macroscopic equation (16.45) becomes:

$$\mathcal{P}_{t+1}(\boldsymbol{\Omega}) = \int \mathrm{d}\boldsymbol{\Omega}'\,\delta\left(\boldsymbol{\Omega} - \frac{\left\langle \boldsymbol{\Omega}(\boldsymbol{\sigma})\, e^{\beta\sum_i \sigma_i h_i(\boldsymbol{\Omega}')}\right\rangle_{\boldsymbol{\sigma}}}{\left\langle e^{\beta\sum_i \sigma_i h_i(\boldsymbol{\Omega}')}\right\rangle_{\boldsymbol{\sigma}}}\right)\mathcal{P}_t(\boldsymbol{\Omega}')$$

This relation again describes deterministic evolution. If at $t = 0$ we know $\boldsymbol{\Omega}$ exactly, this will remain the case for finite timescales and $\boldsymbol{\Omega}$ will evolve according to

$$\boldsymbol{\Omega}(t+1) = \frac{\left\langle \boldsymbol{\Omega}(\boldsymbol{\sigma})\, e^{\beta\sum_i \sigma_i h_i[\boldsymbol{\Omega}(t)]}\right\rangle_{\boldsymbol{\sigma}}}{\left\langle e^{\beta\sum_i \sigma_i h_i[\boldsymbol{\Omega}(t)]}\right\rangle_{\boldsymbol{\sigma}}} \tag{16.48}$$

As with the case of sequential microscopic dynamics, in taking the limit $N \to \infty$ we have to keep in mind that the resulting deterministic theory applies to finite t, and that for sufficiently large times terms of higher order in N do come into play. Compared to the sequential case, the restriction $(n\ln n)/N \to 0$ on the number of macroscopic state variables is less severe; this indicates that also in the sequential case we can probably further relax our condition on n, should the need arise.

Finally, for those macroscopic quantities $\boldsymbol{\Omega}(\boldsymbol{\sigma})$ which are linear in $\boldsymbol{\sigma}$, that is, $\boldsymbol{\Omega}(\boldsymbol{\sigma}) = N^{-1}\sum_i \boldsymbol{\omega}_i\sigma_i$ for a given set of $\boldsymbol{\omega}_i = (\omega_i^1, \ldots, \omega_i^n)$, the remaining spin averages in (16.48) become trivial, giving

$$\boldsymbol{\Omega}(t+1) = \lim_{N\to\infty} \frac{1}{N}\sum_i \boldsymbol{\omega}_i \tanh(\beta h_i(\boldsymbol{\Omega}(t))) \qquad (16.49)$$

Separable models: sublattice magnetizations and overlaps

The separable class of attractor models (16.33), described at the level of sublattice magnetizations (16.34), does indeed have the desired property that all local fields can be written in terms of the macroscopic state variables (the sublattice magnetizations) only. What remains of our conditions for (16.49) to hold is the restriction on the number n of these macroscopic state variables: $\lim_{N\to\infty}(n \ln n)/N = 0$. If all relative sublattice sizes p_η are of the same order in N, as is the case for randomly drawn patterns, and if p once more denotes the number of patterns stored, then this condition again translates into

$$\lim_{N\to\infty} \frac{p}{\ln N} = 0$$

Since the sublattice magnetizations are linear functions of the spins, their evolution in time is now governed by equation (16.49), which acquires the form:

$$m_\eta(t+1) = \tanh\left(\beta \sum_{\eta'} p_{\eta'} Q(\eta,\eta') m_{\eta'}(t)\right) \qquad (16.50)$$

As for sequential dynamics, symmetry of the interaction matrix does not play a role in any of the above analysis.

At the more global level of pattern overlaps $\boldsymbol{m}(\boldsymbol{\sigma})$ (16.40) we obtain autonomous deterministic mappings if the local fields (16.3) can be expressed in terms of $\boldsymbol{m}(\boldsymbol{\sigma})$ only, as for the models (16.39) (or, more generally, for all models in which the interactions are of the form $J_{ij} = \sum_{\mu\le p} f_{i\mu}\xi_j^\mu$), and with the following restriction on the number p of embedded patterns:

$$\lim_{N\to\infty} \frac{p \ln p}{N} = 0$$

For the class of bilinear models (16.39), the evolution in time of the overlap vector $\boldsymbol{m}$, which indeed depends linearly on the spin variables, is governed by (16.49). This now translates into the iterative map:

$$\boldsymbol{m}(t+1) = \langle \boldsymbol{\xi} \tanh(\beta \boldsymbol{\xi}\cdot \boldsymbol{A}\boldsymbol{m}(t))\rangle_{\boldsymbol{\xi}} \qquad \langle f(\boldsymbol{\xi})\rangle_{\boldsymbol{\xi}} = \int \mathrm{d}\boldsymbol{\xi}\, \rho(\boldsymbol{\xi}) f(\boldsymbol{\xi}) \quad (16.51)$$

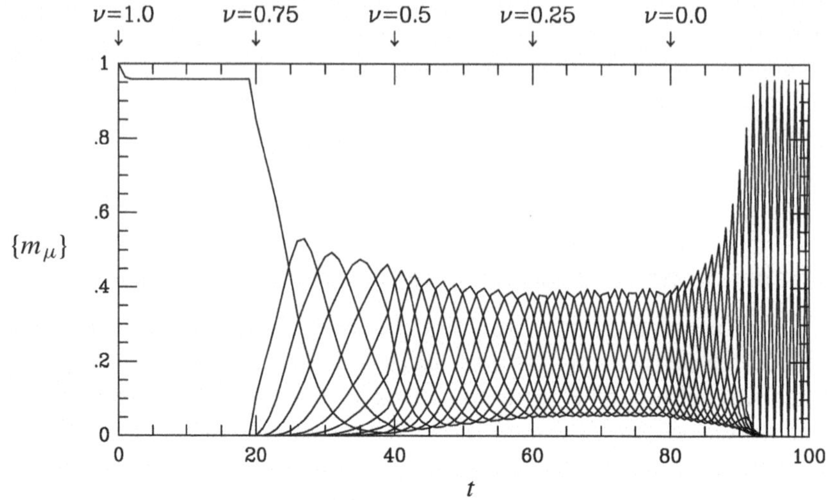

Figure 16.4 Evolution of overlaps $m_\mu(\boldsymbol{\sigma})$, obtained by numerical iteration of the parallel dynamics deterministic macroscopic map, for the bi-linear attractor model $J_{ij} = (\nu/N)\sum_{\mu\nu}\xi_i^\mu\xi_j^\nu + ((1-\nu)/N)\sum_{\mu\nu}\xi_i^{\mu+1}\xi_j^\nu$, with $p = 10$ and $T = 0.5$.

Again symmetry of the interaction matrix is not required. For parallel dynamics it is far more difficult than for sequential dynamics to construct Lyapunov functions and assess under what conditions the macroscopic equations for symmetric systems evolve towards a stable fixed point, but it can still be done. For non-symmetric systems the final macroscopic equations can in principle display all the interesting, but complicated, phenomena of non-conservative non-linear systems. Nevertheless, it is also not uncommon that the macroscopic equations for non-symmetric systems can be mapped by a time-dependent transformation onto the equations for related symmetric systems (mostly variants of the original Hopfield model), such that a thorough analysis is possible. An example of such a model is given below.

As an illustration of the above analysis we show in Figure 16.4 as functions of time the values of the overlap order parameters $\{m_\mu\}$ for $p = 10$ and $T = 0.5$, resulting from numerical iteration of the macroscopic laws (16.51) for the following model:

$$J_{ij} = \frac{\nu}{N}\sum_\mu \xi_i^\mu \xi_j^\mu + \frac{1-\nu}{N}\sum_\mu \xi_i^{\mu+1}\xi_j^\mu \quad (\mu\text{: mod } p)$$

corresponding to

$$A_{\lambda\rho} = \nu\delta_{\lambda\rho} + (1-\nu)\delta_{\lambda,\rho+1} \quad (\lambda, \rho\text{: mod } p)$$

with randomly drawn pattern bits $\xi_i^\mu \in \{-1, 1\}$ The initial state is chosen to be the pure state $m_\mu = \delta_{\mu,1}$. At intervals of $\Delta t = 20$ iterations the parameter ν is reduced in steps of $\Delta\nu = 0.25$ from $\nu = 1$ (where one recovers the symmetric Hopfield model) to $\nu = 0$ (where one obtains a non-symmetric model which processes the p embedded patterns in strict sequential order as a period-p limit cycle).

The analysis of the equation (16.51) for the pure sequence processing case $\nu = 0$ can be greatly simplified by mapping the model onto the ordinary ($\nu = 1$) Hopfield model, using the index permutation symmetries of the pattern distribution, in the following way[31] (all pattern indices are periodic, mod p):

$$m_\mu(t) = M_{\mu-t}(t): \quad M_\mu(t+1) = \langle \xi^{\mu+t+1} \tanh(\beta \sum_\rho \xi^{\rho+1} M_{\rho-t}(t)) \rangle_{\boldsymbol{\xi}}$$

$$= \langle \xi^{\mu+t+1} \tanh(\beta \sum_\rho \xi^{\rho+t+1} M_\rho(t)) \rangle_{\boldsymbol{\xi}}$$

$$= \langle \xi^\mu \tanh(\beta \boldsymbol{\xi} \cdot \boldsymbol{M}(t)) \rangle_{\boldsymbol{\xi}}$$

From this mapping we can immediately infer, in particular, that to each stable macroscopic fixed point attractor of the original Hopfield model there corresponds a stable period-p macroscopic limit cycle attractor in the $\nu = 1$ sequence processing model (e.g. pure states $\leftrightarrow$ pure sequences, mixture states $\leftrightarrow$ mixture sequences), with identical amplitude as a function of temperature. Figure 16.4 shows for $\nu = 0$ (i.e. $t > 80$) a relaxation towards such a pure sequence.

16.4 Exercises

Exercise 16.1. (Markov chains.) In the Markov chains (16.6, 16.9), the kernel $W(\boldsymbol{\sigma}, \boldsymbol{\sigma}')$ gives the probability of making a transition from state $\boldsymbol{\sigma}'$ to state $\boldsymbol{\sigma}$, that is, the probability of finding the system in state $\boldsymbol{\sigma}$ at time $t+1$ if at the previous time t it was in state $\boldsymbol{\sigma}'$. Explain how from this statement the mathematical conditions (16.8) on $W(\boldsymbol{\sigma}, \boldsymbol{\sigma}')$ arise. Verify that they are satisfied for the specific forms of $W(\boldsymbol{\sigma}, \boldsymbol{\sigma}')$ given for sequential and parallel network dynamics in (16.7) and (16.13).

Exercise 16.2. (Transition matrices for small systems.) To get a better feeling for what the transition probabilities $W(\boldsymbol{\sigma}, \boldsymbol{\sigma}')$ look like, consider a very

[31] The mapping discussed here is a special case of a more general duality relating all trajectories $\{\boldsymbol{m}(t)\}$ obtained by iterating the macroscopic laws (16.51) for a given value of the parameter ν to all trajectories $\{\boldsymbol{m}(t)\}$ obtained for the parameter value $1 - \nu$.

simple system, consisting of $N = 2$ neurons with no self-interactions and no external inputs. The fields acting on neuron 1 and 2 are then, respectively,

$$h_1(\boldsymbol{\sigma}) = J_{12}\sigma_2 \qquad h_2(\boldsymbol{\sigma}) = J_{21}\sigma_1$$

where the vector $\boldsymbol{\sigma} = (\sigma_1, \sigma_2)$ collects the states of all neurons as usual. Write down the transition probabilities $W(\boldsymbol{\sigma}, \boldsymbol{\sigma}')$ for both parallel and sequential dynamics. The easiest way to write the result is in the form of a matrix: there are four possible states $\boldsymbol{\sigma}$ of the system (each neuron/spin can be $+1$ or -1). If you number these in some way, you can represent the probabilities $p_t(\boldsymbol{\sigma})$ as a four-dimensional vector, and $W(\boldsymbol{\sigma}, \boldsymbol{\sigma})$ as a 4×4 matrix; the right-hand side of the Markov chains (16.6, 16.9) is then just a product of a matrix and a vector.

Exercise 16.3. (Macroscopic laws for sequential dynamics.) Derive the expansion (16.27).

Exercise 16.4. (Macroscopic laws for sequential dynamics.) Consider the models and methods of Section 16.2, with the separable interaction matrices (16.39). Convince yourself that in the simplest case $p = 1$, where only a single pattern $\boldsymbol{\xi} \in \{-1, 1\}^N$ is stored, and $A_{11} = 1$, the pattern overlap m evolves according to

$$\frac{\mathrm{d}}{\mathrm{d}t} m = \tanh(\beta m) - m$$

For $T > 1$ ($\beta < 1$), the only stationary state is $m = 0$. Linearize the above equation around this state and deduce that, for large times, m is proportional to $\exp(-t/\tau_+(T))$, with the characteristic timescale $\tau_+(T) = 1/(T - 1)$. Note that $\tau_+(T)$ diverges as $T \to 1$ ('critical slowing down').

For $T < 1$, there are three stationary states $-m_*, 0, m_*$, where m_* is the positive solution of $m_* = \tanh(\beta m_*)$. Linearize around these three states. Show that (i) $m = 0$ is an unstable stationary state, and (ii) convergence to the other two stationary states is again exponential, with time constant $\tau_-(T) = 1/[1 - (1 - m_*^2)/T]$. By solving the stationarity condition for small m_*, show that $m_*^2 = 3(1 - T) + \mathcal{O}((1 - T)^2)$ for T close to one, and hence that $\tau_-(T)$ diverges as $\tau_-(T) = 1/[2(1 - T)] + \mathcal{O}(1)$ as $T = 1$ is approached from below.

Finally, consider the case $T = 1$. The only stationary state is again $m = 0$. To find the asymptotic convergence towards this state, use the Taylor expansion $\tanh(m) = m - m^3/3 + \mathcal{O}(m^5)$. Neglect the $\mathcal{O}(m^5)$ term and solve the resulting differential equation for $m(t)$. You should find that $m(t) \approx \frac{1}{2}\sqrt{6/t}$ for large t; note that there is no undetermined proportionality constant in this expression, unlike the other two cases $T > 1$ and $T < 1$.

Exercise 16.5. (Macroscopic laws for parallel dynamics.) Consider the models and methods of Section 16.3, with the separable interaction matrices (16.39). Take the simple case where $p = 1$, but add (uniform) external contributions to the local fields, that is,

$$h_i(\boldsymbol{\sigma}) = \sum_{j=1}^{N} J_{ij}\sigma_j + \vartheta \qquad J_{ij} = \frac{1}{N}\xi_i\xi_j$$

Define the pattern overlap $m(\boldsymbol{\sigma}) = N^{-1}\sum_{i=1}^{N}\xi_i\sigma_i$, and the associated macroscopic probability density

$$\mathcal{P}_t(m) = \sum_{\boldsymbol{\sigma}} p_t(\boldsymbol{\sigma})\delta(m - m(\boldsymbol{\sigma}))$$

Show that this density obeys an iterative equation of the form

$$\mathcal{P}_{t+1}(m) = \int \mathrm{d}m'\,\delta\Big(m - \lim_{N\to\infty}\frac{1}{N}\sum_{i=1}^{N}\xi_i\tanh(\beta\xi_i m' + \beta\vartheta)\Big)\mathcal{P}_t(m')$$

Consider the case where the bits of the pattern $(\xi_1, \ldots, \xi_N)$ are drawn independently at random according to $p(1) = p(-1) = \frac{1}{2}$. Show that the above iterative map describes deterministic overlap evolution, such that

$$m(t+1) = \tfrac{1}{2}\tanh(\beta(m + |\vartheta|)) + \tfrac{1}{2}\tanh(\beta(m - |\vartheta|))$$

Show that the 'no-recall' state $m = 0$ is a fixed point of the dynamics. Use the above deterministic map for $m(t)$ to determine the condition(s) under which $m = 0$ is a stable fixed point. Show that for sufficiently strong external fields ϑ the system will not be able to reconstruct the stored pattern $(\xi_1, \ldots, \xi_N)$. Finally, consider the limit $\beta \to \infty$, where there is no noise in the microscopic dynamics. Solve the macroscopic equation for $m(t)$ for the case where $|\vartheta| > 1$. For the opposite case $|\vartheta| < 1$, solve the equation separately for the three regions (i) $-1 \leq m < -|\vartheta|$, (ii) $-|\vartheta| < m < |\vartheta|$, and (iii) $|\vartheta| < m \leq 1$. What can you see as the advantage of having modest external fields ϑ?

17 Dynamics of online learning in binary perceptrons

17.1 Probabilistic definitions, performance measures

In this chapter we study the dynamics of supervised learning in artificial feedforward neural networks. The basic scenario is identical to that introduced in Part I: a student neural network executes a certain operation $S: \Omega \to R$, which is parametrized by a vector $\boldsymbol{J}$, usually representing synaptic weights and/or neuronal thresholds. Here $\Omega \subseteq \mathbb{R}^N$ denotes the set of all possible questions and R denotes the set of all possible answers. The student is being trained to emulate a given teacher, which executes some as yet unknown operation $T: \Omega \to R$. In order to achieve the objective, the student network S tries gradually to improve its performance by adapting its parameters $\boldsymbol{J}$ according to an iterative procedure, using only input vectors (or questions) $\boldsymbol{\xi}$ which are drawn at random from a fixed training set $D \subseteq \Omega$ of size $|D|$, and the corresponding values of the teacher outputs $T(\boldsymbol{\xi})$ (the correct answers). The iterative procedure, or learning rule, is not allowed to involve any further knowledge of the operation T. As far as the student is concerned the teacher is an oracle, or black box. The only information available about the inner workings of the black box is contained in the various answers $T(\boldsymbol{\xi})$ it provides; see Figure 17.1. For simplicity we assume each question $\boldsymbol{\xi}$ to be equally likely to occur; generalization of what follows to the case where the question probabilities are non-uniform is straightforward.

Again we will attempt to apply statistical mechanical ideas and methods, and try to move away from analysing the dynamics at the microscopic level (which here describes stochastically evolving weights and/or thresholds), in favour of a description of the learning process in terms of autonomous deterministic equations for suitable macroscopic observables. After all, we are usually not interested in knowing the evolution of the full details of the student's synaptic weights and thresholds as such, but rather in knowing the evolving performance of our student network in answering correctly the questions in the training set D and in the full set Ω. This performance will be measured by training and generalization errors, respectively; the latter are indeed *macroscopic* quantities. Our approach in this chapter is

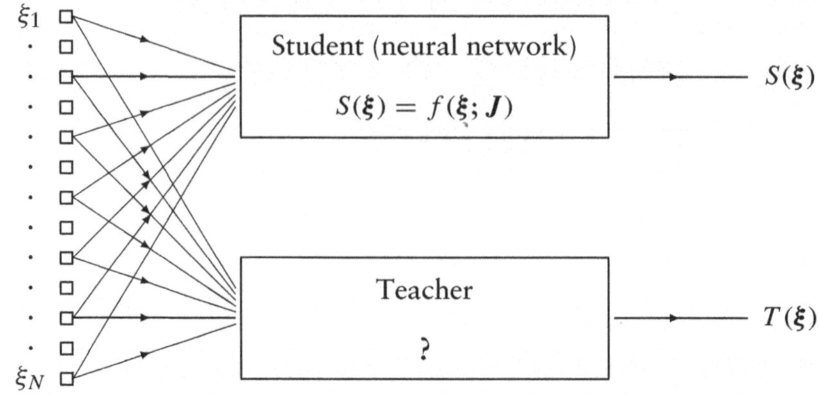

Figure 17.1 The general scenario of supervised learning: a student network S is being trained to perform an operation $T\colon \Omega \to R$ by updating its control parameters $\boldsymbol{J}$ according to an iterative procedure, the learning rule. This rule is allowed to make use only of examples of question/answer pairs $(\boldsymbol{\xi}, T(\boldsymbol{\xi}))$, where $\boldsymbol{\xi} \in D \subseteq \Omega$. The actual teacher operation T that generated the answers $T(\boldsymbol{\xi})$, on the other hand, cannot be observed directly. The goal is to arrive at a situation where $S(\boldsymbol{\xi}) = T(\boldsymbol{\xi})$ for all $\boldsymbol{\xi} \in \Omega$.

therefore very similar to that followed earlier in Section 2.5; the difference is that here we will no longer restrict ourselves to the case of vanishing learning rates. Thus the microscopic learning process remains stochastic, in contrast to Section 2.5. Consequently, our methods will have to be more sophisticated. We will also study more general families of learning rules.

Probabilistic definition of the microscopic process

More specifically, we will consider the following class of learning rules, that is, of recipes for the iterative modification of the student's control parameters $\boldsymbol{J}$, which we will refer to as online learning rules. An input vector $\boldsymbol{\xi}(\ell)$ is drawn independently at each step ℓ from the training set D, followed by a modification of the control parameters $\boldsymbol{J}$:

$$\boldsymbol{J}(\ell+1) = \boldsymbol{J}(\ell) + \boldsymbol{F}[\boldsymbol{\xi}(\ell), \boldsymbol{J}(\ell), T(\boldsymbol{\xi}(\ell))] \tag{17.1}$$

The name 'online' indicates that $\boldsymbol{J}$ is updated after each presentation of a single example, rather than 'offline', that is, after all examples from the training set have been seen. The integer variable $\ell = 0, 1, 2, 3, \ldots$ labels the iteration steps. Since this process is stochastic, we introduce the probability density $p_\ell(\boldsymbol{J})$ of finding parameter vector $\boldsymbol{J}$ at iteration step ℓ. In terms of this microscopic probability density the process (17.1) can again be written in the Markovian form:

$$p_{\ell+1}(\boldsymbol{J}) = \int \mathrm{d}\boldsymbol{J}' W(\boldsymbol{J}, \boldsymbol{J}') p_\ell(\boldsymbol{J}') \tag{17.2}$$

However, the space of all microscopic configurations need now no longer be discrete, so rather than transition probabilities we generally have a *transition probability density*:

$$W(\boldsymbol{J}, \boldsymbol{J}') = \langle \delta(\boldsymbol{J} - \boldsymbol{J}' - \boldsymbol{F}[\boldsymbol{\xi}, \boldsymbol{J}', T(\boldsymbol{\xi})]) \rangle_D \tag{17.3}$$

where $\delta(z)$ denotes the delta-distribution; see Appendix F. The advantage of using online rather than offline (or 'batch') learning rules is a reduction in the amount of calculations that have to be done at each iteration step; the price paid for this reduction is the presence of fluctuations due to the random selection of examples from the training set, with as yet unknown impact on the performance of the system.

We will denote averages over the probability density $p_\ell(\boldsymbol{J})$ as

$$\langle g(\boldsymbol{J}) \rangle = \int \mathrm{d}\boldsymbol{J}\, p_\ell(\boldsymbol{J}) g(\boldsymbol{J})$$

and averages over the full set Ω of possible input vectors and over the training set D, respectively, in the following way:

$$\langle K(\boldsymbol{\xi}) \rangle_\Omega = \frac{1}{|\Omega|} \sum_{\boldsymbol{\xi} \in \Omega} K(\boldsymbol{\xi}) \qquad \langle K(\boldsymbol{\xi}) \rangle_D = \frac{1}{|D|} \sum_{\boldsymbol{\xi} \in D} K(\boldsymbol{\xi})$$

For finite system size N, the average $\langle K(\boldsymbol{\xi}) \rangle_D$ will in general depend on the precise realization of the training set D.

Performance measures

To quantify the goal and the progress of the student one finally defines an error $\mathcal{E}(T(\boldsymbol{\xi}), S(\boldsymbol{\xi})) = \mathcal{E}(T(\boldsymbol{\xi}), f(\boldsymbol{\xi}; \boldsymbol{J}))$, which measures the mismatch between student and correct (teacher) answers for individual questions. The two key quantities of interest in supervised learning are the time-dependent averages of this error measure, calculated over the training set D and the full question set Ω, respectively:

$$\begin{aligned} &\text{training error:} && E_\mathrm{t}(\boldsymbol{J}) = \langle \mathcal{E}(T(\boldsymbol{\xi}), f(\boldsymbol{\xi}; \boldsymbol{J})) \rangle_D \\ &\text{generalization error:} && \mathcal{E}_\mathrm{g}(\boldsymbol{J}) = \langle \mathcal{E}(T(\boldsymbol{\xi}), f(\boldsymbol{\xi}; \boldsymbol{J})) \rangle_\Omega \end{aligned} \tag{17.4}$$

These quantities are stochastic observables, since they are functions of the stochastically evolving vector $\boldsymbol{J}$. Their expectation values over the stochastic process (17.2) are given by

$$\begin{aligned} &\text{mean training error:} && \langle E_{\rm t}\rangle = \langle\langle \mathcal{E}(T(\boldsymbol{\xi}), f(\boldsymbol{\xi};\boldsymbol{J}))\rangle\rangle_D \\ &\text{mean generalization error:} && \langle E_{\rm g}\rangle = \langle\langle \mathcal{E}(T(\boldsymbol{\xi}), f(\boldsymbol{\xi};\boldsymbol{J}))\rangle\rangle_\Omega \end{aligned} \tag{17.5}$$

Note that the prefix 'mean' refers to the stochasticity in the vector $\boldsymbol{J}$; both $\langle E_{\rm t}\rangle$ and $\langle E_{\rm g}\rangle$ will in general still depend on the realization of the training set D.

The training error measures the performance of the student on the questions it could have been confronted with during the learning stage (in the case of online learning the student need not have seen all of them). The generalization error measures the student's performance on the full question set and its minimization is therefore the main target of the process. The quality of a theory describing the dynamics of supervised learning can be measured by the degree to which it succeeds in predicting the values of $\langle E_{\rm t}\rangle$ and $\langle E_{\rm g}\rangle$ as a function of the number of iteration steps ℓ and for arbitrary choices made for the function $\boldsymbol{F}[\cdots]$ that determines the details of the learning rules (17.1).

There are two main classes of situations in the supervised learning arena, which differ fundamentally in their dynamics and in the degree to which we can analyse them mathematically. The first class is the one where the training set D is what we call 'complete': sufficiently large and sufficiently diverse to lead to a learning dynamics which in the limit $N \to \infty$ is identical to that of the situation where $D = \Omega$. For example, in single perceptrons and in multilayer perceptrons with a finite number of hidden nodes one finds, for the case where $\Omega = \{-1, 1\}^N$ and where the members of the training set D are drawn at random from Ω, that completeness of the training set amounts to $\lim_{N\to\infty} N/|D| = 0$. This makes sense: it means that for $N \to \infty$ there will be an infinite number of training examples per adaptable microscopic parameter. For this class of models it is fair to say that the dynamics of learning can be fully analysed in a reasonably simple way. We will restrict ourselves to single perceptrons with various types of learning rules, since they form the most transparent playground for explaining how the mathematical techniques work. For multilayer perceptrons with a finite number of hidden neurons and complete training sets the procedure to be followed is very similar.[32] The picture changes dramatically if we move away from complete training sets and consider those where the number of training examples is proportional to the number of adaptable microscopic

[32] The situation is different if we try to deal with multilayer perceptrons with a number of hidden neurons which scales linearly with the number of input channels N. This still poses an unsolved problem, even in the case of complete training sets.

parameters; in simple perceptrons and in two-layer perceptrons with a finite number of hidden neurons this implies $|D| = \alpha N$ $(0 < \alpha < \infty)$. In those situations one needs much more powerful mathematical tools; we will not deal with such cases here.

17.2 Explicit learning rules

We will now derive explicitly macroscopic dynamical equations that describe the evolution in time for the error in large binary output perceptrons, trained with several online learning rules to perform linearly separable tasks. We restrict ourselves to complete training sets $D = \Omega = \{-1, 1\}^N$. There is consequently no difference between training and generalization error, and we can simply define $E = \langle E_g \rangle = \langle E_t \rangle$.

The family of learning rules

Consider a linearly separable binary classification task T: $\{-1, 1\}^N \to \{-1, 1\}$. It can be regarded as generated by a binary output teacher perceptron with some unknown weight vector $\boldsymbol{B} \in \mathbb{R}^N$, that is, $T(\boldsymbol{\xi}) = \text{sgn}(\boldsymbol{B} \cdot \boldsymbol{\xi})$, normalized according to $|\boldsymbol{B}| = 1$. A student perceptron with output $S(\boldsymbol{\xi}) = \text{sgn}(\boldsymbol{J} \cdot \boldsymbol{\xi})$ (where $\boldsymbol{J} \in \mathbb{R}^N$) is being trained in an online fashion using randomly drawn examples of input vectors $\boldsymbol{\xi} \in \{-1, 1\}^N$ with corresponding teacher answers $T(\boldsymbol{\xi})$. The general picture of Figure 17.1 thus specializes to Figure 17.2. We exploit our knowledge of the perceptron's scaling properties and distinguish between the discrete time unit ℓ in terms of iteration steps, and the scaled time unit $t = \ell/N$. Our goal is to derive well-behaved differential equations in the limit $N \to \infty$, so we require weight

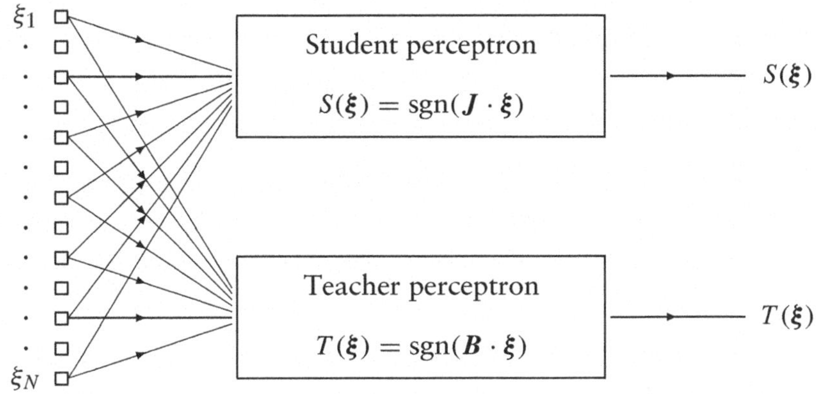

Figure 17.2 A student perceptron S is being trained according to online learning rules to perform a linearly separable operation, generated by some unknown teacher perceptron T.

changes occurring in intervals $\Delta t = N^{-1}$ to be of order $\mathcal{O}(N^{-1})$ as well. In terms of equation (17.1) this implies demanding that $\boldsymbol{F}[\cdots] = \mathcal{O}(N^{-1})$. If, finally, we restrict ourselves to those rules where weight changes are made in the direction of the example vectors, which includes most popular rules, we obtain the generic[33] recipe

$$\boldsymbol{J}(t + \Delta t) = \boldsymbol{J}(t) + \frac{1}{N}\eta(t)\, \boldsymbol{\xi}(t)\mathcal{F}[|\boldsymbol{J}(t)|; \boldsymbol{J}(t) \cdot \boldsymbol{\xi}(t), \boldsymbol{B} \cdot \boldsymbol{\xi}(t)] \qquad (17.6)$$

Here $\eta(t)$ denotes a possibly time-dependent learning rate, and $\boldsymbol{\xi}(t)$ is the input vector selected at time t. The function $\mathcal{F}[\cdots]$ is an as yet arbitrary function of the length of the student weight vector and of the local fields $\boldsymbol{J} \cdot \boldsymbol{\xi}$ and $\boldsymbol{B} \cdot \boldsymbol{\xi}$ of student and teacher. Importantly, however, because the student only observes the teacher output, that is, $\text{sgn}(\boldsymbol{B} \cdot \boldsymbol{\xi}(t))$, the function $\mathcal{F}[\cdots]$ can depend on the sign of the teacher field only, not on its magnitude. For example, for $\mathcal{F}[J; u, v] = \text{sgn}(v)$ we obtain a Hebbian rule, for $\mathcal{F}[J; u, v] = \theta(-uv)\text{sgn}(v)$ we obtain the perceptron learning rule, etc. However, we will develop the theory for arbitrary choices of $\mathcal{F}[\cdots]$; this will allow us not only to compare but even to optimize learning rules.

Finally, note that below we will use the variables (x, y) to denote local fields, rather than (u, v); this is done in order to keep close contact with the conventions in the relevant literature. Note also that from the more general analysis of learning dynamics to be developed in this section one can recover the simpler theory of Section 2.5 (to which it is related via the identification $\epsilon = \eta/N$) by the transformation $t \to t/\eta$, followed by taking the limit $\eta \to 0$.

Deterministic equations for order parameters

We now try to solve the dynamics of the learning process in terms of the two macroscopic observables that played a special role earlier in the perceptron convergence proof (see Section 2.3):

$$Q(t) = \boldsymbol{J}^2(t) \qquad R(t) = \boldsymbol{J}(t) \cdot \boldsymbol{B} \qquad (17.7)$$

At this stage the choice of observables is still no more than intuition-driven guess work. The formal approach, in the spirit of our previous analysis of neuron state dynamics in recurrent networks, would be to derive an expression for the time-dependent probability density $P_t(Q, R) = \langle \delta(Q - Q(t))\delta(R - R(t)) \rangle$. However, it turns out that in the present case there is a short-cut. Squaring (17.6) and taking the inner product of (17.6) with the

[33] One can obviously write down more general rules, and also write the present recipe (17.6) in different ways.

teacher vector $\boldsymbol{B}$ gives, respectively

$$\frac{Q(t+\Delta t)-Q(t)}{\Delta t} = 2\eta(t)\,\boldsymbol{J}(t)\cdot\boldsymbol{\xi}(t)\,\mathcal{F}[|\boldsymbol{J}(t)|;\boldsymbol{J}(t)\cdot\boldsymbol{\xi}(t),\boldsymbol{B}\cdot\boldsymbol{\xi}(t)] + \eta(t)^2\mathcal{F}^2[\cdots]$$

$$\frac{R(t+\Delta t)-R(t)}{\Delta t} = \eta(t)\boldsymbol{B}\cdot\boldsymbol{\xi}(t)\mathcal{F}[\cdots]$$

Here we have used the property $\boldsymbol{\xi}(t)\cdot\boldsymbol{\xi}(t)=N$ and indicated by $[\cdots]$ that the arguments of the function $\mathcal{F}$ are the same in all its three occurrences.

After ℓ discrete update steps we will have accumulated ℓ such modifications, and we thus arrive at:

$$\begin{aligned}\frac{Q(t+\ell\Delta t)-Q(t)}{\ell\Delta t} &= \frac{1}{\ell}\sum_{m=0}^{\ell-1}\frac{Q(t+(m+1)\Delta t)-Q(t+m\Delta t)}{\Delta t}\\ &= \frac{1}{\ell}\sum_{m=0}^{\ell-1}\{2\eta(t+m\Delta t)\boldsymbol{J}(t+m\Delta t)\cdot\boldsymbol{\xi}(t+m\Delta t)\\ &\quad\times\mathcal{F}[|\boldsymbol{J}(t+m\Delta t)|;\boldsymbol{J}(t+m\Delta t)\cdot\boldsymbol{\xi}(t+m\Delta t),\\ &\quad\boldsymbol{B}\cdot\boldsymbol{\xi}(t+m\Delta t)]+\eta^2(t+m\Delta t)\mathcal{F}^2[\cdots]\}\end{aligned}$$

$$\begin{aligned}\frac{R(t+\ell\Delta t)-R(t)}{\ell\Delta t} &= \frac{1}{\ell}\sum_{m=0}^{\ell-1}\frac{R(t+(m+1)\Delta t)-R(t+m\Delta t)}{\Delta t}\\ &= \frac{1}{\ell}\sum_{m=0}^{\ell-1}\{\eta(t+m\Delta t)\boldsymbol{B}\cdot\boldsymbol{\xi}(t+m\Delta t)\mathcal{F}[\cdots]\}\end{aligned}$$

We now use the fact that the weight vector $\boldsymbol{J}$ only changes significantly after $\ell=\mathcal{O}(N)$ updates, where the time t changes by an amount of $\mathcal{O}(1)$. As long as we consider $\ell\ll N$, we can therefore replace $\boldsymbol{J}(t+m\Delta t)$ by $\boldsymbol{J}(t)$ on the right-hand side of the previous equations.[34] An equivalent way of putting this is to say that the distribution of the 'fields' $\boldsymbol{J}(t+m\Delta t)\cdot\boldsymbol{\xi}(t+m\Delta t)$ over the random choice of the $\boldsymbol{\xi}(t+m\Delta t)$ changes only negligibly for $\ell\ll N$. If ℓ itself is nevertheless large enough, the right-hand sides of our evolution equations then simply become averages over the current field distributions.

[34] To see this explicitly, set $\boldsymbol{J}(t+m\Delta)=\boldsymbol{J}(t)+\Delta\boldsymbol{J}$ and abbreviate $\boldsymbol{\xi}(t+m\Delta t)\equiv\boldsymbol{\xi}$. Our replacement changes $(\boldsymbol{J}+\Delta\boldsymbol{J})\cdot\boldsymbol{\xi}$ to $\boldsymbol{J}\cdot\boldsymbol{\xi}$. In the difference $\Delta\boldsymbol{J}\cdot\boldsymbol{\xi}$, each component of $\Delta\boldsymbol{J}$ is at most $\mathcal{O}(m/N)$ because each update causes a change of $\mathcal{O}(1/N)$. But $\boldsymbol{\xi}$ is randomly chosen, so each of the $\mathcal{O}(m/N)$-changes gets a random prefactor of ±1. The typical size of $\Delta\boldsymbol{J}\cdot\boldsymbol{\xi}$ is therefore at most $\mathcal{O}(N^{1/2}m/N)=\mathcal{O}(m/N^{1/2})$, which becomes negligible in the thermodynamic limit.

Formally, we choose to take the two limits $N \to \infty$ and $\ell \to \infty$ in such a way that $\ell/N \to 0$ (e.g. in the form $N \to \infty$ followed by the limit $\ell \to \infty$). Then three welcome simplifications occur:

- The time increment Δt becomes infinitesimally small, and the time t becomes a continuous variable.
- The left-hand sides of the above equations for the evolution of the observables Q and R become temporal derivatives.
- If the learning rate $\eta(t)$ is defined as a continuous function of time t, so that $\eta(t + m\Delta t) \to \eta(t)$, the summations on the right-hand sides of these equations become averages over inputs $\boldsymbol{\xi}$ randomly drawn from the training set $D = \Omega = \{-1, 1\}^N$.

Suppressing time arguments, the result of these combined simplifications can now be written compactly as

$$\frac{\mathrm{d}}{\mathrm{d}t} Q = 2\eta\langle \boldsymbol{J}\cdot\boldsymbol{\xi}\,\mathcal{F}[Q^{1/2}; \boldsymbol{J}\cdot\boldsymbol{\xi}, \boldsymbol{B}\cdot\boldsymbol{\xi}]\rangle_\Omega + \eta^2\langle \mathcal{F}^2[Q^{1/2}; \boldsymbol{J}\cdot\boldsymbol{\xi}, \boldsymbol{B}\cdot\boldsymbol{\xi}]\rangle_\Omega$$

$$\frac{\mathrm{d}}{\mathrm{d}t} R = \eta\langle \boldsymbol{B}\cdot\boldsymbol{\xi}\,\mathcal{F}[Q^{1/2}; \boldsymbol{J}\cdot\boldsymbol{\xi}, \boldsymbol{B}\cdot\boldsymbol{\xi}]\rangle_\Omega$$

As might have been anticipated, the only dependence of the right-hand sides of these expressions on the microscopic variables $\boldsymbol{J} = \boldsymbol{J}(t)$ is via the student fields[35] $\boldsymbol{J}\cdot\boldsymbol{\xi} = Q^{1/2}\hat{\boldsymbol{J}}\cdot\boldsymbol{\xi}$, with $\hat{\boldsymbol{J}} = \hat{\boldsymbol{J}}(t) = \boldsymbol{J}/|\boldsymbol{J}|$. We therefore define the stochastic field variables $x = \hat{\boldsymbol{J}}\cdot\boldsymbol{\xi}$ and $y = \boldsymbol{B}\cdot\boldsymbol{\xi}$ and their joint (time-dependent) probability distribution $P(x, y)$

$$P(x, y) = \langle \delta(x - \hat{\boldsymbol{J}}(t)\cdot\boldsymbol{\xi})\delta(y - \boldsymbol{B}\cdot\boldsymbol{\xi})\rangle_\Omega \tag{17.8}$$

and the associated averages

$$\langle f(x, y)\rangle = \int \mathrm{d}x\mathrm{d}y\, P(x, y) f(x, y) \tag{17.9}$$

The use of brackets without subscripts for joint field averages cannot cause confusion, since such expressions always *replace* averages over Ω, rather than occur simultaneously. Our evolution equations thus take the form

$$\frac{\mathrm{d}}{\mathrm{d}t} Q = 2\eta Q^{1/2}\langle x\mathcal{F}[Q^{1/2}; Q^{1/2}x, y]\rangle + \eta^2\langle \mathcal{F}^2[Q^{1/2}; Q^{1/2}x, y]\rangle \tag{17.10}$$

$$\frac{\mathrm{d}}{\mathrm{d}t} R = \eta\langle y\mathcal{F}[Q^{1/2}; Q^{1/2}x, y]\rangle \tag{17.11}$$

[35] This property of course depends crucially on our choice (17.6) for the form of the learning rules.

We now have a set of evolution equations for the macroscopic order parameters Q and R. Unless we manage to express $P(x, y)$ in terms of these variables, however, these equations do not constitute an actual solution of our problem: we would still be forced to solve the original microscopic dynamical equations in order to find $P(x, y)$ as a function of time and then work out (17.10, 17.11). It is not yet obvious that our equations are closed.

The final stage of the argument is to assume that the joint probability distribution (17.9) has a Gaussian shape, since $\Omega = \{-1, 1\}^N$ and since all $\boldsymbol{\xi} \in \Omega$ contribute equally to the average in (17.9). This will be true in the vast majority of cases; for example, it is true with probability one if the vectors $\boldsymbol{J}$ and $\boldsymbol{B}$ are drawn at random from compact sets like $[-1, 1]^N$, due to the central limit theorem.[36] Gaussian distributions are fully specified by their first- and second-order moments (see Appendix D), which are here calculated trivially using $\langle \xi_i \rangle_\Omega = 0$ and $\langle \xi_i \xi_j \rangle_\Omega = \delta_{ij}$:

$$\langle x \rangle = \sum_i \hat{J}_i \langle \xi_i \rangle_\Omega = 0 \qquad \langle y \rangle = \sum_i B_i \langle \xi_i \rangle_\Omega = 0 \tag{17.12}$$

$$\langle x^2 \rangle = \sum_{ij} \hat{J}_i \hat{J}_j \langle \xi_i \xi_j \rangle_\Omega = 1 \qquad \langle y^2 \rangle = \sum_{ij} B_i B_j \langle \xi_i \xi_j \rangle_\Omega = 1 \tag{17.13}$$

$$\langle xy \rangle = \sum_{ij} \hat{J}_i B_j \langle \xi_i \xi_j \rangle_\Omega = \frac{R}{\sqrt{Q}} \tag{17.14}$$

Upon inverting the covariance matrix of the stochastic fields x and y we then find

$$P(x, y) = \frac{\mathrm{e}^{-(x^2+y^2-2xyR/\sqrt{Q})/2(1-R^2/Q)}}{2\pi\sqrt{1 - R^2/Q}} \tag{17.15}$$

Note that, although we study here a more general class of models (not just the perceptron learning rule) and a broader regime of applicability (not just the limit of vanishing learning rate), the arguments relating to $P(x, y)$ and the final expression (17.15) are fully identical to those in Section 2.5, with the identification $\omega = R/\sqrt{Q}$. The fact that $P(x, y)$ depends on time only through R and Q now ensures that the two equations (17.10, 17.11) do indeed form a *closed* set. Note also that (17.10, 17.11) are deterministic equations. Our derivation thus shows that the fluctuations in the macroscopic observables Q and R vanish in the $N \to \infty$ limit.

Finally, the generalization error E_g—which is here identical to the training error E_t due to $D = \Omega$, and therefore simply denoted by E in

---

[36] It is not true for all choices of $\boldsymbol{J}$ and $\boldsymbol{B}$. A trivial counter-example is $J_k = \delta_{k1}$, less trivial counter-examples are, for example, $J_k = e^{-k}$ and $J_k = k^{-\gamma}$ with $\gamma > \frac{1}{2}$. For a more extensive discussion of the matter see Appendix B.

the following—can also be expressed in terms of our macroscopic observables. We define the error made in a single classification of an input $\boldsymbol{\xi}$ as $\mathcal{E}(T(\boldsymbol{\xi}), S(\boldsymbol{\xi})) = \theta(-(\boldsymbol{B}\cdot\boldsymbol{\xi})(\boldsymbol{J}\cdot\boldsymbol{\xi})) \in \{0,1\}$. This means that the error is 1 if student and teacher disagree in their predictions, that is, if $\text{sgn}(\boldsymbol{J}\cdot\boldsymbol{\xi}) \neq \text{sgn}(\boldsymbol{B}\cdot\boldsymbol{\xi})$, and 0 otherwise. Averaging this error measure over Ω gives the probability of a misclassification for randomly drawn questions $\boldsymbol{\xi} \in \Omega$:

$$E(\boldsymbol{J}(t)) = \langle \theta(-[\boldsymbol{B}\cdot\boldsymbol{\xi}][\boldsymbol{J}(t)\cdot\boldsymbol{\xi}])\rangle_\Omega = \langle \theta(-xy)\rangle$$
$$= \int_0^\infty\int_0^\infty \mathrm{d}x\mathrm{d}y[P(x,-y) + P(-x,y)]$$

The integral, with the distribution $P(x,y)$ as given in (17.15), can be done analytically (see Appendix D) and produces the simple expression

$$E = \frac{1}{\pi}\arccos\left(\frac{R}{\sqrt{Q}}\right) \tag{17.16}$$

This result, which had also been encountered and used in Section 2.5, has a transparent geometric interpretation as illustrated in Figure 17.3. Input patterns $\boldsymbol{\xi}$ are classified by student and teacher according to whether they fall on one or the other side of the $(N-1)$-dimensional hyperplanes $\boldsymbol{J}\cdot\boldsymbol{\xi} = 0$ and $\boldsymbol{B}\cdot\boldsymbol{\xi} = 0$, respectively. If $\vartheta = \arccos(R/\sqrt{Q})$ denotes the angle between $\boldsymbol{J}$ and $\boldsymbol{B}$, the fraction of input space on which student and teacher disagree about the classification is then just $E = \vartheta/\pi$. This assumes that the projections of the $\boldsymbol{\xi}$ onto the plane spanned by $\boldsymbol{J}$ and $\boldsymbol{B}$ are isotropically distributed. If we exclude pathological cases such as those from

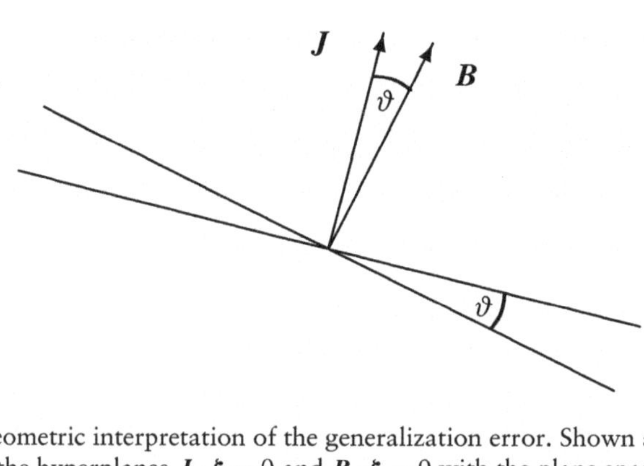

Figure 17.3 Geometric interpretation of the generalization error. Shown are the intersections of the hyperplanes $\boldsymbol{J}\cdot\boldsymbol{\xi} = 0$ and $\boldsymbol{B}\cdot\boldsymbol{\xi} = 0$ with the plane spanned by $\boldsymbol{J}$ and $\boldsymbol{B}$. If ϑ denotes the angle between $\boldsymbol{J}$ and $\boldsymbol{B}$, and if the input data are distributed isotropically, the fraction of input space on which student and teacher disagree about the classification is expected to be given by $E = \vartheta/\pi$.

footnote 36, this is indeed true: the distribution of the projection is isotropic and Gaussian.

It is clear from the above that, like R and Q, the generalization error evolves deterministically for $N \to \infty$. We have thus achieved our goal: we have derived a closed set of deterministic equations for a small number (two) of macroscopic observables, valid for $N \to \infty$, and these observables determine the generalization error at any time.

Since the operation performed by the student does not depend on the length $|\boldsymbol{J}|$ of its weight vector, and since both R and Q involve $|\boldsymbol{J}|$, we will often find it convenient later to switch from R and Q to another equivalent pair of observables:

$$J = |\boldsymbol{J}| = \sqrt{Q} \qquad \omega = \boldsymbol{B} \cdot \hat{\boldsymbol{J}} = R/\sqrt{Q} \tag{17.17}$$

Using the simple relations $(\mathrm{d}/\mathrm{d}t)Q = 2J(\mathrm{d}/\mathrm{d}t)J$ and $(\mathrm{d}/\mathrm{d}t)R = J(\mathrm{d}/\mathrm{d}t)\omega + \omega(\mathrm{d}/\mathrm{d}t)J$ we then find the compact expressions

$$\frac{\mathrm{d}}{\mathrm{d}t}J = \eta\langle x\mathcal{F}[J; Jx, y]\rangle + \frac{\eta^2}{2J}\langle \mathcal{F}^2[J; Jx, y]\rangle \tag{17.18}$$

$$\frac{\mathrm{d}}{\mathrm{d}t}\omega = \frac{\eta}{J}\langle (y - \omega x)\mathcal{F}[J; Jx, y]\rangle - \frac{\omega\eta^2}{2J^2}\langle \mathcal{F}^2[J; Jx, y]\rangle \tag{17.19}$$

The local field distribution reads

$$P(x, y) = \frac{\mathrm{e}^{-(x^2+y^2-2\omega xy)/2(1-\omega^2)}}{2\pi\sqrt{1-\omega^2}} \tag{17.20}$$

and the generalization error becomes

$$E = \frac{1}{\pi}\arccos(\omega) \tag{17.21}$$

We will sometimes use this last relation to convert the macrosopic evolution equations (17.18, 17.19) to yet another set of equivalent observables, namely, J and E.

Hebbian learning with constant learning rate

We will now work out our general result (17.18–17.20) for specific members of the general class (17.6) of online learning rules. The simplest non-trivial choice is the Hebbian rule, obtained for $\mathcal{F}[J; Jx, y] = \mathrm{sgn}(y)$, with a constant learning rate η:

$$\boldsymbol{J}(t + \Delta t) = \boldsymbol{J}(t) + \frac{\eta}{N}\boldsymbol{\xi}(t)\mathrm{sgn}(\boldsymbol{B} \cdot \boldsymbol{\xi}(t)) \tag{17.22}$$

Equations (17.18) and (17.19), describing the macroscopic dynamics generated by (17.22) in the limit $N \to \infty$, now become

$$\frac{\mathrm{d}}{\mathrm{d}t}J = \eta\langle x\,\mathrm{sgn}(y)\rangle + \frac{\eta^2}{2J} \qquad \frac{\mathrm{d}}{\mathrm{d}t}\omega = \frac{\eta}{J}\langle |y| - \omega x\,\mathrm{sgn}(y)\rangle - \frac{\omega\eta^2}{2J^2}$$

The integrals in these equations can be calculated analytically (see Appendix D) and we get

$$\frac{\mathrm{d}}{\mathrm{d}t}J = \omega\eta\sqrt{\frac{2}{\pi}} + \frac{\eta^2}{2J} \qquad \frac{\mathrm{d}}{\mathrm{d}t}\omega = (1-\omega^2)\frac{\eta}{J}\sqrt{\frac{2}{\pi}} - \frac{\omega\eta^2}{2J^2}$$

Thus, after eliminating the observable ω in favour of E using equation (17.21), we arrive at the following closed differential equations in terms of J and E:

$$\frac{\mathrm{d}}{\mathrm{d}t}J = \eta\cos(\pi E)\sqrt{\frac{2}{\pi}} + \frac{\eta^2}{2J} \tag{17.23}$$

$$\frac{\mathrm{d}}{\mathrm{d}t}E = -\frac{\eta\sin(\pi E)}{\pi J}\sqrt{\frac{2}{\pi}} + \frac{\eta^2}{2\pi J^2\tan(\pi E)} \tag{17.24}$$

The flow in the (E, J) plane described by these equations is drawn in Figure 17.4, which is obtained by numerical solution of (17.23, 17.24). From (17.23) we also have that $\mathrm{d}J/\mathrm{d}t > 0\ \forall t \geq 0$. From (17.24) it follows that $\mathrm{d}E/\mathrm{d}t = 0$ along the line

$$J_c(E) = \frac{\eta\cos(\pi E)}{2\sin^2(\pi E)}\sqrt{\frac{\pi}{2}}$$

which is drawn as a dashed line in Figure 17.4. Clearly, although $\lim_{t\to\infty} E = 0$, the evolution of the error E can be non-monotonic, allowing for an initial increase in E if the initial length J of the student's weight vector is small.

Let us now investigate the temporal properties of the solution (17.23, 17.24) in more detail, and work out the prediction for the asymptotic decay of the generalization error. For small values of E equations (17.23, 17.24) yield

$$\frac{\mathrm{d}}{\mathrm{d}t}J = \eta\sqrt{\frac{2}{\pi}} + \frac{\eta^2}{2J} + \mathcal{O}(E^2) \tag{17.25}$$

$$\frac{\mathrm{d}}{\mathrm{d}t}E = -\frac{\eta E}{J}\sqrt{\frac{2}{\pi}} + \frac{\eta^2}{2\pi^2 J^2 E} + \mathcal{O}\left(\frac{E^3}{J}, \frac{E}{J^2}\right) \tag{17.26}$$

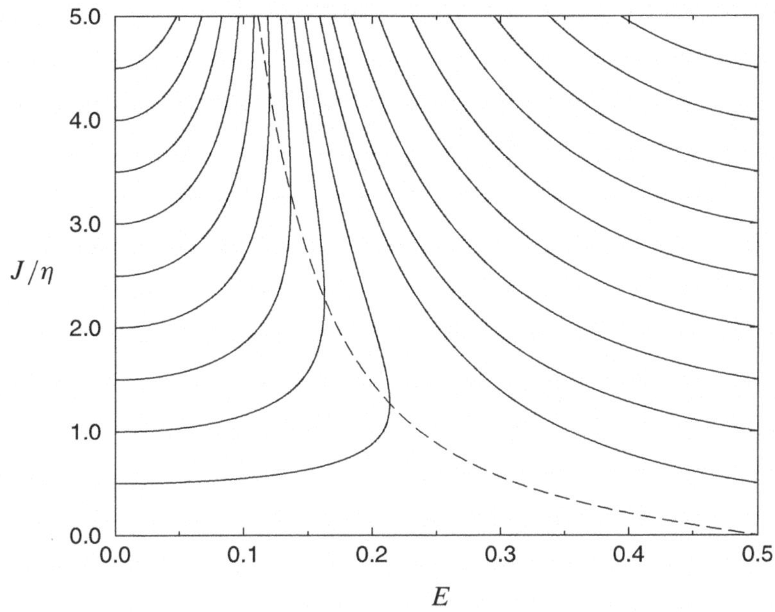

Figure 17.4 Flow in the (E, J) plane generated by the Hebbian learning rule with constant learning rate η, in the limit $N \to \infty$. Dashed: the line where $\mathrm{d}E/\mathrm{d}t = 0$ (note that $\mathrm{d}J/\mathrm{d}t > 0$ for any (E, J)). The flow is asymptotically seen to give $E \to 0$ and $J \to \infty$, for all initial conditions.

From (17.25) we infer that $J \sim \eta t\sqrt{2/\pi}$ for $t \to \infty$. Substitution of this asymptotic solution into equation (17.26) subsequently gives

$$\frac{\mathrm{d}}{\mathrm{d}t}E = -\frac{E}{t} + \frac{1}{4\pi E t^2} + \mathcal{O}\left(\frac{E^3}{t}, \frac{E}{t^2}\right) \quad (t \to \infty) \tag{17.27}$$

We insert the ansatz $E = At^{-\alpha}$ into equation (17.27) and obtain the solution $A = 1/\sqrt{2\pi}$, $\alpha = 1/2$. This implies that, in the limit $N \to \infty$, online Hebbian learning with complete training sets produces an asymptotic decay of the generalization error of the form

$$E \sim \frac{1}{\sqrt{2\pi t}} \quad (t \to \infty) \tag{17.28}$$

Figures 17.7, 17.8, and 17.9 below show the theoretical results of this section together with the results of doing numerical simulations of the learning rule (17.22) and with similar results for other online learning rules with constant learning rates. The agreement between theory and simulations is quite convincing.

Perceptron learning with constant learning rate

Our second application of the closed trio of macroscopic laws (17.18–17.20) is obtained upon making the choice $\mathcal{F}[J; Jx, y] = \theta(-xy)\text{sgn}(y)$ in equation (17.6), with constant learning rate η, which produces the perceptron learning algorithm:

$$\boldsymbol{J}(t+\Delta t) = \boldsymbol{J}(t) + \frac{\eta}{N}\boldsymbol{\xi}(t)\theta(-[\boldsymbol{B}\cdot\boldsymbol{\xi}(t)][\boldsymbol{J}(t)\cdot\boldsymbol{\xi}(t)])\text{sgn}(\boldsymbol{B}\cdot\boldsymbol{\xi}(t)) \quad (17.29)$$

In other words: the student weights are updated in accordance with the Hebbian rule only when $\text{sgn}(\boldsymbol{B}\cdot\boldsymbol{\xi}) = -\text{sgn}(\boldsymbol{J}\cdot\boldsymbol{\xi})$, that is, when student and teacher are not in agreement about the output. Equations (17.18, 17.19) now become

$$\frac{\mathrm{d}}{\mathrm{d}t}J = \eta\langle x\text{sgn}(y)\theta(-xy)\rangle + \frac{\eta^2}{2J}\langle\theta(-xy)\rangle$$
$$\frac{\mathrm{d}}{\mathrm{d}t}\omega = \frac{\eta}{J}\langle[|y| - \omega x\text{sgn}(y)]\theta(-xy)\rangle - \frac{\omega\eta^2}{2J^2}\langle\theta(-xy)\rangle$$

with the averages being over $P(x, y)$ as given by (17.20). As before, the various Gaussian integrals occurring in these expressions can be done analytically (see Appendix D), which results in

$$\frac{\mathrm{d}}{\mathrm{d}t}J = -\frac{\eta(1-\omega)}{\sqrt{2\pi}} + \frac{\eta^2}{2\pi J}\arccos(\omega)$$
$$\frac{\mathrm{d}}{\mathrm{d}t}\omega = \frac{\eta(1-\omega^2)}{\sqrt{2\pi}\,J} - \frac{\omega\eta^2}{2\pi J^2}\arccos(\omega) \quad (17.30)$$

Elimination of ω using (17.21) then gives us the equivalent dynamical equations in terms of the pair (J, E):

$$\frac{\mathrm{d}}{\mathrm{d}t}J = -\frac{\eta(1-\cos(\pi E))}{\sqrt{2\pi}} + \frac{\eta^2 E}{2J} \quad (17.31)$$

$$\frac{\mathrm{d}}{\mathrm{d}t}E = -\frac{\eta\sin(\pi E)}{\pi\sqrt{2\pi}\,J} + \frac{\eta^2 E}{2\pi J^2\tan(\pi E)} \quad (17.32)$$

Figure 17.5 shows the flow in the (E, J) plane, obtained by numerical solution of (17.31, 17.32). The two lines where $\mathrm{d}J/\mathrm{d}t = 0$ and where $\mathrm{d}E/\mathrm{d}t = 0$ are found to be $J_{c,1}(E)$ and $J_{c,2}(E)$, respectively:

$$J_{c,1}(E) = \eta\sqrt{\frac{\pi}{2}}\frac{E}{1-\cos(\pi E)}, \qquad J_{c,2}(E) = \eta\sqrt{\frac{\pi}{2}}\frac{E\cos(\pi E)}{1-\cos^2(\pi E)}$$

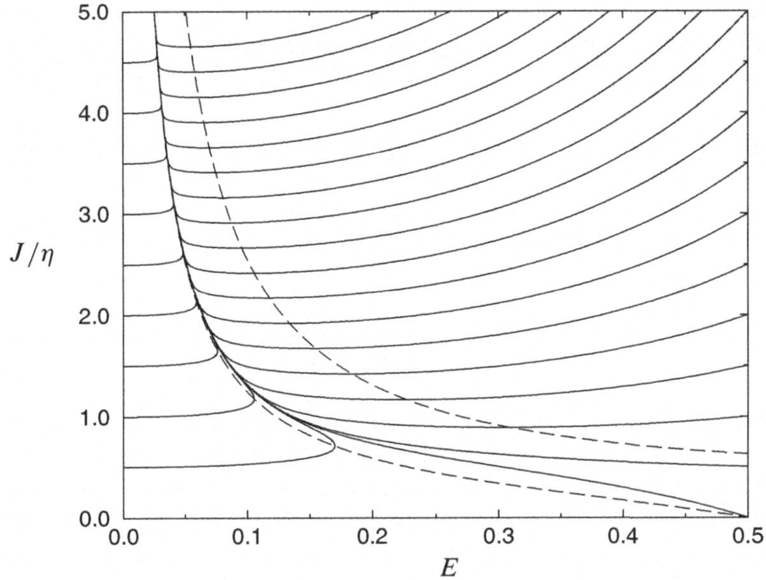

Figure 17.5 Flow in the (E, J) plane generated by the perceptron learning rule with constant learning rate η, in the limit $N \to \infty$. Dashed: the two lines where $\mathrm{d}J/\mathrm{d}t = 0$ (top) and $\mathrm{d}E/\mathrm{d}t = 0$ (bottom), respectively. Note that the flow is attracted into the gully between these two dashed lines, and asymptotically gives $E \to 0$ and $J \to \infty$.

For $E \in [0, 1/2]$ one always has $J_{c,1}(E) \geq J_{c,2}(E)$, with equality only if $(J, E) = (\infty, 0)$. Figure 17.5 shows that the flow is drawn into the gully between the curves $J_{c,1}(E)$ and $J_{c,2}(E)$.

As with the Hebbian rule we now wish to investigate the asymptotic behaviour of the generalization error. To do this we expand equations (17.31, 17.32) for small E:

$$\frac{\mathrm{d}}{\mathrm{d}t}J = -\frac{\eta\pi^2 E^2}{2\sqrt{2\pi}} + \frac{\eta^2 E}{2J} + \mathcal{O}(E^4)$$

$$\frac{\mathrm{d}}{\mathrm{d}t}E = -\frac{\eta E}{\sqrt{2\pi}\,J} + \frac{\eta^2}{2\pi^2 J^2} - \frac{\eta^2 E^2}{6J^2} + \mathcal{O}(E^3)$$

For small E and large t we know that $J \sim J_{c,1}(E) \sim 1/E$. Making the ansatz $J = A/E$, and hence $\mathrm{d}E/\mathrm{d}t = -(E^2/A)(\mathrm{d}J/\mathrm{d}t)$, now leads to a situation where we have two equivalent differential equations for E:

$$\frac{\mathrm{d}}{\mathrm{d}t}E = \frac{\eta\pi^2 E^4}{2\sqrt{2\pi}\,A} - \frac{\eta^2 E^4}{2A^2} + \mathcal{O}(E^6)$$

$$\frac{\mathrm{d}}{\mathrm{d}t}E = -\frac{\eta E^2}{\sqrt{2\pi}\,A} + \frac{\eta^2 E^2}{2\pi^2 A^2} + \mathcal{O}(E^4)$$

Since both must describe the same dynamics, the leading term of the second expression should be identical to that of the first, that is, $\mathcal{O}(E^4)$, giving us the condition $A = \eta\sqrt{2\pi}/2\pi^2$. Substitution of this condition into the first expression for $\mathrm{d}E/\mathrm{d}t$ then leads us to

$$\frac{\mathrm{d}}{\mathrm{d}t}E = -\frac{1}{2}\pi^3 E^4 + \mathcal{O}(E^5) \quad (t \to \infty)$$

which has the solution

$$E \sim \left(\frac{2}{3}\right)^{1/3} \pi^{-1} t^{-1/3} \quad (t \to \infty) \tag{17.33}$$

We find, somewhat surprisingly, that in large systems ($N \to \infty$) the online perceptron learning rule is asymptotically much slower in converging towards the desired $E = 0$ state than the simpler online Hebbian rule. This will be different, however, if we allow for time-dependent learning rates. Figures 17.7–17.9 below show the theoretical results on the perceptron rule together with the results of numerical simulations and together with similar results for other online learning rules. Again the agreement between theory and experiment is quite satisfactory.

AdaTron learning with constant learning rate

As our third application we analyse the macroscopic dynamics of the so-called AdaTron learning rule, corresponding to the choice $\mathcal{F}[J; Jx, y] = |Jx|\theta(-xy)\mathrm{sgn}(y)$ in the general recipe (17.6). As in the perceptron rule, modifications are made only when student and teacher are in disagreement; here, however, the modification made is proportional to the magnitude of the student's local field. Students are punished in proportion to their confidence in the wrong answer. The rationale is that wrong student answers $S(\boldsymbol{\xi}) = \mathrm{sgn}(\boldsymbol{J} \cdot \boldsymbol{\xi})$ with large values of $|\boldsymbol{J} \cdot \boldsymbol{\xi}|$ require more rigorous corrections to $\boldsymbol{J}$ than those with small values of $|\boldsymbol{J} \cdot \boldsymbol{\xi}|$. The learning rule thus reads

$$\boldsymbol{J}(t + \Delta t) = \boldsymbol{J}(t) + \frac{\eta}{N}\boldsymbol{\xi}(t)|\boldsymbol{J}(t) \cdot \boldsymbol{\xi}(t)|\theta(-[\boldsymbol{B} \cdot \boldsymbol{\xi}(t)][\boldsymbol{J}(t) \cdot \boldsymbol{\xi}(t)])\mathrm{sgn}(\boldsymbol{B} \cdot \boldsymbol{\xi}(t)) \tag{17.34}$$

Working out the general equations (17.18, 17.19) for this case gives

$$\frac{\mathrm{d}}{\mathrm{d}t}J = \eta J\langle x|x|\,\mathrm{sgn}(y)\theta(-xy)\rangle + \frac{1}{2}\eta^2 J\langle x^2\theta(-xy)\rangle$$

$$\frac{\mathrm{d}}{\mathrm{d}t}\omega = \eta\langle |xy|\theta(-xy)\rangle - \eta\omega\langle x|x|\,\mathrm{sgn}(y)\theta(-xy)\rangle - \frac{1}{2}\omega\eta^2\langle x^2\theta(-xy)\rangle$$

All averages over $P(x, y)$ can once more be done analytically (see Appendix D), giving the explicit macroscopic flow equations:

$$\frac{\mathrm{d}}{\mathrm{d}t}J = \frac{J}{\omega}\left(\eta - \frac{\eta^2}{2}\right)I_2(\omega) \qquad \frac{\mathrm{d}}{\mathrm{d}t}\omega = \eta I_1(\omega) - \left(\eta - \frac{\eta^2}{2}\right)I_2(\omega)$$

with the two shorthands

$$I_1(\omega) = \frac{(1-\omega^2)^{3/2}}{\pi} - \frac{\omega(1-\omega^2)}{\pi}\arccos(\omega) + \frac{\omega^2\sqrt{1-\omega^2}}{\pi} - \frac{\omega^3}{\pi}\arccos(\omega)$$

$$I_2(\omega) = -\frac{\omega(1-\omega^2)}{\pi}\arccos(\omega) + \frac{\omega^2\sqrt{1-\omega^2}}{\pi} - \frac{\omega^3}{\pi}\arccos(\omega)$$

The usual translation from equations for the pair (J, ω) into equivalent equations in terms of the pair (J, E), following (17.21), turns out to simplify matters considerably, giving

$$\frac{\mathrm{d}}{\mathrm{d}t}J = J\left(\frac{\eta^2}{2} - \eta\right)\left[E - \frac{\cos(\pi E)\sin(\pi E)}{\pi}\right] \tag{17.35}$$

$$\frac{\mathrm{d}}{\mathrm{d}t}E = -\frac{\eta\sin^2(\pi E)}{\pi^2} + \frac{\eta^2 E}{2\pi\tan(\pi E)} - \frac{\eta^2\cos^2(\pi E)}{2\pi^2} \tag{17.36}$$

The flow described by the equations (17.35, 17.36) is shown in Figure 17.6, for the case $\eta = 1$. In contrast with the online Hebbian and the perceptron learning rules, we here observe from the equations (17.35, 17.36) that the learning rate η cannot be eliminated from the macroscopic laws by a re-scaling of the weight vector length J. Moreover, the state $E = 0$ is stable only for $\eta < 3$, in which case $\mathrm{d}E/\mathrm{d}t < 0$ for all t. For $\eta < 2$ one has $\mathrm{d}J/\mathrm{d}t < 0$ for all t, for $\eta = 2$ one has $J(t) = J(0)$ for all t, and for $2 < \eta < 3$ we have $\mathrm{d}J/\mathrm{d}t > 0$ for all t.

For small values of the error E equation (17.36) reduces to

$$\frac{\mathrm{d}}{\mathrm{d}t}E = \left(\frac{\eta^2}{3} - \eta\right)E^2 + \mathcal{O}(E^4)$$

giving

$$E \sim \frac{3t^{-1}}{\eta(3-\eta)} \qquad (t \to \infty) \tag{17.37}$$

For $\eta = 1$, which gives the standard representation of the AdaTron algorithm, we find $E \sim \frac{3}{2}t^{-1}$. Note from equation (17.35) that for the

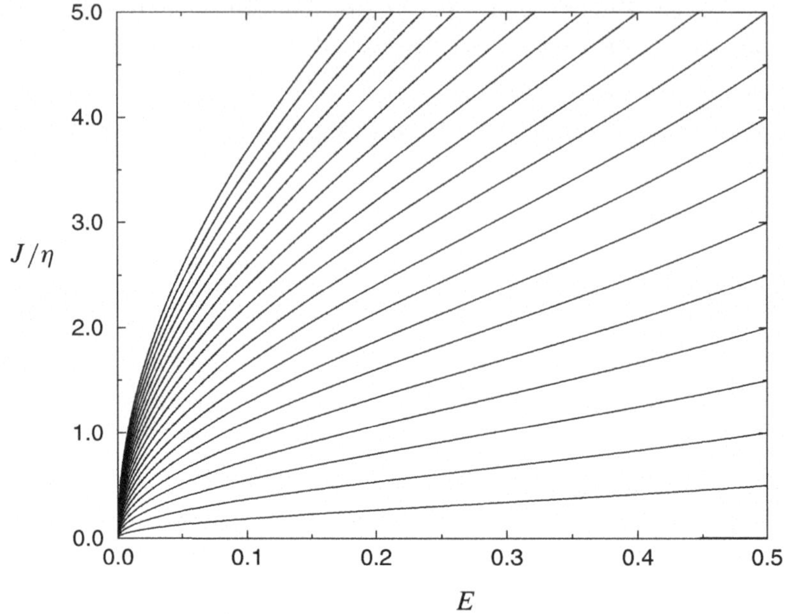

Figure 17.6 Flow in the (E, J) plane generated by the AdaTron learning rule with constant learning rate $\eta = 1$, in the limit $N \to \infty$. Here it is impossible to have $\mathrm{d}E/\mathrm{d}t = 0$ or $\mathrm{d}J/\mathrm{d}t = 0$.

AdaTron rule there is a special value for η which normalizes the length J of the student's weight vector at all times, being $\eta = 2$, which again gives $E \sim \frac{3}{2}t^{-1}$. The optimal value for η, however, is $\eta = \frac{3}{2}$ in which case we find $E \sim \frac{4}{3}t^{-1}$ (see (17.37)).

Theory versus simulations

We close this section by comparing the dynamics described by the various macroscopic flow equations with measurements of the error E during numerical simulations of the various (microscopic) stochastic learning rules discussed so far. This will serve to support the analysis and its implicit and explicit assumptions, but also to illustrate how the three learning rules compare to each other. Figures 17.7 and 17.8 show the initial stage of the learning processes, for initializations corresponding to random guessing ($E = 0.5$) and almost correct classification (E small), respectively. Note that for the perceptron and AdaTron rules, starting at precisely $E = 0$ produces a stationary state in finite systems. The solutions of the flow equations (solid lines) were obtained by numerical iteration. The initial increase in the error E following initialization with small values, as observed for the Hebbian and perceptron rule, can be understood as follows. The error depends only on the orientation of the weight vector $\boldsymbol{J}$, not on its length J. This means that the modifications generated by the Hebbian and perceptron learning

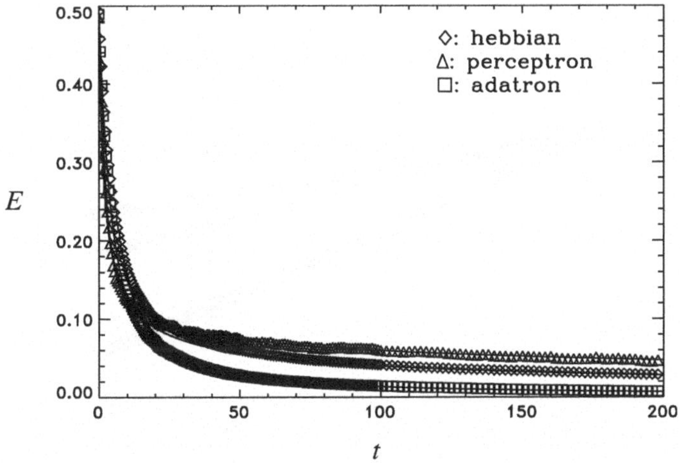

Figure 17.7 Evolution in time of the generalization error E as measured during numerical simulations, with $N = 1000$ neurons, of three different online learning rules: Hebbian (diamonds), perceptron (triangles), and AdaTron (squares). Initial state: $E(0) = \frac{1}{2}$ (random guessing) and $J(0) = 1$. Learning rate: $\eta = 1$. The solid lines give for each learning rule the prediction of the $N = \infty$ theory, obtained by numerical solution of the flow equations for (E, J).

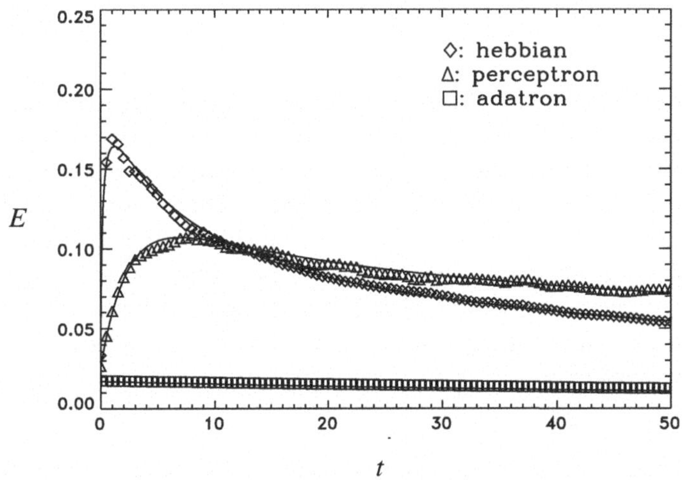

Figure 17.8 Evolution in time of the generalization error E as measured during numerical simulations, with $N = 1000$ neurons, of three different online learning rules: Hebbian (diamonds), perceptron (triangles), and AdaTron (squares). Initial state: $E(0) \approx 0.025$ and $J(0) = 1$. Learning rate: $\eta = 1$. The solid lines give for each learning rule the prediction of the $N = \infty$ theory, obtained by numerical solution of the flow equations for (E, J).

rules, which in those particular recipes are of uniform magnitude, generate large changes in E when J is small, but small changes in E when J is large, with corresponding effects on the stability of low E states. The AdaTron rule, in contrast, involves weight changes which scale with the length J,

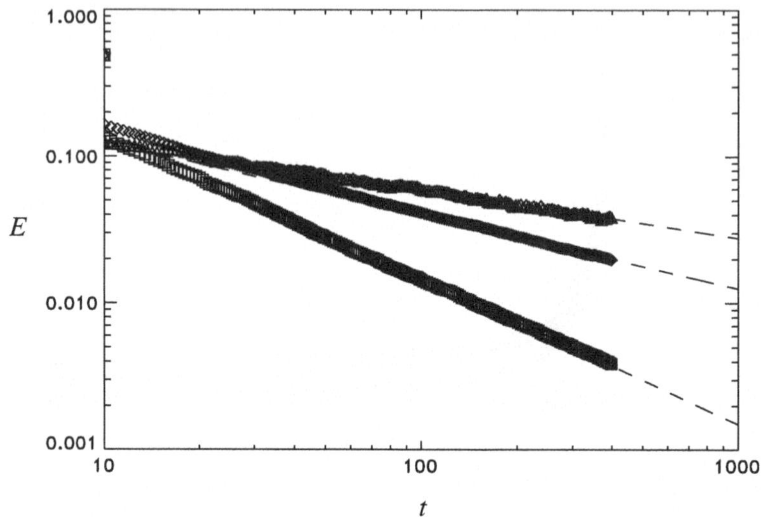

Figure 17.9 Asymptotic behaviour of the generalization error E measured during numerical simulations, with $N = 1000$, of three different online learning rules: Hebbian (diamonds, middle curve), perceptron (triangles, upper curve), and AdaTron (squares, lower curve). Initial state: $E(0) = \frac{1}{2}$ and $J(0) = 1$. Learning rate: $\eta = 1$. The dashed lines give for each learning rule the corresponding power law predicted by the $N = \infty$ theory (equations (17.28, 17.33, 17.37), respectively).

so that the stability of the $E = 0$ state does not depend on the value of J. Figure 17.9 shows the asymptotic relaxation of the error E, in a log–log plot, together with the three corresponding asymptotic power law predictions (17.28, 17.33, 17.37). All simulations were carried out with networks of $N = 1000$ neurons; we see that this is already sufficiently large for the $N = \infty$ theory to apply. The teacher weight vectors $\boldsymbol{B}$ were in all cases drawn at random from $[-1, 1]^N$ and then normalized to unit length. We conclude that the statistical mechanical theory describes the simulations essentially perfectly.

17.3 Optimized learning rules

We now set out to use our macroscopic equations in 'reverse mode'. Rather than calculate the macroscopic dynamics for a given choice of learning rule, we will try to find learning rules that optimize the macroscopic dynamical laws, in the sense that they produce the fastest decay towards the desired $E = 0$ state. As a bonus it will turn out that in many cases we can even solve the corresponding macroscopic differential equations analytically, and find explicit expressions for error $E(t)$, or rather its inverse $t(E)$.

Time-dependent learning rates

First we illustrate how modifying existing learning rules in a simple way, by just allowing for suitably chosen time-dependent learning rates $\eta(t)$, can already lead to a drastic improvement in the asymptotic behaviour of the error E. We will consider two specific choices of time-dependent learning rates for the perceptron rule. Without loss of generality we can always put $\eta(t) = K(t)J(t)$ in our dynamic equations (for notational convenience we will drop the explicit time argument of K). This choice will enable us to decouple the dynamics of J from that of the generalization error E. For the perceptron rule we then find equation (17.32) being replaced by

$$\frac{\mathrm{d}}{\mathrm{d}t}E = -\frac{K\sin(\pi E)}{\pi\sqrt{2\pi}} + \frac{K^2 E}{2\pi\tan(\pi E)}$$

which gives for small E

$$\frac{\mathrm{d}}{\mathrm{d}t}E = -\frac{KE}{\sqrt{2\pi}} + \frac{K^2}{2\pi^2} + \mathcal{O}(K^2E^2)$$

In order to obtain $E \to 0$ for $t \to \infty$ it is clear that we need to choose our time-dependent learning rate such that $K \to 0$. Applying the ansätze $E = A/t^\alpha$ and $K = B/t^\beta$ for the asymptotic forms in the previous equation produces

$$-\alpha A t^{-\alpha-1} = \frac{-ABt^{-\alpha-\beta}}{\sqrt{2\pi}} + \frac{B^2 t^{-2\beta}}{2\pi^2} + \mathcal{O}(t^{-2\alpha-2\beta})$$

and so $\alpha = \beta = 1$ and $A = B^2/[\pi\sqrt{2\pi}(B - \sqrt{2\pi})]$. Our aim is to obtain the fastest approach to the $E = 0$ state, so we wish to maximize α (for which we found $\alpha = 1$) and subsequently minimize A. The value of B for which A is minimized is $B = 2\sqrt{2\pi}$, in which case we obtain the error decay given by

$$\eta \sim \frac{2J\sqrt{2\pi}}{t}: \qquad E \sim \frac{4}{\pi t} \quad (t \to \infty) \tag{17.38}$$

This is clearly a great improvement over the result for the perceptron rule with constant η, that is, equation (17.33); in fact it is the fastest error relaxation we have derived so far.

Let us now move on to an alternative choice for the time-dependent learning rate for the perceptron. According to equation (17.31), there is one specific recipe for $\eta(t)$ such that the length J of the student's weight vector will remain constant, given by

$$\eta = \sqrt{\frac{2}{\pi}}\frac{J}{E}(1 - \cos(\pi E)) \tag{17.39}$$

Making this choice converts equation (17.32) for the evolution of E into

$$\frac{\mathrm{d}}{\mathrm{d}t}E = -\frac{(1 - \cos(\pi E))^2}{\pi^2 E \sin(\pi E)} \tag{17.40}$$

Equation (17.40) can be written in the form $\mathrm{d}t/\mathrm{d}E = g(E)$, so that $t(E)$ becomes a simple integral which can be done analytically, with the result

$$t(E) = \frac{\pi E + \sin(\pi E)}{1 - \cos(\pi E)} - \frac{\pi E_0 + \sin(\pi E_0)}{1 - \cos(\pi E_0)} \tag{17.41}$$

This can also be verified directly by substitution into (17.40). Expansion of (17.41) and (17.39) for small E then gives the asymptotic behaviour also encountered in (17.38):

$$\eta \sim \frac{2J\sqrt{2\pi}}{t}: \qquad E \sim \frac{4}{\pi t} \quad (t \to \infty) \tag{17.42}$$

It might appear that implementation of the recipe (17.39) is in practice impossible, since it involves information which is not available to the student perceptron, namely the instantaneous error E. However, since we know (17.41) we can simply calculate the required $\eta(t)$ explicitly as a function of time.

One has to be somewhat careful in extrapolating results such as those obtained in this section. For instance, choosing the time-dependent learning rate (17.39) enforces the constraint $\boldsymbol{J}^2(t) = 1$ in the macroscopic equations for $N \to \infty$. This is not identical to choosing $\eta(t)$ in the original equation (17.6) such as to enforce $\boldsymbol{J}^2(t + \Delta t) = \boldsymbol{J}^2(t)$ at the level of individual iteration steps, as can be seen by working out the dynamical laws. The latter case would correspond to the *microscopically fluctuating* choice

$$\eta(t) = -2\frac{\boldsymbol{J}(t)\cdot\boldsymbol{\xi}(t)}{\mathcal{F}[|\boldsymbol{J}(t)|; \boldsymbol{J}(t)\cdot\boldsymbol{\xi}(t), \boldsymbol{B}\cdot\boldsymbol{\xi}(t)]} \quad \text{if } \mathcal{F}[|\boldsymbol{J}(t)|; \boldsymbol{J}(t)\cdot\boldsymbol{\xi}(t), \boldsymbol{B}\cdot\boldsymbol{\xi}(t)] \neq 0$$

If we now choose, for example, $\mathcal{F}[J; Jx, y] = \theta(-xy)\mathrm{sgn}(y)$, implying $\eta(t) = 2|\boldsymbol{J}(t)\cdot\boldsymbol{\xi}(t)|$, we find by insertion into (17.6) that the perceptron rule with 'hard' weight normalization at each iteration step via adaptation of the learning rate is identical to the AdaTron rule with constant learning rate $\eta = 2$. We know therefore that in this case one obtains $E \sim 3/2t$, whereas for the perceptron rule with 'soft' weight normalization via (17.39) (see the analysis above) one obtains $E \sim 4/\pi t$. This shows that the two procedures certainly are not equivalent.

Spherical online learning rules

We arrive in a natural way at the question of how to find the optimal time-dependent learning rate for any given learning rule, or more generally, of how to find the optimal learning rule. This involves variational calculations in two-dimensional flows because our macroscopic equations are defined in terms of the evolving pair (J, E). Such calculations would be much simpler if our macroscopic equations were just one-dimensional, for example, describing only the evolution of the error E with a stationary or simply irrelevant value of the length J. Often it will turn out that for finding the optimal learning rate or the optimal learning rule the problem can indeed be reduced to a one-dimensional one. To be able to obtain results also for those cases where this reduction does not happen we will now construct so-called spherical learning rules, where $\boldsymbol{J}^2(t) = 1$ for all t. This can be arranged in several ways.

Our first method will be to add to the general rule (17.6) a term proportional to the instantaneous weight vector $\boldsymbol{J}$, whose sole purpose is to achieve the normalization constraint $\boldsymbol{J}^2 = 1$:

$$\boldsymbol{J}(t+\Delta t) = \boldsymbol{J}(t) + \frac{1}{N}\{\eta(t)\boldsymbol{\xi}(t)\mathcal{F}[|\boldsymbol{J}(t)|; \boldsymbol{J}(t)\cdot\boldsymbol{\xi}(t), \boldsymbol{B}\cdot\boldsymbol{\xi}(t)] - \lambda(t)\boldsymbol{J}(t)\} \tag{17.43}$$

The evolution of the two observables $Q(\boldsymbol{J})$ and $R(\boldsymbol{J})$ (17.7) is now given by

$$\begin{aligned}\frac{Q(t+\Delta t) - Q(t)}{\Delta t} &= -2\lambda(t)Q(t) + 2\eta(t)\boldsymbol{J}(t)\cdot\boldsymbol{\xi}(t)\\ &\quad \times \mathcal{F}[|\boldsymbol{J}(t)|; \boldsymbol{J}(t)\cdot\boldsymbol{\xi}(t), \boldsymbol{B}\cdot\boldsymbol{\xi}(t)] + \eta^2(t)\mathcal{F}^2[\cdots]\\ &\quad + \mathcal{O}(N^{-1})\\ \frac{R(t+\Delta t) - R(t)}{\Delta t} &= -\lambda(t)R(t) + \eta(t)\boldsymbol{B}\cdot\boldsymbol{\xi}(t)\mathcal{F}[\cdots]\end{aligned}$$

with $\Delta t = N^{-1}$, as before. Following the procedure of Section 17.2 to arrive at the $N \to \infty$ limit of the dynamical equations for Q and R then leads us to

$$\begin{aligned}\frac{\mathrm{d}}{\mathrm{d}t}Q &= 2\eta Q^{1/2}\langle x\mathcal{F}[Q^{1/2}; Q^{1/2}x, y]\rangle + \eta^2\langle\mathcal{F}^2[Q^{1/2}; Q^{1/2}x, y]\rangle - 2\lambda Q\\ \frac{\mathrm{d}}{\mathrm{d}t}R &= \eta\langle y\mathcal{F}[Q^{1/2}; Q^{1/2}x, y]\rangle - \lambda R\end{aligned}$$

where we have dropped the explicit time arguments as usual. We now choose the newly introduced function $\lambda(t)$ such that $Q(t) = 1$ for all $t \geq 0$. This ensures that $R(t) = \omega(t) = \hat{\boldsymbol{J}}(t) \cdot \boldsymbol{B}$ and gives, via $\mathrm{d}Q/\mathrm{d}t = 0$, an explicit recipe for $\lambda(t)$:

$$\lambda = \eta\langle x\mathcal{F}[1;x,y]\rangle + \tfrac{1}{2}\eta^2\langle \mathcal{F}^2[1;x,y]\rangle$$

This can be substituted into the equation for $\mathrm{d}\omega/\mathrm{d}t = \mathrm{d}(R/\sqrt{Q})/\mathrm{d}t$, which follows from the above expressions for $\mathrm{d}R/\mathrm{d}t$ and $\mathrm{d}Q/\mathrm{d}t$, to give

$$\frac{\mathrm{d}}{\mathrm{d}t}\omega = \eta\left\langle (y - \omega x)\mathcal{F}[1;x,y] - \frac{1}{2}\omega\eta^2\mathcal{F}^2[1;x,y]\right\rangle \tag{17.44}$$

The averages are, as usual, defined with respect to the Gaussian joint field distribution (17.20). The latter depends only on ω, so that equation (17.44) is indeed autonomous.

A second method to arrange the constraint $\boldsymbol{J}^2 = 1$ is to explicitly normalize the weight vector $\boldsymbol{J} = \hat{\boldsymbol{J}}$ after each modification step, that is,

$$\begin{aligned}\hat{\boldsymbol{J}}(t+\Delta t) &= \frac{\hat{\boldsymbol{J}}(t) + (1/N)\eta(t)\boldsymbol{\xi}(t)\mathcal{F}[1;\hat{\boldsymbol{J}}(t)\cdot\boldsymbol{\xi}(t),\boldsymbol{B}\cdot\boldsymbol{\xi}(t)]}{|\hat{\boldsymbol{J}}(t) + (1/N)\eta(t)\boldsymbol{\xi}(t)\mathcal{F}[1;\hat{\boldsymbol{J}}(t)\cdot\boldsymbol{\xi}(t),\boldsymbol{B}\cdot\boldsymbol{\xi}(t)]|}\\ &= \hat{\boldsymbol{J}}(t) + \frac{1}{N}\eta(t)[\boldsymbol{\xi}(t) - \hat{\boldsymbol{J}}(t)(\hat{\boldsymbol{J}}(t)\cdot\boldsymbol{\xi}(t))]\mathcal{F}[1;\hat{\boldsymbol{J}}(t)\cdot\boldsymbol{\xi}(t),\boldsymbol{B}\cdot\boldsymbol{\xi}(t)]\\ &\quad - \frac{1}{2N}\eta^2(t)\hat{\boldsymbol{J}}(t)\mathcal{F}^2[1;\hat{\boldsymbol{J}}(t)\cdot\boldsymbol{\xi}(t),\boldsymbol{B}\cdot\boldsymbol{\xi}(t)] + \mathcal{O}(N^{-2})\end{aligned} \tag{17.45}$$

The evolution of the observable $\omega(t) = \hat{\boldsymbol{J}}(t)\cdot\boldsymbol{B}$ is thus given by

$$\begin{aligned}\frac{\omega(t+\Delta t) - \omega(t)}{\Delta t} &= \eta(t)\,[x(t) - \omega(t)x(t)]\,\mathcal{F}[1;x(t),y(t)]\\ &\quad - \frac{1}{2}\omega(t)\eta^2(t)\mathcal{F}^2[1;x(t),y(t)] + \mathcal{O}(N^{-1})\end{aligned}$$

Following the procedure of Section 17.2 then leads to

$$\frac{\mathrm{d}}{\mathrm{d}t}\omega = \eta\left\langle (y - \omega x)\mathcal{F}[1;x,y] - \frac{1}{2}\omega\eta^2\mathcal{F}^2[1;x,y]\right\rangle \tag{17.46}$$

which is seen to be identical to equation (17.44).

Finally we may convert equation (17.44) into a dynamical equation for the error E, using (17.21), which gives the end result

$$\frac{\mathrm{d}}{\mathrm{d}t}E = -\frac{\eta\langle[y - \cos(\pi E)x]\mathcal{F}[1;x,y]\rangle}{\pi\sin(\pi E)} + \frac{\eta^2\langle\mathcal{F}^2[1;x,y]\rangle}{2\pi\tan(\pi E)} \tag{17.47}$$

with averages defined with respect to the distribution (17.20), in which $\omega = \cos(\pi E)$.

In summary, for spherical models described by either of the equivalent classes of online rules (17.43) or (17.45), the evolution of the error E is for $N \to \infty$ described by a single first-order non-linear differential equation, rather than a pair of coupled non-linear differential equations. This will allow us to push the analysis further, but the price we pay is that of a loss in generality.

Optimal time-dependent learning rates

We wish to optimize the approach to the $E = 0$ state of our macroscopic equations, by choosing a suitable time-dependent learning rate. Let us distinguish between the possible situations we can find ourselves in. If our learning rule is of the general form (17.6), that is, without spherical normalization, we have two coupled macroscopic equations:

$$\frac{\mathrm{d}}{\mathrm{d}t}J = \eta\langle x\mathcal{F}[J; Jx, y]\rangle + \frac{\eta^2}{2J}\langle \mathcal{F}^2[J; Jx, y]\rangle \tag{17.48}$$

$$\frac{\mathrm{d}}{\mathrm{d}t}E = -\frac{\eta\langle [y - \cos(\pi E)x]\,\mathcal{F}[J; Jx, y]\rangle}{J\pi\,\sin(\pi E)} + \frac{\eta^2\langle \mathcal{F}^2[J; Jx, y]\rangle}{2\pi J^2\tan(\pi E)} \tag{17.49}$$

These are obtained by combining (17.18, 17.19) with (17.21). The probability distribution (17.20) with which the averages are computed depends on E only, not on J. If, on the other hand, we complement the rule (17.6) with weight vector normalization as in (17.43) or (17.45) (the spherical rules), we obtain a single equation for E only:

$$\frac{\mathrm{d}}{\mathrm{d}t}E = -\frac{\eta\langle [y - \cos(\pi E)x]\mathcal{F}[1; x, y]\rangle}{\pi\,\sin(\pi E)} + \frac{\eta^2\langle \mathcal{F}^2[1; x, y]\rangle}{2\pi\,\tan(\pi E)} \tag{17.50}$$

Since equation (17.50) is autonomous—there are no dynamical variables other than E—the optimal choice of the function $\eta(t)$ which generates the fastest decay of the error E is obtained by simply minimizing the temporal derivative of the error *at each time-step*:

$$\forall t \geq 0\colon\quad \frac{\partial}{\partial\eta(t)}\left(\frac{\mathrm{d}}{\mathrm{d}t}E\right) = 0 \tag{17.51}$$

which is called the 'greedy' recipe. Note, however, that the same is true for equation (17.49) if we restrict ourselves to rules with the property that $\mathcal{F}[J; Jx, y] = \gamma(J)\mathcal{F}[1; x, y]$ for some function $\gamma(J)$, such as the Hebbian

($\gamma(J) = 1$), perceptron ($\gamma(J) = 1$), and AdaTron ($\gamma(J) = J$) rules. This specific property can also be written as

$$\frac{\partial}{\partial x}\frac{\mathcal{F}[J;Jx,y]}{\mathcal{F}[1;x,y]} = \frac{\partial}{\partial y}\frac{\mathcal{F}[J;Jx,y]}{\mathcal{F}[1;x,y]} = 0 \tag{17.52}$$

For rules which obey (17.52) we can simply write the time-dependent learning rate as $\eta = \tilde{\eta}J/\gamma(J)$, such that equations (17.48, 17.49) acquire the following form:

$$\frac{\mathrm{d}}{\mathrm{d}t}\ln J = \tilde{\eta}\langle x\mathcal{F}[1;x,y]\rangle + \frac{1}{2}\tilde{\eta}^2\langle \mathcal{F}^2[1;x,y]\rangle \tag{17.53}$$

$$\frac{\mathrm{d}}{\mathrm{d}t}E = -\frac{\tilde{\eta}\langle[y-\cos(\pi E)x]\mathcal{F}[1;x,y]\rangle}{\pi\sin(\pi E)} + \frac{\tilde{\eta}^2\langle \mathcal{F}^2[1;x,y]\rangle}{2\pi\tan(\pi E)} \tag{17.54}$$

In these cases, precisely since we are free to choose the function $\tilde{\eta}(t)$ as we wish, the evolution of J decouples from our problem of optimizing the evolution of E. For learning rules where $\mathcal{F}[J;Jx,y]$ truly depends on J on the other hand, that is, where (17.52) does not hold, optimization of the error relaxation is considerably more difficult, and is likely to depend on the particular time t for which one wants to minimize $E(t)$. We will not deal with such cases here.

If the greedy recipe applies (for spherical rules and for ordinary ones with the property (17.52)) then working out the derivative in (17.51) immediately gives us

$$\tilde{\eta}(t)_{\text{opt}} = \frac{\langle[y-\cos(\pi E)x]\mathcal{F}[1;x,y]\rangle}{\cos(\pi E)\langle \mathcal{F}^2[1;x,y]\rangle} \tag{17.55}$$

Insertion of this choice into equation (17.47) then leads to

$$\left.\frac{\mathrm{d}}{\mathrm{d}t}E\right|_{\text{opt}} = -\frac{\langle[y-\cos(\pi E)x]\mathcal{F}[1;x,y]\rangle^2}{2\pi\sin(\pi E)\cos(\pi E)\langle \mathcal{F}^2[1;x,y]\rangle} \tag{17.56}$$

These and subsequent expressions we will write in terms of $\tilde{\eta}$, defined as $\tilde{\eta}(t) = \eta(t)$ for the spherical learning rules and as $\tilde{\eta}(t) = \eta(t)J(t)/\gamma(J(t))$ for the non-spherical learning rules. We will now work out the details of the results (17.55, 17.56) for the familiar choices for the function $\mathcal{F}[\cdots]$: the Hebbian, perceptron, and AdaTron rules.

For the ordinary and spherical Hebbian rules, corresponding to $\mathcal{F}[J;Jx,y] = \text{sgn}(y)$, the various Gaussian integrals in (17.55, 17.56) are the same as those we have already performed in the case of constant learning rate η. Substitution of the outcomes of the integrals (see Appendix D) into the equations (17.55, 17.56) gives

$$\tilde{\eta}_{\rm opt} = \sqrt{\frac{2}{\pi}\frac{\sin^2(\pi E)}{\cos(\pi E)}} \qquad \left.\frac{\mathrm{d}}{\mathrm{d}t}E\right|_{\rm opt} = -\frac{\sin^3(\pi E)}{\pi^2\cos(\pi E)}$$

The equation for the error E can be solved explicitly, giving

$$t(E) = \tfrac{1}{2}\pi\sin^{-2}(\pi E) - \tfrac{1}{2}\pi\sin^{-2}(\pi E_0) \tag{17.57}$$

as can be verified by explicit substitution. The asymptotic behaviour of the process follows from expansion of (17.57) for small E, and gives

$$E_{\rm opt} \sim \frac{1}{\sqrt{2\pi t}} \qquad \tilde{\eta}_{\rm opt} \sim \sqrt{\frac{\pi}{2}\frac{1}{t}} \qquad (t \to \infty)$$

We conclude that, for the Hebbian rule, asymptotically there is nothing to be gained by choosing the optimal time-dependent learning rate, since the same asymptotic form for E was also obtained in (17.28) for constant η. Note that the property $\mathcal{F}[J; Jx, y] = \mathcal{F}[1; x, y]$ of the Hebbian recipe guarantees that the result (17.57) applies to both the ordinary and the spherical Hebbian rule. The only difference between the two cases is in the definition of $\tilde{\eta}$: for the ordinary (non-spherical) version $\tilde{\eta}(t) = \eta(t)/J(t)$, whereas for the spherical version $\tilde{\eta}(t) = \eta(t)$.

We move on to the (ordinary and spherical) perceptron learning rules, where $\mathcal{F}[J; Jx, y] = \theta(-xy)\mathrm{sgn}(y)$, with time-dependent learning rates $\eta(t)$ which we aim to optimize. As in the Hebbian case all integrals occurring in (17.55, 17.56) after substitution of the present choice of $\mathcal{F}[\cdots]$ have been performed already (see Appendix D). Insertion of the results of these integrals into (17.55, 17.56) gives

$$\tilde{\eta}_{\rm opt} = \frac{\sin^2(\pi E)}{\sqrt{2\pi}E\cos(\pi E)} \qquad \left.\frac{\mathrm{d}}{\mathrm{d}t}E\right|_{\rm opt} = -\frac{\sin^3(\pi E)}{4\pi^2 E\cos(\pi E)}$$

Again the non-linear differential equation describing the evolution of the error E can be solved exactly:

$$t(E) = \frac{2[\pi E + \sin(\pi E)\cos(\pi E)]}{\sin^2(\pi E)} - \frac{2[\pi E_0 + \sin(\pi E_0)\cos(\pi E_0)]}{\sin^2(\pi E_0)} \tag{17.58}$$

Expansion of (17.58) for small E gives the asymptotic behaviour

$$E_{\text{opt}} \sim \frac{4}{\pi t} \qquad \tilde{\eta}_{\text{opt}} \sim \frac{2\sqrt{2\pi}}{t} \qquad (t \to \infty)$$

This is identical to that found in the beginning of this section, that is, equations (17.38, 17.42), where we explored the consequences of making two simple ad hoc choices for the time-dependent learning rate (since $\tilde{\eta} = \eta/J$). As with the Hebbian rule, the property $\mathcal{F}[J; Jx, y] = \mathcal{F}[1; x, y]$ of the perceptron recipe guarantees that the result (17.58) applies to both the ordinary and the spherical version.

Finally we try to optimize the learning rate for the spherical AdaTron learning rule, corresponding to the choice $\mathcal{F}[J; Jx, y] = |Jx|\theta(-xy)\text{sgn}(y)$. Working out the averages in (17.55, 17.56) again does not require doing any new integrals. Using those already encountered in analysing the AdaTron rule with constant learning rate (to be found in Appendix D), we obtain

$$\tilde{\eta}_{\text{opt}} = \frac{\sin^3(\pi E)}{\pi}\left[E\cos(\pi E) - \frac{\cos^2(\pi E)\sin(\pi E)}{\pi}\right]^{-1}$$

$$\left.\frac{\mathrm{d}}{\mathrm{d}t}E\right|_{\text{opt}} = -\frac{\sin^5(\pi E)}{2\pi^2\cos(\pi E)}\left[\frac{1}{\pi E - \cos(\pi E)\sin(\pi E)}\right]$$

Note that in both versions, ordinary and spherical, of the AdaTron rule we simply have $\tilde{\eta}(t) = \eta(t)$. It will no longer come as a surprise that also this equation for the evolution of the error allows for analytical solution:

$$t(E) = \frac{\pi}{8}\left[\frac{4\pi E - \sin(4\pi E)}{\sin^4(\pi E)} - \frac{4\pi E_0 - \sin(4\pi E_0)}{\sin^4(\pi E_0)}\right] \tag{17.59}$$

Asymptotically we find, by expanding (17.59) for small E, a relaxation of the form

$$E_{\text{opt}} \sim \frac{4}{3t} \qquad \tilde{\eta}_{\text{opt}} \sim \frac{3}{2} \qquad (t \to \infty)$$

So for the AdaTron rule the asymptotic behaviour for optimal time-dependent learning rate η is identical to that found for the optimal *constant* learning rate η, which is indeed $\eta = \frac{3}{2}$, see (17.37). As with the previous two rules, the property $\mathcal{F}[J; Jx, y] = J\mathcal{F}[1; x, y]$ of the AdaTron recipe guarantees that the result (17.57) applies to both the ordinary and the spherical version.

It is quite remarkable that the simple perceptron learning rule, which was at the bottom of the league among the three learning rules considered so far in the case of constant learning rates, all of a sudden comes out at the top as soon as we allow for optimized time-dependent learning rates. It is in addition quite satisfactory that in a number of cases one can actually find an explicit expression for the relation $t(E)$ between the duration of the learning stage and the generalization error achieved, that is, equations (17.41, 17.57–17.59).

Optimal online learning rules

We need not restrict our optimization attempts to varying the learning rate η only, but we can also vary the full form $\eta\mathcal{F}[J; Jx, y]$ of the learning rule. The aim, as always, is to minimize the generalization error, but there will be limits to what is achievable. So far all examples of online learning rules we have studied gave an asymptotic relaxation of the error of the form $E \sim t^{-q}$ with $q \leq 1$. It can be shown using general probabilistic arguments that

$$\lim_{t\to\infty} tE(t) \geq 0.44\ldots \tag{17.60}$$

No online learning rule for binary systems[37] can violate (17.60). On the other hand, we have already encountered several rules with at least the optimal power $E \sim t^{-1}$. The optimal online learning rule is thus one which gives asymptotically $E \sim A/t$, but with the smallest value of A possible.

The function $\mathcal{F}[J; Jx, y]$ in the learning rules is allowed to depend only on the *sign* of the teacher field $y = \boldsymbol{B} \cdot \boldsymbol{\xi}$, not on its magnitude, since otherwise it would describe a situation where considerably more than just the answers $T(\boldsymbol{\xi}) = \text{sgn}(\boldsymbol{B} \cdot \boldsymbol{\xi})$ of the teacher are used for updating the parameters of the student. One can easily see that using unavailable information indeed violates (17.60). Suppose, for instance, we were to consider spherical online rules, that is, (17.43) or (17.45), and make the forbidden choice

$$\eta\mathcal{F}[1; x, y] = \frac{y - \cos(\pi E)x}{\cos(\pi E)}$$

We would then find for the corresponding equation (17.50) describing the evolution of the error E for $N \to \infty$:

$$\frac{\mathrm{d}}{\mathrm{d}t}E = -\frac{\langle [y - \cos(\pi E)x]^2 \rangle}{2\pi \sin(\pi E)\cos(\pi E)}$$

[37] This will be different, however, for graded-response perceptrons.

with the averages as always calculated with the distribution (D.5). From this it follows, using the Gaussian integrals done in Appendix D, that

$$\frac{\mathrm{d}}{\mathrm{d}t}E = -\frac{\tan(\pi E)}{2\pi}$$

This produces exponential asymptotic decay of the error, since $\tan(\pi E) = \pi E + \mathcal{O}(E^3)$, and thus indeed violates (17.60).

Taking into account the restrictions on available information, and anticipating the form subsequent expressions will take, we write the function $\mathcal{F}[J; Jx, y]$ (which we will vary, and also allow to have an explicit time-dependence[38]) in the following form

$$\eta\mathcal{F}[J; Jx, y] = \begin{cases} J\mathcal{F}_+(x,t), & \text{if } y > 0 \\ J\mathcal{F}_-(x,t), & \text{if } y < 0 \end{cases} \tag{17.61}$$

If our learning rule is of the general form (17.6), without spherical normalization, the coupled equations (17.48, 17.49) describe the macroscopic dynamics. For the spherical rules (17.43, 17.45) we have the single macroscopic equation (17.50). Both (17.49) and (17.50) now acquire the form

$$\frac{\mathrm{d}}{\mathrm{d}t}E = -\frac{1}{\pi\sin(\pi E)}\Big[\langle(y-\omega x)\theta(y)\mathcal{F}_+(x,t)\rangle + \langle(y-\omega x)\theta(-y)\mathcal{F}_-(x,t)\rangle$$
$$-\frac{1}{2}\omega\langle\theta(y)\mathcal{F}_+^2(x,t)\rangle - \frac{1}{2}\omega\langle\theta(-y)\mathcal{F}_-^2(x,t)\rangle\Big] \tag{17.62}$$

with the usual shorthand $\omega = \cos(\pi E)$ and with averages calculated with the time-dependent distribution (17.20). To simplify notation we now introduce the two functions

$$\int \mathrm{d}y\;\theta(y)P(x,y) = \Omega(x,t) \qquad \int \mathrm{d}y\;\theta(y)(y-\omega x)P(x,y) = \Delta(x,t)$$

and hence, using the symmetry $P(x,y) = P(-x,-y)$, equation (17.62) acquires the compact form

$$\frac{\mathrm{d}}{\mathrm{d}t}E = -\frac{1}{\pi\sin(\pi E)}\int \mathrm{d}x\left[\Delta(x,t)\mathcal{F}_+(x,t) - \frac{1}{2}\omega\Omega(x,t)\mathcal{F}_+^2(x,t)\right]$$
$$-\frac{1}{\pi\sin(\pi E)}\int \mathrm{d}x\left[-\Delta(-x,t)\mathcal{F}_-(x,t) - \frac{1}{2}\omega\Omega(-x,t)\mathcal{F}_-^2(x,t)\right] \tag{17.63}$$

[38] By allowing for an explicit time-dependence, we can drop the dependence on J in $\mathcal{F}[J; Jx, y]$ if we wish, without loss of generality, since J is itself just some function of time.

Since there is only one dynamical variable, the error E, our optimization problem is solved by the greedy recipe which here involves functional derivatives:

$$\forall x,\ \forall t:\quad \frac{\delta}{\delta\mathcal{F}_+(x,t)}\left(\frac{\mathrm{d}}{\mathrm{d}t}E\right)=\frac{\delta}{\delta\mathcal{F}_-(x,t)}\left(\frac{\mathrm{d}}{\mathrm{d}t}E\right)=0$$

with the solution

$$\mathcal{F}_+(x,t)=\frac{\Delta(x,t)}{\omega\Omega(x,t)}\qquad \mathcal{F}_-(x,t)=-\frac{\Delta(-x,t)}{\omega\Omega(-x,t)}=-\mathcal{F}_+(-x,t)$$

Substitution of this solution into (17.63) gives the corresponding law describing the optimal error evolution of (ordinary and spherical) online rules:

$$\left.\frac{\mathrm{d}}{\mathrm{d}t}E\right|_{\mathrm{opt}}=-\frac{1}{\pi\sin(\pi E)\cos(\pi E)}\int \mathrm{d}x\,\frac{\Delta^2(x,t)}{\Omega(x,t)}$$

Explicit calculation of the integrals $\Delta(x,t)$ and $\Omega(x,t)$ (see Appendix D) gives:

$$\Delta(x,t)=\frac{\sin(\pi E)}{2\pi}\,e^{-x^2/2\sin^2(\pi E)}$$

$$\Omega(x,t)=\frac{e^{-x^2/2}}{2\sqrt{2\pi}}[1+\mathrm{erf}(x/\sqrt{2}\tan(\pi E))]$$

with which we finally obtain an explicit expression for the optimal form of the learning rule, via (17.61), as well as for the dynamical law describing the corresponding error evolution:

$$\eta\mathcal{F}[J;Jx,y]_{\mathrm{opt}}=\sqrt{\frac{2}{\pi}}\,\frac{J\tan(\pi E)e^{-x^2/2\tan^2(\pi E)}}{1+\mathrm{sgn}(xy)\mathrm{erf}(|x|/\sqrt{2}\tan(\pi E))}\tag{17.64}$$

$$\left.\frac{\mathrm{d}}{\mathrm{d}t}E\right|_{\mathrm{opt}}=-\frac{\tan^2(\pi E)}{\pi^2\sqrt{2\pi}}\int \mathrm{d}x\,\frac{e^{-x^2[1+\cos^2(\pi E)]/2\cos^2(\pi E)}}{1+\mathrm{erf}(x/\sqrt{2})}\tag{17.65}$$

The asymptotic form of the error relaxation towards the $E=0$ state follows from expansion of equation (17.65) for small E, which gives

$$\frac{\mathrm{d}}{\mathrm{d}t}E=-E^2\int \mathrm{d}x\,\frac{e^{-x^2}}{\sqrt{2\pi}[1+\mathrm{erf}(x/\sqrt{2})]}+\mathcal{O}(E^4)$$

so that we can conclude that the optimum asymptotic decay for online learning rules, whether spherical or non-spherical, is given by $E\sim A/t$ for

$t \to \infty$, with

$$A^{-1} = \int \mathrm{d}x \, \frac{e^{-x^2}}{\sqrt{2\pi}[1 + \mathrm{erf}(x/\sqrt{2})]}$$

Numerical evaluation of this integral, which is somewhat delicate due to the behaviour of the integrand for $x \to -\infty$, finally gives

$$E \sim \frac{0.883\ldots}{t} \qquad (t \to \infty)$$

It is instructive to investigate briefly the form of the optimal learning rule (17.64) for large values of E (as in the initial stages of learning processes) and for small values of E (as in the final stages of learning processes). Initially we find

$$\lim_{E \uparrow 1/2} \frac{\eta \mathcal{F}[J; Jx, y]_{\mathrm{opt}}}{\tan(\pi E)} = J\sqrt{\frac{2}{\pi}}\mathrm{sgn}(y)$$

which describes a Hebbian-type learning rule with diverging learning rate (note that $\tan(\pi E) \to \infty$ for $E \uparrow \frac{1}{2}$). In contrast, in the final stages the optimal learning rule (17.64) acquires the form

$$\begin{aligned}\lim_{E \downarrow 0} \eta \mathcal{F}[J; Jx, y]_{\mathrm{opt}} &= \frac{J|x|}{\sqrt{\pi}}\theta(-xy)\,\mathrm{sgn}(y) \lim_{z \to \infty} \frac{e^{-z^2}}{z[1 - \mathrm{erf}(z)]} \\ &= J|x|\theta(-xy)\mathrm{sgn}(y)\end{aligned}$$

which is the AdaTron learning rule with learning rate $\eta = 1$.[39]

In Figures 17.10 (short times and ordinary axes) and 17.11 (large times and log–log axes) we finally compare the evolution of the error for the optimal online learning rule (17.64) with the two online learning rules which so far were found to give the fastest relaxation: the perceptron rule with normalizing time-dependent learning rate, giving the error (17.41), and the perceptron rule with optimal time-dependent learning rate which yields the error (17.58). This is in order to assess whether choosing the optimal online learning rule (17.64) rather than its simpler competitors is actually worth the effort. The curves for the optimal online rule were obtained by numerical solution of equation (17.65).

[39] The reason that, in spite of the asymptotic equivalence of the two rules, the optimal rule does not asymptotically give the same relaxation of the error E as the AdaTron rule is as follows. In order to determine the asymptotics one has to take the limit $E \to 0$ in the full macroscopic differential equation for E, which, in addition to the function $\mathcal{F}[\cdots]$ defining the learning rule, involves also the Gaussian probability distribution (D.5). The latter depends on E in a non-trivial way, especially near $E = 0$.

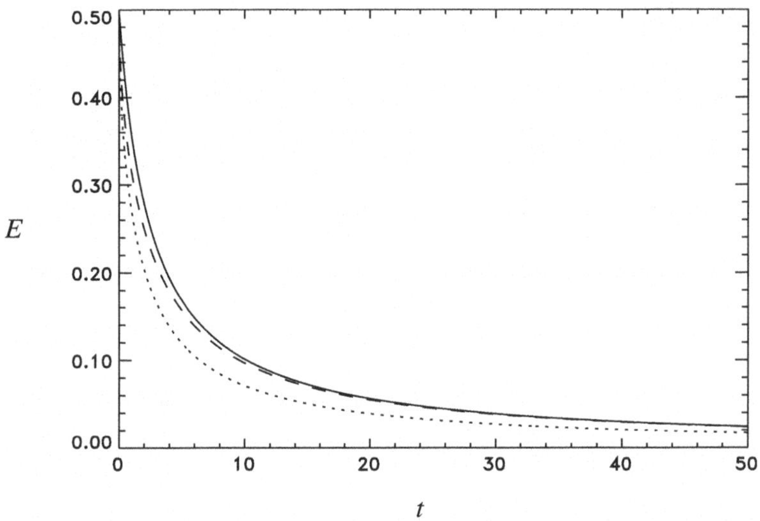

Figure 17.10 Evolution of the error E for three online learning rules: perceptron rule with a learning rate such that $J(t) = 1$ for all $t \geq 0$ (solid line), perceptron rule with optimal learning rate (dashed line), and the optimal spherical learning rule (dotted line). Initial state: $E(0) = \frac{1}{2}$ and $J(0) = 1$. The curves for the perceptron rules are given by (17.41) and (17.58). The curve for the optimal spherical rule was obtained by numerical solution of equation (17.65).

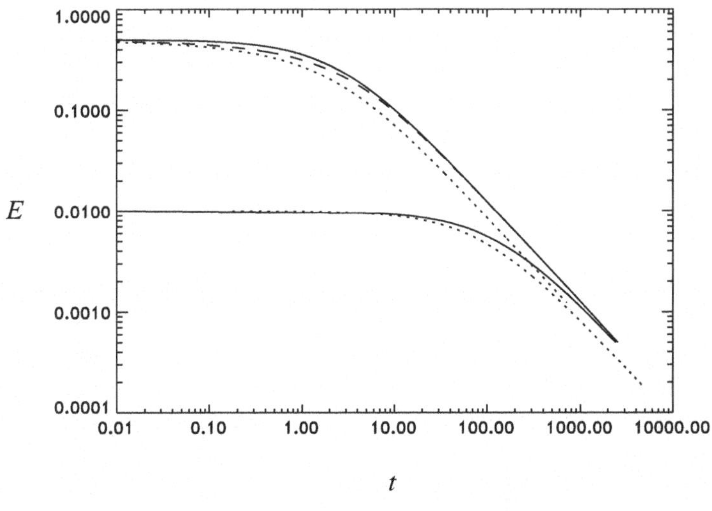

Figure 17.11 Evolution of the error E for the online perceptron rule with a learning rate such that $J(t) = 1$ for all $t \geq 0$ (solid line), the online perceptron rule with optimal learning rate (dashed line), and the optimal spherical online learning rule (dotted line). Initial states: $(J, E) = (1, \frac{1}{2})$ (upper curves), and $(J, E) = (1, \frac{1}{100})$ (lower curves). The curves for the perceptron rules are given by (17.41) and (17.58). The curves for the optimal spherical rule were obtained by numerical solution of equation (17.65).

Summary in a table

We close this section with an overview of some of the results on online learning in perceptrons derived so far. The upper part of this table contains results for specific learning rules with arbitrary constant learning rates η (first column), optimal constant learning rate η (second column), and where possible, a time-dependent learning rate $\eta(t)$ chosen to realize the normalization $J(t) = 1$ for all t. The lower part of the table gives results for specific learning rules with optimized time dependent learning rates $\eta(t)$, as well as lower bounds on the asymptotic generalization error.

17.4 Exercises

Exercise 17.1. (Relation with the earlier infinitesimal learning rate theory.) If for the macroscopic laws describing online learning, as derived in the present section, we re-define our time to be measured in units of the learning rate η, this implies switching to the new time variable $s = \eta t$. Transform the equations (17.30) for the perceptron rule into the language of s, and show that subsequently taking the limit $\eta \to 0$ reproduces the theory developed earlier in Section 2.5, that is, equations (2.57).

Exercise 17.2. (Learning dynamics for generalized perceptron/AdaTron rules.) Consider a perceptron with N inputs and weight vector $\boldsymbol{J} \in \mathbb{R}^N$, which is trained in an online fashion to perform a task generated by a teacher perceptron with weight vector $\boldsymbol{B} \in \mathbb{R}^N$ (with $|\boldsymbol{B}| = 1$). The learning rule used is the following generalization of the perceptron ($k = 0$) and AdaTron ($k = 1$) rules:

$$\boldsymbol{J}(t+\Delta t) = \boldsymbol{J}(t) + \frac{\eta}{N}\boldsymbol{\xi}(t)\mathrm{sgn}(\boldsymbol{B}\cdot\boldsymbol{\xi}(t))|\boldsymbol{J}(t)\cdot\boldsymbol{\xi}(t)|^k\theta(-[\boldsymbol{B}\cdot\boldsymbol{\xi}(t)][\boldsymbol{J}(t)\cdot\boldsymbol{\xi}(t)])$$

with $k \geq 0$. The vector $\boldsymbol{\xi}(t) \in \{-1, 1\}^N$ denotes the input vector drawn at random from $\{-1, 1\}^N$, with uniform probabilities, at time t. $\theta(z)$ is the step function, and $\Delta t = N^{-1}$. Define the macroscopic observables $J = |\boldsymbol{J}|$ and $\omega = \boldsymbol{B}\cdot\boldsymbol{J}/J$. Show that in the limit $N \to \infty$ they obey the following deterministic laws:

$$\frac{\mathrm{d}}{\mathrm{d}t}J = -\eta J^k\langle |x|^{k+1}\theta(-xy)\rangle + \frac{1}{2}\eta^2 J^{2k-1}\langle x^{2k}\theta(-xy)\rangle$$

$$\frac{\mathrm{d}}{\mathrm{d}t}\omega = \eta J^{k-1}\langle(|y| + \omega|x|)\,|x|^k\theta(-xy)\rangle - \frac{1}{2}\omega\eta^2 J^{2k-2}\langle x^{2k}\theta(-xy)\rangle$$

Generalization error in perceptrons with online learning rules

	Constant learning rate η		Variable η
Rule	Asymptotic decay, constant η	Optimal asymptotic decay, constant η	η chosen to normalize J
Hebbian	$E \sim \frac{1}{\sqrt{2\pi}} t^{-1/2}$ for $\eta > 0$	$E \sim \frac{1}{\sqrt{2\pi}} t^{-1/2}$ for $\eta > 0$	N/A
Perceptron	$E \sim \left(\frac{2}{3}\right)^{1/3} \pi^{-1} t^{-1/3}$ for $\eta > 0$	$E \sim \left(\frac{2}{3}\right)^{1/3} \pi^{-1} t^{-1/3}$ for $\eta > 0$	$E \sim \frac{4}{\pi} t^{-1}$
AdaTron	$E \sim \left(\frac{3}{3\eta - \eta^2}\right) t^{-1}$ for $0 < \eta < 3$	$E \sim \frac{4}{3} t^{-1}$ for $\eta = \frac{3}{2}$	$E \sim \frac{3}{2} t^{-1}$

Optimal generalization

	Optimal time-dependent learning rate η	
Rule	Generalization error for optimal time-dependent η	Asymptotics
Hebbian	$t = \frac{\pi}{2}\left[\frac{1}{\sin^2(\pi E)} - \frac{1}{\sin^2(\pi E_0)}\right]$	$E \sim \frac{1}{\sqrt{2\pi}} t^{-1/2}$
Perceptron	$t = 2\left[\frac{\pi E + \sin(\pi E)\cos(\pi E)}{\sin^2(\pi E)} - \frac{\pi E_0 + \sin(\pi E_0)\cos(\pi E_0)}{\sin^2(\pi E_0)}\right]$	$E \sim \frac{4}{\pi} t^{-1}$
AdaTron	$t = \frac{\pi}{8}\left[\frac{4\pi E - \sin(4\pi E)}{\sin^4(\pi E)} - \frac{4\pi E_0 - \sin(4\pi E_0)}{\sin^4(\pi E_0)}\right]$	$E \sim \frac{4}{3} t^{-1}$
Lower bound for online learning (asymptotics of the optimal learning rule)		$E \sim 0.88 t^{-1}$
Lower bound for any learning rule		$E \sim 0.44 t^{-1}$

Assume the field statistics to be described by (17.20), and show that

$$\frac{\mathrm{d}}{\mathrm{d}t}J = -\eta J^k \mathcal{J}(\omega, k+1) + \frac{1}{2}\eta^2 J^{2k-1}\mathcal{J}(\omega, 2k)$$
$$\frac{\mathrm{d}}{\mathrm{d}t}\omega = \eta J^{k-1}\left[\mathcal{I}(\omega, k+1) + \omega\mathcal{J}(\omega, k+1)\right] - \frac{1}{2}\omega\eta^2 J^{2k-2}\mathcal{J}(\omega, 2k)$$

in which $\mathcal{J}(\omega, \ell)$ and $\mathcal{I}(\omega, \ell)$ denote the following integrals:

$$\mathcal{J}(\omega, \ell) = \int_0^\infty \int_0^\infty \frac{\mathrm{d}x\mathrm{d}y}{\pi\sqrt{1-\omega^2}} e^{-(x^2+y^2+2\omega xy)/2(1-\omega^2)} x^\ell$$

$$\mathcal{I}(\omega, \ell) = \int_0^\infty \int_0^\infty \frac{\mathrm{d}x\mathrm{d}y}{\pi\sqrt{1-\omega^2}} e^{-(x^2+y^2+2\omega xy)/2(1-\omega^2)} yx^{\ell-1}$$

Now choose the learning rate η to be time-dependent in such a way as to normalize $\boldsymbol{J}$: $J(t)=1$ for all $t \geq 0$ (assume $J(0)=1$). Show that this results in the following law for the remaining observable ω:

$$\frac{1}{2}\frac{\mathrm{d}}{\mathrm{d}t}\omega = \frac{\mathcal{J}(\omega, k+1)\mathcal{I}(\omega, k+1)}{\mathcal{J}(\omega, 2k)}$$

By using the relation $\omega = \cos(\pi E)$ and retaining only the leading contributions for $E \to 0$ in the two integrals above, show that asymptotically the error decays as

$$E \sim C_k t^{-1} \quad (t \to \infty)$$

and give an expression for C_k.

18 Dynamics of online gradient descent learning

In this chapter we consider learning in systems with continuous real-valued outputs, rather than those with binary outputs as in the previous chapter. A natural way of constructing learning algorithms for such systems is by gradient descent on some appropriate error measure. This error measure should tell us by how much student and teacher output differ. A popular choice is the squared deviation between actual and desired outputs; carrying out gradient descent on this measure for multilayer networks yields the well-known error backpropagation algorithm. The results of our analysis are therefore of relevance to practical neural network learning. For simplicity, here we only analyse learning in continuous output *perceptrons*, that is, systems without hidden layers; the case of networks with a single hidden layer containing a finite number of neurons can also be treated, but requires rather more complicated algebra.

18.1 Online gradient descent

Definition of microscopic learning rule

We modify the scenario from the previous chapter as follows. For a given input $\boldsymbol{\xi}$ (drawn randomly from $D = \Omega \subseteq \{-1,1\}^N$, as before), let us assume that both the teacher output $T(\boldsymbol{\xi})$ and the student output $S(\boldsymbol{\xi}) = f(\boldsymbol{\xi};\boldsymbol{J})$ are real-valued rather than binary. Here $\boldsymbol{J}$ is the student weight vector as before, but we now let the student output depend on $\boldsymbol{J}$ in a smooth (differentiable) way. Similarly, let us assume that the error measure $\mathcal{E}(T(\boldsymbol{\xi}), S(\boldsymbol{\xi})) = \mathcal{E}(T(\boldsymbol{\xi}), f(\boldsymbol{\xi};\boldsymbol{J}))$ is differentiable with respect to the student output $S(\boldsymbol{\xi})$, and hence also with respect to $\boldsymbol{J}$. Then a natural way to construct a learning algorithm is by *gradient descent* on the error made for the current training example:

$$\boldsymbol{J}(t+\Delta t) = \boldsymbol{J}(t) - \frac{\eta}{N}\nabla_{\boldsymbol{J}}\mathcal{E}(T(\boldsymbol{\xi}(t)), f(\boldsymbol{\xi}(t);\boldsymbol{J}(t))) \qquad (18.1)$$

As before, we define the time $t = \ell/N$ as the rescaled iteration number $\ell = 0, 1, \ldots$, with $\Delta t = 1/N$. The learning rate η is similarly scaled by

N to give sensible behaviour in the limit $N \to \infty$, and taken to be time-independent (for simplicity). A very common choice for the error measure is the simple squared deviation, $\mathcal{E}(T,S) = \frac{1}{2}(T-S)^2$. With this choice, our learning rule becomes

$$\boldsymbol{J}(t+\Delta t) = \boldsymbol{J}(t) - \frac{\eta}{N}[f(\boldsymbol{\xi}(t);\boldsymbol{J}(t)) - T(\boldsymbol{\xi}(t))]\nabla_{\boldsymbol{J}} f(\boldsymbol{\xi}(t);\boldsymbol{J}(t)) \quad (18.2)$$

which is the backpropagation algorithm, as defined earlier in Section 2.4. Recall that the name derives from the way in which the gradient $\nabla_{\boldsymbol{J}} f$ is calculated in multilayer networks, by propagating it backwards from the output unit where it is measured towards the inputs, using the chain rule.

Let us now specialize to the case of perceptron (i.e. single layer) students and teachers. The input–output relations then take the form

$$T(\boldsymbol{\xi}) = g(\boldsymbol{B}\cdot\boldsymbol{\xi}) \qquad S(\boldsymbol{\xi}) = f(\boldsymbol{\xi};\boldsymbol{J}) = g(\boldsymbol{J}\cdot\boldsymbol{\xi}) \quad (18.3)$$

with some sigmoidal transfer function $g(\cdot)$, which is assumed to be identical for student and teacher. This transforms (18.2) into

$$\boldsymbol{J}(t+\Delta t) = \boldsymbol{J}(t) - \frac{\eta}{N}\boldsymbol{\xi}(t)[g(\boldsymbol{J}(t)\cdot\boldsymbol{\xi}(t)) - g(\boldsymbol{B}\cdot\boldsymbol{\xi}(t))]g'(\boldsymbol{J}(t)\cdot\boldsymbol{\xi}(t)) \quad (18.4)$$

Derivation of closed macroscopic laws

Equation (18.4) is seen to have the same form as the general learning rule (17.6) analysed in the last chapter, provided we set $\mathcal{F}[J;x,y] = -[g(x)-g(y)]g'(x)$. Simply by translating the results (17.10) and (17.11), we can therefore immediately write down the equations governing the time evolution of the observables $R = \boldsymbol{J}\cdot\boldsymbol{B}$ and $Q = \boldsymbol{J}^2$ in the thermodynamic limit for the present problem. However, here it will prove useful to define the student's local field in terms of the *unnormalized* student weight vector $\boldsymbol{J}$, that is, as $x = \boldsymbol{J}\cdot\boldsymbol{\xi}$, rather than in terms of the *normalized* one as in the previous chapter. This eliminates some factors of $Q^{1/2}$ which we would otherwise have to carry around; it also makes sense intuitively, because in the current scenario the length of the weight vector $\boldsymbol{J}$ does affect the student outputs, in contrast to the previous binary perceptron case. We thus get

$$\frac{\mathrm{d}}{\mathrm{d}t}R = -\eta\langle y[g(x)-g(y)]g'(x)\rangle \quad (18.5)$$

$$\frac{\mathrm{d}}{\mathrm{d}t}Q = -2\eta\langle x[g(x)-g(y)]g'(x)\rangle + \eta^2\langle[g(y)-g(x)]^2[g'(x)]^2\rangle \quad (18.6)$$

with averages in (18.5, 18.6) that are now defined with respect to the redefined field distribution

$$P(x, y) = \langle \delta(x - \boldsymbol{J} \cdot \boldsymbol{\xi}) \delta(y - \boldsymbol{B} \cdot \boldsymbol{\xi}) \rangle_\Omega \tag{18.7}$$

Because we are dealing with the case of complete training sets, the average in this definition is over all possible input vectors $\boldsymbol{\xi}$, sampled with uniform probability from $\Omega = \{-1, 1\}^N$. As in the previous chapter, we now assume that $P(x, y)$ has a Gaussian shape; this is true except for rather pathological choices of $\boldsymbol{J}$ and $\boldsymbol{B}$ as discussed before. $P(x, y)$ is therefore determined by its first and second-order moments, that is, by the means and covariances of x and y. Using $\langle \xi_i \rangle_\Omega = 0$ and $\langle \xi_i \xi_j \rangle_\Omega = \delta_{ij}$, we find these without much effort, in analogy with (17.12–17.14) in the previous chapter,

$$\langle x \rangle = \langle y \rangle = 0 \qquad \langle x^2 \rangle = Q \qquad \langle xy \rangle = R \qquad \langle y^2 \rangle = 1 \tag{18.8}$$

As before, we have assumed here that the teacher weight vector is normalized, that is, $\boldsymbol{B}^2 = 1$. After inverting the covariance matrix given by (18.8), we then find for $P(x, y)$

$$P(x, y) = \frac{1}{2\pi\sqrt{Q - R^2}} e^{-(x^2 - 2Rxy + Qy^2)/2(Q - R^2)} \tag{18.9}$$

Because this only depends on R and Q, the equations (18.5, 18.6, 18.9) constitute a closed system of differential equations for the evolution of the macroscopic observables R and Q. The generalization error is also determined by R and Q alone, via the distribution $P(x, y)$:

$$E = \tfrac{1}{2}\langle [g(\boldsymbol{B} \cdot \boldsymbol{\xi}) - g(\boldsymbol{J} \cdot \boldsymbol{\xi})]^2 \rangle_\Omega = \tfrac{1}{2}\langle [g(y) - g(x)]^2 \rangle \tag{18.10}$$

To find the time dependence of R, Q, and E we now need to carry out the averages over x and y. In order to be able to do this analytically, we make the following choice for the transfer function:

$$g(z) = 2\int_0^z Du = \operatorname{erf}(z/\sqrt{2}) \tag{18.11}$$

with the shorthand $Du = (2\pi)^{-1/2} e^{-(1/2)u^2}$, and where $\operatorname{erf}(x)$ denotes the error function as before. The function $g(z)$ is certainly sigmoidal, in the sense that it produces bounded outputs (between -1 and $+1$) and increases monotonically with z. It is also not too different from the $\tanh(z)$ transfer functions that are used frequently in applications, and one may assume that the slight differences between the two choices will not cause qualitative differences in the results. With the above choice of $g(\cdot)$, all averages over x and y in equations (18.5, 18.6) can be calculated analytically, and one finds

$$\frac{\mathrm{d}}{\mathrm{d}t}R = \eta r(R, Q) \tag{18.12}$$

$$\frac{\mathrm{d}}{\mathrm{d}t}Q = \eta q_1(R, Q) + \eta^2 q_2(R, Q) \tag{18.13}$$

with

$$r(R, Q) = \frac{2}{\pi}\frac{1}{1+Q}\left[\frac{1+Q-R^2}{\sqrt{2(1+Q)-R^2}} - \frac{R}{\sqrt{1+2Q}}\right] \tag{18.14}$$

$$q_1(R, Q) = \frac{4}{\pi}\frac{1}{1+Q}\left[\frac{R}{\sqrt{2(1+Q)-R^2}} - \frac{Q}{\sqrt{1+2Q}}\right] \tag{18.15}$$

$$q_2(R, Q) = \frac{4}{\pi^2}\frac{1}{\sqrt{1+2Q}}\left[\arcsin\left(\frac{Q}{1+3Q}\right) + \arcsin\left(\frac{1+2(Q-R^2)}{2(1+2Q-R^2)}\right) - 2\arcsin\left(\frac{R}{\sqrt{1+3Q}\sqrt{2(1+2Q-R^2)}}\right)\right] \tag{18.16}$$

These first-order differential equations can now be solved numerically, and from the values of R and Q the generalization error can be calculated; for our choice (18.11) of transfer function, the latter takes the relatively simple form

$$E = \frac{1}{6} - \frac{2}{\pi}\arcsin\left(\frac{R}{\sqrt{2(1+Q)}}\right) + \frac{1}{\pi}\arcsin\left(\frac{Q}{1+Q}\right) \tag{18.17}$$

Behaviour of the macroscopic laws

Figure 18.1 shows examples for the evolution of E with the (scaled) number of learning steps $t = \ell/N$. We see that for small enough learning rates η the system converges to $E = 0$, and that the speed of convergence increases with η. As η becomes larger, however, convergence slows down again, and finally for η larger than some critical value $\eta_c \approx 4$ the systems stops converging to $E = 0$ altogether; perfect generalization is not obtained even after an infinite number of learning steps per student weight.

To understand these observations, let us analyse the asymptotic behaviour of the system in some more detail. The numerical data show that for small enough η, convergence to a state with $E = 0$ does indeed occur. For monotonic transfer functions $g(\cdot)$—the case which we treat here—it follows from (18.10) that zero generalization error can be obtained only

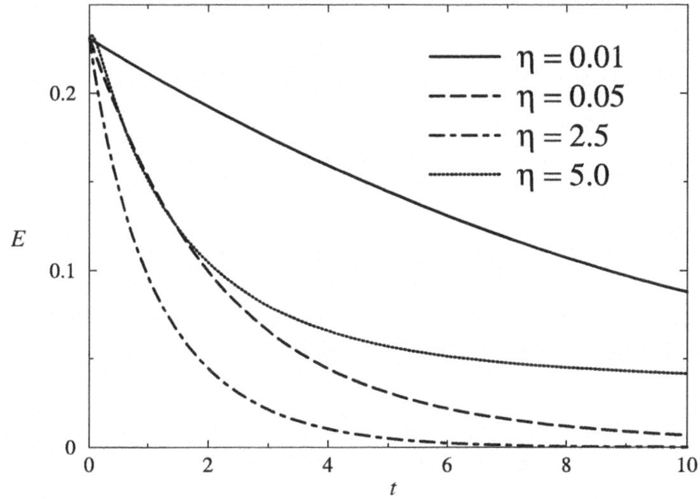

Figure 18.1 Evolution of generalization error E versus the rescaled number of learning steps $t = \ell/N$, for the different values of η shown. The initial values of the macroscopic observables were in all cases: $R(0) = 0$, $Q(0) = 1/4$.

if x and y are identical with probability one. This means that we need to have $\langle (x-y)^2 \rangle = 0$, and hence $R = Q = 1$. It is easy to show that this is a fixed point of the dynamics (18.12, 18.13); the numerical solution also confirms that R and Q both tend to 1 for small η. We now linearize around this particular stationary point, setting $R = 1 - \delta r$ and $Q = 1 - \delta q$ and expanding (18.12, 18.13) to first order in δr and δq. This yields

$$\frac{\mathrm{d}}{\mathrm{d}t}\begin{pmatrix}\delta r\\ \delta q\end{pmatrix} = \boldsymbol{M}\begin{pmatrix}\delta r\\ \delta q\end{pmatrix}, \quad \boldsymbol{M} = -c\tilde{\eta}\begin{pmatrix} 4 & -\frac{3}{2} \\ -4(1-3\tilde{\eta}) & 3(1-2\tilde{\eta})\end{pmatrix} \tag{18.18}$$

where

$$c = \frac{2\sqrt{5}}{9} \qquad \tilde{\eta} = \frac{\eta}{\eta_{\mathrm{c}}} \qquad \eta_{\mathrm{c}} = \pi\sqrt{\frac{5}{3}} = 4.05577\ldots \tag{18.19}$$

The notation η_{c} here is deliberately suggestive; we will see in a moment that η_{c} is actually the critical learning rate. The eigenvalues $\{\lambda_1, \lambda_2\}$ and associated eigenvectors $\{\mathbf{e}_1, \mathbf{e}_2\}$ of the matrix $\boldsymbol{M}$ can be calculated, and turn out to be

$$\lambda_1 = -6c\tilde{\eta}(1-\tilde{\eta}) \qquad \mathbf{e}_1 = \begin{pmatrix} 1 \\ -\frac{4}{3}+4\tilde{\eta} \end{pmatrix}$$

$$\lambda_2 = -c\tilde{\eta} \qquad \mathbf{e}_2 = \begin{pmatrix} 1 \\ 2 \end{pmatrix} \tag{18.20}$$

Using these, we deduce from (18.18) that the asymptotic time evolution of δr and δq can be written as

$$\begin{pmatrix} \delta r \\ \delta q \end{pmatrix} = C_1 e^{\lambda_1 t}\mathbf{e}_1 + C_2 e^{\lambda_2 t}\mathbf{e}_2 \tag{18.21}$$

Here C_1 and C_2 are two constants that will depend on the initial conditions.

The eigenvalues λ_1 and λ_2 are shown in Figure 18.2 as a function of η. In order for the stationary point $R = Q = 1$ around which we are expanding to be stable, we need both these eigenvalues to be negative (compare (18.21)), which leads to the condition $\eta < \eta_c$. For $\eta > \eta_c$, on the other hand, λ_1 is positive, the stationary point is unstable, and the system will no longer converge to a state where $E = 0$. This justifies the interpretation of η_c as the critical learning rate.

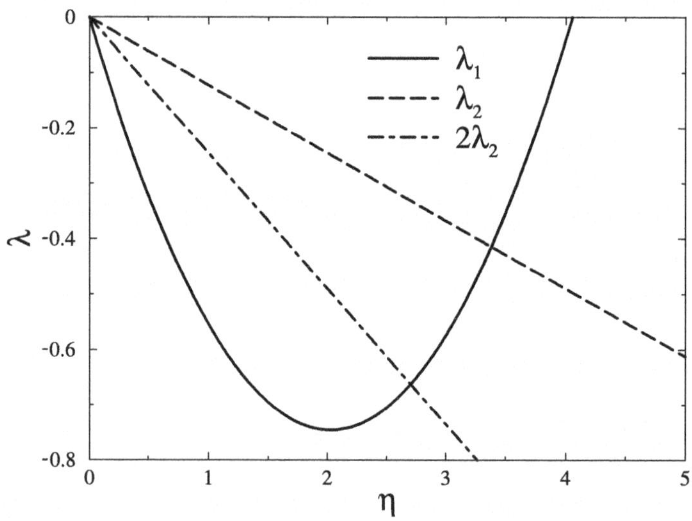

Figure 18.2 The values of the two eigenvalues $\{\lambda_1, \lambda_2\}$ that govern the dynamics around the fixed point $R = Q = 1$, which corresponds to perfect learning, as functions of the learning rate η. For the asymptotic decay of E, λ_1 and $2\lambda_2$ (rather than λ_2 itself) turn out to be relevant; see the main text.

The eigenvalues $\lambda_{1,2}$ also provide information on the speed of convergence. For $\eta < \eta_c$, we see from (18.21) that R and Q converge exponentially to their limiting values, with a decay rate given by $\min\{-\lambda_1, -\lambda_2\}$; the least negative eigenvalue is dominant asymptotically, because it gives the slowest convergence. As the critical learning rate is approached, one has $-\lambda_1 \sim \eta_c - \eta$ and hence the decay time—which is the inverse of the decay rate—diverges as $1/(\eta_c - \eta)$. In physics, this type of phenomenon is called critical slowing down. Precisely at the critical learning rate, that is, for $\eta = \eta_c$, we have power law rather than exponential convergence; here one can show that both R and Q approach their limiting values as $\sim 1/t$, that is, via power law relaxation.

An intuitive interpretation of what happens at the critical learning rate is provided by the following analogy. Assume there is only a single student weight, which is adapted by gradient descent on a parabolic (quadratic) error measure. If the learning rate is too high, the gradient descent steps can overshoot the minimum of the parabola and land on the other side, further away from the minimum than where it was previously. This obviously prevents convergence, and leads to larger and larger moduli of the weight. In the perceptron case, matters are somewhat more complicated because the error measure is bounded whenever the transfer function $g(\cdot)$ is. For our choice of $g(\cdot)$, one can show that R and Q still tend to finite limits (which are >1) for $\eta_c < \eta < \pi/\arcsin(1/3)$, and only actually diverge for even larger values of η.

Finally, let us analyse the asymptotic behaviour of the generalization error in the regime of sub-critical learning rates, that is, when $\eta < \eta_c$. Expanding (18.17) for small values of δr and δq we find

$$E = \frac{2\delta r - \delta q}{\pi\sqrt{3}} + \mathcal{O}(\delta r^2, \delta r \delta q, \delta q) \tag{18.22}$$

From the asymptotic behaviour (18.21) of δr and δq, we see that the first term in (18.22) will give contributions that decay as $\exp(\lambda_1 t)$ and $\exp(\lambda_2 t)$, while the quadratic terms exhibit time dependencies of the form $\exp(2\lambda_1 t)$, $\exp((\lambda_1 + \lambda_2)t)$, and $\exp(2\lambda_2 t)$. However, due to the specific form of the eigenvector $\mathbf{e}_2$, see (18.20), the linear contribution proportional to $\exp(\lambda_2 t)$ drops out. Hence we are left with terms with decay rates $-\lambda_1$, $-2\lambda_2$, $-\lambda_1 - \lambda_2$, and $-2\lambda_1$ (and higher order terms that decay even faster). The last two of these are always larger than the first one, and so we have the final result that the asymptotic decay rate of the generalization error E is given by $\min\{-\lambda_1, -2\lambda_2\}$; the dependence of these two rates on η is shown in Figure 18.2. We read off that the fastest asymptotic convergence of the generalization error E occurs when $\lambda_1 = 2\lambda_2$; from (18.20) it follows that this happens for the learning rate $\eta = \frac{2}{3}\eta_c$. Note, however, that this specific value of η optimizes only the asymptotic convergence rate; the initial decay of $E(t)$ can be faster for other values of η.

18.2 Learning from noisy examples

The scenario which we have considered so far is rather idealized, in that we assumed that the outputs provided by the teacher are noise free. In practice, training data are often *noisy*. We therefore now consider the more general case where the teacher output for training example $\boldsymbol{\xi}(t)$ is $g(\boldsymbol{B}\cdot\boldsymbol{\xi}(t)) + \epsilon_t$, with ϵ_t some additive noise variable. We make the natural assumptions that the distribution of ϵ_t is the same for all t, and that ϵ_t and $\epsilon_{t'}$ are independent for $t \neq t'$. Intuitively, this means that the noise process that corrupts our data does not change over time and that it has no memory carrying over from one example to the next. Our gradient descent learning rule now takes the following form, with the shorthand $\mathcal{G}[x, T] = [g(x) - T]g'(x)$:

$$\boldsymbol{J}(t+\Delta t) = \boldsymbol{J}(t) - \frac{\eta}{N}\boldsymbol{\xi}(t)\mathcal{G}[\boldsymbol{J}(t)\cdot\boldsymbol{\xi}(t), g(\boldsymbol{B}(t)\cdot\boldsymbol{\xi}(t)) + \epsilon_t] \qquad (18.23)$$

We once more follow the procedure in Section 17.2, setting $Q(t) = \boldsymbol{J}^2(t)$ and $R(t) = \boldsymbol{B}\cdot\boldsymbol{J}(t)$. Taking the scalar product of (18.23) with $\boldsymbol{B}$ gives us

$$\frac{R(t+\Delta t) - R(t)}{\Delta t} = -\eta\boldsymbol{B}\cdot\boldsymbol{\xi}(t)\mathcal{G}[\boldsymbol{J}(t)\cdot\boldsymbol{\xi}(t), g(\boldsymbol{B}\cdot\boldsymbol{\xi}(t)) + \epsilon_t] \qquad (18.24)$$

while by taking the scalar product of (18.23) with itself we get

$$\frac{Q(t+\Delta t) - Q(t)}{\Delta t} = -2\eta\boldsymbol{J}(t)\cdot\boldsymbol{\xi}(t)\mathcal{G}[\cdots] + \eta^2\mathcal{G}^2[\cdots] \qquad (18.25)$$

where we have used $\boldsymbol{\xi}(t)\cdot\boldsymbol{\xi}(t) = N$. One can now make the transition to the continuous time limit by accumulating ℓ discrete learning steps, and taking the limits $\ell \to \infty$, $N \to \infty$ in such a way that $\ell/N \to 0$. This allows us to replace the left-hand sides of (18.24) and (18.25) by time derivatives, and the right-hand sides by averages over the random quantities involved. These averages are now over all $\boldsymbol{\xi} \in \{-1, 1\}^N$ *and* over the noise variables ϵ_t. The inputs $\boldsymbol{\xi}$ again enter only through the fields $x = \boldsymbol{J}\cdot\boldsymbol{\xi}$ and $y = \boldsymbol{B}\cdot\boldsymbol{\xi}$, and after inserting explicitly the definition of $\mathcal{G}[x, T]$ we end up with

$$\frac{\mathrm{d}}{\mathrm{d}t}R = -\eta\langle y[g(x) - g(y) - \epsilon]g'(x)\rangle_{x,y,\epsilon} \tag{18.26}$$

$$\frac{\mathrm{d}}{\mathrm{d}t}Q = -2\eta\langle x[g(x) - g(y) - \epsilon]g'(x)\rangle_{x,y,\epsilon} + \eta^2\langle[g(x) - g(y) - \epsilon]^2[g'(x)]^2\rangle_{x,y,\epsilon} \tag{18.27}$$

The averages in (18.26, 18.27) are over the distribution (18.7) of the fields x and y, and over the noise ϵ, which is independent of x and y. We now assume that the noise has mean zero, since a nonzero mean can always be absorbed by adding it to the teacher's transfer function, and some finite variance which we will denote by σ^2. Because the noise ϵ appears only in linear and quadratic terms, the noise averages have become trivial; linear terms simply drop out. This gives us the final form for the equations of motion for R and Q, where we drop the subscripts on the averages again, since they are now over x and y as before:

$$\frac{\mathrm{d}}{\mathrm{d}t}R = -\eta\langle y[g(x) - g(y)]g'(x)\rangle \tag{18.28}$$

$$\frac{\mathrm{d}}{\mathrm{d}t}Q = -2\eta\langle x[g(x) - g(y)]g'(x)\rangle + \eta^2\langle[g(x) - g(y)]^2[g'(x)]^2\rangle + \eta^2\sigma^2\langle[g'(x)]^2\rangle \tag{18.29}$$

Comparison with (18.5, 18.6) shows that, at the macroscopic level of description and for $N \to \infty$, the only effect of the noise in the teacher outputs is to add an extra term to $\mathrm{d}Q/\mathrm{d}t$. As expected, this term is proportional to the strength of the noise as measured by the variance σ^2. As soon as there is any noise at all (i.e. as soon as $\sigma^2 > 0$), this additional term is positive, which means that the optimal solution $R = Q = 1$ can no longer be a stationary state. The asymptotic generalization error, as reached in the limit $t \to \infty$, must therefore be nonzero. Its actual value depends on η and σ^2. In general, it cannot be calculated analytically and has to be obtained from a numerical solution of the stationarity conditions for R and Q. For small noise levels σ^2, however, the stationary state will be close to $R = Q = 1$. One can therefore again linearize the equations of motion for small values of $\delta r = 1 - R$ and $\delta q = 1 - Q$, and find their stationary values. Focusing as before on the case of the transfer function $g(z) = \mathrm{erf}(z/\sqrt{2})$, and inserting the stationary values δr and δq into the linearized expression for the generalization error (18.22), one then obtains

$$E(t \to \infty) = \frac{\sqrt{5}}{6}\sigma^2 \frac{\eta/\eta_\mathrm{c}}{1 - \eta/\eta_\mathrm{c}} + \mathcal{O}(\eta^2\sigma^4) \tag{18.30}$$

This illustrates an important point: the effect of noisy training inputs on the asymptotic generalization performance depends not only on σ^2, but also on the learning rate η. The optimal value of $E(t \to \infty)$ is obtained for $\eta \to 0$; this remains true also for larger values of σ^2, even though the above expansion for small σ^2 can then no longer be used. This means that there is actually a tradeoff between the asymptotic value of E and the speed with which it is reached. For small learning rate η, the asymptotic convergence rate is proportional to η, and so the corresponding timescale $\sim 1/\eta$ diverges for $\eta \to 0$. In practice, one therefore often strikes a compromise by using time-dependent learning rates when learning from noisy data. Initially, a relatively large value of η is used in order to achieve fast convergence; then η is gradually reduced to zero ($\eta(t) \sim 1/t$ can be shown to be optimal asymptotically, see Exercise 18.3) to get good asymptotic generalization performance.

18.3 Exercises

Exercise 18.1. (Verification of details in derivations.) Confirm that $R = Q = 1$ is a stationary state of the equations of motion (18.12, 18.16). Derive the linearized equation of motion (18.18)—this is not difficult conceptually, but involves a fair bit of algebra. Calculate the eigenvalues and eigenvectors of the matrix $\boldsymbol{M}$; see (18.20) for the result. Also verify the linearized representation of the generalization error (18.22). Finally, show from the condition $\lambda_1 = 2\lambda_2$ that the learning rate that optimizes the asymptotic convergence rate is indeed given by $\eta = (2/3)\eta_c$.

Exercise 18.2. (Learning dynamics in the presence of teacher noise.) Work out the final term in (18.29) (which is due to the noise in the training outputs) explicitly for $g(z) = \text{erf}(z/\sqrt{2})$; you should find the result $\eta^2\sigma^2(2/\pi)\times(1+2Q)^{-1/2}$. Expand this expression to first order in $\delta q = 1-Q$. Combining the result with (18.18) for the noise free case, show that the linearized equations of motion in the presence of noise are given by

$$\frac{\mathrm{d}}{\mathrm{d}t}\begin{pmatrix}\delta r\\ \delta q\end{pmatrix} = \tilde{\boldsymbol{M}}\begin{pmatrix}\delta r\\ \delta q\end{pmatrix} - \begin{pmatrix}0\\ d\end{pmatrix}, \quad \tilde{\boldsymbol{M}} = \boldsymbol{M} - \begin{pmatrix}0 & 0\\ 0 & d/3\end{pmatrix}$$

where $d = 2\eta^2\sigma^2/(\pi\sqrt{3})$. By setting the left-hand sides to zero, obtain the stationary values of δr and δq as

$$\begin{pmatrix}\delta r\\ \delta q\end{pmatrix} = -\boldsymbol{M}^{-1}\begin{pmatrix}0\\ d\end{pmatrix} + \mathcal{O}(\eta^2\sigma^4) = -\frac{\pi\sqrt{15}}{1-\tilde{\eta}}\,\tilde{\eta}\sigma^2\begin{pmatrix}1/4\\ 2/3\end{pmatrix} + \mathcal{O}(\eta^2\sigma^4)$$

You can do this either by inverting $\tilde{\boldsymbol{M}}$ explicitly, or by noting that the relative deviation between the elements of $\tilde{\boldsymbol{M}}$ and $\boldsymbol{M}$ is of order $\mathcal{O}(\eta\sigma^2)$. Finally, confirm expression (18.30) by inserting your result into the linearized representation of the generalization error (18.22).

Exercise 18.3. (Linear student and teacher.) Apply the formalism in Section 18.2 for learning by continuous output perceptrons in the presence of teacher output noise to the case of a linear transfer function, that is, to $g(z) = z$. Show that the differential equations for R and Q simplify to

$$\frac{\mathrm{d}}{\mathrm{d}t} R = -\eta R + \eta$$

$$\frac{\mathrm{d}}{\mathrm{d}t} Q = 2\eta(1-\eta)R + \eta(\eta - 2)Q + \eta^2(1+\sigma^2)$$

and that the generalization error becomes $E = \frac{1}{2}(1 - 2R + Q)$. Show from the definitions of R and Q that $R^2 \leq Q$ and that $Q \geq 0$. Use these inequalities to show that E is always non-negative, and that it achieves its minimal value for $R = Q = 1$. Find the stationary state (R_*, Q_*) of the dynamical equations; show that the generalization error in this state is given by

$$E_* = \frac{\eta\sigma^2}{2(2-\eta)}$$

Deduce that the stationary state is not accessible (because it violates one of the constraints $R^2 \leq Q$, $Q \geq 0$) for $\eta > 2$. Starting from your expressions for $\mathrm{d}R/\mathrm{d}t$ and $\mathrm{d}Q/\mathrm{d}t$, find an expression for $\mathrm{d}E/\mathrm{d}t$. You should find that this is a linear differential equation. Find its general solution, and the value of η which gives the fastest convergence of E to its asymptotic value. Next solve the equations for R and Q explicitly. The equation for $R(t)$ is simple; to get $Q(t)$, you can simply combine the results for $R(t)$ and $E(t)$. Draw a flow diagram in the R–Q plane, separately for values of η below and above 2. From the second diagram you should see explicitly how the stationary point becomes physically inaccessible.

Assume from now on that $\sigma^2 > 0$. Why does it make sense to reduce η to zero for $t \to \infty$, in spite of your previous claims? Find the optimal $\eta(t)$; since the aim is to minimize E, the optimal $\eta(t)$ is the one that maximizes $|\mathrm{d}E/\mathrm{d}t|$ for any given t. Show that this gives $\eta(t) = 2E(t)/[2E(t) + \sigma^2]$. For this choice of $\eta(t)$, integrate the differential equation for $E(t)$ to get $-\ln E + \sigma^2/(2E) = t +$ constant. When $E \to 0$, the first term on the left-hand side can be neglected compared to the second one; hence show that the optimal learning rate is of the form $\eta(t) \sim 1/t$ for large t.

Exercise 18.4. (Mismatched student and teacher.) Extend the formalism of Section 18.2 to the case where the transfer function of the teacher, $h(z)$, is different from that of the student, $g(z)$. Derive the dynamical equations for R and Q in the limit $N \to \infty$; the only change compared to the case of identical transfer functions should be the replacement of $g(y)$ by $h(y)$ everywhere. Specialize to the case of a linear student, that is, $g(z) = z$, and a teacher with a small non-linearity, that is, $h(z) = z + az^2$. Perform the averages over x and y in the dynamical equations explicitly. You will need the result that for zero mean Gaussian random variables $\langle z^4 \rangle = 3\langle z^2 \rangle^2$ (you may want to show this yourself, or see Appendix D). Show that at the macroscopic level the 'unlearnability', that is, the mismatch between student and teacher transfer functions, just acts as extra noise source, giving an increased effective noise level of $\sigma^2 + 3a^2$.

19 Notes and suggestions for further reading

In carrying out dynamical studies such as those in the previous three chapters one always relies on general background knowledge of stochastic processes (at the microscopic level of description), and of non-linear dynamical systems (at the level of deterministic macroscopic observables); recommended general textbooks on these topics are the ones by van Kampen [79] and by Khalil [81], respectively. In contrast to the situation in equilibrium, however (see Part V), it is difficult to give references to textbooks on the specific problems that we have been concerned with here, viz. the processes of operation in recurrent networks and of learning in layered ones. Such books appear to be surprisingly hard to find, partly, it seems, because dynamical studies only got started seriously towards 1990 (whereas many neural network textbooks were written immediately before then).

The first to analyse the dynamics of recurrent neural networks at the level of macroscopic observables appears to have been Amari in 1977 [82]. His ideas were worked out further and generalized in [83] and [84]. Amari's method was based on approximating the distribution of the local fields in recurrent networks by a Gaussian one, followed by an analysis of the evolution of the moments of this Gaussian distribution. In Chapter 16 we have discussed only those cases where, as a result of restricting oneself to small numbers of stored patterns, the fields are fully deterministic (so that we do not need to calculate field distributions), allowing for exact closed equations. This simplifying property was discovered and exploited by several authors in the late 1980s, see, for example, [85–87]. An alternative class of models that allow for a relatively simple derivation of exact closed macroscopic laws are the so-called asymmetrically extremely diluted networks, see, for example, Derrida *et al.* [88] or the review by Kree and Zippelius [89]; here the field distributions are indeed Gausssian. The problem originally addressed by Amari (fully and symmetrically connected networks with a number of stored patterns that is no longer small), in contrast, was found to be solvable without resorting to approximations only via the more demanding generating functional analysis formalism; the first to take this route were Rieger *et al.* [90] and Horner *et al.* [91]. Examples of alternative (and simpler but approximate) methods, developed in roughly the same period, are [92] and [93]. A relatively recent review of the analysis of the dynamics of recurrent neural networks, including many of the above distinct and complementary model types and analytical approaches (and also others), is [94].

The application of statistical mechanical methods, which the calculation of dynamical equations for macroscopic observables from stochastic microscopic laws represents, to learning processes in neural networks was largely initiated by the equilibrium analysis of Gardner [95, 96], to be discussed in Chapter 22. Many subsequent *dynamical* studies were influenced significantly by the early two papers [97] and [98]. Early studies can be traced via the review papers [99–101]; a more recent review is [102]. The online learning algorithms for training perceptrons as considered in Chapter 17 were introduced by Rosenblatt [5] (the perceptron rule), Vallet [103] (the Hebbian rule), and Anlauf and Biehl [104] (the AdaTron rule), although at the time they were not yet studied with the methods described here. Kinzel and Rujan were the first to derive, in embryonic form, closed equations for the observables $\boldsymbol{J}^2$ and $\boldsymbol{J} \cdot \boldsymbol{B}$ in perceptrons [105]. Many of the results derived in Chapter 17 can be found in [106–108]. The lower bound $E_g \sim 0.44\ldots t^{-1}$ for online learning rules was derived in [109]. The systematic optimization of learning rules to achieve the fastest decay of the generalization error in perceptrons was introduced by Kinouchi and Caticha [106].

The approach to online learning by gradient descent described in Chapter 18 was pioneered by Biehl and Schwarze [110] and generalized to multilayer neural networks by Saad and Solla [111]. A useful overview of later developments is the collection [112] of contributions to a workshop on online learning.

Finally, just like in the case of the dynamics of recurrent networks one has a parameter regime where the problem demands more sophisticated methods (operation close to saturation, that is, with large numbers of stored patterns, see Chapter 21), also in the dynamics of learning one has such a regime. In the latter case one finds that more advanced methods are required as soon as the size of the training set is of the same order as the number of dynamic variables (i.e. the synaptic weights), such that the data must inevitably be re-cycled in the learning process. Examples of papers where these more complicated scenarios are studied are [113–116].

Part V Equilibrium statistical mechanics of neural networks

Statistical mechanical techniques are employed in those cases where the microscopic dynamical equations of a given many-particle system are too complicated to be solved directly and explicitly for all times. In the preceding part of this book we used *non-equilibrium* statistical mechanical techniques to avoid having to solve our stochastic equations at the microscopic level, by instead first deriving stochastic equations for suitable macroscopic observables, which could then be solved much more easily than the microscopic ones (at least in the limit of an infinite system size). Whenever this method applies, whether in studying the operation or the learning of neural systems, it leads to closed and deterministic dynamical laws for macroscopic quantities.

In *equilibrium* statistical mechanics the route towards a deterministic macroscopic theory is different: here one focuses on those stochastic processes which evolve towards an equilibrium state, where the so-called detailed balance property holds. This property is a mathematical condition that rules out the existence of microscopic probability currents in the stationary state, and enables us to write down the microscopic equilibrium state probabilities of our system in explicit form. Put differently, in such systems we are able to solve the microscopic stochastic equations after all, but only in a stationary state. This then serves as the starting point for the derivation of macroscopic laws, in the limit of an infinite system size. This route is in one sense more limited than the non-equilibrium one, in that we can at most find a macroscopic theory describing specific systems in equilibrium; there will be no description of how the system will get there. In another sense it is more powerful: one finds that the interactions between the microscopic elements can be much more complicated, compared to the situation in non-equilibrium studies, without impairing our ability to derive the macroscopic laws.

We first discuss applications of equilibrium statistical mechanics in the domain of recurrent neural networks (where the condition for evolution towards detailed balance equilibrium translates into restrictions on the synaptic matrices), allowing us to study the operation of such systems as associative memories not only at modest storage levels but also when they operate close to saturation. Furthermore, one finds that also certain problems in learning theory (especially those related to settling questions regarding the *existence* of weights and thresholds required for layered networks to solve a given problem) can be mapped onto an equilibrium statistical mechanical calculation; this latter application domain is known as Gardner theory. Both types of applications will involve a mathematical method, replica theory, which has been developed to deal with the complexities induced by randomness or disorder in the microscopic system parameters.

20 Basics of equilibrium statistical mechanics

Rather than explaining the ideas and methods of equilibrium statistical mechanics in an abstract setting, we illustrate them directly in the context of neural network models. In Section 16.1 we defined our basic model for the operation of recurrent networks with binary units. Their dynamics was found as a process of stochastic alignment of spin variables $\sigma_i \in \{-1, 1\}$, representing the neurons, to local fields h_i. This takes the form of a Markov chain, for both parallel and sequential state updates:

$$p_{t+1}(\boldsymbol{\sigma}) = \sum_{\boldsymbol{\sigma}'} W(\boldsymbol{\sigma}, \boldsymbol{\sigma}') p_t(\boldsymbol{\sigma}') \tag{20.1}$$

with the transition matrices (16.7) and (16.13), respectively, and with $\boldsymbol{\sigma} \in \{-1, 1\}^N$. In general, Markov processes can have quite complex behaviour, including limit cycles, absorbing states etc. However, we will see that the processes we are interested in are ergodic, and the probability distribution $p_t(\boldsymbol{\sigma})$ of a finite system is guaranteed to converge to a unique stationary distribution $p_\infty(\boldsymbol{\sigma})$ for $t \to \infty$. If, in addition, the interaction matrix J_{ij} is symmetric, the dynamics obey what is known as detailed balance. The resulting stationary state is then called an equilibrium state, and $p_\infty(\boldsymbol{\sigma})$ has the form of a Boltzmann distribution, the consequences of which can be analysed using the formalism of equilibrium statistical mechanics. These concepts and properties will be explained and derived in the present chapter. We conclude with a simple example, which will illustrate the subtle but important issue of the order of the two limits $N \to \infty$ and $t \to \infty$ and its relation to phase transitions.

20.1 Stationary distributions and ergodicity

Ergodicity

The main property of our transition matrices which ensures convergence to a unique stationary distribution is that they describe Markovian processes that are ergodic, except in the special limit $\beta \to \infty$ to be discussed separately in Section 20.2. Intuitively, ergodicity means that all possible states $\boldsymbol{\sigma}$ of the network are connected to each other; for any two microscopic states $\boldsymbol{\sigma}$ and $\boldsymbol{\sigma}'$ there is a chain of allowed microscopic transitions that allows us to go from $\boldsymbol{\sigma}$ to $\boldsymbol{\sigma}'$. If we are prepared to wait long enough, the probability will then spread out over all states, whatever initial distribution $p_0(\boldsymbol{\sigma})$ we start from. More formally, a Markov process is ergodic if, whatever the initial conditions $p_0(\boldsymbol{\sigma})$, there exists a time τ such that

$$p_t(\boldsymbol{\sigma}) > 0 \quad \text{for all } \boldsymbol{\sigma} \text{ and all } t \geq \tau \tag{20.2}$$

For parallel dynamics (16.6) just one iteration is needed for ensuring that all probabilities $p_t(\boldsymbol{\sigma})$ are positive: $\tau_{\text{par}} = 1$. For sequential dynamics (16.9), at most N iterations are needed since we can reach any state from any other by at most N spin flips, hence $\tau_{\text{seq}} = N$.

By repeated iteration of (20.1) one may write the solution $p_t(\boldsymbol{\sigma})$ of the Markov chain as $p_t(\boldsymbol{\sigma}) = \sum_{\boldsymbol{\sigma}''} W^t(\boldsymbol{\sigma}, \boldsymbol{\sigma}'') p_0(\boldsymbol{\sigma}'')$, where W^t denotes the tth matrix power of the $2^N \times 2^N$ transition matrix W. If we then choose the initial conditions $p_0(\boldsymbol{\sigma}'') = \delta_{\boldsymbol{\sigma}', \boldsymbol{\sigma}''}$ for some arbitrary $\boldsymbol{\sigma}' \in \{-1, 1\}^N$, we find $p_t(\boldsymbol{\sigma}) = W^t(\boldsymbol{\sigma}, \boldsymbol{\sigma}')$. It now follows, in view of (20.2), that an ergodic system must obey

$$W^t(\boldsymbol{\sigma}, \boldsymbol{\sigma}') > 0 \quad \text{for all } \boldsymbol{\sigma}, \boldsymbol{\sigma}' \text{ and all } t \geq \tau \tag{20.3}$$

Here the time τ, which characterizes the minimum number of transitions required to connect arbitrary microscopic states, is the one referred to in (20.2). Since, in turn, property (20.2) is an immediate consequence of (20.3), the two can be regarded as equivalent definitions of ergodicity.

Existence of a stationary distribution

Let us consider ergodic Markov processes of the type (20.1), with some $2^N \times 2^N$ transition matrix W with entries $W(\boldsymbol{\sigma}, \boldsymbol{\sigma}')$. Conservation of probability guarantees that the transition matrix has a left eigenvector (namely the vector $\boldsymbol{u} = (1, 1, \ldots, 1)$) with eigenvalue one:

$$\sum_{\boldsymbol{\sigma}} u(\boldsymbol{\sigma}) W(\boldsymbol{\sigma}, \boldsymbol{\sigma}') = \sum_{\boldsymbol{\sigma}} W(\boldsymbol{\sigma}, \boldsymbol{\sigma}') = 1 = u(\boldsymbol{\sigma}')$$

Now, for any finite-dimensional matrix W, the spectrum of left eigenvalues is identical to the spectrum of right eigenvalues, since

$$\det(W - \lambda \mathbf{1}) = \det(W - \lambda \mathbf{1})^{\dagger}$$

We can therefore be sure that there exists also at least one non-trivial right eigenvector ϕ with eigenvalue one, that is, with

$$\sum_{\sigma'} W(\sigma,\sigma')\phi(\sigma') = \phi(\sigma) \tag{20.4}$$

We next prove that for ergodic systems (20.2) there exists an eigenvector of the type (20.4) with positive components only (since the components must represent probabilities, we must demand they be non-negative). To do so we first define S_+, S_0, and S_- as the sets of all system states $\boldsymbol{\sigma} \in \{-1,1\}^N$ for which $\phi(\boldsymbol{\sigma}) > 0$, $=0$, and < 0, respectively. From (20.4) we can derive, by summation over either all $\boldsymbol{\sigma} \in S_+$ or over all $\boldsymbol{\sigma} \in S_-$, respectively, the following two equations:

$$\sum_{\sigma\in S_+} \phi(\sigma) = \sum_{\sigma\in S_+}\Big[\sum_{\sigma'\in S_+} W(\sigma,\sigma')\phi(\sigma') + \sum_{\sigma'\in S_-} W(\sigma,\sigma')\phi(\sigma')\Big]$$

$$\sum_{\sigma\in S_-} \phi(\sigma) = \sum_{\sigma\in S_-}\Big[\sum_{\sigma'\in S_+} W(\sigma,\sigma')\phi(\sigma') + \sum_{\sigma'\in S_-} W(\sigma,\sigma')\phi(\sigma')\Big]$$

or, after relabelling $\boldsymbol{\sigma} \to \boldsymbol{\sigma}'$ on the left-hand sides,

$$\sum_{\sigma'\in S_+}\Big[1 - \sum_{\sigma\in S_+} W(\sigma,\sigma')\Big]\phi(\sigma') = \sum_{\sigma\in S_+}\sum_{\sigma'\in S_-} W(\sigma,\sigma')\phi(\sigma') \tag{20.5}$$

$$\sum_{\sigma'\in S_-}\Big[1 - \sum_{\sigma\in S_-} W(\sigma,\sigma')\Big]\phi(\sigma') = \sum_{\sigma\in S_-}\sum_{\sigma'\in S_+} W(\sigma,\sigma')\phi(\sigma') \tag{20.6}$$

By construction, all terms on the left-hand side of (20.5) are non-negative, while those on the right-hand side are all non-positive. Similarly, all terms on the left-hand side of (20.6) are non-positive, while those on the right-hand side are all non-negative. It follows that both sides of both equations (20.5, 20.6) must be zero. Let us now focus on the implications for the left-hand sides of (20.5, 20.6), which are, respectively:

$$\text{for all } \sigma' \in S_+: \quad \sum_{\sigma\in S_+} W(\sigma,\sigma') = 1$$

$$\text{for all } \sigma' \in S_-: \quad \sum_{\sigma\in S_-} W(\sigma,\sigma') = 1$$

Since $\sum_{\sigma} W(\sigma,\sigma') = 1$ for *any* state σ' (probability conservation), this statement, in turn, implies that

$$\text{for all } \sigma' \in S_+, \quad \sigma \notin S_+: \quad W(\sigma,\sigma') = 0$$

$$\text{for all } \sigma' \in S_-, \quad \sigma \notin S_-: \quad W(\sigma,\sigma') = 0$$

We conclude that our stochastic process allows for only two types of transitions away from states $\sigma' \in S_+ \bigcup S_-$, namely

$$\sigma' \in S_- \to \sigma \in S_- \qquad \sigma' \in S_+ \to \sigma \in S_+$$

Since ϕ is a non-trivial eigenvector, we know that either S_+ or S_- is not empty (or even both). Now suppose S_+ is not empty. Given that our systems are ergodic (20.2) and that starting from a state in S_+ we can never go to a state outside S_+, it follows immediately that S_+ must then contain *all* states. In other words: if ϕ has positive components, then *all* its components must be positive. Similarly, if S_- is not empty, it must contain all states: if ϕ has negative components, then *all* its components must be negative. Since from any solution ϕ of (20.4) with only negative components we can obtain one with only positive components by switching $\phi \to -\phi$ (which can then be properly normalized so that its components sum to one), we have proven the existence of a non-trivial stationary probability distribution.

Convergence and uniqueness

We now turn to the evolution in time of the difference ψ_t between two individual probability distributions p_t^a and p_t^b, which are obtained as a result of iterating (20.1) from different initial conditions a and b. Due to the linearity of the problem, ψ_t is itself again a solution of (20.1):

$$\psi_t(\sigma) = p_t^a(\sigma) - p_t^b(\sigma) \qquad \psi_{t+1}(\sigma) = \sum_{\sigma'} W(\sigma,\sigma')\psi_t(\sigma)$$

Thinking again of $\psi_t(\sigma)$ as the components of a 2^N-dimensional vector ψ_t, and of $W(\sigma,\sigma')$ as the entries of a $2^N \times 2^N$ matrix $\boldsymbol{W}$, we can simply write $\psi_{t+1} = \boldsymbol{W}\psi_t$. At all times and for all σ we have $\psi_t(\sigma) \in [-1,1]$, simply because all entries $W(\sigma,\sigma')$ represent transition probabilities. So the sequence ψ_t $(t = 0,1,2,\ldots)$ is bounded. Since $\sum_{\sigma} p_t^a(\sigma) = \sum_{\sigma} p_t^b(\sigma) = 1$

for all $t \geq 0$, we also know that

$$\sum_{\sigma} \psi_t(\sigma) = 0 \quad \text{for all } t \geq 0 \tag{20.7}$$

We will show below that $\lim_{t\to\infty} \psi_t(\sigma) = 0$ for all σ individually. If we now choose $p_0^b(\sigma)$ to be the stationary distribution $p_\infty(\sigma)$, whose existence we have already demonstrated, we know that $p_t^b(\sigma) = p_\infty(\sigma)$ for all $t \geq 0$, so that the asymptotic vanishing of ψ_t translates into

$$\lim_{t\to\infty} p_t(\sigma) = p_\infty(\sigma) \quad \text{for all } \sigma \in \{-1, 1\}^N \tag{20.8}$$

This holds for all solutions $p_t(\sigma)$ of the ergodic Markov chain (20.1), since $p_0^a(\sigma)$ could be chosen arbitrarily. This gives the desired result: the probability distribution $p_t(\sigma)$ will converge to p_∞ for $t \to \infty$, from any initial condition $p_0(\sigma)$. The existence of more than one stationary probability distribution $\{p_\infty(\sigma)\}$ would lead to a contradiction in (20.8), and is therefore ruled out.

To prove that $\lim_{t\to\infty} \psi_t(\sigma) = 0$ for all σ, we generalize the construction that we employed in proving existence of a stationary distribution. We again divide the set $\{-1, 1\}^N$ of all micro-states into subsets, now depending on the sign of the components $\psi_t(\sigma)$. However, since (in contrast to ϕ) the vector ψ_t is not invariant with time, these sets will here be time-dependent as well. We define

$$\begin{aligned}
S_+(\psi) &= \quad \text{all} \quad \sigma \in \{-1, 1\}^N \quad \text{with } \psi(\sigma) > 0 \\
S_0(\psi) &= \quad \text{all} \quad \sigma \in \{-1, 1\}^N \quad \text{with } \psi(\sigma) = 0 \\
S_-(\psi) &= \quad \text{all} \quad \sigma \in \{-1, 1\}^N \quad \text{with } \psi(\sigma) < 0
\end{aligned}$$

We define the following function of ψ:

$$U(\psi) = \sum_{\sigma} |\psi(\sigma)| = \sum_{\sigma \in S_+(\psi)} \psi(\sigma) - \sum_{\sigma \in S_-(\psi)} \psi(\sigma)$$

It is clearly bounded from below, $U(\psi) \geq 0$. If for ψ we now substitute the solution of the time evolution equation $\psi_{t+1} = \boldsymbol{W}\psi_t$, we find that U is also decreasing monotonically with time, until a stage is reached where $U(\psi) = 0$. This can be seen as follows. In any single iteration step $\psi \to \boldsymbol{W}\psi$

we have

$$
\begin{aligned}
U(\boldsymbol{W}\psi) - U(\psi) \\
&= \sum_{\sigma\in S_+(\boldsymbol{W}\psi)} (\boldsymbol{W}\psi)(\boldsymbol{\sigma}) - \sum_{\sigma\in S_+(\psi)} \psi(\boldsymbol{\sigma}) \\
&\quad - \sum_{\sigma\in S_-(\boldsymbol{W}\psi)} (\boldsymbol{W}\psi)(\boldsymbol{\sigma}) + \sum_{\sigma\in S_-(\psi)} \psi(\boldsymbol{\sigma}) \\
&= - \sum_{\sigma'\in S_+(\psi)} |\psi(\boldsymbol{\sigma}')| \Big[1 - \sum_{\sigma\in S_+(\boldsymbol{W}\psi)} W(\boldsymbol{\sigma},\boldsymbol{\sigma}') \Big] \\
&\quad - \sum_{\sigma'\in S_-(\psi)} |\psi(\boldsymbol{\sigma}')| \sum_{\sigma\in S_+(W\psi)} W(\boldsymbol{\sigma},\boldsymbol{\sigma}') \\
&\quad - \sum_{\sigma'\in S_-(\psi)} |\psi(\boldsymbol{\sigma}')| \Big[1 - \sum_{\sigma\in S_-(\boldsymbol{W}\psi)} W(\boldsymbol{\sigma},\boldsymbol{\sigma}') \Big] \\
&\quad - \sum_{\sigma'\in S_+(\psi)} |\psi(\boldsymbol{\sigma}')| \sum_{\sigma\in S_-(\boldsymbol{W}\psi)} W(\boldsymbol{\sigma},\boldsymbol{\sigma}') \\
&= - \sum_{\sigma'\in S_+(\psi)} |\psi(\boldsymbol{\sigma}')| \Big[2 \sum_{\sigma\in S_-(\boldsymbol{W}\psi)} W(\boldsymbol{\sigma},\boldsymbol{\sigma}') + \sum_{\sigma\in S_0(\boldsymbol{W}\psi)} W(\boldsymbol{\sigma},\boldsymbol{\sigma}') \Big] \\
&\quad - \sum_{\sigma'\in S_-(\psi)} |\psi(\boldsymbol{\sigma}')| \Big[2 \sum_{\sigma\in S_+(\boldsymbol{W}\psi)} W(\boldsymbol{\sigma},\boldsymbol{\sigma}') + \sum_{\sigma\in S_0(\boldsymbol{W}\psi)} W(\boldsymbol{\sigma},\boldsymbol{\sigma}') \Big] \\
&\leq 0
\end{aligned}
\tag{20.9}
$$

Since $U(\psi)$ is also bounded from below, it must tend to a limit: $\lim_{t\to\infty} U(\psi_t) = U_\infty \geq 0$ exists. We now prove that this limit must be $U_\infty = 0$.

Let τ denote the time required for all states to be connected by an allowed transition, in the sense of the ergodicity definition (20.3). Since our process is assumed ergodic, we know that

$$\exists W_0 \in (0,1): \quad \boldsymbol{W}^\tau(\boldsymbol{\sigma},\boldsymbol{\sigma}') > W_0 2^{-N} \quad \text{for all } \boldsymbol{\sigma},\boldsymbol{\sigma}' \in \{-1,1\}^N \tag{20.10}$$

The specific factor 2^{-N} will prove convenient. The inequality $W_0 > 0$ follows directly from (20.3), whereas $W_0 < 1$ follows by summing the inequality (20.10) over all $\boldsymbol{\sigma}$ for fixed $\boldsymbol{\sigma}'$. We can now repeat the above steps leading to our expression (20.9), but now applied to the change in U

after τ iterations, viz. $U(\boldsymbol{W}^\tau\psi) - U(\psi)$. This gives simply

$$\begin{aligned}
U(\boldsymbol{W}^\tau\psi) - U(\psi) = -\sum_{\sigma'\in S_+(\psi)} |\psi(\sigma')| \Bigg[2 \sum_{\sigma\in S_-(\boldsymbol{W}^\tau\psi)} \boldsymbol{W}^\tau(\sigma,\sigma') \\
+ \sum_{\sigma\in S_0(\boldsymbol{W}^\tau\psi)} \boldsymbol{W}^\tau(\sigma,\sigma')\Bigg] - \sum_{\sigma'\in S_-(\psi)} |\psi(\sigma')| \\
\times \Bigg[2 \sum_{\sigma\in S_+(\boldsymbol{W}^\tau\psi)} \boldsymbol{W}^\tau(\sigma,\sigma') + \sum_{\sigma\in S_0(\boldsymbol{W}^\tau\psi)} \boldsymbol{W}^\tau(\sigma,\sigma')\Bigg]
\end{aligned}$$

We may now use (20.10) to write

$$\begin{aligned}
U(\boldsymbol{W}^\tau\psi) - U(\psi) \leq -W_0 2^{-N} \sum_{\sigma\in S_+(\psi)} |\psi(\sigma)| \left[2|S_-(\boldsymbol{W}^\tau\psi)| + |S_0(\boldsymbol{W}^\tau\psi)|\right] \\
- W_0 2^{-N} \sum_{\sigma\in S_-(\psi)} |\psi(\sigma)| \left[2|S_+(\boldsymbol{W}^\tau\psi)| + |S_0(\boldsymbol{W}^\tau\psi)|\right]
\end{aligned}$$

From (20.7) it follows that always $\sum_{\sigma\in S_+(\psi)} |\psi(\sigma)| = \sum_{\sigma\in S_+(\psi)} |\psi(\sigma)| = \frac{1}{2}U(\psi)$. Therefore

$$\begin{aligned}
U(\boldsymbol{W}^\tau\psi) - U(\psi) &\leq -W_0 U(\psi) 2^{-N}[|S_-(\boldsymbol{W}^\tau\psi)| + \tfrac{1}{2}|S_0(\boldsymbol{W}^\tau\psi)|] \\
&\quad - W_0 U(\psi) 2^{-N}[|S_+(\boldsymbol{W}^\tau\psi)| + \tfrac{1}{2}|S_0(\boldsymbol{W}^\tau\psi)|] \\
&= -W_0 U(\psi) 2^{-N}[|S_-(\boldsymbol{W}^\tau\psi)| + |S_+(\boldsymbol{W}^\tau\psi)| + |S_0(\boldsymbol{W}^\tau\psi)|] \\
&= -W_0 U(\psi)
\end{aligned}$$

We conclude that $U(\boldsymbol{W}^\tau\psi) \leq (1 - W_0)U(\psi)$. Thus also $U(\psi_\tau) \leq (1 - W_0)U(\psi_0)$, and (upon repeating the argument ℓ times): $U(\psi_{\ell\tau}) \leq (1 - W_0)^\ell U(\psi_0)$. Taking the limit $\ell \to \infty$, together with the lower bound $U(\psi_{\ell\tau}) \geq 0$, gives the desired result: $\lim_{t\to\infty} U(\psi_t) = 0$. Given definition (20.1), we can now indeed be sure that $\lim_{t\to\infty} \psi_t(\sigma) = 0$ for all $\sigma \in \{-1, 1\}^N$. This completes our proof. Ergodic Markov processes have a unique stationary distribution to which they will converge from any initial distribution over states.

20.2 Detailed balance and interaction symmetry

Definition of detailed balance

In the previous section, we have shown that for our Markov process models describing the operation of recurrent neural networks, there is a well-defined and unique stationary distribution $p_\infty(\boldsymbol{\sigma})$ over the 2^N possible microscopic states $\boldsymbol{\sigma}$, which is reached in the limit $t \to \infty$ (at fixed N). This distribution is determined by the stationarity condition

$$\text{for all } \boldsymbol{\sigma} \in \{-1,1\}^N: \quad p_\infty(\boldsymbol{\sigma}) = \sum_{\boldsymbol{\sigma}'} W(\boldsymbol{\sigma},\boldsymbol{\sigma}')p_\infty(\boldsymbol{\sigma}')$$

While it is reassuring that p_∞ exists, to calculate it we would have to solve this system of 2^N linear equations for the 2^N values $p_\infty(\boldsymbol{\sigma})$, subject to the conditions $p_\infty(\boldsymbol{\sigma}) \geq 0$ and $\sum_{\boldsymbol{\sigma}} p_\infty(\boldsymbol{\sigma}) = 1$. This seems rather a hopeless task.

However, for some Markov processes the stationary distribution obeys the following stronger condition:

$$W(\boldsymbol{\sigma},\boldsymbol{\sigma}')p_\infty(\boldsymbol{\sigma}') = W(\boldsymbol{\sigma}',\boldsymbol{\sigma})p_\infty(\boldsymbol{\sigma}) \quad \text{for all } \boldsymbol{\sigma},\boldsymbol{\sigma}' \in \{-1,1\}^N \tag{20.11}$$

Such Markov processes are said to obey *detailed balance*, and (20.11) is called the detailed balance condition. By summing (20.11) over all $\boldsymbol{\sigma}'$, and using the normalization of the transition probabilities, $\sum_{\boldsymbol{\sigma}'} W(\boldsymbol{\sigma}',\boldsymbol{\sigma}) = 1$ for all $\boldsymbol{\sigma}$, we see that any distribution $p_\infty(\boldsymbol{\sigma})$ which obeys (20.11) is necessarily stationary; the converse is not true.

Detailed balance is a special feature which greatly simplifies the calculation of the stationary probability distribution $p_\infty(\boldsymbol{\sigma})$. It states that, in addition to the probability distribution being stationary, the latter describes *equilibrium* in the sense that there is no net probability current between any two microscopic system states $\boldsymbol{\sigma}$ and $\boldsymbol{\sigma}'$. A useful analogy is an electric network. If we identify the nodes of this electric network with the possible microscopic states $\boldsymbol{\sigma}$, and the charge at each node with the probability for that state, then stationarity means that the currents flowing into and out of each node add up to zero, so that there is no net current into or out of the node. In equilibrium, that is, if we also have detailed balance, the currents do not just add up to zero: they are actually all zero individually.

We now show that, in our model of network operation as stochastic alignment of the spins (or neurons) σ_i to the local fields $h_i(\boldsymbol{\sigma})$ given in equation (16.3), detailed balance holds if and only if the neural interactions are symmetric, that is, if $J_{ij} = J_{ji}$ for all neuron pairs (i, j). A slight proviso is that for sequential dynamics there must also be no self-interactions, that is,

$J_{ii} = 0$ for all i. We consider the cases of parallel and sequential dynamics separately.

Parallel dynamics

For parallel dynamics the transition matrix is given by (16.7) and the detailed balance condition (20.11) becomes

$$\frac{e^{\beta\sum_{i=1}^{N}\sigma_i h_i(\boldsymbol{\sigma}')}\,p_\infty(\boldsymbol{\sigma}')}{\prod_{i=1}^{N}\cosh(\beta h_i(\boldsymbol{\sigma}'))} = \frac{e^{\beta\sum_{i=1}^{N}\sigma_i' h_i(\boldsymbol{\sigma})}\,p_\infty(\boldsymbol{\sigma})}{\prod_{i=1}^{N}\cosh(\beta h_i(\boldsymbol{\sigma}))} \quad \text{for all } \boldsymbol{\sigma},\boldsymbol{\sigma}' \qquad (20.12)$$

Our transition matrix (16.7) indeed describes an ergodic system, that is, from any initial state $\boldsymbol{\sigma}$ one can reach any final state $\boldsymbol{\sigma}'$ with nonzero probability in a finite number of steps (in this case: one). As a consequence all stationary probabilities $p_\infty(\boldsymbol{\sigma})$ must be nonzero. Without loss of generality we can therefore put:

$$p_\infty(\boldsymbol{\sigma}) = e^{\beta[\sum_{i=1}^{N}\vartheta_i\sigma_i + K(\boldsymbol{\sigma})]}\prod_{i=1}^{N}\cosh(\beta h_i(\boldsymbol{\sigma})) \qquad (20.13)$$

which, in combination with the definition (16.3) of the local fields $h_i(\boldsymbol{\sigma})$, simplifies the detailed balance condition to:

$$K(\boldsymbol{\sigma}) - K(\boldsymbol{\sigma}') = \sum_{ij=1}^{N}\sigma_i(J_{ij} - J_{ji})\sigma_j' \quad \text{for all } \boldsymbol{\sigma},\boldsymbol{\sigma}' \qquad (20.14)$$

Now, if the interactions are symmetric, the right-hand side of (20.14) is zero, and so (20.14) can be satisfied by simply choosing $K(\boldsymbol{\sigma}) = K$ (a constant). Hence our Markov process obeys the detailed balance condition with respect to the probability distribution

$$p_\infty(\boldsymbol{\sigma}) = e^{\beta K}\, e^{\beta\sum_{i=1}^{N}\vartheta_i\sigma_i}\prod_{i=1}^{N}\cosh(\beta h_i(\boldsymbol{\sigma})) \qquad (20.15)$$

and $p_\infty(\boldsymbol{\sigma})$ is therefore the (unique, because of ergodicity) equilibrium distribution; the actual value of K is determined from the normalization of p_∞. Interaction symmetry implies detailed balance.

Conversely, let us assume that detailed balance holds, that is, that there is a function $K(\boldsymbol{\sigma})$ obeying (20.14). If we now take a uniform average of (20.14) over the 2^N states $\boldsymbol{\sigma}'$, the right-hand side becomes zero and we obtain:

$$K(\boldsymbol{\sigma}) = \langle K(\boldsymbol{\sigma}') \rangle_{\boldsymbol{\sigma}'} \quad \text{for all } \boldsymbol{\sigma}$$

This implies that K must again be a constant. But then (20.14) implies

$$\sum_{ij=1}^{N} \sigma_i (J_{ij} - J_{ji}) \sigma'_j = 0 \quad \text{for all } \boldsymbol{\sigma}, \boldsymbol{\sigma}'$$

For $2^{N-1} \geq N$ (or: $N \geq 2$) the vector pairs $(\boldsymbol{\sigma}, \boldsymbol{\sigma}')$ span the space of all $N \times N$ matrices and so it follows that $J_{ij} = J_{ji}$ for all i, j. For $N = 1$, this is automatically true (since $J_{11} = J_{11}$).

In summary: for parallel dynamics as defined by (16.7), interaction symmetry implies detailed balance and vice versa. If detailed balance holds, the equilibrium distribution is given by (20.15).

Sequential dynamics without self-interactions

Now consider the case of sequential dynamics without self-interactions; $J_{ii} = 0$ for all i. Because of the form of the transition matrix (16.13), the detailed balance condition (20.11) is then non-trivial only if either $\boldsymbol{\sigma}' = F_i \boldsymbol{\sigma}$ for some i, or $\boldsymbol{\sigma}' = \boldsymbol{\sigma}$. For all other state pairs $(\boldsymbol{\sigma}', \boldsymbol{\sigma})$, the transition probabilities are zero, so both sides of (20.11) vanish. In the case where $\boldsymbol{\sigma}' = \boldsymbol{\sigma}$, the two sides are also trivially equal. Thus we only have to consider the case $\boldsymbol{\sigma}' = F_i \boldsymbol{\sigma}$, where (20.11) simplifies to:

$$\frac{e^{-\beta (F_i \sigma_i) h_i (F_i \boldsymbol{\sigma})} p_\infty(F_i \boldsymbol{\sigma})}{\cosh(\beta h_i (F_i \boldsymbol{\sigma}))} = \frac{e^{-\beta \sigma_i h_i (\boldsymbol{\sigma})} p_\infty(\boldsymbol{\sigma})}{\cosh(\beta h_i (\boldsymbol{\sigma}))} \quad \text{for all } \boldsymbol{\sigma} \text{ and all } i$$

Because of the absence of self-interactions, the local field acting on σ_i, viz.

$$h_i(\boldsymbol{\sigma}) = \sum_{k \neq i} J_{ik} \sigma_k + \vartheta_i \tag{20.16}$$

is independent of σ_i. So $h_i(\boldsymbol{\sigma}) = h_i(F_i \boldsymbol{\sigma})$, and the detailed balance condition becomes

$$e^{-\beta (F_i \sigma_i) h_i (F_i \boldsymbol{\sigma})} p_\infty(F_i \boldsymbol{\sigma}) = e^{-\beta \sigma_i h_i (\boldsymbol{\sigma})} p_\infty(\boldsymbol{\sigma}) \quad \text{for all } \boldsymbol{\sigma} \text{ and all } i \tag{20.17}$$

As discussed previously, the sequential transition matrix (16.13) describes an ergodic system; we can get from any initial state $\boldsymbol{\sigma}$ to any desired final state $\boldsymbol{\sigma}'$ with nonzero probability in at most N iterations. Since all stationary probabilities $p_\infty(\boldsymbol{\sigma})$ must therefore be nonzero, we can write:

$$p_\infty(\boldsymbol{\sigma}) = \exp\left[\beta\left(\sum_k \vartheta_k\sigma_k + \frac{1}{2}\sum_{k\neq l}\sigma_k J_{kl}\sigma_l + K(\boldsymbol{\sigma})\right)\right] \tag{20.18}$$

This simplifies (20.17) to

$$g_i(F_i\boldsymbol{\sigma}) = g_i(\boldsymbol{\sigma}) \quad \text{for all } \boldsymbol{\sigma} \text{ and all } i \tag{20.19}$$

where

$$g_i(\boldsymbol{\sigma}) = -\sigma_i h_i(\boldsymbol{\sigma}) + \sum_k \vartheta_k\sigma_k + \frac{1}{2}\sum_{k\neq l}\sigma_k J_{kl}\sigma_l + K(\boldsymbol{\sigma})$$

The detailed balance condition (20.19) requires that $g_i(\boldsymbol{\sigma})$ be independent of σ_i, so we separate off terms not involving σ_i. Inserting $h_i(\boldsymbol{\sigma})$ from (20.16), this gives

$$\begin{aligned} g_i(\boldsymbol{\sigma}) &= -\sum_{k\neq i}\sigma_i J_{ik}\sigma_k + \sum_{k\neq i}\vartheta_k\sigma_k + \frac{1}{2}\sum_{k\neq l, k\neq i, l\neq i}\sigma_k J_{kl}\sigma_l \\ &\quad + \frac{1}{2}\sum_{k\neq i}\sigma_k J_{ki}\sigma_i + \frac{1}{2}\sum_{l\neq i}\sigma_i J_{il}\sigma_l + K(\boldsymbol{\sigma}) \\ &= \text{terms not involving } \sigma_i + \frac{1}{2}\sum_{k\neq i}\sigma_i(J_{ki} - J_{ik})\sigma_k + K(\boldsymbol{\sigma}) \end{aligned}$$

The detailed balance condition (20.19) thus becomes, after cancelling all terms that are independent of σ_i,

$$K(F_i\boldsymbol{\sigma}) - K(\boldsymbol{\sigma}) = \sigma_i\sum_{k\neq i}(J_{ki} - J_{ik})\sigma_k \quad \text{for all } \boldsymbol{\sigma} \text{ and all } i \tag{20.20}$$

We have shown, therefore, that for sequential dynamics without self-interactions detailed balance holds if and only if a function $K(\boldsymbol{\sigma})$ obeying (20.20) exists.

We can now prove our statement that detailed balance implies interaction symmetry and vice versa. Assume first that detailed balance holds. Since

(20.20) is then obeyed for all $\boldsymbol{\sigma}$, it also holds for all $F_j\boldsymbol{\sigma}$ (where $j \neq i$):

$$K(F_iF_j\boldsymbol{\sigma}) - K(F_j\boldsymbol{\sigma}) = \sigma_i \sum_{k\neq i}(J_{ki} - J_{ik})F_j\sigma_k$$
$$= \sigma_i \sum_{k\neq i}(J_{ki} - J_{ik})\sigma_k - 2\sigma_i(J_{ji} - J_{ij})\sigma_j$$

Subtracting (20.20) from this, we get

$$K(F_iF_j\boldsymbol{\sigma}) - K(F_i\boldsymbol{\sigma}) - K(F_j\boldsymbol{\sigma}) + K(\boldsymbol{\sigma}) = -2\sigma_i(J_{ji} - J_{ij})\sigma_j$$

Because the left-hand side is symmetric under permutation of the pair (i, j), so must be the right-hand side. This implies that the interactions must be symmetric, $J_{ij} = J_{ji}$ for all (i, j), as we wanted to show.

Conversely, if the interactions are symmetric, the detailed balance condition (20.20) has a trivial solution, namely $K(\boldsymbol{\sigma}) = K$ (a constant). Thus detailed balance holds and the corresponding equilibrium distribution is, from (20.18),

$$p_\infty(\boldsymbol{\sigma}) = e^{\beta K}\, e^{-\beta H(\boldsymbol{\sigma})} \quad \text{with} \quad H(\boldsymbol{\sigma}) = -\frac{1}{2}\sum_{ij=1}^{N} \sigma_i J_{ij}\sigma_j - \sum_{i=1}^{N} \vartheta_i\sigma_i \tag{20.21}$$

In summary: for sequential dynamics without self-interactions, interaction symmetry implies detailed balance and vice versa. If detailed balance holds, the equilibrium distribution is given by (20.21).

Sequential dynamics with self-interactions

In this final case the situation is considerably more complicated. In principle, detailed balance may now hold for both symmetric and non-symmetric systems. However, one can show that such cases must be pathological ones, since only for very specific choices for the matrix elements $\{J_{ij}\}$ can the corresponding requirements be met (e.g. in systems with self-interactions *only*).

Zero noise dynamics for symmetric interactions

Let us briefly mention the special case $\beta \to \infty$ where the dynamics of our network is deterministic, at least up to the random choice of site for an update in the sequential dynamics case. We then no longer have ergodicity, but can still often say something about the long time (i.e. $t \to \infty$) behaviour of the system, by constructing appropriate Lyapunov functions, that is, functions of the dynamic state variables which decreases monotonically and are bounded from below. This approach has been explored in Part I of the book. As would be expected from our discussion of detailed balance above, systems with symmetric interactions are the simplest, and these are indeed the ones for which we were able to find Lyapunov functions in Section 3.2.

20.3 Equilibrium statistical mechanics: concepts, definitions

Hamiltonians

So far we have seen that the evolution of our networks is described by Markov processes which are ergodic, and which must therefore converge to a unique stationary distribution $p_\infty(\boldsymbol{\sigma})$ over the possible microscopic states $\boldsymbol{\sigma}$. If the Markov process obeys detailed balance, which is the case if the interactions J_{ij} are symmetric (and if, for sequential dynamics, there are no self-interactions), the stationary distribution represents equilibrium and we write it as $p_{\text{eq}}(\boldsymbol{\sigma})$. For symmetric models we have found the form of p_{eq} explicitly:

$$p_{\text{eq}}(\boldsymbol{\sigma}) = \frac{1}{Z} e^{-\beta H(\boldsymbol{\sigma})} \tag{20.22}$$

where Z is a normalization constant (which we previously wrote as $e^{-\beta K}$), and the function $H(\boldsymbol{\sigma})$ is called the Hamiltonian. For sequential dynamics, from (20.21) we have

$$H(\boldsymbol{\sigma}) = -\frac{1}{2}\sum_{ij=1}^{N} \sigma_i J_{ij}\sigma_j - \sum_{i=1}^{N} \vartheta_i\sigma_i \tag{20.23}$$

For parallel dynamics, p_{eq} can still be written in the form (20.22), but with a different Hamiltonian $H(\boldsymbol{\sigma})$, which follows from (20.15) as

$$H(\boldsymbol{\sigma}) = -\sum_{i=1}^{N} \vartheta_i\sigma_i - \frac{1}{\beta}\sum_{i=1}^{N} \ln 2\cosh(\beta h_i(\boldsymbol{\sigma})) \tag{20.24}$$

Since here the function $H(\boldsymbol{\sigma})$ depends on the noise parameter β, in contrast to (20.23) and to 'normal' physical systems, the function in (20.24) is in fact usually called a pseudo-Hamiltonian.

Partition function and free energy

In statistical mechanics, distributions of the form (20.22) are called *Boltzmann distributions*. The normalization constant

$$Z = \sum_{\sigma} e^{-\beta H(\sigma)} \tag{20.25}$$

is called the *partition function* or sum over states; the notation Z comes from the German word for this, 'Zustandssumme'. Statistical mechanics was originally developed for systems of point particles obeying the laws of classical mechanics, hence the name, and the general theory shows that the equilibrium behaviour at *temperature* $T = 1/\beta$ of any system is described by a Boltzmann distribution, where the Hamiltonian represents the energy of the system. Our Hamiltonian for sequential dynamics, equation (20.23), is called the Ising Hamiltonian, and its first part corresponds in physics terminology to the interaction energy between the spins, while the second part represents the energy of the spins in an external field. The Hamiltonian (20.24) has no equally direct interpretation as an energy.

We will mostly be interested in averages over the distribution p_{eq}:

$$\langle f \rangle_{\text{eq}} = \sum_{\sigma} f(\sigma) p_{\text{eq}}(\sigma) = \frac{1}{Z} \sum_{\sigma} f(\sigma) e^{-\beta H(\sigma)}$$

of certain observables $f(\sigma)$, which are simply functions of the network state σ, over the equilibrium distribution. For this purpose, it is useful to define the *free energy*

$$F = -T \ln Z = -\frac{1}{\beta} \ln Z \tag{20.26}$$

If we can calculate F, then by taking derivatives we can also get the required averages. This can be seen as follows. If the Hamiltonian depends on a parameter λ, then the derivative of F with respect to λ is given by

$$\frac{\partial F}{\partial \lambda} = -\frac{1}{\beta Z} \frac{\partial Z}{\partial \lambda} = -\frac{1}{\beta Z} \sum_{\sigma} \left(-\beta \frac{\partial H(\sigma)}{\partial \lambda} \right) e^{-\beta H(\sigma)} = \left\langle \frac{\partial H}{\partial \lambda} \right\rangle_{\text{eq}} \tag{20.27}$$

For example, if in the case of sequential dynamics we apply this relation to $\lambda \equiv \vartheta_i$ and $\lambda \equiv J_{ij}$, we obtain

$$-\frac{\partial F}{\partial \vartheta_i} = \langle \sigma_i \rangle_{\text{eq}} \qquad -\frac{\partial F}{\partial J_{ij}} = \langle \sigma_i \sigma_j \rangle_{\text{eq}}$$

As an aside we note that, in the case of parallel dynamics, the averages generated by the same derivatives are more complicated,

$$-\frac{\partial F}{\partial \vartheta_i} = \langle \sigma_i \rangle_{\text{eq}} + \langle \tanh(\beta h_i(\boldsymbol{\sigma})) \rangle_{\text{eq}}$$

$$-\frac{\partial F}{\partial J_{ij}} = \langle \sigma_i \tanh(\beta h_j(\boldsymbol{\sigma})) \rangle_{\text{eq}} + \langle \sigma_j \tanh(\beta h_i(\boldsymbol{\sigma})) \rangle_{\text{eq}} \quad \text{for } i \neq j$$

$$-\frac{\partial F}{\partial J_{ii}} = \langle \sigma_i \tanh(\beta h_i(\boldsymbol{\sigma})) \rangle_{\text{eq}}$$

reflecting the different structure of the Hamiltonian (20.24).

More generally, the equilibrium average of any arbitrary observable $f(\boldsymbol{\sigma})$ can be obtained by adding suitable generating terms to the Hamiltonian, taking a derivative of the free energy, and then setting the generating terms back to zero:

$$H(\boldsymbol{\sigma}) \to H(\boldsymbol{\sigma}) + \lambda f(\boldsymbol{\sigma}) \qquad \langle f \rangle_{\text{eq}} = \lim_{\lambda \to 0} \frac{\partial F}{\partial \lambda}$$

While its derivatives are useful for calculating averages, the free energy is also an interesting quantity in its own right. By averaging the relation $H(\boldsymbol{\sigma}) + T \ln p_{\text{eq}}(\boldsymbol{\sigma}) = -T \ln Z$ (which holds for all $\boldsymbol{\sigma}$, as follows from (20.22)) over the equilibrium distribution, one finds

$$F = E - TS \qquad \text{where } E = \langle H \rangle_{\text{eq}}, \quad S = -\sum_{\boldsymbol{\sigma}} p_{\text{eq}}(\boldsymbol{\sigma}) \ln p_{\text{eq}}(\boldsymbol{\sigma}) \qquad (20.28)$$

Here E, the average of the Hamiltonian H, is simply the (average) energy, while S is the *entropy* of the equilibrium distribution, a concept which we have encountered before in Part III of this book devoted to information theory and its applications.[40] If the Hamiltonian is independent of β, both terms in (20.28) can be written in terms of derivatives of F with respect to β (see Exercise 20.1):

$$E = -\frac{\partial \ln Z}{\partial \beta} = \frac{\partial(\beta F)}{\partial \beta} \qquad S = \beta(E - F) = \beta^2 \frac{\partial F}{\partial \beta} \qquad (20.29)$$

[40] Note that the information entropy (or Shannon entropy) was defined in terms of digital rather than natural logarithms, and thus differs from the present convention by a factor $1/\ln 2$.

If we extend (20.28) and use it to define the free energy for any general distribution $p(\boldsymbol{\sigma})$ over states $\boldsymbol{\sigma}$,

$$F[p(\boldsymbol{\sigma})] = \langle H \rangle - TS$$
$$\text{where } \langle H \rangle = \sum_{\boldsymbol{\sigma}} p(\boldsymbol{\sigma}) H(\boldsymbol{\sigma}), \quad S = -\sum_{\boldsymbol{\sigma}} p(\boldsymbol{\sigma}) \ln p(\boldsymbol{\sigma}) \tag{20.30}$$

then one also finds that the Boltzmann distribution $p_{\text{eq}}(\boldsymbol{\sigma})$ is the distribution that actually minimizes $F[p(\boldsymbol{\sigma})]$. This provides an alternative interpretation of the effect of the temperature T on the equilibrium distribution $p_{\text{eq}}(\boldsymbol{\sigma})$. The entropy S has its maximal value $N \ln 2$ when $p(\boldsymbol{\sigma}) = 1/2^N$, a uniform distribution over all states $\boldsymbol{\sigma}$; in this sense, minimization of the term $-TS$ in the free energy $F[p(\boldsymbol{\sigma})]$ favours disorder. The *minimal* value of S is 0, and is achieved for a distribution $p(\boldsymbol{\sigma})$ which gives nonzero probability only to a single state $\boldsymbol{\sigma}$. The first term in the free energy, $\langle H \rangle$, on the other hand, favours order: it prefers distributions $p(\boldsymbol{\sigma})$ which give weight only to the states of minimum energy $H(\boldsymbol{\sigma})$, the so-called *ground states*. The temperature T determines the tradeoff between these two contributions: for large T, more disorder results, while for small T the entropic contribution becomes unimportant and the tendency is to minimize the average energy. This agrees with our earlier interpretation of $T = 1/\beta$ as a noise parameter.

Constrained free energy

We can also extend the concept of a free energy to that of a so-called constrained free energy, in order to obtain information about the *distribution* of values of observables $m(\boldsymbol{\sigma})$ in an equilibrium situation, rather than just their averages. The observables we will normally be interested in are macroscopic in the sense that they describe the overall behaviour of the system. An example would be the average neuron activity $m(\boldsymbol{\sigma}) = N^{-1} \sum_i \sigma_i$, whereas the activity of an individual neuron, σ_i, is a *microscopic* observable. The probability of $m(\boldsymbol{\sigma})$ taking a certain value $\tilde{m}$ can be written as

$$P(\tilde{m}) = \langle \delta(\tilde{m} - m(\boldsymbol{\sigma})) \rangle_{\text{eq}} = \sum_{\boldsymbol{\sigma}} p_{\text{eq}}(\boldsymbol{\sigma}) \delta(\tilde{m} - m(\boldsymbol{\sigma}))$$

using the δ-distribution (see Appendix F). That this is a sensible definition can be seen from the fact that it gives the correct average of any function $f(m(\boldsymbol{\sigma}))$:

$$\int d\tilde{m}\, P(\tilde{m}) f(\tilde{m}) = \int d\tilde{m}\, \langle \delta(\tilde{m} - m(\boldsymbol{\sigma})) \rangle_{\text{eq}} f(\tilde{m})$$
$$= \left\langle \int d\tilde{m}\, \delta(\tilde{m} - m(\boldsymbol{\sigma})) f(\tilde{m}) \right\rangle_{\text{eq}} = \langle f(m(\boldsymbol{\sigma})) \rangle_{\text{eq}}$$

Using the Boltzmann form (20.22) of the equilibrium distribution, we can now rewrite $P(\tilde{m})$ as

$$P(\tilde{m}) = \frac{1}{Z}\sum_{\sigma}\delta(\tilde{m} - m(\boldsymbol{\sigma}))e^{-\beta H(\boldsymbol{\sigma})} = \frac{Z(\tilde{m})}{Z} = e^{-\beta(F(\tilde{m})-F)} \qquad (20.31)$$

where

$$Z(\tilde{m}) = \sum_{\sigma}\delta(\tilde{m} - m(\boldsymbol{\sigma}))e^{-\beta H(\boldsymbol{\sigma})} \qquad F(\tilde{m}) = -T\ln Z(\tilde{m})$$

are the constrained partition function and free energy, respectively. We have chosen the name 'constrained' here because the sum over states defining $Z(\tilde{m})$ is constrained to those states $\boldsymbol{\sigma}$ which give the correct value of $m(\boldsymbol{\sigma})$.

In the notation up to now, we have distinguished the observable $m(\boldsymbol{\sigma})$, a function of $\boldsymbol{\sigma}$, from its desired value $\tilde{m}$. To make things more concise, we will follow convention and henceforth drop the tilde on $\tilde{m}$, writing the definitions of the constrained partition function and free energy, for example, simply as

$$Z(m) = \sum_{\sigma}\delta(m - m(\boldsymbol{\sigma}))e^{-\beta H(\boldsymbol{\sigma})} \qquad F(m) = -T\ln Z(m) \qquad (20.32)$$

The fact that the same symbol m is used for the observable $m(\boldsymbol{\sigma})$ and its value m should not cause confusion; which one is meant is clear from whether the function argument $\boldsymbol{\sigma}$ is given or not. Finally, we note that the definition (20.32) can be extended straightforwardly to a constrained free energy that depends on the values of any finite number of observables $m_1(\boldsymbol{\sigma}),\ldots,m_k(\boldsymbol{\sigma})$.

Thermodynamic limit, fluctuations, and saddle point integration

As mentioned earlier, statistical mechanics focuses on the limit of large systems, $N \to \infty$. This is called the *thermodynamic limit*, for mainly historical reasons. For systems of particles obeying the laws of classical mechanics, it turns out that in this limit the free energy F, the (average) energy $E = \langle H\rangle_{\text{eq}}$, and the entropy are *extensive*: they are, for large N, proportional to N. Considering the case of the energy, the underlying intuitive idea is that there is a well-defined energy per particle, and that if we make our system twice as large, then the total energy will simply double. More precisely, the free energy being extensive means that the limit $f = \lim_{N\to\infty} F/N$ exists, so that for large N we can write $F = Nf$ up to terms which are negligible by comparison, being either independent of N or increasing more slowly than linearly with N. Such finite-size corrections are (nearly) always neglected in statistical mechanics.

For the models of network operation that we will consider, we will similarly find that F, E, and S will be proportional to N in the thermodynamic limit, so that we can write, for example, $F = Nf$. For suitable macroscopic observables $m(\boldsymbol{\sigma})$, the same scaling with N applies to the constrained free energies $F(m) = Nf(m)$. The corresponding partition functions $Z = e^{-\beta F} = e^{-N\beta f}$ and $Z(m) = e^{-N\beta f(m)}$ are thus *exponential* in N. From the N-dependence of $F(m) = Nf(m)$ we can draw an important conclusion regarding the fluctuations of m across the equilibrium distribution. Let us assume that m is normalized such that its range of typical values does not depend on N, and let us consider the simplest case where $f(m)$ has a single (local and global) minimum at $m = m^*$. Expanding $f(m)$ to second order around this minimum, we find from (20.31) that

$$P(m) = e^{-N\beta[f(m)-f]} \approx e^{-N\beta[f(m^*)-f]-N\beta f''(m^*)(m-m^*)^2/2}$$

This is a Gaussian distribution of width $\mathcal{O}(N^{-(1/2)})$, centred on m^* (the symbol $\mathcal{O}(\cdots)$ is, as always, read as 'of the order of' and indicates the dependence on N or other variables while ignoring constant prefactors and terms which are negligible by comparison). We see that only values of m for which $m - m^* = \mathcal{O}(1/\sqrt{N})$ have a significant probability of occurring. For $N \to \infty$, the fluctuations of m vanish, m takes the value m^* with probability one, and m^* is therefore also the average value of m. Hence, in the thermodynamic limit suitably chosen macroscopic observables take deterministic values. This is the intuitive reason why we consider this limit: fluctuations average out and vanish for $N \to \infty$, and this makes calculations feasible which would otherwise be impossible.

The thermodynamic limit also produces a corresponding simplification in the calculation of the free energy. Suppose we have managed to find the constrained free energy per neuron/spin/particle, $f(m)$. Then, from (20.32), the unconstrained partition function is given by

$$Z = \int dm\, Z(m) = \int dm\, e^{-N\beta f(m)}$$

As always, integrals without explicitly written limits run from $-\infty$ to ∞; if m cannot assume all of these values, the 'impossible' ones are automatically excluded because they give $Z(m) = 0$. For large N, the integrand is very sharply peaked around the minimum m^* of $f(m)$. Expanding to second order around this minimum, we obtain

$$Z \approx \int dm\, e^{-N\beta f(m^*)}\, e^{-N\beta f''(m^*)(m-m^*)^2/2} = e^{-N\beta f(m^*)} \sqrt{\frac{2\pi}{N\beta f''(m^*)}}$$

and thus the free energy (per neuron) becomes

$$f = -\frac{1}{N\beta} \ln Z \approx f(m^*) - \frac{\ln[2\pi/\beta f''(m^*)] - \ln N}{2N\beta} \to f(m^*) \quad (N \to \infty)$$

(often the thermodynamic limit $N \to \infty$ is understood to be taken even if not written explicitly). So the free energy f per neuron is simply the value of $f(m)$ at its minimum. We will often use this so-called 'saddle-point integration' technique to calculate free energies. It applies to all integrals with integrands which are exponential in some large parameter, and gives the general result

$$\lim_{N\to\infty} -\frac{1}{N} \ln \int \mathrm{d}x\, e^{-Ng(x)} = \min_x g(x) \tag{20.33}$$

Such integrals can therefore be evaluated by finding the stationary points of $g(x)$ and selecting the one with the smallest value of g. Under suitable conditions, this result even holds when these stationary points are in the complex plane; the fact that stationary points of a function of a complex variable always have the structure of a saddle point gives the technique its name. For further discussion of the saddle point method see Appendix I.

20.4 A simple example: storing a single pattern

Reduction to calculating the density of states

To show how the above definitions and concepts of statistical mechanics are applied in practice, let us consider a neural network with uniform interactions J_{ij}, no self-interactions, and zero external fields:

$$J_{ij} = J_{ji} = \frac{J}{N} \ (i \neq j), \qquad \vartheta_i = 0 \tag{20.34}$$

We will see that this recipe can be thought of as storing a pattern of all $+1$s (or all -1s) in the network. In physics terminology, the system defined by (20.34) is called an 'infinite range ferromagnet'. The name 'infinite range' comes from the fact that if we imagine arranging the neurons/spins in space, there is an interaction between them independently of how far apart they are.

We focus on the case of sequential dynamics. Accounting for the fact that there are no self-interactions, the relevant Ising Hamiltonian (20.23) can then be written as

$$H(\boldsymbol{\sigma}) = -\frac{J}{2N}\left(\sum_{ij}\sigma_i\sigma_j - \sum_i \sigma_i^2\right) = -\frac{NJ}{2}m^2(\boldsymbol{\sigma}) + \frac{J}{2}$$

with the average neuron activity, or 'magnetization' of the spins,

$$m(\boldsymbol{\sigma}) = \frac{1}{N}\sum_k \sigma_k$$

The second term in the Hamiltonian is $\mathcal{O}(1)$, that is, does not scale with N, and only gives a corresponding $\mathcal{O}(1)$ factor $e^{-\beta J/2}$ in the partition function and thus an additive contribution to the free energy F which is also $\mathcal{O}(1)$, namely $J/2$. This can be neglected compared to the dominant $\mathcal{O}(N)$ contribution, so we can write directly

$$Z = \sum_{\boldsymbol{\sigma}} e^{N\beta J m^2(\boldsymbol{\sigma})/2 + \mathcal{O}(1)} \qquad F = -T \ln Z \tag{20.35}$$

The fact that the Hamiltonian depends on $\boldsymbol{\sigma}$ only through $m(\boldsymbol{\sigma})$ suggests the introduction of the constrained partition function and free energy for m:

$$\begin{aligned} Z = \int \mathrm{d}m\, Z(m), \quad Z(m) &= \sum_{\boldsymbol{\sigma}} e^{N\beta J m^2(\boldsymbol{\sigma})/2 + \mathcal{O}(1)} \delta(m - m(\boldsymbol{\sigma})) \\ &= e^{N\beta J m^2/2 + \mathcal{O}(1)} \sum_{\boldsymbol{\sigma}} \delta(m - m(\boldsymbol{\sigma})) \end{aligned} \tag{20.36}$$

Using saddle point integration, the free energy per neuron in the thermodynamic limit is then

$$f = \min_m f(m), \quad f(m) = -\lim_{N\to\infty} \frac{T}{N} \ln Z(m) = -\frac{1}{2}Jm^2 - Ts(m) \tag{20.37}$$

where

$$s(m) = \lim_{N\to\infty} \frac{1}{N} \ln \mathcal{D}(m) \qquad \mathcal{D}(m) = \sum_{\boldsymbol{\sigma}} \delta(m - m(\boldsymbol{\sigma})) \tag{20.38}$$

From the last definition, we see that $\mathcal{D}(m) = e^{Ns(m)}$ (to leading order in N) basically counts the number of states $\boldsymbol{\sigma}$ with a given value of $m(\boldsymbol{\sigma})$. It is therefore often called the 'density of states', and $s(m)$ the (normalized) log-density of states. Comparing (20.37) with (20.28), and noting that the first term in $f(m)$ is just $H(m(\boldsymbol{\sigma}))/N$, apart from vanishing terms, the normalized

Hamiltonian for the given value of m, gives an alternative interpretation of $s(m)$ as a constrained entropy per neuron.

Calculation of the density of states

To evaluate $s(m)$, we use the integral representation of the δ-function (see Appendix F). We choose the integration variable in this representation as Nx rather than x; this guarantees that we will be left with an integral which can be evaluated by saddle point integration:

$$\delta(m - m(\boldsymbol{\sigma})) = \int \frac{N\mathrm{d}x}{2\pi}\, e^{\mathrm{i}Nx[m-m(\boldsymbol{\sigma})]} = \int \frac{N\mathrm{d}x}{2\pi}\, e^{\mathrm{i}Nxm-\mathrm{i}x\sum_i \sigma_i} \tag{20.39}$$

The point in using (20.39) is to relocate $m(\boldsymbol{\sigma}) = N^{-1}\sum_i \sigma_i$ into the exponent; this gives an expression which factorizes over the different σ_i, so that the sum over states can be carried out. Let us look at this idea of *factorization* in more detail. Suppose we are trying to work out the sum $\sum_{\boldsymbol{\sigma}} f(\boldsymbol{\sigma})$. For general $f(\boldsymbol{\sigma})$, this is hard. But if f factorizes over the different σ_i, that is, if $f(\boldsymbol{\sigma}) = f_1(\sigma_1) \times f_2(\sigma_2) \times \ldots \times f_N(\sigma_N)$, we can make progress. First note that the sum over $\boldsymbol{\sigma}$ corresponds to summing over the possible values ± 1 for each spin:

$$\sum_{\boldsymbol{\sigma}} f(\boldsymbol{\sigma}) = \sum_{\sigma_1=\pm 1} \cdots \sum_{\sigma_N=\pm 1} f_1(\sigma_1) \times \ldots \times f_N(\sigma_N)$$

Now σ_N only appears in $f_N(\sigma_N)$, and we can therefore sum over it:

$$\sum_{\boldsymbol{\sigma}} f(\boldsymbol{\sigma}) = \sum_{\sigma_1=\pm 1} \cdots \sum_{\sigma_{N-1}=\pm 1} f_1(\sigma_1) \times \ldots \times f_{N-1}(\sigma_{N-1}) \Big(\sum_{\sigma_N=\pm 1} f_N(\sigma_N) \Big)$$

We can repeat the same process for all other spins, $\sigma_{N-1}, \sigma_{N-2}, \ldots, \sigma_1$ and get the general expression for a factorized sum

$$\sum_{\boldsymbol{\sigma}} f_1(\sigma_1) \times \ldots \times f_N(\sigma_N) = \Big(\sum_{\sigma_1=\pm 1} f_1(\sigma_1) \Big) \Big(\sum_{\sigma_2=\pm 1} f_2(\sigma_2) \Big) \cdots \Big(\sum_{\sigma_N=\pm 1} f_N(\sigma_N) \Big)$$

or in short

$$\sum_{\boldsymbol{\sigma}} \prod_i f_i(\sigma_i) = \prod_i \Big(\sum_{\sigma_i} f_i(\sigma_i) \Big) \tag{20.40}$$

Applying this to the sum over $\boldsymbol{\sigma}$ of (20.39) which gives us the density of states (20.38), we have

$$\begin{aligned}\mathcal{D}(m) &= \sum_{\boldsymbol{\sigma}} \int \frac{N\mathrm{d}x}{2\pi}\, e^{\mathrm{i}Nxm - \mathrm{i}x\sum_i \sigma_i} = \int \frac{N\mathrm{d}x}{2\pi}\, e^{\mathrm{i}Nxm} \sum_{\boldsymbol{\sigma}} e^{-\mathrm{i}x\sum_i \sigma_i} \\ &= \int \frac{N\mathrm{d}x}{2\pi}\, e^{\mathrm{i}Nxm} \sum_{\boldsymbol{\sigma}} \prod_i e^{-\mathrm{i}x\sigma_i} = \int \frac{N\mathrm{d}x}{2\pi}\, e^{\mathrm{i}Nxm} \prod_i \Big(\sum_{\sigma_i=\pm 1} e^{-\mathrm{i}x\sigma_i} \Big) \\ &= \int \frac{N\mathrm{d}x}{2\pi}\, e^{\mathrm{i}Nxm} [2\cos(x)]^N = \int \frac{N\mathrm{d}x}{2\pi}\, e^{N[\mathrm{i}xm + \ln 2\cos(x)]} \end{aligned} \tag{20.41}$$

The stationary point of the exponent is given by

$$\mathrm{i}m - \tan x = 0 \;\Rightarrow\; x = \arctan(\mathrm{i}m) = \mathrm{i}\,\mathrm{artanh}\,(m)$$

So, upon evaluating the integral by saddle point integration and using the relations $\cos(\mathrm{i}\alpha) = \cosh(\alpha)$, $\cosh(\alpha) = [1 - \tanh^2(\alpha)]^{-1/2}$ and $\mathrm{artanh}\,(\alpha) = \frac{1}{2}\ln[(1+\alpha)/(1-\alpha)]$, we arrive at

$$\begin{aligned} s(m) &= \frac{1}{N}\ln \mathcal{D}(m) = -m\,\mathrm{artanh}\,(m) + \ln 2\cosh(\,\mathrm{artanh}\,(m)) \\ &= -\frac{1+m}{2}\ln\left(\frac{1+m}{2}\right) - \frac{1-m}{2}\ln\left(\frac{1-m}{2}\right) \end{aligned} \tag{20.42}$$

This result for the constrained entropy (or log density of states) per neuron makes sense: to get the desired value of m, each spin σ_i must be ± 1 with probability $(1 \pm m)/2$, and $s(m)$ is just the entropy of a distribution over two possible states with these probabilities (see Equation (12.3)).

Properties and interpretation of the solution

The result of our modest calculation is that the constrained free energy and free energy are (20.37), with $s(m)$ given by (20.42). If $J < 0$ (the so-called anti-ferromagnetic case), both terms in $f(m)$ are minimized for $m = 0$, so this is the single minimum of $f(m)$ at all T (see Figure 20.1, right). We therefore focus now on the case of a ferromagnetic coupling, $J > 0$. Here the first (energetic) term in $f(m)$ favours large values of $|m|$, that is, ordered states, while the second (entropic) term favours the most disordered state $m = 0$. Correspondingly, as shown in Figure 20.1 (left), $f(m)$ has a single minimum at $m = 0$ for large T, where the entropic term is dominant, but develops two minima as T is lowered. This is reflected in the condition

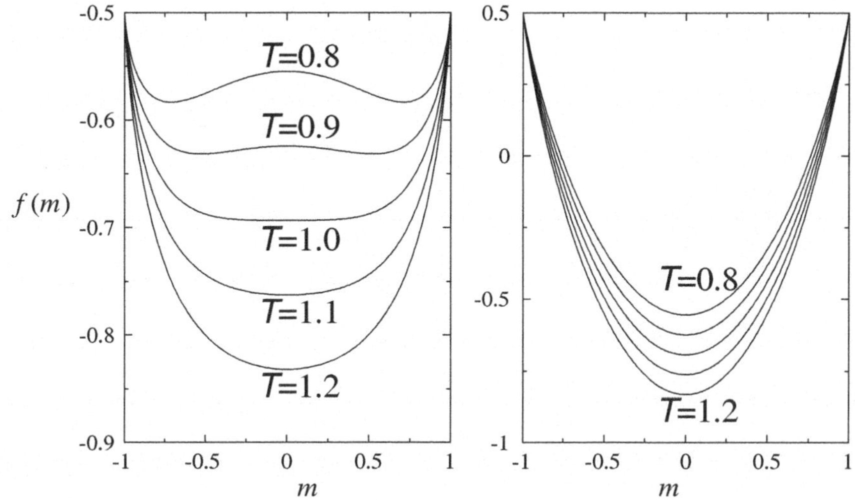

Figure 20.1 The constrained free energies $f(m)$ for the infinite-range ferromagnet with sequential dynamics, for the ferromagnetic case $J > 0$ (left, $J = 1$) and the anti-ferromagnetic case $J < 0$ (right, $J = -1$). In each graph a sequence of decreasing temperatures T is shown from bottom to top, corresponding to increasing values of $\beta = 1/T$.

$f'(m) = 0$ for the stationary points of $f(m)$. Using

$$s'(m) = -\frac{1}{2}\ln\left(\frac{1+m}{1-m}\right) = -\operatorname{artanh}(m)$$

one finds that the extremal condition $f'(m) = 0$ is equivalent to

$$m = \tanh(\beta J m) \tag{20.43}$$

This equation for m is called the 'Curie–Weiss' equation in the context of magnetism. As shown in Figure 20.2, it has a single solution $m = 0$ for large $T = 1/\beta$, but develops three solutions for low T. The transition between the two regimes takes place at $\beta J = 1$. This is clear graphically by looking at Figure 20.2. Nonzero solutions appear at the point where the graphs of m and $\tanh(\beta J m)$ have the same slope at the origin. More explicitly, expanding the function tanh around $m = 0$, equation (20.43) gives

$$m = \beta J m - \tfrac{1}{3}(\beta J)^3 m^3 + \mathcal{O}(m^5)$$

Neglecting the higher order terms, we can write the nonzero m solutions as

$$m^2 = 3(\beta J - 1)/(\beta J)^3$$

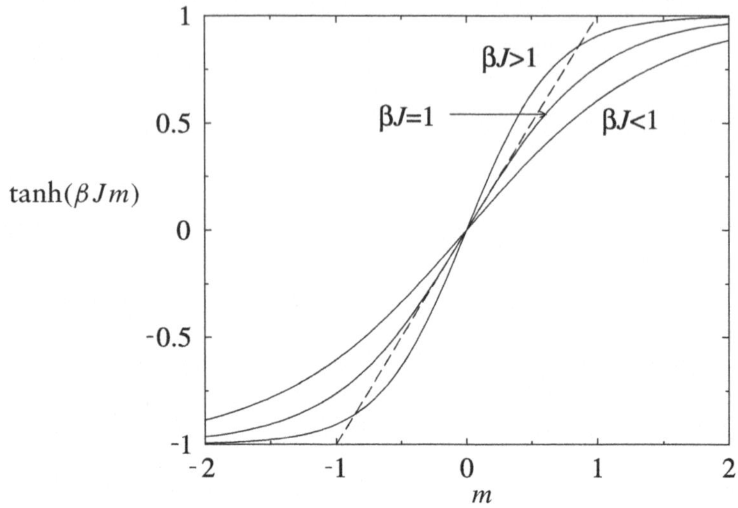

Figure 20.2 Graphical solution of the Curie–Weiss equation (20.43), viz. $m = \tanh(\beta Jm)$. Solid lines show the function $\tanh(\beta Jm)$ for different values of βJ. Dashed: the diagonal which this function must intersect. For $\beta J < 1$, $m = 0$ is the only solution; for larger values of βJ, there are two additional solutions m_β and $-m_\beta$.

We find two nonzero solutions for $\beta J > 1$. For βJ close to (and above) 1 these are, to leading order in $\beta J - 1$, given by

$$m = \pm\sqrt{3(\beta J - 1)} + \cdots$$

Denoting the transition (or 'critical') temperature by $T_c = 1/\beta_c = J$, and expanding $\beta J - 1 = (J - T)/T \approx (J - T)/J = (T_c - T)/T_c$ to leading order in $T_c - T$, this can also be written in the more conventional form

$$m = \pm\sqrt{3(T_c - T)/T_c}$$

Thus, the magnetization, or average neuron activity, has (initially) a square-root dependence on the deviation of T from T_c for $T < T_c$. For $T > T_c$, on the other hand, the above analysis suggests that the only stationary point of $f(m)$, that is, the only solution of the Curie–Weiss equation (20.43), is $m = 0$. This can also be shown more rigorously, by using the relation $\mathrm{d}\tanh(z)/\mathrm{d}z = 1 - \tanh^2(z)$ to write

$$|\tanh(z)| = \tanh(|z|) = \int_0^{|z|} \mathrm{d}z'[1 - \tanh^2(z')] \leq |z| \tag{20.44}$$

(which is obvious graphically; see Figure 20.2). If m is a solution of the Curie–Weiss equation, this gives

$$|m| = |\tanh(\beta J m)| \le \beta J |m|$$

which for $\beta J < 1$ (i.e. for $T > T_c$) is possible only for $m = 0$, as claimed.

Finally, we note that (20.43) has a simple intuitive interpretation. If spin i is updated at time t, then from our basic update equation (16.2) its value at time $t + 1$ is on average

$$\langle \sigma_i(t+1) \rangle = \tanh(\beta h_i(\boldsymbol{\sigma}(t))) \tag{20.45}$$

In equilibrium, both sides must be equal on average because the probability distribution over states is stationary, so

$$\langle \sigma_i \rangle_{\text{eq}} = \langle \tanh(\beta h_i(\boldsymbol{\sigma})) \rangle_{\text{eq}} \tag{20.46}$$

For our choice of interactions (20.34), the local fields are

$$h_i(\boldsymbol{\sigma}) = \frac{J}{N} \sum_{j \neq i} \sigma_j = J m(\boldsymbol{\sigma}) + \mathcal{O}(1/N) \tag{20.47}$$

and we recognize equation (20.43) simply as the average of (20.46) over i.

20.5 Phase transitions and ergodicity breaking

Ergodicity breaking for sequential dynamics

Let us consider in more detail the equilibrium distribution of the magnetization m in the above example of the long-range ferromagnet, again with $J > 0$. For $T > T_c = J$, the function $f(m)$ has a single minimum. Hence $P(m) \sim \exp(-N\beta f(m))$ has a single maximum at $m = m^* = 0$; because this maximum is very sharp, of width $\mathcal{O}(1/\sqrt{N})$, we also have $\langle m(\boldsymbol{\sigma}) \rangle_{\text{eq}} = m^* = 0$. The same conclusion can be reached using the relation (20.27) to find this average. We replace

$$H(\boldsymbol{\sigma}) = -\frac{N}{2} J m^2(\boldsymbol{\sigma}) + \mathcal{O}(1) \to -\frac{N}{2} J m^2(\boldsymbol{\sigma}) + N\lambda m(\boldsymbol{\sigma}) + \mathcal{O}(1) \tag{20.48}$$

where the factor N in front of the extra term ensures that it is $\mathcal{O}(N)$, and will remain relevant in the thermodynamic limit compared to the first term.

This replacement is seen to carry through to the constrained free energy (per neuron/spin), which becomes

$$f(m;\lambda) = -\tfrac{1}{2}Jm^2 + \lambda m - Ts(m) \tag{20.49}$$

This new function will have a minimum at some $m^*(\lambda)$, which then gives the free energy per neuron

$$f(\lambda) = \min_m f(m;\lambda) = f(m^*(\lambda);\lambda)$$

Applying (20.27) we now have

$$\frac{\partial N f(\lambda)}{\partial \lambda} = \left\langle \frac{\partial H}{\partial \lambda} \right\rangle_{\text{eq}} = N\langle m(\boldsymbol{\sigma})\rangle_{\text{eq}} \Rightarrow \langle m(\boldsymbol{\sigma})\rangle_{\text{eq}} = \frac{\partial f(\lambda)}{\partial \lambda}$$

where all derivatives are to be evaluated at $\lambda = 0$ if we wish to return to our original model. The chain rule gives

$$\frac{\partial f(\lambda)}{\partial \lambda} = \frac{\partial f(m^*(\lambda);\lambda)}{\partial m}\frac{\mathrm{d}}{\mathrm{d}\lambda}m^*(\lambda) + \frac{\partial f(m^*(\lambda);\lambda)}{\partial \lambda}$$

The first term on the right-hand side is zero due to the stationarity condition for the free energy, $\partial f(m;\lambda)/\partial m = 0$ at $m = m^*(\lambda)$. In the second term we may use $\partial f(m;\lambda)/\partial\lambda = m$, so that altogether

$$\langle m(\boldsymbol{\sigma})\rangle_{\text{eq}} = m^*(\lambda) \tag{20.50}$$

Evaluating this at $\lambda = 0$ indeed gives $\langle m(\boldsymbol{\sigma})\rangle_{\text{eq}} = m^*$, as before.

Now consider the regime $T < T_c$. Here the constrained free energy $f(m)$ has two distinct minima $m^* = \pm m_\beta$, where m_β is the positive solution of the stationarity condition (20.43). Hence $P(m) \sim \exp(-N\beta f(m))$ has two narrow peaks at those two values. However, because of the symmetry $m \to -m$ of $f(m)$, $P(m)$ is likewise symmetric about the origin, so the average value of $m(\boldsymbol{\sigma})$ is

$$\langle m(\boldsymbol{\sigma})\rangle_{\text{eq}} = 0 \tag{20.51}$$

What is the meaning of this average over the two peaks of $P(m)$? Let us return to the beginning of our analysis: the equilibrium distribution $p_{\text{eq}}(\boldsymbol{\sigma})$ over network states $\boldsymbol{\sigma}$ is the unique stationary distribution to which any network of *fixed* size N will converge if we wait long enough. The distribution $P(m)$, derived from $p_{\text{eq}}(\boldsymbol{\sigma})$, tells us which values of m we would observe if we monitored the operation of such a network, once it has reached its stationary state. Mostly, m would be close to $\pm m_\beta$, but over time it could and would flip between these two values, giving on average $\langle m(\boldsymbol{\sigma})\rangle_{\rm eq} = 0$. Our analysis leading to (20.51) thus corresponds to taking the infinite time limit $t \to \infty$ *first*, and *then* the thermodynamic limit $N \to \infty$ of large system size.

How relevant is this order of taking the limits in practice? This depends on how long we would have to wait to see the network flip between the two preferred values of $m(\boldsymbol{\sigma})$. It turns out that this time is generically *exponential* in N. This follows from the exponential form of $P(m) \sim \exp(-N\beta f(m))$: to go from $m = +m_\beta$ to $m = -m_\beta$, the system has to pass through the exponentially unlikely values of m in between; we therefore have to wait for an exponentially long time for this transition to occur by chance. But this means that, even for moderate values of N ($N = 1000$, say) we will in practice never see such transitions, because we would have to wait for an astronomically long time: $e^{1000} \approx 10^{400}$, which even if we set our time unit to 10^{-15} s, say (the order of the fastest atomic processes) is still unimaginably much longer than the age of the universe.[41] The network will thus get stuck in one of the two preferred values of m at long but not exponentially long times t. For $N \to \infty$ at fixed t it will do so with probability one. The parts of the equilibrium distribution associated with the opposite value of $m(\boldsymbol{\sigma})$ are effectively inaccessible on such timescales: ergodicity is broken by the limit $N \to \infty$, and the system can only explore part of its phase space. Formally, to see this *ergodicity breaking*, we have taken $N \to \infty$ first and then $t \to \infty$; the above discussion shows that this limit is the one that is relevant for the behaviour of large networks on practical timescales.

For $T < T_c$, and in the thermodynamic limit $N \to \infty$, we have seen that $m(\boldsymbol{\sigma})$ will converge to either $+m_\beta$ or $-m_\beta$ at long times; which one of these will depend on the initial conditions. This is entirely consistent with our dynamical analysis in Chapter 16, where we showed that for $N \to \infty$ and sequential dynamics, m evolves in time according to the deterministic equation

$$\frac{\mathrm{d}}{\mathrm{d}t}m = \tanh(\beta J m) - m \tag{20.52}$$

which indeed has as its stable fixed points exactly $m^* = \pm m_\beta$. These two values of m are associated with different *ergodic sectors* or *components* into which phase space is split, and correspond to the different local minima of $f(m)$. If we plot the equilibrium value of m as a function of T, it bifurcates at $T = T_c$ into the two different values in the low temperature regime. We have what is called a *phase transition* from a 'paramagnetic' (disordered, $m = 0$) phase at high T to a 'ferromagnetic' (ordered) phase with $m \neq 0$ at

[41] According to the latest estimates the age of the universe is about 13.7×10^9y $\approx 4\times10^{17}$ s.

low T. The fact that the transition of m from zero to nonzero values indicates the onset of order justifies our use of the term *order parameter* for m. Transitions where the order parameter is a continuous function of T are called second order, while those with a discontinuous jump of the order parameter are called first order. For $T \to 0$ (i.e. $\beta \to \infty$), m converges to ± 1; this is clear from the Curie–Weiss equation (20.43), with $\tanh(\beta J m) \to \text{sgn}(m)$. It also agrees with our general discussion in Section 20.3: at zero temperature, the equilibrium distribution p_{eq} only gives weight to the ground states $\boldsymbol{\sigma}$ which minimize the Hamiltonian $H(\boldsymbol{\sigma})$. For our present model, because $H(\boldsymbol{\sigma}) = -NJm^2(\boldsymbol{\sigma})/2 + \mathcal{O}(1)$, these are the states with $m(\boldsymbol{\sigma}) = \pm 1$, that is, where either $\sigma_i = +1$ for all i, or $\sigma_i = -1$ for all i. These states are also called *attractors*: the network is 'attracted' to one of them (depending, again, on the initial conditions) in the long time limit (at $T = 0$).

As an aside, we note that in the present case the method of calculating averages using the trick (20.27) can also give us information about ergodicity breaking. The relation (20.50),

$$\langle m(\boldsymbol{\sigma}) \rangle_{\text{eq}} = m^*(\lambda)$$

still holds, but now the limit $\lambda \to 0$ is no longer unique. For $\lambda < 0$, the minimum of $f(m; \lambda)$ (equation (20.49)) is located at a positive value of m, while for $\lambda > 0$ it is at a negative value, so

$$m^*(\lambda \to 0^-) = +m_\beta \qquad m^*(\lambda \to 0^+) = -m_\beta$$

and we recover precisely the averages of $m(\boldsymbol{\sigma})$ in the two ergodic sectors. The special feature that causes the ergodicity breaking to show up in the limit $\lambda \to 0$ is the fact that both ergodic components (local minima of $f(m)$) have the same free energy; any infinitesimal λ is sufficient to select between these two degenerate minima. The same would not happen for local minima with different values of $f(m)$; but these would still locate ergodic sectors of phase space in which the system would be trapped in the thermodynamic limit.

Ergodicity breaking for parallel dynamics

The general approach to the analysis of the infinite-range ferromagnet (20.34) with parallel dynamics is very similar to that for sequential dynamics. For the case of ferromagnetic couplings ($J > 0$), we will see that also the results are identical; for $J < 0$, there are some subtle differences.

Using (20.47), the pseudo-Hamiltonian (20.24) becomes

$$H(\boldsymbol{\sigma}) = -\frac{1}{\beta}\sum_{i=1}^{N} \ln 2\cosh(\beta J m(\boldsymbol{\sigma}) - \beta J\sigma_i/N)$$
$$= -NT \ln 2\cosh(\beta J m(\boldsymbol{\sigma})) + \mathcal{O}(1)$$

Going through exactly the same steps as for the sequential case, we then find the constrained free energy (per neuron or spin) as a function of magnetization m:

$$f(m) = -T \ln 2\cosh(\beta J m) - Ts(m)$$

and the free energy $f = \min_m f(m)$. The stationary (saddle point) condition $f'(m) = 0$ now gives

$$m = \tanh(\beta J \tanh(\beta J m)) \tag{20.53}$$

The solutions of this equation again obey a Curie–Weiss law. This can be seen as follows. The definition $\hat{m} = \tanh(\beta|J|m)$ transforms (20.53) into

$$m = \tanh(\beta|J|\hat{m}) \qquad \hat{m} = \tanh(\beta|J|m)$$

from which one derives

$$0 \leq (m - \hat{m})^2 = (m - \hat{m})[\tanh(\beta|J|\hat{m}) - \tanh(\beta|J|m)] \leq 0$$

This immediately implies that $m = \hat{m}$, so

$$m = \tanh(\beta|J|m) \tag{20.54}$$

For $J > 0$, we therefore have the same results as for sequential dynamics: a phase transition occurs at $T_c = J$, from a paramagnetic phase $m = 0$ to a ferromagnetic phase where phase space is broken into two ergodic components with the values $m = \pm m_\beta$.

For $J < 0$, there are differences. Whereas in the sequential case we found $m = 0$ for all T, for parallel dynamics the behaviour is the same as for $J > 0$ (because $f(m)$ depends only on $|J|$), with $m = \pm m_\beta$ for $T < T_c$. Here m_β is the positive solution of $m = \tanh(\beta|J|m)$. This can be understood from the different dynamics. In the sequential case, equation (20.52) shows that, for $J < 0$, the system is always driven towards the fixed point $m = 0$. In the parallel case, on the other hand, we know that (for $N \to \infty$, as usual) $m(t)$ evolves according to

$$m(t+1) = \tanh(\beta J m(t)) \tag{20.55}$$

(see Section 16.3). For $J < 0$ and $T < |J|$, $m(t)$ will now approach the limit cycle $m(t) = m_\beta(-1)^t$, or its twin brother $m(t) = -m_\beta(-1)^t$. Ergodicity breaking manifests itself in the fact that only one these two limit cycles is chosen. For large but finite N, on the other hand, if we were prepared to wait for very long times, we would occasionally see transitions between the two cycles. As a consequence, at any given (long) time t, we could only predict that m would be close to either $+m_\beta$ or $-m_\beta$, but not which one.

Stepping back—the general strategy

The analysis of the infinite-range ferromagnet in the previous sections shows the general ingredients of a statistical mechanics analysis of equilibrium network operation. One first finds the Hamiltonian for a given choice of interactions J_{ij} and external fields ϑ_i, which will often (but not always) be expressible in terms of a finite number of order parameters. One then introduces the density of states for these order parameters, and calculates it using integral representations for the delta functions constraining the order parameters to their required values. The log-density of states gives the constrained entropy, and combining this with the known Hamiltonian gives the constrained free energy. One then locates the local minima of the constrained free energy. For $N \to \infty$, the system will stay in one of the ergodic components of phase space (which one is determined by the initial condition) which these local minima represent. The values of the order parameters at these local minima are those that will be observed in the limit of long but not exponentially long times. On exponentially long timescales, on the other hand, the system would equilibrate fully. Only the lowest (global) minimum of the constrained free energy would then remain relevant, and this would determine the so-called 'thermodynamic' value of the unconstrained free energy f.

20.6 Exercises

Exercise 20.1. (Completion of proofs.) Derive the expressions (20.29) for energy and entropy in terms of temperature derivatives of the free energy, starting from the definition of the partition function and for a generic (β-independent) Hamiltonian. Prove that $F[p(\sigma)]$ of (20.30) is minimized when $p(\sigma)$ takes the Boltzmann form; you will need a Lagrange multiplier to enforce the constraint that $\sum_{\boldsymbol{\sigma}} p(\boldsymbol{\sigma}) = 1$. Fill in the details of the calculation of $s(m)$, equation (20.42), for the infinite-range ferromagnet. Show that $s'(m) = -\operatorname{artanh}(m)$.

Exercise 20.2. (Parallel dynamics Hamiltonian and partition function.) Consider the parallel dynamics process (20.1, 16.7), with symmetric interactions $\{J_{ij}\}$. Show also that $\lim_{\beta\to\infty} H(\boldsymbol{\sigma}) = L(\boldsymbol{\sigma})$, where the Hamiltonian is given by (20.24) and $L(\boldsymbol{\sigma})$ denotes the zero noise Lyapunov function (3.8) of the parallel dynamics. Show that the partition function $Z = \sum_{\boldsymbol{\sigma}} \exp(-\beta H(\boldsymbol{\sigma}))$ can also be written as

$$Z = \sum_{\boldsymbol{\sigma}} \sum_{\boldsymbol{\sigma}'} \exp\left[-\beta \left(-\frac{1}{2} \sum_{ij=1}^{N} \sigma_i J_{ij} \sigma'_j - \frac{1}{2} \sum_{ij=1}^{N} \sigma'_i J_{ij} \sigma_j \right.\right.$$
$$\left.\left. - \sum_{i=1}^{N} \vartheta_i \sigma_i - \sum_{i=1}^{N} \vartheta_i \sigma'_i \right) \right]$$

Exercise 20.3. (Parallel dynamics Hopfield model with $p = 1$.) Consider the parallel dynamics process (20.1, 16.7). For a given state $\boldsymbol{\sigma}$ at time t, denote averages over the state $\boldsymbol{\sigma}'$ at time $t + 1$ by $\langle f(\boldsymbol{\sigma}')\rangle = \sum_{\boldsymbol{\sigma}'} f(\boldsymbol{\sigma}')W(\boldsymbol{\sigma}', \boldsymbol{\sigma})$. Show that $\langle \sigma'_i \rangle = \tanh(\beta h_i(\boldsymbol{\sigma}))$; this is equation (20.45), which also holds for sequential dynamics when neuron i is the one chosen for the update. Derive the analogous result for $\langle \sigma'_i \sigma'_j \rangle$. Apply these results to the overlap $m(\boldsymbol{\sigma}) = N^{-1} \sum_{i=1}^{N} \xi_i \sigma_i$ of the state $\boldsymbol{\sigma}$ with a pattern $\boldsymbol{\xi} = (\xi_1, \ldots \xi_N) \in \{-1, 1\}^N$, in order to find $\langle m(\boldsymbol{\sigma}')\rangle$, $\langle m^2(\boldsymbol{\sigma}')\rangle$ and the variance $\langle m^2(\boldsymbol{\sigma}')\rangle - [\langle m(\boldsymbol{\sigma}')\rangle]^2$. Show that the latter is less than N^{-1}.

Consider now the Hopfield model with $p = 1$, which has $J_{ij} = (J/N)\xi_i\xi_j$ and $\vartheta_i = 0$. This is essentially the infinite-range ferromagnet covered in this chapter, up to the transformation $\sigma_i \to \xi_i\sigma_i$. Use your earlier results to show that, for $N \to \infty$, m evolves deterministically according to $m(t+1) = \tanh[\beta J m(t)]$; this is (20.55). Depending on the sign and modulus of βJ, work out the implications for the time evolution of $m(t)$, particularly at long times t.

The same method can also be used to analyse the dynamics of simple models that do not have detailed balance. Consider, for example, $J_{ij} = N^{-1}\nu_i\xi_j$, $\vartheta_i = 0$, with $\nu_i \in \{-1, 1\}$, and derive the evolution equation for $m(t)$ in this case. (Hint: The ν_i should appear only through the parameter $\alpha = N^{-1}\sum_i \nu_i\xi_i$.) Compare your results with those in Chapter 16, in particular to (16.44) and its analogue for sequential dynamics, equations (16.23, 16.24).

Exercise 20.4. (Combinatorial derivation of density of states.) An alternative derivation of $s(m)$ can be given using some combinatorics. To carry out the sum over states $\boldsymbol{\sigma}$ in the partition function (20.35) we have to count how many states there are for each possible value of $m(\boldsymbol{\sigma})$. For finite N, we can write $m(\boldsymbol{\sigma}) = 2n/N - 1$, where n is the number of spins which are in state $+1$. The number of states with a given n is just a binomial coefficient, and so

$$Z = \sum_{n=0}^{N} \binom{N}{n} e^{N\beta J(2n/N-1)^2/2+\mathcal{O}(1)}$$

Write the binomial coefficient in terms of factorials, and use the Stirling approximation (see next exercise) to show that, for large N,

$$\frac{1}{N} \ln \binom{N}{n} = s(m)|_{m=2n/N-1}$$

where $s(m)$ is the constrained entropy as calculated previously in (20.42). Insert this into the previous result for Z and convert the sum over n into an integral over $m = 2n/N - 1$, which is justified for $N \to \infty$. Show that

$$Z = \int_{-1}^{1} \mathrm{d}m \; e^{N[\beta J m^2/2+s(m)]}$$

up to factors that only make a negligible contribution to $N^{-1} \ln Z$ in the limit $N \to \infty$. Finally, derive equation (20.37) by saddle point integration.

Exercise 20.5. (Stirling's formula.) The Stirling approximation is an approximation for large factorials,

$$k! \approx \sqrt{2\pi k} \left(\frac{k}{e}\right)^k \qquad (k \to \infty)$$

This holds asymptotically, in the sense that the relative error of the approximation goes to zero for $k \to \infty$ (in other words, the ratio of the left- and right-hand side tends to one). Test the quality of the approximation for a few values of k; you should find reasonable agreement for $k > 12$ or so. Then derive it, as follows. The factorial can be written in terms of the Gamma-function integral:

$$k! = \Gamma(k+1) = \int_0^\infty \mathrm{d}x \; x^k e^{-x}$$

You can show this by induction, using integration by parts for the induction step. By a change of integration variable to $y = x/k$, find

$$k! = k^{k+1} \int_0^\infty \mathrm{d}y \; e^{k(\ln y - y)}$$

Expand the exponent around its maximum, to second order. With this approximation, and extending the integration range to $y \in \mathbb{R}$ (why is this justified?), you are left with an integral which should give you the desired result.

Exercise 20.6. (Solution by Gaussian linearization.) Another way of solving the infinite-range ferromagnet and similar models is via so-called Gaussian linearization, which applies when the Hamiltonian is quadratic in one or more order parameters. First add a generating term $\lambda \sum_i \sigma_i = N\lambda m(\boldsymbol{\sigma})$ to the Hamiltonian, as in (20.48), to deduce the average value of $m(\boldsymbol{\sigma})$ later. This gives for (20.35)

$$Z = \sum_{\sigma} e^{\beta J(\sum_i \sigma_i)^2/2N - \beta\lambda \sum_i \sigma_i + \mathcal{O}(1)}$$

Now use

$$\int \frac{dz}{\sqrt{2\pi\sigma^2}}\, e^{-z^2/2\sigma^2} e^{xz} = e^{x^2\sigma^2/2}$$

to write Z as

$$Z = \int \frac{dz}{\sqrt{2\pi\beta J/N}} \sum_{\sigma} e^{-Nz^2/2\beta J + (z-\beta\lambda)\sum_i \sigma_i + \mathcal{O}(1)}$$

Note that the scaling of the variance $\sigma^2 = \beta J/N$ with N has been chosen such that both terms in the exponent are of order N. The sum over states now factorizes over the different i and you should get

$$Z = \int \frac{dz}{\sqrt{2\pi\beta J/N}}\, e^{-Nz^2/2\beta J + N \ln 2\cosh(z-\beta\lambda) + \mathcal{O}(1)} \tag{20.56}$$

Then show by saddle point integration that

$$f = \lim_{N\to\infty} \frac{F}{N} = \min_z \left\{ \frac{z^2}{2\beta^2 J} - T \ln 2\cosh(z - \beta\lambda) \right\}$$

Show that at $\lambda = 0$, the saddle point condition for z is

$$z = \beta J \tanh(z) \tag{20.57}$$

Differentiate f with respect to λ at $\lambda = 0$, and show that $\langle m(\sigma)\rangle_{\text{eq}} = \tanh(z)$, and hence that (20.57) is equivalent to the Curie–Weiss law (20.43).

Exercise 20.7. (Ergodicity breaking in networks with parallel dynamics.) Consider the infinite-range ferromagnet with parallel dynamics. Consider the probability $W(\boldsymbol{\sigma}', \boldsymbol{\sigma})$ that the system will be in state $\boldsymbol{\sigma}'$ at time $t+1$ if it was in state $\boldsymbol{\sigma}$ at time t. Anticipating that this will depend exponentially on N, define

$$w_{\text{particular}}(\boldsymbol{\sigma}', \boldsymbol{\sigma}) = -\frac{1}{N} \ln W(\boldsymbol{\sigma}', \boldsymbol{\sigma})$$

and show that, for large N, the right-hand side depends on the new state $\boldsymbol{\sigma}'$ and the previous state $\boldsymbol{\sigma}$ only through their respective magnetizations $m' = m(\boldsymbol{\sigma}')$ and $m = m(\boldsymbol{\sigma})$. You should find

$$w_{\text{particular}}(\boldsymbol{\sigma}', \boldsymbol{\sigma}) = -\beta J m m' + \ln 2 \cosh(\beta J m)$$

As suggested by the subscript, $\exp(-N w_{\text{particular}}(\boldsymbol{\sigma}', \boldsymbol{\sigma}))$ gives the probability of landing in any *particular* state $\boldsymbol{\sigma}'$ with magnetization m' at time $t+1$. If we want the probability of landing in *any* state with magnetization m', we have to multiply with the number of states with that particular magnetization, which is (see Exercise 20.4)

$$\binom{N}{N(1+m')/2} \approx e^{N s(m')} \quad (N \to \infty)$$

Terms which are not exponential in N have been neglected on the right-hand side, as usual. Show that for large N the probability of landing in a state with magnetization m' at time $t+1$, given that the magnetization at time t was m, is

$$e^{-N w(m', m)} \quad \text{with} \quad w(m', m) = -s(m') - \beta J m m' + \ln 2 \cosh(\beta J m)$$

It follows that for $N \to \infty$ only values of m' for which $w(m', m)$ is minimal have a significant probability of occurring at time $t+1$. Determine where this minimum is, by differentiating with respect to m'. Hence confirm that, in the thermodynamic limit, the magnetization follows the deterministic evolution equation

$$m' = \tanh(\beta J m) \tag{20.58}$$

as stated in equation (20.55). Specialize to $J > 0$ now. Iterate the evolution equation (20.58) numerically, starting from different starting values of m. For large temperature (small β), you should observe convergence to $m = 0$, whatever the initial conditions. For larger $\beta > 1/J$, you should see convergence to one of two nonzero values of m, depending on the initial condition. What determines which of the two values you converge to, and why do the limiting values of m satisfy the Curie–Weiss law (20.43)?

For large β, the limiting value of m depends on the initial conditions (ergodicity breaking). Let us try to understand how this is linked to the thermodynamic limit $N \to \infty$. Call m_β the positive solution of the Curie–Weiss equation (20.43) (for $J > 0$, and $\beta > 1/J$). Assume we are initially in a state with magnetization $m = m_\beta$. What is the probability of being in a state with $m' = -m_\beta$, the other (stable) solution of the Curie–Weiss law, at the next time step, for large but finite N? The inverse of this probability gives us an estimate for the number of time steps one would have to wait to actually see this transition. Confirm that for large N, we have to wait an exponentially long time for the system to become *ergodic*, that is, for it to explore the whole of its phase space. Choose some reasonable values for β and J and calculate how many time steps we would need to wait for $N = 100, 1000, 10000$. Explain why the strict ergodicity breaking described by the thermodynamic limit $N \to \infty$ really is relevant for describing the behaviour of large, but not necessarily enormous, systems on realistic timescales.

21 Network operation: equilibrium analysis

In this chapter we restrict ourselves to networks which obey detailed balance, so that we know the equilibrium probability distribution and equilibrium statistical mechanics applies. We will only consider the case of sequential dynamics; the results for parallel dynamics can be derived along very similar lines, and are largely identical. To have detailed balance, we thus assume that the interaction matrix J_{ij} is symmetric and that there are no self-interactions ($J_{ii} = 0$ for all i). We will study in detail the Hopfield model, which is the archetypical model for describing the functioning of symmetric neural networks as associative memories. The basic ideas behind such systems, based on the creation of attractors in the microscopic state space, was introduced and illustrated already in Section 3.3.

To make the connection with the models and preliminary analyses in Section 3.3 more explicit, and re-phrase them in equilibrium statistical mechanical terms, let us return to the early example (3.16), where a single pattern $\boldsymbol{\xi} \in \{-1, 1\}^N$ was stored in an infinite-range network, via

$$J_{ij} = \frac{1}{N}\xi_i\xi_j \ \ (i \neq j), \qquad J_{ii} = 0, \qquad \vartheta_i = 0 \tag{21.1}$$

The Ising Hamiltonian (20.23) for this system is seen to be

$$H(\boldsymbol{\sigma}) = -\frac{1}{2}\sum_{ij=1}^{N} \sigma_i J_{ij}\sigma_j - \sum_{i=1}^{N} \vartheta_i\sigma_i = -\frac{N}{2}\left(\frac{1}{N}\sum_i \xi_i\sigma_i\right)^2 + \frac{1}{2}$$

It is essentially the same as that of the infinite-range ferromagnet of Section 20.4, up to the so-called gauge transformation $\sigma_i \rightarrow \xi_i\sigma_i$. Its ground states are those for which $N^{-1}\sum_i \xi_i\sigma_i = \pm 1$; this requires either $\boldsymbol{\sigma} = \boldsymbol{\xi}$, or $\boldsymbol{\sigma} = -\boldsymbol{\xi}$. At $T = 0$, that is, in the noise-free limit, the equilibrium distribution $p_{\text{eq}}(\boldsymbol{\sigma})$ will assign probability $\frac{1}{2}$ to each of these two states. Due to ergodicity breaking, the network will then converge to one of these two states, dependent on the initial condition. For this simple model, and for $T = 0$ only, the same conclusion could also be reached using the Lyapunov function of Section 3.2. Below we will apply the more powerful tools of equilibrium statistical mechanics to the more complicated attractor-based recurrent neural network models, for which the simpler methods of Section 3.3 would no longer be inadequate.

21.1 Hopfield model with finite number of patterns

Definition

The Hopfield model is obtained by generalizing the recipe (21.1) to the case of an arbitrary number p of patterns:

$$J_{ij} = \frac{1}{N} \sum_{\mu=1}^{p} \xi_i^\mu \xi_j^\mu \qquad \vartheta_i = 0 \tag{21.2}$$

For now we consider the case where the number of patterns p remains finite in the thermodynamic limit $N \to \infty$, so that $p/N \to 0$. The case of extensive p, where $p = N\alpha$, is more complicated and is left for later. Remembering that there are no self-interactions, the Ising Hamiltonian (20.23) can then be written as

$$\begin{aligned} H(\boldsymbol{\sigma}) &= -\frac{1}{2N} \sum_{\mu=1}^{p} \sum_{i,j} \sigma_i \xi_i^\mu \sigma_j \xi_j^\mu + \frac{1}{2N} \sum_{\mu=1}^{p} \sum_{i} \sigma_i^2 (\xi_i^\mu)^2 \\ &= -\frac{N}{2} \sum_{\mu=1}^{p} m_\mu^2(\boldsymbol{\sigma}) + \frac{1}{2} p \end{aligned} \tag{21.3}$$

with the pattern overlaps

$$m_\mu(\boldsymbol{\sigma}) = \frac{1}{N} \sum_{i=1}^{N} \xi_i^\mu \sigma_i \tag{21.4}$$

Each of these p overlaps measures the resemblance between the current microscopic network state $\boldsymbol{\sigma}$ and one particular pattern.

Free energy and saddle point equations

The partition function and free energy are, by definition,

$$Z = \sum_{\boldsymbol{\sigma}} e^{-\beta H(\boldsymbol{\sigma})} \qquad F = -T \ln Z$$

The Hamiltonian depends on $\boldsymbol{\sigma}$ only through the pattern overlaps m_μ, so we choose these as our order parameters and define the corresponding constrained partition function. Introducing the shorthand notation $\boldsymbol{m} = (m_1, \ldots, m_p)$, and discarding the $\mathcal{O}(1)$ term $p/2$ from the Hamiltonian,

we have

$$Z = \int \mathrm{d}\boldsymbol{m}\ Z(\boldsymbol{m}) \qquad Z(\boldsymbol{m}) = e^{N\beta \boldsymbol{m}^2/2}\,\mathcal{D}(\boldsymbol{m}) \tag{21.5}$$

with the density of states:

$$\mathcal{D}(\boldsymbol{m}) = \sum_{\sigma} \delta\left(\boldsymbol{m} - \boldsymbol{m}(\boldsymbol{\sigma})\right)$$

Note that the δ-function occurring here is a p-dimensional one, that is, a product of p ordinary δ-functions:

$$\delta\left(\boldsymbol{m} - \boldsymbol{m}(\boldsymbol{\sigma})\right) = \prod_{\mu=1}^{p} \delta(m_\mu - m_\mu(\boldsymbol{\sigma}))$$

So we also need p integration variables $\boldsymbol{x} = (x_1, \ldots, x_p)$ to represent these δ-functions as integrals. As usual, these are scaled such as to produce extensive terms in the exponent. Writing $\boldsymbol{\xi}_i = (\xi_i^1, \ldots, \xi_i^p)$, we have

$$\begin{aligned}\mathcal{D}(\boldsymbol{m}) &= \left(\frac{N}{2\pi}\right)^p \int \mathrm{d}\boldsymbol{x}\ e^{\mathrm{i}N\boldsymbol{x}\cdot\boldsymbol{m}} \sum_{\sigma} e^{-\mathrm{i}\sum_{i=1}^{N}\sigma_i \boldsymbol{\xi}_i\cdot\boldsymbol{x}} \\ &= \left(\frac{N}{2\pi}\right)^p \int \mathrm{d}\boldsymbol{x}\ \exp(N[\mathrm{i}\boldsymbol{x}\cdot\boldsymbol{m} + \langle \ln 2\cos\left(\boldsymbol{\xi}\cdot\boldsymbol{x}\right)\rangle_{\boldsymbol{\xi}}])\end{aligned}$$

with the abbreviation

$$\langle g(\boldsymbol{\xi})\rangle_{\boldsymbol{\xi}} = \frac{1}{N}\sum_{i=1}^{N} g(\boldsymbol{\xi}_i) \tag{21.6}$$

The log-density of states, that is, the constrained entropy, can now be evaluated by saddle point integration:

$$s(\boldsymbol{m}) = \ \mathrm{extr}_{\boldsymbol{x}}\ s(\boldsymbol{m},\boldsymbol{x}) \qquad s(\boldsymbol{m},\boldsymbol{x}) = \mathrm{i}\boldsymbol{x}\cdot\boldsymbol{m} + \langle \ln 2\cos\left(\boldsymbol{\xi}\cdot\boldsymbol{x}\right)\rangle_{\boldsymbol{\xi}} \tag{21.7}$$

From (21.5), the free energy (per neuron/spin) is then

$$f = -\lim_{N\to\infty}\frac{T}{N}\ln\int \mathrm{d}\boldsymbol{m}\ e^{-N\beta f(\boldsymbol{m})} = \min_{\boldsymbol{m}} f(\boldsymbol{m}) \tag{21.8}$$

with the constrained free energy

$$f(\boldsymbol{m}) = -\tfrac{1}{2}\boldsymbol{m}^2 - Ts(\boldsymbol{m}) \tag{21.9}$$

To identify the ergodic components, we need to find the stationary points of $f(\boldsymbol{m})$, which are given by the conditions

$$\frac{\partial f(\boldsymbol{m})}{\partial m_\mu} = -m_\mu - T\frac{\partial s(\boldsymbol{m})}{\partial m_\mu} = 0 \quad (\mu = 1, \ldots, p) \tag{21.10}$$

Finding the derivative $\partial s(\boldsymbol{m})/\partial m_\mu$ may seem difficult at first because the saddle point condition for the x_μ, viz.

$$\frac{\partial}{\partial x_\mu} s(\boldsymbol{m}, \boldsymbol{x}) = 0 \Rightarrow \mathrm{i}\boldsymbol{m} = \langle \boldsymbol{\xi} \tan(\boldsymbol{\xi} \cdot \boldsymbol{x}) \rangle_{\boldsymbol{\xi}} \tag{21.11}$$

cannot be solved explicitly for $\boldsymbol{x}$. But this is not actually a problem, as can be seen by an argument similar to the one that lead us to (20.50). If we write the solution of (21.11) as $\boldsymbol{x}(\boldsymbol{m})$, then $s(\boldsymbol{m}) = s(\boldsymbol{m}, \boldsymbol{x}(\boldsymbol{m}))$ and

$$\begin{aligned}\frac{\partial s(\boldsymbol{m})}{\partial m_\mu} &= \sum_{\nu=1}^{p} \frac{\partial s(\boldsymbol{m}, \boldsymbol{x}(\boldsymbol{m}))}{\partial x_\nu} \frac{\partial x_\nu(\boldsymbol{m})}{\partial m_\mu} + \frac{\partial s(\boldsymbol{m}, \boldsymbol{x}(\boldsymbol{m}))}{\partial m_\mu} \\ &= \frac{\partial s(\boldsymbol{m}, \boldsymbol{x}(\boldsymbol{m}))}{\partial m_\mu} = \mathrm{i}x_\mu\end{aligned}$$

The terms with the unknown derivatives $\partial x_\nu(\boldsymbol{m})/\partial m_\mu$ do not contribute, because of the saddle point condition for $\boldsymbol{x}$. Inserting this into (21.10), we see that the conditions for a stationary point of $f(\boldsymbol{m})$ are

$$\boldsymbol{x} = \mathrm{i}\beta\boldsymbol{m} \qquad \mathrm{i}\boldsymbol{m} = \langle \boldsymbol{\xi} \tan(\boldsymbol{\xi} \cdot \boldsymbol{x}) \rangle_{\boldsymbol{\xi}} \tag{21.12}$$

These are equivalent to $\boldsymbol{x} = \mathrm{i}\beta\boldsymbol{m}$ and

$$\boldsymbol{m} = \langle \boldsymbol{\xi} \tanh(\beta\boldsymbol{\xi} \cdot \boldsymbol{m}) \rangle_{\boldsymbol{\xi}} \tag{21.13}$$

The saddle point value of $\boldsymbol{x}$ is purely imaginary, as was the case for the infinite-range ferromagnet of Section 20.4. We refer to (21.13) as the saddle point equation for the order parameters $\boldsymbol{m}$; the alternative name 'stationarity condition' is less common.

As far as the derivation of saddle point equations is concerned, the above analysis illustrates a general point. It does not matter whether we find our saddle point equations in different stages for different subsets of variables—as done above: we first found the saddle point condition for $\boldsymbol{x}$, inserted the solution $\boldsymbol{x}(\boldsymbol{m})$ into $s(\boldsymbol{m}, \boldsymbol{x})$, and then worked out the saddle point condition for $\boldsymbol{m}$—or for all variables simultaneously. Indeed, equation (21.12) is what we would have obtained if we had looked directly for the extrema of

$$f(\boldsymbol{m}, \boldsymbol{x}) = -\tfrac{1}{2}\boldsymbol{m}^2 - Ts(\boldsymbol{m}, \boldsymbol{x}) \tag{21.14}$$

with respect to $\boldsymbol{x}$ and $\boldsymbol{m}$.

Yet another method for obtaining the saddle point equation (21.13) for $\boldsymbol{m}$ is to use $\boldsymbol{x} = \mathrm{i}\beta\boldsymbol{m}$ to eliminate the so-called 'conjugate order parameters' $\boldsymbol{x}$ from $f(\boldsymbol{m}, \boldsymbol{x})$. Using (21.7), this gives

$$\tilde{f}(\boldsymbol{m}) = \tfrac{1}{2}\boldsymbol{m}^2 - T\langle \ln 2\cosh(\beta\boldsymbol{\xi}\cdot\boldsymbol{m})\rangle_{\boldsymbol{\xi}} \tag{21.15}$$

The notation $\tilde{f}(\boldsymbol{m})$ is meant to emphasize that, for general $\boldsymbol{m}$, this is *not* the constrained free energy $f(\boldsymbol{m})$, equation (21.9), because we have incorrectly used the saddle point conditions for $\boldsymbol{m}$ rather than those for $\boldsymbol{x}$ to eliminate $\boldsymbol{x}$. Nevertheless, *at* a saddle point $\boldsymbol{m}$ of the true constrained free energy f (where $\boldsymbol{x} = \mathrm{i}\beta\boldsymbol{m}$ from (21.12)), we do have $f(\boldsymbol{m}) = \tilde{f}(\boldsymbol{m})$. Moreover, by differentiating (21.15) we see that the stationary points of $\tilde{f}(\boldsymbol{m})$ obey (21.13). So f and $\tilde{f}$ have identical saddle points. This conclusion can be checked more generally, and in summary we can state: one is allowed to use the 'wrong' saddle point conditions to eliminate the conjugate order parameters, as long as one bears in mind that the resulting function only has physical significance (as a constrained free energy) *at* its saddle points. We will call $\tilde{f}$ the 'pseudo-free energy'.

The rest of the programme from here on is clear: we need to find the solutions of the saddle point equation (21.13) as a function of temperature T, and then check whether they are stable in the sense that they are local minima of $f(\boldsymbol{m})$.

Self-averaging

Before we proceed, however, let us emphasize another important property of the free energy given by equations (21.7–21.9) and of the corresponding saddle point equation (21.13). Both depend on the patterns to be stored only through the statistics of the $\boldsymbol{\xi}_i = (\xi_i^1, \ldots, \xi_i^p)$, as already suggested by the notation (21.6). Each of the N vectors $\boldsymbol{\xi}_i$ can only take on a finite number of values (namely 2^p), so the average $\langle g(\boldsymbol{\xi})\rangle_{\boldsymbol{\xi}}$ is simply an average over these values, weighted by their relative frequencies.

Let us now assume that the p patterns are drawn randomly and independently from some distribution. The simplest case, on which we focus in the following, is that where this distribution is uniform over all the 2^N possible patterns. Each of the N pattern bits ξ_i^μ of a given pattern μ then takes on its two different values ± 1 with equal probability. For a given sample of p such patterns, we can then simply go through the list of the $\{\boldsymbol{\xi}_i\}$ for $i = 1, \ldots, N$, and count the relative frequencies of the 2^p different values that they can have. Because of the assumed pattern distributions, these relative frequencies should all be roughly equal, but for finite N, there will be deviations from this depending on the details of the sample. However, for $N \to \infty$ and by the definition of probability as the limit of a frequency count, all relative frequencies will become exactly equal with probability one, *independently* of the particular sample of patterns. Since only these relative frequencies affect the value of the free energy and the saddle point equations derived from it, we conclude that the free energy is *self-averaging* in the thermodynamic limit: it only depends on the distribution of patterns, but not on which particular set of patterns we have sampled from this distribution.

This property will be crucial when we extend the analysis of the Hopfield model to an extensive number of patterns. It is then no longer possible to calculate the free energy for a given set of patterns as we have done above; but an average over all sets of patterns from a given distribution *can* be calculated. Self-averaging guarantees that this average gives meaningful results: the average free energy is the same as that for any particular set of patterns, with probability one in the thermodynamic limit.

A note on terminology is in order here. Because the patterns are random samples from some distribution, they are often thought of as 'disorder' affecting the operation of the network. This disorder is imposed from the outside onto the network, and remains fixed while it operates. For this reason, it is more specifically referred to as 'quenched disorder' (quenching a molten metal essentially means freezing it, and thus fixing its structure). The average over patterns is therefore also called 'quenched average' or 'disorder average'. This kind of disorder is to be distinguished from the 'annealed' or 'thermal' disorder that we have already encountered in the operation of a network (the stochasticity in the evolving microscopic variables), for fixed patterns and hence interactions.

Analysis of saddle point equations: mixture states

As explained above, for randomly drawn patterns all possible values of the $\boldsymbol{\xi}_i$ have the same relative frequencies; this applies with probability one in the limit $N \to \infty$, whatever the particular set of patterns chosen. So we can evaluate the averages over the $\{\boldsymbol{\xi}_i\}$ simply as

$$\langle g(\boldsymbol{\xi}) \rangle_{\boldsymbol{\xi}} = 2^{-p} \sum_{\boldsymbol{\xi} \in \{-1,1\}^p} g(\boldsymbol{\xi})$$

In particular,

$$\langle \xi_\mu \rangle_{\boldsymbol{\xi}} = 0 \qquad \langle \xi_\mu \xi_\nu \rangle_{\boldsymbol{\xi}} = \delta_{\mu\nu} \tag{21.16}$$

The average over a product of two pattern bits is nonzero only when $\mu = \nu$, in which case we get $\xi_\mu^2 = 1$. Similarly, for a product of four bits the average equals one if we can pair up the indices into two pairs or if all four are equal, giving

$$\langle \xi_\mu \xi_\nu \xi_\rho \xi_\lambda \rangle_{\boldsymbol{\xi}} = \delta_{\mu\nu}\delta_{\rho\lambda} + \delta_{\mu\rho}\delta_{\nu\lambda} + \delta_{\mu\lambda}\delta_{\nu\rho} - 2\delta_{\mu\nu}\delta_{\nu\rho}\delta_{\rho\lambda} \tag{21.17}$$

The last term here prevents us from over-counting in the case where all four indices are equal. As for the infinite-range ferromagnet, we suspect that nonzero solutions $\boldsymbol{m}$ of the saddle point equation (21.13) will bifurcate continuously from the trivial solution $\boldsymbol{m} = 0$, as we lower the temperature.

We first establish an upper bound for the temperature $T = 1/\beta$ at which this bifurcation occurs. Taking the scalar product of (21.13) with $\boldsymbol{m}$ and using the inequality $|\tanh(z)| \le |z|$ (equation (20.44)) together with (21.16) gives

$$\begin{aligned} \boldsymbol{m}^2 &= \langle (\boldsymbol{\xi} \cdot \boldsymbol{m}) \tanh(\beta \boldsymbol{\xi} \cdot \boldsymbol{m}) \rangle_{\boldsymbol{\xi}} = \langle |\boldsymbol{\xi} \cdot \boldsymbol{m}| |\tanh(\beta \boldsymbol{\xi} \cdot \boldsymbol{m})| \rangle_{\boldsymbol{\xi}} \\ &\le \beta \langle (\boldsymbol{\xi} \cdot \boldsymbol{m})^2 \rangle_{\boldsymbol{\xi}} = \beta \sum_{\mu\nu} m_\mu m_\nu \langle \xi_\mu \xi_\nu \rangle_{\boldsymbol{\xi}} = \beta \boldsymbol{m}^2 \end{aligned} \tag{21.18}$$

which for $\beta < 1$ is possible only for $\boldsymbol{m} = 0$. So for $T > 1$ the only solution of (21.13) is the paramagnetic state $\boldsymbol{m} = 0$. To find the bifurcation of nonzero solutions at $T = 1$, we expand (21.13) for small $|\boldsymbol{m}|$ in powers of $\tau = \beta - 1$ and use (21.16, 21.17):

$$\begin{aligned} m_\mu &= \sum_\nu \beta \langle \xi_\mu \xi_\nu \rangle_{\boldsymbol{\xi}} m_\nu - \frac{1}{3} \beta^3 \sum_{\nu\rho\lambda} \langle \xi_\mu \xi_\nu \xi_\rho \xi_\lambda \rangle_{\boldsymbol{\xi}} m_\nu m_\rho m_\lambda + \mathcal{O}(\boldsymbol{m}^5) \\ &= (1+\tau) m_\mu + m_\mu \left(-\boldsymbol{m}^2 + \frac{2}{3} m_\mu^2 \right) + \mathcal{O}(\boldsymbol{m}^5, \tau \boldsymbol{m}^3) \end{aligned}$$

In the second line, we have anticipated that the values of the $\{m_\mu\}$ will be $\mathcal{O}(\tau^{1/2})$ for small τ, so that in $\beta^3 = (1+\tau)^3 = 1 + 3\tau + \cdots$ we only need to keep the leading term; the first neglected term is $\mathcal{O}(\tau \boldsymbol{m}^3)$ and thus of the same order as the $\mathcal{O}(\boldsymbol{m}^5)$ terms that we are discarding anyway. Neglecting now all the higher order terms, we have

$$m_\mu (\tau - \boldsymbol{m}^2 + \tfrac{2}{3} m_\mu^2) = 0$$

which gives, for each μ:

$$m_\mu = 0 \quad \text{or} \quad 0 = \tau - \boldsymbol{m}^2 + \tfrac{2}{3} m_\mu^2$$

The solutions are of the form $m_\mu \in \{-a, 0, a\}$, with $a = \sqrt{3(\boldsymbol{m}^2 - \tau)/2}$. If we denote by n the number of nonzero components in the vector $\boldsymbol{m}$, we have therefore $\boldsymbol{m}^2 = na^2$. Thus $a^2 = \frac{3}{2}(\boldsymbol{m}^2 - \tau) = \frac{3}{2}(na^2 - \tau)$, from which we find $a = \sqrt{3\tau/(3n-2)}$ and so

$$m_\mu = 0 \quad \text{or} \quad m_\mu = \pm \left(\frac{3}{3n-2} \right)^{1/2} \tau^{1/2}$$

This confirms the anticipated $\tau^{1/2}$ scaling. The above saddle points are called *mixture states*, since they correspond to microscopic network states that are correlated equally with a finite number n of the stored patterns (or their negatives). Without loss of generality we can always perform transformations on the set of stored patterns (permutations and reflections $\boldsymbol{\xi}^{\mu} \to -\boldsymbol{\xi}^{\mu}$) such that these mixture states acquire the form

$$\boldsymbol{m} = m_n(\overbrace{1, \ldots, 1}^{n \text{ times}}, \overbrace{0, \ldots, 0}^{p-n \text{ times}}) \qquad m_n = \left(\frac{3}{3n-2}\right)^{1/2} (\beta - 1)^{1/2} + \cdots \tag{21.19}$$

With a more complicated dependence of $m_n = m_n(T)$ on temperature T, these states are in fact valid saddle points at any $T < 1$, as can be verified by substitution of (21.19) as an *ansatz* into (21.13). By setting $M = \sum_{\nu \leq n} \xi_{\nu}$ we then find that (21.13) reduces to

$$\begin{aligned} \mu \leq n: \quad m_n &= \langle \xi_{\mu} \tanh(\beta m_n M) \rangle_{\boldsymbol{\xi}} \\ \mu > n: \quad 0 &= \langle \xi_{\mu} \tanh(\beta m_n M) \rangle_{\boldsymbol{\xi}} \end{aligned} \tag{21.20}$$

The second equation is automatically satisfied since ξ_{μ} only appears outside the tanh. The first equation leads to a condition determining the amplitude m_n of the mixture states:

$$m_n = \frac{1}{n} \langle M \tanh(\beta m_n M) \rangle_{\boldsymbol{\xi}} \tag{21.21}$$

The corresponding values of the (pseudo-) free energy $\tilde{f}(\boldsymbol{m})$ (equation (21.15)), to be denoted by f_n, are

$$f_n = \tfrac{1}{2} n m_n^2 - T \langle \ln 2 \cosh(\beta m_n M) \rangle_{\boldsymbol{\xi}} \tag{21.22}$$

As explained at the end of Section 21.1, because we are considering saddle points, $\tilde{f}(\boldsymbol{m})$ actually gives the true constrained free energy. This is why we are allowed to omit the tilde on f_n.

Stability of saddle points

The relevant question at this stage is whether the saddle points found above are stable in the sense that they correspond to local minima of the constrained free energy $f(\boldsymbol{m})$. To check this, we need to find the matrix of second derivatives of $f(\boldsymbol{m})$ at the saddle points and check whether it is positive definite. The procedure is slightly complicated because of the dependence of the saddle point values of $\boldsymbol{x}$ on $\boldsymbol{m}$ which we only know implicitly. Fortunately, however, it turns out in this case (and many others) that saddle points which are local minima of $f(\boldsymbol{m})$ are also local minima of the pseudo-free energy $\tilde{f}(\boldsymbol{m})$. So we can consider the matrix of second derivatives of $\tilde{f}$, as given by (21.15):

$$D_{\mu\nu} = \frac{\partial^2 \tilde{f}}{\partial m_\mu \partial m_\nu} = \delta_{\mu\nu} - \beta\langle \xi_\mu \xi_\nu [1 - \tanh^2(\beta \boldsymbol{\xi} \cdot \boldsymbol{m})]\rangle_{\boldsymbol{\xi}} \qquad (21.23)$$

and our saddle points will be stable if this is positive definite. In the trivial saddle point $\boldsymbol{m} = 0$ we have $D_{\mu\nu} = \delta_{\mu\nu}(1 - \beta)$, so at $T = 1$ this state destabilizes. In a mixture state of the type (21.19) the second derivative becomes:

$$D^{(n)}_{\mu\nu} = \delta_{\mu\nu} - \beta\langle \xi_\mu \xi_\nu [1 - \tanh^2(\beta m_n M)]\rangle_{\boldsymbol{\xi}} \qquad (21.24)$$

Due to the symmetries in the problem, the eigenspaces and eigenvalues of the matrix $D^{(n)}$ can be calculated. One finds three distinct eigenspaces:

	Eigenspace	Eigenvalue
I:	$\boldsymbol{x} = (0, \ldots, 0, x_{n+1}, \ldots, x_p)$	$1 - \beta(1 - Q)$
II:	$\boldsymbol{x} = (1, \ldots, 1, 0, \ldots, 0)$	$1 - \beta(1 - Q + (1 - n)R)$
III:	$\boldsymbol{x} = (x_1, \ldots, x_n, 0, \ldots, 0),\ \sum_\mu x_\mu = 0$	$1 - \beta(1 - Q + R)$

with

$$Q = \langle \tanh^2(\beta m_n M)\rangle_{\boldsymbol{\xi}} \qquad R = \langle \xi_1 \xi_2 \tanh^2(\beta m_n M)\rangle_{\boldsymbol{\xi}}$$

Eigenspace *III* and the quantity R only come into play for $n > 1$. The matrix $D^{(n)}$ is positive definite if all its eigenvalues are positive, so we can concentrate on the smallest eigenvalue. For $n = 1$ this is *I*. For $n > 1$, one can show that R is positive, and so the relevant eigenvalue is *III*. We can then also combine Q and R into one single average, which reduces to a trivial expression for $n = 2$. Altogether, the conditions for the n-mixture states to be stable become

$$n = 1: \quad 1 - \beta[1 - \tanh^2(\beta m_1)] > 0$$

$$n = 2: \quad 1 - \beta > 0$$

$$n \geq 3: \quad 1 - \beta\left[1 - \left\langle \tanh^2\left(\beta m_n \sum_{\rho=3}^{n} \xi_\rho\right)\right\rangle_{\boldsymbol{\xi}}\right] > 0$$

The pure $n = 1$ states, correlated with one pattern only, are the desired solutions. They turn out to be stable for all $T < 1$, since partial differentiation with respect to β of the $n = 1$ amplitude equation (21.21) gives

$$m_1 = \tanh(\beta m_1) \quad \Rightarrow \quad 1 - \beta[1 - \tanh^2(\beta m_1)] = \frac{m_1[1 - \tanh^2(\beta m_1)]}{\partial m_1/\partial \beta} > 0$$

(Looking at the graphical solution of $m_1 = \tanh(\beta m_1)$ shown in Figure 20.2, it is clear that $\text{sgn}(m_1) = \text{sgn}(\partial m_1/\partial \beta)$). The $n = 2$ mixtures, on the other hand, are always unstable. For $n \geq 3$ we have to solve the amplitude equation (21.21) numerically to evaluate their stability. The result is shown in Figure 21.1, together with the corresponding free energies f_n (21.22). It turns out that only for odd n will there be a critical temperature below which the n-mixture states are local minima of $f(\boldsymbol{m})$. From Figure 21.1 we can also conclude that, in terms of the network functioning as an associative

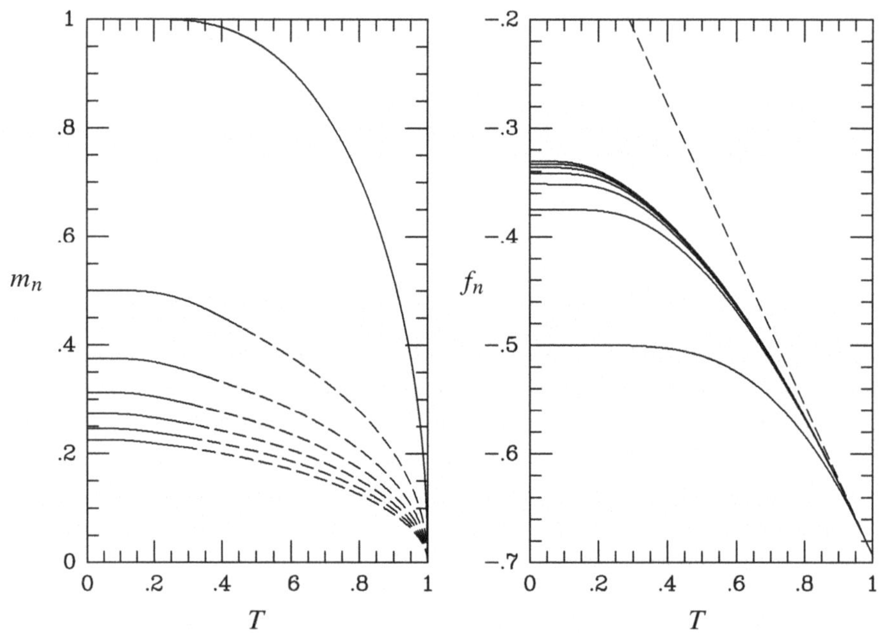

Figure 21.1 Left picture: amplitudes m_n of the mixture states of the Hopfield model as a function of temperature. From top to bottom: $n = 1, 3, 5, 7, 9, 11, 13$. Solid: region where they are stable, that is, local minima of $f(\boldsymbol{m})$. Dashed: region where they are unstable. Right picture: corresponding free energies f_n. From bottom to top: $n = 1, 3, 5, 7, 9, 11, 13$. Dashed line: free energy of the paramagnetic state $\boldsymbol{m} = 0$, shown for comparison.

memory, noise is actually beneficial in the sense that it can be used to eliminate the unwanted $n > 1$ ergodic components while retaining the relevant ones, that is, the pure $n = 1$ states.

In fact the overlap equation (21.13) do also allow for stable solutions different from the n-mixture states discussed here. These solutions are in turn found to be continuously bifurcating mixtures of the mixture states. However, for random (or uncorrelated) patterns they come into existence only near $T = 0$ and play a marginal role; phase space is dominated by the odd n-mixture states.

Simulation results that illustrate the functioning of the Hopfield model as an associative memory, and the description of the pattern recall process in terms of overlaps, were already shown earlier in Figures 3.2–3.4 of Section 3.3.

21.2 Introduction to replica theory: the SK model

Definition and motivation

The method of analysis presented so far breaks down if p no longer remains finite for $N \to \infty$, but scales as $p = \alpha N$ with $\alpha > 0$. In (21.7, 21.8), we can then no longer evaluate the constrained entropy and free energy by saddle point integration, since the dimension of the integral involved diverges at the same time as the exponent of the integrand (see Exercise 21.7). The number of ground states of the Hamiltonian (21.3) and the number of ergodic components will diverge, and we will encounter phenomena reminiscent of so-called spin glasses. As a consequence we will need corresponding methods of analysis, in the present case the replica method. As an introduction to this, we consider the so-called Sherrington–Kirkpatrick (SK) spin glass model.

We can motivate the form of the interactions in this model from the large $\alpha = p/N$ limit of the Hopfield model (21.2). In the case of randomly drawn patterns, the law of large numbers tells us that the couplings J_{ij} $(i \neq j)$ then become Gaussian random variables, with zero mean

$$\overline{J_{ij}} = \frac{1}{N} \sum_{\mu} \overline{\xi_i^\mu \xi_j^\mu} = 0$$

(because the pattern bits are uncorrelated for $i \neq j$) and covariances

$$\overline{J_{ij} J_{k\ell}} = \frac{1}{N^2} \sum_{\mu\nu} \overline{\xi_i^\mu \xi_j^\mu \xi_k^\nu \xi_\ell^\nu} = \begin{cases} \alpha/N, & \text{for } (k,\ell) = (i,j) \text{ or } (j,i) \\ 0, & \text{otherwise} \end{cases} \tag{21.25}$$

Here we have introduced the notation $\overline{\cdots}$ for averages over the patterns, that is, the quenched disorder. The choice of interactions in the SK model,

$$J_{ij} = J_{ji} = (1 - \delta_{ij})\left(\frac{J_0}{N} + \frac{J}{\sqrt{N}} z_{ij}\right), \qquad \overline{z_{ij}} = 0, \ \overline{z_{ij}^2} = 1 \qquad (21.26)$$

in which the z_{ij} $(i < j)$ are independent Gaussian random variables, is very similar, except for the addition of a ferromagnetic contribution J_0/N; the parameter J would correspond[42] to $\sqrt{\alpha}$. We will forget about external fields ϑ_i for the moment. Alternatively one could view the prescription (21.26), after a simple gauge transformation where $\sigma_i \to \xi_i \sigma_i$ for all i, as referring to a recurrent network in which a single pattern $\boldsymbol{\xi} = (\xi_1, \ldots, \xi_N)$ has been stored, with embedding strength J_0, on a background of zero average random Gaussian synapses.[43] In the latter case

$$J_{ij} = J_{ji} = (1 - \delta_{ij})\left(\frac{J_0}{N} \xi_i \xi_j + \frac{J}{\sqrt{N}} z_{ij}\right), \qquad \overline{z_{ij}} = 0, \ \overline{z_{ij}^2} = 1 \quad (21.27)$$

For the choice (21.26), the Ising Hamiltonian H (20.23), corresponding to sequential dynamics, that is, to the Markov chain with transition matrix (16.13), becomes

$$H(\boldsymbol{\sigma}) = -\frac{J_0}{N} \sum_{i<j} \sigma_i \sigma_j - \frac{J}{\sqrt{N}} \sum_{i<j} \sigma_i \sigma_j z_{ij} \qquad (21.28)$$

Anticipating self-averaging, and because we clearly cannot calculate the free energy for every given microscopic realization of the interactions $\{J_{ij}\}$, our aim is now to calculate the disorder-averaged free energy

$$\bar{F} = -T\,\overline{\ln Z} \qquad Z = \sum_{\boldsymbol{\sigma}} e^{-\beta H(\boldsymbol{\sigma})} \qquad (21.29)$$

The replica trick: general strategy

In the form (21.29), the disorder average is difficult to carry out, because we have to average the logarithm of a sum and cannot pull the average inside the logarithm. However, we can use the following trick to transform

[42] There are further differences, however, in loop-correlations of higher order such as $\overline{J_{ij} J_{jk} J_{ki}}$. They vanish in the SK model, but take the value α/N^{s-1} for loops of length s in the Hopfield model. Also, apart from the removal of the self-interactions, the interaction matrix in the Hopfield matrix is non-negative definite, whereas that of the SK model has both positive and negative eigenvalues.

[43] Note that the gauge transformation $\sigma_i \to \sigma_i \xi_i$ would also imply that $z_{ij} \to z_{ij} \xi_i \xi_j$, but for $\xi_i \in \{-1, 1\}$ the moments of the new z_{ij} are simply identical to those of the old z_{ij}.

the average of the logarithm into an average of powers of the partition function Z. Expanding Z^n for small n, we have

$$Z^n = e^{n \ln Z} = 1 + n \ln Z + \mathcal{O}(n^2) \tag{21.30}$$

Taking the disorder average, this shows that

$$\overline{\ln Z} = \lim_{n \to 0} \frac{1}{n}(\overline{Z^n} - 1) \tag{21.31}$$

An alternative form is often more convenient for calculations. If we first take the disorder average of (21.30) and then take the logarithm, we have

$$\ln \overline{Z^n} = \ln(1 + n\,\overline{\ln Z} + \mathcal{O}(n^2)) = n\,\overline{\ln Z} + \mathcal{O}(n^2)$$

and so

$$\overline{\ln Z} = \lim_{n \to 0} \frac{1}{n} \ln \overline{Z^n} \tag{21.32}$$

Crucially, the disorder average now appears *inside* the logarithm on the right-hand side. The so-called replica trick now consists in evaluating the averages $\overline{Z^n}$ for integer values of n, and taking the limit $n \to 0$ afterwards, under the assumption—which to date is only beginning to be justified rigorously in non-trivial cases—that the resulting expression is correct for non-integer values of n as well. The integer powers of Z are written as a product of terms, each of which can be interpreted as an equivalent copy, or 'replica', of the original system. The disorder-averaged free energy now becomes

$$\begin{aligned}\bar{F} &= -\lim_{n \to 0} \frac{T}{n} \ln \overline{Z^n} = -\lim_{n \to 0} \frac{T}{n} \ln \overline{\sum_{\sigma^1} e^{-\beta H(\sigma^1)} \times \cdots \times \sum_{\sigma^n} e^{-\beta H(\sigma^n)}} \\ &= -\lim_{n \to 0} \frac{T}{n} \ln \left(\sum_{\sigma^1 \ldots \sigma^n} \overline{e^{-\beta \sum_{a=1}^{n} H(\sigma^a)}} \right)\end{aligned}$$

Henceforth, indices $a, b, \ldots$ from near the beginning of the alphabet will label replicas, for example, $a = 1, \ldots, n$. The general strategy now is to carry out the disorder average of the exponential and to write the result in the form

$$e^{-\beta \Phi(\sigma^1 \ldots \sigma^n)} = \overline{e^{-\beta \sum_{a=1}^{n} H(\sigma^a)}}$$

$\Phi(\boldsymbol{\sigma}^1 \cdots \boldsymbol{\sigma}^n)$ is called the 'replicated Hamiltonian', because it arises from the sum of the Hamiltonians of the individual replicas. Note that the average over the disorder, which acts on all replicas equally, will produce interaction terms in Φ which couple the different replicas. The free energy is now

$$\bar{F} = -\lim_{n\to 0} \frac{T}{n} \ln\left(\sum_{\boldsymbol{\sigma}^1 \cdots \boldsymbol{\sigma}^n} e^{-\beta\Phi(\boldsymbol{\sigma}^1 \cdots \boldsymbol{\sigma}^n)} \right)$$

Assuming that the order of the limits $N \to \infty$ and $n \to 0$ can be interchanged, we can now write the thermodynamic limit of the disorder-averaged free energy per spin as

$$\bar{f} = \lim_{N\to\infty} \frac{\bar{F}}{N} = \lim_{n\to 0} \frac{1}{n} \left[\lim_{N\to\infty} \left(-\frac{T}{N} \right) \ln\left(\sum_{\boldsymbol{\sigma}^1 \cdots \boldsymbol{\sigma}^n} e^{-\beta\Phi(\boldsymbol{\sigma}^1 \cdots \boldsymbol{\sigma}^n)} \right) \right] \tag{21.33}$$

The term in square brackets is now of exactly the same form as the free energy of a system without quenched disorder, and can be calculated using the same method: we (i) identify which order parameters the (replicated) Hamiltonian Φ depends on, (ii) introduce the corresponding density of states using δ-functions, and (iii) evaluate the final result using saddle point integration. In the end, we then divide by n and take the limit $n \to 0$. At this point, one has to make assumptions about how the saddle point values of the order parameters behave for $n \to 0$. We will only explore the simplest assumption of this kind, called 'replica symmetry'.

Application to the SK model

To calculate the replicated Hamiltonian, we use the following abbreviation for the Gaussian measure: $Dz = (2\pi)^{-1/2}\, e^{-z^2/2} \mathrm{d}z$. We now note the important identity (which was also the basis of the Gaussian linearization trick encountered earlier in Exercise 20.6):

$$\int Dz\, e^{xz} = e^{x^2/2} \tag{21.34}$$

For the Hamiltonian (21.28), application of (21.34) allows us to write

$$\overline{e^{-\beta \sum_{a=1}^{n} H(\boldsymbol{\sigma}^a)}} = e^{(\beta J_0/N) \sum_{i<j} \sum_a \sigma_i^a \sigma_j^a} \prod_{i<j} \left(\int Dz\, e^{(\beta J z/\sqrt{N}) \sum_a \sigma_i^a \sigma_j^a} \right)$$

$$= e^{(\beta J_0/2N) \sum_a \sum_{i\neq j} \sigma_i^a \sigma_j^a + (\beta^2 J^2/4N) \sum_{ab} \sum_{i\neq j} \sigma_i^a \sigma_j^a \sigma_i^b \sigma_j^b}$$

The replicated Hamiltonian is therefore

$$\Phi(\boldsymbol{\sigma}^1 \cdots \boldsymbol{\sigma}^n) = -\frac{J_0}{2N} \sum_a \sum_{i \neq j} \sigma_i^a \sigma_j^a - \frac{\beta J^2}{4N} \sum_{ab} \sum_{i \neq j} \sigma_i^a \sigma_j^a \sigma_i^b \sigma_j^b$$

and we can clearly see in the second term how the disorder average has coupled the different replicas. If we now complete the sums over sites in this expression,

$$\sum_{i \neq j} \sigma_i^a \sigma_j^a = \Big(\sum_i \sigma_i^a\Big)^2 - N \qquad \sum_{i \neq j} \sigma_i^a \sigma_j^a \sigma_i^b \sigma_j^b = \Big(\sum_i \sigma_i^a \sigma_i^b\Big)^2 - N$$

we can write (using the shorthand $\{\boldsymbol{\sigma}\} \equiv \boldsymbol{\sigma}^1 \cdots \boldsymbol{\sigma}^n$)

$$\Phi(\{\boldsymbol{\sigma}\}) = -\frac{NJ_0}{2} \sum_a m_a^2(\{\boldsymbol{\sigma}\}) - \frac{N\beta J^2}{4} \sum_{ab} q_{ab}^2(\{\boldsymbol{\sigma}\}) + \mathcal{O}(1) \qquad (21.35)$$

with the order parameters

$$q_{ab}(\{\boldsymbol{\sigma}\}) = \frac{1}{N} \sum_i \sigma_i^a \sigma_i^b \qquad m_a(\{\boldsymbol{\sigma}\}) = \frac{1}{N} \sum_i \sigma_i^a \qquad (21.36)$$

So we can write the disorder-averaged free energy per spin (21.33) as

$$\bar{f} = -\lim_{n \to 0} \frac{T}{Nn} \ln \int \mathrm{d}\boldsymbol{m} \mathrm{d}\boldsymbol{q}\, \mathcal{D}(\boldsymbol{q}, \boldsymbol{m})\, e^{N[(\beta J_0/2) \sum_a m_a^2 + (\beta^2 J^2/4) \sum_{ab} q_{ab}^2]} \qquad (21.37)$$

where the limit $N \to \infty$ is not written explicitly (but is understood to be taken, so that subleading terms in N may be discarded), and the density of states is

$$\begin{aligned}
\mathcal{D}(\boldsymbol{q}, \boldsymbol{m}) \\
&= \sum_{\{\boldsymbol{\sigma}\}} \prod_{ab} \delta\Big(q_{ab} - \frac{1}{N} \sum_i \sigma_i^a \sigma_i^b\Big) \prod_a \delta\Big(m_a - \frac{1}{N} \sum_i \sigma_i^a\Big) \\
&= \sum_{\{\boldsymbol{\sigma}\}} \Big(\frac{N}{2\pi}\Big)^{n^2+n} \int \mathrm{d}\hat{\boldsymbol{q}} \mathrm{d}\hat{\boldsymbol{m}}\, e^{\mathrm{i}N \sum_{ab} \hat{q}_{ab}(q_{ab} - \sum_i \sigma_i^a \sigma_i^b/N) + \mathrm{i}N \sum_a \hat{m}_a (m_a - \sum_i \sigma_i^a/N)}
\end{aligned}$$

The integrations in (21.37) and in $\mathcal{D}(\boldsymbol{q}, \boldsymbol{m})$ are over the $n \times n$ matrices $\boldsymbol{q}$ and $\hat{\boldsymbol{q}}$ and over the n-vectors $\boldsymbol{m}$ and $\hat{\boldsymbol{m}}$. The sum over states now factorizes over the different sites i as usual, and we are left with a sum over the states of a single n-replicated spin $\boldsymbol{\sigma} = (\sigma^1, \ldots, \sigma^n)$; this notation replaces our earlier use of $\boldsymbol{\sigma}$ as an N-component vector describing the state of an individual network:

$$\mathcal{D}(\boldsymbol{q},\boldsymbol{m}) = \left(\frac{N}{2\pi}\right)^{n^2+n} \int \mathrm{d}\hat{\boldsymbol{q}}\mathrm{d}\hat{\boldsymbol{m}}\; e^{\mathrm{i}N\sum_{ab}\hat{q}_{ab}q_{ab}+\mathrm{i}N\sum_a \hat{m}_a m_a} \times \left(\sum_{\boldsymbol{\sigma}} e^{-\mathrm{i}\sum_{ab}\hat{q}_{ab}\sigma^a\sigma^b-\mathrm{i}\sum_a\hat{m}_a\sigma^a}\right)^N \tag{21.38}$$

Inserting this expression into (21.37), and evaluating the integrals by saddle point integration gives for the free energy

$$\bar{f} = \lim_{n\to 0}\ \mathrm{extr}\, f(\boldsymbol{q},\boldsymbol{m};\hat{\boldsymbol{q}},\hat{\boldsymbol{m}}) \tag{21.39}$$

where

$$f(\boldsymbol{q},\boldsymbol{m};\hat{\boldsymbol{q}},\hat{\boldsymbol{m}}) = -\frac{J_0}{2n}\sum_a m_a^2 - \frac{\beta J^2}{4n}\sum_{ab} q_{ab}^2 - \frac{T}{n}\Big[\mathrm{i}\sum_{ab}\hat{q}_{ab}q_{ab} + \mathrm{i}\sum_a \hat{m}_a m_a + \ln\Big(\sum_{\boldsymbol{\sigma}} e^{-\mathrm{i}\sum_{ab}\hat{q}_{ab}\sigma^a\sigma^b-\mathrm{i}\sum_a\hat{m}_a\sigma^a}\Big)\Big] \tag{21.40}$$

We recognize in the first two terms the replicated Hamiltonian (21.35), up to the $1/n$ factors, while the term in square brackets is the log density of states (21.38), up to terms which are negligible for $N \to \infty$. The saddle point conditions for $\{q_{ab}\}$ and $\{m_a\}$ are found to be

$$\hat{q}_{ab} = \tfrac{1}{2}\mathrm{i}\beta^2 J^2 q_{ab} \qquad \hat{m}_a = \mathrm{i}\beta J_0 m_a \tag{21.41}$$

while those for $\{\hat{q}_{ab}\}$ and $\{\hat{m}_a\}$ give

$$q_{ab} = \frac{\sum_{\boldsymbol{\sigma}} \sigma^a\sigma^b \kappa(\boldsymbol{\sigma})}{\sum_{\boldsymbol{\sigma}} \kappa(\boldsymbol{\sigma})} \tag{21.42}$$

$$m_a = \frac{\sum_{\boldsymbol{\sigma}} \sigma^a \kappa(\boldsymbol{\sigma})}{\sum_{\boldsymbol{\sigma}} \kappa(\boldsymbol{\sigma})} \tag{21.43}$$

where

$$\kappa(\boldsymbol{\sigma}) = \exp\Big(-\mathrm{i}\sum_{ab}\hat{q}_{ab}\sigma^a\sigma^b - \mathrm{i}\sum_a \hat{m}_a\sigma^a\Big)$$

Using (21.41) to eliminate the conjugate parameters $\hat{\boldsymbol{m}}$ and $\hat{\boldsymbol{q}}$ simplifies κ to

$$\kappa(\boldsymbol{\sigma}) = \exp\left(\frac{1}{2}\beta^2 J^2 \sum_{ab} q_{ab}\sigma^a\sigma^b + \beta J_0 \sum_a m_a\sigma^a\right) \tag{21.44}$$

The saddle point equations (21.42, 21.43) for the order parameter $\boldsymbol{q}$ and $\boldsymbol{m}$ are now closed: the conjugate order parameters no longer appear. They have the form of averages of $\sigma^a\sigma^b$ and σ^a, respectively, over all possible states of the n-replicated single-site spin $\boldsymbol{\sigma}$. Given the original definition (21.36) of the order parameters, this is quite plausible. The weight factor for these averages is given by $\kappa(\boldsymbol{\sigma})$; the denominators in (21.42, 21.43) are just the normalizing factor for the averages. Because $(\sigma^a)^2 = 1$, the diagonal elements of $\boldsymbol{q}$ are always $q_{aa} = 1$; again, this was to be expected from the definition (21.36) of these order parameters. For high temperatures, $\beta = T^{-1} \to 0$, we obtain $\kappa(\boldsymbol{\sigma}) = 1$ and hence the trivial result

$$q_{ab} = \delta_{ab} \qquad m_a = 0$$

Assuming a continuous transition to a non-trivial state as the temperature is lowered, we can expand the saddle point equations (21.42, 21.43) in powers of $\boldsymbol{q}$ and $\boldsymbol{m}$ and look for bifurcations. This gives (for $a \neq b$, and using the fact that averages over odd powers of σ^a vanish):

$$q_{ab} = \beta^2 J^2 q_{ab} + \cdots \qquad m_a = \beta J_0 m_a + \cdots \tag{21.45}$$

Therefore we expect second-order transitions either at $T = J_0$ (if $J_0 > J$) or at $T = J$ (if $J > J_0$). The remaining programme is as follows. For $T < \max\{J_0, J\}$, find the saddle point $(\boldsymbol{q}, \boldsymbol{m})$ which minimizes $f(\boldsymbol{q}, \boldsymbol{m}; \hat{\boldsymbol{q}}, \hat{\boldsymbol{m}})$, and take the limit $n \to 0$. The latter is in fact the most complicated part of the procedure.

As at the end of Section 21.1, we could have also got the saddle point equations (21.42, 21.43) from a pseudo-free energy. The latter is obtained by using (21.41) to eliminate the conjugate order parameters from $f(\boldsymbol{q}, \boldsymbol{m}; \hat{\boldsymbol{q}}, \hat{\boldsymbol{m}})$:

$$\begin{aligned}\tilde{f}(\boldsymbol{q}, \boldsymbol{m}) = {} & \frac{J_0}{2n}\sum_a m_a^2 + \frac{\beta J^2}{4n}\sum_{ab} q_{ab}^2 \\ & - \frac{T}{n}\ln\left(\sum_{\boldsymbol{\sigma}} \exp\left(\frac{1}{2}\beta^2 J^2 \sum_{ab} q_{ab}\sigma^a\sigma^b + \beta J_0 \sum_a m_a\sigma^a\right)\right)\end{aligned} \tag{21.46}$$

As explained earlier, $\tilde{f}$ coincides with the true constrained free energy $f(\boldsymbol{q}, \boldsymbol{m})$ at its saddle points, but not generally elsewhere.

Physical interpretation of saddle points

In order to get a better idea of how to select saddle points, we now turn to a different although equivalent version of the replica trick (21.32) that allows us to attach a physical meaning to the saddle point parameters $(\boldsymbol{m}, \boldsymbol{q})$. This version transforms (as yet arbitrary) averages with a given weight factor W, according to

$$\begin{aligned}\frac{\sum_{\boldsymbol{\sigma}} g(\boldsymbol{\sigma})W(\boldsymbol{\sigma})}{\sum_{\boldsymbol{\sigma}} W(\boldsymbol{\sigma})} &= \frac{\sum_{\boldsymbol{\sigma}} g(\boldsymbol{\sigma})W(\boldsymbol{\sigma})[\sum_{\boldsymbol{\sigma}} W(\boldsymbol{\sigma})]^{n-1}}{[\sum_{\boldsymbol{\sigma}} W(\boldsymbol{\sigma})]^n} \\ &= \lim_{n\to 0} \sum_{\boldsymbol{\sigma}} g(\boldsymbol{\sigma})W(\boldsymbol{\sigma})\Big[\sum_{\boldsymbol{\sigma}} W(\boldsymbol{\sigma})\Big]^{n-1} \\ &= \lim_{n\to 0} \sum_{\boldsymbol{\sigma}^1\ldots\boldsymbol{\sigma}^n} g(\boldsymbol{\sigma}^1)\prod_{a=1}^{n} W(\boldsymbol{\sigma}^a) \\ &= \lim_{n\to 0} \frac{1}{n}\sum_b \sum_{\boldsymbol{\sigma}^1\ldots\boldsymbol{\sigma}^n} g(\boldsymbol{\sigma}^b)\prod_{a=1}^{n} W(\boldsymbol{\sigma}^a)\end{aligned} \tag{21.47}$$

The trick again consists in evaluating this quantity for *integer* n, whereas the relevant limit refers to non-integer n.

We now use the above identity to write the distribution $P(m)$ of the magnetization in the SK model in equilibrium as

$$\begin{aligned}P(m) &= \frac{\sum_{\boldsymbol{\sigma}} \delta(m - N^{-1}\sum_i \sigma_i)\, e^{-\beta H(\boldsymbol{\sigma})}}{\sum_{\boldsymbol{\sigma}} e^{-\beta H(\boldsymbol{\sigma})}} \\ &= \lim_{n\to 0} \frac{1}{n}\sum_b \sum_{\boldsymbol{\sigma}^1\ldots\boldsymbol{\sigma}^n} \delta\Big(m - \frac{1}{N}\sum_i \sigma_i^b\Big)\prod_a e^{-\beta H(\boldsymbol{\sigma}^a)}\end{aligned}$$

If we average this distribution over the disorder, we find identical expressions to those encountered in evaluating the disorder averaged free energy. By inserting again delta-functions constraining the values of the order parameters $\boldsymbol{q}$ and $\boldsymbol{m}$, we arrive at the saddle point integration (21.39) and find

$$\overline{P(m)} = \lim_{n\to 0} \frac{1}{n}\sum_b \delta\,(m - m_b) \tag{21.48}$$

where $\{m_b\}$ refers to the relevant solution of (21.42, 21.43).

Similarly we can imagine *two* systems $\boldsymbol{\sigma}$ and $\boldsymbol{\sigma}'$ with identical realizations of the interactions $\{J_{ij}\}$, both in thermal equilibrium. We now use the replica identity to rewrite the distribution $P(q)$ for the mutual overlap between the micro-states of the two systems

$$P(q) = \frac{\sum_{\boldsymbol{\sigma},\boldsymbol{\sigma}'} \delta(q - N^{-1}\sum_i \sigma_i \sigma_i')\, e^{-\beta H(\boldsymbol{\sigma}) - \beta H(\boldsymbol{\sigma}')}}{\sum_{\boldsymbol{\sigma},\boldsymbol{\sigma}'} e^{-\beta H(\boldsymbol{\sigma}) - \beta H(\boldsymbol{\sigma}')}}$$

$$= \lim_{n\to 0} \frac{1}{n(n-1)} \sum_{b\neq c} \sum_{\boldsymbol{\sigma}^1 \cdots \boldsymbol{\sigma}^n} \delta\left(q - \frac{1}{N}\sum_i \sigma_i^b \sigma_i^c\right) \prod_a e^{-\beta H(\boldsymbol{\sigma}^a)}$$

Averaging over the disorder again leads to the saddle point integration (21.39), and we find

$$\overline{P(q)} = \lim_{n\to 0} \frac{1}{n(n-1)} \sum_{b\neq c} \delta(q - q_{bc}) \qquad (21.49)$$

where $\{q_{bc}\}$ refers to the relevant solution of (21.42, 21.43).

We can now partly interpret the saddle point parameters $(\boldsymbol{m}, \boldsymbol{q})$, since the shape of $\overline{P(q)}$ and $\overline{P(m)}$ gives direct information on the structure of phase space with respect to ergodicity. The crucial observation is that for an ergodic system one always has

$$P(m) = \delta\left(m - \frac{1}{N}\sum_i \langle \sigma_i \rangle_{\text{eq}}\right) \qquad P(q) = \delta\left(q - \frac{1}{N}\sum_i \langle \sigma_i \rangle_{\text{eq}}^2\right) \qquad (21.50)$$

If, on the other hand, there are L ergodic components in our system, within each of which we have microstate probabilities proportional to $\exp(-\beta H)$ and corresponding averages $\langle \cdots \rangle_\ell$, and if we denote the probability of finding the system in component ℓ by W_ℓ, we find for $P(q)$ and $P(m)$:

$$P(m) = \sum_{\ell=1}^{L} W_\ell \delta\left(m - \frac{1}{N}\sum_i \langle \sigma_i \rangle_\ell\right)$$

$$P(q) = \sum_{\ell,\ell'=1}^{L} W_\ell W_{\ell'} \delta\left(q - \frac{1}{N}\sum_i \langle \sigma_i \rangle_\ell \langle \sigma_i \rangle_{\ell'}\right)$$

We see that for ergodic systems both $P(m)$ and $P(q)$ are δ-functions, whereas for systems with a finite number of ergodic components they are composed of a finite sum of δ-functions. A diverging number (in the limit $N \to \infty$) of ergodic components, however, generally leads to distributions with continuous pieces. If we combine this interpretation with our results

(21.48, 21.49) we find that ergodicity is equivalent to the relevant saddle point being of the form:

$$q_{ab} = \delta_{ab} + q(1 - \delta_{ab}) \qquad m_a = m \tag{21.51}$$

Replica symmetric solution

The ansatz (21.51) for the order parameters (which we found to be equivalent to assuming our system to be ergodic) is called the 'replica symmetry' (RS) ansatz, because it has the property that order parameters do not change if we permute the replica indices arbitrarily. The physical meaning of m and q is provided by (21.50):

$$m = \frac{1}{N}\sum_i \overline{\langle \sigma_i \rangle_{\text{eq}}} \qquad q = \frac{1}{N}\sum_i \overline{\langle \sigma_i \rangle_{\text{eq}}^2} \tag{21.52}$$

Given the definition (21.36) of the order parameters q_{ab} and m_a, this result also makes intuitive sense: the disorder average arises simply because such an average was already contained in the definition of the replicated Hamiltonian Φ.

Insertion of the above RS ansatz (21.51) into the equations (21.42, 21.43, 21.46) gives

$$\tilde{f}(q, m) = -\frac{1}{4}\beta J^2(1-q)^2 + \frac{1}{2}J_0 m^2 - \frac{T}{n}\ln \sum_{\boldsymbol{\sigma}} \tilde{\kappa}(\boldsymbol{\sigma}) + \mathcal{O}(n)$$

$$q = \frac{\sum_{\boldsymbol{\sigma}} \sigma^1 \sigma^2 \tilde{\kappa}(\boldsymbol{\sigma})}{\sum_{\boldsymbol{\sigma}} \tilde{\kappa}(\boldsymbol{\sigma})} \qquad m = \frac{\sum_{\boldsymbol{\sigma}} \sigma^1 \tilde{\kappa}(\boldsymbol{\sigma})}{\sum_{\boldsymbol{\sigma}} \tilde{\kappa}(\boldsymbol{\sigma})}$$

with

$$\tilde{\kappa}(\boldsymbol{\sigma}) = \exp\left(\frac{1}{2}q\beta^2 J^2 \Big(\sum_a \sigma^a\Big)^2 + \beta J_0 m \sum_a \sigma^a\right)$$

To perform the summations over $\boldsymbol{\sigma}$, we linearize the terms $\left(\sum_a \sigma^a\right)^2$ with the identity (21.34) (this is the by now familiar Gaussian linearization trick). In the free energy and in the denominators of the saddle point equations, we then get

$$\begin{aligned}\sum_{\boldsymbol{\sigma}} e^{(q\beta^2 J^2/2)(\sum_a \sigma^a)^2 + \beta J_0 m \sum_a \sigma^a} &= \sum_{\boldsymbol{\sigma}} \int Dz\, e^{\sum_a (\beta J_0 m + \beta J z\sqrt{q})\sigma^a} \\ &= \int Dz\, [2\cosh(\beta J_0 m + \beta J z\sqrt{q})]^n\end{aligned} \tag{21.53}$$

The solutions m and q of the RS saddle point equations turn out to have well defined limits for $n \to 0$, so we can also take this limit directly in the (pseudo-) free energy. We then get

$$\begin{aligned}\lim_{n\to 0} \tilde{f}(q,m) = &-\frac{1}{4}\beta J^2(1-q)^2 + \frac{1}{2}J_0 m^2\\ &- T\lim_{n\to 0}\frac{1}{n}\ln\int Dz\,[2\cosh(\beta J_0 m + \beta J z\sqrt{q})]^n\end{aligned}$$

The integral over z in the last line, being properly normalized, can now be interpreted as an average (over a Gaussian random variable z with zero mean and unit variance). This enables us to use the replica identity (21.32)—which holds for any average, not just a disorder average—in reverse, to get

$$\lim_{n\to 0}\tilde{f}(q,m) = -\frac{1}{4}\beta J^2(1-q)^2 + \frac{1}{2}J_0 m^2 - T\int Dz\,\ln 2\cosh(\beta J_0 m + \beta J z\sqrt{q}) \tag{21.54}$$

Similarly, again using Gaussian linearization we can evaluate the numerators in the saddle point equations (21.42, 21.43), abbreviating $\Xi = \beta J_0 m + \beta J z\sqrt{q}$:

$$\sum_{\sigma}\sigma^1\sigma^2\, e^{(q\beta^2J^2/2)(\sum_a\sigma^a)^2 + \beta J_0 m\sum_a\sigma^a} = \int Dz\,[2\sinh(\Xi)]^2[2\cosh(\Xi)]^{n-2}$$

$$\sum_{\sigma}\sigma^1\, e^{(q\beta^2J^2/2)(\sum_a\sigma^a)^2 + \beta J_0 m\sum_a\sigma^a} = \int Dz\,[2\sinh(\Xi)][2\cosh(\Xi)]^{n-1}$$

and obtain in the $n \to 0$ limit, using (21.53),

$$q = \int Dz\,\tanh^2(\beta(J_0 m + Jz\sqrt{q})) \tag{21.55}$$

$$m = \int Dz\,\tanh(\beta(J_0 m + Jz\sqrt{q})) \tag{21.56}$$

We note that, rather than deriving the saddle point equations (21.55, 21.56) by taking the $n \to 0$ limit of the nonzero-n saddle point equations (21.42, 21.43), as was done here, we could also have found them as the saddle point conditions of the $n \to 0$ (pseudo-) free energy (21.54); see Exercise 21.9. This shortcut is often useful in replica calculations. Comparing (21.56) with the Curie–Weiss equation (20.43), we also see that the only difference is the integral (average) over z; the term involving z is proportional to J, so we can interpret this average as a consequence of the quenched disorder in the couplings (21.26).

Upon linearizing (21.55, 21.56) for small q and m, one now finds the following continuous bifurcations of non-trivial solutions of the RS saddle point equations (see Exercise 21.10):

	at	from	to
$J_0 > J$:	$T = J_0$	$m = q = 0$	$m \neq 0,\ q > 0$
$J_0 < J$:	$T = J$	$m = q = 0$	$m = 0,\ q > 0$
$T < \max\{J_0, J\}$:	$J_0 = (1 - q)/T$	$m = 0,\ q > 0$	$m \neq 0,\ q > 0$

So, within our replica symmetric analysis we have found that the SK model has three phases: a paramagnetic phase (P) with $m = q = 0$, a ferromagnetic phase (F) with both m and q nonzero, and a new phase with $m = 0$ but $q \neq 0$, which is called a 'spin glass' (SG) phase. The location of two of the phase boundaries is given by $T = J_0$ and $T = J$, respectively; the third one is obtained by solving numerically the equations $T = J_0(1 - q)$ and (21.55, 21.56). One then arrives at the phase diagram shown in Figure 21.2. The case where there is no disorder ($J \to 0$, i.e., $J_0/J \to \infty$) reproduces our earlier results for the infinite-range ferromagnet, where we found a paramagnetic and a ferromagnetic phase, with a transition at $T = J_0$. As the strength of the disorder increases (J_0/J decreases), we can now have a transition from the ferromagnetic to a SG phase. The nature of this SG phase is rather peculiar. There is local order, in the sense that the average local magnetizations $\langle \sigma_i \rangle_{eq}$ are nonzero; this follows from (21.52) and from

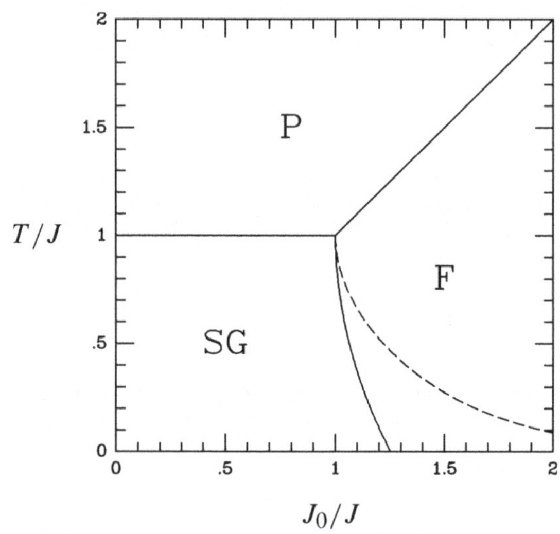

Figure 21.2 Phase diagram of the SK model, as obtained from the RS solution. P: paramagnetic phase, $m = q = 0$. SG: spin glass phase, $m = 0$, $q > 0$. F: ferromagnetic phase, $m \neq 0$, $q > 0$. Solid lines: phase transitions. Dashed: the AT instability, where the RS solution becomes unstable. For $J_0/J < 1$ this instability coincides with the P→SG transition line $T/J = 1$.

the fact that q is nonzero. Nevertheless, there is no global order in the conventional sense: the overall magnetization $m = N^{-1}\sum_i \langle\sigma_i\rangle_{\text{eq}}$ is zero (m is self-averaging, so (21.52) also holds without the disorder average). The name 'glass' comes from the analogy with ordinary (i.e. window) glass: there, the local arrangements of the atoms is also ordered, as in a crystal, but globally there is no crystalline order.

We have not yet checked the stability of the saddle points that we have calculated. If this is done, it turns out (see below) that below the dashed line in Figure 21.2 our RS saddle points are actually unstable. This region includes the whole part of the phase diagram for which we had found a spin glass phase, so our predictions for this phase should not be trusted; nevertheless, the presence of the instability itself does indicate that a SG phase must exist at low temperatures.

Breaking of replica symmetry: the AT instability

If for the RS solution we calculate the disorder-averaged entropy $\bar{S} = \beta^2\partial\bar{F}/\partial\beta$, we find that for small temperatures it becomes negative. It follows from the information-theoretic definition (20.28) that this cannot happen (see Chapter 12), so the RS solution must be incorrect in the low temperature region. The reason for this is that the RS ansatz (21.51) no longer corresponds to the correct physical saddle point of $\tilde{f}(\boldsymbol{q},\boldsymbol{m})$, (21.46), for low temperatures. If saddle points without RS bifurcate continuously from the RS, we can locate the occurrence of this 'replica symmetry breaking' (RSB) by studying the effect on $\tilde{f}(\boldsymbol{q},\boldsymbol{m})$ of small fluctuations around the RS solution. It was shown by de Almeida and Thouless that the 'dangerous' fluctuations are of the form

$$q_{ab} \to \delta_{ab} + q(1-\delta_{ab}) + \eta_{ab} \qquad \sum_b \eta_{ab} = 0 \qquad (21.57)$$

in which q is the solution of (21.55), $|\eta_{ab}| \ll 1$, $\eta_{aa} = 0$ and $\eta_{ab} = \eta_{ba}$. We can calculate the resulting change in $\tilde{f}(\boldsymbol{q},\boldsymbol{m})$, away from the RS value $\tilde{f}(\boldsymbol{q}_{\text{RS}},\boldsymbol{m}_{\text{RS}})$, the leading order of which must be quadratic in the fluctuations $\{\eta_{ab}\}$ since the RS solution (21.55, 21.56) is a saddle point:

$$\tilde{f}(\boldsymbol{q},\boldsymbol{m}) - \tilde{f}(\boldsymbol{q}_{\text{RS}},\boldsymbol{m}_{\text{RS}}) = \frac{\beta J^2}{4n}\sum_{a\neq b}\eta_{ab}^2 - \frac{\beta^3 J^4}{8n}\sum_{a\neq b}\sum_{c\neq d}\eta_{ab}\eta_{cd}G_{abcd} + \cdots$$

with

$$G_{abcd} = \frac{\sum_{\sigma} \sigma^a\sigma^b\sigma^c\sigma^d\, e^{(q\beta^2J^2/2)(\sum_a\sigma^a)^2 + \beta m J_0\sum_a\sigma^a}}{\sum_{\sigma} e^{(q\beta^2J^2/2)(\sum_a\sigma^a)^2 + \beta m J_0\sum_a\sigma^a}} \qquad (21.58)$$

Because of the index permutation symmetry in the spin-average (21.58), we can write for any $a \neq b$ and $c \neq d$:

$$G_{abcd} = \delta_{ac}\delta_{bd} + \delta_{ad}\delta_{bc} + G_4(1-\delta_{ac})(1-\delta_{bd})(1-\delta_{ad})(1-\delta_{bc})$$
$$+ G_2[\delta_{ac}(1-\delta_{bd}) + \delta_{bd}(1-\delta_{ac}) + \delta_{ad}(1-\delta_{bc}) + \delta_{bc}(1-\delta_{ad})]$$

with

$$G_\ell = \frac{\int Dz \tanh^\ell(\beta(J_0 m + Jz\sqrt{q}))\cosh^n(\beta(J_0 m + Jz\sqrt{q}))}{\int Dz \cosh^n(\beta(J_0 m + Jz\sqrt{q}))}$$

Only terms which involve precisely two δ-functions can contribute to our expansion for $\tilde{f}(\boldsymbol{q},\boldsymbol{m})$, because of the requirements $a \neq b$ and $c \neq d$, and due to $\sum_b \eta_{ab} = 0$. As a result we obtain:

$$\tilde{f}(\boldsymbol{q},\boldsymbol{m}) - \tilde{f}(\boldsymbol{q}_{\mathrm{RS}},\boldsymbol{m}_{\mathrm{RS}}) = \frac{\beta J^2}{4n}[1-\beta^2 J^2(1-2G_2+G_4)]\sum_{a\neq b}\sum_{c\neq d}\eta_{ab}^2 + \cdots$$

The condition for the RS solution to minimize $\tilde{f}(\boldsymbol{q},\boldsymbol{m})$, if compared to the so called 'replicon' fluctuations (21.57), is therefore

$$1 > \beta^2 J^2 \lim_{n\to 0}(1-2G_2+G_4)$$

After taking the limit in the quantities G_ℓ this condition can be written as

$$1 > \beta^2 J^2 \int Dz \cosh^{-4}(\beta J_0 m + \beta J z\sqrt{q}) \tag{21.59}$$

The so-called AT line in the phase diagram, where this condition ceases to be met, indicates a phase transition to a SG state where ergodicity is broken (i.e. to a state where the distribution $\overline{P(q)}$ in (21.49) is no longer a δ-function). It is shown in Figure 21.2 (following numerical evaluation) as a dashed line for $J_0/J > 1$, and coincides with the line $T/J = 1$ for $J_0 < 1$.

21.3 Hopfield model with an extensive number of patterns

Having dealt with the SK model as a 'warm-up' for replica calculations, we now return to the Hopfield model with an extensive number of patterns stored, that is, with $p = \alpha N$ in (21.2). Although we can still write the log density of states and the free energy in the form (21.7, 21.8), this will not be of help since here it involves integrals over an extensive (i.e. $\mathcal{O}(N)$) number of variables, so that saddle point integration does not apply. Instead, following the approach of the SK spin glass model, we assume that the free energy is self-averaging, so that we can average it over the distribution of the patterns with the help of the replica trick:

$$\bar{F} = -T \lim_{n\to 0} \frac{1}{n} \ln \overline{Z^n} = -\lim_{n\to 0} \frac{T}{n} \ln \Big(\sum_{\sigma^1 \ldots \sigma^n} \overline{e^{-\beta \sum_{a=1}^n H(\sigma^a)}} \Big)$$

Again, Roman characters $a, b, \ldots$ will be used to label replicas ($a = 1, \ldots, n$) while Greek indices will be used for the pattern labels ($\mu = 1, \ldots, p$). The pattern components $\{\xi_i^\mu\}$, of which there are now αN^2, are assumed to be drawn independently at random from $\{-1, 1\}$, as usual.

Replica calculation of the disorder-averaged free energy

By analogy with the case of a finite number of patterns, we anticipate that the ergodic components of our system will be characterized by the pattern overlap order parameters m_μ (21.4), and that for large N only a finite number ℓ of these overlaps will be nonzero (while the others will be of order $N^{-1/2}$, similar to the overlap values one would find for randomly chosen micro-states). Since all patterns are equivalent in the calculation, we may choose the ℓ 'nominated' patterns with which the system has non-vanishing overlap as $\mu = 1, \ldots, \ell$. To draw out the analogy with the case of a finite number of stored patterns, it is useful to keep the nominated patterns $\boldsymbol{\xi}^1, \ldots, \boldsymbol{\xi}^\ell$ fixed at first, and average only over the disorder that is responsible for the complications: the non-nominated (or 'non-condensed') patterns $\boldsymbol{\xi}^{\ell+1}, \ldots, \boldsymbol{\xi}^p$. As in the SK case we denote this disorder average by $\overline{\cdots}$. To calculate the replicated Hamiltonian, we first rewrite $H(\boldsymbol{\sigma})$ as

$$H(\boldsymbol{\sigma}) = -\frac{1}{2N} \sum_{\mu \le \ell} \Big(\sum_i \sigma_i \xi_i^\mu \Big)^2 - \frac{1}{2N} \sum_{\mu > \ell} \Big(\sum_i \sigma_i \xi_i^\mu \Big)^2 + \frac{p}{2}$$

taking account of the absence of self-interactions, as usual. The disorder average defining the replicated Hamiltonian is then

$$\overline{e^{-\beta \sum_{a=1}^n H(\sigma^a)}} = e^{(\beta/2N) \sum_{\mu\le\ell} \sum_a (\sum_i \sigma_i^a \xi_i^\mu)^2 - Nn\beta\alpha/2} \, \overline{e^{(\beta/2N) \sum_a \sum_{\mu>\ell} (\sum_i \sigma_i^a \xi_i^\mu)^2}} \tag{21.60}$$

The disorder average over the non-nominated patterns is now seen to factorize:

$$\overline{e^{(\beta/2N)\sum_a\sum_{\mu>\ell}(\sum_i \sigma_i^a\xi_i^\mu)^2}} = \left[\overline{e^{(1/2)\sum_a(\sqrt{\beta/N}\sum_i\sigma_i^a\xi_i)^2}}\right]^{p-\ell}$$

The square in the exponent still couples the variables ξ_i at different sites i, so we need to use Gaussian linearization (21.34), with n auxiliary Gaussian integration variables $z = (z_1, \ldots, z_n)$ to linearize the exponent:

$$\begin{aligned}\overline{e^{(1/2)\sum_a(\sqrt{\beta/N}\sum_i\sigma_i^a\xi_i)^2}} &= \int Dz\, \overline{e^{\sqrt{\beta/N}\sum_a z_a\sum_i\sigma_i^a\xi_i}} \\ &= \int Dz \prod_i \cosh\left(\sqrt{\beta/N}\sum_a z_a\sigma_i^a\right)\end{aligned}$$

To simplify this, one writes the product as $\exp[\sum_i \ln\cosh(\cdots)]$ and expands in the argument of the ln cosh. The leading term is of $\mathcal{O}(1/N)$ and, when summed over i, gives a contribution of $\mathcal{O}(1)$. The next term only gives a negligible correction of $\mathcal{O}(1/N)$ to the sum, so

$$\prod_i \cosh\left(\sqrt{\beta/N}\sum_a z_a\sigma_i^a\right) = e^{(\beta/2N)\sum_{ab} z_a z_b \sum_i \sigma_i^a\sigma_i^b + \mathcal{O}(1/N)}$$

When we raise this to the power $p-\ell$, the $\mathcal{O}(1/N)$ term in the exponent only results in an overall $\mathcal{O}(1)$ factor. Replacing $p-\ell$ by p also gives a factor of the same order, so altogether

$$\overline{e^{(\beta/2N)\sum_a\sum_{\mu>\ell}(\sum_i \sigma_i^a\xi_i^\mu)^2}} = \left[\int Dz\, e^{(\beta/2N)\sum_{ab} z_a z_b\sum_i\sigma_i^a\sigma_i^b}\right]^p \times \mathcal{O}(1)$$

Inserting this into (21.60), we obtain the replicated Hamiltonian (with, as in the calculation of the SK model, $\{\boldsymbol{\sigma}\} \equiv \boldsymbol{\sigma}^n \cdots \boldsymbol{\sigma}^n$)

$$\begin{aligned}\Phi(\{\boldsymbol{\sigma}\}) &= -\frac{1}{\beta}\ln \overline{e^{-\beta\sum_{a=1}^n H(\boldsymbol{\sigma}^a)}} \\ &= -\frac{1}{2N}\sum_{\mu\le\ell}\sum_a\Big(\sum_i\sigma_i^a\xi_i^\mu\Big)^2 + \frac{1}{2}Nn\alpha \\ &\quad - NT\alpha\ln\int Dz\, e^{(\beta/2N)\sum_{ab}z_a z_b\sum_i\sigma_i^a\sigma_i^b} + \mathcal{O}(1)\end{aligned}$$

This function depends on $\{\boldsymbol{\sigma}\}$ only through the following order parameters:

$$q_{ab}(\{\boldsymbol{\sigma}\}) = \frac{1}{N}\sum_i \sigma_i^a \sigma_i^b \qquad m_\mu^a(\{\boldsymbol{\sigma}\}) = \frac{1}{N}\sum_i \sigma_i^a \xi_i^\mu \tag{21.61}$$

These are nearly identical to those (21.36) of the SK model, except that instead of a single magnetization order parameter m_a we now have the ℓ nominated pattern overlaps m_μ^a for each replica a. We can further simplify Φ by carrying out the n-dimensional Gaussian integral over z; this factorizes in the standard way after an appropriate orthogonal transformation of the integration variables z, with the result:

$$\ln \int Dz\, e^{(\beta/2)\sum_{ab} z_a z_b q_{ab}} = -\frac{1}{2}\ln\det(\mathbf{I} - \beta \boldsymbol{q}) \tag{21.62}$$

in which $\mathbf{I}$ denotes the $n \times n$ identity matrix. So the replicated Hamiltonian becomes

$$\begin{aligned}\frac{1}{N}\Phi(\{\boldsymbol{\sigma}\}) &= -\frac{1}{2}\sum_\mu\sum_a (m_\mu^a(\{\boldsymbol{\sigma}\}))^2 + \frac{1}{2}n\alpha \\ &\quad + \frac{1}{2}T\alpha\ln\det(\mathbf{I} - \beta\boldsymbol{q}(\{\boldsymbol{\sigma}\})) + \mathcal{O}\left(\frac{1}{N}\right)\end{aligned} \tag{21.63}$$

Here and in the following all sums and products over μ run from 1 to ℓ unless stated otherwise. From our discussion at the beginning of Section 21.2, one would expect that (21.63) should, in the limit $\alpha \to \infty$, become identical to the replicated Hamiltonian (21.35) of the SK model without the ferromagnetic part, that is, with $J_0 = 0$. This can indeed be shown to be the case; see Exercise 21.11.

By direct analogy with the SK model, we can now write the disorder-averaged asymptotic free energy per spin (21.33) as

$$\begin{aligned}\bar{f} = &-\lim_{N\to\infty}\lim_{n\to 0}\frac{T}{Nn}\ln\int \mathrm{d}\boldsymbol{q}\,\mathrm{d}\boldsymbol{m}\,\mathcal{D}(\boldsymbol{q},\boldsymbol{m}) \\ &\times \exp\left(N\left[\frac{\beta}{2}\sum_\mu\sum_a (m_\mu^a)^2 - \frac{n\alpha\beta}{2} - \frac{\alpha}{2}\ln\det(\mathbf{I} - \beta\boldsymbol{q})\right]\right)\end{aligned} \tag{21.64}$$

with the density of states

$$\begin{aligned}\mathcal{D}(\boldsymbol{q},\boldsymbol{m}) &= \sum_{\{\sigma\}}\prod_{ab}\delta\Big(q_{ab}-\frac{1}{N}\sum_i\sigma_i^a\sigma_i^b\Big)\prod_{a\mu}\delta\Big(m_\mu^a-\frac{1}{N}\sum_i\sigma_i^a\xi_i^\mu\Big)\\ &= \sum_{\{\sigma\}}\Big(\frac{N}{2\pi}\Big)^{n^2+n\ell}\int \mathrm{d}\hat{\boldsymbol{q}}\,\mathrm{d}\hat{\boldsymbol{m}}\; e^{\mathrm{i}N\sum_{ab}\hat{q}_{ab}\left[q_{ab}-(1/N)\sum_i\sigma_i^a\sigma_i^b\right]}\\ &\quad\times e^{\mathrm{i}N\sum_{a\mu}\hat{m}_\mu^a\left[m_\mu^a-(1/N)\sum_i\sigma_i^a\xi_i^\mu\right]}\end{aligned}$$

where $\boldsymbol{m}$ and $\hat{\boldsymbol{m}}$ now stand for the $n\times\ell$ matrices with entries $\{m_\mu^a\}$ and $\{\hat{m}_\mu^a\}$. The sum over states now factorizes over the different sites i as usual, and we are left with a sum over the states of a single n-replicated spin, which we denote by $\boldsymbol{\sigma}=(\sigma^1,\ldots,\sigma^n)$ as before. This gives

$$\begin{aligned}\mathcal{D}(\boldsymbol{q},\boldsymbol{m}) = \Big(\frac{N}{2\pi}\Big)^{n^2+n\ell}&\int \mathrm{d}\hat{\boldsymbol{q}}\,\mathrm{d}\hat{\boldsymbol{m}}\; e^{\mathrm{i}N\sum_{ab}\hat{q}_{ab}q_{ab}+\mathrm{i}N\sum_{a\mu}\hat{m}_\mu^a m_\mu^a}\\ &\times\prod_i\Big(\sum_{\boldsymbol{\sigma}}e^{-\mathrm{i}\sum_{ab}\hat{q}_{ab}\sigma^a\sigma^b-\mathrm{i}\sum_{a\mu}\hat{m}_\mu^a\sigma^a\xi_i^\mu}\Big)\end{aligned}\tag{21.65}$$

The product can be expressed as $\prod_i(\cdots)=\exp[\sum_i\ln(\cdots)]$, and the sum over i in the exponent then written as N times an average over the vectors $\boldsymbol{\xi}_i=(\xi_i^1,\ldots,\xi_i^\ell)$, using notation analogous to (21.6):

$$\langle g(\boldsymbol{\xi})\rangle_{\boldsymbol{\xi}} = \frac{1}{N}\sum_i g(\boldsymbol{\xi}_i) = 2^{-\ell}\sum_{\boldsymbol{\xi}\in\{-1,1\}^\ell} g(\boldsymbol{\xi})$$

Self-averaging ensures that the second equality holds in the thermodynamic limit $N\to\infty$, because of our assumption that the patterns are chosen randomly. If we insert the resulting expression for $\mathcal{D}(\boldsymbol{q},\boldsymbol{m})$ into (21.64) and evaluate the integrals by saddle point integration we get for the free energy

$$\bar{f} = \lim_{n\to 0}\ \mathrm{extr}\, f(\boldsymbol{q},\boldsymbol{m};\hat{\boldsymbol{q}},\hat{\boldsymbol{m}})\tag{21.66}$$

where

$$f(\boldsymbol{q},\boldsymbol{m};\hat{\boldsymbol{q}},\hat{\boldsymbol{m}}) = -\frac{1}{2n}\sum_{\mu}\sum_{a}(m_{\mu}^{a})^2 + \frac{1}{2}\alpha + \frac{T\alpha}{2n}\ln\det(\mathbf{1}-\beta\boldsymbol{q})$$
$$-\frac{T}{n}\Bigg[\mathrm{i}\sum_{ab}\hat{q}_{ab}q_{ab} + \mathrm{i}\sum_{a\mu}\hat{m}_{\mu}^{a}m_{\mu}^{a}$$
$$+\left\langle\ln\left(\sum_{\boldsymbol{\sigma}} e^{-\mathrm{i}\sum_{ab}\hat{q}_{ab}\sigma^a\sigma^b-\mathrm{i}\sum_{a\mu}\hat{m}_{\mu}^{a}\sigma^a\xi^{\mu}}\right)\right\rangle_{\boldsymbol{\xi}}\Bigg] \qquad (21.67)$$

We recognize in the first terms the replicated Hamiltonian (21.63), up to the $1/n$ factors, while the last term in square brackets is the log density of states (21.65), up to terms which are negligible for $N \to \infty$. Variation of the conjugate order parameters $\{\hat{q}_{ab}\}$, $\{\hat{m}_a^{\mu}\}$ in (21.67) gives the following saddle point equations:

$$m_a^{\mu} = \left\langle\frac{\sum_{\boldsymbol{\sigma}}\sigma^a\xi^{\mu}\kappa(\boldsymbol{\sigma})}{\sum_{\boldsymbol{\sigma}}\kappa(\boldsymbol{\sigma})}\right\rangle_{\boldsymbol{\xi}} \qquad (21.68)$$

$$q_{ab} = \left\langle\frac{\sum_{\boldsymbol{\sigma}}\sigma^a\sigma^b\kappa(\boldsymbol{\sigma})}{\sum_{\boldsymbol{\sigma}}\kappa(\boldsymbol{\sigma})}\right\rangle_{\boldsymbol{\xi}} \qquad (21.69)$$

where

$$\kappa(\boldsymbol{\sigma}) = \exp\left(-\mathrm{i}\sum_{ab}\hat{q}_{ab}\sigma^a\sigma^b - \mathrm{i}\sum_{a\mu}\hat{m}_{\mu}^{a}\sigma^a\xi^{\mu}\right)$$

Not unexpectedly, in view of our previous analysis of the SK model, these equations take the form of averages over $\boldsymbol{\sigma}$ and $\boldsymbol{\xi}$, weighted by $\kappa(\boldsymbol{\sigma})$. In agreement with the order parameter definition (21.61), the diagonal elements of $\boldsymbol{q}$ are always $q_{aa} = 1$.

Similarly, demanding stationarity of (21.67) with respect to the remaining order parameters $\{q_{ab}\}$, $\{m_a^{\mu}\}$ gives the conditions

$$\hat{q}_{ab} = \frac{1}{2}\mathrm{i}\alpha\beta\left[\frac{\int \mathrm{d}\boldsymbol{z}\, z_a z_b\, e^{-\boldsymbol{z}\cdot(\mathbf{1}-\beta\boldsymbol{q})\boldsymbol{z}/2}}{\int \mathrm{d}\boldsymbol{z}\, e^{-\boldsymbol{z}\cdot(\mathbf{1}-\beta\boldsymbol{q})\boldsymbol{z}/2}}\right] = \frac{1}{2}\mathrm{i}\alpha\beta(\mathbf{1}-\beta\boldsymbol{q})^{-1}{}_{ab} \qquad (21.70)$$

$$\hat{m}_a^{\mu} = \mathrm{i}\beta m_{\mu}^{a} \qquad (21.71)$$

In deriving (21.70), we used (21.62) in reverse to evaluate the derivative of $\ln\det(\mathbf{1}-\beta\boldsymbol{q})$ with respect to q_{ab}. Equation (21.71) can be used to eliminate the conjugate order parameters $\hat{\boldsymbol{m}}$, simplifying $\kappa(\boldsymbol{\sigma})$ to

$$\kappa(\boldsymbol{\sigma}) = \exp\left(-\mathrm{i}\sum_{ab}\hat{q}_{ab}\sigma^a\sigma^b + \beta\sum_{a\mu}m_{\mu}^{a}\sigma^a\xi^{\mu}\right)$$

Note that the diagonal elements $\hat{q}_{aa}$ drop out of (21.68, 21.69), because they just contribute constant factors to $\kappa(\boldsymbol{\sigma})$. Their values are simply given as functions of the remaining parameters by (21.70).

As for the SK model, we can also use (21.71) to eliminate the $\hat{\boldsymbol{m}}$ from the free energy (21.67); this gives a pseudo-free energy which coincides with the true free energy at its saddle points:

$$\tilde{f}(\boldsymbol{m},\boldsymbol{q},\hat{\boldsymbol{q}}) = \frac{1}{2n}\sum_{\mu}\sum_{a}(m_{\mu}^{a})^{2} + \frac{\alpha}{2} + \frac{T\alpha}{2n}\ln\det(\mathbf{1}-\beta\boldsymbol{q})$$
$$-\frac{T}{n}\left[\mathrm{i}\sum_{ab}\hat{q}_{ab}q_{ab} + \left\langle \ln\left(\sum_{\boldsymbol{\sigma}} e^{-\mathrm{i}\sum_{ab}\hat{q}_{ab}\sigma^{a}\sigma^{a}+\beta\sum_{a\mu}m_{\mu}^{a}\sigma^{a}\xi^{\mu}}\right)\right\rangle_{\boldsymbol{\xi}}\right] \tag{21.72}$$

Before proceeding with a full analysis of the saddle point equations (21.68–21.70) using a RS ansatz, we make a few tentative statements on the phase diagram. For $\beta = 0$ we obtain the trivial paramagnetic solution $q_{ab} = \delta_{ab}$, $\hat{q}_{ab} = 0$, $m_{a}^{\mu} = 0$. We can identify continuous bifurcations to a non-trivial state by expanding the saddle point equations to first order in the relevant parameters:

$$m_{\mu}^{a} = \beta m_{\mu}^{a} + \cdots \qquad q_{ab} = -2\mathrm{i}\hat{q}_{ab} + \cdots \quad (a \neq b)$$
$$\hat{q}_{ab} = \frac{\mathrm{i}}{2}\frac{\alpha\beta}{1-\beta}\left[\delta_{ab} + \frac{\beta}{1-\beta}q_{ab}(1-\delta_{ab})\right] + \cdots$$

By combining the equations for $\boldsymbol{q}$ and $\hat{\boldsymbol{q}}$ we obtain (for $a \neq b$)

$$q_{ab} = \alpha\left(\frac{\beta}{1-\beta}\right)^{2} q_{ab} + \cdots$$

Therefore we expect a second-order transition when $\alpha\beta^2/(1-\beta)^2 = 1$, that is, at $T = 1 + \sqrt{\alpha}$, from the trivial state to a spin glass state where $\boldsymbol{m} = 0$ but $\boldsymbol{q} \neq 0$.

Physical interpretation of saddle points

We proceed once more along the lines of the SK model. If we apply the alternative version (21.47) of the replica trick to the Hopfield model, we can write the distribution of the ℓ overlaps $\boldsymbol{m} = (m_1, \ldots, m_\ell)$ in equilibrium as

$$P(\boldsymbol{m}) = \lim_{n\to 0}\frac{1}{n}\sum_{b}\sum_{\boldsymbol{\sigma}^{1}\ldots\boldsymbol{\sigma}^{n}}\delta\left(\boldsymbol{m} - \frac{1}{N}\sum_{i}\sigma_{i}^{b}\boldsymbol{\xi}_{i}\right)\prod_{a}e^{-\beta H(\boldsymbol{\sigma}^{a})}$$

with $\boldsymbol{\xi}_i = (\xi_i^1, \ldots, \xi_i^\ell)$. Averaging this distribution over the disorder leads to expressions identical to those encountered in evaluating the disorder averaged free energy. By inserting the same delta-functions we arrive once more at the saddle point integration (21.66, 21.72), and find

$$\overline{P(\boldsymbol{m})} = \lim_{n\to 0} \frac{1}{n} \sum_b \delta(\boldsymbol{m} - \boldsymbol{m}^b) \tag{21.73}$$

where $\boldsymbol{m}^b = (m_1^b, \ldots, m_\ell^b)$ refers to the relevant solution of (21.68–21.70).

Similarly we imagine two systems $\boldsymbol{\sigma}$ and $\boldsymbol{\sigma}'$ with identical realizations of the interactions $\{J_{ij}\}$, both in thermal equilibrium, and use (21.47) to rewrite the distribution $P(q)$ for the mutual overlap between the microstates of the two systems as

$$P(q) = \lim_{n\to 0} \frac{1}{n(n-1)} \sum_{b\neq c} \sum_{\boldsymbol{\sigma}^1 \cdots \boldsymbol{\sigma}^n} \delta\left(q - \frac{1}{N}\sum_i \sigma_i^b \sigma_i^c\right) \prod_a e^{-\beta H(\boldsymbol{\sigma}^a)}$$

Averaging over the disorder again leads to the saddle point integration (21.66, 21.72), and we find

$$\overline{P(q)} = \lim_{n\to 0} \frac{1}{n(n-1)} \sum_{b\neq c} \delta(q - q_{bc}) \tag{21.74}$$

where $\{q_{bc}\}$ refers to the relevant solution of (21.68–21.70).

Finally, we analyse the physical meaning of the conjugate parameters $\{\hat{q}_{ab}\}$ for $a \neq b$. We will do this in more detail, it being rather specific for the Hopfield model and slightly different from the derivations above. Again we imagine two systems $\boldsymbol{\sigma}$ and $\boldsymbol{\sigma}'$ with identical interactions $\{J_{ij}\}$, both in thermal equilibrium. We now use (21.47) to evaluate the covariance, rescaled by an appropriate factor N (since non-nominated overlaps are by definition individually of order $\mathcal{O}(N^{-1/2})$), of the overlaps corresponding to non-nominated patterns:

$$\begin{aligned} r &= \frac{N}{p-\ell} \overline{\sum_{\mu=\ell+1}^{p} \left\langle \frac{1}{N}\sum_i \sigma_i \xi_i^\mu \right\rangle_{\text{eq}} \left\langle \frac{1}{N}\sum_i \sigma_i' \xi_i^\mu \right\rangle_{\text{eq}}} \\ &= \lim_{n\to 0} \frac{N}{n(n-1)} \sum_{b\neq c} \sum_{\boldsymbol{\sigma}^1 \cdots \boldsymbol{\sigma}^n} \overline{\left(\frac{1}{N}\sum_i \sigma_i^b \xi_i^p\right)\left(\frac{1}{N}\sum_i \sigma_i^c \xi_i^p\right) \prod_a e^{-\beta H(\boldsymbol{\sigma}^a)}} \end{aligned} \tag{21.75}$$

Here we have used the equivalence of all such non-nominated patterns. We next perform the same manipulations as in calculating the free energy.

The disorder average involves

$$
\begin{aligned}
&\overline{\left(\frac{1}{\sqrt{N}}\sum_i \sigma_i^b \xi_i^p\right)\left(\frac{1}{\sqrt{N}}\sum_i \sigma_i^c \xi_i^p\right) e^{(\beta/2N)\sum_a \sum_{\mu>\ell}(\sum_i \sigma_i^a \xi_i^\mu)^2}} \\
&\quad = \left[\int Dz\, \overline{e^{\sqrt{\beta/N}\sum_a z_a \sum_i \sigma_i^a \xi_i}}\right]^{p-\ell-1} \frac{1}{\beta}\int Dz \frac{\partial^2}{\partial z_b \partial z_c}\, \overline{e^{\sqrt{\beta/N}\sum_a z_a \sum_i \sigma_i^a \xi_i}} \\
&\quad = \left[\int Dz\, \overline{e^{\sqrt{\beta/N}\sum_a z_a \sum_i \sigma_i^a \xi_i}}\right]^{p-\ell-1} \frac{1}{\beta}\int Dz\, z_b z_c\, \overline{e^{\sqrt{\beta/N}\sum_a z_a \sum_i \sigma_i^a \xi_i}}
\end{aligned}
$$

after an integration by parts. We thus finally obtain an expression which involves the surface (21.72):

$$
\begin{aligned}
r &= \frac{1}{\beta}\lim_{n\to 0}\frac{1}{n(n-1)} \\
&\quad \times \sum_{b\neq c}\lim_{N\to\infty}\left\{\left(\int \mathrm{d}\boldsymbol{m}\mathrm{d}\boldsymbol{q}\mathrm{d}\hat{\boldsymbol{q}}\left[\frac{\int \mathrm{d}\boldsymbol{z}\, z_b z_c\, e^{-\boldsymbol{z}\cdot(\boldsymbol{1}-\beta\boldsymbol{q})\boldsymbol{z}/2}}{\int \mathrm{d}\boldsymbol{z}\, e^{-\boldsymbol{z}\cdot(\boldsymbol{1}-\beta\boldsymbol{q})\boldsymbol{z}/2}}\right] e^{-\beta n N \tilde{f}(\boldsymbol{m},\boldsymbol{q},\hat{\boldsymbol{q}})}\right)\right. \\
&\quad \left.\times \left(\int \mathrm{d}\boldsymbol{m}\mathrm{d}\boldsymbol{q}\mathrm{d}\hat{\boldsymbol{q}}\, e^{-\beta n N \tilde{f}(\boldsymbol{m},\boldsymbol{q},\hat{\boldsymbol{q}})}\right)^{-1}\right\}
\end{aligned}
$$

The normalization of the above integral over $\{\boldsymbol{m}, \boldsymbol{q}, \hat{\boldsymbol{q}}\}$ (i.e. the appearance of the integral in the denominator) follows from using the replica procedure to rewrite unity. The integration being dominated by the extrema of $\tilde{f}$, we can now use the saddle point equation (21.70) to arrive at

$$
\lim_{n\to 0}\frac{1}{n(n-1)}\sum_{b\neq c}\hat{q}_{bc} = \frac{\mathrm{i}}{2}\alpha\beta^2 r \tag{21.76}
$$

The result (21.76) thus provides a physical interpretation of the order parameters $\{\hat{q}_{ab}\}$, via (21.75), in terms of the uncondensed overlaps.

We know that assuming ergodicity implies that the distributions $\overline{P(q)}$ and $\overline{P(\boldsymbol{m})}$ are δ-functions. This is equivalent to the relevant saddle point being of the RS form:

$$
m_\mu^a = m_\mu \qquad q_{ab} = \delta_{ab} + q(1-\delta_{ab}) \qquad \hat{q}_{ab} = \tfrac{1}{2}\mathrm{i}\alpha\beta^2[R\delta_{ab} + r(1-\delta_{ab})] \tag{21.77}
$$

which is the replica symmetry (RS) ansatz for the Hopfield model. The RS form for $\{q_{ab}\}$ and $\{m_\mu^a\}$ is a direct consequence of the corresponding distributions being δ-functions, whereas the RS form for $\{\hat{q}_{ab}\}$ subsequently follows from (21.70). The physical meaning of m_μ and q is

$$m_\mu = \overline{\langle m_\mu(\boldsymbol{\sigma})\rangle_{\rm eq}} \qquad q = \frac{1}{N}\sum_i \overline{\langle \sigma_i\rangle_{\rm eq}^2}$$

The parameter R appearing in (21.77) can be related to the order parameter q, via (21.70). We do not give the explicit form because R will disappear from our analysis shortly.

RS free energy and saddle point equations

We now explore the consequences of the RS ansatz (21.77) for the saddle point. The relatively simple form of this ansatz allows us to diagonalize the matrix $\boldsymbol{\Lambda} = \mathbf{1} - \beta\boldsymbol{q}$ which we encountered in the saddle point problem:

$$\Lambda_{ab} = [1-\beta(1-q)]\delta_{ab} - \beta q$$

Eigenspace:	Eigenvalue:	Multiplicity:
$\boldsymbol{x} = (1,\ldots,1)$	$1-\beta(1-q)-\beta qn$	1
$\sum_a x_a = 0$	$1-\beta(1-q)$	$n-1$

so that

$$\begin{aligned}\ln\det\boldsymbol{\Lambda} &= \ln(1-\beta(1-q)-\beta qn) + (n-1)\ln(1-\beta(1-q)) \\ &= n\left[\ln(1-\beta(1-q)) - \frac{\beta q}{1-\beta(1-q)}\right] + \mathcal{O}(n^2)\end{aligned}$$

Inserting the RS ansatz (21.77) for the saddle point into (21.72) and using the above expression for the determinant and the shorthand $\boldsymbol{m} = (m_1,\ldots,m_\ell)$ gives us

$$\begin{aligned}\tilde{f}(\boldsymbol{m}_{\rm RS},\boldsymbol{q}_{\rm RS},\hat{\boldsymbol{q}}_{\rm RS}) &= \frac{1}{2}\boldsymbol{m}^2 + \frac{1}{2}\alpha[1+\beta r(1-q)] \\ &\quad + \frac{1}{2}T\alpha\left[\ln(1-\beta(1-q)) - \frac{\beta q}{1-\beta(1-q)}\right] \\ &\quad - \frac{T}{n}\left\langle \ln\sum_{\boldsymbol{\sigma}} e^{\beta\boldsymbol{m}\cdot\boldsymbol{\xi}\sum_a\sigma^a + (\alpha r\beta^2/2)(\sum_a\sigma^a)^2}\right\rangle_{\boldsymbol{\xi}} + \mathcal{O}(n)\end{aligned}$$

Following closely the calculation for the SK model leading to (21.54), we now linearize the squares in the spin averages with (21.34). We then carry out the sum over the replicated spin $\boldsymbol{\sigma}$ and take the limit $n \to 0$ using the replica trick (21.32) in reverse. This gives the asymptotic disorder-averaged free energy per spin of the RS solution:

$$\begin{aligned}\bar{f}_{\rm RS} &= \lim_{n\to 0} \tilde{f}(\boldsymbol{m}_{\rm RS}, \boldsymbol{q}_{\rm RS}, \hat{\boldsymbol{q}}_{\rm RS}) \\ &= \frac{1}{2}\boldsymbol{m}^2 + \frac{\alpha}{2}\left[1 + \beta r(1-q) + T\ln(1-\beta(1-q)) - \frac{q}{1-\beta(1-q)}\right] \\ &\quad - T\int Dz \langle \ln[2\cosh(\beta(\boldsymbol{m}\cdot\boldsymbol{\xi} + z\sqrt{\alpha r}))]\rangle_{\boldsymbol{\xi}} \qquad (21.78)\end{aligned}$$

The saddle point equations for $\boldsymbol{m}$, q, and r can be obtained either by inserting the RS ansatz (21.77) into (21.68–21.70) and taking the $n \to 0$ limit, or by finding the stationary points of the RS expression (21.78). The latter route is the fastest one. After performing integrations by parts where appropriate, we obtain the final result:

$$\boldsymbol{m} = \int Dz\, \langle \boldsymbol{\xi} \tanh(\beta(\boldsymbol{m}\cdot\boldsymbol{\xi} + z\sqrt{\alpha r}))\rangle_{\boldsymbol{\xi}} \qquad (21.79)$$

$$q = \int Dz\, \langle \tanh^2(\beta(\boldsymbol{m}\cdot\boldsymbol{\xi} + z\sqrt{\alpha r}))\rangle_{\boldsymbol{\xi}} \qquad (21.80)$$

$$r = \frac{q}{[1-\beta(1-q)]^2} \qquad (21.81)$$

It is reassuring to see that from equation (21.79) one recovers for $\alpha = 0$ our previous result (21.13) for a finite number of patterns. As in the SK model, the average over the Gaussian variable z represents the effect of the disorder, which here arises from the non-condensed (or non-nominated) patterns $\mu = \ell+1, \ldots, N$, that is from those that have an $\mathcal{O}(N^{-1/2})$ overlap with the network state $\boldsymbol{\sigma}$.

Analysis of RS order parameter equations and phase diagram

We first establish an upper bound for the temperature $T = 1/\beta$ for non-trivial solutions of the set of equations (21.79–21.81) to exist. Following a line of reasoning similar to that leading to (21.18), one can show that $\boldsymbol{m} = 0$ for $T > 1$. In this temperature regime, we can then obtain from (21.80, 21.81), using $\tanh^2(x) \leq x^2$ and $0 \leq q \leq 1$:

$$q = 0 \quad \text{or} \quad q \leq 1 + \sqrt{\alpha} - T$$

We conclude from this that $q = 0$ for $T > 1 + \sqrt{\alpha}$. Linearization of (21.79, 21.80) for small q and $\boldsymbol{m}$ shows the continuous bifurcations as

T is decreased:

	at	from	to
$\alpha > 0$:	$T = 1 + \sqrt{\alpha}$	$\boldsymbol{m} = 0,\ q = 0$	$\boldsymbol{m} = 0,\ q > 0$
$\alpha = 0$:	$T = 1$	$\boldsymbol{m} = 0,\ q = 0$	$\boldsymbol{m} \neq 0,\ q > 0$

where the $\alpha = 0$ result corresponds simply to our earlier results for an intensive (i.e. order $\mathcal{O}(N^0)$) number of patterns. We see that the upper bound $T = 1 + \sqrt{\alpha}$ is actually the critical temperature that indicates a continuous transition to a SG state, where there is no significant alignment of the spins in the direction of one particular pattern, but still a certain degree of local freezing. Since $\boldsymbol{m} = 0$ for $T > 1$, this SG state persists at least down to $T = 1$. The quantitative details of the SG state are obtained by inserting $\boldsymbol{m} = 0$ into (21.80, 21.81), since (21.79) is fulfilled automatically. If one analyses the stability of the saddle point describing the SG phase *within the RS ansatz*,[44] one finds an important difference between the previously studied case $\alpha = 0$ and the present case $\alpha > 0$: the $\boldsymbol{m} = 0$ spin glass solution is now *stable* within RS for all $T < 1 + \sqrt{\alpha}$. In terms of information processing this implies that for $\alpha > 0$ an initial state must have a certain nonzero overlap with a pattern to evoke a final state with $\boldsymbol{m} \neq 0$, in order to avoid ending up in the $\boldsymbol{m} = 0$ spin glass state. In contrast, for $\alpha = 0$, the state with $\boldsymbol{m} = 0$ is unstable for $T < 1$, so *any* initial state will eventually lead to a final state with $\boldsymbol{m} \neq 0$.

Next we consider the *retrieval states*, that is, the solutions with $\boldsymbol{m} \neq 0$. The impact on the saddle point equations (21.79, 21.80) of having $\alpha > 0$ is seen to be a smoothing of the hyperbolic tangent by convolution with a Gaussian kernel. The latter can be viewed as noise caused by interference between the attractors, that is, between the different patterns stored. The natural strategy for solving (21.79, 21.80) is therefore to make an ansatz for the nominated overlaps $\boldsymbol{m}$ of the mixture state type (21.19). Insertion of this second ansatz into the saddle point equations does indeed lead to self-consistent solutions. One can solve numerically the remaining equations for the amplitudes of the mixture states, and then evaluate their stability, in essentially the same way as for $\alpha = 0$. The calculations are just more involved. It then turns out that mixtures of an even number of patterns are again unstable for any T and α, whereas odd mixtures can become locally stable for sufficiently small T and small α. Among the mixture states, the pure states, where the vector $\boldsymbol{m}$ has only one nonzero component, are

[44] As the discussion in Section 21.3 shows, the SG phase is actually unstable if non-replica symmetric variations of the order parameters are taken into account. Nevertheless, as in the case of the SK model, the presence of this instability itself shows that there is a SG phase in the region of the phase diagram that we have calculated, even if its properties are not accurately described by the replica symmetric solution.

the first to stabilize as the temperature is lowered. We will study these pure states in more detail.

Inserting the pure state ansatz $\boldsymbol{m} = m(1, 0, \ldots, 0)$ into our RS equations gives us

$$m = \int Dz \tanh\left(\beta\left[m + \frac{z\sqrt{\alpha q}}{1-\beta(1-q)}\right]\right) \tag{21.82}$$

$$q = \int Dz \tanh^2\left(\beta\left[m + \frac{z\sqrt{\alpha q}}{1-\beta(1-q)}\right]\right) \tag{21.83}$$

$$\tilde{f} = \frac{1}{2}m^2 + \frac{1}{2}\alpha\left[(1-q)\frac{1+\beta(1-q)(\beta-2)}{[1-\beta(1-q)]^2} + \frac{1}{\beta}\ln(1-\beta(1-q))\right] - T\int Dz \ln\left(2\cosh\left(\beta\left[m + \frac{z\sqrt{\alpha q}}{1-\beta(1-q)}\right]\right)\right) \tag{21.84}$$

These equations look like we have just inserted $\xi_1 = 1$ everywhere, rather than averaged over $\xi_1 = \pm 1$. The reason is that for states of the form $\boldsymbol{m} = m(1, 0, \ldots, 0)$ the saddle point equations (21.79–21.81) and the free energy per spin (21.78) are actually independent of ξ_1. To see this, we note that for $\xi_1 = \pm 1$, one has $\xi_1 \tanh(x) = \tanh(\xi_1 x)$. This transformation also gives $\xi_1 z$ instead of z inside the integral. But then one can transform the integration variable to $z' = \xi_1 z$ (which leaves the Gaussian measure unaffected, as it is symmetric under $z \to -z$) and obtain a result which is the same for $\xi_1 = 1$ and $\xi_1 = -1$.

If we solve the equations (21.82, 21.83) numerically for different values of α, and calculate the corresponding free energies (21.84) for the pure states and the SG state $\boldsymbol{m} = 0$, we obtain Figure 21.3. For $\alpha > 0$ the non-trivial solution m for the amplitude of the pure state disappears *discontinuously* as the temperature is raised, defining a transition temperature $T_M(\alpha)$. Once the pure state appears, it turns out to be locally stable within the RS ansatz. Its free energy $\tilde{f}$, however, remains larger than the one corresponding to the spin glass state, until the temperature is further reduced to below a second transition temperature $T_c(\alpha)$. For $T < T_c(\alpha)$ the pure states are therefore the equilibrium states in the thermodynamic sense.

By drawing the above transition lines in the (α, T) plane, together with the line $T_g(\alpha) = 1 + \sqrt{\alpha}$ which signals the transition from the paramagnetic to the SG state, we obtain the RS phase diagram of the Hopfield model, depicted in Figure 21.4. Strictly speaking, the line T_M would appear meaningless in the thermodynamic picture, only the saddle point that minimises $\tilde{f}$ being relevant. However, we have to keep in mind the physics behind the formalism (see Section 20.5). The occurrence of multiple locally stable saddle points is the manifestation of ergodicity breaking in the limit $N \to \infty$. For times which are not exponentially long, the thermodynamic analysis,

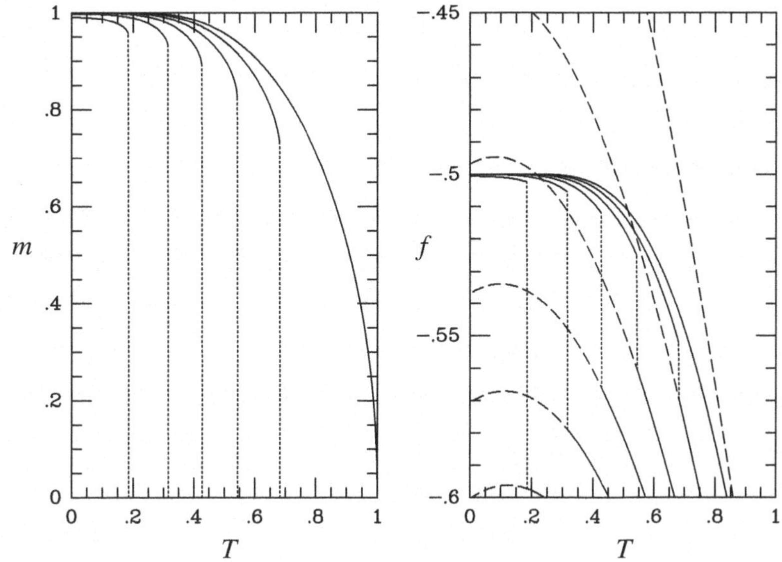

Figure 21.3 Left picture: RS amplitudes m of the pure states of the Hopfield model as a function of temperature. From top to bottom: $\alpha = 0.000 \ldots 0.125$ ($\Delta\alpha = 0.025$). Right picture, solid lines: free energies of the pure states. From top to bottom: $\alpha = 0.000 \ldots 0.125$ ($\Delta\alpha = 0.025$). Dashed lines and their solid continuations: free energies of the spin glass state $\boldsymbol{m} = 0$ for the same values of α, shown for comparison.

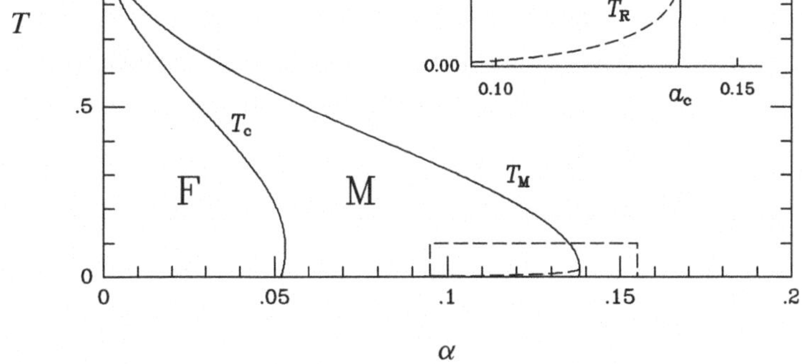

Figure 21.4 Phase diagram of the Hopfield model. P: paramagnetic phase, $m = q = 0$. SG: spin glass phase, $m = 0$, $q > 0$. F: pattern recall phase, where the pure states with $m \neq 0$ and $q > 0$ minimize f. In region M, the pure states are local but not global minima of f. Dashed: the AT instability for the retrieval solutions (T_R). Inset: close-up of the low temperature region.

based on ergodicity, therefore applies only within a single ergodic component. As a result, each locally stable saddle point is indeed relevant for appropriate initial conditions and finite timescales.

Zero temperature, storage capacity

The storage capacity α_c of the Hopfield model is defined as the largest α for which locally stable pure states still exist. The critical temperature $T_M(\alpha)$, where the pure states appear as the noise level T is lowered, decreases monotonically with α, and the storage capacity is reached for[45] $T = 0$. Before we can put $T \to 0$ in (21.82, 21.83), however, we have to rewrite these equations in terms of quantities with well defined $T \to 0$ limits, since $q \to 1$. A suitable quantity turns out to be $C = \beta(1-q)$, which must obey $0 \leq C \leq 1$ for the free energy (21.78) to exist. The saddle point equations can now be written in the following form:

$$m = \int Dz \tanh\left(\beta\left(m + \frac{z\sqrt{\alpha q}}{1-C}\right)\right)$$

$$C = \frac{\partial}{\partial m}\int Dz \tanh\left(\beta\left(m + \frac{z\sqrt{\alpha q}}{1-C}\right)\right)$$

in which the limit $T \to 0$ simply corresponds to replacing $\tanh(\beta x) \to \text{sgn}(x)$ and $q \to 1$. After taking this limit, we perform the Gaussian integral and find

$$m = \text{erf}\left(\frac{m(1-C)}{\sqrt{2\alpha}}\right) \qquad C = (1-C)\sqrt{\frac{2}{\alpha\pi}}\, e^{-m^2(1-C)^2/2\alpha} \tag{21.85}$$

This set can be reduced further to a single transcendental equation, upon introducing the variable $x = m(1-C)/\sqrt{2\alpha}$, as follows. Multiplying the equation for C by m gives $mC = 2x\, e^{-x^2}/\sqrt{\pi}$. Subtracting this from $m = \text{erf}(x)$ yields $m(1-C) = x\sqrt{2\alpha}$ on the left-hand side and thus

$$x\sqrt{2\alpha} = F(x) \qquad F(x) = \text{erf}(x) - \frac{2x}{\sqrt{\pi}}\, e^{-x^2} \tag{21.86}$$

Equation (21.86) is then solved numerically (see Figure 21.5). Since $F(x)$ is anti-symmetric, the solutions come in pairs $(x, -x)$, reflecting the symmetry of the Hamiltonian of the system with respect to an overall spin-flip $\boldsymbol{\sigma} \to -\boldsymbol{\sigma}$. For $\alpha < \alpha_c \sim 0.138$ there do indeed exist pure state solutions $x \neq 0$.

[45] Here we neglect the low temperature re-entrance peculiarities in the phase diagram (Figure 21.4) arising from the AT instability discussed below.

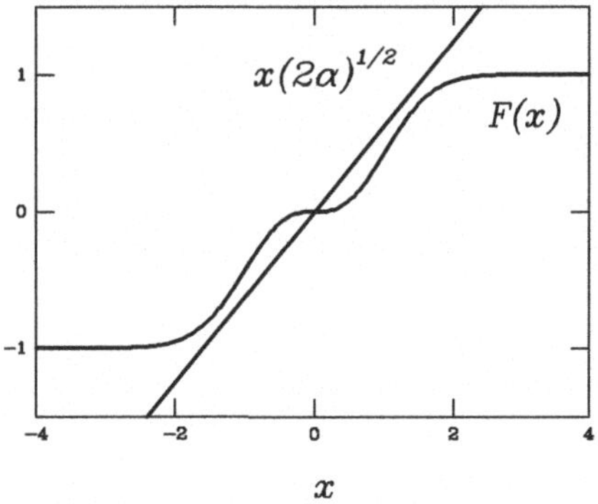

Figure 21.5 Solution of the transcendental equation $F(x) = x\sqrt{2\alpha}$; x is related to the pattern overlap by $m = \text{erf}(x)$. The storage capacity $\alpha_c \sim 0.138$ of the Hopfield model is the largest α for which solutions $x \neq 0$ exist.

For $\alpha > \alpha_c$ there is only the SG solution $x = 0$. Given a solution x of (21.86), the zero temperature values for the order parameters follow from

$$\lim_{T\to 0} m = \text{erf}(x) \qquad \lim_{T\to 0} C = \left(1 + \sqrt{\frac{\alpha\pi}{2}}\, e^{x^2}\right)^{-1}$$

(The second expression is obtained by solving (21.85), in the form $C = (1-C)\sqrt{2/\alpha\pi}\, e^{-x^2}$, for C.) With these values we can then also find the zero temperature limit of our expression (21.84) for the free energy:

$$\lim_{T\to 0} \tilde{f} = \frac{1}{2}\text{erf}^2(x) + \frac{1}{\pi}\, e^{-x^2} - \frac{2}{\pi}\left(e^{-x^2} + \sqrt{\frac{\alpha\pi}{2}}\right)\left(x\sqrt{\pi}\,\text{erf}(x) + e^{-x^2}\right)$$

Comparison of the values for $\lim_{T\to 0} \tilde{f}$ thus obtained, for the pure state $m > 0$ versus those of the SG state $m = 0$ leads to Figure 21.6, which clearly shows that for sufficiently small α the pure states are the true ground states of the system.

Let us summarize the main quantitative conclusions that can now be drawn about information recall in the Hopfield model with an extensive number $p = \alpha N$ of stored patterns, within the RS ansatz of the replica formalism. We saw that for sufficiently small values of the storage ratio, roughly $\alpha < 0.138$, and low noise levels T, patterns can indeed be recalled. Moreover, the recall overlap m is in fact seen to be very close to its maximum value; one finds that $m > 0.97$ in the limit $T \to 0$, even at the onset of recall (see Figure 21.6). This value implies that in such macroscopic (recall) states the percentage of recall errors made by the network, that is, the percentage of spins where $\sigma_i = -\xi_i^\mu$ (given that pattern μ is recalled) is below 1.5%.

Breaking of replica symmetry: the AT Instability

As in the case of the SK spin glass model, the above RS solution generates negative entropies at sufficiently low temperatures, indicating that RS must

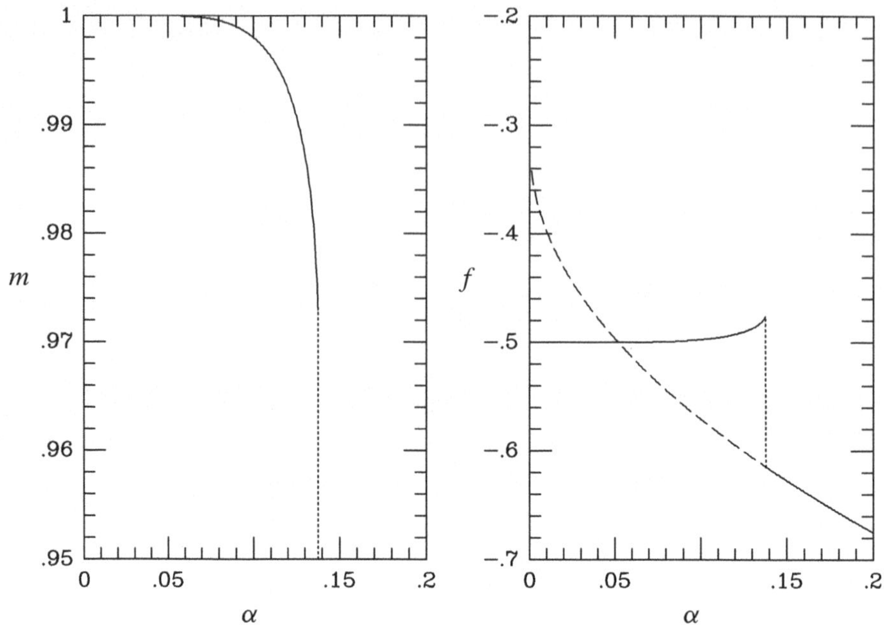

Figure 21.6 Left picture: RS amplitudes m of the pure states of the Hopfield model for $T = 0$ as a function of $\alpha = p/N$. The location of the discontinuity, where m vanishes, defines the storage capacity $\alpha_c \approx 0.138$. Note the vertical scale: even just below α_c, m is still within 3% of perfect retrieval. Right picture, solid line: $T = 0$ free energy f of the pure states. Dashed line and solid continuation: $T = 0$ free energy of the SG state $\boldsymbol{m} = 0$, for comparison.

be broken. If saddle points without replica symmetry bifurcate continuously from the RS one, we can locate the RS breaking by studying the effect on $\tilde{f}(\boldsymbol{m}, \boldsymbol{q}, \hat{\boldsymbol{q}})$ (21.72) of small (so-called 'replicon') fluctuations around the RS solution, following de Almeida and Thouless:

$$
\begin{aligned}
&q_{ab} \to \delta_{ab} + q(1 - \delta_{ab}) + \eta_{ab} \\
&\eta_{ab} = \eta_{ba} \qquad \eta_{aa} = 0 \qquad \sum_a \eta_{ab} = 0
\end{aligned}
\tag{21.87}
$$

The small perturbation of $\boldsymbol{q}$ induces a similar change in the conjugate parameters $\hat{\boldsymbol{q}}$ through equation (21.70):

$$
\begin{aligned}
&\hat{q}_{ab} \to \tfrac{1}{2}\mathrm{i}\alpha\beta^2[R\delta_{ab} + r(1 - \delta_{ab}) + \hat{\eta}_{ab}] \\
&\hat{\eta}_{ab} = \frac{1}{2} \sum_{cd} \eta_{cd}(g_{abcd} - g_{ab}g_{cd})
\end{aligned}
$$

with

$$g_{abcd} = \frac{\int \mathrm{d}z\, z_a z_b z_c z_d\, e^{-z\cdot(\mathbf{1}-\beta \boldsymbol{q}_{\mathrm{RS}})z/2}}{\int \mathrm{d}z\, e^{-z\cdot(\mathbf{1}-\beta \boldsymbol{q}_{\mathrm{RS}})z/2}} \qquad g_{ab} = \frac{\int \mathrm{d}z\, z_a z_b\, e^{-z\cdot(\mathbf{1}-\beta \boldsymbol{q}_{\mathrm{RS}})z/2}}{\int \mathrm{d}z\, e^{-z\cdot(\mathbf{1}-\beta \boldsymbol{q}_{\mathrm{RS}})z/2}}$$

Wick's theorem (which expresses higher order moments of Gaussian variables in terms of the second-order ones, see, e.g., [117]) can now be used to write everything in terms of second moments of the Gaussian integrals only:

$$g_{abcd} = g_{ab}g_{cd} + g_{ac}g_{bd} + g_{ad}g_{bc}$$

With this we can express the replicon variation in $\hat{\boldsymbol{q}}$, using the symmetry of $\{\eta_{ab}\}$ and the saddle point equation (21.70), as

$$\begin{aligned}
\hat{\eta}_{ab} &= \sum_{cd} g_{ac}\eta_{cd}g_{db} \\
&= \beta^2 \sum_{c\neq d} [R\delta_{ac} + r(1-\delta_{ac})]\eta_{cd}[R\delta_{db} + r(1-\delta_{db})] \\
&= \beta^2 (R-r)^2 \eta_{ab}
\end{aligned} \tag{21.88}$$

(since only those terms can contribute which involve precisely two δ-symbols, as a consequence of $\sum_a \eta_{ab} = 0$).

We can now calculate the resulting change in $\tilde{f}(\boldsymbol{m}, \boldsymbol{q}, \hat{\boldsymbol{q}})$, away from the RS value $\tilde{f}(\boldsymbol{m}_{\mathrm{RS}}, \boldsymbol{q}_{\mathrm{RS}}, \hat{\boldsymbol{q}}_{\mathrm{RS}})$, the leading order of which must be quadratic in the fluctuations $\{\eta_{ab}\}$ since the RS solution (21.79–21.81) is a saddle point:

$$\begin{aligned}
\tilde{f}(\boldsymbol{m}_{\mathrm{RS}}, \boldsymbol{q}, \hat{\boldsymbol{q}}) = \tilde{f}(\boldsymbol{m}_{\mathrm{RS}}, \boldsymbol{q}_{\mathrm{RS}}, \hat{\boldsymbol{q}}_{\mathrm{RS}}) + \frac{1}{\beta n}\Bigg[&\frac{1}{2}\alpha \ln\left(\frac{\det(\mathbf{1}-\beta(\boldsymbol{q}_{\mathrm{RS}}+\boldsymbol{\eta}))}{\det(\mathbf{1}-\beta \boldsymbol{q}_{\mathrm{RS}})}\right) \\
&- \mathrm{i}\,\mathrm{tr}(\hat{\boldsymbol{q}}_{\mathrm{RS}}\boldsymbol{\eta}) + \frac{1}{2}\alpha\beta^2\,\mathrm{tr}(\hat{\boldsymbol{\eta}}\boldsymbol{\eta} + \hat{\boldsymbol{\eta}}\boldsymbol{q}_{\mathrm{RS}}) \\
&- \left\langle \ln\left(\frac{\sum_{\sigma} e^{\beta\boldsymbol{\xi}\cdot\boldsymbol{m}_{\mathrm{RS}}\sum_a \sigma^a - \mathrm{i}\sigma\cdot(\hat{\boldsymbol{q}}_{\mathrm{RS}}+\mathrm{i}\alpha\beta^2\hat{\boldsymbol{\eta}}/2)\sigma}}{\sum_{\sigma} e^{\beta\boldsymbol{\xi}\cdot\boldsymbol{m}_{\mathrm{RS}}\sum_a \sigma^a - \mathrm{i}\sigma\cdot\hat{\boldsymbol{q}}_{\mathrm{RS}}\sigma}}\right)\right\rangle_{\boldsymbol{\xi}}\Bigg]
\end{aligned} \tag{21.89}$$

This expression looks more awkward than it actually is. Evaluation is greatly simplified by the fact that the matrices $\boldsymbol{q}_{\mathrm{RS}}$ and $\boldsymbol{\eta}$ commute, which is a direct consequence of the properties (21.87) of the replicon fluctuations and the form of the replica-symmetric saddle point. If we define the $n \times n$ matrix $\boldsymbol{P}$ to be the projection onto the uniform state $(1, \ldots, 1)$, we have

$P_{ab} = 1/n$ and thus the relations

$$\begin{aligned}
&\boldsymbol{q}_{\text{RS}} = (1-q)\mathbf{1} + nq\boldsymbol{P}, \qquad \boldsymbol{P}\eta = \eta\boldsymbol{P} = 0 \\
&\boldsymbol{q}_{\text{RS}}\eta = \eta\boldsymbol{q}_{\text{RS}} = (1-q)\eta \\
&(\mathbf{1} - \beta\boldsymbol{q}_{\text{RS}})^{-1} = \frac{\mathbf{1}}{1-\beta(1-q)} \\
&\qquad + \frac{\beta nq\boldsymbol{P}}{[1-\beta(1-q)-\beta nq][1-\beta(1-q)]}
\end{aligned} \tag{21.90}$$

We can now simply expand the relevant terms, using the identity $\ln(\det \boldsymbol{M}) = \text{tr}(\ln \boldsymbol{M})$:

$$\begin{aligned}
&\ln\left(\frac{\det(\mathbf{1} - \beta(\boldsymbol{q}_{\text{RS}} + \eta))}{\det(\mathbf{1} - \beta\boldsymbol{q}_{\text{RS}})}\right) \\
&= \text{tr}\ln(\mathbf{1} - \beta\eta(\mathbf{1} - \beta\boldsymbol{q}_{\text{RS}})^{-1}) \\
&= \text{tr}\left[-\beta\eta(\mathbf{1} - \beta\boldsymbol{q}_{\text{RS}})^{-1} - \frac{1}{2}\beta^2[\eta(\mathbf{1} - \beta\boldsymbol{q}_{\text{RS}})^{-1}]^2\right] + \mathcal{O}(\eta^3) \\
&= -\frac{1}{2}\frac{\beta^2}{[1-\beta(1-q)]^2}\text{tr}(\eta^2) + \mathcal{O}(\eta^3)
\end{aligned} \tag{21.91}$$

Finally we address the remaining term in (21.89), again using the RS saddle point equations (21.79–21.81) where appropriate:

$$\begin{aligned}
&\left\langle \ln\left(\left\{\sum_{\sigma} e^{\beta\xi\cdot\boldsymbol{m}_{\text{RS}}\sum_a \sigma^a - \text{i}\sigma\cdot\hat{\boldsymbol{q}}_{\text{RS}}\sigma}\left[1 + \frac{1}{2}\alpha\beta^2\boldsymbol{\sigma}\cdot\hat{\eta}\boldsymbol{\sigma} + \frac{1}{8}\alpha^2\beta^4(\boldsymbol{\sigma}\cdot\hat{\eta}\boldsymbol{\sigma})^2 + \cdots\right]\right\}\right.\right. \\
&\qquad \times \left.\left.\left(\sum_{\sigma} e^{\beta\xi\cdot\boldsymbol{m}_{\text{RS}}\sum_a \sigma^a - \text{i}\sigma\cdot\hat{\boldsymbol{q}}_{\text{RS}}\sigma}\right)^{-1}\right)\right\rangle_{\xi} \\
&= \frac{1}{2}\alpha\beta^2\text{tr}(\hat{\eta}\boldsymbol{q}_{\text{RS}}) + \frac{1}{8}\alpha^2\beta^4\sum_{abcd}\hat{\eta}_{ab}\hat{\eta}_{cd}(G_{abcd} - H_{abcd}) + \cdots
\end{aligned} \tag{21.92}$$

with

$$G_{abcd} = \left\langle \frac{\sum_{\sigma}\sigma^a\sigma^b\sigma^c\sigma^d\, e^{\beta\xi\cdot\boldsymbol{m}_{\text{RS}}\sum_a \sigma^a - \text{i}\sigma\cdot\hat{\boldsymbol{q}}_{\text{RS}}\sigma}}{\sum_{\sigma} e^{\beta\xi\cdot\boldsymbol{m}_{\text{RS}}\sum_a \sigma^a - \text{i}\sigma\cdot\hat{\boldsymbol{q}}_{\text{RS}}\sigma}} \right\rangle_{\xi}$$

$$H_{abcd} = \left\langle \frac{\sum_{\sigma}\sigma^a\sigma^b\, e^{\beta\xi\cdot\boldsymbol{m}_{\text{RS}}\sum_a \sigma^a - \text{i}\sigma\cdot\hat{\boldsymbol{q}}_{\text{RS}}\sigma}}{\sum_{\sigma} e^{\beta\xi\cdot\boldsymbol{m}_{\text{RS}}\sum_a \sigma^a - \text{i}\sigma\cdot\hat{\boldsymbol{q}}_{\text{RS}}\sigma}} \frac{\sum_{\sigma}\sigma^c\sigma^d\, e^{\beta\xi\cdot\boldsymbol{m}_{\text{RS}}\sum_a \sigma^a - \text{i}\sigma\cdot\hat{\boldsymbol{q}}_{\text{RS}}\sigma}}{\sum_{\sigma} e^{\beta\xi\cdot\boldsymbol{m}_{\text{RS}}\sum_a \sigma^a - \text{i}\sigma\cdot\hat{\boldsymbol{q}}_{\text{RS}}\sigma}} \right\rangle_{\xi}$$

Inserting the ingredients (21.88, 21.90–21.92) into expression (21.89) and rearranging terms shows that the linear terms indeed cancel and that the term involving H_{abcd} does not contribute (since the elements H_{abcd} do not depend on the indices for $a \neq b$ and $c \neq d$). We are thus just left with:

$$
\begin{aligned}
&\tilde{f}(\boldsymbol{m}_{\mathrm{RS}}, \boldsymbol{q}, \hat{\boldsymbol{q}}) - \tilde{f}(\boldsymbol{m}_{\mathrm{RS}}, \boldsymbol{q}_{\mathrm{RS}}, \hat{\boldsymbol{q}}_{\mathrm{RS}}) \\
&\quad = \frac{1}{\beta n}\left[-\frac{1}{4}\frac{\alpha\beta^2}{[1-\beta(1-q)]^2}\,\mathrm{tr}(\eta^2) + \frac{1}{2}\alpha\beta^4(R-r)^2\,\mathrm{tr}(\eta^2)\right. \\
&\qquad \left. -\frac{1}{8}\alpha^2\beta^8(R-r)^4\sum_{abcd}\eta_{ab}\eta_{cd}G_{abcd}\right] + \cdots
\end{aligned}
$$

Because of the index permutation symmetry in the spin-average we can write for $a \neq b$ and $c \neq d$:

$$
\begin{aligned}
G_{abcd} &= \delta_{ac}\delta_{bd} + \delta_{ad}\delta_{bc} + G_4(1-\delta_{ac})(1-\delta_{bd})(1-\delta_{ad})(1-\delta_{bc}) \\
&\quad + G_2\{\delta_{ac}(1-\delta_{bd}) + \delta_{bd}(1-\delta_{ac}) + \delta_{ad}(1-\delta_{bc}) + \delta_{bc}(1-\delta_{ad})\}
\end{aligned}
$$

with

$$
G_\ell = \left\langle \frac{\int Dz\,\tanh^\ell(\beta(\boldsymbol{m}\cdot\boldsymbol{\xi} + z\sqrt{\alpha r}))\cosh^n(\beta(\boldsymbol{m}\cdot\boldsymbol{\xi} + z\sqrt{\alpha r})}{\int Dz\,\cosh^n(\beta(\boldsymbol{m}\cdot\boldsymbol{\xi} + z\sqrt{\alpha r})} \right\rangle_{\boldsymbol{\xi}}
$$

Only those terms which involve precisely two δ-functions can contribute, because of the replicon properties (21.87). As a result:

$$
\begin{aligned}
&\tilde{f}(\boldsymbol{m}_{\mathrm{RS}}, \boldsymbol{q}, \hat{\boldsymbol{q}}) - \tilde{f}(\boldsymbol{m}_{\mathrm{RS}}, \boldsymbol{q}_{\mathrm{RS}}, \hat{\boldsymbol{q}}_{\mathrm{RS}}) \\
&\quad = \frac{1}{\beta n}\mathrm{tr}(\eta^2)\left[-\frac{1}{4}\frac{\alpha\beta^2}{[1-\beta(1-q)]^2} + \frac{1}{2}\alpha\beta^4(R-r)^2\right. \\
&\qquad \left. -\frac{1}{4}\alpha^2\beta^8(R-r)^4(1-2G_2+G_4)\right] + \cdots
\end{aligned}
$$

Since $\mathrm{tr}(\eta^2) = \sum_{ab}\eta_{ab}^2$, the condition for the RS solution to minimize $\tilde{f}(\boldsymbol{m}, \boldsymbol{q}, \hat{\boldsymbol{q}})$, if compared to the replicon fluctuations, is therefore

$$
-\frac{1}{[1-\beta(1-q)]^2} + 2\beta^2(R-r)^2 - \alpha\beta^6(R-r)^4(1-2G_2+G_4) > 0 \tag{21.93}
$$

After taking the limit in the expressions G_ℓ and after evaluating

$$\lim_{n\to 0} R = \frac{1}{\beta}\lim_{n\to 0} g_{aa} = \lim_{n\to 0}\frac{1}{n\beta}\frac{\int \mathrm{d}\mathbf{z}\, z^2\, e^{-\mathbf{z}\cdot(\mathbf{1}-\beta \boldsymbol{q}_{\mathrm{RS}})\mathbf{z}/2}}{\int \mathrm{d}\mathbf{z}\, e^{-\mathbf{z}\cdot(\mathbf{1}-\beta \boldsymbol{q}_{\mathrm{RS}})\mathbf{z}/2}}$$

$$= \lim_{n\to 0}\frac{1}{n\beta}\left[\frac{n-1}{1-\beta(1-q)} + \frac{1}{1-\beta(1-q+nq)}\right]$$

$$= \frac{1}{\beta}\frac{1-\beta+2\beta q}{[1-\beta(1-q)]^2}$$

and using (21.81), the condition (21.93) can be written as

$$1 > \frac{\alpha\beta^2}{[1-\beta(1-q)]^2}\int Dz\langle \cosh^{-4}(\beta(\boldsymbol{m}\cdot\boldsymbol{\xi} + z\sqrt{\alpha r}))\rangle_{\boldsymbol{\xi}} \qquad (21.94)$$

The AT line in the phase diagram, where this condition ceases to be met, indicates a second-order transition to a spin glass state where ergodicity is broken in the sense that the distribution $\overline{P(q)}$ from (21.74) is no longer a δ-function.

In the paramagnetic regime of the phase diagram, that is, $\boldsymbol{m} = q = 0$, the AT condition reduces precisely to $T > T_g = 1 + \sqrt{\alpha}$. Therefore we can be sure that the paramagnetic solution is stable. The AT line coincides with the boundary between the paramagnetic and SG phase. Numerical evaluation of (21.94) shows that the RS–SG solution remains unstable for all $T < T_g$, but that the retrieval solution $\boldsymbol{m} \neq 0$ is unstable only for very low temperatures $T < T_R$ (see Figure 21.4).

21.4 Exercises

Exercise 21.1. (Constrained-free energy versus pseudo-free energy.) For the infinite range ferromagnet studied in Section 20.4, we could use the same trick as for the Hopfield model (Section 21.1) to define a pseudo-free energy $\tilde{f}(m)$. Leaving the saddle point value of x in (20.41) undetermined, we can obtain the free energy as the stationary point of

$$f(m,x) = -\tfrac{1}{2}Jm^2 - \mathrm{i}Txm - T\ln(2\cos(x))$$

with respect to variation of m and x; see the discussion before equation (21.14). The stationarity (saddle point) condition for m gives

$$-Jm - \mathrm{i}Tx = 0 \Rightarrow x = \mathrm{i}\beta Jm$$

Using this to find x (rather than m, as we should if we were really evaluating the saddle point with respect to m) and inserting the result into $f(m, x)$, gives the pseudo-free energy

$$\tilde{f}(m) = \tfrac{1}{2}Jm^2 - T\ln(2\cosh(\beta Jm))$$

Plot this function versus m for different values of T, along with the true constrained free energy $f(m)$ (equations (20.37) and (20.42)). You should find, in agreement with the general discussion after (21.15), that $\tilde{f}$ and f are different in general, but agree in the values at their stationary points.

Exercise 21.2. (Hopfield model with $p = 2$.) Consider the Hopfield model with $p = 2$, for randomly chosen patterns. Use the fact that $\cosh(x) = \cosh(-x)$ to confirm that the (pseudo-)free energy (21.15) becomes

$$\begin{aligned}\tilde{f}(m_1, m_2) = \tfrac{1}{2}(m_1^2 + m_2^2) - \tfrac{1}{2}T\ln(2\cosh(\beta(m_1 + m_2)))\\ - \tfrac{1}{2}T\ln(2\cosh(\beta(m_1 - m_2)))\end{aligned}$$

Plot this as a function of m_1 and m_2, for different T. For $T < 1$ you should see nine stationary points. Which ones are stable (local minima) and unstable (saddle points or local maxima), and does this agree with our discussion of the stability of mixture states? We have discussed the appearance of retrieval states ($\boldsymbol{m} \neq 0$) by expanding the saddle point condition (21.13) for small $\boldsymbol{m}$. Equivalently, one can of course expand the (pseudo-) free energy $\tilde{f}(\boldsymbol{m})$ around $\boldsymbol{m} = 0$. Do this expansion, to second order in $\boldsymbol{m}$, for (i) the concrete example $p = 2$ above, and (ii) generally for the case of p random patterns. Either way, you should find that the point $\boldsymbol{m} = 0$ becomes unstable, that is, ceases to be a local minimum, at $T = 1$. Note: In principle, one should use the true constrained free energy $f(\boldsymbol{m})$—see next problem—to analyse stability. However, it turns out that using the pseudo-free energy $\tilde{f}(\boldsymbol{m})$, as suggested, actually gives the correct results. Compare with the discussion before equation (21.23).

Exercise 21.3. (More on the Hopfield model with $p = 2$.) In the Hopfield model with a finite number p of patterns, it is generally not possible to give an explicit expression for the log-density of states $s(\boldsymbol{m})$, see equation (21.7), because the saddle point condition (21.11) for $\boldsymbol{x}$ cannot be solved explicitly for $\boldsymbol{x}$. However, for $p = 2$, this can be done. Proceed as follows. Anticipating that $\boldsymbol{x}$ will be imaginary, set $\boldsymbol{x} = i\hat{\boldsymbol{m}}$. Show that $s(\boldsymbol{m}) = \text{extr}_{\hat{\boldsymbol{m}}} s(\boldsymbol{m}, \hat{\boldsymbol{m}})$ with

$$s(\boldsymbol{m}, \hat{\boldsymbol{m}}) = -m_1\hat{m}_1 - m_2\hat{m}_2 + \frac{1}{N}\sum_i \ln(2\cosh(\xi_i^1\hat{m}_1 + \xi_i^2\hat{m}_2))$$

Use the symmetry of the function cosh to write its argument as $\hat{m}_1+\xi_i^1\xi_i^2\hat{m}_2$; carry out the sum over i to get

$$s(\boldsymbol{m},\hat{\boldsymbol{m}}) = -m_1\hat{m}_1 - m_2\hat{m}_2 + \tfrac{1}{2}(1+\alpha)\ln(2\cosh(\hat{m}_1+\hat{m}_2)) + \tfrac{1}{2}(1-\alpha)\ln(2\cosh(\hat{m}_1-\hat{m}_2))$$

where $\alpha = N^{-1}\sum_i \xi_i^1\xi_i^2$. Now write down the extremum conditions with respect to variation of $(\hat{m}_1, \hat{m}_2)$ and solve them explicitly. Insert the solution into $s(\boldsymbol{m},\hat{\boldsymbol{m}})$ and rearrange the expression to show that the end result is of the simple form

$$s(m_1,m_2) = \tfrac{1}{2}(1+\alpha)s_1(m_+) + \tfrac{1}{2}(1-\alpha)s_1(m_-)$$

where $m_\pm = (m_1 \pm m_2)/(1\pm\alpha)$ and $s_1(m) = -[(1+m)/2]\ln[(1+m)/2] - [(1-m)/2]\ln[(1-m)/2]$ is the density of states that we found for $p=1$. There must be a simple explanation for such a simple result. Construct an explanation from the fact that m_1+m_2 (respectively m_1-m_2) only depends on the spins/neurons σ_i at the sites i where $\xi_i^1=\xi_i^2$ (respectively $\xi_i^1\neq\xi_i^2$). Finally, use your explicit expression for $s(\boldsymbol{m})$ in (21.9) to get the explicit constrained free energy $f(\boldsymbol{m})$. Compare this with the pseudo-free energy from the previous exercise; you may want to repeat some of the analysis there. Also derive the equations for stationary points of $f(\boldsymbol{m})$ and show that they are equivalent to (21.13), as they should be.

Exercise 21.4. (Stability of mixture states.) We saw that n-mixture states in the Hopfield model are never stable for even n. It is not trivial to find a simple explanation for this, but you can get some insight by focusing on the limit of $T\to 0$. Consider the first part of (21.20), which can be written as

$$\begin{aligned} m_n &= \langle \xi^1 \tanh[\beta m_n(\xi_1 + M')]\rangle_{\boldsymbol{\xi}} \\ &= \tfrac{1}{2}\langle\tanh[\beta m_n(M'+1)]\rangle_{M'} - \tfrac{1}{2}\langle\tanh[\beta m_n(M'-1)]\rangle_{M'} \end{aligned}$$

where $M' = \sum_{\nu=2}^{n}\xi_\nu$. Note that M' can only take integer values in the range $-n+1, -n+3, \ldots, n-1$. In the limit $\beta\to\infty$, show that the equation for m_n becomes

$$m_n = \tfrac{1}{2}\text{Prob}[M'=-1] + \text{Prob}[M'=0] + \tfrac{1}{2}\text{Prob}[M'=1]$$

Using the fact that, for random patterns, $\text{Prob}[M'=k]$ is directly related to a binomial distribution, show that

$$m_n = 2^{1-n}\binom{n-1}{\lfloor n/2\rfloor}$$

where $\lfloor z \rfloor$ ('floor') is the largest integer $\leq z$. Deduce that $m_{2k} = m_{2k+1}$, that is, the pattern overlap for an even mixture is 'as bad' as that of the odd mixture with one additional pattern. Consider also the corresponding free energies $f_n = -\frac{1}{2}nm_n^2$ (there is no entropic contribution, since we are looking at $T = 0$). Show that f_{2k} decreases as k increases, while f_{2k+1} increases as k increases. Hint: Consider ratios such as f_{2k}/f_{2k+2}. Finally, use the Stirling approximation to show that both sequences of free energies converge to $-1/\pi$ for large k. This implies that all f_{2k} are *larger* than $-1/\pi$, while all f_{2k+1} are *smaller*. At $T = 0$, any even mixture state thus has a higher free energy than an odd mixture state. The result does not say anything about the stability of the even mixture states, but at least it suggests that the even mixtures are systematically worse than the odd mixtures.

Exercise 21.5. (Hopfield model with biased patterns.) Consider the Hopfield model with a finite number of *biased* patterns, where the pattern bits are still drawn independently from each other, but where now the probability of drawing ± 1 is $(1 \pm a)/2$ rather than $1/2$ (as for unbiased patterns). For the case $p = 2$, show that the pseudo-free energy is now

$$\tilde{f}(m_1, m_2) = \tfrac{1}{2}(m_1^2 + m_2^2) - \tfrac{1}{2}(1 + a^2)T\ln(2\cosh(\beta(m_1 + m_2))) \\ - \tfrac{1}{2}(1 - a^2)T\ln(2\cosh(\beta(m_1 - m_2)))$$

Plot this against m_1 and m_2. Experimenting with different values of a and T, try to guess at what temperature retrieval states, that is, stationary points with nonzero $\boldsymbol{m}$, first appear. How are m_1 and m_2 in the retrieval states related? Now try to find the answers to these questions analytically, for general p, by expanding the pseudo-free energy (21.15) to second order around $\boldsymbol{m} = 0$ (as in Exercise 21.2). To do this, first show that

$$\langle \xi^\mu \xi^\nu \rangle = a^2 + (1 - a^2)\delta_{\mu\nu}$$

by considering the two cases $\mu = \nu$ and $\mu \neq \nu$ separately. Using this result, you should find

$$\tilde{f}(\boldsymbol{m}) = -T\ln 2 + \tfrac{1}{2}\boldsymbol{m} \cdot \boldsymbol{M}\boldsymbol{m} + \mathcal{O}(\boldsymbol{m}^4)$$

where $\boldsymbol{M}$ is a $p \times p$ matrix whose diagonal and off-diagonal entries equal $1 - \beta$ and $-\beta a^2$, respectively. Show that this matrix has eigenvalues $1 - \beta(1 - a^2)$, with degeneracy $(p - 1)$, and $1 - \beta[1 + (p - 1)a^2]$ (non-degenerate). Use the fact that the second eigenvalue is always smaller than the first to show that the state $\boldsymbol{m} = 0$ becomes unstable (thus leading to the appearance of retrieval states) at the temperature $T_c = 1 + (p - 1)a^2$. Compare this with your earlier guess. Finally, the eigenvector of $\boldsymbol{m}$ corresponding to the eigenvalue which becomes zero at $T = T_c$ tells you in which direction in $\boldsymbol{m}$-space the retrieval states will bifurcate from the state with $\boldsymbol{m} = 0$. Deduce from this that near T_c, retrieval states obey $m_1 = m_2 = \cdots = m_p$, and compare this once more with your earlier empirical observations. To which simpler model does the Hopfield model with biased patterns reduce for $a \to 1$? Use this relationship to check that your answers to the previous parts of the question are indeed sensible in this limit.

Exercise 21.6. (Generalized Hopfield model.) Consider a generalized Hopfield model for a finite number p of patterns, with non-diagonal interactions

$$J_{ij} = \frac{1}{N} \sum_{\mu,\nu=1}^{p} \xi_i^\mu A_{\mu\nu} \xi_j^\nu$$

The $A_{\mu\nu}$ are the elements of a positive definite symmetric $p \times p$ matrix $\boldsymbol{A}$. Note that for $A_{\mu\nu} = \delta_{\mu\nu}$, the standard Hopfield model is recovered. Show that, up to negligible $\mathcal{O}(1)$ terms, the Hamiltonian for this model can be written as

$$H = -\frac{N}{2} \sum_{\mu\nu} m_\mu(\boldsymbol{\sigma}) A_{\mu\nu} m_\nu(\boldsymbol{\sigma})$$

with the pattern overlaps $m_\mu(\boldsymbol{\sigma}) = N^{-1} \sum_{i=1}^{N} \xi_i^\mu \sigma_i$ defined as usual. Show that

$$Z = \int \mathrm{d}\boldsymbol{m}\, e^{N\beta \boldsymbol{m}\cdot\boldsymbol{A}\boldsymbol{m}/2} \mathcal{D}(\boldsymbol{m})$$

where $\boldsymbol{m} = (m_1, \ldots, m_p)$ and where $\mathcal{D}(\boldsymbol{m})$ is the density of states. Repeat for the present model the analysis that we went through for the original Hopfield model; in particular, show that the free energy per neuron f is here given by the stationary point(s) of

$$f(\boldsymbol{m}, \boldsymbol{x}) = -\tfrac{1}{2}\boldsymbol{m} \cdot \boldsymbol{A}\boldsymbol{m} - \mathrm{i}T\boldsymbol{x} \cdot \boldsymbol{m} - T\langle \ln(2\cos(\boldsymbol{\xi} \cdot \boldsymbol{x}))\rangle_{\boldsymbol{\xi}}$$

and that the saddle point conditions are $\boldsymbol{m} = \langle \boldsymbol{\xi} \tanh(\beta\boldsymbol{\xi} \cdot \boldsymbol{A}\boldsymbol{m})\rangle_{\boldsymbol{\xi}}$. What is the physical interpretation of the fact that these equations can have multiple solutions at small values of $T = \beta^{-1}$? Using the same trick that led to equation (21.18), show that $\boldsymbol{m} \cdot \boldsymbol{A}\boldsymbol{m} \leq \beta\langle(\boldsymbol{\xi} \cdot \boldsymbol{A}\boldsymbol{m})^2\rangle_{\boldsymbol{\xi}}$. For the case of random patterns, deduce that

$$\boldsymbol{m} \cdot \boldsymbol{A}(\beta\boldsymbol{A} - \mathbf{1})\boldsymbol{m} \geq 0$$

Find from this the smallest temperature below which non-trivial saddle points $\boldsymbol{m}$ can exist.

Exercise 21.7. (Saddle point integration for an extensive number of order parameters.) Suppose we have a system of N spins or neurons which is described by p order parameters $\boldsymbol{m} = (m_1, \ldots, m_p)$. Suppose also that we have been able to work out the constrained free energy per spin and that it is given by

$$f(\boldsymbol{m}) = \frac{1}{2p}\boldsymbol{m}^2 = \frac{1}{2p}\sum_{\mu=1}^{p} m_\mu^2$$

Our goal now is to find the free energy, which by definition of the constrained free energy is given by

$$f = -\frac{T}{N}\ln\int \mathrm{d}\boldsymbol{m}\, e^{-N\beta f(\boldsymbol{m})}$$

For the quadratic $f(\boldsymbol{m})$ assumed here, one can do the p-dimensional integral exactly, since it just factorizes into p Gaussian integrals. Thus show that

$$f = -\frac{Tp}{2N}\ln\left(\frac{2\pi Tp}{N}\right)$$

Compare this with the result you get if you evaluate the integral by saddle point (SP) integration. Confirm that SP gives the correct result in the thermodynamic limit $N \to \infty$ when p is finite, but that it is incorrect when p is extensive (i.e. when $p = \alpha N$ for some nonzero $\alpha > 0$). Intuition: SP neglects the fluctuations of the order parameters around their most likely value. This is fine if there are only a finite number of order parameters, but for an extensive number, the contributions from the fluctuations add up such as to remain non-negligible even for $N \to \infty$.

Exercise 21.8. (Bifurcations in the SK model.) Perform explicitly the small-$\boldsymbol{m}$ and small-$\boldsymbol{q}$ expansion of the (finite-n) saddle point equations (21.42–21.44) for the SK model. Proceed as follows. First show, by treating terms involving q_{aa} separately, that

$$\kappa(\boldsymbol{\sigma}) = \exp\left(\tfrac{1}{2}n\beta^2 J^2\right)\tilde{\kappa}(\boldsymbol{\sigma})$$

where

$$\tilde{\kappa}(\boldsymbol{\sigma}) = \exp\left(\frac{1}{2}\beta^2 J^2 \sum_{a\neq b} q_{ab}\sigma^a\sigma^b + \beta J_0 \sum_a m_a\sigma^a\right)$$

Convince yourself that equations (21.42, 21.43) hold with κ replaced by $\tilde{\kappa}$ everywhere. Now expand $\tilde{\kappa}$ to first order in the m_a and q_{ab} ($a \neq b$), and carry out the sums over $\boldsymbol{\sigma}$ occurring in (21.42, 21.43). Note that $\sum_{\boldsymbol{\sigma}}$ of any product containing an odd number of spins is zero (e.g. $\sum_{\boldsymbol{\sigma}} \sigma^a = 0$), and that products of an even number of spins are nonzero only if each spin occurs an even number of times (e.g. $\sum_{\boldsymbol{\sigma}} \sigma^a\sigma^b = 2^n\delta_{ab}$). These arguments parallel those leading to equations (21.16, 21.17). Your results should agree with the equations (21.45). Also try to do the next order of the expansion.

Exercise 21.9. (RS saddle point equations of the SK model.) Confirm the statement after equation (21.56): find the conditions for the RS free energy (21.54) to be stationary with respect to variation of m and q. For m you should directly get (21.56), whereas for q you should find

$$\frac{1}{2}\beta J^2(1-q) = \frac{J}{2\sqrt{q}} \int \frac{\mathrm{d}z}{2\pi}\, e^{-z^2/2} z \tanh(\beta(J_0 m + Jz\sqrt{q}))$$

where the Gaussian measure Dz has been written out explicitly. Now use integration by parts (differentiate the tanh, and integrate the remainder of the integrand) to bring this into the following form (which is equivalent to (21.55)):

$$1 - q = \int \frac{\mathrm{d}z}{2\pi}\, e^{-z^2/2}[1 - \tanh^2(\beta(J_0 m + Jz\sqrt{q}))]$$

Exercise 21.10. (Bifurcations of RS saddle points in the SK model.) The bifurcations at $T = J$ and $T = J_0$ were already dealt with in a previous exercise, without the assumption of RS. You can of course also get these bifurcations within RS, by expanding equations (21.55, 21.56) for small m and q; try this. You should find that at the bifurcation to the ferromagnetic phase, $q \propto m^2$. The third bifurcation, at $T = J_0(1-q)$, is from a phase with $q > 0$, $m = 0$ to one with $q > 0$ and $m \neq 0$. To find this third bifurcation, expand equation (21.56) for small m. Use the Taylor expansion of tanh to show

$$\tanh(\beta(Jz\sqrt{q}+J_0 m)) = \tanh(\beta Jz\sqrt{q}) + m\beta J_0[1-\tanh^2(\beta Jz\sqrt{q})] + \mathcal{O}(m^2)$$

Integrating over Dz should then give you $m = m\beta J_0(1-q) + \cdots$. Make sure you understand why this implies a bifurcation at $T = J_0(1-q)$. Show also that the neglected higher order terms are $\mathcal{O}(m^3)$ (rather than $\mathcal{O}(m^2)$). Hint: Think about how a change of sign of m affects the right-hand sides of equations (21.55, 21.56).

Exercise 21.11. (Link between solutions of SK model and of Hopfield model.) From our discussion at the beginning of Section 21.2, one would expect that the replicated Hamiltonian (21.63) of the Hopfield model should, in the limit $\alpha \to \infty$, become identical to that (21.35) of the SK model without the ferromagnetic part, that is, with $J_0 = 0$. In this exercise we check this. In (21.25), we found that for $\alpha \to \infty$ the couplings $J_{ij} = J_{ji}$ of the Hopfield model become independent Gaussian random variables, with zero mean and variance α/N. In the SK model with $J_0 = 0$, this variance is given by J^2/N. To find a correspondence with the SK model, we therefore need to consider a Hopfield model with rescaled non-diagonal couplings

$$J_{ij} = \frac{J}{N\sqrt{\alpha}} \sum_{\mu=1}^{p} \xi_i^\mu \xi_j^\mu$$

with $J_{ii} = 0$ as usual. Work through the calculation of the replicated Hamiltonian with these couplings; you should find, instead of (21.63),

$$\frac{1}{N}\Phi(\{\sigma\}) = -\frac{J}{2\sqrt{\alpha}} \sum_\mu \sum_a (m_\mu^a(\{\sigma\}))^2 + \frac{nJ\sqrt{\alpha}}{2} + \frac{T\alpha}{2} \ln\det\left(\mathbf{1} - \frac{\beta J}{\sqrt{\alpha}} \boldsymbol{q}(\{\sigma\})\right)$$

Write the eigenvalues of the matrix $\boldsymbol{q}(\{\sigma\})$ as $Q_1, \ldots, Q_n$. Show that the last ('ln det') term equals

$$\sum_\gamma \ln\left(1 - \frac{\beta J}{\sqrt{\alpha}} Q_\gamma\right)$$

Expand this to second order in the Q_γ, to show that

$$\begin{aligned}
\frac{T\alpha}{2} \ln\det\left(\mathbf{1} - \frac{\beta J}{\sqrt{\alpha}} \boldsymbol{q}(\{\sigma\})\right) &= \sum_\gamma \left(-\frac{J\sqrt{\alpha}}{2} Q_\gamma - \frac{\beta J^2}{4} Q_\gamma^2\right) + \mathcal{O}(\alpha^{-1/2}) \\
&= -\frac{J\sqrt{\alpha}}{2} \operatorname{tr} \boldsymbol{q}(\{\sigma\}) - \frac{\beta J^2}{4} \operatorname{tr} \boldsymbol{q}^2(\{\sigma\}) \\
&\quad + \mathcal{O}(\alpha^{-1/2})
\end{aligned}$$

Deduce from definition (21.61) that $\operatorname{tr} \boldsymbol{q}(\{\sigma\}) = n$, and hence that for $\alpha \to \infty$

$$\frac{1}{N}\Phi(\{\sigma\}) = -\frac{\beta J^2}{4} \operatorname{Tr} \boldsymbol{q}^2(\{\sigma\})$$

This is the same as the replicated SK Hamiltonian (21.35) with $J_0 = 0$, as anticipated.

22 Gardner theory of task realizability

Our convergence proofs and dynamical analyses of learning processes have so far always relied on the *existence* of a solution, that is, on the existence of a specific allocation of values to the network's parameters (synapses and thresholds) such that the resulting network faithfully generates the correct outputs for the input data presented in the learning stage. This guaranteed that we could regard the input–output relationships to be learned as having been generated by a suitable 'teacher network', a property on which our methods have relied quite heavily. Here we turn to the following complementary question: how can we predict beforehand whether certain families of tasks are indeed solvable by the architecture at hand, without actually constructing the teacher network?

In the previous chapters we have described the application of statistical mechanical techniques in the analysis of the stochastic process that represents the operation of recurrent neural networks with binary neurons and *fixed* neuronal interactions. One can easily convince oneself that the various learning algorithms that we have defined and studied can be regarded as stochastic processes (see Chapter 17), but, in contrast to network operation, they will almost never obey detailed balance. This would suggest that here there is no role for equilibrium statistical mechanics. Yet, perhaps somewhat surprisingly, it was shown by Gardner [95, 96] that equilibrium statistical mechanics can find fruitful applications also in learning theory. More specifically, it provides systematic methods for answering the questions posed in the previous paragraph.

22.1 The space of interactions

Proving existence of solutions by calculating volumes and free energies

Suppose we wish to determine the existence or otherwise of the solution $\boldsymbol{w}^\star$ of a mathematical problem that can be written as a set of equations or inequalities to be satisfied by a vector or group of variables $\boldsymbol{w} \in \mathcal{G} \subseteq \mathbb{R}^N$. We denote by $\mathcal{G}$ the space of $\boldsymbol{w}$ values appropriate for the problem at hand.

Let p be the number of constraints to be satisfied by $\boldsymbol{w}$. In order not to complicate matters too much, we suppose that the constraints are all of the same type. Of particular interest is the regime where the number p of constraints is proportional to the number N of adjustable parameters (the components w_i of $\boldsymbol{w}$), that is, where $p = \alpha N$. It is expected that solutions to a problem will exist if $\alpha \ll 1$, as this implies that the number of constraints per adjustable parameter is small, whereas solutions become less and less likely to exist if the number of constraints per adjustable parameter becomes much larger than 1, that is, if $\alpha \gg 1$.

This phenomenon is well known in linear algebra. For instance, suppose we want to solve p linear equations of the form

$$\sum_{i=1}^{N} A_{\mu i} w_i = b_\mu \qquad \mu = 1, \ldots, p$$

with a given $p \times N$ matrix $\boldsymbol{A} = \{A_{\mu i}\}$ and a given right-hand side $\boldsymbol{b} = \{b_\mu\} \in \mathbb{R}^p$. This problem is typically underconstrained if the number p of equations is smaller than N, that is, for $\alpha < 1$, in which case there are infinitely many solutions $\boldsymbol{w}$; these form an $(N - p)$-dimensional vector space. Conversely, the problem is typically overconstrained if the number of equations is larger than N, so that $\alpha > 1$, and no solution exists. Precisely *at* $\alpha = 1$ the number of solutions is exactly 1, if the matrix $\boldsymbol{A}$ is non-singular.

In the terminology of statistical mechanics one is tempted to call $\alpha = \alpha_c = 1$ a phase transition point of the problem. While it is true that statistical mechanics is not needed to solve the problem of the existence of solutions in the case of linear equations, there are situations where rigorous mathematical theorems are not available in the same way, and statistical mechanics tools do prove useful to decide existence problems of the type just discussed.

The way in which statistical mechanics can be brought into play is as follows. One begins by introducing non-negative error measures $\{E_\mu(\boldsymbol{w})\}$ signifying whether or not a given constraint μ is violated by $\boldsymbol{w}$ via

$$\begin{aligned} E_\mu(\boldsymbol{w}) &> 0 \quad \text{if constraint } \mu \text{ is violated} \\ E_\mu(\boldsymbol{w}) &= 0 \quad \text{if constraint } \mu \text{ is satisfied} \end{aligned}$$

In terms of this definition, a problem imposing p constraints on the N-components of a parameter vector $\boldsymbol{w}$ will have a solution in which all constraints are satisfied if and only if

$$\min_{\boldsymbol{w} \in \mathcal{G}} \left\{ \sum_{\mu=1}^{p} E_\mu(\boldsymbol{w}) \right\} = 0 \tag{22.1}$$

Within a statistical mechanics framework, this problem can be decided as follows. Introduce the sum of single-constraint error measures as the

Hamiltonian of a system with the N components w_i of the parameter vector $\boldsymbol{w}$ as its degrees of freedom,

$$H(\boldsymbol{w}) = \sum_{\mu=1}^{p} E_\mu(\boldsymbol{w}) \tag{22.2}$$

and consider the Boltzmann distribution corresponding to this Hamiltonian,

$$p(\boldsymbol{w}) = \frac{1}{Z}\, e^{-\beta H(\boldsymbol{w})} \tag{22.3}$$

in which β denotes an inverse temperature as usual. The normalization constant Z in (22.3) is a partition function,

$$Z = \int_{\mathcal{G}} \mathrm{d}\boldsymbol{w}\, e^{-\beta H(\boldsymbol{w})} \tag{22.4}$$

We assume that the partition function exists for all finite N; this can be achieved if necessary by assuming $\mathcal{G}$ to be a bounded subset of $\mathbb{R}^N$. From (22.4) a free energy (per degree of freedom) is obtained in the usual way

$$f(\beta) = -(\beta N)^{-1} \ln Z \tag{22.5}$$

At inverse temperature β, the average energy per degree of freedom in this system is

$$E(\beta) = \frac{\partial}{\partial\beta}[\beta f(\beta)] = \frac{1}{N}\langle H(\boldsymbol{w})\rangle = \frac{1}{N}\sum_{\mu=1}^{p}\langle E_\mu(\boldsymbol{w})\rangle \tag{22.6}$$

in which $\langle\cdots\rangle$ denotes an average over the Boltzmann distribution (22.3).

We now use the fact that in the $\beta \to \infty$ limit the Boltzmann distribution (22.3) gives all weight to configurations $\boldsymbol{w}$ which minimize the Hamiltonian. The p constraints on the parameters can therefore be satisfied, and the problem has a solution, if and only if

$$E_0 = \lim_{\beta\to\infty} E(\beta) = \min_{\boldsymbol{w}\in\mathcal{G}}\{H(\boldsymbol{w})/N\} = 0 \tag{22.7}$$

that is, if the system's ground state energy vanishes. In other words

$$\text{a solution } \boldsymbol{w}^\star \in \mathcal{G} \text{ exists} \iff E_0 = \min_{\boldsymbol{w}\in\mathcal{G}}\{H(\boldsymbol{w})/N\} = 0 \tag{22.8}$$

The existence of a solution to a problem defined in terms of constraints is thus decided by whether the ground state energy of a statistical mechanical system is zero or nonzero.

When applying the general framework just described to investigate learning in neural netwoks, we find ourselves doing equilibrium statistical mechanics calculations and integrals in the space $\mathcal{G}$ of the adjustable parameters $\boldsymbol{w}$ of these systems, which are usually synaptic interactions and thresholds. This space is called the 'space of interactions', or 'Gardner space' after [95].

Disorder: the composition of the data set

As was the case in our previous applications of equilibrium statistical mechanics to neural information processing systems, there is usually also disorder in the problem: here this would be the detailed realization of a given data set D, relative to which one has defined the error measure. Let us reflect this in our notation by putting $H(\boldsymbol{w}) \to H(\boldsymbol{w}|D)$, and accordingly writing

$$f(\beta|D) = -(\beta N)^{-1} \ln \int_{\mathcal{G}} \mathrm{d}\boldsymbol{w}\, e^{-\beta H(\boldsymbol{w}|D)} \tag{22.9}$$

As was the case with the attractor networks in which an extensive number of patterns was stored, we are therefore faced also here with the task of calculating the free energy per degree of freedom for a system in which the Hamiltonian contains disorder; this is usually impossible.

However, normally we are not interested in our system's performance on a specific data set, but rather in its generic performance on a certain *family* (or ensemble) of data sets, characterized only in statistical terms. We can then average expression (22.9) over all microscopic realizations of the data D drawn from our ensemble. Furthermore, experience tells us that in the infinite system size limit $N \to \infty$ the free energy per degree of freedom should be self-averaging, that is, independent of the realization of the disorder (i.e. of the data set D), in which case it would coincide with its disorder average. Thus we would expect that

$$f(\beta|D) = -(\beta N)^{-1} \ln Z(D) = -(\beta N)^{-1} \ln \int_{\mathcal{G}} \mathrm{d}\boldsymbol{w}\, e^{-\beta H(\boldsymbol{w}|D)} \tag{22.10}$$

converges to its disorder average in the limit of large system size:

$$f(\beta|D) \;\to\; \bar{f}(\beta) = -\lim_{N\to\infty} \frac{1}{\beta N} \overline{\ln Z(D)} \tag{22.11}$$

as N becomes large. Here $\overline{\cdots} = \sum_D p_D \ldots$ denotes an average over the ensemble of data sets, with p_D giving the likelihood of individual realizations of the data D in the ensemble.

In this language then, the learning task is called *typically* solvable if the average ground state energy over the data ensemble (also denoted by $\bar{E}_0$)

satisfies

$$\bar{E}_0 = \lim_{N\to\infty} \min_{\boldsymbol{w}\in\mathcal{G}} N^{-1}\overline{H(\boldsymbol{w}|D)} = \lim_{N\to\infty} \lim_{\beta\to\infty} N^{-1}\overline{\langle H(\boldsymbol{w}|D)\rangle} = 0 \qquad (22.12)$$

The average ground state energy is obtained from the quenched free energy $\bar{f}(\beta)$ defined by (22.11) as

$$\bar{E}_0 = \lim_{\beta\to\infty} \frac{\partial}{\partial\beta}[\beta\bar{f}(\beta)] \qquad (22.13)$$

It is useful to rephrase this finally in terms of the single constraint error measures as

$$\bar{E}_0 = \alpha \lim_{N\to\infty} \min_{\boldsymbol{w}\in\mathcal{G}} \left\{ \frac{1}{\alpha N} \sum_{\mu=1}^{\alpha N} \overline{E_\mu(\boldsymbol{w}|D)} \right\} \qquad (22.14)$$

If we assume $E_\mu(\boldsymbol{w}|D) = \mathcal{O}(1)$, the condition

$$\text{a solution } \boldsymbol{w}^\star \in \mathcal{G} \text{ exists} \iff \bar{E}_0 = 0 \qquad (22.15)$$

says that we call a problem solvable if the average fraction of unsatisfied constraints approaches zero in the large system limit. (Stronger conditions can be imposed if need be by turning to what is known in statistical mechanics as a micro-canonical description.)

Yes-or-no error measures and version space

The most transparent situations are those where it is natural and easy to define a binary error measure $E_\mu(\boldsymbol{w}|D) \in \{0, 1\}$, that is, $\boldsymbol{w}$ satisfies the μth constraint in a given data set D when $E_\mu(\boldsymbol{w}|D) = 0$, whereas the constraint is violated if $E_\mu(\boldsymbol{w}|D) = 1$. This would be the natural setup for information processing systems with discrete-output neurons (e.g. McCulloch–Pitts ones), such as perceptrons and recurrent networks of binary neurons. When $E_\mu(\boldsymbol{w}|D) \in \{0, 1\}$ we can write the (data dependent) partition function $Z(D)$ as

$$\begin{aligned} Z(D) &= \int_{\mathcal{G}} \mathrm{d}\boldsymbol{w}\, e^{-\beta\sum_\mu E_\mu(\boldsymbol{w}|D)} \\ &= \int_{\mathcal{G}} \mathrm{d}\boldsymbol{w} \prod_\mu [1 - E_\mu(\boldsymbol{w}|D) + e^{-\beta} E_\mu(\boldsymbol{w}|D)] \end{aligned} \qquad (22.16)$$

In the limit $\beta \to \infty$ the last term in each of the square brackets in the above product will vanish, and the product will be zero for all $\boldsymbol{w}$ which violate one or more constraints. In this limit, contributions to the partition function therefore only come from those $\boldsymbol{w}$ which satisfy all the constraints.

This subset of the parameter space is called the *version space*, and the zero temperature limit of the partition function is nothing but the volume $V(D)$ of the version space,

$$V(D) = \lim_{\beta\to\infty} Z(D) = \int_{\mathcal{G}} \mathrm{d}\boldsymbol{w} \prod_{\mu} [1 - E_\mu(\boldsymbol{w}|D)] \tag{22.17}$$

The volume is expected to scale exponentially with the system size, that is, $V(D) = e^{N\Psi(D)}$, so the quantity of interest is

$$\Psi(D) = \lim_{\beta\to\infty} \frac{1}{N} \ln Z(D)$$

This is, up to a factor minus β, the zero temperature limit of a free energy per degree of freedom, and like the latter is expected to be self-averaging. It therefore makes sense to define

$$\Psi = \overline{\Psi(D)} = \lim_{N\to\infty} \frac{1}{N} \overline{\ln V(D)} \tag{22.18}$$

We then see that there are two qualitatively different possible situations:

$$\Psi = -\infty: \quad \text{no solutions with probability one} \tag{22.19}$$

$$\Psi = \text{finite}: \quad \text{solutions exist with probability one} \tag{22.20}$$

Our problem of determining whether solutions exist has thus for large systems been reduced to the calculation of the quantity Ψ in (22.18). When data are few, one expects to have a finite value for Ψ, that is, a non-negligible version space with many solutions. As one increases the number of data and/or the complexity of the task, however, one expects to find at some stage a divergence $\Psi \downarrow -\infty$. This defines a critical point marking the breakdown of solvability, which can in many cases be calculated explicitly.

22.2 Capacity of perceptrons—definition and toy example

Let us illustrate the application of the above theoretical results to real problems. We turn to the limited but transparent domain of binary perceptrons, carrying out the usual linear separations $S: \Omega \subseteq \{-1,1\}^N \to \{-1,1\}$ defined by $S(\boldsymbol{\xi}) = \mathrm{sgn}(\boldsymbol{J}\cdot\boldsymbol{\xi} + \vartheta)$. This type of system is asked to carry out a binary classification task, defined by a set D of data which consist of p input vectors $\boldsymbol{\xi}^\mu \in \mathbb{R}^N$ with corresponding outputs $t_\mu \in \{-1,1\}$:

$$D = \{(\boldsymbol{\xi}^1, t_1), \ldots, (\boldsymbol{\xi}^p, t_p)\}$$

We are not told whether these data are linearly separable. If we were to draw our data D simply at random, we should expect the problem to be linearly separable only for sufficiently small p. It will turn out that for $N \to \infty$ and $\boldsymbol{\xi}^\mu \in \{-1, 1\}^N$ this random data separation problem is solvable by a perceptron if and only if $\lim_{N\to\infty} p/N < 2$. This result had been found earlier by elementary methods [118]; here we will derive it from our equilibrium statistical mechanical formalism.

The condition of linear separability

We found in Chapter 8 that the sufficient and necessary condition for our data to be classified correctly by a perceptron with parameters $(\boldsymbol{J}, \vartheta)$, with all input vectors at a distance larger than $\kappa > 0$ from the separating plane, can be written in terms of the stability parameters:

$$\forall \mu \leq p: \quad t_\mu(\boldsymbol{J} \cdot \boldsymbol{\xi}^\mu + \vartheta)/|\boldsymbol{J}| > \kappa \tag{22.21}$$

As in Chapter 8 we wish to eliminate the degree of freedom which consists in rescaling all parameters according to $(\boldsymbol{J}, \vartheta) \to \lambda(\boldsymbol{J}, \vartheta)$, with $\lambda > 0$; such rescaling leaves us with exactly the same operation. We do this by insisting on the normalization $\boldsymbol{J}^2 = N$, so $J_i = \mathcal{O}(N^0)$ on average. We also re-write the threshold ϑ as $\vartheta = J_0\sqrt{N}$, with $J_0 = \mathcal{O}(N^0)$, and require that $|J_0| \leq \Lambda$ (for some $\Lambda \geq 0$). This converts the above definitions into the following:

$$S(\boldsymbol{\xi}) = \mathrm{sgn}(N^{-1/2}\boldsymbol{J} \cdot \boldsymbol{\xi} + J_0) \qquad \boldsymbol{J}^2 = N \qquad |J_0| \leq \Lambda \tag{22.22}$$

Each allowed choice of $(\boldsymbol{J}, J_0)$ now represents a distinct perceptron. The Gardner space $\mathcal{G}$ for the present problem is therefore defined as

$$\mathcal{G} = \{(\boldsymbol{J}, J_0) \in \mathbb{R}^{N+1} | \boldsymbol{J}^2 = N, \ |J_0| \leq \Lambda\} \tag{22.23}$$

The parameter Λ is introduced to ensure that the condition $\int_{\mathcal{G}} \mathrm{d}\boldsymbol{J}\mathrm{d}J_0 < \infty$ will be met; it can be chosen arbitrarily large. The sufficient and necessary condition for a perceptron $(\boldsymbol{J}, J_0) \in \mathcal{G}$ to solve the task D, with some prescribed minimal distance κ between input vectors and the separating plane to act as a safety margin (the stability), becomes

$$\begin{array}{l}\text{correct separation by } (\boldsymbol{J}, J_0) \in \mathcal{G} \\ \text{with stability } > \kappa\end{array} \iff \gamma_\mu(\boldsymbol{J}, J_0|D) > \kappa \quad \forall \mu \leq p \tag{22.24}$$

in which the stability parameters now take the following simpler form:

$$\gamma_\mu(\boldsymbol{J}, J_0|D) = t_\mu(N^{-1/2}\boldsymbol{J} \cdot \boldsymbol{\xi}^\mu + J_0) \tag{22.25}$$

So far we have only done preparatory work, similar to the steps taken in Chapter 8, except that here we have ensured that our microscopic variables all obey $J_i = \mathcal{O}(N^0)$ for $N \to \infty$. This is required,[46] since the role of the parameters $\boldsymbol{w}$ of our general theory is here played by $(\boldsymbol{J}, J_0) \in \mathcal{G}$. In order to apply the results (22.19, 22.20) to our perceptron capacity problem, we need scalar error measures $E_\mu(\boldsymbol{J}, J_0|D) \in \{0, 1\}$ which tell us whether or not a perceptron $(\boldsymbol{J}, J_0) \in \mathcal{G}$ separates correctly data point $\boldsymbol{\xi}^\mu$ with error margin $\kappa > 0$. For this we can choose

$$E_\mu(\boldsymbol{J}, J_0|D) = 1 - \theta(\gamma_\mu(\boldsymbol{J}, J_0|D) - \kappa) \tag{22.26}$$

The volume $V(D)$ of version space as defined in (22.17), that is, of the regions in $\mathcal{G}$ where $\sum_\mu E_\mu(\boldsymbol{J}, J_0|D) = 0$ (or, equivalently, where $\prod_\mu [1 - E_\mu(\boldsymbol{J}, J_0|D)] = 1$), now becomes

$$\begin{aligned} V(D) &= \int_{\mathcal{G}} \mathrm{d}\boldsymbol{J}\mathrm{d}J_0 \prod_{\mu=1}^{p} \theta(\gamma_\mu(\boldsymbol{J}, J_0|D) - \kappa) \\ &= \int_{-\Lambda}^{\Lambda} \mathrm{d}J_0 \int \mathrm{d}\boldsymbol{J}\; \delta(\boldsymbol{J}^2 - N) \prod_{\mu=1}^{p} \theta(\gamma_\mu(\boldsymbol{J}, J_0|D) - \kappa) \\ &= \int \frac{\mathrm{d}z}{2\pi}\, e^{-\mathrm{i}zN} \int \mathrm{d}\boldsymbol{J}\; e^{\mathrm{i}z\boldsymbol{J}^2} \int_{-\Lambda}^{\Lambda} \mathrm{d}J_0 \prod_{\mu=1}^{p} \theta(\gamma_\mu(\boldsymbol{J}, J_0|D) - \kappa) \end{aligned} \tag{22.27}$$

According to (22.19, 22.20), our remaining task boils down to calculating from (22.27) the quantity $\Psi = \lim_{N\to\infty} N^{-1}\overline{\ln V(D)}$.

A toy problem: orthogonal inputs

Before turning to the non-trivial case of fully random data, let us first, by way of illustration, inspect the simpler problem where the input vectors $\boldsymbol{\xi}^\mu \in \mathbb{R}^N$ of the data D are orthogonal, that is, where $\boldsymbol{\xi}^\mu \cdot \boldsymbol{\xi}^\nu = N\delta_{\mu\nu}$. This obviously limits the analysis to $p \le N$. Now we may use the p normalized vectors $\hat{\mathbf{e}}^\mu = \boldsymbol{\xi}^\mu/\sqrt{N}$ as a basis in $\mathbb{R}^N$, so that $\boldsymbol{J} \cdot \boldsymbol{\xi}^\mu = \sqrt{N} J_\mu$ and

$$\begin{aligned} V(D) &= \int \frac{\mathrm{d}z}{2\pi}\, e^{-\mathrm{i}zN} \int \mathrm{d}\boldsymbol{J}\; e^{\mathrm{i}z\boldsymbol{J}^2} \int_{-\Lambda}^{\Lambda} \mathrm{d}J_0 \prod_{\mu=1}^{p} \theta(t_\mu(J_\mu + J_0) - \kappa) \\ &= \int \mathrm{d}z\; e^{-\mathrm{i}zN} \left(\int \mathrm{d}J\; e^{\mathrm{i}zJ^2}\right)^{N-p} \int_{-\Lambda}^{\Lambda} \mathrm{d}J_0 \prod_{\mu=1}^{p} \int \mathrm{d}J\; e^{\mathrm{i}zJ^2} \theta(t_\mu(J + J_0) - \kappa) \end{aligned}$$

[46] We have to insist on the components of $\boldsymbol{w}$ scaling as N^0 in order to ensure that volumes $\int \mathrm{d}\boldsymbol{w}$ in $\mathbb{R}^N$ scale exponentially in N.

If we write the number of outputs that equal $t_\mu = \pm 1$ as $\frac{1}{2}p(1 \pm \gamma)$, and define $\alpha = p/N$, we obtain an expression which confirms that the relevant volume does indeed generically scale exponentially with the system size N:

$$V(D) = \int \mathrm{d}z\, e^{N\Phi(z,\kappa)} \qquad \Psi = \mathrm{extr}_z \Phi(z,\kappa) \tag{22.28}$$

with

$$\begin{aligned}\Phi(z,\kappa) &= -\mathrm{i}z + (1-\alpha)\ln \int \mathrm{d}J\, e^{\mathrm{i}zJ^2} + \frac{1}{N}\ln \int_{-\Lambda}^{\Lambda} \mathrm{d}J_0 \\ &\quad\times \left(\int_{\kappa - J_0}^{\infty} \mathrm{d}J\, e^{\mathrm{i}zJ^2}\right)^{(1/2)(1+\gamma)\alpha N} \left(\int_{\kappa + J_0}^{\infty} \mathrm{d}J\, e^{\mathrm{i}zJ^2}\right)^{(1/2)(1-\gamma)\alpha N} \\ &= -\mathrm{i}z + (1-\alpha)\ln \int \mathrm{d}J\, e^{\mathrm{i}zJ^2} + \frac{1}{2}\alpha \\ &\quad\times \mathrm{extr}_{|J_0|<\Lambda} \left\{(1+\gamma)\ln \int_{\kappa - J_0}^{\infty} \mathrm{d}J\, e^{\mathrm{i}zJ^2} + (1-\gamma)\ln \int_{\kappa + J_0}^{\infty} \mathrm{d}J\, e^{\mathrm{i}zJ^2}\right\}\end{aligned}$$

Let us, for simplicity, specialize further to the case $\gamma = 0$ (i.e. output values $t_\mu = 1$ occur with the same frequency as those with $t_\mu = -1$), where the extremization with respect to the perceptron's threshold J_0 simply gives $J_0 = 0$, so that

$$\Phi(z,\kappa) = -\mathrm{i}z + (1-\alpha)\ln \int \mathrm{d}J\, e^{\mathrm{i}zJ^2} + \alpha \ln \int_{\kappa}^{\infty} \mathrm{d}J\, e^{\mathrm{i}zJ^2} \tag{22.29}$$

This form suggests that the relevant saddle-point in (22.28) will be purely imaginary, so we put $z = \mathrm{i}u^2$ with $u \in \mathbb{R}$ and positive (the square ensures that the integrals exist):

$$\begin{aligned}\Phi(\mathrm{i}u^2,\kappa) &= u^2 + (1-\alpha)\ln \int \mathrm{d}J\, e^{-u^2J^2} + \alpha \ln \int_{\kappa}^{\infty} \mathrm{d}J\, e^{-u^2J^2} \\ &= u^2 - \ln(u/\sqrt{\pi}) - \alpha \ln 2 + \alpha \ln(1 - \mathrm{erf}(\kappa u))\end{aligned} \tag{22.30}$$

Extremization of Φ, as required by (22.28), gives the saddle-point equation

$$u = F(u) \qquad F(u) = \frac{1}{2u} + \frac{\alpha\kappa}{\sqrt{\pi}} \frac{e^{-\kappa^2u^2}}{1 - \mathrm{erf}(\kappa u)} \tag{22.31}$$

The function $F(u)$ in (22.31) is always positive, descending initially from the singularity $F(0) = \infty$. If α and κ are both positive, then $F(u)$ has a positive minimum for some positive u and subsequently increases once more towards $F(\infty) = \infty$, approaching the asymptotic form $F(u) \sim \alpha\kappa^2 u$

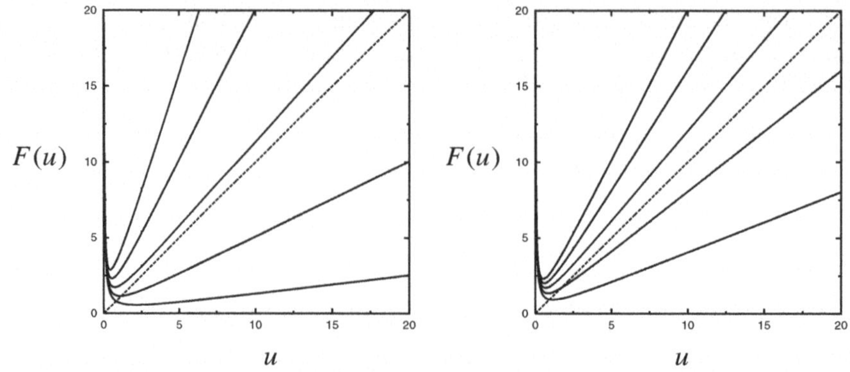

Figure 22.1 The function $F(u)$ as appearing in the saddle-point equation (22.31) for the classification capacity (at required stability $\kappa > 0$) of a perceptron with data D consisting of $p = \alpha N$ orthogonal input vectors $\boldsymbol{\xi}^{\mu}$ and randomly drawn outputs $t_{\mu} \in \{-1, 1\}$. Left: solid lines show $F(u)$ for $\alpha = \frac{1}{2}$ and $\kappa \in \{\frac{1}{2}, 1, \frac{3}{2}, 2, \frac{5}{2}, 3\}$ (from bottom to top). Right: solid lines show $F(u)$ for $\kappa = 2$ and $\alpha \in \{0.1, 0.2, 0.3, 0.4, 0.5, 0.6\}$ (from bottom to top). Dashed: the diagonal which $F(u)$ has to intersect to solve $F(u) = u$. Finite solutions of the equation $F(u) = u$ (representing a non-vanishing volume of solutions to the classification problem) are seen to exist only for sufficiently small α and κ.

for $u \to \infty$. See also Figure 22.1. It follows that there will be a finite positive solution of equation (22.31), and hence a finite value for Ψ (so that solutions exist of our perceptron classification problem, with probability one) if and only if $\alpha\kappa^2 < 1$. At $\alpha\kappa^2 = 1$ this finite solution ceases to exist. Hence the classification capacity $\alpha_c(\kappa)$ for a prescribed classification stability κ is given by

$$\alpha_c(\kappa) = \kappa^{-2} \tag{22.32}$$

(with $\alpha \leq 1$, for orthogonal input vectors to exist). This curve is shown in Figure 22.2, together with the corresponding result for random input data to be derived below. We see that for $\kappa < 1$ the data are always separable, for any value of $\alpha \leq 1$. For $\kappa > 1$, however, the increasing demands of classification stability can only be met at the cost of a reduction of the number of data points to be classified, that is, $\alpha_c(\kappa) < 1$.

22.3 Capacity of perceptrons—random inputs

Replica analysis in Gardner space

For random (and hence non-orthogonal) input vectors we can no longer get away with the simple calculation that worked for orthogonal input vectors. Now we have to carry out the disorder average in $\Psi = \lim_{N\to\infty} N^{-1}\overline{\ln V(D)}$ explicitly, which can be done with the replica method, as introduced in Section 21.2. For simplicity we will deal only with perceptrons without

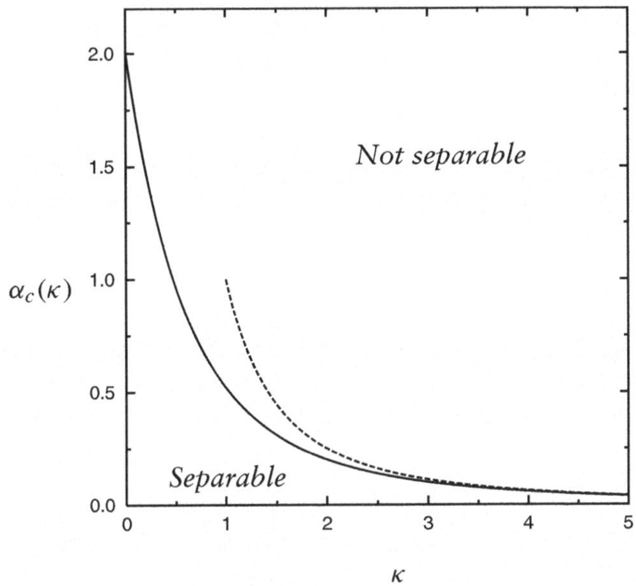

Figure 22.2 Asymptotic classification capacity $\alpha_c(\kappa)$ of a perceptron, for data sets D consisting of $p = \alpha N$ input vectors $\boldsymbol{\xi}^\mu \in \mathbb{R}^N$ with corresponding random binary outputs t^μ (independently drawn, with equal probabilities for outputs $t^\mu = \pm 1$), versus the required classification stability κ. Solid line: randomly drawn input vectors $\boldsymbol{\xi}^\mu \in \{-1, 1\}^N$. Dashed line: orthogonal input vectors $\boldsymbol{\xi}^\mu \cdot \boldsymbol{\xi}^\nu = N\delta_{\mu\nu}$ (with $\alpha \leq 1$). The linear separations are possible with probability one for $N \to \infty$ only for $\alpha < \alpha_c(\kappa)$, that is, below the lines.

thresholds, that is, $J_0 = 0$, where the expression (22.27) for the volume $V(D)$ of version space takes the form

$$V(D) = \int \frac{\mathrm{d}z}{2\pi}\, e^{-\mathrm{i}zN} \int \mathrm{d}\boldsymbol{J}\, e^{\mathrm{i}z\boldsymbol{J}^2} \prod_{\mu=1}^{p} \theta(N^{-1/2} t^\mu \boldsymbol{J} \cdot \boldsymbol{\xi}^\mu - \kappa) \qquad (22.33)$$

We consider randomly drawn binary input vectors $\boldsymbol{\xi}^\mu \in \{-1, 1\}^N$ and randomly drawn corresponding outputs $t_\mu \in \{-1, 1\}$ with all components taking the values ± 1 with equal probabilities. In the disorder average defining Ψ we may then use the gauge transformation $\boldsymbol{\xi}^\mu \to t_\mu \boldsymbol{\xi}^\mu$ to eliminate the output variables,[47] giving

$$\Psi = \lim_{N\to\infty} \frac{1}{N} \overline{\left[\ln \int \mathrm{d}z\, e^{\mathrm{i}zN} \int \mathrm{d}\boldsymbol{J}\, e^{-\mathrm{i}z\boldsymbol{J}^2} \prod_{\mu=1}^{p} \theta(N^{-1/2} \boldsymbol{J} \cdot \boldsymbol{\xi}^\mu - \kappa) \right]} \qquad (22.34)$$

[47] This would generally not have been possible in the presence of thresholds, or for data sets D where the input components and the outputs do not have equal probabilities for ± 1.

Now we apply the replica identity $\overline{\ln Z} = \lim_{n\to 0} n^{-1} \ln \overline{Z^n}$, and write Z^n as an n-fold integral, that is, we replace $[\int \mathrm{d}z\mathrm{d}\boldsymbol{J}\, g(z,\boldsymbol{J})]^n = \int \prod_{a=1}^n [\mathrm{d}z_a \mathrm{d}\boldsymbol{J}^a\, g(z_a,\boldsymbol{J}^a)]$:

$$\Psi = \lim_{N\to\infty} \lim_{n\to 0} \frac{1}{nN} \ln \int \prod_a [\mathrm{d}z_a \mathrm{d}\boldsymbol{J}^a\, e^{\mathrm{i}z_a N - \mathrm{i}z_a(\boldsymbol{J}^a)^2}] \overline{\prod_a \prod_{\mu=1}^{p} \theta\Big(\frac{\boldsymbol{J}^a\cdot\boldsymbol{\xi}^\mu}{\sqrt{N}} - \kappa\Big)} \tag{22.35}$$

To proceed with (22.35) we need to evaluate the disorder average of a product of step functions. To do this, we use an integral representation for $\theta(u)$, which follows from the integral representation of the δ-function via $\theta'(u) = \delta(u)$:

$$\begin{aligned}\theta(y-\kappa) &= \int_{-\infty}^{y-\kappa} \mathrm{d}\lambda\, \delta(\lambda) = \int_{-\infty}^{y-\kappa} \mathrm{d}\lambda \int \frac{\mathrm{d}x}{2\pi}\, e^{\mathrm{i}x\lambda} \\ &= \int_{-\infty}^{-\kappa} \mathrm{d}\lambda \int \frac{\mathrm{d}x}{2\pi}\, e^{\mathrm{i}x(y+\lambda)} = \int \frac{\mathrm{d}\lambda \mathrm{d}x}{2\pi}\, \theta(\lambda-\kappa)\, e^{\mathrm{i}x(\lambda-y)}\end{aligned}$$

This is equivalent to using a δ-function for 'transporting' the variable y (which contains the disorder) out of the argument of $\theta(y-\kappa)$. In (22.35) we have np step functions, so we need np new integration variables. As in the case of orthogonal inputs, we will choose $p = \alpha N$, with $\alpha = \mathcal{O}(N^0)$. For large N we then find for the term containing the disorder average

$$\begin{aligned}\Xi &= \overline{\prod_a \prod_{\mu=1}^{p} \theta\Big(\frac{\boldsymbol{J}^a\cdot\boldsymbol{\xi}^\mu}{\sqrt{N}} - \kappa\Big)} \\ &= \int \prod_{a\mu} \Big(\frac{\mathrm{d}\lambda_\mu^a \mathrm{d}x_\mu^a}{2\pi}\, \theta(\lambda_\mu^a - \kappa) e^{\mathrm{i}x_\mu^a \lambda_\mu^a}\Big)\, \overline{e^{-\mathrm{i}\sum_{i\mu} \xi_i^\mu \sum_a J_i^a x_\mu^a/\sqrt{N}}} \\ &= \int \prod_{a\mu} \Big(\frac{\mathrm{d}\lambda_\mu^a \mathrm{d}x_\mu^a}{2\pi}\, \theta(\lambda_\mu^a - \kappa) e^{\mathrm{i}x_\mu^a \lambda_\mu^a}\Big) \prod_{i\mu} \cos\Big(\frac{\sum_a J_i^a x_\mu^a}{\sqrt{N}}\Big) \\ &= \int \prod_{a\mu} \Big(\frac{\mathrm{d}\lambda_\mu^a \mathrm{d}x_\mu^a}{2\pi}\, \theta(\lambda_\mu^a - \kappa) e^{\mathrm{i}x_\mu^a \lambda_\mu^a}\Big) e^{-\sum_{i\mu}(\sum_a J_i^a x_\mu^a)^2/2N + \mathcal{O}(N^0)} \\ &= \Big[\int \prod_a \Big(\frac{\mathrm{d}\lambda_a \mathrm{d}x_a}{2\pi}\, \theta(\lambda_a - \kappa) e^{\mathrm{i}x_a \lambda_a}\Big) e^{-\sum_{ab} x_a x_b \sum_i J_i^a J_i^b/2N + \mathcal{O}(N^{-1})}\Big]^p\end{aligned} \tag{22.36}$$

Proceeding by analogy with the arguments in Section 21.2, we insert (22.36) into (22.35) and isolate the n^2 quantities $N^{-1}\sum_i J_i^a J_i^b$ via suitable

δ-functions, that is, by inserting

$$1 = \prod_{ab} \int \mathrm{d}q_{ab}\, \delta\Big(q_{ab} - \frac{1}{N}\sum_i J_i^a J_i^b\Big)$$
$$= \prod_{ab} \int \frac{\mathrm{d}q_{ab}\,\mathrm{d}\hat{q}_{ab}}{2\pi/N}\, e^{\mathrm{i}N\hat{q}_{ab}(q_{ab}-\boldsymbol{J}^a\cdot\boldsymbol{J}^b/N)}$$

This results in, with $z = \{z_a\}$, and $\boldsymbol{q} = \{q_{ab}\}$ and $\hat{\boldsymbol{q}} = \{\hat{q}_{ab}\}$,

$$\begin{aligned}
\Psi = {} & \lim_{N\to\infty}\lim_{n\to 0} \frac{1}{nN} \ln \int \mathrm{d}z\,\mathrm{d}\boldsymbol{q}\,\mathrm{d}\hat{\boldsymbol{q}}\; e^{\mathrm{i}N(\sum_a z_a + \sum_{ab}\hat{q}_{ab}q_{ab}) + \mathcal{O}(\ln N)} \\
& \times \left\{ \int \prod_a \left[\frac{\mathrm{d}\lambda_a\,\mathrm{d}x_a}{2\pi}\,\theta(\lambda_a-\kappa)e^{\mathrm{i}x_a\lambda_a}\right] e^{-\sum_{ab} x_a q_{ab} x_b/2} \right\}^p \\
& \times \int \Big(\prod_a \mathrm{d}\boldsymbol{J}^a\Big) e^{-\mathrm{i}\sum_a z_a (\boldsymbol{J}^a)^2 - \mathrm{i}\sum_{ab}\hat{q}_{ab}\boldsymbol{J}^a\cdot\boldsymbol{J}^b} \\
= {} & \lim_{N\to\infty}\lim_{n\to 0} \frac{1}{nN} \ln \int \mathrm{d}z\mathrm{d}\boldsymbol{q}\mathrm{d}\hat{\boldsymbol{q}}\; e^{\mathrm{i}N(\sum_a z_a + \sum_{ab}\hat{q}_{ab}q_{ab}) + \mathcal{O}(\ln N)} \\
& \times \left\{ \int \prod_a \left[\frac{\mathrm{d}\lambda_a\mathrm{d}x_a}{2\pi}\,\theta(\lambda_a-\kappa)e^{\mathrm{i}x_a\lambda_a}\right] e^{-\sum_{ab} x_a q_{ab} x_b/2} \right\}^p \\
& \times \left[\int \Big(\prod_a \mathrm{d}J_a\Big) e^{-\mathrm{i}\sum_a z_a J_a^2 - \mathrm{i}\sum_{ab} J_a\hat{q}_{ab}J_b} \right]^N
\end{aligned} \tag{22.37}$$

After exchanging the order of the two limits $n \to 0$ and $N \to \infty$ in the by now familiar manner, and using $p = \alpha N$ with α remaining finite for $N \to \infty$, we end up once more with an integral to be evaluated by steepest descent:

$$\begin{aligned}
\Psi = {} & \lim_{n\to 0} \frac{1}{n} \mathrm{extr}_{z,\boldsymbol{q},\hat{\boldsymbol{q}}} \Big\{ \mathrm{i}\sum_a z_a + \mathrm{i}\sum_{ab}\hat{q}_{ab}q_{ab} \\
& + \alpha \ln \int \prod_a \left[\frac{\mathrm{d}\lambda_a\mathrm{d}x_a}{2\pi}\,\theta(\lambda_a-\kappa)e^{\mathrm{i}x_a\lambda_a}\right] e^{-\sum_{ab} x_a q_{ab} x_b/2} \\
& + \ln \int \Big(\prod_a \mathrm{d}J_a\Big) e^{-\mathrm{i}\sum_{ab} J_a(\hat{q}_{ab}+z_a\delta_{ab})J_b} \Big\}
\end{aligned} \tag{22.38}$$

Anticipating the form of the relevant extremum, we write $\hat{q}_{ab} = -\frac{1}{2}\mathrm{i}k_{ab} - z_a\delta_{ab}$. Carrying out the two Gaussian integrals in (22.38) (see Appendix D) then gives

$$\Psi = \frac{1}{2}(1-\alpha)\ln(2\pi) + \lim_{n\to 0}\frac{1}{n}\mathrm{extr}_{z,\boldsymbol{q},\boldsymbol{k}}\Bigg\{ \mathrm{i}\sum_a z_a(1-q_{aa}) + \frac{1}{2}\sum_{ab} k_{ab}q_{ab}$$

$$+\alpha \ln \int \prod_a [\mathrm{d}\lambda_a \theta(\lambda_a - \kappa)] e^{-\sum_{ab}\lambda_a(\boldsymbol{q}^{-1})_{ab}\lambda_b/2}$$

$$-\frac{1}{2}\alpha \ln\det \boldsymbol{q} - \frac{1}{2}\ln\det\boldsymbol{k}\Bigg\}$$

Extremization with respect to the $\{z_a\}$ recovers what can be recognized as the built-in spherical constraint $\sum_i J_i^2 = N$, $q_{aa} = 1$ for all a, leaving

$$\Psi = \frac{1}{2}(1-\alpha)\ln(2\pi) + \lim_{n\to 0}\frac{1}{n}\mathrm{extr}_{\boldsymbol{q},\boldsymbol{k}}\Bigg\{\frac{1}{2}\sum_a k_{aa} + \frac{1}{2}\sum_{a\neq b} k_{ab}q_{ab} - \frac{1}{2}\alpha\ln\det\boldsymbol{q}$$

$$-\frac{1}{2}\ln\det\boldsymbol{k} + \alpha\ \ln\int_\kappa^\infty\Big(\prod_a \mathrm{d}\lambda_a\Big)e^{-\sum_{ab}\lambda_a(\boldsymbol{q}^{-1})_{ab}\lambda_b/2}\Bigg\} \quad (22.39)$$

Replica symmetry

At this stage we make the replica symmetric (RS) ansatz, which in the case of an underlying stochastic process would have been equivalent to assuming ergodicity but which here boils down to assuming that the version space $V(D) \in \mathcal{G}$ is connected. As in Section 21.2 it takes the form

$$q_{ab} = \delta_{ab} + q(1-\delta_{ab}) \qquad k_{ab} = K\delta_{ab} + k(1-\delta_{ab})$$

Both these RS matrices have the following eigenvectors: $\boldsymbol{x} = (1,\ldots,1)$ giving a first eigenvalue with multiplicity one, and any vector in the orthogonal space $(1,\ldots,1)^\perp$ giving a second eigenvalue with mutiplicity $n-1$. It follows that

$$\det\boldsymbol{k} = (K-k+nk)(K-k)^{n-1} = (K-k)^n\left(1+\frac{nk}{K-k}\right)$$

$$\det\boldsymbol{q} = (1-q+nq)(1-q)^{n-1} = (1-q)^n\left(1+\frac{nq}{1-q}\right)$$

$$(\boldsymbol{q}^{-1})_{ab} = \frac{\delta_{ab}}{1-q} - \frac{q}{(1-q)(1-q+nq)}$$

We use these RS identities to simplify our general expression (22.39). In addition we introduce a further Gaussian integral to linearize the quadratic exponent in the integral over $\{\lambda_a\}$, using the familiar shorthand

$Dz = (2\pi)^{-1/2} e^{-z^2/2}$. This gives us the value of Ψ for replica symmetric solutions, with extremization now over the triplet $\{q, K, k\}$:

$$
\begin{aligned}
2\Psi_{\mathrm{RS}} =& (1-\alpha)\ln(2\pi) + \mathrm{extr}\Bigg\{ K - kq - \ln(K-k) - \frac{k}{K-k} - \alpha\ln(1-q) \\
& - \frac{\alpha q}{1-q} + 2\alpha \lim_{n\to 0}\frac{1}{n}\ln\int_{\kappa}^{\infty}\Big(\prod_a \mathrm{d}\lambda_a\Big) \\
& \times e^{-\sum_a \lambda_a^2/[2(1-q)] + q(\sum_a \lambda_a)^2/[2(1-q)(1-q+nq)]}\Bigg\} \\
=& (1-\alpha)\ln(2\pi) + \mathrm{extr}\Bigg\{ K - kq - \ln(K-k) - \frac{k}{K-k} - \alpha\ln(1-q) \\
& - \frac{\alpha q}{1-q} + 2\alpha \lim_{n\to 0}\frac{1}{n}\ln\int Dz \\
& \times \left[\int_{\kappa}^{\infty}\mathrm{d}\lambda\, e^{-\lambda^2/[2(1-q)] + z\sqrt{q}\lambda/\sqrt{(1-q)(1-q+nq)}}\right]^n\Bigg\} \\
=& (1-\alpha)\ln(2\pi) + \mathrm{extr}\Bigg\{ K - kq - \ln(K-k) - \frac{k}{K-k} - \alpha\ln(1-q) \\
& - \frac{\alpha q}{1-q} + 2\alpha\int Dz\, \ln\int_{\kappa}^{\infty}\mathrm{d}\lambda\, e^{-\lambda^2/[2(1-q)] + z\sqrt{q}\lambda/(1-q)}\Bigg\} \qquad (22.40)
\end{aligned}
$$

The term with the integral in the last line contains only q, so that the extermization with respect to K and k has become trivial, giving the two saddle-point equations $(K-k)^2 = K - 2k$ and $k = -q(K-k)^2$. As we have to reject $K = k = 0$ for Ψ_{RS} to exist, the relevant solution is

$$K = (1-2q)/(1-q)^2 \qquad k = -q/(1-q)^2 \qquad (22.41)$$

Insertion of (22.41) into (22.40) subsequently leaves us with a transparent expression that is to be extremized only with respect to the remaining order parameter $q \in [0, 1]$. In this expression one can also carry out a simple transformations on the integration variable λ, viz. $\lambda = z\sqrt{q} + t\sqrt{2(1-q)}$, to write the remaining integral in terms of the error function

$$\mathrm{erf}(x) = \frac{2}{\sqrt{\pi}}\int_0^x \mathrm{d}t\, e^{-t^2}$$

The final result is: $\Psi_{\text{RS}} = \text{extr}_q \Psi_{\text{RS}}(q)$, with

$$\Psi_{\text{RS}}(q) = \frac{1}{2} + \frac{1}{2}(1-2\alpha)\ln 2 + \frac{1}{2}\ln\pi + \frac{1}{2}\ln(1-q) + \frac{q}{2(1-q)} + \alpha\int Dz\,\ln\left[1-\text{erf}\left(\frac{\kappa - z\sqrt{q}}{\sqrt{2(1-q)}}\right)\right] \tag{22.42}$$

The classification capacity

It is clear from expression (22.42) that one has a finite value for Ψ_{RS} (and hence linear classification of the random data D is possible with probability one) as long as the relevant extremum has $q < 1$. The classification capacity of our system is therefore defined by the condition that $q = 1$ at the saddle-point, which will give us a relation between the control parameters α and κ, that is, an expression for the critical relative size $\alpha_c(\kappa)$ of the data set (as in the simpler toy example of orthogonal input vectors). The saddle-point equation for q, as obtained by putting $\partial\Psi_{\text{RS}}(q)/\partial q = 0$, is found to take the following form:

$$q = \frac{\alpha\sqrt{2(1-q)}}{\sqrt{\pi q}}\int Dz\,[1-\text{erf}(u)]^{-1}e^{-u^2}(\kappa\sqrt{q} - z) \tag{22.43}$$

with the shorthand $u = (\kappa - z\sqrt{q})/\sqrt{2(1-q)}$. The transition where classifications cease to exist occurs when the solution of (22.43) is indeed $q = 1$. Hence $\alpha_c(\kappa)$ is to be solved from

$$1 = \alpha_c(\kappa)\sqrt{\frac{2}{\pi}}\int Dz\,(\kappa - z)\,\lim_{q\uparrow 1}\{\sqrt{1-q}[1-\text{erf}(u)]^{-1}e^{-u^2}\} \tag{22.44}$$

The remaining limit in (22.44) is most easily calculated by putting $q = 1-\epsilon^2$, where $\epsilon \to 0$. One may then write

$$u = \frac{\kappa - z}{\epsilon\sqrt{2}} + \frac{z\epsilon}{2\sqrt{2}} + \mathcal{O}(\epsilon^3)$$

and

$$1 = \alpha_c(\kappa)\sqrt{\frac{2}{\pi}}\int Dz\,(\kappa - z) \times \lim_{\epsilon\to 0}\left\{\frac{\epsilon\,\exp[-((\kappa-z)/(\epsilon\sqrt{2}) + z\epsilon/(2\sqrt{2}) + \mathcal{O}(\epsilon^3))^2]}{1-\text{erf}((\kappa-z)/(\epsilon\sqrt{2}) + z\epsilon/(2\sqrt{2}) + \mathcal{O}(\epsilon^3))}\right\} \tag{22.45}$$

The result of the limit $\epsilon \to 0$ in (22.45) depends crucially on the value of $\kappa - z$. For $\kappa - z < 0$ one has a finite denominator and a vanishing numerator, giving $\lim_{\epsilon \to 0}\{\cdots\} = 0$. For $\kappa - z > 0$, however, both numerator and denominator go to zero for $\epsilon \to 0$, and one may use the asymptotic behaviour of the error function [1], viz.

$$\mathrm{erf}(x) = 1 - \frac{1}{x\sqrt{\pi}} e^{-x^2}(1 + \mathcal{O}(x^{-2})) \quad (x \to \infty)$$

to obtain $\lim_{\epsilon \to 0}\{\cdots\} = (\kappa - z)\sqrt{\pi/2}$. In combination we may therefore write $\lim_{\epsilon \to 0}\{\cdots\} = (\kappa - z)\theta(\kappa - z)\sqrt{\pi/2}$, and find (22.45) reducing to

$$1 = \alpha_c(\kappa) \int_{-\infty}^{\kappa} Dz\, (\kappa - z)^2$$

This can also be written in the remarkably simple and elegant form

$$\alpha_c(\kappa) = \left[\int_{-\kappa}^{\infty} Dz\, (\kappa + z)^2\right]^{-1} \tag{22.46}$$

In (22.46), which is shown above in Figure 22.2 together with our earlier expression for data with orthogonal input vectors and random outputs, we have found the perceptron's classification capacity for random binary data, as a function of the required stability κ. As expected, $\alpha_c(\kappa)$ decreases monotonically with κ; the larger the requested separation margins, the smaller the number of data that can be classified. In the limit $\kappa \to 0$ one obtains the absolute upper limit for classification, $\alpha_c(0) = 2$. For small values of α, that is, when the number of data points to be classified is moderate, one would anticipate that the differences between random or orthogonal input vectors should become small. Figure 22.2 confirms that this intuition is indeed correct.

One should note that, since any fully connected recurrent networks of N binary neurons functioning as associative memories (as studied, e.g. in Chapter 21) is mathematically equivalent to a collection of N perceptrons acting in parallel, the result (22.46) also applies to such recurrent networks. It follows that the maximum number of random patterns that can be stored as fixed point attractors in recurrent networks of binary neurons (without thresholds, without noise, and without further constraints of any kind[48]) also scales with N as $p_{\max}/N = 2$.

[48] This latter condition is relevant, since it can be shown that in order to satisfy the upper bound $\alpha_c = 2$ in an associative memory one needs non-symmetric synapses, that is, $J_{ij} \neq J_{ji}$.

23 Notes and suggestions for further reading

Many interesting phenomena relevant to the information *processing* capabilities of neural networks are clearly dynamical in nature, and can therefore not be investigated by techniques of equilibrium statistical mechanics because these concentrate on stationary states. However, for a large class of problems one is simply forced to accept this limitation in scope because their full dynamics turns out to be far too complicated to unravel with the analytical techniques currently available. As the present part of the book has demonstrated, a number of interesting properties of neural networks can nevertheless be investigated in some detail using equilibrium theory.

Equilibrium statistical mechanics has a long history dating back to seminal work of Maxwell, Boltzmann, and Gibbs in the nineteenth and early twentieth century. It provides a rich arsenal of concepts and techniques for studying stationary states of systems containing many interacting degrees of freedom; these can be applied to neural networks—natural and artificial—once the restriction of symmetric synaptic interactions is imposed.

As we saw, the stochastic dynamics of a set of recursively coupled binary neurons constitutes a Markov chain. Our demonstration of the existence and uniqueness of stationary distributions for such processes closely follows the reasoning of van Kampen [79]. In a more abstract setting these results, which concern the largest eigenvalue and the corresponding eigenvector of stochastic matrices, were proven by Perron for positive, and by Frobenius for non-negative matrices; they are therefore often jointly referred to as the Perron–Frobenius theorem. The interested reader will find proofs of these theorems and further results about stochastic matrices in [119].

Although the modelling of associative memories in terms of networks of interacting neurons has in itself a long history (see notes on Part I), the applicability of equilibrium statistical mechanics techniques for studying their collective behaviour was firmly established only through the work of Little and Shaw [8, 120], Hopfield [14], and Peretto [121]. The full analysis of the equilibrium properties of the Hopfield model is due to Amit, Gutfreund, and Sompolinsky, both for the case of finitely many stored patterns [122], and for the much more demanding case of extensive loading [123, 124]. The latter requires the use of replicas as we saw. Replica identities for averaging logarithms were used already in the 1930s [125];

however, they began to have a major impact in the world of physics only much later through the work of Edwards and Anderson [126] on spin glasses. A detailed account of the replica method and in particular its application to the study of the Sherrington–Kirkpatrick model [127] can be found in the book by Mézard *et al.* [128].

As explained in Section 21.3, the replica symmetric approximation used by Amit *et al.* in their study of the Hopfield model is unstable against a spontaneous breaking of the permutation symmetry among replicas at low temperatures. An instability of this kind was first revealed by de Alemeida and Thouless [129] for the SK model; our analysis of the AT instabilities of the SK and Hopfield models in Sections 21.2 and 21.3 follows their reasoning. The effects of replica symmetry breaking are rather pronounced in the SK model; correct descriptions of phases with broken replica symmetry were first obtained through the pioneering work of Parisi in the early 1980s, which is documented in detail in [128].

There was at first some doubt about the true value for the zero temperature storage capacity of the Hopfield model, as its value determined within a replica symmetric approximation, $\alpha_c = \alpha_c^{\mathrm{RS}} \approx 0.1379$, was found to differ from that obtained via numerical simulations, $\alpha_c^{\mathrm{sim}} \approx 0.144$. The discrepancy was initially put down to effects of replica symmetry breaking, which were not included in the analysis of Amit *et al.* [123, 124]. However, it is now known that the effects of replica symmetry breaking are rather weak in the retrieval phase of the Hopfield model and cannot be held responsible for the discrepancy: calculations based on retrieval phases with broken replica symmetry [130] suggest that the correct value for the storage capacity is $\alpha_c^{\mathrm{RSB}} \approx 0.1382$ and thus very close indeed to the value determined in a replica symmetric approximation. The deviation from the initial numerical results is now thought to be due to a combination of strong finite size effects and inappropriate ways of performing the average over the disorder in the numerical simulations.

Once Hopfield's original model was properly understood, modifications were proposed and investigated with respect to *all* defining characteristics of the original proposal. These include (i) parallel instead of sequential dynamics [131], (ii) different pattern statistics, for example, with low levels of activity [132, 133], or hierarchically correlated data [134, 135], (iii) different forms of synaptic interactions, for example, based on the correlation matrix between the stored patterns [136], (iv) neurons which can take more than two discrete [137] or continuously many states [138], as well as sets of states having a different symmetry [139], and finally (v) sparse or asymmetric connectivity of the interactions, an extreme version being [88]. Studies of models with asymmetric interactions do of course require non-equilibrium techniques; alternatively they can and have been studied by numerical simulations. The main point of all these investigations has been to delineate the capabilities and limitations and the degree of universality of neural information processing systems. The fact that, qualitatively, the basic functionality of recursively coupled networks does indeed survive these—sometimes drastic—modifications has been taken as an indication that the essence of associative memory is captured by this type of modelling.

Several excellent books and reviews providing further details are available; let us mention the monographs [22–24, 140], the reviews in [141] and [142], and the collections [21] of reference material and [20] of reprints of older research papers. General textbooks on statistical mechanics are [143–145].

The networks analysed in the first two chapters of the present part of the book store a given set of patterns by encoding them in synaptic couplings *according to a fixed prescription*, and we analysed the probability distribution over the *states* of the network. The Gardner theory of task realizability [95, 146] takes a rather different view. It starts from a given task, such as storage of a pattern set in a recursive network, or classification of patterns in a perceptron. One then considers an ensemble of networks dealing with this task that is characterized by a probability distribution over the *set of couplings* rather than the network states. We only discussed one of the simplest questions that one may ask of such an ensemble, namely whether coupling configurations *exist* that solve the given task without errors; if no such configuration exists, no conceivable learning algorithm could be successful. We saw that this question can be answered by looking at the zero temperature limit of a suitably defined free energy, which for binary classification perceptrons is closely related to the volume of the space of solutions. This problem is already sufficiently rich to illustrate many of the technical issues that arise.

Many other questions can of course be asked. The properties of an ensemble of networks solving a given task, not perfectly but with a certain fraction of errors was studied by Gardner and Derrida [96]; in this case one does not take the zero temperature limit in the free energy calculation. Of some interest is also the case where the set of couplings is itself discrete. This was investigated by Krauth and Mézard [147], who demonstrated that a randomly classified pattern set is typically no longer linearly separable by a perceptron with binary couplings once the number of patterns increases beyond $p_{\max} \approx 0.83N$. Recall that the corresponding figure for perceptrons with continuous weights was $p_{\max} = 2N$.

On a cautionary note we add that the *existence* of solutions for a given task tells us nothing about our ability to actually find them. For instance, for the task of finding a linear separation of p randomly classified N-component patterns using a perceptron with binary weights, Horner [148] demonstrated that algorithms with a complexity scaling polynomially in system size are not likely to find solutions at *any* nonzero value of p/N in the large system limit, despite the fact that solutions are known to exist up to $p_{\max} \approx 0.83N$ [147].

Another issue arises when a classification that is to be learnt is not *random* but provided by a rule, for example, by a teacher perceptron. Such a classification is obviously always learnable by a student perceptron, if it has the same architecture as the teacher and the latter is noise-free. The interesting question now concerns the generalization ability, studied within an ensemble of student perceptrons, and in particular its scaling with the size of the training data set. Here students are assumed to be trained *on the whole set*, rather than adapting their weights in an online fashion as examples come in. This problem was first analysed by Opper *et al.* [149] and generalized in [97]. The generalization error for the maximal margin classifier was found to decrease at a rate inversely proportional to the size of the training set—a behaviour which, as we saw earlier, can be achieved in an online learning mode only by properly adapting the learning rate.

A wealth of interesting results has been obtained since the early 1990s using Gardner's interaction space approach. Let us specifically mention Virasoro's work [150] on predicting the effects of brain lesions. He demonstrated that after learning hierarchically organized data—items grouped into classes of comparatively large similarity within classes, and greater dissimilarity between classes—the class information contained in each pattern enjoys a greater embedding stability than the information that identifies a pattern as a specific member of a class. As a consequence, brain lesions that randomly destroy or disturb a certain fraction of synapses after learning will lead to the effect that the *specific* information is lost first, and the class information only when destructions become more severe. An example of the ensuing kind of malfunctioning is provided by the prosopagnosia syndrome—characterized by the ability to recognize faces as faces, without being able to distinguish between individual faces. The analysis reveals that this kind of malfunctioning must *typically* be expected when injury occurs to networks storing hierarchically organized data. This result is particularly interesting because it relies on very few assumptions apart from the basic starting point that memory resides in the synaptic organization of a network. For further results obtained within the Gardner approach we refer to the reviews of Opper and Kinzel [101], Watkin *et al.* [100], and Györgyi and Tishby [151], or the recent book by Engel and van den Broeck [152].

Appendix A: Probability theory in a nutshell

We define 'events' $\boldsymbol{x}$ as n-dimensional vectors, drawn from some event set $A \subseteq \mathbb{R}^n$. We associate with each event $\boldsymbol{x} \in A$ a real-valued and non-negative probability $p(\boldsymbol{x}) \geq 0$.

A.1 Discrete event sets

Definitions and conventions

If A is discrete and countable, each component x_i of $\boldsymbol{x}$ can only assume values from a discrete set A_i so $A \subseteq A_1 \otimes A_2 \otimes \cdots \otimes A_n$. We do not write event sets explicitly where the meaning is clear; for example, $\sum_{x_i}$ will mean $\sum_{x_i \in A_i}$, and $\sum_{\boldsymbol{x}}$ will mean $\sum_{\boldsymbol{x} \in A}$, etc. No problems arise as long as the arguments of $p(\cdots)$ are symbols; only if and when we evaluate probabilities for explicit values of the arguments will we need to indicate to which components of $\boldsymbol{x}$ such values are assigned. The probabilities are normalized according to $\sum_{\boldsymbol{x}} p(\boldsymbol{x}) = 1$.

Interpretation of probability

Imagine a system which generates events $\boldsymbol{x} \in A$ sequentially, giving the infinite series $\boldsymbol{x}_1, \boldsymbol{x}_2, \boldsymbol{x}_3, \ldots$. We choose an arbitrary one-to-one index mapping $\pi\colon \{1, 2, \ldots\} \to \{1, 2, \ldots\}$, and one particular event $\boldsymbol{x} \in A$ (in that order), and calculate for the M sequence elements $\{\boldsymbol{x}_{\pi(1)}, \ldots, \boldsymbol{x}_{\pi(M)}\}$ the frequency $f_M(\boldsymbol{x})$ with which the particular event $\boldsymbol{x}$ occurred:

$$f_M(\boldsymbol{x}) = \frac{1}{M} \sum_{m=1}^{M} \delta_{\boldsymbol{x}, \boldsymbol{x}_{\pi(m)}} \qquad \begin{cases} \delta_{\boldsymbol{x},\boldsymbol{y}} = 1 & \text{if } \boldsymbol{x} = \boldsymbol{y} \\ \delta_{\boldsymbol{x},\boldsymbol{y}} = 0 & \text{if } \boldsymbol{x} \neq \boldsymbol{y} \end{cases}$$

We define *random events* as those generated by a system as above with the property that for each one-to-one index map π, for each event $\boldsymbol{x} \in A$ the frequency of occurrence $f_M(\boldsymbol{x})$ tends to a limit as $M \to \infty$. This limit is then defined as the 'probability' associated with $\boldsymbol{x}$:

$$\forall \boldsymbol{x} \in A: \quad p(\boldsymbol{x}) = \lim_{M\to\infty} f_M(\boldsymbol{x})$$

Since $f_M(\boldsymbol{x}) \geq 0$ for each $\boldsymbol{x}$, and since $\sum_{\boldsymbol{x}} f_M(\boldsymbol{x}) = 1$ for any M, it follows that $p(\boldsymbol{x}) \geq 0$ and that $\sum_{\boldsymbol{x}} p(\boldsymbol{x}) = 1$ (as it should).

Marginal and conditional probabilities, statistical independence

The so-called 'marginal probabilities' are obtained from $p(\boldsymbol{x}) = p(x_1, \ldots, x_n)$ upon summing over individual components of $\boldsymbol{x} = (x_1, \ldots, x_n)$:

$$p(x_1, \ldots, x_{\ell-1}, x_{\ell+1}, \ldots, x_n) = \sum_{x_\ell} p(x_1, \ldots, x_n) \tag{A.1}$$

In particular we obtain (after repeating this procedure $n-1$ times):

$$p(x_i) = \sum_{x_1,\ldots,x_{i-1},x_{i+1},\ldots,x_n} p(x_1, \ldots, x_n) \tag{A.2}$$

Marginal probabilities are normalized. This follows by combining their definition (A.1) with the basic normalization $\sum_{\boldsymbol{x}} p(\boldsymbol{x}) = 1$, for example,

$$\sum_{x_1,\ldots,x_{\ell-1},x_{\ell+1},\ldots,x_n} p(x_1, \ldots, x_{\ell-1}, x_{\ell+1}, \ldots, x_n) = 1 \qquad \sum_{x_i} p(x_i) = 1$$

For any two disjunct subsets $\{i_1, \ldots, i_k\}$ and $\{j_1, \ldots, j_\ell\}$ of the index set $\{1, \ldots, n\}$ (with necessarily $k + \ell \leq n$) we next define the conditional probability

$$p(x_{i_1}, \ldots, x_{i_k} | x_{j_1}, \ldots, x_{j_\ell}) = \frac{p(x_{i_1}, \ldots, x_{i_k}, x_{j_1}, \ldots, x_{j_\ell})}{p(x_{j_1}, \ldots, x_{j_\ell})} \tag{A.3}$$

Expression (A.3), Bayes' rule, gives the probability that the k components $\{i_1, \ldots, i_k\}$ of $\boldsymbol{x}$ take the values $\{x_{i_1}, \ldots, x_{i_k}\}$, given the knowledge that the ℓ components $\{j_1, \ldots, j_\ell\}$ take the values $\{x_{j_1}, \ldots, x_{j_\ell}\}$.

The concept of statistical independence now follows naturally. Loosely speaking, statistical independence means that conditioning in the sense defined above does not affect any of the marginal probabilities. Thus the n events $\{x_1, \ldots, x_n\}$ are said to be statistically independent if for *any* two disjunct subsets $\{i_1, \ldots, i_k\}$ and $\{j_1, \ldots, j_\ell\}$ of $\{1, \ldots, n\}$ we have

$$p(x_{i_1}, \ldots, x_{i_k} | x_{j_1}, \ldots, x_{j_\ell}) = p(x_{i_1}, \ldots, x_{i_k})$$

This can be shown to be equivalent to saying

$$\{x_1,\ldots,x_n\} \text{ are independent:} \quad \begin{array}{l} p(x_{i_1},\ldots,x_{i_k}) = p(x_{i_1})p(x_{i_2})\cdots p(x_{i_k}) \\ \text{for every subset } \{i_1,\ldots,i_k\} \subseteq \{1,\ldots,n\} \end{array} \tag{A.4}$$

A.2 Continuous event sets

Definitions and conventions

Here the event set A is no longer countable. Each component x_i of $\boldsymbol{x}$ can assume values from a continuous set $A_i = \{x \in \mathbb{R} | \, \exists \boldsymbol{x} \in A \text{ with } x_i = x\}$, and $A \subseteq A_1 \otimes A_2 \otimes \cdots \otimes A_n$. As before we drop explicit reference to sets where possible; for example, $\int \mathrm{d}x_i$ will mean $\int_{A_i} \mathrm{d}x_i$ and $\int \mathrm{d}\boldsymbol{x}$ will mean $\int_A \mathrm{d}\boldsymbol{x}$, etc. The function $p(\boldsymbol{x})$ is now to be interpreted as a *probability density*, which is accordingly normalized via integration: $\int \mathrm{d}\boldsymbol{x}\; p(\boldsymbol{x}) = 1$.

Interpretation of probability

Again we imagine a system which generates events $\boldsymbol{x} \in A$ sequentially, giving $\boldsymbol{x}_1, \boldsymbol{x}_2, \ldots$. We define boxes (hypercubes) $B(\boldsymbol{x}, \boldsymbol{\Delta})$ in $\mathbb{R}^n$ as follows:

$$B(\boldsymbol{x}, \boldsymbol{\Delta}) = \{\boldsymbol{y} \in \mathbb{R}^n \,|\, x_i \le y_i < x_i + \Delta_i \text{ for all } i\}$$

in which all $\Delta_i > 0$. The volume of such a box is simply $\prod_{i=1}^n \Delta_i$. We choose an arbitrary one-to-one index mapping π: $\{1,2,\ldots\} \to \{1,2,\ldots\}$, and one particular event $\boldsymbol{x} \in A$ (in that order), and calculate for the M sequence elements $\{\boldsymbol{x}_{\pi(1)},\ldots,\boldsymbol{x}_{\pi(M)}\}$ the frequency $f_M(\boldsymbol{x}, \boldsymbol{\Delta})$ with which events were generated which happened to lie in box $B(\boldsymbol{x}, \boldsymbol{\Delta})$:

$$f_M(\boldsymbol{x}, \boldsymbol{\Delta}) = \frac{1}{M}\sum_{m=1}^{M} I(\boldsymbol{x}_{\pi(m)}; \boldsymbol{x}, \boldsymbol{\Delta}) \qquad \begin{cases} I(\boldsymbol{y}; \boldsymbol{x}, \boldsymbol{\Delta}) = 1 & \text{if } \boldsymbol{y} \in B(\boldsymbol{x}, \boldsymbol{\Delta}) \\ I(\boldsymbol{y}; \boldsymbol{x}, \boldsymbol{\Delta}) = 0 & \text{if } \boldsymbol{y} \notin B(\boldsymbol{x}, \boldsymbol{\Delta}) \end{cases}$$

We define *random events* as those generated by a system as above with the property that for each one-to-one index map π, for each box $B(\boldsymbol{x}, \boldsymbol{\Delta})$ the frequency of occurrence $f_M(\boldsymbol{x}, \boldsymbol{\Delta})$ tends to a limit as $M \to \infty$. This limit is then used to define the 'probability density' $p(\boldsymbol{x})$ associated with $\boldsymbol{x}$:

$$\forall \boldsymbol{x} \in A: \quad p(\boldsymbol{x}) = \lim_{\boldsymbol{\Delta}\to 0} \frac{\lim_{M\to\infty} f_M(\boldsymbol{x}, \boldsymbol{\Delta})}{\prod_{i=1}^n \Delta_i}$$

provided this limit exists. Since $f_M(\boldsymbol{x}, \boldsymbol{\Delta}) \geq 0$ for each $\boldsymbol{x}$, and since $\int \mathrm{d}\boldsymbol{x}\, f_M(\boldsymbol{x}, \boldsymbol{\Delta}) = \prod_{i=1}^n \Delta_i$ for any M, it follows that $p(\boldsymbol{x}) \geq 0$ and that $\int \mathrm{d}\boldsymbol{x}\, p(\boldsymbol{x}) = 1$, as it should.

Marginal and conditional probability densities, statistical independence

The marginal probabilities are now obtained by integrating (as opposed to summing) over individual components of $\boldsymbol{x} = (x_1, \ldots, x_n)$:

$$p(x_1, \ldots, x_{\ell-1}, x_{\ell+1}, \ldots, x_n) = \int \mathrm{d}x_\ell\, p(x_1, \ldots, x_n) \tag{A.5}$$

In particular we obtain, upon repeating this procedure:

$$p(x_i) = \int \mathrm{d}x_1 \ldots \mathrm{d}x_{i-1}\mathrm{d}x_{i+1} \ldots \mathrm{d}x_n\, p(x_1, \ldots, x_n) \tag{A.6}$$

Again, marginal probabilities are normalized, but now in the sense of integration. This follows as before by combining their definition (A.5) with the basic normalization $\int \mathrm{d}\boldsymbol{x}\, p(\boldsymbol{x}) = 1$, for example,

$$\int \mathrm{d}x_1 \ldots \mathrm{d}x_{\ell-1}\mathrm{d}x_{\ell+1} \ldots \mathrm{d}x_n\, p(x_1, \ldots, x_{\ell-1}, x_{\ell+1}, \ldots, x_n) = 1$$

$$\int \mathrm{d}x_i\, p(x_i) = 1$$

For any two disjoint subsets $\{i_1, \ldots, i_k\}$ and $\{j_1, \ldots, j_\ell\}$ of the index set $\{1, \ldots, n\}$ we next define the conditional probability density

$$p(x_{i_1}, \ldots, x_{i_k} | x_{j_1}, \ldots, x_{j_\ell}) = \frac{p(x_{i_1}, \ldots, x_{i_k}, x_{j_1}, \ldots, x_{j_\ell})}{p(x_{j_1}, \ldots, x_{j_\ell})} \tag{A.7}$$

It gives the probability density for the k components $\{i_1, \ldots, i_k\}$, given the knowledge that the ℓ components $\{j_1, \ldots, j_\ell\}$ take the values $\{x_{j_1}, \ldots, x_{j_\ell}\}$.

Statistical independence can as before be defined in the following way:

$$\{x_1, \ldots, x_n\} \text{ are independent:} \quad \begin{array}{l} p(x_{i_1}, \ldots, x_{i_k}) = p(x_{i_1})p(x_{i_2}) \cdots p(x_{i_k}) \\ \text{for every subset } \{i_1, \ldots, i_k\} \subseteq \{1, \ldots, n\} \end{array} \tag{A.8}$$

A.3 Averages of specific random variables

We define 'random variables' as arbitrary functions $F(\boldsymbol{x})$ of random events $\boldsymbol{x} \in A$. We define *averages* or *expectation values* or *mean values* $\langle F(\boldsymbol{x})\rangle$ of random variables $F(\boldsymbol{x})$ as follows:

$$\begin{aligned} &\text{discrete random variables:} && \langle F(\boldsymbol{x})\rangle = \textstyle\sum_{\boldsymbol{x}} p(\boldsymbol{x})F(\boldsymbol{x}) \\ &\text{continuous random variables:} && \langle F(\boldsymbol{x})\rangle = \textstyle\int \mathrm{d}\boldsymbol{x}\; p(\boldsymbol{x})F(\boldsymbol{x}) \end{aligned} \tag{A.9}$$

Let us now turn to the definitions and properties of a number of relevant (discrete or continuous) random variables and averages. Note that in general one cannot be sure beforehand (without explicit proof) that the following averages will actually exist (i.e. are finite):

average: $\mu_i = \langle x_i\rangle$

variance: $\sigma_i^2 = \langle x_i^2\rangle - \langle x_i\rangle^2$

σ_i^2 is non-negative, since $\langle x_i^2\rangle - \langle x_i\rangle^2 = \langle (x_i - \langle x_i\rangle)^2\rangle$. This also shows that $\sigma_i^2 = 0$ implies that $x_i = x_i'$ for any two events $\boldsymbol{x} \in A$ and $\boldsymbol{x}' \in A$ with nonzero probabilities.

covariance matrix: $C_{ij} = \langle x_i x_j\rangle - \langle x_i\rangle\langle x_j\rangle$

Note that $C_{ii} = \sigma_i^2$. The covariance matrix is symmetric so all eigenvalues are real. It is also non-negative definite (so all eigenvalues are non-negative), since it can be written as $\langle x_i x_j\rangle - \langle x_i\rangle\langle x_j\rangle = \langle (x_i - \langle x_i\rangle)(x_j - \langle x_j\rangle)\rangle$, from which it follows that

$$\text{for any } \boldsymbol{z} \in \mathbb{R}^n\text{:}\quad \boldsymbol{z}\cdot\boldsymbol{C}\boldsymbol{z} = \left\langle \left[\sum_{i=1}^{n} z_i(x_i - \langle x_i\rangle)\right]^2\right\rangle \geq 0$$

moments: $\langle x_{i_1}^{m_{i_1}} x_{i_2}^{m_{i_2}}, \ldots, x_{i_k}^{m_{i_k}}\rangle$, with $m_{i_\ell} \in \{0, 1, 2, 3, \ldots\}$

characteristic function: For a single random variable x, the characteristic function is defined as $\phi(k) = \langle e^{\mathrm{i}kx}\rangle$. The functional dependence of this on k encapsulates all the moments; this follows by Taylor-expanding the exponential: $\phi(k) = 1 + \mathrm{i}k\langle x\rangle - \frac{1}{2}k^2\langle x^2\rangle + \cdots$. Also, by writing out $\phi(k)$ explicitly as

$$\phi(k) = \int \mathrm{d}x\; p(x)\, e^{\mathrm{i}kx}$$

one sees that it is just the Fourier transform of the probability distribution $p(x)$. Applying the inverse Fourier transform (see Appendix F) means that we can retrieve $p(x)$ if we know $\phi(k)$:

$$p(x) = \int \frac{dk}{2\pi} \phi(k) e^{-ikx}$$

Thus—at least for sufficiently well-behaved probability distributions—knowledge of the characteristic function is equivalent to knowing $p(x)$. The above arguments generalize to the case of several random variables: here one defines $\phi(\boldsymbol{k}) = \langle \exp(i \sum_{i=1}^{n} k_i x_i) \rangle$ and the inverse Fourier transform gives

$$p(\boldsymbol{x}) = \int \left(\prod_{i=1}^{n} \frac{dk_i}{2\pi} \right) \phi(\boldsymbol{k}) e^{-i \sum_{i=1}^{n} k_i x_i}$$

Appendix B: Conditions for the central limit theorem to apply

We first give a simple *necessary* condition for a random variable to have a Gaussian probability distribution. This is followed by Lindeberg's Theorem, which gives a *sufficient* condition for an infinite sum of independent random variables to have a Gaussian probability distribution. We then apply both results to expressions of the form $\sum_{i=1}^{N} W_i x_i$, in which the $x_i \in \{-1, 1\}$ are independent zero average random variables.

B.1 Moment condition

Consider a zero average random variable Y, described by a Gaussian probability distribution

$$p(y) = \frac{1}{\sigma\sqrt{2\pi}}\, e^{-y^2/2\sigma^2}$$

All odd moments are zero, that is, $\langle y^{2m+1}\rangle = 0$, due to the symmetry $p(y) = p(-y)$. All even moments $\langle y^{2m}\rangle$ can be expressed in terms of the width σ of this distribution. For instance,

$$\begin{aligned}
\langle y^2\rangle &= \int \frac{\mathrm{d}y}{\sigma\sqrt{2\pi}}\, y^2\, e^{-y^2/2\sigma^2} \\
&= (2\pi\sigma^2)^{-1/2} \lim_{x\to 1/2\sigma^2} \int \mathrm{d}y\, y^2\, e^{-xy^2} \\
&= -(2\pi\sigma^2)^{-1/2} \lim_{x\to 1/2\sigma^2} \frac{\mathrm{d}}{\mathrm{d}x} \int \mathrm{d}y\, e^{-xy^2} \\
&= -(2\pi\sigma^2)^{-1/2} \lim_{x\to 1/2\sigma^2} \frac{\mathrm{d}}{\mathrm{d}x} \sqrt{\pi}\, x^{-1/2} \\
&= \sigma^2
\end{aligned}$$

(where we used $\int dy\, e^{-y^2/2} = \sqrt{2\pi}$, see Appendix D). We obtain in a similar way:

$$\begin{aligned}\langle y^4\rangle &= \int \frac{dy}{\sigma\sqrt{2\pi}}\, y^4\, e^{-y^2/2\sigma^2} = (2\pi\sigma^2)^{-1/2} \lim_{x\to 1/2\sigma^2} \int dy\, y^4\, e^{-xy^2} \\ &= (2\pi\sigma^2)^{-1/2} \lim_{x\to 1/2\sigma^2} \frac{d^2}{dx^2} \int dy\, e^{-xy^2} \\ &= (2\pi\sigma^2)^{-1/2} \lim_{x\to 1/2\sigma^2} \frac{d^2}{dx^2} \sqrt{\pi}\, x^{-1/2} = 3\sigma^2\end{aligned}$$

A necessary condition for y to have a Gaussian probability distribution is thus $\langle y^4\rangle = 3\langle y^2\rangle^2$.

We now choose $y_N = \sum_{i=1}^N W_i x_i \left(\sum_{i=j}^N W_j^2\right)^{-1/2}$, where the $x_k \in \{-1, 1\}$ are independent random variables with $\langle x_k\rangle = 0$. A necessary condition for y_N to have a Gaussian probability distribution for $N \to \infty$ is then

$$\lim_{N\to\infty} \frac{\sum_{ijk\ell=1}^n W_i W_j W_k W_\ell \langle x_i x_j x_k x_\ell\rangle}{\left(\sum_{i=1}^N W_i^2\right)^2} = 3$$

With the help of the identity $\langle x_i x_j x_k x_\ell\rangle = \delta_{ij}\delta_{k\ell} + \delta_{ik}\delta_{j\ell} + \delta_{i\ell}\delta_{jk} - 2\delta_{ij}\delta_{k\ell}\delta_{ik}$ we find the previous condition simplifying to

$$\lim_{N\to\infty} \frac{\sum_{i=1}^N W_i^4}{\left(\sum_{j=1}^N W_j^2\right)^2} = 0 \tag{B.1}$$

B.2 Lindeberg's theorem

Let $X_1, X_2, X_3, \ldots$ be a sequence of independent random variables such that $\langle x_k\rangle = 0$ and $\langle x_k^2\rangle = \sigma_k^2$. Let $p_k(x)$ denote the distribution function of X_k and define $S_N = \sum_{i=1}^N x_i$, so that

$$\langle S_N\rangle = 0 \qquad s_N^2 = \langle S_N^2\rangle = \sigma_1^2 + \sigma_2^2 + \cdots + \sigma_N^2$$

Suppose now that the so-called Lindeberg condition is satisfied, that is,

$$\text{for each } t > 0: \quad \lim_{N\to\infty} \frac{1}{s_N^2} \sum_{k=1}^n \int_{|x|\geq ts_N} dx\, x^2 p_k(x) = 0 \tag{B.2}$$

then the distribution of the normalized sum S_N/s_N tends to the zero average and unit variance Gaussian distribution as $N \to \infty$. For the proof of this theorem see, for example, [76, 77].

We now apply this theorem to the choice $X_i = W_i x_i$, where the $x_k \in \{-1, 1\}$ are independent random variables with $\langle x_k \rangle = 0$. Thus $\sigma_k^2 = W_k^2$ for each k. Lindeberg's condition (B.2) now reads:

$$\text{for each } t > 0: \quad \lim_{N\to\infty} \frac{\sum_{i=1}^N W_i^2 \theta\left(|W_i| - t\sqrt{\sum_{j=1}^N W_j^2}\right)}{\sum_{i=1}^N W_i^2} = 0$$

We can simplify this condition further. Upon defining $v_k = W_k / \sqrt{\sum_{j=1}^N W_j^2}$ it can be written as

$$\text{for each } \epsilon > 0: \quad \lim_{N\to\infty} \sum_{i=1}^N v_i^2 \theta(v_i^2 - \epsilon) = 0$$

We note that all nonzero terms in this sum obey ${v_k}^2 \geq \epsilon$. Since also ${v_k}^2 \leq 1$, it now follows that

$$\epsilon \sum_{k=1}^N \theta(v_k^2 - \epsilon) \leq \sum_{k=1}^N v_k^2 \theta(v_k^2 - \epsilon) \leq \sum_{k=1}^N \theta(v_k^2 - \epsilon)$$

This tells us that here the Lindeberg condition is equivalent to:

$$\text{for each } \epsilon > 0: \quad \lim_{N\to\infty} \sum_{i=1}^N \theta(v_i^2 - \epsilon) = 0$$

In terms of the original variables W_i this reads:

$$\text{for each } \epsilon > 0: \quad \lim_{N\to\infty} \sum_{i=1}^N \theta\left(W_i^2 - \epsilon \sum_{k=1}^N W_k^2\right) = 0 \qquad \text{(B.3)}$$

Appendix C: Some simple summation identities

Here we give, without proof, some useful identities dealing with the summation of simple series which are encountered in the various examples and exercises:

$$\sum_{k=1}^{n} k = \frac{1}{2}n(n+1) \tag{C.1}$$

$$\sum_{k=1}^{n} k^2 = \frac{1}{6}n(n+1)(2n+1) \tag{C.2}$$

$$\sum_{k=1}^{\infty} \frac{1}{k^2} = \frac{1}{6}\pi^2 \tag{C.3}$$

$$\sum_{k=1}^{\infty} \frac{1}{k^4} = \frac{11}{180}\pi^4 \tag{C.4}$$

$$\sum_{k=1}^{\infty} \frac{1}{k} = \infty \tag{C.5}$$

$$\sum_{k=0}^{n} z^k = \frac{1-z^{n+1}}{1-z} \quad (z \neq 1) \tag{C.6}$$

Appendix D: Gaussian integrals and probability distributions

In this appendix we derive some properties of symmetric positive definite matrices $\boldsymbol{A}$, their associated Gaussian probability distributions in $\mathbb{R}^N$ and integrals of the following general form (for simple functions f):

$$I = \int \mathrm{d}\boldsymbol{x}\; f(\boldsymbol{x}) e^{-\boldsymbol{x}\cdot\boldsymbol{A}\boldsymbol{x}/2}$$

We calculate explicitly several integrals of this type, with specific choices of the matrix $\boldsymbol{A}$, that we encounter in the various chapters of this book.

D.1 General properties of Gaussian integrals

Real, symmetric, positive definite matrices

The symmetric $N \times N$ matrix $\boldsymbol{A}$ is assumed to be positive definite, that is, $\boldsymbol{x} \cdot \boldsymbol{A}\boldsymbol{x} > 0$ for all $\boldsymbol{x} \in \mathbb{R}^N$ with $|\boldsymbol{x}| \neq 0$. The characteristic polynomial $\det(\boldsymbol{A} - \lambda\mathbb{1})$ is of order N, so there will be N (possibly complex) solutions λ (where some may coincide) of the eigenvalue problem

$$\boldsymbol{A}\boldsymbol{x} = \lambda\boldsymbol{x}, \quad \boldsymbol{x} \neq 0 \tag{D.1}$$

We denote complex conjugation of complex numbers z in the usual way: if $z = a + ib$ (where $a, b \in \mathbb{R}$), then $z^* = a - ib$ and $|z|^2 = z^*z \in \mathbb{R}$. We denote the unit matrix in $\mathbb{R}^N$ by $\mathbb{1}$, so $\mathbb{1}_{ij} = \delta_{ij}$.

Proposition 1. All eigenvalues of the matrix $\boldsymbol{A}$ are real.

Proof. We simply take the inner product in (D.1) with the conjugate vector $\boldsymbol{x}^*$, which gives

$$\sum_{i,j=1}^{N} x_i^* A_{ij} x_j = \lambda \sum_{i=1}^{N} |x_i|^2$$

We use the symmetry of A, and substitute $A_{ij} \to \frac{1}{2}(A_{ij} + A_{ji})$:

$$\lambda = \frac{1}{2} \frac{\sum_{ij} x_i^*(A_{ij} + A_{ji})x_j}{\sum_{i=1}^{N} |x_i|^2} = \frac{1}{2} \frac{\sum_{ij} A_{ij}(x_i^* x_j + x_i x_j^*)}{\sum_{i=1}^{N} |x_i|^2}$$

Since $(x_i^* x_j + x_i x_j^*)^* = x_i x_j^* + x_i^* x_j = x_i^* x_j + x_i x_j^*$, the above fraction is entirely real-valued, so $\lambda \in \mathbb{R}$. □

Proposition 2. All eigenvectors can be chosen real-valued.

Proof. For a given eigenvalue λ the corresponding eigenvectors $\boldsymbol{x}$ are the solutions of (D.1). We separate real and imaginary parts of every eigenvector:

$$\boldsymbol{x} = \mathrm{Re}\,\boldsymbol{x} + \mathrm{i}\,\mathrm{Im}\,\boldsymbol{x} \qquad \mathrm{Re}\,\boldsymbol{x} = \frac{1}{2}(\boldsymbol{x} + \boldsymbol{x}^*) \qquad \mathrm{Im}\,\boldsymbol{x} = \frac{1}{2\mathrm{i}}(\boldsymbol{x} - \boldsymbol{x}^*)$$

with $\mathrm{Re}\,\boldsymbol{x} \in \mathbb{R}^N$ and $\mathrm{Im}\,\boldsymbol{x} \in \mathbb{R}^N$. Taking the complex conjugate of equation (D.1) gives us $\boldsymbol{A}\boldsymbol{x}^* = \lambda \boldsymbol{x}^*$ (since λ is real). Thus, if $\boldsymbol{x}$ is an eigenvector with eigenvalue λ, so is $\boldsymbol{x}^*$; complex eigenvectors always come in conjugate pairs. But by adding to equation (D.1) its conjugate, and by similarly subtracting the conjugate, it follows that if $\boldsymbol{x}$ and $\boldsymbol{x}^*$ are eigenvectors, then so are $\mathrm{Re}\,\boldsymbol{x}$ and $\mathrm{Im}\,\boldsymbol{x}$. Since the space spanned by $\boldsymbol{x}$ and $\boldsymbol{x}^*$ is the same as the space spanned by $\mathrm{Re}\,\boldsymbol{x}$ and $\mathrm{Im}\,\boldsymbol{x}$, we are always allowed to choose the equivalent real-valued pair $\mathrm{Re}\,\boldsymbol{x}$ and $\mathrm{Im}\,\boldsymbol{x}$. □

Proposition 3. All eigenvalues λ are positive.

Proof. We can derive this property directly from the eigenvalue equation (D.1) by taking the inner product with $\boldsymbol{x}$: $\lambda = (\boldsymbol{x} \cdot \boldsymbol{A}\boldsymbol{x})/(\boldsymbol{x}^2) > 0$, since $\boldsymbol{A}$ is positive definite and $\boldsymbol{x}$ is real and nonzero. □

Proposition 4. For every linear subspace $L \subseteq \mathbb{R}^N$ the following holds:

$$\text{if } AL \subseteq L \text{ then also } AL^{\perp} \subseteq L^{\perp}$$

in which $L^{\perp}$ denotes the orthogonal complement, that is, $\mathbb{R}^N = L \oplus L^{\perp}$.

Proof. For each $\boldsymbol{x} \in L$ and $\boldsymbol{y} \in L^{\perp}$ we find $(\boldsymbol{x} \cdot \boldsymbol{A}\boldsymbol{y}) = (\boldsymbol{y} \cdot \boldsymbol{A}\boldsymbol{x}) = 0$ (since $\boldsymbol{A}\boldsymbol{x} \in L$ and $\boldsymbol{y} \in L^{\perp}$). Therefore $\boldsymbol{A}\boldsymbol{y} \in L^{\perp}$, which completes the proof. □

Proposition 5. We can construct a complete orthogonal basis in $\mathbb{R}^N$ of A-eigenvectors.

Proof. Consider two eigenvectors $\boldsymbol{x}_a$ and $\boldsymbol{x}_b$ of $\boldsymbol{A}$, corresponding to different eigenvalues:

$$\boldsymbol{A}\boldsymbol{x}_a = \lambda_a \boldsymbol{x}_a \qquad \boldsymbol{A}\boldsymbol{x}_b = \lambda_b \boldsymbol{x}_b \qquad \lambda_a \neq \lambda_b$$

We now form:

$$\begin{aligned} 0 &= (\boldsymbol{x}_a \cdot \boldsymbol{A}\boldsymbol{x}_b) - (\boldsymbol{x}_a \cdot \boldsymbol{A}\boldsymbol{x}_b) = (\boldsymbol{x}_a \cdot \boldsymbol{A}\boldsymbol{x}_b) - (\boldsymbol{x}_b \cdot \boldsymbol{A}\boldsymbol{x}_a) \\ &= \lambda_b(\boldsymbol{x}_a \cdot \boldsymbol{x}_b) - \lambda_a(\boldsymbol{x}_b \cdot \boldsymbol{x}_a) = (\lambda_a - \lambda_b)(\boldsymbol{x}_a \cdot \boldsymbol{x}_b) \end{aligned}$$

Since $\lambda_a \neq \lambda_b$ it follows that $\boldsymbol{x}_a \cdot \boldsymbol{x}_b = 0$: eigenspaces corresponding to different eigenvalues are mutually orthogonal. If all eigenvalues are distinct, this completes the proof, since in that case there will be N eigenvalues with corresponding eigenvectors $\boldsymbol{x} \neq 0$. Since these N eigenvectors are proven to be orthogonal, after normalization $\boldsymbol{x} \to \boldsymbol{x}/|\boldsymbol{x}|$ they form a complete orthogonal basis.

In order to deal with degenerate eigenvalues we need the previous Property 4. For every symmetric $N \times N$ matrix we know: if $A\boldsymbol{x} = \lambda \boldsymbol{x}$, then $\forall \boldsymbol{y}$ with $\boldsymbol{x} \cdot \boldsymbol{y} = 0$: $(A\boldsymbol{y}) \cdot \boldsymbol{x} = 0$. Having found such an eigenvector $\boldsymbol{x}$ for a given eigenvalue λ (not unique in the case of a degenerate eigenvalue), a new reduced $(N-1) \times (N-1)$ matrix can be constructed by restricting ourselves to the subspace $\boldsymbol{x}^{\perp}$. The new matrix is again symmetric, the eigenvalue polynomial is of order $N-1$ (and contains all the previous roots except for one corresponding to the eigenvector just eliminated), and we can repeat the argument. This shows that there *must* be N orthogonal eigenvectors, which we can normalize and use as a basis in $\mathbb{R}^N$. □

The final consequence of the above facts is that there exist a set of vectors $\{\hat{\boldsymbol{e}}^i\}$, where $i = 1, \ldots, N$ and $\hat{\boldsymbol{e}}^i \in \mathbb{R}^N$ for all i, with the following properties:

$$\boldsymbol{A}\hat{\boldsymbol{e}}^i = \lambda_i \hat{\boldsymbol{e}}^i, \quad \lambda_i \in \mathbb{R}, \quad \lambda_i > 0, \quad \hat{\boldsymbol{e}}^i \cdot \hat{\boldsymbol{e}}^j = \delta_{ij} \tag{D.2}$$

We can now bring $\boldsymbol{A}$ onto diagonal form by a simple unitary transformation $\boldsymbol{U}$, which we construct from the components of the normalized eigenvectors $\hat{\boldsymbol{e}}$: $U_{ij} = \hat{e}^j_i$. We denote the transpose of $\boldsymbol{U}$ by $\boldsymbol{U}^\dagger$, $U^\dagger_{ij} = U_{ji}$, and show that $\boldsymbol{U}$ is indeed unitary, that is, $\boldsymbol{U}^\dagger \boldsymbol{U} = \boldsymbol{U}\boldsymbol{U}^\dagger = \mathbf{1}$:

$$\begin{aligned} \sum_j (\boldsymbol{U}^\dagger \boldsymbol{U})_{ij} x_j &= \sum_{jk} U_{ki} U_{kj} x_j = \sum_{jk} \hat{e}^i_k \hat{e}^j_k x_j = \sum_j \delta_{ij} x_j = x_i \\ \sum_j (\boldsymbol{U}\boldsymbol{U}^\dagger)_{ij} x_j &= \sum_{jk} U_{ik} U_{jk} x_j = \sum_{jk} \hat{e}^k_i \hat{e}^k_j x_j = \sum_k \hat{e}^k_i (\hat{\boldsymbol{e}}^k \cdot \boldsymbol{x}) = x_i \end{aligned}$$

(since $\{\hat{\boldsymbol{e}}^\ell\}$ is a complete orthogonal basis). From $\boldsymbol{U}$ being unitary it follows that $\boldsymbol{U}$ and $\boldsymbol{U}^\dagger$ leave inner products, and therefore also lengths, invariant:

$$\boldsymbol{Ux}\cdot\boldsymbol{Uy}=\boldsymbol{x}\cdot\boldsymbol{U}^\dagger\boldsymbol{Uy}=\boldsymbol{x}\cdot\boldsymbol{y}\qquad \boldsymbol{U}^\dagger\boldsymbol{x}\cdot\boldsymbol{U}^\dagger\boldsymbol{y}=\boldsymbol{x}\cdot\boldsymbol{UU}^\dagger\boldsymbol{y}=\boldsymbol{x}\cdot\boldsymbol{y}$$

We can see explicitly that $\boldsymbol{U}$ indeed brings $\boldsymbol{A}$ into diagonal form:

$$(\boldsymbol{U}^\dagger\boldsymbol{AU})_{ij}=\sum_{kl=1}^{N}U^\dagger_{ik}A_{kl}U_{lj}=\sum_{kl=1}^{N}\hat{e}^i_kA_{kl}\hat{e}^j_l=\lambda_j\sum_{k=1}^{N}\hat{e}^i_k\hat{e}^j_k=\lambda_j\delta_{ij}\qquad\text{(D.3)}$$

Note that the inverse $\boldsymbol{A}^{-1}$ of the matrix $\boldsymbol{A}$ exists, and can be written as follows:

$$(\boldsymbol{A}^{-1})_{ij}=\sum_{k=1}^{N}\lambda_k^{-1}\hat{e}^k_i\hat{e}^k_j\qquad\text{(D.4)}$$

To prove that this is indeed the inverse of $\boldsymbol{A}$, we just work out for any $\boldsymbol{x}\in\mathbb{R}^N$ the two expressions

$$(\boldsymbol{AA}^{-1}\boldsymbol{x})_i=\sum_{kj=1}^{N}A_{ik}\sum_{\ell=1}^{N}\lambda_\ell^{-1}\hat{e}^\ell_k\hat{e}^\ell_jx_j=\sum_{\ell=1}^{N}\hat{e}^\ell_i(\hat{\boldsymbol{e}}^\ell\cdot\boldsymbol{x})=x_i$$

(again since $\{\hat{\boldsymbol{e}}^\ell\}$ forms a complete orthogonal basis), and

$$(\boldsymbol{A}^{-1}\boldsymbol{Ax})_i=\sum_{kj=1}^{N}\sum_{\ell=1}^{N}\lambda_\ell^{-1}\hat{e}^\ell_i\hat{e}^\ell_kA_{kj}x_j=\sum_{\ell=1}^{N}\hat{e}^\ell_i(\hat{\boldsymbol{e}}^\ell\cdot\boldsymbol{x})=x_i$$

Multivariate Gaussian integrals

We have now established all the required tools to turn to a simple analysis of the Gaussian integrals associated with positive definite symmetric matrices:

$$I=\int\mathrm{d}\boldsymbol{x}\ f(\boldsymbol{x})e^{-\boldsymbol{x}\cdot\boldsymbol{Ax}/2}\qquad\text{(D.5)}$$

The simplest such integral is obtained for $f(\boldsymbol{x})=1$ and $N=1$:

$$\int\mathrm{d}x\ e^{-x^2/2}=\sqrt{2\pi}\qquad\text{(D.6)}$$

(for a proof of (D.6) see the last part of this appendix). For $f(\boldsymbol{x})=1$ and $N>1$ we can do the integral (D.5) by using the previous results on the diagonalizability of the matrix $\boldsymbol{A}$. We put $\boldsymbol{x} = \boldsymbol{U}\boldsymbol{z}$ (since $\boldsymbol{U}$ leaves inner products invariant, we are guaranteed that $\mathrm{d}\boldsymbol{x} = \mathrm{d}\boldsymbol{z}$):

$$\int \mathrm{d}\boldsymbol{x}\, e^{-\boldsymbol{x}\cdot\boldsymbol{A}\boldsymbol{x}/2} = \int \mathrm{d}\boldsymbol{z}\, e^{-\boldsymbol{z}\cdot\boldsymbol{U}^{\dagger}\boldsymbol{A}\boldsymbol{U}\boldsymbol{z}/2} = \prod_{\ell=1}^{N}\left(\int \mathrm{d}z\, e^{-\lambda_\ell z^2/2}\right)$$
$$= \left(\prod_{\ell=1}^{N}\frac{1}{\sqrt{\lambda_\ell}}\right)\left(\int \mathrm{d}z\, e^{-z^2/2}\right)^{N} = \frac{(2\pi)^{N/2}}{\sqrt{\det \boldsymbol{A}}} \qquad \text{(D.7)}$$

Here we have used the fact that the determinant of $\boldsymbol{A}$ is invariant under rotations, so it can be evaluated with $\boldsymbol{A}$ in diagonal form, giving the product of its N eigenvalues.

Let us turn next to less trivial choices for $f(\boldsymbol{x})$. Due to the symmetry of the integrand in (D.5) under reflection $\boldsymbol{x} \to -\boldsymbol{x}$, the integral reduces to zero for $f(\boldsymbol{x}) = x_i$. For the choice $f(\boldsymbol{x}) = x_i x_j$ we use the following trick:

$$\int \mathrm{d}\boldsymbol{x}\, x_i x_j\, e^{-\boldsymbol{x}\cdot\boldsymbol{A}\boldsymbol{x}/2} = \lim_{\boldsymbol{b}\to 0} \frac{\partial^2}{\partial b_i \partial b_j} \int \mathrm{d}\boldsymbol{x}\, e^{-\boldsymbol{x}\cdot\boldsymbol{A}\boldsymbol{x}/2+\boldsymbol{b}\cdot\boldsymbol{x}} \qquad \text{(D.8)}$$

The integral on the right-hand side can be evaluated by completing the square in the exponent and then shifting the integration variable:

$$\int \mathrm{d}\boldsymbol{x}\, e^{-\boldsymbol{x}\cdot\boldsymbol{A}\boldsymbol{x}/2+\boldsymbol{b}\cdot\boldsymbol{x}} = \int \mathrm{d}\boldsymbol{x}\, e^{-(\boldsymbol{x}-\boldsymbol{A}^{-1}\boldsymbol{b})\cdot\boldsymbol{A}(\boldsymbol{x}-\boldsymbol{A}^{-1}\boldsymbol{b})/2+\boldsymbol{b}\cdot\boldsymbol{A}^{-1}\boldsymbol{b}/2}$$
$$= \frac{(2\pi)^{N/2}}{\sqrt{\det \boldsymbol{A}}}\, e^{\boldsymbol{b}\cdot\boldsymbol{A}^{-1}\boldsymbol{b}/2} \qquad \text{(D.9)}$$

Thus, carrying out the differentiations in (D.8) gives

$$\frac{\sqrt{\det \boldsymbol{A}}}{(2\pi)^{N/2}} \int \mathrm{d}\boldsymbol{x}\, x_i x_j\, e^{-\boldsymbol{x}\cdot\boldsymbol{A}\boldsymbol{x}/2} = \lim_{\boldsymbol{b}\to 0}\,[(\boldsymbol{A}^{-1})_{ij} + (\boldsymbol{A}^{-1}\boldsymbol{b})_i(\boldsymbol{A}^{-1}\boldsymbol{b})_j]e^{\boldsymbol{b}\cdot\boldsymbol{A}^{-1}\boldsymbol{b}/2}$$
$$= (\boldsymbol{A}^{-1})_{ij} \qquad \text{(D.10)}$$

D.2 Gaussian probability distributions

Simple Gaussian (or 'normal') probability distributions

A single random variable x is said to have a Gaussian probability distribution (or probability density) with mean μ and variance σ^2 if

$$p(x) = \frac{e^{-(x-\mu)^2/2\sigma^2}}{\sqrt{2\pi\sigma^2}}, \qquad x \in \mathbb{R} \qquad \text{(D.11)}$$

This expression is properly normalized, as follows from our elementary Gaussian integral (D.6) above:

$$\int \mathrm{d}x\, p(x) = \int \frac{\mathrm{d}x}{\sigma\sqrt{2\pi}}\, e^{-(x-\mu)^2/2\sigma^2} = \int \frac{\mathrm{d}z}{\sqrt{2\pi}}\, e^{-z^2/2} = 1$$

To work out the moments of (D.11), one can start from the identity

$$\langle (x-\mu)^n \rangle = \int \frac{\mathrm{d}x}{\sigma\sqrt{2\pi}} (x-\mu)^n e^{-(x-\mu)^2/2\sigma^2} = \sigma^n \int \frac{\mathrm{d}z}{\sqrt{2\pi}}\, z^n e^{-z^2/2}$$

For n odd the result is zero. For n even one finds:

$$\begin{aligned}
\langle (x-\mu)^{2m} \rangle &= \sigma^{2m}(-1)^m \lim_{y\to 1/2} \frac{\mathrm{d}^m}{\mathrm{d}y^m} \int \frac{\mathrm{d}z}{\sqrt{2\pi}}\, e^{-yz^2} \\
&= \frac{\sigma^{2m}}{\sqrt{2}}(-1)^m \lim_{y\to 1/2} \frac{\mathrm{d}^m}{\mathrm{d}y^m}\, y^{-1/2} \\
&= \frac{\sigma^{2m}}{\sqrt{2}} \lim_{y\to 1/2} \left(\frac{1}{2} \times \frac{3}{2} \times \cdots \times \frac{2m-1}{2}\right) y^{-(1/2)-m} \\
&= \sigma^{2m}(1 \times 3 \times \cdots \times (2m-1))
\end{aligned} \qquad \text{(D.12)}$$

With (D.12), together with $\langle (x-\mu)^n \rangle = 0$ for all odd n, one can generate the various moments iteratively. For example:

$$\begin{aligned}
\langle x-\mu \rangle &= 0 & &\Rightarrow & \langle x \rangle &= \mu \\
\langle (x-\mu)^2 \rangle &= \sigma^2 & &\Rightarrow & \langle x^2 \rangle &= \mu^2 + \sigma^2 \\
\langle (x-\mu)^3 \rangle &= 0 & &\Rightarrow & \langle x^3 \rangle &= \mu^3 + 3\mu\sigma^2 \\
\langle (x-\mu)^4 \rangle &= 3\sigma^4 & &\Rightarrow & \langle x^4 \rangle &= 3(\mu^2+\sigma^2)^2 - 2\mu^4
\end{aligned}$$

In addition, relations such as $\langle (x-\mu)^4 \rangle = 3\langle (x-\mu)^2 \rangle^2$ can often serve as a quick test to see whether an unknown distribution could be Gaussian.

Multivariate Gaussian probability distributions

A collection of N random variables $\boldsymbol{x} = (x_1, \ldots, x_N)$ are said to have a zero-mean (joint) Gaussian probability distribution if

$$p(\boldsymbol{x}) = \frac{\sqrt{\det \boldsymbol{A}}}{(2\pi)^{N/2}}\, e^{-\boldsymbol{x}\cdot\boldsymbol{A}\boldsymbol{x}/2}, \quad \boldsymbol{x} \in \mathbb{R}^N$$

From (D.7) we see that this expression is properly normalized. As discussed above, the symmetry of the distribution implies that all the means vanish, $\langle x_i \rangle = 0$. The covariances follow from (D.10): $\langle x_i x_j \rangle = (\boldsymbol{A}^{-1})_{ij}$.

It follows that a zero-mean Gaussian distribution is fully determined by its covariances. Writing the covariance matrix as $\boldsymbol{C}$, one therefore normally represents such distributions in the form

$$p(\boldsymbol{x}) = \frac{1}{(2\pi)^{N/2}(\det \boldsymbol{C})^{1/2}}\, e^{-\boldsymbol{x}\cdot\boldsymbol{C}^{-1}\boldsymbol{x}/2}$$

where we have used $\det \boldsymbol{C} = 1/\det \boldsymbol{A}$.

We can also immediately work out the characteristic function of a Gaussian distribution, using the integral (D.9):

$$\langle e^{\mathrm{i}\boldsymbol{k}\cdot\boldsymbol{x}}\rangle = e^{-\boldsymbol{k}\cdot\boldsymbol{C}\boldsymbol{k}/2} \tag{D.13}$$

Thus, the characteristic function of a Gaussian distribution is again Gaussian.

These above results generalize easily to the case of nonzero means, by setting $\boldsymbol{y} = \boldsymbol{x} + \boldsymbol{\mu}$. The probability distribution of $\boldsymbol{y}$ is then

$$p(\boldsymbol{y}) = \frac{1}{(2\pi)^{N/2}(\det \boldsymbol{C})^{1/2}}\, e^{-(\boldsymbol{y}-\boldsymbol{\mu})\cdot\boldsymbol{C}^{-1}(\boldsymbol{y}-\boldsymbol{\mu})/2} \tag{D.14}$$

with $\langle y_i\rangle = \mu_i$ and $\langle y_i y_j\rangle = \mu_i\mu_j + C_{ij}$. The characteristic function is, using (D.13)

$$\langle e^{\mathrm{i}\boldsymbol{k}\cdot\boldsymbol{y}}\rangle = e^{\mathrm{i}\boldsymbol{k}\cdot\boldsymbol{\mu}}\langle e^{\mathrm{i}\boldsymbol{k}\cdot\boldsymbol{x}}\rangle = e^{\mathrm{i}\boldsymbol{k}\cdot\boldsymbol{\mu}-\boldsymbol{k}\cdot\boldsymbol{C}\boldsymbol{k}/2} \tag{D.15}$$

and hence again of a Gaussian form.

Linear combinations of Gaussian random variables

Often one needs to deal with sums or, more generally, linear combinations of Gaussian random variables. Let us suppose $\boldsymbol{x}$ is Gaussian distributed with mean $\boldsymbol{\mu}$ and covariance matrix $\boldsymbol{C}$. Now consider a set of M linear combinations $y_i = \sum_{j=1}^{N} L_{ij}x_j$ $(i = 1, \ldots, M)$, or $\boldsymbol{y} = \boldsymbol{L}\boldsymbol{x}$ in matrix notation. The characteristic function of the new variables $\boldsymbol{y}$ can be expressed in terms of that of the $\boldsymbol{x}$:

$$\begin{aligned}\langle e^{\mathrm{i}\boldsymbol{k}\cdot\boldsymbol{y}}\rangle &= \langle e^{\mathrm{i}\boldsymbol{k}\cdot\boldsymbol{L}\boldsymbol{x}}\rangle = \langle e^{\mathrm{i}(\boldsymbol{L}^{\dagger}\boldsymbol{k})\cdot\boldsymbol{x}}\rangle = e^{\mathrm{i}(\boldsymbol{L}^{\dagger}\boldsymbol{k})\cdot\boldsymbol{\mu}-(\boldsymbol{L}^{\dagger}\boldsymbol{k})\cdot\boldsymbol{C}\boldsymbol{L}^{\dagger}\boldsymbol{k}/2}\\ &= e^{\mathrm{i}\boldsymbol{k}\cdot\boldsymbol{L}\boldsymbol{\mu}-\boldsymbol{k}\cdot(\boldsymbol{L}\boldsymbol{C}\boldsymbol{L}^{\dagger})\boldsymbol{k}/2}\end{aligned}$$

Comparison with (D.15) shows that the $\boldsymbol{y}$ once more have a Gaussian distribution: linear combinations of Gaussian random variables are again Gaussian. The means and covariances of the distribution are seen to be $\langle y_i\rangle = (\boldsymbol{L}\boldsymbol{\mu})_i$ and $\langle y_i y_j\rangle = (\boldsymbol{L}\boldsymbol{C}\boldsymbol{L}^{\dagger})_{ij}$; these latter identities could of course also have been worked out directly by inserting the definition of the y_i.

Conditional Gaussian distributions

A final useful tool concerns the distribution of a subset of Gaussian variables $\boldsymbol{y} \in \mathbb{R}^N$ from a larger set $(\boldsymbol{x}, \boldsymbol{y})$, when the values of the $\boldsymbol{x} \in \mathbb{R}^M$ are known; this is the conditional distribution of $\boldsymbol{y}$ given $\boldsymbol{x}$. Let us assume that the joint distribution of $\boldsymbol{x}$ and $\boldsymbol{y}$ is a zero-mean Gaussian, with a covariance matrix which we write in block form as

$$\boldsymbol{C} = \begin{pmatrix} \boldsymbol{C}_{xx} & \boldsymbol{C}_{xy} \\ \boldsymbol{C}_{xy} & \boldsymbol{C}_{yy} \end{pmatrix}, \qquad \boldsymbol{C}^{-1} = \begin{pmatrix} \boldsymbol{D}_{xx} & \boldsymbol{D}_{xy} \\ \boldsymbol{D}_{yx} & \boldsymbol{D}_{yy} \end{pmatrix} \tag{D.16}$$

where $\boldsymbol{C}_{xy} = \boldsymbol{C}_{yx}^{\dagger}$ and $\boldsymbol{D}_{xy} = \boldsymbol{D}_{yx}^{\dagger}$ because covariance matrices are symmetric. Thus we have

$$p(\boldsymbol{x}, \boldsymbol{y}) = [(2\pi)^{N+M} \det \boldsymbol{C}]^{-1/2} \exp\left(-\frac{1}{2}\begin{pmatrix} \boldsymbol{x} \\ \boldsymbol{y} \end{pmatrix} \cdot \boldsymbol{C}^{-1}\begin{pmatrix} \boldsymbol{x} \\ \boldsymbol{y} \end{pmatrix}\right) \tag{D.17}$$

$$p(\boldsymbol{x}) = [(2\pi)^{M} \det \boldsymbol{C}_{xx}]^{-1/2} \exp\left(-\tfrac{1}{2}\boldsymbol{x} \cdot (\boldsymbol{C}_{xx})^{-1}\boldsymbol{x}\right) \tag{D.18}$$

From Bayes' rule, the required conditional distribution is $p(\boldsymbol{y}|\boldsymbol{x}) = p(\boldsymbol{x}, \boldsymbol{y})/p(\boldsymbol{x})$, which is here found to take the form

$$\begin{aligned} p(\boldsymbol{y}|\boldsymbol{x}) &= \left[\frac{(2\pi)^{N+M} \det \boldsymbol{C}}{(2\pi)^{M} \det \boldsymbol{C}_{xx}}\right]^{-1/2} \exp\left(\frac{1}{2}\boldsymbol{x} \cdot (\boldsymbol{C}_{xx})^{-1}\boldsymbol{x} - \frac{1}{2}\begin{pmatrix} \boldsymbol{x} \\ \boldsymbol{y} \end{pmatrix} \cdot \boldsymbol{C}^{-1}\begin{pmatrix} \boldsymbol{x} \\ \boldsymbol{y} \end{pmatrix}\right) \\ &= \frac{1}{Y(\boldsymbol{x})} \exp\left(-\frac{1}{2}\boldsymbol{x} \cdot \boldsymbol{D}_{xy}\boldsymbol{y} - \frac{1}{2}\boldsymbol{y} \cdot \boldsymbol{D}_{yx}\boldsymbol{x} - \frac{1}{2}\boldsymbol{y} \cdot \boldsymbol{D}_{yy}\boldsymbol{y}\right) \end{aligned} \tag{D.19}$$

in which the ($\boldsymbol{y}$-independent) factor $Y(\boldsymbol{x})$ can be calculated *a posteriori* from the normalization requirement $\int \mathrm{d}\boldsymbol{y}\, p(\boldsymbol{y}|\boldsymbol{x}) = 1$ for all $\boldsymbol{x} \in \mathbb{R}^M$. Recalling that $\boldsymbol{D}_{xy} = \boldsymbol{D}_{yx}^{\dagger}$, we can complete the square in the exponent, dropping yet another term dependent only on $\boldsymbol{x}$ (which changes the previous normalization factor $Y(\boldsymbol{x})$ into a new one, say $Z(\boldsymbol{x})$):

$$p(\boldsymbol{y}|\boldsymbol{x}) = \frac{1}{Z(\boldsymbol{x})} \exp\left(-\frac{1}{2}(\boldsymbol{y} + \boldsymbol{D}_{yy}^{-1}\boldsymbol{D}_{yx}\boldsymbol{x}) \cdot \boldsymbol{D}_{yy}(\boldsymbol{y} + \boldsymbol{D}_{yy}^{-1}\boldsymbol{D}_{yx}\boldsymbol{x})\right) \tag{D.20}$$

This shows that $p(\boldsymbol{y}|\boldsymbol{x})$ is again Gaussian, with mean $-\boldsymbol{D}_{yy}^{-1}\boldsymbol{D}_{yx}\boldsymbol{x}$ and with covariance matrix $\boldsymbol{D}_{yy}^{-1}$. It remains to write these in terms of the covariance matrix $\boldsymbol{C}$ rather than its inverse $\boldsymbol{C}^{-1}$, using the results for block matrix inverses derived in Appendix E. Referring back to (D.16), we find from (E.6) that $\boldsymbol{D}_{yy} = (\boldsymbol{C}_{yy} - \boldsymbol{C}_{yx}\boldsymbol{C}_{xx}^{-1}\boldsymbol{C}_{xy})^{-1}$, so the covariance matrix of $p(\boldsymbol{y}|\boldsymbol{x})$ is

$$\boldsymbol{D}_{yy}^{-1} = \boldsymbol{C}_{yy} - \boldsymbol{C}_{yx}\boldsymbol{C}_{xx}^{-1}\boldsymbol{C}_{xy}$$

This makes sense. The first term is the covariance matrix of the unconditional distribution $p(\boldsymbol{y})$. The second, negative, term reduces the fluctuations of the $\boldsymbol{y}$ because our knowledge of $\boldsymbol{x}$ ties down the values of $\boldsymbol{y}$ to some extent. How large the reduction in fluctuations is depends on the correlation of $\boldsymbol{x}$ and $\boldsymbol{y}$ (as it should be): for $\boldsymbol{C}_{xy} = 0$ the variables $\boldsymbol{x}$ and $\boldsymbol{y}$ are uncorrelated, and therefore—since we are dealing with Gaussian distributions—actually independent, so that in that case $p(\boldsymbol{y}|\boldsymbol{x}) = p(\boldsymbol{y})$.

Finally, for the conditional mean of $\boldsymbol{y}$ given $\boldsymbol{x}$, defined as $\int \mathrm{d}\boldsymbol{y}\, \boldsymbol{y} p(\boldsymbol{y}|\boldsymbol{x})$, we see from (E.6) that $-\boldsymbol{D}_{yy}^{-1}\boldsymbol{D}_{yx}\boldsymbol{x} = \boldsymbol{C}_{yx}\boldsymbol{C}_{xx}^{-1}\boldsymbol{x}$. Summarizing the properties of the conditional Gaussian distribution, we have

$$\langle y_i \rangle_{\boldsymbol{x}} = (\boldsymbol{C}_{yx}\boldsymbol{C}_{xx}^{-1}\boldsymbol{x})_i \tag{D.21}$$

$$\langle y_i y_j \rangle_{\boldsymbol{x}} - \langle y_i \rangle_{\boldsymbol{x}} \langle y_j \rangle_{\boldsymbol{x}} = (\boldsymbol{C}_{yy} - \boldsymbol{C}_{yx}\boldsymbol{C}_{xx}^{-1}\boldsymbol{C}_{xy})_{ij} \tag{D.22}$$

where the subscript $\langle \cdots \rangle_{\boldsymbol{x}}$ is used to indicate the conditioning on $\boldsymbol{x}$. The result for the conditional mean again makes intuitive sense: if $\boldsymbol{x}$ and $\boldsymbol{y}$ are uncorrelated, then the conditional mean is identical to that of the unconditioned distribution $p(\boldsymbol{y})$, that is, zero. Otherwise the conditional mean is linearly dependent on the values of $\boldsymbol{x}$ and proportional to $\boldsymbol{C}_{yx}$.

D.3 A list of specific Gaussian integrals

Finally we calculate explicitly the various Gaussian integrals which we encounter throughout this book. To allow for the efficient use of these integral calculations for reference purposes, we first give a compact list of results, and include their derivations in a separate subsection.

We use the notation $\langle f(x,y) \rangle = \int \mathrm{d}x\mathrm{d}y\, f(x,y)P(x,y)$ for those integrals that can be interpreted as averages over the bivariate Gaussian distribution

$$P(x,y) = \frac{1}{2\pi\sqrt{1-\omega^2}}\, e^{-(x^2+y^2-2xy\omega)/2(1-\omega^2)} \tag{D.23}$$

Both marginals of (D.23) are unit-variance Gaussian distributions:

$$p(x) = \int \mathrm{d}y\, P(x,y) = \frac{e^{-x^2/2}}{\sqrt{2\pi}}, \qquad p(y) = \int \mathrm{d}x\, P(x,y) = \frac{e^{-y^2/2}}{\sqrt{2\pi}} \tag{D.24}$$

Without creating ambiguities, we can therefore use a similar notation in the integrals to follow below for averages involving only the unit variance Gaussians, viz. $\langle f(x) \rangle = \int \mathrm{d}x\, f(x)p(x)$ and $\langle g(y) \rangle = \int \mathrm{d}y\, g(y)p(y)$.

Results of integrals

$$I_0 = \int dx\, e^{-x^2/2} = \sqrt{2\pi} \tag{D.25}$$

$$I_1 = \langle |y| \rangle = \sqrt{\frac{2}{\pi}} \tag{D.26}$$

$$I_2 = \langle x\, \mathrm{sgn}(y) \rangle = \omega \sqrt{\frac{2}{\pi}} \tag{D.27}$$

$$I_3 = \langle \theta(-xy) \rangle = \frac{1}{\pi} \arccos(\omega) \tag{D.28}$$

$$I_4 = \langle x\, \mathrm{sgn}(y)\, \theta(-xy) \rangle = \frac{\omega - 1}{\sqrt{2\pi}} \tag{D.29}$$

$$I_5 = \langle |y| \theta(-xy) \rangle = \frac{1 - \omega}{\sqrt{2\pi}} \tag{D.30}$$

$$I_6 = \langle x^2 \theta(-xy) \rangle = \frac{1}{\pi} \arccos(\omega) - \frac{\omega\sqrt{1-\omega^2}}{\pi} \tag{D.31}$$

$$I_7 = \langle |x|\, |y|\, \theta(-xy) \rangle = \frac{\sqrt{1-\omega^2}}{\pi} - \frac{\omega}{\pi} \arccos(\omega) \tag{D.32}$$

$$I_8(x) = \int dy\, \theta(y) P(x, y) = \frac{e^{-x^2/2}}{2\sqrt{2\pi}} \left[1 + \mathrm{erf}\left(\frac{\omega x}{\sqrt{2}\sqrt{1-\omega^2}} \right) \right] \tag{D.33}$$

$$I_9(x) = \int dy\, \theta(y)(y - \omega x) P(x, y) = \frac{\sqrt{1-\omega^2}}{2\pi} e^{-x^2/2(1-\omega^2)} \tag{D.34}$$

Corresponding derivations

I_0**:** In order to calculate I_0 one squares the integral, and evaluates the square using polar coordinates ($x_1 = r\cos\phi, x_2 = r\sin\phi$). This gives

$$I_0^2 = \int dx_1 dx_2\, e^{-(x_1^2+x_2^2)/2} = \int_0^{2\pi} d\phi \int_0^{\infty} dr\, r e^{-r^2/2} = 2\pi[-e^{-r^2/2}]_0^{\infty} = 2\pi$$

□

I_1**:** One may verify the expression given for I_1 by writing

$$I_1 = 2 \int_0^{\infty} \frac{dy}{\sqrt{2\pi}} y\, e^{-y^2/2} = \sqrt{\frac{2}{\pi}} \int_0^{\infty} dy \left(-\frac{\partial}{\partial y} \right) e^{-(1/2)y^2} = \sqrt{\frac{2}{\pi}}$$

□

***I*$_2$:** The integral I_2 can be calculated as follows:

$$I_2 = \int \frac{\mathrm{d}x\mathrm{d}y}{2\pi\sqrt{1-\omega^2}}\, \mathrm{sgn}(y)\, e^{-(y^2-2\omega xy)/2(1-\omega^2)} \left(-(1-\omega^2)\frac{\partial}{\partial x}\right) e^{-x^2/2(1-\omega^2)}$$

$$= \int \frac{\mathrm{d}x\mathrm{d}y}{2\pi\sqrt{1-\omega^2}}\, e^{-(x^2+y^2-2\omega xy)/2(1-\omega^2)} \omega y\, \mathrm{sgn}(y) = \omega\langle |y|\rangle = \omega\sqrt{\frac{2}{\pi}}$$

where I_1 has been used in the last step. □

***I*$_3$:** Integral I_3 is first written as

$$I_3 = \int_0^\infty \int_0^\infty \frac{\mathrm{d}x\mathrm{d}y}{\pi\sqrt{1-\omega^2}}\, e^{-(x^2+y^2+2\omega xy)/2(1-\omega^2)}$$

$$= \frac{\sqrt{1-\omega^2}}{\pi} \int_0^\infty \int_0^\infty \mathrm{d}x\mathrm{d}y\, e^{-(x^2+y^2+2\omega xy)/2}$$

In polar coordinates $(x, y) = r(\cos\phi, \sin\phi)$ this becomes

$$I_3 = \frac{\sqrt{1-\omega^2}}{\pi} \int_0^{\pi/2} \mathrm{d}\phi \int_0^\infty \mathrm{d}r\, r e^{-r^2[1+\omega\sin(2\phi)]/2}$$

$$= \frac{\sqrt{1-\omega^2}}{\pi} \int_0^{\pi/2} \frac{\mathrm{d}\phi}{1+\omega\sin(2\phi)}$$

The substitution $x = \tan(\phi)$ turns the last integral into

$$I_3 = \frac{\sqrt{1-\omega^2}}{\pi} \int_0^\infty \frac{\mathrm{d}x}{1+2\omega x+x^2}$$

Using partial fractions one obtains

$$I_3 = \frac{1}{2\pi \mathrm{i}} \ln\left[\frac{1+\mathrm{i}\sqrt{1-\omega^2}/\omega}{1-\mathrm{i}\sqrt{1-\omega^2}/\omega}\right] = \frac{1}{\pi}\arctan\left(\frac{\sqrt{1-\omega^2}}{\omega}\right) = \frac{1}{\pi}\arccos(\omega)$$

□

I_4: Next we turn to I_4 where we write

$$\begin{aligned} I_4 &= -\frac{1-\omega^2}{\pi}\int_0^\infty \mathrm{d}x\, x\, e^{-x^2/2}\int_0^\infty \mathrm{d}y\, e^{-(y+\omega x)^2/2+\omega^2x^2/2} \\ &= \frac{1}{\pi}\int_0^\infty \mathrm{d}x \left(\frac{\partial}{\partial x} e^{-(1-\omega^2)x^2/2}\right)\int_{\omega x}^\infty \mathrm{d}y\, e^{-y^2/2} \\ &= \frac{1}{\pi}\left\{\left[e^{-(1-\omega^2)x^2/2}\int_{\omega x}^\infty \mathrm{d}y\, e^{-y^2/2}\right]_0^\infty + \omega\int_0^\infty \mathrm{d}x\, e^{-x^2/2}\right\} \\ &= \frac{1}{\pi}\left(-\sqrt{\frac{\pi}{2}}+\omega\sqrt{\frac{\pi}{2}}\right) = \frac{\omega-1}{\sqrt{2\pi}} \end{aligned}$$

□

I_5: This integral can be converted into an expression which is identical to the previous one, except for interchanging x and y:

$$I_5 = \frac{1-\omega^2}{\pi}\int_0^\infty \mathrm{d}y\, y\, e^{-y^2/2}\int_0^\infty \mathrm{d}x\, e^{-(x+\omega y)^2/2+\omega^2y^2/2} = \frac{1-\omega}{\sqrt{2\pi}}$$

following the algebra used in the evaluation of I_4, with x and y exchanged. □

I_6: Integral I_6 is somewhat more difficult. Using a rescaling of x and y similar to that employed in the computation of I_3, we first write

$$\begin{aligned} I_6 &= \frac{(1-\omega^2)^{3/2}}{\pi}\int_0^\infty\int_0^\infty \mathrm{d}x\mathrm{d}y\, x^2\, e^{-(x^2+y^2+2xy\omega)/2} \\ &= \frac{(1-\omega^2)^{3/2}}{2\pi}\int_0^\infty\int_0^\infty \mathrm{d}x\mathrm{d}y(x^2+y^2)\, e^{-(x^2+y^2+2xy\omega)/2} \end{aligned}$$

We now switch to polar coordinates $(x,y) = r(\cos\phi, \sin\phi)$, and substitute $t = \frac{1}{2}r^2[1+\omega\sin(2\phi)]$, followed by rescaling $2\phi \to \phi$, to get

$$\begin{aligned} I_6 &= \frac{(1-\omega^2)^{3/2}}{2\pi}\int_0^{\pi/2}\mathrm{d}\phi\int_0^\infty \mathrm{d}r\, r^3\, e^{-(r^2+\omega r^2\sin 2\phi)/2} \\ &= \frac{(1-\omega^2)^{3/2}}{\pi}\int_0^{\pi/2}\frac{\mathrm{d}\phi}{(1+\omega\sin(2\phi))^2}\int_0^\infty \mathrm{d}t\, t\, e^{-t} \\ &= \frac{(1-\omega^2)^{3/2}}{2\pi}\int_0^{\pi}\frac{\mathrm{d}\phi}{(1+\omega\sin\phi)^2} \end{aligned}$$

To calculate the latter integral we define the following family of integrals:

$$\tilde{I}_n = \int_0^\pi \frac{\mathrm{d}\phi}{(1+\omega\sin\phi)^n}$$

These integrals obey

$$\omega\frac{\mathrm{d}}{\mathrm{d}\omega}\tilde{I}_n - n\tilde{I}_{n+1} = -n\tilde{I}_n$$

so

$$\tilde{I}_2 = \tilde{I}_1 + \omega\frac{\mathrm{d}}{\mathrm{d}\omega}\tilde{I}_1 \qquad \tilde{I}_1 = \frac{2}{\sqrt{1-\omega^2}}\arccos(\omega)$$

(where we used the integral already encountered when evaluating I_3). We now find

$$I_6 = \frac{(1-\omega^2)^{3/2}}{2\pi}\tilde{I}_2 = \frac{1}{\pi}\arccos(\omega) - \frac{\omega\sqrt{1-\omega^2}}{\pi} \qquad \square$$

***I*$_7$:** We turn to I_7. Here we write, using rescaled variables as in I_3 and I_6,

$$I_7 = \frac{(1-\omega^2)^{3/2}}{\pi}\int_0^\infty\int_0^\infty \mathrm{d}x\mathrm{d}y\, xy\, e^{-(x^2+y^2+2xy\omega)/2}$$

We use polar coordinates, the substitution $t = \frac{1}{2}r^2[1+\omega\sin(2\phi)]$ and the rescaling $2\phi \to \phi$ to proceed as in the calculation of I_6:

$$\begin{aligned} I_7 &= \frac{(1-\omega^2)^{3/2}}{2\pi}\int_0^\pi \mathrm{d}\phi\, \frac{\sin\phi}{(1+\omega\sin\phi)^2} \\ &= -\frac{(1-\omega^2)^{3/2}}{2\pi}\frac{\mathrm{d}\tilde{I}_1}{\mathrm{d}\omega} = \frac{\sqrt{1-\omega^2}}{\pi} - \frac{\omega}{\pi}\arccos(\omega), \end{aligned}$$

where we have used $\tilde{I}_1$ as introduced while evaluating I_6. $\square$

***I*$_8$:** The integral I_8 can be evaluated simply by completing the square in the exponent:

$$\begin{aligned} I_8(x) &= \int_0^\infty \frac{\mathrm{d}y}{2\pi\sqrt{1-\omega^2}} e^{-(x^2+y^2-2xy\omega)/2(1-\omega^2)} \\ &= \frac{e^{-x^2/2}}{\sqrt{2\pi}}\int_0^\infty \frac{\mathrm{d}y\, e^{-(y-\omega x)^2/2(1-\omega^2)}}{\sqrt{2\pi(1-\omega^2)}} = \frac{e^{-x^2/2}}{2\sqrt{2\pi}}\left[1+\mathrm{erf}\left(\frac{\omega x}{\sqrt{2}\sqrt{1-\omega^2}}\right)\right] \end{aligned}$$

$\square$

***I*$_9$:** Our final integral is again relatively easy to work out. The result follows from

$$I_9(x) = -\frac{\sqrt{1-\omega^2}}{2\pi}\int_0^\infty \mathrm{d}y\, \frac{\partial}{\partial y}e^{-(x^2+y^2-2xy\omega)/2(1-\omega^2)} = \frac{\sqrt{1-\omega^2}}{2\pi}e^{-x^2/2(1-\omega^2)}$$

$\square$

Appendix E: Matrix identities

E.1 Block inverses

In the treatment of Gaussian processes, or when considering conditional Gaussian distributions, we often need to invert block matrices of the following form

$$M = \begin{pmatrix} A & B \\ C & D \end{pmatrix}$$

Writing the inverse in the same block structure,

$$M^{-1} = \begin{pmatrix} A' & B' \\ C' & D' \end{pmatrix}$$

we see that the condition $M^{-1}M = \mathbf{1}$ is equivalent to

$$A'A + B'C = \mathbf{1}, \quad A'B + B'D = 0, \quad C'A + D'C = 0, \quad C'B + D'D = \mathbf{1}$$

where we are abusing the symbol $\mathbf{1}$ to denote the identity matrix of the appropriate size in each case since there is no risk of ambiguity. Solving the second of the above four conditions gives $B' = -A'BD^{-1}$; inserting into the first one then leads to $A' = (A - BD^{-1}C)^{-1}$ and this can be inserted into the expression for B'. The sub-matrices C' and D' can be determined similarly, and overall we have

$$A' = (A - BD^{-1}C)^{-1} \tag{E.1}$$

$$-B' = (A - BD^{-1}C)^{-1}BD^{-1} \tag{E.2}$$

$$-C' = (D - CA^{-1}B)^{-1}CA^{-1} \tag{E.3}$$

$$D' = (D - CA^{-1}B)^{-1} \tag{E.4}$$

Note that the matrix inverses that appear here are all of square matrices, and are therefore well-defined (assuming that the relevant matrices are actually invertible, otherwise there is no point in the present exercise in the first place).

E.2 The Woodbury formula

It would be helpful if we could unpack the inverses that appear above yet further. For $\boldsymbol{A}'$, for example, we need, upon setting $\boldsymbol{L} = -\boldsymbol{D}^{-1}$, the inverse $(\boldsymbol{A} + \boldsymbol{BLC})^{-1}$. This can be evaluated using the Woodbury formula:

$$(\boldsymbol{A} + \boldsymbol{BLC})^{-1} = \boldsymbol{A}^{-1} - \boldsymbol{A}^{-1}\boldsymbol{B}(\boldsymbol{L}^{-1} + \boldsymbol{CA}^{-1}\boldsymbol{B})^{-1}\boldsymbol{CA}^{-1} \tag{E.5}$$

The important feature of this result is that it allows us to change the dimensionality of the inverse required. If we denote the size of $\boldsymbol{A}$ by $m \times m$ and that of $\boldsymbol{L}$ by $n \times n$, then $\boldsymbol{B}$ and $\boldsymbol{C}$ are $m \times n$ and $n \times m$ matrices, respectively. The inverse on the left-hand side of (E.5) is that of an $m \times m$ matrix, while on the right we have the inverse of an $n \times n$ matrix. If m is larger than n, then it will clearly be more efficient to evaluate the inverse using the latter form.

To prove the Woodbury formula (E.5), one simply multiplies the right-hand side by the matrix to be inverted, which gives

$$\begin{aligned}
&\boldsymbol{A}^{-1}(\boldsymbol{A} + \boldsymbol{BLC}) - \boldsymbol{A}^{-1}\boldsymbol{B}(\boldsymbol{L}^{-1} + \boldsymbol{CA}^{-1}\boldsymbol{B})^{-1}\boldsymbol{CA}^{-1}(\boldsymbol{A} + \boldsymbol{BLC})\\
&= \mathbf{1} + \boldsymbol{A}^{-1}\boldsymbol{BLC} - \boldsymbol{A}^{-1}\boldsymbol{B}(\boldsymbol{L}^{-1} + \boldsymbol{CA}^{-1}\boldsymbol{B})^{-1}\boldsymbol{C}(\mathbf{1} + \boldsymbol{A}^{-1}\boldsymbol{BLC})\\
&= \mathbf{1} + \boldsymbol{A}^{-1}\boldsymbol{B}[\boldsymbol{L} - (\boldsymbol{L}^{-1} + \boldsymbol{CA}^{-1}\boldsymbol{B})^{-1}(\mathbf{1} + \boldsymbol{CA}^{-1}\boldsymbol{BL})]\boldsymbol{C}\\
&= \mathbf{1} + \boldsymbol{A}^{-1}\boldsymbol{B}(\boldsymbol{L}^{-1} + \boldsymbol{CA}^{-1}\boldsymbol{B})^{-1}[(\boldsymbol{L}^{-1} + \boldsymbol{CA}^{-1}\boldsymbol{B})\boldsymbol{L} - (\mathbf{1} + \boldsymbol{CA}^{-1}\boldsymbol{BL})]\boldsymbol{C}\\
&= \mathbf{1}
\end{aligned}$$

A useful special case of the Woodbury formula is obtained for the extreme situation $n = 1$, where $\boldsymbol{B}$ and $\boldsymbol{C}$ become vectors $\boldsymbol{b}$ and $\boldsymbol{c}$, and $\boldsymbol{L}$ becomes a scalar which we can set to unity (because any other value could be absorbed into either $\boldsymbol{B}$ or $\boldsymbol{C}$). Using appropriate vector notation for $\boldsymbol{B}$ and $\boldsymbol{C}$ we then have

$$(\boldsymbol{A} + \boldsymbol{bc}^{\dagger})^{-1} = \boldsymbol{A}^{-1} - \frac{\boldsymbol{A}^{-1}\boldsymbol{bc}^{\dagger}\boldsymbol{A}^{-1}}{1 + \boldsymbol{c} \cdot \boldsymbol{A}^{-1}\boldsymbol{b}}$$

Here $\boldsymbol{bc}^{\dagger}$ denotes the matrix with entries $(\boldsymbol{bc}^{\dagger})_{ij} = b_i c_j$.

Finally, by applying the Woodbury formula to the above result (E.1)–(E.4) for block matrix inverses, one finds—after a little rearranging for $\boldsymbol{B}'$ and $\boldsymbol{C}'$—the following useful alternative forms:

$$\begin{aligned}
\boldsymbol{A}' &= (\boldsymbol{A} - \boldsymbol{BD}^{-1}\boldsymbol{C})^{-1} = \boldsymbol{A}^{-1} + \boldsymbol{A}^{-1}\boldsymbol{B}(\boldsymbol{D} - \boldsymbol{CA}^{-1}\boldsymbol{B})^{-1}\boldsymbol{CA}^{-1}\\
-\boldsymbol{B}' &= (\boldsymbol{A} - \boldsymbol{BD}^{-1}\boldsymbol{C})^{-1}\boldsymbol{BD}^{-1} = \boldsymbol{A}^{-1}\boldsymbol{B}(\boldsymbol{D} - \boldsymbol{CA}^{-1}\boldsymbol{B})^{-1}\\
-\boldsymbol{C}' &= (\boldsymbol{D} - \boldsymbol{CA}^{-1}\boldsymbol{B})^{-1}\boldsymbol{CA}^{-1} = \boldsymbol{D}^{-1}\boldsymbol{C}(\boldsymbol{A} - \boldsymbol{BD}^{-1}\boldsymbol{C})^{-1}\\
\boldsymbol{D}' &= (\boldsymbol{D} - \boldsymbol{CA}^{-1}\boldsymbol{B})^{-1} = \boldsymbol{D}^{-1} + \boldsymbol{D}^{-1}\boldsymbol{C}(\boldsymbol{A} - \boldsymbol{BD}^{-1}\boldsymbol{C})^{-1}\boldsymbol{BD}^{-1}
\end{aligned} \tag{E.6}$$

Appendix F: The δ-distribution

F.1 Definition

There are several ways of introducing the δ-distribution. Here we will go for an intuitive definition first, and a formal one later. We define the δ-distribution as the probability distribution $\delta(x)$ corresponding to a random variable in the limit where the randomness in the variable vanishes. If x is 'distributed' around zero, this implies

$$\int dx\, f(x)\delta(x) = f(0) \quad \text{for any function } f$$

The problem arises when we want to actually write down an expression for $\delta(x)$. Intuitively one could think of writing something like

$$\delta(x) = \lim_{\Delta\to 0} G_\Delta(x) \qquad G_\Delta(x) = \frac{1}{\Delta\sqrt{2\pi}}\, e^{-x^2/2\Delta^2} \tag{F.1}$$

This is not a true function in a mathematical sense; $\delta(x)$ is zero for $x \neq 0$ and $\delta(0) = \infty$. The way to interpret and use expressions like (F.1) is to realize that $\delta(x)$ only has a meaning when appearing inside an integration. One then takes the limit $\Delta \to 0$ *after* performing the integration. Upon adopting this convention, we can use (F.1) to derive the following properties (for sufficiently well-behaved and differentiable functions[49] f):

$$\int dx\, \delta(x) f(x) = \lim_{\Delta\to 0} \int dx\, G_\Delta(x) f(x) = \lim_{\Delta\to 0} \int \frac{dx}{\sqrt{2\pi}}\, e^{-x^2/2} f(\Delta x) = f(0)$$

$$\begin{aligned}\int dx\, \delta'(x) f(x) &= \lim_{\Delta\to 0} \int dx \left\{ \frac{d}{dx}[G_\Delta(x) f(x)] - G_\Delta(x) f'(x) \right\} \\ &= \lim_{\Delta\to 0} [G_\Delta(x) f(x)]_{-\infty}^{\infty} - f'(0) = -f'(0)\end{aligned}$$

[49] The conditions on the so-called 'test-functions' f can be properly formalized; this not being a book on distribution theory, we just concentrate on the basic ideas and properties.

These statements can be summarized in and generalized to the single expression:

$$\int dx\, f(x) \frac{d^n}{dx^n}\delta(x) = (-1)^n \lim_{x\to 0} \frac{d^n}{dx^n} f(x) \quad (n = 0, 1, 2, \ldots) \tag{F.2}$$

Equivalently we can take the result (F.2) as our definition of the δ-distribution.

F.2 $\delta(x)$ as solution of the Liouville equation

Next we prove that the δ-distribution can be used to represent the solution of the so-called Liouville equation:

$$\frac{\partial}{\partial t} P_t(x) = -\frac{\partial}{\partial x}[P_t(x)F(x)] \tag{F.3}$$

The general solution of (F.3) is

$$P_t(x) = \int dx_0\, P_0(x_0)\delta(x - x^\star(t; x_0)) \tag{F.4}$$

in which $x^\star(t; x_0)$ is the solution of the ordinary differential equation

$$\frac{d}{dt} x^\star(t; x_0) = F(x^\star(t; x_0)), \qquad x^\star(0; x_0) = x_0 \tag{F.5}$$

In particular, if $P_0(x_0)$ is a δ-distribution in x_0, the general solution will remain a δ-distribution in x for all times: $P_t(x) = \delta(x - x^\star(t; x_0))$. The proof of (F.4) proceeds by showing that both sides of (F.3) give the same result inside integrals if we insert the proposed solution (F.4).

$$\int dx\, f(x)\left\{\frac{\partial}{\partial t} P_t(x) + \frac{\partial}{\partial x}[P_t(x)F(x)]\right\}$$

$$= \frac{d}{dt}\left[\int dx\, f(x)P_t(x)\right] + [f(x)P_t(x)F(x)]_{x=-\infty}^{x=\infty} - \int dx\, P_t(x)F(x)f'(x)$$

$$= \int dx_0\, P_0(x_0)\left[\frac{\partial}{\partial t} f(x^\star(t; x_0)) - F(x^\star(t; x_0))f'(x^\star(t; x_0))\right]$$

$$= \int dx_0\, P_0(x_0)f'(x^\star(t; x_0))\left[\frac{d}{dt}x^\star(t; x_0) - F(x^\star(t; x_0))\right] = 0$$

For an alternative proof without test functions, one can differentiate (F.4) using the chain rule to get

$$\begin{aligned}\frac{\partial}{\partial t}P_t(x) &= \int \mathrm{d}x_0\, P_0(x_0)\left[-\frac{\mathrm{d}}{\mathrm{d}t}x^*(t;x_0)\right]\frac{\partial}{\partial x}\delta(x-x^*(t;x_0))\\ &= -\frac{\partial}{\partial x}\int \mathrm{d}x_0\, P_0(x_0)F(x^*(t;x_0))\delta(x-x^*(t;x_0))\\ &= -\frac{\partial}{\partial x}\left[F(x)\int \mathrm{d}x_0\, P_0(x_0)\delta(x-x^*(t;x_0))\right]\\ &= -\frac{\partial}{\partial x}[F(x)P_t(x)]\end{aligned}$$

F.3 Representations, relations, and generalizations

We can use the definitions of Fourier transforms and inverse Fourier transforms to obtain an integral representation of the δ-distribution:

$$\begin{aligned}\mathcal{F}\colon\quad f(x)\to\hat{f}(k)\qquad &\hat{f}(k)=\int \mathrm{d}x\, e^{-2\pi ikx}f(x)\\ \mathcal{F}^{-1}\colon\quad \hat{f}(k)\to f(x)\qquad &f(x)=\int \mathrm{d}k\, e^{2\pi ikx}\hat{f}(k)\end{aligned}$$

In combination these relations give the identity:

$$f(x)=\int \mathrm{d}k\, e^{2\pi ikx}\int \mathrm{d}y\, e^{-2\pi iky}f(y)$$

Application to $f(x)=\delta(x)$ gives:

$$\delta(x)=\int \mathrm{d}k\, e^{2\pi ikx}=\int\frac{\mathrm{d}k}{2\pi}e^{ikx} \tag{F.6}$$

Another useful relation is the following one, which relates the δ-distribution to the step-function:

$$\delta(x)=\frac{\mathrm{d}}{\mathrm{d}x}\theta(x) \tag{F.7}$$

This we prove by showing that both have the same effect inside an integration (with an arbitrary test-function):

$$\int \mathrm{d}x \left[\delta(x) - \frac{\mathrm{d}}{\mathrm{d}x}\theta(x)\right] f(x)$$

$$= f(0) - \lim_{\epsilon\to 0}\int_{-\epsilon}^{\epsilon} \mathrm{d}x \left\{\frac{\mathrm{d}}{\mathrm{d}x}[\theta(x)f(x)] - f'(x)\theta(x)\right\}$$

$$= f(0) - \lim_{\epsilon\to 0}[f(\epsilon) - 0] + \lim_{\epsilon\to 0}\int_0^{\epsilon} \mathrm{d}x\ f'(x) = 0$$

Third we can inspect the effect of performing a continuously differentiable and invertible[50] transformation g on a variable that occurs inside a δ-distribution, giving rise to the following identity:

$$\delta(g(x) - g(a)) = \frac{\delta(x-a)}{|g'(a)|} \tag{F.8}$$

Again this is proved by showing that both sides have the same effect inside an integration, with an arbitrary test-function f (noting the extra term $\mathrm{sgn}(g'(x))$, which reflects the possible exchange of integration boundaries):

$$\int_{-\infty}^{\infty} \mathrm{d}x\ f(x)\left[\delta(g(x) - g(a)) - \frac{\delta(x-a)}{|g'(a)|}\right]$$

$$= \int_{-\infty}^{\infty} \mathrm{d}x\ g'(x)\left[\frac{f(x)}{g'(x)}\right]\delta(g(x) - g(a)) - \frac{f(a)}{|g'(a)|}$$

$$= \int_{g(-\infty)}^{g(\infty)} \mathrm{d}k\left[\frac{f(g^{\mathrm{inv}}(k))}{g'(g^{\mathrm{inv}}(k))}\right]\delta(k - g(a)) - \frac{f(a)}{|g'(a)|}$$

$$= \int_{g(-\infty)}^{g(\infty)} \mathrm{d}k\left[\frac{f(a)}{g'(a)}\right]\delta(k - g(a)) - \frac{f(a)}{|g'(a)|}$$

$$= \int_{-\infty}^{\infty} \mathrm{d}k\ \mathrm{sgn}(g'(a))\left[\frac{f(a)}{g'(a)}\right]\delta(k - g(a)) - \frac{f(a)}{|g'(a)|} = 0$$

Finally, the following generalization is straightforward:

$$\boldsymbol{x} \in \mathrm{I\!R}^N:\quad \delta(\boldsymbol{x}) = \prod_{i=1}^{N} \delta(x_i) \tag{F.9}$$

[50] Note that it follows from g being invertible that $g'(x)$ cannot ever change sign.

Appendix G: Inequalities based on convexity

In this appendix we derive a number of inequalities which play an important role in information theory, especially in establishing the various proofs of the mathematical properties of entropy-based information measures. We will first have to define what we mean by convexity and strict convexity:

Definition. A function f is called convex on the open interval (a,b) if

$$\begin{aligned}&(\forall x_1, x_2 \in (a,b),\ x_1 \neq x_2)(\forall \lambda \in [0,1]):\\ &\quad f((1-\lambda)x_1 + \lambda x_2) \leq (1-\lambda) f(x_1) + \lambda f(x_2)\end{aligned} \tag{G.1}$$

Definition. A function f is called strictly convex on the open interval (a,b) if

$$\begin{aligned}&(\forall x_1, x_2 \in (a,b),\ x_1 \neq x_2)(\forall \lambda \in [0,1]):\\ &\quad f((1-\lambda)x_1 + \lambda x_2) < (1-\lambda) f(x_1) + \lambda f(x_2)\end{aligned} \tag{G.2}$$

except for $\lambda = 0$ and $\lambda = 1$, where one trivially has equality in (G.2).

Next we show how that for twice differentiable functions convexity is a direct consequence of having a strictly non-negative second derivative. When applicable, this is usually a far quicker way to demonstrate that a given function is (strictly) convex than by proving the inequalities (G.1, G.2) directly:

Proposition. If a function f is twice differentiable on the open interval (a,b) and if $f''(x) \geq 0$ for all $x \in (a,b)$, then f is convex. If $f''(x) > 0$ for all $x \in (a,b)$, then f is strictly convex.

Proof. Without loss of generality we may choose $a < x_1 < x_2 < b$, and evaluate for $0 < \lambda < 1$:

$$\begin{aligned}&f((1-\lambda)x_1 + \lambda x_2) - (1-\lambda) f(x_1) - \lambda f(x_2)\\ &\quad = f(x_1 + \lambda(x_2 - x_1)) - f(x_1) - \lambda(f(x_2) - f(x_1))\\ &\quad = \int_{x_1}^{x_1+\lambda(x_2-x_1)} \mathrm{d}y\, f'(y) - \lambda \int_{x_1}^{x_2} \mathrm{d}y\, f'(y)\end{aligned}$$

$$= \lambda(x_2 - x_1) \int_0^1 dz\, f'(x_1 + z\lambda(x_2 - x_2))$$

$$- \lambda(x_2 - x_1) \int_0^1 dz\, f'(x_1 + z(x_2 - x_1))$$

$$= -\lambda(x_2 - x_1) \int_0^1 dz\, [f'(x_1 + z(x_2 - x_1)) - f'(x_1 + z\lambda(x_2 - x_2))]$$

$$= -\lambda(x_2 - x_1) \int_0^1 dz \int_{x_1+z\lambda(x_2-x_2)}^{x_1+z(x_2-x_1)} dy\, f''(y) \leq 0$$

We thus conclude that f is convex. Finally, if the stronger statement $f''(x) > 0$ for all $x \in (a, b)$ is true, then we can replace '≤ 0' by the stronger statement '<0' in the last step, so f is strictly convex. This completes the proof. □

The converse statement is also true, but will not be used in this book. Finally we turn to the main subject of this appendix, two important inequalities based on convexity: Jenssen's inequality and the so-called log-sum inequality.

Jenssen's inequality: If a function f is convex on the open interval (a, b), and $x \in (a, b)$ is a random variable, then

$$\langle f(x)\rangle \geq f(\langle x\rangle) \qquad \text{(G.3)}$$

Furthermore, if f is strictly convex on the open interval (a, b), then the equality in (G.3) holds if and only if x is a constant.

Proof for discrete random variables: We use induction with respect to the number n of values that the random variable x can take, that is, $x \in A = \{x_1, \ldots, x_n\}$. Since f is convex and since $\sum_{i=1}^n p(x_i) = 1$ the statement (G.3) is clearly true for $n = 2$:

$$n = 2: \quad \langle f(x)\rangle = p(x_1)f(x_1) + [1 - p(x_1)]f(x_2)$$

$$\geq f(p(x_1)x_1 + [1 - p(x_1)]x_2) = f(\langle x\rangle)$$

Next we assume (G.3) to be true for a given value of n and prove that it must then also be true for the value $n + 1$:

$$\langle f(x)\rangle = \sum_{i=1}^{n+1} p(x_i)f(x_i) = \sum_{i=1}^{n} p(x_i)f(x_i) + p(x_{n+1})f(x_{n+1})$$

We define for $i \in \{1,\ldots,n\}$ the auxiliary probabilities $\hat{p}(x_i)$:

$$\hat{p}(x_i) = \frac{p(x_i)}{\sum_{j=1}^{n} p(x_j)}, \quad \hat{p}(x_i) \in [0,1], \quad \sum_{i=1}^{n} \hat{p}(x_i) = 1$$

with which we obtain, using convexity of f, validity of (G.3) for $|A| = n$, as well as the normalization $\sum_{i=1}^{n+1} p(x_i) = 1$:

$$\begin{aligned}
\langle f(x)\rangle &= \left[\sum_{j=1}^{n} p(x_j)\right] \sum_{i=1}^{n} \hat{p}(x_i) f(x_i) + p(x_{n+1}) f(x_{n+1}) \\
&\geq \left[\sum_{j=1}^{n} p(x_j)\right] f\left(\sum_{i=1}^{n} \hat{p}(x_i) x_i\right) + \left[1 - \sum_{j=1}^{n} p(x_j)\right] f(x_{n+1}) \\
&\geq f\left(\left[\sum_{j=1}^{n} p(x_j)\right] \sum_{i=1}^{n} \hat{p}(x_i) x_i + \left[1 - \sum_{j=1}^{n} p(x_j)\right] x_{n+1}\right) \\
&= f\left(\sum_{i=1}^{n+1} p(x_i) x_i\right) = f(\langle x\rangle)
\end{aligned}$$

Finally, suppose that f is strictly convex and suppose that we find an equality in (G.3). Then we know that at each step in the above derivation where the convexity inequality (G.1) was used, the corresponding value of $\lambda \in [0,1]$ in (G.1) must have been either 0 or 1. Inspection of the relevant inequalities in the above induction proof shows that $\forall i \in \{1,\ldots,n\}$: $p(x_i) \in \{0,1\}$. Since probabilities are normalized we find that precisely one of the n probabilities $p(x_i)$ is 1 and the others are 0; hence x is a constant, which completes the proof. □

Proof for continuous random variables: We will here treat averages involving continuous random variables as limits of averages involving discrete ones (whereby integrals are written as limits of summations):

$$\begin{aligned}
\langle f(x)\rangle - f(\langle x\rangle) &= \int_a^b \mathrm{d}x\, p(x) f(x) - f\left(\int_a^b \mathrm{d}x\, p(x) x\right) \\
&= \lim_{n\to\infty} \left\{\frac{b-a}{n} \sum_{i=1}^{n} p(x_i) f(x_i) - f\left(\frac{b-a}{n} \sum_{i=1}^{n} p(x_i) x_i\right)\right\}
\end{aligned}$$

where

$$x_i = a + \left(i - \frac{1}{2}\right)\frac{b-a}{n}$$

Again we define suitable auxiliary probabilities with built-in and n-independent normalization:

$$\hat{p}(x_i) = \frac{p(x_i)}{\sum_{j=1}^{n} p(x_j)}, \quad \hat{p}(x_i) \in [0,1], \quad \sum_{i=1}^{n} \hat{p}(x_i) = 1$$

so that we can use the validity of (G.3) for discrete random variables, as proven already:

$$\begin{aligned}
\langle f(x)\rangle - f(\langle x\rangle) &= \lim_{n\to\infty} \left\{ \frac{b-a}{n} \left[\sum_{i=1}^{n} p(x_i)\right] \sum_{j=1}^{n} \hat{p}(x_j) f(x_j) \right. \\
&\quad \left. - f\left(\frac{b-a}{n} \sum_{i=1}^{n} p(x_i) x_i\right)\right\} \\
&\geq \lim_{n\to\infty} \left\{ \frac{b-a}{n} \left[\sum_{i=1}^{n} p(x_i)\right] f\left(\sum_{j=1}^{n} \hat{p}(x_j) x_j\right) \right. \\
&\quad \left. - f\left(\frac{b-a}{n} \left[\sum_{i=1}^{n} p(x_i)\right] \sum_{i=1}^{n} \hat{p}(x_i) x_i\right)\right\} \\
&= 0
\end{aligned}$$

In the last step we have used the properties $\lim_{n\to\infty}[(b-a)/n]\sum_{i=1}^{n} p(x_i) = \int_a^b \mathrm{d}x\, p(x) = 1$ as well as

$$\begin{aligned}
\lim_{n\to\infty} \sum_{i=1}^{n} \hat{p}(x_i) x_i &= \lim_{n\to\infty} \frac{[(b-a)/n]\sum_{i=1}^{n} p(x_i) x_i}{[(b-a)/n]\sum_{j=1}^{n} p(x_j)} \\
&= \frac{\lim_{n\to\infty}[(b-a)/n]\sum_{i=1}^{n} p(x_i) x_i}{\lim_{n\to\infty}[(b-a)/n]\sum_{j=1}^{n} p(x_j)} = \langle x\rangle
\end{aligned}$$

Finally, if f is strictly convex and we obtain an equality in (G.3), we know from the discrete case that for any finite value of n the random variable x must be a constant, which must then also be true if we take the above continuum limit $n \to \infty$. This completes our proof. □

The log–sum inequality, which we will turn to now, is a direct consequence of Jenssen's inequality. The only preparatory work needed is introducing the convention

$$0 \ln 0 = \lim_{\epsilon \downarrow 0} \epsilon \ln \epsilon = 0 \tag{G.4}$$

and showing that the function $f(x) = \ln(1/x)$ is strictly convex on the interval $(0, \infty)$:

$$x \in (0, \infty): \quad \frac{\mathrm{d}^2}{\mathrm{d}x^2} f(x) = \frac{1}{x^2} > 0 \quad \Rightarrow \quad f \text{ is strictly convex on } (0, \infty)$$

In particular we can now apply Jenssen's theorem (G.3) to f.

Log–sum inquality: If $a_i, b_i \in [0, \infty)$, with $\sum_{i=1}^n a_i > 0$ and $\sum_{i=1}^n b_i > 0$, then:

$$\sum_{i=1}^n a_i \ln\left(\frac{a_i}{b_i}\right) \geq \left(\sum_{i=1}^n a_i\right) \ln\left(\frac{\sum_{j=1}^n a_j}{\sum_{j=1}^n b_j}\right) \tag{G.5}$$

with equality if and only if $(\exists \lambda > 0)$: $b_i = \lambda a_i$ $(\forall i \in \{1, \ldots, n\})$.

Proof. We define the new variables $x_i = b_i/a_i$, with associated probabilities

$$p(x_i) = \frac{a_i}{\sum_{j=1}^n a_j}, \qquad p(x_i) \in [0, 1], \qquad \sum_{i=1}^n p(x_i) = 1$$

Note that (G.5) is trivially true as soon as $(\exists i)$: $b_i = 0$ and $a_i/b_i \neq 0$ (since in that case the left-hand side of the inequality diverges, whereas the right-hand side remains finite). Therefore we may restrict ourselves to those cases where $b_i = 0$ always implies $a_i/b_i = 0$, so that $a_i \ln(a_i/b_i) = 0$. According to (G.3) the convexity of the function $f(x) = \ln(1/x)$ allows us to write

$$\begin{aligned}
\sum_{i=1}^n a_i \ln\left(\frac{a_i}{b_i}\right) &= \left(\sum_{i=1}^n a_i\right) \sum_{i=1}^n p(x_i) \ln(1/x_i) \\
&\geq \left(\sum_{i=1}^n a_i\right) \ln\left(\frac{1}{\sum_{j=1}^n p(x_j) x_j}\right) \\
&= \left(\sum_{i=1}^n a_i\right) \ln\left(\frac{\sum_{j=1}^n a_j}{\sum_{i=1}^n a_i (b_i/a_i)}\right) \\
&= \left(\sum_{i=1}^n a_i\right) \ln\left(\frac{\sum_{j=1}^n a_j}{\sum_{i=1}^n b_i}\right)
\end{aligned}$$

Finally, as soon as we find an equality in (G.5), we immediately know that the variables $x_i = b_i/a_i$ in the above derivation must all be identical (since $\ln(1/x)$ is strictly convex). In other words: $(\exists \lambda)$: $b_i = \lambda a_i$ for all i. Since both $a_i \geq 0$ and $b_i \geq 0$ (with $\sum_i a_i > 0$ and $\sum_i b_i > 0$) this constant λ must be positive. This completes the proof. □

Appendix H: Metrics for parametrized probability distributions

H.1 Local distance definitions

Let us inspect the demands to be placed on distance measures $d(\boldsymbol{\theta}, \boldsymbol{\theta}')$ in the parameter space underlying parametrized probability distributions (where $\boldsymbol{\theta} \in \mathbb{R}^L$), not necessarily given by the Euclidean recipe $d^2(\boldsymbol{\theta}, \boldsymbol{\theta}') = |\boldsymbol{\theta} - \boldsymbol{\theta}'|^2 = \sum_i (\theta_i - \theta_i')^2$. We obviously require

$$d(\boldsymbol{\theta}, \boldsymbol{\theta}') \geq 0, \qquad d(\boldsymbol{\theta}, \boldsymbol{\theta}) = 0, \qquad d(\boldsymbol{\theta}, \boldsymbol{\theta}') = d(\boldsymbol{\theta}', \boldsymbol{\theta}) \quad \text{for all } \boldsymbol{\theta}, \boldsymbol{\theta}' \in \mathbb{R}^L \tag{H.1}$$

as well as the triangular inequality

$$d(\boldsymbol{\theta}, \boldsymbol{\theta}') + d(\boldsymbol{\theta}', \boldsymbol{\theta}'') \geq d(\boldsymbol{\theta}, \boldsymbol{\theta}'') \quad \text{for all } \boldsymbol{\theta}, \boldsymbol{\theta}', \boldsymbol{\theta}'' \in \mathbb{R}^L \tag{H.2}$$

We will at first consider small parameter differences: $\boldsymbol{\theta}' = \boldsymbol{\theta} + \Delta\boldsymbol{\theta}$ with $|\Delta\boldsymbol{\theta}| \ll 1$. If our distance measure is well-behaved we can expand

$$\begin{aligned} d^2(\boldsymbol{\theta}, \boldsymbol{\theta} + \Delta\boldsymbol{\theta}) = &\sum_i \Delta\theta_i \left. \frac{\partial d^2(\boldsymbol{\theta}, \boldsymbol{\theta}')}{\partial \theta_i'} \right|_{\boldsymbol{\theta}' = \boldsymbol{\theta}} \\ &+ \frac{1}{2} \sum_{ij} \Delta\theta_i \Delta\theta_j \left. \frac{\partial^2 d^2(\boldsymbol{\theta}, \boldsymbol{\theta}')}{\partial \theta_i' \partial \theta_j'} \right|_{\boldsymbol{\theta}' = \boldsymbol{\theta}} + \mathcal{O}(|\Delta\boldsymbol{\theta}|^3) \end{aligned}$$

The zeroth order term is absent due to $d(\boldsymbol{\theta}, \boldsymbol{\theta}) = 0$. In view of (H.1) we know that the term linear in $\Delta\boldsymbol{\theta}$ must also be zero, since otherwise we could always violate $d(\boldsymbol{\theta}, \boldsymbol{\theta}') \geq 0$ by choosing $\Delta\theta_i = -\epsilon(\partial d^2(\boldsymbol{\theta}, \boldsymbol{\theta}')/\partial\theta_i')|_{\boldsymbol{\theta}' = \boldsymbol{\theta}}$ with ϵ sufficiently small. Thus any well behaved distance measure must locally be of the form

$$d^2(\boldsymbol{\theta}, \boldsymbol{\theta}') = \sum_{ij} (\theta_i - \theta_i')\, g_{ij}(\boldsymbol{\theta})\, (\theta_j - \theta_j') + \mathcal{O}(|\boldsymbol{\theta} - \boldsymbol{\theta}'|^3) \tag{H.3}$$

in which the $L \times L$ matrix $\boldsymbol{g}(\boldsymbol{\theta})$ is symmetric, that is, $g_{ij}(\boldsymbol{\theta}) = g_{ji}(\boldsymbol{\theta})$, and positive definite due to the non-negativity of D, since in the case of negative eigenvalues we could choose our $\Delta\boldsymbol{\theta}$ proportional to the corresponding eigenvector and again violate $d(.,.) \geq 0$. The Euclidean metric is just the simplest case, where $g_{ij}(\boldsymbol{\theta}) = \delta_{ij}$ for all $\boldsymbol{\theta}$. Note that in (H.3) we could equally well put $g_{ij}(\boldsymbol{\theta}) \to g_{ij}(\boldsymbol{\theta}')$, since this would only generate (irrelevant) higher order terms.

H.2 The triangular inequality

We now show that any metric of the form (H.3), with positive definite $\boldsymbol{g}(\boldsymbol{\theta})$, satisfies the triangular inequality. For any triplet of vectors $\{\boldsymbol{\theta}, \boldsymbol{\theta}', \boldsymbol{\theta}''\}$, with $\boldsymbol{\theta} - \boldsymbol{\theta}' = \epsilon \boldsymbol{v}$ and $\boldsymbol{\theta}' - \boldsymbol{\theta}'' = \epsilon \boldsymbol{w}$ and $0 < \epsilon \ll 1$, we obtain

$$
\begin{aligned}
&[d(\boldsymbol{\theta},\boldsymbol{\theta}') + d(\boldsymbol{\theta}',\boldsymbol{\theta}'')]^2 - d^2(\boldsymbol{\theta},\boldsymbol{\theta}'') \\
&= d^2(\boldsymbol{\theta},\boldsymbol{\theta}') + d^2(\boldsymbol{\theta}',\boldsymbol{\theta}'') + 2d(\boldsymbol{\theta},\boldsymbol{\theta}')d(\boldsymbol{\theta}',\boldsymbol{\theta}'') - d^2(\boldsymbol{\theta},\boldsymbol{\theta}'') \\
&= \epsilon^2 \sum_{ij} g_{ij}(\boldsymbol{\theta})[v_i v_j + w_i w_j - (v_i + w_i)(v_j + w_j)] \\
&\quad + 2\epsilon^2 \Big[\sum_{ij} v_i g_{ij}(\boldsymbol{\theta}) v_j\Big]^{1/2} \Big[\sum_{ij} w_i g_{ij}(\boldsymbol{\theta}) w_j\Big]^{1/2} + \mathcal{O}(\epsilon^3) \\
&= 2\epsilon^2 \Big[\sum_{ij} v_i g_{ij}(\boldsymbol{\theta}) v_j\Big]^{1/2} \Big[\sum_{ij} w_i g_{ij}(\boldsymbol{\theta}) w_j\Big]^{1/2} - 2\epsilon^2 \sum_{ij} v_i g_{ij}(\boldsymbol{\theta}) w_j + \mathcal{O}(\epsilon^3)
\end{aligned}
$$

where we have used the symmetry of $\boldsymbol{g}(\boldsymbol{\theta})$. We next switch to the basis in $\mathbb{R}^L$ where $\boldsymbol{g}(\boldsymbol{\theta})$ is diagonal (the eigenvalues of $\boldsymbol{g}(\boldsymbol{\theta})$ are written as g_n), whereby $(\boldsymbol{v}, \boldsymbol{w}) \to (\hat{\boldsymbol{v}}, \hat{\boldsymbol{w}})$:

$$
\begin{aligned}
&[d(\boldsymbol{\theta},\boldsymbol{\theta}') + d(\boldsymbol{\theta}',\boldsymbol{\theta}'')]^2 - d^2(\boldsymbol{\theta},\boldsymbol{\theta}'') \\
&\qquad = 2\epsilon^2 \Big(\sum_n g_n \hat{v}_n^2\Big)^{1/2} \Big(\sum_n g_n \hat{w}_n^2\Big)^{1/2} - 2\epsilon^2 \sum_n g_n \hat{v}_n \hat{w}_n + \mathcal{O}(\epsilon^3)
\end{aligned}
$$

Note that the eigenvalues $\{g_n\}$ and the vectors $\hat{\boldsymbol{v}}$ and $\hat{\boldsymbol{w}}$ will depend on $\boldsymbol{\theta}$, due to the dependence of $\boldsymbol{g}(\boldsymbol{\theta})$ on $\boldsymbol{\theta}$. Finally we define the new vectors $\boldsymbol{x}$ and $\boldsymbol{y}$ (which are again $\boldsymbol{\theta}$-dependent), with components $x_n = \hat{v}_n\sqrt{g_n}$ and $y_n = \hat{w}_n\sqrt{g_n}$:

$$
[d(\boldsymbol{\theta},\boldsymbol{\theta}') + d(\boldsymbol{\theta}',\boldsymbol{\theta}'')]^2 - d^2(\boldsymbol{\theta},\boldsymbol{\theta}'') = 2\epsilon^2\left(|\boldsymbol{x}||\boldsymbol{y}| - \boldsymbol{x}\cdot\boldsymbol{y}\right) + \mathcal{O}(\epsilon^3)
$$

which, due to the Schwarz inequality $|\boldsymbol{x} \cdot \boldsymbol{y}| \leq |\boldsymbol{x}||\boldsymbol{y}|$, completes the proof that locally the triangular inequality $d(\boldsymbol{\theta}, \boldsymbol{\theta}') + d(\boldsymbol{\theta}', \boldsymbol{\theta}'') \geq d(\boldsymbol{\theta}, \boldsymbol{\theta}'')$ indeed holds.

H.3 Global distance definitions

Given the local metric (H.3), one obtains the length A of a path $\{\boldsymbol{\theta}(t)\}$ through parameter space, with $t_0 \leq t \leq t_1$, simply by integrating over the locally defined distance:

$$A = \int_{t_0}^{t_1} \mathrm{d}t\, L\left(\boldsymbol{\theta}(t), \frac{\mathrm{d}}{\mathrm{d}t}\boldsymbol{\theta}(t)\right), \quad L\left(\boldsymbol{\theta}(t), \frac{\mathrm{d}}{\mathrm{d}t}\boldsymbol{\theta}(t)\right) = \left[\frac{\mathrm{d}}{\mathrm{d}t}\boldsymbol{\theta}(t) \cdot \boldsymbol{g}(\boldsymbol{\theta}(t)) \frac{\mathrm{d}}{\mathrm{d}t}\boldsymbol{\theta}(t)\right]^{1/2} \tag{H.4}$$

Any finite distance $d(\boldsymbol{\theta}, \boldsymbol{\theta}')$ is now defined as the length A of the *shortest* path $\{\boldsymbol{\theta}(t)\}$ with $\boldsymbol{\theta}(t_0) = \boldsymbol{\theta}$ and $\boldsymbol{\theta}(t_1) = \boldsymbol{\theta}'$. This (special) path, which is a so-called 'geodesic', is calculated by extremization of the expression in (H.4) by functional variation of the path $\{\boldsymbol{\theta}(t)\}$, subject to the constraints that $\delta\boldsymbol{\theta}(t_0) = \delta\boldsymbol{\theta}(t_1) = 0$:

$$\begin{aligned}
\delta A &= \sum_i \int_{t_0}^{t_1} \mathrm{d}t \left[\delta\theta_i(t) \frac{\partial L}{\partial \theta_i(t)} + \frac{\mathrm{d}}{\mathrm{d}t}\delta\theta_i(t)\, \frac{\partial L}{\partial(\mathrm{d}\theta_i(t)/\mathrm{d}t)}\right] \\
&= \sum_i \int_{t_0}^{t_1} \mathrm{d}t\, \delta\theta_i(t) \frac{\partial L}{\partial \theta_i(t)} + \sum_i \left[\delta\theta_i(t) \frac{\partial L}{\partial(\mathrm{d}\theta_i(t)/\mathrm{d}t)}\right]_{t_0}^{t_1} \\
&\quad - \sum_i \int_{t_0}^{t_1} \mathrm{d}t\, \delta\theta_i(t)\, \frac{\mathrm{d}}{\mathrm{d}t} \frac{\partial L}{\partial(\mathrm{d}\theta_i(t)/\mathrm{d}t)} \\
&= \sum_i \int_{t_0}^{t_1} \mathrm{d}t\, \delta\theta_i(t) \left\{\frac{\partial L}{\partial \theta_i(t)} - \frac{\mathrm{d}}{\mathrm{d}t}\left[\frac{\partial L}{\partial(\mathrm{d}\theta_i(t)/\mathrm{d}t)}\right]\right\}
\end{aligned}$$

Therefore, the extremal path is a solution of the equation

$$\frac{\partial L}{\partial \theta_i(t)} = \frac{\mathrm{d}}{\mathrm{d}t}\left[\frac{\partial L}{\partial(\mathrm{d}\theta_i(t)/\mathrm{d}t)}\right] \tag{H.5}$$

with the function L as given in (H.4). It is a trivial exercise to show that in the case of Euclidean geometry, $g_{ij}(\boldsymbol{\theta}) = \delta_{ij}$, the shortest path is always the Euclidean straight line $\boldsymbol{\theta}(t) = [(t_1 - t)\boldsymbol{\theta}(t_0) + (t - t_0)\boldsymbol{\theta}(t_1)]/(t_1 - t_0)$.

Appendix I: Saddle-point integration

The objective of steepest descent (or 'saddle-point') integration in its simplest form is to deal with integrals of the following type, with $\boldsymbol{x} \in \mathbb{R}^p$, with continuous functions $f(\boldsymbol{x})$ and $g(\boldsymbol{x})$, of which f is bounded from below, and with $N \in \mathbb{R}$ positive and large:

$$I_N[f,g] = \int_{\mathbb{R}^p} \mathrm{d}\boldsymbol{x}\ g(\boldsymbol{x}) e^{-Nf(\boldsymbol{x})} \tag{I.1}$$

We first take $f(\boldsymbol{x})$ to be real-valued; this is the simplest case, for which finding the asymptotic behaviour of (I.1) as $N \to \infty$ goes back to Laplace. We assume that $f(\boldsymbol{x})$ can be expanded in a Taylor series around its minimum $f(\boldsymbol{x}^\star)$, which we assume to be unique, that is,

$$f(\boldsymbol{x}) = f(\boldsymbol{x}^\star) + \frac{1}{2}\sum_{ij=1}^{p} A_{ij}(x_i - x_i^\star)(x_j - x_j^\star) + \mathcal{O}(|\boldsymbol{x} - \boldsymbol{x}^\star|^3) \tag{I.2}$$

$$A_{ij} = \left.\frac{\partial^2 f}{\partial x_i \partial x_j}\right|_{\boldsymbol{x}^\star}$$

Provided the integral (I.1) exists, insertion of (I.2) into (I.1) followed by the transformation $\boldsymbol{x} = \boldsymbol{x}^\star + \boldsymbol{y}/\sqrt{N}$ gives

$$\begin{aligned} I_N[f,g] &= e^{-Nf(\boldsymbol{x}^\star)} \int_{\mathbb{R}^p} \mathrm{d}\boldsymbol{x}\ g(\boldsymbol{x}) e^{-N\sum_{ij}(x_i - x_i^\star)A_{ij}(x_j - x_j^\star)/2 + \mathcal{O}(N|\boldsymbol{x}-\boldsymbol{x}^\star|^3)} \\ &= N^{-(p/2)} e^{-Nf(\boldsymbol{x}^\star)} \int_{\mathbb{R}^p} \mathrm{d}\boldsymbol{y}\ g\left(\boldsymbol{x}^\star + \frac{\boldsymbol{y}}{\sqrt{N}}\right) e^{-\sum_{ij} y_i A_{ij} y_j/2 + \mathcal{O}(|\boldsymbol{y}|^3/\sqrt{N})} \end{aligned} \tag{I.3}$$

From this latter expansion, and given the assumptions made, we can obtain two important identities, both of which we use regularly in this book:

$$\begin{aligned} -\lim_{N\to\infty} \frac{1}{N} \ln \int_{\mathbb{R}^p} \mathrm{d}\boldsymbol{x}\ e^{-Nf(\boldsymbol{x})} &= -\lim_{N\to\infty} \frac{1}{N} \ln I_N[f,1] \\ &= f(\boldsymbol{x}^\star) + \lim_{N\to\infty} \left[\frac{p \ln N}{2N} - \frac{1}{N} \ln \int_{\mathbb{R}^p} \mathrm{d}\boldsymbol{y}\ e^{-\sum_{ij} y_i A_{ij} y_j/2 + \mathcal{O}(|\boldsymbol{y}|^3/\sqrt{N})}\right] \\ &= f(\boldsymbol{x}^\star) = \min_{\boldsymbol{x}\in\mathbb{R}^p} f(\boldsymbol{x}) \end{aligned} \tag{I.4}$$

and

$$\lim_{N\to\infty} \frac{\int \mathrm{d}\boldsymbol{x}\, g(\boldsymbol{x}) e^{-Nf(\boldsymbol{x})}}{\int \mathrm{d}\boldsymbol{x}\, e^{-Nf(\boldsymbol{x})}} = \lim_{N\to\infty} \frac{I_N[f,g]}{I_N[f,1]}$$

$$= \lim_{N\to\infty} \left[\frac{\int_{\mathrm{IR}^p} \mathrm{d}\boldsymbol{y}\, g(\boldsymbol{x}^\star + \boldsymbol{y}/\sqrt{N}) e^{-\sum_{ij} y_i A_{ij} y_j/2 + \mathcal{O}(|\boldsymbol{y}|^3/\sqrt{N})}}{\int_{\mathrm{IR}^p} \mathrm{d}\boldsymbol{y}\, e^{-\sum_{ij} y_i A_{ij} y_j/2 + \mathcal{O}(|\boldsymbol{y}|^3/\sqrt{N})}} \right]$$

$$= \frac{g(\boldsymbol{x}^\star)(2\pi)^{p/2}/\sqrt{\det \boldsymbol{A}}}{(2\pi)^{p/2}/\sqrt{\det \boldsymbol{A}}} = g(\boldsymbol{x}^\star)$$

$$= g(\mathrm{argmin}_{\boldsymbol{x}\in\mathrm{IR}^p} f(\boldsymbol{x})) \tag{I.5}$$

The situation becomes more complicated when we allow the dimension p of our integrations to depend on N. Provided the ratio p/N goes to zero sufficiently fast as $N \to \infty$, one can still prove the above identities, but much more care will be needed in dealing with correction terms.

In those cases where the function $f(\boldsymbol{x})$ is complex, it is much less clear how to calculate the asymptotic form of (I.1). The correct procedure to be followed here is to deform the integration paths in the complex plane (using Cauchy's theorem) such that along the deformed path the imaginary part of the function $f(\boldsymbol{x})$ is constant, and preferably (if possible) zero. In the models analysed in this book we can be sure on physical grounds that a path where $f(\boldsymbol{x}) \in \mathrm{IR}$ can always be found. Having succeeded, one can then proceed using Laplace's argument and find the leading order in N of our integral in the usual manner by extremization of the real part of $f(\boldsymbol{x})$. In combination one finds that our integrals will thus again be dominated by an extremum of the (complex) function $f(\boldsymbol{x})$, but since f is generally complex we can no longer interpret this extremum as a minimum:

$$-\lim_{N\to\infty} \frac{1}{N} \ln \int_{\mathrm{IR}^p} \mathrm{d}\boldsymbol{x} e^{-Nf(\boldsymbol{x})} = \mathrm{extr}_{\boldsymbol{x}\in\mathrm{IR}^p} f(\boldsymbol{x}) \tag{I.6}$$

$$\lim_{N\to\infty} \frac{\int \mathrm{d}\boldsymbol{x} g(\boldsymbol{x}) e^{-Nf(\boldsymbol{x})}}{\int \mathrm{d}\boldsymbol{x} e^{-Nf(\boldsymbol{x})}} = g(\mathrm{argextr}_{\boldsymbol{x}\in\mathrm{IR}^p} f(\boldsymbol{x})) \tag{I.7}$$

Whereas the Laplace method for real functions $f(\boldsymbol{x})$ is relatively straightforward, the precise mathematical details of the full saddle-point method (including the subtleties in the correct deformation of integration paths, the question of under which conditions a path with $f(\boldsymbol{x}) \in \mathrm{IR}$ exists, etc.) are more involved. For these the reader will therefore have to be referred to textbooks on methods in mathematical physics or on perturbation methods (e.g. see [153]).

References

[1] M Abramowitz and I A Stegun. *Handbook of Mathematical Functions*. Dover, New York, 1972.

[2] A M Turing. On computable numbers, with an application to the Entscheidungsproblem. *Proc. Lond. Math. Soc. (Series 2)*, 42:230–265, 1936.

[3] W S McCulloch and W H Pitts. A logical calculus of the ideas immanent in nervous activity. *Bull. Math. Biophys.*, 5:115–133, 1943.

[4] D O Hebb. *The Organization of Behaviour*. Wiley, New York, 1949.

[5] F Rosenblatt. The perceptron: a probabilistic model for information storage and organization in the brain. *Psychol. Rev.*, 65:386–408, 1958.

[6] F Rosenblatt. *Principles of Neurodynamics*. Spartan, New York, 1969.

[7] M L Minsky and S A Papert. *Perceptrons (expanded edition, 1988)*. MIT Press, Cambridge, MA, 1969.

[8] W A Little. The existence of persistent states in the brain. *Math. Biosci.*, 19:101–120, 1974.

[9] B G Cragg and H N V Temperley. Memory: the analogy with ferromagnetic hysteresis. *Brain*, 78:304–316, 1955.

[10] A L Hodgkin and A F Huxley. A quantitative description of membrane current and its application to conduction and excitation in nerve. *J. Physiol. Lond.*, 117:500–544, 1952.

[11] T Kohonen. Correlation matrix memories. *IEEE Trans. Comput. C*, 21:353–359, 1972.

[12] S I Amari. Learning patterns and pattern sequences by self-organizing nets of threshold elements. *IEEE Trans. Comput. C*, 21:1197–1206, 1972.

[13] W K Taylor. Electrical simulation of some nervous system functional activities. In C Cherry, editor, *Information Theory*, pp. 314–328. Butterworths, London, 1956.

[14] J J Hopfield. Neural networks and physical systems with emergent collective computational abilities. *Proc. Natl. Acad. Sci. USA*, 79:2554–2558, 1982.

[15] T Kohonen. *Self-Organization and Associative Memory*. Springer Verlag, Berlin, 1984.

[16] D E Rumelhart and J L McClelland (Eds.). *Parallel Distributed Processing I & II*. MIT Press, Cambridge, MA, 1986.

[17] P Werbos. *The Roots of Backpropagation: From Ordered Derivatives to Neural Networks and Political Forecasting*. Wiley, New York, 1994.

[18] Y Kuramoto. *Chemical Oscillations, Waves and Turbulence*. Springer Verlag, Berlin, 1984.

[19] W Gerstner and W Kistler. *Spiking Neuron Models*. Cambridge University Press, Cambridge, 2002.

[20] J A Anderson and E Rosenfeld (Eds.). *Neurocomputing—Foundations of Research*. MIT Press, Cambridge, MA, 1988.

[21] M A Arbib (Ed.). *The Handbook of Brain Theory and Neural Networks (2nd Ed.)* MIT Press, Cambridge, MA, 2003.

[22] D J Amit. *Modelling Brain Function*. Cambridge University Press, Cambridge, 1989.

[23] J A Hertz, R G Palmer, and A S Krogh. *Introduction to the Theory of Neural Computation*. Addison-Wesley, Redwood City, CA, 1991.

[24] P Peretto. *An Introduction to the Modeling of Neural Networks*. Cambridge University Press, Cambridge, 1992.

[25] S Haykin. *Neural Networks: a Comprehensive Foundation (2nd Ed.)*. Prentice Hall, Englewood Cliffs, NJ, 1998.

[26] T Kohonen. *Self-Organizing Maps*. Springer Verlag, Berlin, 1995.

[27] T Ritter, H Martinetz, and K Schulten. *Neural Computation and Self-Organizing Maps*. Addison-Wesley, Reading, MA, 1992.

[28] S I Amari. Topographic organization of nerve fields. *Bull. Math. Biol.*, 42:339–364, 1980.

[29] T Kohonen. Self-organized formation of topologically correct feature maps. *Biol. Cybern.*, 43:59–69, 1982.

[30] Z Ghahramani. Unsupervised learning. In O Bousquet, G Raetsch, and U von Luxburg, editors, *Advanced Lectures on Machine Learning, Lecture Notes in Artificial Intelligence 3176*. Springer Verlag, Berlin, 2004.

[31] S L Lauritzen. *Graphical Models*. Oxford University Press, Oxford, 1996.

[32] E Castillo, J M Gutierrez, and A S Hadi. *Expert Systems and Probabilistic Network Models*. Springer Verlag, Berlin, 1997.

[33] F V Jensen. *Bayesian Networks and Decision Graphs*. Springer Verlag, Berlin, 2001.

[34] C M Bishop, M Svensen, and C K I Williams. Gtm: the generative topographic mapping. *Neural Computation*, 10:215–234, 1998.

[35] C M Bishop. *Neural Networks for Pattern Recognition*. Oxford University Press, Oxford, 1995.

[36] B D Ripley. *Pattern Recognition and Neural Networks*. Cambridge University Press, Cambridge, 1996.

[37] D J C MacKay. Bayesian interpolation. *Neural Computation*, 4:415–447, 1992.

[38] D J C MacKay. A practical Bayesian framework for backpropagation networks. *Neural Computation*, 4:448–472, 1992.

[39] D J C MacKay. The evidence framework applied to classification networks. *Neural Computation*, 4:720–736, 1992.

[40] D J C MacKay. Probable networks and plausible predictions—a review of practical Bayesian methods for supervised neural networks. *Network: Computation in Neural Systems*, 6:469–505, 1995.

[41] R M Neal. *Bayesian Learning for Neural Networks*. Springer, New York, 1996.

[42] D J C MacKay. *Information Theory, Inference, and Learning Algorithms*. Cambridge University Press, Cambridge, 2004.

[43] C K I Williams. Prediction with Gaussian processes: from linear regression to linear prediction and beyond. In M I Jordan, editor, *Learning and Inference in Graphical Models*, pp. 159–261. Kluwer Academic, Amsterdam, 1998.

[44] R M Neal. Priors for infinite networks. Technical report, University of Toronto, 1994. Available by anonymous ftp from: `ftp.cs.toronto.edu`, file `/pub/radford/pin.ps.Z`.

[45] C K I Williams and C E Rasmussen. Gaussian processes for regression. In D S Touretzky, M C Mozer, and M E Hasselmo, editors, *Advances in Neural Information Processing Systems 8*, pp. 514–520. Cambridge, MA, 1996. MIT Press.

[46] M Seeger. Gaussian processes for machine learning. *Int. J. Neural Systs.*, 14:69–106, 2004.

[47] V Vapnik. *Statistical Learning Theory*. Wiley, New York, 1998.

[48] V N Vapnik. *The Nature of Statistical Learning Theory (2nd Ed.)*. Springer Verlag, Berlin, 2000.

[49] N Cristiani and J Shawe-Taylor. *An Introduction to Support Vector Machines*. Cambridge University Press, Cambridge, 2000.
[50] M Anthony and N Biggs. *Computational Learning Theory*. Cambridge Tracts in Theoretical Computer Science (30). Cambridge University Press, Cambridge, 1992.
[51] M J Kearns and U V Vazirani. *An Introduction to Computational Learning Theory*. MIT Press, Cambridge, MA, 1994.
[52] T M Mitchell. *Machine Learning*. WCB/McGraw-Hill, Boston, MA, 1997.
[53] M Anthony and P Bartlett. *Neural Network Learning: Theoretical Foundations*. Cambridge University Press, Cambridge, 1999.
[54] D A McAllester. Some PAC-bayesian theorems. In *COLT: Proceedings of the Workshop on Computational Learning Theory*, pp. 230–234, Morgan Kaufmann, San Francisco, CA, 1998.
[55] Schölkopf B and Smola A. *Learning with Kernels*. MIT Press, Cambridge, MA, 2002.
[56] J Shawe-Taylor and N Cristianini. *Kernel Methods for Pattern Analysis*. Cambridge University Press, Cambridge, 2004.
[57] C E Shannon. A mathematical theory of communication. *Bell Sys. Tech. Journal*, 27:379–423, 623–656, 1948.
[58] C E Shannon. *Shannon's original 1948 paper is available on the internet at* `http://cm.bell-labs.com/cm/ms/what/shannonday/shannon1948.pdf`.
[59] C E Shannon and W W Weaver. *The Mathematical Theory of Communication*. University of Illinois Press, Urbana, IL, 1949.
[60] H Nyquist. Certain factors affecting telegraph speed. *Bell Sys. Tech. Journal*, 3:324–346, 1924.
[61] R V Hartley. Transmission of information. *Bell Sys. Tech. Journal*, 7:535–563, 1928.
[62] N Wiener. *Cybernetics*. MIT Press, Cambridge, MA, 1948.
[63] N Wiener. *Extrapolation, Interpolation and Smoothing of Stationary Time Series*. MIT Press, Cambridge, MA, 1949.
[64] A Y Khinchin. *Mathematical Foundations of Information Theory*. Dover, New York, 1957.
[65] L Brillouin. *Science and Information Theory*. Academic Press, New York, 1962.
[66] T M Cover and J A Thomas. *Elements of Information Theory*. Wiley, New York, 1991.
[67] R A Fisher. Theory of statistical estimation. *Proc. Cambridge Phil. Society*, 22:700–725, 1925.
[68] E T Jaynes. Information theory and statistical mechanics. *Phys. Rev.*, 106:620–630, 1957.
[69] E T Jaynes. Information theory and statistical mechanics. *Phys. Rev.*, 108:171–190, 1957.
[70] E T Jaynes. Where do we stand on maximum entropy. In R Levin and M Tribus, editors, *The Maximum Entropy Formalism*, pp. 15–118. MIT Press, Cambridge, MA, 1979.
[71] D H Ackley, G E Hinton, and T J Sejnowski. A learning algorithm for Boltzmann machines. *Cognit. Sci.*, 9:147–169, 1985.
[72] G E Hinton and T J Sejnowski. Learning and relearning in Boltzmann machines. In D E Rumelhart and J L McClelland, editors, *Parallel Distributed Processing, Vol 1*, pp. 159–261. MIT Press, Cambridge, MA, 1986.
[73] G Deco and D Obradovic. *An Information-Theoretic Approach to Neural Computing*. Springer Verlag, London, 1996.
[74] S I Amari. Natural gradient works efficiently in learning. *Neural Comp.*, 10:251–276, 1998.

[75] M K Murray and J W Rice. *Differential Geometry and Statistics*. Chapman and Hall, London, 1993.

[76] W Feller. *An Introduction to Probability Theory and Its Applications, Vol. I*. Wiley, New York, 1957.

[77] W Feller. *An Introduction to Probability Theory and Its Applications, Vol. II*. Wiley, New York, 1966.

[78] C W Gardiner. *Handbook of Stochastic Methods*. Springer Verlag, Berlin, 1990.

[79] N G van Kampen. *Stochastic Processes in Physics and Chemistry (2nd Ed.)*. North-Holland, Amsterdam, 1992.

[80] V N Vapnik. *Estimation of Dependences Based on Empirical Data*. Springer Verlag, Berlin, 1982.

[81] H K Khalil. *Nonlinear Systems*. MacMillan, New York, 1992.

[82] S I Amari. Neural theory of association and concept formation. *Biol. Cybern.*, 26:175–185, 1977.

[83] S I Amari and K Maginu. Statistical neurodynamics of associative memory. *Neural Networks*, 1:63–73, 1988.

[84] M Okada. A hierarchy of macrodynamical equations for associative memory. *Neural Networks*, 8:833–838, 1995.

[85] J Buhmann and K Schulten. Noise-driven temporal association in neural networks. *Europhys. Lett.*, 4:1205–1209, 1987.

[86] U Riedel, R Kühn, and J L van Hemmen. Temporal sequences and chaos in neural nets. *Phys. Rev. A*, 38:1105–1108, 1988.

[87] A C C Coolen and T W Ruijgrok. Image evolution in Hopfield networks. *Phys. Rev. A*, 38:4253–4255, 1988.

[88] B Derrida, E Gardner, and A Zippelius. An exactly solvable asymmetric neural network model. *Europhys. Lett.*, 4:167–173, 1987.

[89] R Kree and A Zippelius. Asymmetrically diluted neural networks. In R Domany, J L van Hemmen, and K Schulten, editors, *Models of Neural Networks I*, pp. 193–212. Springer Verlag, Berlin, 1991.

[90] H Rieger, M Schreckenberg, and J Zittartz. Glauber dynamics of neural network models. *J. Phys. A: Math. Gen.*, 21:L263–L267, 1988.

[91] H Horner, D Bormann, M Frick, H Kinzelbach, and A Schmidt. Transients and basins of attraction in neural network models. *Z. Phys. B*, 76:381–398, 1989.

[92] R D Henkel and M Opper. Distribution of internal fields and dynamics of neural networks. *Europhys. Lett.*, 11:403–408, 1990.

[93] A C C Coolen and D Sherrington. Order parameter flow in the fully connected Hopfield model near saturation. *Phys. Rev. E*, 49:1921–1934, 1994.

[94] A C C Coolen. Statistical mechanics of recurrent neural networks II: Dynamics. In F Moss and S Gielen, editors, *Handbook of Biological Physics IV*, pp. 597–662. Elsevier Science, Amsterdam, 2001.

[95] E Gardner. The space of interactions in neural network models. *J. Phys. A: Math. Gen.*, 21:257–270, 1988.

[96] E Gardner and B Derrida. Optimal storage properties of neural networks models. *J. Phys. A: Math. Gen.*, 21:271–284, 1988.

[97] H Seung, H S Sompolinsky, and N Tishby. Statistical mechanics of learning from examples. *Phys. Rev. A*, 45:6056–6091, 1992.

[98] A Krogh and J A Hertz. Generalization in a linear perceptron in the presence of noise. *J. Phys. A: Math. Gen.*, 25:1135–1147, 1992.

[99] W Kinzel and M Opper. Dynamics of learning. In R Domany, J L van Hemmen, and K Schulten, editors, *Models of Neural Networks I*, pp. 149–171. Springer Verlag, Berlin, 1991.

[100] T L H Watkin, A Rau, and M Biehl. The statistical mechanics of learning a rule. *Rev. Mod. Phys.*, 65:499–556, 1993.

[101] M Opper and W Kinzel. Physics of generalization. In R Domany, J L van Hemmen, and K Schulten, editors, *Models of Neural Networks III*, pp. 151–209. Springer Verlag, Berlin, 1994.

[102] C W H Mace and A C C Coolen. Statistical mechanical analysis of the dynamics of learning in perceptrons. *Statistics and Computing*, 8:55–88, 1998.

[103] F Vallet. The Hebb rule for learning separable Boolen functions: learning and generalization. *Europhys. Lett.*, 8:747–751, 1989.

[104] J K Anlauf and M Biehl. The AdaTron, an adaptive perceptron algorithm. *Europhys. Lett.*, 10:687–692, 1989.

[105] W Kinzel and P Rujan. Improving a network generalization ability by selecting examples. *Europhys. Lett.*, 13:473–477, 1990.

[106] O Kinouchi and N Caticha. Optimal generalization in perceptrons. *J. Phys. A: math. Gen.*, 25:6243–6250, 1992.

[107] M Biehl and H Schwarze. On-line learning of a time-dependent rule. *Europhys. Lett.*, 20:733–738, 1992.

[108] M Biehl and P Riegler. Online learning with a perceptron. *Europhys. Lett.*, 28(7):525–530, 1994.

[109] M Opper and D Haussler. Generalization performance of Bayes optimal classification algorithm for learning a perceptron. *Phys. Rev. Lett.*, 66:2677–2680, 1991.

[110] M Biehl and H Schwarze. Learning by online gradient descent. *Journal of Physics A: Math. Gen.*, 28:643–656, 1995.

[111] D Saad and S A Solla. Exact solution for online learning in multilayer neural networks. *Phys. Rev. Lett.*, 74:4337–4340, 1995.

[112] D Saad (Ed.). *On-Line Learning in Neural Networks*. Cambridge University Press, Cambridge, 1998.

[113] H C Rae, P Sollich, and A C C Coolen. On-line learning with restricted training sets: an exactly solvable case. *J. Phys. A: Math. Gen.*, 32:3321–3339, 1999.

[114] A C C Coolen and D Saad. Dynamics of learning with restricted training sets. *Phys. Rev. E*, 62:5444–5487, 2000.

[115] J A F Heimel and A C C Coolen. Supervised learning with restricted traing sets: a generating functional analysis. *J. Phys. A: Math. Gen.*, 34:9009–9026, 2001.

[116] P Luo and K Y M Wong. Cavity approach to noisy learning in nonlinear perceptrons. *Phys. Rev. E*, 64:061912, 2001.

[117] J Zinn-Justin. *Quantum Field Theory and Critical Phenomena*. Oxford University Press, Oxford, 1993.

[118] T Cover. Geometrical and statistical properties of systems of linear inequalities with applications in pattern recognition. *IEEE Trans. Elect. Comput.*, 14:326–334, 1965.

[119] F R Gantmacher. *Applications of the Theory of Matrices*. Interscience, New York, 1959.

[120] W A Little and G L Shaw. A statistical theory of short and long term memory. *Behav. Biol.*, 14:115–133, 1975. Reprinted in [20].

[121] P Peretto. Collective properties of neural networks: a statistical physics approach. *Biol. Cybern.*, 50:51–62, 1984.

[122] D J Amit, H Gutfreund, and H Sompolinsky. Spin-glass models of neural networks. *Phys. Rev. A*, 32:1007–1018, 1985.

[123] D J Amit, H Gutfreund, and H Sompolinsky. Storing infinite number of patterns in a spin-glass model of neural networks. *Phys. Rev. Lett.*, 55:1530–1533, 1985.

[124] D Amit, H Gutfreund, and H Sompolinsky. Statistical mechanics of neural networks near saturation. *Annals Physics*, 173:30–67, 1987.

[125] G H Hardy, J E Littlewood, and G Pólya. *Inequalities*. Cambridge University Press, Cambridge, 1934.

[126] S F Edwards and P W Anderson. Theory of spin glasses. *J. Phys. F*, 5:965–974, 1975.

[127] D Sherrington and S Kirkpatrick. Solvable model of a spin glass. *Phys. Rev. Lett.*, 35:1792–1796, 1975.

[128] M Mézard, G Parisi, and M A Virasoro. *Spin-Glass Theory and Beyond*. World Scientific, Singapore, 1987.

[129] J R L de Almeida and D J Thouless. Stability of the Sherrington–Kirkpatrick solution of a spin-glass model. *J. Phys. A*, 11:983–990, 1978.

[130] H Steffan and R Kühn. Replica symmetry breaking in attractor neural network models. *Z. Phys. B*, 95:249–260, 1994.

[131] J F Fontanari and R Koeberle. Information storage and retrieval in synchronous neural networks. *Phys. Rev. A*, 36:2475–2477, 1987.

[132] D Amit, H Gutfreund, and H Sompolinsky. Information storage in neural networks with low levels of activity. *Phys. Rev. A*, 35:2293–2303, 1987.

[133] H Horner. Neural networks with low levels of activity: Ising vs. McCulloch–Pitts neurons. *Z. Phys. B*, 75:133–136, 1989.

[134] A Krogh and J A Hertz. Mean field analysis of hierarchical associative networks with magnetization. *J. Phys. A*, 21:2211–2224, 1988.

[135] S Bös, R Kühn, and J L van Hemmen. Martingale approach to neural networks with hierarchically structured information. *Z. Phys. B*, 71:261–271, 1988.

[136] I Kanter and H Sompolinsky. Associative recall of memory without errors. *Phys. Rev. A*, 35:380–392, 1987.

[137] H Rieger. Storing an extensive number of grey-toned patterns in a neural network using multistate neurons. *J. Phys. A*, 23:L1273–L1279, 1990.

[138] R Kühn and S Bös. Statistical mechanics for neural networks with continuous dynamics. *J. Phys. A*, 23:831–857, 1993.

[139] I Kanter. Potts-glass models of neural networks. *Phys. Rev. A*, 37:2739–2742, 1988.

[140] H Nishimori. *Statistical Physics of Spin Glasses and Information Processing*. Oxford University Press, Oxford, 2001.

[141] E Domany, J L van Hemmen, and K Schulten (Eds.). *Models of Neural Networks I*. Springer Verlag, Berlin, 1991.

[142] A C C Coolen. Statistical mechanics of recurrent neural networks I: Statics. In F Moss and S Gielen, editors, *Handbook of Biological Physics IV*, pp. 531–596. Elsevier Science, Amsterdam, 2001.

[143] J M Yeomans. *Statistical Mechanics of Phase Transitions*. Oxford University Press, Oxford, 1992.

[144] M Plischke and B Bergersen. *Equilibrium Statistical Mechanics*. World Scientific, Singapore, 1994.

[145] S K Ma. *Statistical Mechanics*. World Scientific, Singapore, 1985.

[146] E Gardner. Maximum storage capacity in neural networks. *Europhys. Lett.*, 4:481–485, 1987.

[147] W Krauth and M Mézard. Storage capacity of memory networks with binary couplings. *J. Phys. France*, 50:3057–3066, 1989.

[148] H Horner. Dynamics of learning for the binary perceptron problem. *Z. Phys. B*, 86:291–308, 1992.

[149] M Opper, W Kinzel, J Kleinz, and R Nehl. On the ability of the optimal perceptron to generalize. *J. Phys. A: Math. Gen.*, 23:L581–L586, 1990.

[150] M A Virasoro. The effect of synapses destruction on categorization in neural networks. *Europhys. Lett.*, 7:293–298, 1988.

[151] G Györgyi and N Tishby. Statistical theory of learning a rule. In W K Theumann and R Koeberle, editors, *Neural Networks and Spin Glasses*. World Scientific, Singapore, 1990.

[152] A Engel and C van den Broeck. *Statistical Mechanics of Learning*. Cambridge University Press, Cambridge, 2001.

[153] E J Hinch. *Perturbation Methods*. Cambridge University Press, Cambridge, 1991.

Index

The manufacturer's authorised representative in the EU for product safety is Oxford University Press España S.A. of El Parque Empresarial San Fernando de Henares, Avenida de Castilla, 2 - 28830 Madrid (www.oup.es/en or product.safety@oup.com). OUP España S.A. also acts as importer into Spain of products made by the manufacturer.
Printed and bound by CPI Group (UK) Ltd, Croydon, CR0 4YY
14/09/2026
02216290-0011